Kerrie Meyler
Pete Zerger
Marcus Oh
Anders Bengtsson
Kurt Van Hoecke

with Romuald Gauvin
Nicholas J. Dattil

System Center 2012 Orchestrator

UNLEASHED

SAMS | 800 East 96th Street, Indianapolis, Indiana 46240 USA

System Center 2012 Orchestrator Unleashed

ISBN-13: 978-0-672-33610-2

ISBN-10: 0-672-33610-3

Library of Congress Control Number: 2013943417

Printed in the United States of America

First Printing September 2013

Trademarks

Warning and Disclaimer

Bulk Sales

Sams Publishing offers excellent discounts on this book when ordered in quantity for bulk purchases or special sales. For more information, please contact

U.S. Corporate and Government Sales
1-800-382-3419
corpsales@pearsontechgroup.com

For sales outside of the U.S., please contact

International Sales
international@pearsoned.com

Editor-in-Chief
Greg Wiegand

Executive Editor
Neil Rowe

Development Editor
Mark Renfrow

Managing Editor
Kristy Hart

Senior Project Editor
Lori Lyons

Project Editor
Katie Matejka

Copy Editor
Krista Hansing

Indexer
Erika Millen

Proofreader
Sarah Kearns

Technical Editor
Jeff Fanjoy

Editorial Assistant
Cindy Teeters

Cover Compositor
Mark Shirar

Senior Compositor
Gloria Schurick

Contents at a Glance

Table of Contents

Foreword

I have seen automation defined as the use of machines, controls, and information technologies to optimize the productivity in the production of goods and delivery of services.

In today's modern data centers, this statement is both true and a requirement that allows your IT people the assets to work on strategic initiatives and spend less time on repetitive, mundane tasks that can be susceptible to human error. On the other hand, automation will not achieve these gains in and of itself, as data centers across the globe are built, managed, and sustained using a multitude of workloads that provide a service to users and customers. Enter *integration*—when automation and integration intersect, IT departments are provided the tools necessary to reach into disparate systems and essentially get them to "talk" to one another using well-defined workflows or *runbooks* as we sometimes call them. These runbooks allow IT staff to compose highly available, flexible automation and integration touch-points across business processes that span a multitude of workloads on various platforms.

Designing, publishing, and executing these workflows is simple using System Center 2012 SP 1 Orchestrator, a System Center 2012 SP 1 component. Orchestrator allows IT staff to deploy *integration packs* for all the System Center components as well as third-party workloads such as HP, IBM, VMware, and also other Microsoft workloads outside System Center such as Active Directory, Exchange, FTP, REST, and Windows Azure. Composing these workflows is easy using the Orchestrator Runbook Designer, which provides the user with a simple WYSIWYG graphical interface for dragging and dropping activities into a sequence that makes sense to your defined business process. Once enabled, these workflows can be manually triggered from the designer or invoked from another system such as System Center Service Manager. Users also have the ability to execute these workflows from our RESTful web service without requiring the Runbook Designer. Combine this designer with a highly available SQL Server backend and runbook servers that are able to scale out, and you have an enterprise-ready automation and integration tool that is simple to use and powerful enough to automate away business processes within your organization.

The demand for automation and integration has been quickly trending upward in IT. No matter whom you talk to, from large to small, automating business processes is becoming more prevalent in organizations around the world. This book intends to instruct IT administrators on how to use System Center 2012 Orchestrator to integrate and automate their existing business processes using a friendly, easy-to-use WYSIWYG designer with ready-to-import integration packs that cover a multitude of workloads essential to your business. The authors asked me to provide the Foreword for the book; and I can't think of a better-suited group of individuals who are able to produce this type of documentation, examples, and real-world scenarios to help you take advantage of this powerful System Center 2012 component.

Justin Incarnato, Senior Program Manager
Cloud and Enterprise Division, Microsoft

About the Authors

Kerrie Meyler, System Center MVP for Cloud and Datacenter Management, is the lead author of numerous System Center books in the Unleashed series. This includes *System Center Operations Manager 2007 Unleashed* (2008), *System Center Configuration Manager 2007 Unleashed* (2009), *System Center Operations Manager 2007 R2 Unleashed* (2010), *System Center Opalis Integration Server 6.3 Unleashed* (2011), *System Center Service Manager 2010 Unleashed* (2011), *System Center 2012 Configuration Manager Unleashed* (2012), and *System Center 2012 Operations Manager Unleashed* (2013). She is an independent consultant and trainer with more than 15 years of Information Technology experience. Kerrie has presented on System Center technologies at TechEd NA and MMS.

Pete Zerger is a consultant, author, speaker, and System Center Cloud and Datacenter Management MVP focusing on System Center management, private cloud, and data center automation solutions. He is a frequent speaker at Microsoft conferences, and writes articles for a variety of technical magazines including *Microsoft TechNet*. Pete is a contributing author for several books, including *System Center Opalis Integration Server 6.3 Unleashed* (2011), *PowerShell 2.0 Bible* (Wiley, 2011), and *System Center 2012 Operations Manager Unleashed* (2013). He is also the co-founder of SystemCenterCentral.com, a popular web community providing information, news, and support for System Center technologies. In 2008, Pete founded the System Center Virtual User Group, a group dedicated to sharing System Center knowledge with users worldwide.

Marcus Oh, System Center Cloud and Datacenter Management MVP, is a senior technical manager for a large telecommunications provider, running directory services and management infrastructure for ~30,000 systems. He has been an MVP since 2004 in System Center, specializing in Configuration Manager, Operations Manager, and Orchestrator. Marcus has written numerous articles for technology websites and blogs on Orchestrator and other System Center components at http://marcusoh.blogspot.com. He coauthored *Professional SMS 2003, MOM 2005, and WSUS* (Wrox, 2006), was a contributing author to *System Center Opalis Integration Server 6.3 Unleashed* (2011), and coauthored *System Center 2012 Configuration Manager Unleashed* (2012). Marcus is also the president of the Atlanta Systems Management User Group (http://www.atlsmug.com) and a board member of the Deskside Management Forum.

Anders Bengtsson is a Microsoft senior premier field engineer focusing on System Center. He has written a number of System Center training courses, including the Service Manager 2010 and Operations Manager 2007 advanced courses for Microsoft Learning. He was a coauthor for *System Center Service Manager 2010 Unleashed* (2011). Before joining Microsoft, Anders was a Microsoft MVP from 2007-2010 for his work in the System Center community, including more than 10,000 posts in news groups and forums. Anders has presented and worked at numerous Microsoft conferences and events, including MMS and Microsoft TechEd NA and EMEA.

Kurt Van Hoecke, System Center Cloud and Datacenter Management MVP, is a managing consultant at Inovativ Belgium. He focuses on the System Center product suite, including Orchestrator, Service Manager, and Configuration Manager. Kurt was a contributing author to *System Center Service Manager 2010 Unleashed* (2011) and blogs for System Center User Group Belgium and AuthoringFriday, where he shares his field experiences and discusses how to extend the built-in functionality of the System Center components.

About the Contributors

Romuald Gauvin, System Center Cloud and Datacenter Management MVP, manages a consulting company dedicated to orchestration and cloud projects. Previously in charge of development at Opalis Inc., Romuald began consulting in 2000. He has worked on automation and orchestration projects using Opalis/Orchestrator for more than 15 years. Romuald regularly shares his experiences on orchestration project approaches, methodology, and technical aspects during seminars with Microsoft, the French System Center user group, and at Microsoft TechDays.

Nicholas J. Dattilo is a consultant with Acceleres, a Microsoft Silver Partner for Management and Virtualization. He has worked with a wide range of clients to help them implement and optimize System Center Orchestrator and Service Manager. Nick frequently contributes to the monthly Acceleres Presents! webcasts on service delivery and automation.

Dedication

To those IT professionals worldwide interested in automation and using System Center, and the System Center Cloud and Data Center Management MVPs.

Acknowledgments

Writing a book is an all-encompassing and time-consuming project, and this book certainly meets that description. The authors and contributors would like to offer appreciation to those who helped with *System Center 2012 Orchestrator Unleashed.*

Thank you to Didier Leclercq of Aezan, to ClearPointe Technology for lab assistance and to John Joyner for environment support, and to Justin Incarnato of Microsoft. Jeff Fanjoy, also of Microsoft, was invaluable as our technical editor.

Thanks also go to the staff at Pearson, in particular to Neil Rowe, who has worked with us since with *Microsoft Operations Manger 2005 Unleashed* (Sams, 2006).

We Want to Hear from You!

As the reader of this book, *you* are our most important critic and commentator. We value your opinion and want to know what we're doing right, what we could do better, what areas you'd like to see us publish in, and any other words of wisdom you're willing to pass our way.

We welcome your comments. You can email or write to let us know what you did or didn't like about this book—as well as what we can do to make our books better.

Please note that we cannot help you with technical problems related to the topic of this book.

When you write, please be sure to include this book's title and author as well as your name and email address. We will carefully review your comments and share them with the author and editors who worked on the book.

Email: consumer@samspublishing.com

Mail: Sams Publishing
ATTN: Reader Feedback
800 East 96th Street
Indianapolis, IN 46240 USA

Reader Services

Visit our website and register this book at informit.com/register for convenient access to any updates, downloads, or errata that might be available for this book.

Introduction

In December 2009, Opalis Software, Inc. became a wholly owned subsidiary of Microsoft Corporation. Opalis, a leader in information technology process automation (ITPA) and run book automation (RBA), was best known for its Opalis Integration Server (OIS) software. As Brad Anderson said at the time, the acquisition was a pivotal piece for delivering on Microsoft's dynamic data center initiative, as it brought together Opalis Software's deep data center automation expertise with the integrated physical and virtualized data center management capabilities provided by Microsoft System Center (http://blogs.technet.com/b/systemcenter/archive/2009/12/11/microsoft-acquires-opalis-software.aspx).

As part of the acquisition, Opalis Software released OIS 6.2.2, a remediated version of 6.2.1. In November 2010, Microsoft released OIS 6.3, which became the "last OIS." Microsoft then further integrated OIS into System Center 2012 and rebranded it as System Center Orchestrator. Orchestrator enables Microsoft to integrate process automation into its vision of the data center.

ITPA is a powerful capability that can assist in streamlining IT operations by removing much of the overhead associated with manual responses to IT problems, whereas BPA concentrates on automating processes linked to the core business of an enterprise; these are often linked to data management. System Center Orchestrator, which incorporates an easy-to-use, drag-and-drop user interface, enables you to capture and document processes that encompass an entire IT organization. This is a core building block for the future of IT and is the foundation for the automation necessary to deliver cloud computing—self-adjusting tools of computing resources that can be tuned based on real-time events.

This book is divided into four sections:

Part I, "Orchestrator Overview and Concepts," includes an introduction to Orchestrator and discusses its history, internals, architectural concepts, and design concepts. These topics are discussed in Chapter 1, "Orchestration, Integration, and Automation," Chapter 2, "What's New in System Center 2012 Orchestrator," Chapter 3, "Looking Inside System Center 2012 Orchestrator," and Chapter 4, "Architectural Design."

Part II, "Installation and Implementation," steps through the installation process and discusses implementing Orchestrator:

- Chapter 5, "Installing System Center 2012 Orchestrator," covers installation and OIS 6.3 migration.
- Chapter 6, "Using System Center 2012 Orchestrator," provides an overview of how to use this System Center component.
- Chapter 7, "Runbook Basics," covers the anatomy of a runbook and introduces the different types of activities included with Orchestrator 2012.
- Chapter 8, "Advanced Runbook Concepts," goes deeper into runbook concepts, including scheduling, invoking child runbooks, looping, junctions, working with data, error handling, computer groups, variables, and counters.
- Chapter 9, "Standard Activities," provides additional depth on the Orchestrator standard activities.
- Chapter 10, "Runbook and Configuration Best Practices," covers best practices for runbooks and configuration.
- Chapter 11, "Security and Administration," discusses the Orchestrator security model, and user roles and security.

Part III, "Integration Packs and the OIT," focuses on integrating System Center Orchestrator into the data center through integration packs. IPs are software components that plug into the larger Orchestrator framework, and are designed around a series of atomic tasks targeted to a specific application. Orchestrator IPs are discussed in Chapter 12, "Orchestrator Integration Packs." The System Center IPs are discussed in greater depth in the following chapters:

- Chapter 13, "Integration with System Center Operations Manager"
- Chapter 14, "Integration with System Center Service Manager"
- Chapter 15, "Integration with System Center Configuration Manager"
- Chapter 16, "Integration with System Center Virtual Machine Manager"
- Chapter 17, "Integration with System Center Data Protection Manager"

Chapter 18, "Integration with Windows Azure," goes into depth on the Windows Azure IP, introduced with System Center 2012 Service Pack 1.

Chapter 19, "Runbook Automation in the Data Center and the Cloud," takes the Azure and System Center IPs to the next level by presenting examples that integrate objects from these IPs together in workflows and also incorporate PowerShell to achieve true end-to-end automation. Just in case you still don't have all the objects you need to accomplish your own integrations, Chapter 20, "The Orchestrator Integration Toolkit," gives you the tools to create your own IPs using the Orchestrator Integration Toolkit, also known as the OIT.

By this time, you should have all the tools necessary to become an Orchestrator expert. The last section of the book includes three appendices. Appendix A, "Community

Solutions and Tools," includes resources developed by the community, Appendix B, "Reference URLs," incorporates useful references you can use for further information, and Appendix C, "Available Online," is a guide to supplementary resources offered with the book that you can download from Pearson's website at http://www.informit.com/store/product.aspx?isbn=9780672336102.

This book provides in-depth reference and technical information about System Center 2012 Orchestrator SP 1, as well as information on orchestrating with System Center and third-party products through integration packs. The material will be of interest to those shops using System Center, Orchestrator, and anyone interested in ITPA.

Microsoft announced System Center 2012 R2 at TechEd in early June 2013. This release, slated for general availability by the end of the year, provides parity between Microsoft's data center software and its public cloud portfolio. As such, there are minimal changes planned to Orchestrator 2012 beyond updates to the Azure and VMM IPs, a new IP for SharePoint, support for Windows Server 2012 R2, and updates to the Orchestrator installation program for installing the new Service Management Automation (SMA) web service and runbook workers. The SMA feature is also interesting in that it provides a glimpse to where Microsoft may go with cloud-based automation.

Disclaimers and Fine Print

There are several disclaimers. Microsoft is continually improving and enhancing its products. This means the information provided is probably outdated the moment the book goes to print.

In addition, the moment Microsoft considers code development on any product complete, they begin working on a cumulative update, service pack, or future release; as the authors continue to work with the product, it is likely yet another one or two wrinkles will be discovered! The authors and contributors of *System Center 2012 Orchestrator Unleashed* have made every attempt to present information that is accurate and current as known at the time. Updates and corrections will be provided as errata on the InformIT website at http://www.informit.com/store/system-center-2012-orchestrator-unleashed-9780672336102.

Thank you for purchasing *System Center 2012 Orchestrator Unleashed*. The authors hope it is worth your while!

PART I

Orchestrator Overview and Concepts

IN THIS PART

CHAPTER 1

Orchestration, Integration, and Automation

IN THIS CHAPTER

- Orchestration, ITIL, and MOF
- Integration, Automation, Orchestration: The Differences
- Positioning of Orchestrator in System Center 2012
- Typical Use Cases
- Managing a Project
- Example: Orchestrating a VM Deployment

Information technology's (IT) expansion in recent decades has enabled companies to define business-driven applications that can help improve their performance. With IT services now regarded as key to the growth of organizations, the health and availability of these services is critical. This realization has led to routine procedures to check system availability, determine whether these systems are running correctly, verify whether data processing occurred as expected last night, and so on. These procedures and checks to ensure availability and health become increasingly complex as IT's role in the business continues to grow.

As part of this growth in the role of IT and the expansion of distributed computing in the mid-1990s, Opalis Robot, the grandfather of System Center Orchestrator, came into existence. (See Chapter 2, "What's New in System Center 2012 Orchestrator," for a detailed history of Orchestrator.) The goal of Robot was to help IT teams manage routine procedures more efficiently and be able to react quickly to events (unexpected behaviors). Opalis Robot was an implementation of run book automation (RBA) software, which helps organizations manage runbooks of routine procedures.

The need for IT management activities remains unchanged today: IT must focus on delivering services to companies and ensuring that those services are available. These activities include tools and management processes such as the IT Information Library (ITIL). As IT continues to evolve, these are evolving as well.

Automation, the focus of System Center Orchestrator, includes additional approaches such as business process automation (BPA) and IT process automation (ITPA):

- BPA concentrates on automating processes linked to the core business of an enterprise and often processes linked to data management. As an example, a process could perform a daily extraction of new customers registered on a website, convert those into a CSV file, send the file by email to a person in charge of data quality to check validity, and then import the file into customer relationship management (CRM) software.
- ITPA focuses on orchestrating and integrating tools, people, and processes through automated workflows dedicated to IT activities. Those activities can be all types of routine IT procedures, such as deployment (virtual machine creation, application deployment, and so on) and configuration updates.

This chapter discusses integration, automation, and orchestration from an IT management point of view. It shows how System Center and Orchestrator can help you extend best practices of ITIL and the Microsoft Operations Framework (MOF), and how Orchestrator can help you integrate, automate, and orchestrate your IT environment.

Orchestration, ITIL, and MOF

If you have already started an ITIL project in your organization, you have probably spent a considerable amount of time defining processes, process owners, and change policies. Improving quality in your organization can be a challenging task and requires an initial investment in time and resources.

ITIL is widely accepted as an international standard of best practices for operations management. Those ITIL projects are excellent opportunities to gain benefits from orchestration. As you inventory your processes, you can identify technical operations that appear regularly. For example, orchestration perfectly fits a scenario with multiple individuals collaborating to treat a user request. This could be delivering a new server or application or updating a user quota.

MOF is closely related to ITIL, and both describe best practices for IT service management (ITSM) processes. ITIL is generally accepted as the "best practices" for the industry. Because it is technology agnostic, it is a foundation that can be adopted and adapted to meet the specific needs of various IT organizations. Although Microsoft chose to adopt ITIL as a standard for its own IT operations for its descriptive guidance, the company designed MOF to provide prescriptive guidance for effective design, implementation, and support of Microsoft technologies. MOF is a set of publications that provide both descriptive (what to do, when, and why) and prescriptive (how to do) guidance on ITSM. The key focus in developing MOF was providing a framework specifically geared toward managing Microsoft technologies.

MOF v4 now incorporates Microsoft's previously existing Microsoft Solutions Framework (MSF), providing guidance for application development solutions. The combined framework provides guidance throughout the IT life cycle, as Figure 1.1 shows.

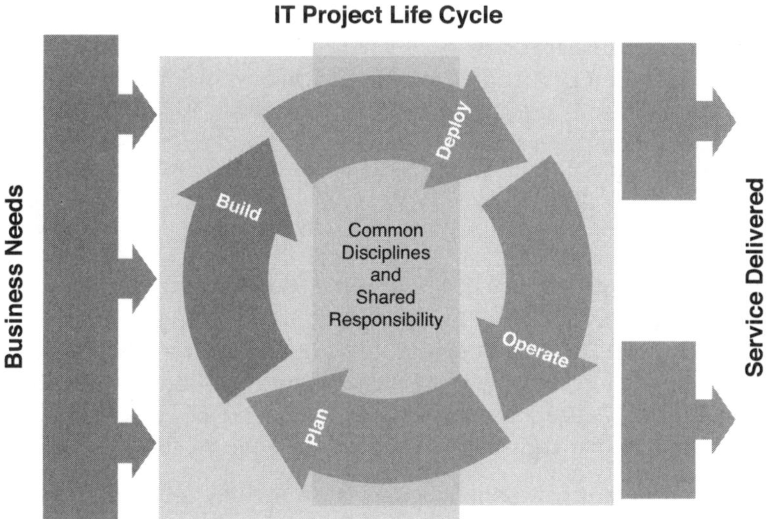

FIGURE 1.1 The IT lifecycle.

At its core, MOF is a collection of best practices, principles, and models. It provides direction on achieving reliability, availability, supportability, and manageability of mission-critical production systems by focusing on solutions and services that use Microsoft products and technologies. MOF extends ITIL by including guidance and best practices derived from the experience of Microsoft's internal operations groups, partners, and customers worldwide. MOF aligns with and builds on the ITSM practices documented within ITIL, thus enhancing the supportability built on Microsoft's products and technologies.

The authors recommend taking a new look at your ITIL processes to identify potentials for orchestration. You will gain valuable returns while ensuring that all processes are realized according to your ITIL definition—and you will save time on orchestrated actions.

Integration, Automation, Orchestration: The Differences

As an IT Pro, you might at some point face situations in which you need to do the following:

- Regularly check the availability of an application, server, or process
- Set up new servers, applications, file shares, and services

- React to an event in the system
- Verify that applications have run correctly, but lack the time to do so
- Respond to a call from a user on something that is not working as expected

This list just touches the surface of what regularly occurs in IT. This is just one place where integration, automation, and orchestration can help. If you have been exposed to marketing material on Orchestrator or its predecessor, Opalis Integration Server (OIS), you have probably heard these terms more than once. The next sections discuss these concepts and the differences in their approaches.

About Integration

The first step in saving time and ensuring efficiency, and also popularized by UNIX administrators, is using scripts. Instead of having to perform a sequence of tasks manually, you can use scripts to include those sequences in a single operation. You then launch a single command and check just one result—you can even ask your developers to create a special program to assist with this. A script also provides an audit trail of exactly what occurred so that you do not have to manually type commands or perform console clicks.

Here's an example of when incorporating a script is beneficial: launching a backup from the command line on different servers.

- You first write a script that takes the targeted server as a parameter and launches the backup with the appropriate parameters.
- You then write another script to launch this backup on all your servers.
- You can even script your processes so that applications stop before the backup and restart when the backup is complete, all backup files are moved to a remote location, monitoring stops and then restarts during the operation, and so on. Here you are integrating an entire process—involving different servers and applications—in a single command.

The popularity of scripting languages, particularly PowerShell, shows how efficient scripting is. Scripting is easy to access, requires few skills to get started, and is quick to implement. Not surprisingly, IT teams develop scripts dedicated to their activities at so-called silos, organized around server management, virtualization, network, database, and so on. These are known as inner-silo integration scripts. However, anyone who writes or uses scripts also knows that scripts bring their own challenges:

- Scripts are usually written for a specific purpose, so they do not take advantage of sharing and generalization.
- Scripts are frequently not documented or are under documented, making them difficult to maintain.

- Various people can write and exploit scripting in different ways and at different times, without centralized coordination or reporting required.
- Error checking is poorly implemented—errors typically are checked during execution, and manual corrections are made as necessary.
- Scripts frequently must be rewritten when applications change or new ones need to be added to the sequence.
- As processes evolve, script complexity grows and can become difficult to manage.

Although scripts are useful for starting integration and saving time on simple processes, they are difficult to manage over time and across teams. You need to connect these scripts across teams and silos.

As applied to System Center Orchestrator, integration is the connection created between Orchestrator and an integration service on the application or applications to be automated and orchestrated.

Using Automation

After you create task sequences (scripts or programs) to begin the integration process, automation is the second step. Automation enables these task sequences to be launched at the proper moment. Batch schedulers (known as CronTab in the UNIX world) typically handle this work. For every device you manage and system you maintain, there seem to be at least that many other solutions available to do the job. Keeping up with all this without automation can be challenging.

Schedulers enable you to launch a backup script at the proper time. Using the example of the backup task in the previous section, the batch scheduler lets you initiate a backup every Saturday night. Those batch schedulers are useful for daily routine procedures and give you flexibility in several areas:

- Launching your scripts at the correct time
- Launching scripts in response to different events, such as file creation/modification/deletion, process start/end, a new entry in the event log, and so on
- Launching one script when another has finished, enabling you to chain your scripts
- Managing central launches of all your scripts

However, difficulties remain in several areas:

- Managing scripts, evolutions, versioning, and so on
- Managing error checking

To address the general needs of running day-to-day routine procedures, most IT organizations incorporate batch schedulers. All teams (network, server, database, and such) plan their own operations to manage their services. These batch schedulers work well for all standard and routine procedures, but they lack the agility to evolve and dynamically answer to team or user requests. You would hardly align them in a cloud-oriented architecture!

Automation is the programmed execution of tasks within and between your applications. It involves processes such as BPA and ITPA.

About Orchestration

Because IT teams are organized by their specialty and responsibilities, they are usually seen as silos, as Figure 1.2 illustrates.

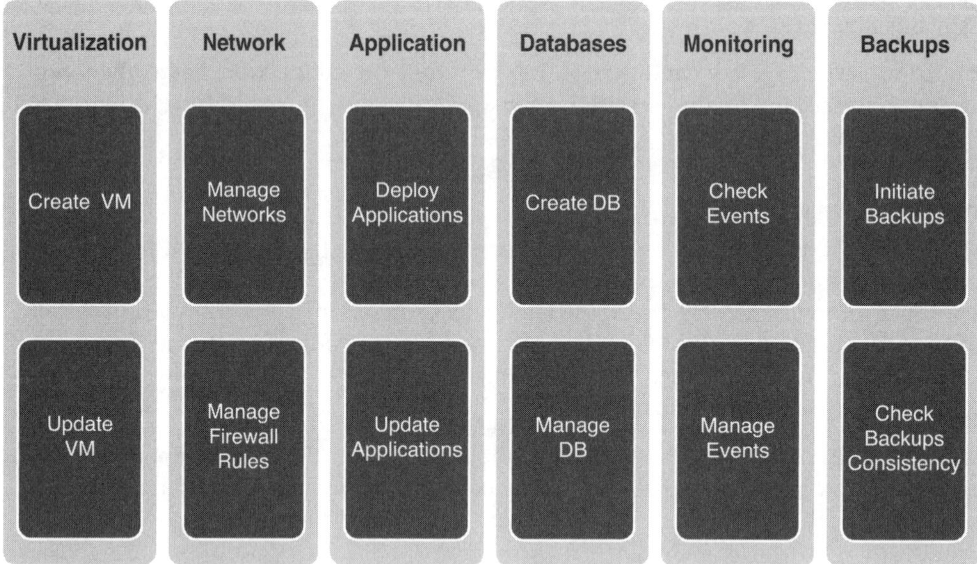

FIGURE 1.2 IT silos.

Here every team deals with its own business and has little communication with other teams. Processes are typically seen as inner-silo processes. This type of organization arises because every silo requires specific skills and specialists.

How would you deal with cross-silo processes in this organization? As a simple use case, consider the backup and reboot of an infrastructure dedicated to a specific web-oriented application. Here is the procedure:

- Stop monitoring.
- Create a temporary maintenance page for new users.

- Stop front-facing web servers and start backups.
- Stop application servers and start backups.
- Back up databases and then stop servers.
- Ensure that the backups occurred correctly, or raise an alarm.
- Restart the servers and applications in the right order (database, application, front ends).
- Check that each component is working properly.
- Restart monitoring.

Correctly completing this procedure requires dealing with many different teams and waiting for each team to develop its own process. The global procedure thus needs a considerable amount of time because of synchronization between teams—individuals from all teams must be available at the same time.

This is where orchestration helps, by organizing a full process across different silos and verifying that each step is complete before moving to the next. Orchestration is the external management of an application or applications. It can be thought of as the coordinator of a complex process, as Figure 1.3 shows. Orchestration ensures that all processes in different silos start at the correct time and behave as expected, and it conducts each process in the global process.

Benefits of Orchestration

Using orchestration, you can take your organization to a new level with the capabilities to do the following:

- Conduct evolved cross-silo routine procedures
- Analyze and react to root causes of specific events across silos
- Create user- or business-oriented services based on sophisticated interaction between applications
- Save manpower in conducting procedures
- Shorten delays because all steps are synchronized

Orchestration enables you to address IT management through global and business-meaningful processes, regardless of what they are involved with technically.

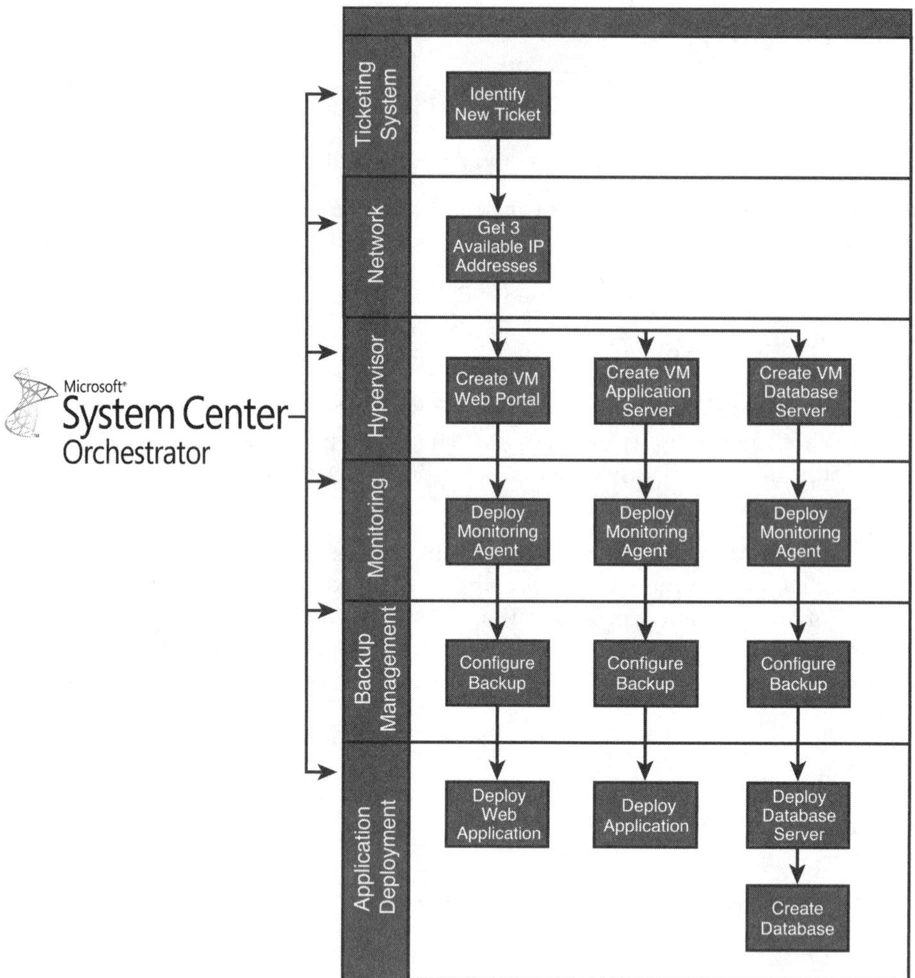

FIGURE 1.3 Orchestrating processes across silos.

What can you expect? The questions are always the same when you discover a new technology:

- What will it do for me?
- How easy is it to get access to this new technology?
- Is it worth it?

To help answer these questions, the next section discusses what you can expect from an orchestration project. Keep in mind that where your organization begins in its use of orchestration depends on a number of factors, including these:

- **Priorities:** These are your current issues and needs, along with your goals for the next several years.
- **Internal support skills:** Consider the state of your service or help desk.
- **ITIL implementation:** How far are you on the path to ITIL and how important is it to your organization? This includes policies for incident, change, and release management.

How Orchestration Can Help

You can expect four types of benefits from an orchestration project:

- **Improved process quality and consistency:** You can consistently provide your users with the correct delivery process. Quality and consistency are often issues when delivering a procedure to an IT team. People tend to adapt the procedure to their individual needs, habits, or availability.

  When modeled in System Center Orchestrator, all your processes are handled in the same exact manner. This ensures consistency across all instances of a certain process.

- **Reduced routine workload and higher level of expertise for your team:** As you automate processes, you remove associated work from your team. This lets team members orchestrate their day-to-day routine tasks to focus on items of more value, such as event analysis, complex scenarios, new procedures, and runbook development.

- **Reduced delays of delivery to service requests:** Delays can be reduced in two areas:

  - **Capability to quickly consider a user request:** After an IT service is orchestrated, it can start processing user requests immediately and without waiting for someone to be available to address them. This means that the service can start as soon as a request is identified and mandatory resources are available.

  - **Synchronicity of all actions across silos:** In a classical human delivery model, delays arise between the time one team finishes its part of the job and the time the next team in the next silo begins its part.

  With tasks orchestrated, actions in all silos start synchronously. When the first series of tasks completes, the next set initiates. This ensures that the entire scenario is completed with the shortest possible delays, and without waiting between steps.

- **Capability to move to high request volumes and cloud compliancy:** When moving to automated service delivery, especially for cloud services, user requests increase dramatically. You cannot expect to manage these manually using a traditional approach. With orchestration, requests are addressed as soon as they occur or as soon as Information Systems can address them.

  At some point, you might face 10,000 user requests, yet your Information Systems group can handle only 100 concurrently. With orchestrated processes, you can narrow the number of requests treated in parallel to the maximum your infrastructure can handle.

What Not to Expect with Orchestration

As discussed in the previous section, you can expect much from orchestration in all IT operations and cloud services. However, do not expect that starting an orchestration project or using System Center 2012 Orchestrator will deliver instant nirvana:

- Orchestrator does not define your processes. This is the first challenge you face after you decide to orchestrate your processes: Running Orchestrator does not instantly give you orchestrated processes.

  Processes, day-to-day operations, and IT services are your responsibility. System Center Orchestrator does not know anything about these areas and does not provide a methodology to organize them. It merely gives you the opportunity to automate and orchestrate those processes.

  This means that an orchestration project and a good implementation require you to understand your processes, define synchronization between tasks/steps, and check that these behave as expected.

- Orchestrator does not natively orchestrate everything. After seeing the integrated features, which are easy to use through a simple graphical interface, people might expect that they will find Orchestrator activities for everything. That is not the case.

  Activities in Orchestrator are interfaces to different systems, such as supervisory tools, configuration management, virtualization, databases, and enterprise resource planning (ERP) software. Although the System Center Orchestrator community is growing and is developing many integration packs (IPs) to extend Orchestrator functionality, third-party software organizations such as Hewlett-Packard and BMC Software must develop Orchestrator interfaces to their software.

  Connections exist to work with Microsoft management systems, such as all System Center 2012 components. Still needed are new and up-to-date interfaces to integrate with other recognized and widely implemented solutions such as HP OVO, BMC Remedy, and Nagios.

  Meanwhile, web services, PowerShell, and the command line are there to help you integrate your existing environment. You might even consider developing your own integration packs incorporating those commands.

Positioning of Orchestrator in System Center 2012

System Center, a brand name for Microsoft's management platform, represents a means to integrate system management tools and technologies to help you with systems operations, troubleshooting, and planning.

The System Center 2012 product includes Operations Manager, Configuration Manager, Virtual Machine Manager, Service Manager, Data Protection Manager, Orchestrator, Endpoint Protection, App Controller, and Advisor. System Center Advisor, now offered at no additional cost to users of Microsoft server products, offers configuration-monitoring cloud services for Microsoft SQL Server, SharePoint, Exchange, Lync Server, and Windows

Server deployments; expect the list of monitored products to continue to grow. Microsoft's System Center 2012 cloud and data center solutions provide a common management toolset for your private and public cloud applications and services to help you deliver IT as a service to your business.

System Center builds on Microsoft's Dynamic Systems Initiative (DSI), which is designed to deliver simplicity, automation, and flexibility in the data center across the IT environment. Microsoft System Center components share the following DSI-based characteristics:

- Ease of use and deployment
- Based on industry and customer knowledge
- Scalability (both up to the largest enterprises and down to the smallest organizations)

Figure 1.4 illustrates the relationship between the System Center 2012 components and MOF.

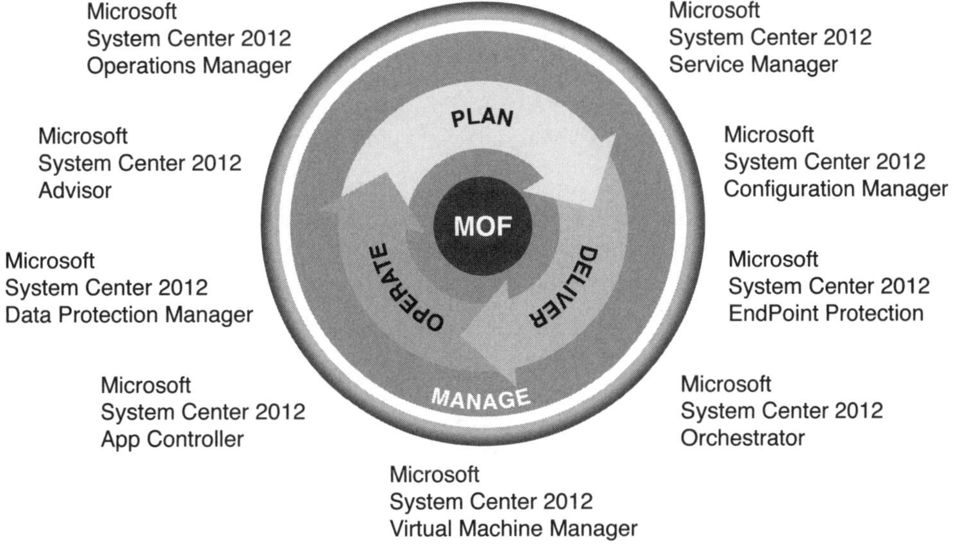

FIGURE 1.4 MOF with System Center components.

Orchestrator, the runbook automation component and the "glue" of System Center 2012, plays a central role in System Center, as Figure 1.5 shows. The right side of the figure shows the IT team, with the well-known System Center components: Virtual Machine Manager, Operations Manager, Configuration Manager, and Data Protection Manager. These are the typical tools you use to manage your infrastructure, whether it is physical, virtual, or already in a private or public cloud. Orchestrator is a powerful support tool for these IT teams because it helps in deploying and configuring, or supervising and administrating, the infrastructure.

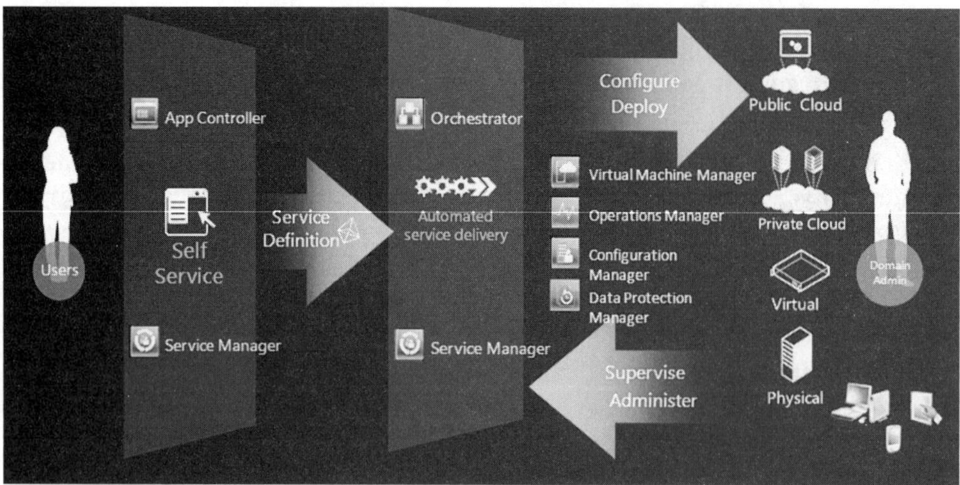

FIGURE 1.5 Orchestrator's role in System Center.

Orchestrator can be a great tool to automate all your IT configurations and deployments, such as when performing virtual machine (VM) creation and network integration; creating user accounts in Active Directory, Exchange, and third-party applications; or, depending on your infrastructure usage, moving a VM to a private cloud.

For operations, Orchestrator helps you supervise and administer your infrastructure. As an example, if all nodes from a SharePoint cluster are at about 80% utilization, you can use Orchestrator to create and integrate a new VM in the cluster. Orchestrator can also help you perform a server reboot by moving the target server to Operations Manager maintenance mode, protecting your SLA obligations before disconnecting users, starting a backup, and then restarting the server.

Integration with Service Manager becomes effortless as well. In fact, after your IT deployment and configuration processes are orchestrated, you can expose them to your entire IT team through a service catalog. You can easily set up this service catalog in Service Manager, which uses the System Center Service Manager IP to initiate the correct processes within Orchestrator. You can then take advantage of the entire service request lifecycle management within Service Manager. Orchestrator can update a request as closed if delivery or configuration was successful or, in case of errors, escalate the request to your team.

After your standard delivery and configuration processes are orchestrated and exposed, the next logical step is to expose those services to your users. Service Manager hides the technical complexity for users; you need to follow up on requests only when errors occur. This lets you offer services to your users at any time, without having to hire new people and manage them across time zones.

This architecture enables you to deliver those services to your users without day-to-day incremental work for your team, providing a high level of quality with very short delays.

You can even get statistics on the number of requests from your users, average delivery delays, and so on. This is a very modern way to manage IT services and align them to business needs.

Finally, App Controller enables you to publish an application in a cloud environment, particularly Windows Azure, and obtain a global view about all related resources, wherever they are in the cloud or on your own IT environment.

Orchestrator plays a central role in System Center: It organizes and synchronizes all operations based on user requests, as well as events in your IT system. System Center Orchestrator helps you deliver the right service, with the shortest delay to your users, while also dramatically reducing the workload for your team.

Typical Use Cases

Orchestration can accomplish a lot, but as with anything new in your IT toolbox, you must determine where to start. Figure 1.6 shows typical use cases you can implement in your organization to begin orchestration. The next sections discuss them in more detail.

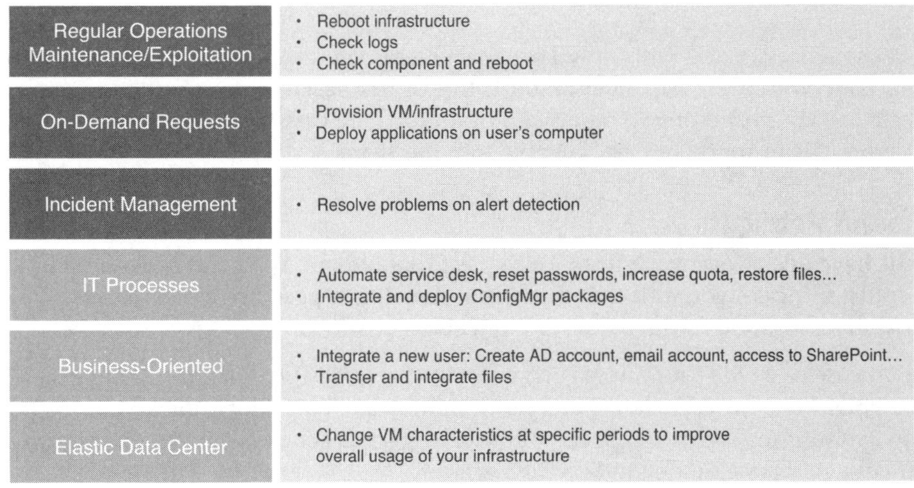

FIGURE 1.6 Typical use cases for System Center Orchestrator.

Regular Maintenance and Daily Operations

IT requires regular performance of many operations to maintain healthy and efficient IT systems. These operations include deleting old temporary files, reindexing databases, and so on. To save time, you can easily create runbooks that will perform those operations for you at the proper time.

A typical example is an application infrastructure reboot that does the following:

- Waits for a maintenance period
- Sets servers in maintenance mode
- Disables new user connections
- Disconnects all connected users
- Shuts down front-end servers
- Starts application server backups and ensures backup integrity
- Shuts down application servers
- Starts database server backups and ensures backup integrity
- Reboots database servers
- Starts application and then front-end servers
- Checks that the application is running correctly
- Re-enables user connections
- Takes servers out of maintenance mode

Because those processes deal with only IT management, you can define them easily with your team. The production implementation is free of risk because processes are triggered and reported to your team only. These types of projects are easy to accomplish with System Center Orchestrator and are valuable for your team.

On-Demand Requests

You might have operations to perform on request that are not as regular as your daily operations. In this case, you wait for an external signal to trigger a complex process. You typically need to respond to the request as quickly as possible.

This could be delivery of IT resources such as VMs, shares, restore operations, application deployment, a new server in a Configuration Manager collection, and so on. In these cases, you can wait for events to appear and then trigger runbooks yourself, or you can expose them as a service catalog in Service Manager.

Incident Management

Incidents differ from problems from an ITIL viewpoint because you know how to recognize them and then respond to them. Even better, you can easily create runbooks that check your systems for events related to an incident. This is accomplished using logs or Windows event log checking, events in Operations Manager, and so on. You can even correlate events from different sources to identify an incident. When an incident is identified, you can automate corrective actions such as restarting an application or a service, deleting temporary files, and such.

You can extend this principle of analysis and corrective action to any type of event and corrective action, particularly if you need to interact with different systems.

IT Process Automation

IT process automation typically consists of requests from users to IT teams. You can identify them easily with a service desk team through an analysis of user requests. Here are some examples:

- Unlock a user account
- Reset a password
- Increase disk quota
- Restore a file from a backup
- Deploy an application on a user computer

Here automation can save your team a considerable amount of time and help deliver user services more efficiently.

Business-Oriented Processes Automation

Those processes are extensions of IT processes and focus on the organization's activity. Here you are looking for increases in company productivity rather than IT increases in efficiency.

This could be all the tasks necessary to set up a new user: creating an AD account, creating an Exchange account, setting up a storage resource in the data center nearest where the user will be located, providing access to SharePoint folders based on the user's job, and so on. In addition, you must delete all the user's accesses when he or she leaves the organization.

Your company could have orders coming from different stores worldwide. Order integrity can be checked using a specific tool. After validating, you can pass the order to another application that integrates all orders in your production system. These types of applications can be quite useful if your company has many offices worldwide. You simply ensure that all orders or information are treated exactly the same, regardless of where they come from. Alternatively, you can imagine delivering information or triggering operations to many remote locations.

Elastic Data Center

Increasing the size of your data center is generally easy, from a technical point of view (although not necessarily in terms of budget). However, you might be able to better utilize resources by provisioning them when needed and releasing them when they are no longer required.

For example, in a data center, some servers are frequently used during peak times and other servers are used only in nonpeak periods. Using Orchestrator, you can reduce virtual

CPUs and memory during nonpeak times and increase those resources during peak times. This lets you adjust your data center usage more efficiently, based on resources needed at certain times.

Managing a Project

Beyond any typical use cases, it is important for you is to be able to identify projects within your organization and orchestrate them. Four key steps can make your orchestration process a success. Figure 1.7 displays these steps, and the following sections cover them in more detail.

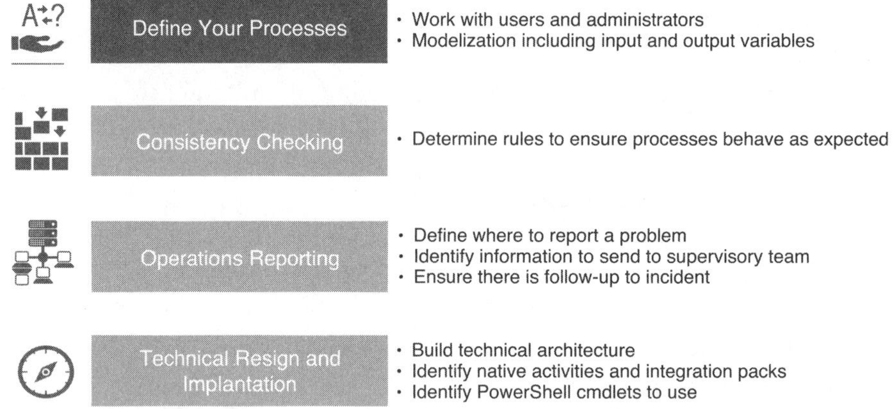

FIGURE 1.7 Steps in an Orchestrator project.

Define Your Processes

You first must reach an agreement with your users on the service you will deliver. What is the purpose of your process? Will it improve quality of your delivery, reduce delays for users, and/or save you time? Remember that you are targeting users' processes, meaning that you must deliver the service they expect; otherwise, your orchestration will be useless.

After identifying your process, describe it. Include all the steps and interactions with infrastructure, applications, and so on. Then define inputs needed from users and results, as well as feedback to send them. Microsoft Visio can be a very useful tool for this task.

Even if you are comfortable with what you want to orchestrate, the authors encourage you to describe the process to identify interactions with users as well as your team. For example, VM generation is a simple process, but integrating the VM with the right task sequence and according to business usage is more complex.

Consistency Checking

For every process, determine how to ensure that it is executed correctly. In this step, you reproduce what people working in teams are doing: One person executes an operation, and another team member checks the operation's results.

For instance, you can check execution details of your process, such as whether the VM you created has the expected number of virtual processors, memory, and hard drives. Another example is checking the number of files a program generates. When sharing files between systems, check the number of files to transfer from one location to another and the associated amount of data.

Report on Operations

Now that you have identified rules to ensure that your process has executed, consider whether the results are as expected. You must report this fact to the appropriate person or team. A series of simple questions can help determine this:

- What should be reported? All execution details? Only warnings and errors?
- Who should be warned? User, supervision team, application team, someone else?
- What contextual information must be sent to understand what is occurring?
- How do you ensure follow-up for errors?

Technical Implementation

At this point, your process is well defined, you are able to describe the rules to identify a correct behavior or an unexpected one, and you know how to send warnings/alarms if problems arise. You can now implement your process within Orchestrator. This book helps you do so in the right manner with, for example, Chapter 9, "Standard Activities," and Chapter 13, "Integration with System Center Operations Manager" through Chapter 18, "Integration with Windows Azure," is your reference to interact with all System Center components and Windows Azure. Chapter 12, "Orchestrator Integration Packs," introduces you to other activities available through the other available IPs, extending the standard activities available in System Center Orchestrator.

Example: Orchestrating a VM Deployment

The example in this section demonstrates the different steps in orchestrating a process. In this example, a virtual machine is created and configured upon user request.

Figure 1.8 describes the process details of delivering this VM with roles defined in the user request and ensuring that all elements are up-to-date and configured as expected. Here's how it works:

- A user request in Service Manager triggers the process. After the request is validated, the information is stored and Orchestrator can identify this request later (such as at night, when less activity occurs).

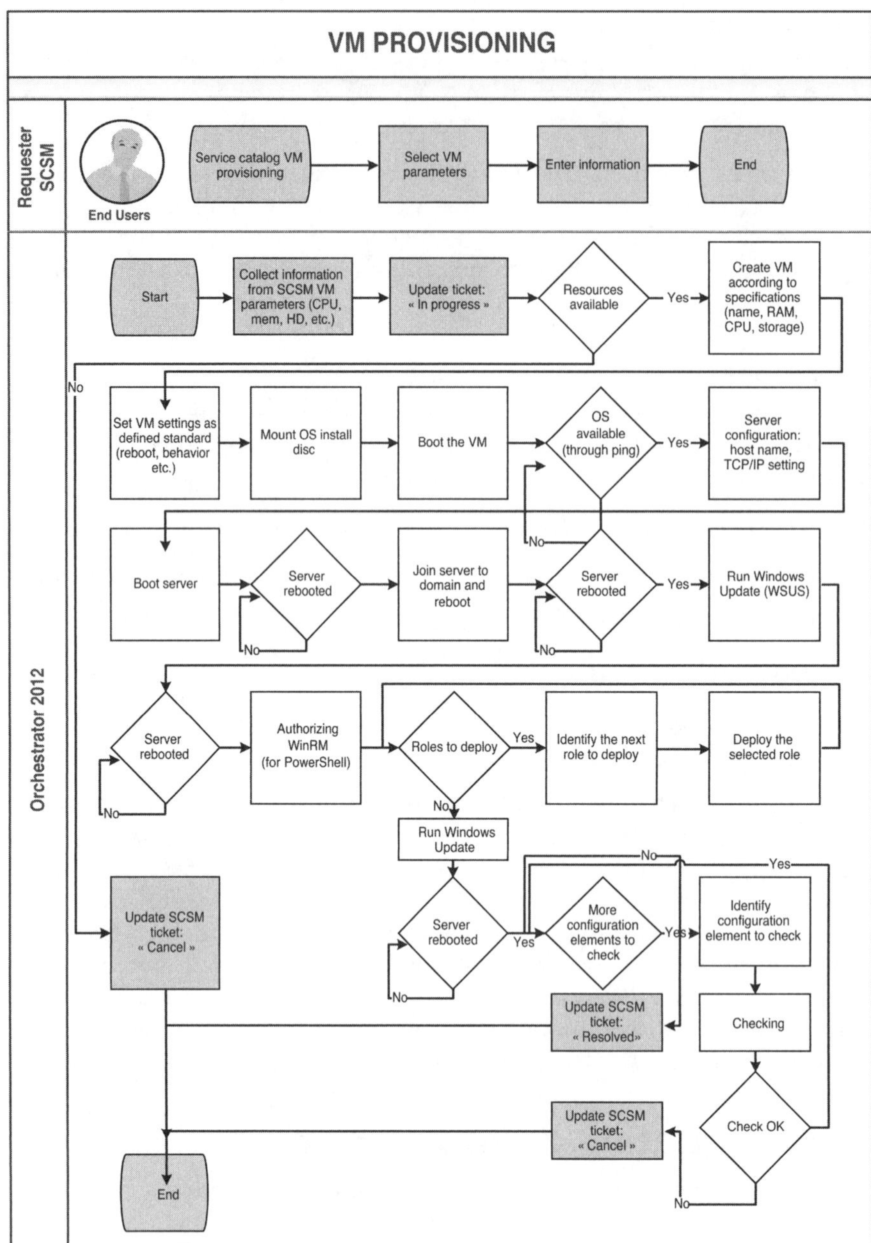

FIGURE 1.8 VM delivery process.

- Before creating anything, the Orchestrator process checks whether resources are available to create the machine, particularly whether enough storage is available.
    - If resources are available, the VM is created within Virtual Machine Manager (or any virtualization software) with the requested parameters (CPU, memory,

disk size, and other specifications). The OS install disk is mounted, and the VM is booted.

- If resources are insufficient, the Service Manager ticket is updated to Cancel status.

- When the server answers to a ping request, it is considered available and its server configuration can be updated. After a new reboot, the server can join a target production domain. After the domain join, the server is rebooted again and WinRM is authorized, enabling you to remotely run PowerShell on the VM.

  Roles can now be deployed and configured using PowerShell commands from System Center Orchestrator. After all roles are deployed, another Windows update is performed through Windows Software Update Services (WSUS).

- When all configuration actions are completed, the last part of the process is to confirm that everything is configured as expected. If this is the case, the ticket status is updated to Resolved; otherwise, it updates to Cancel.

This process shows that many operations surround the creation of a simple VM to manage the correct configuration of roles and integration in your network and domain. Based on your security rules, you might have even more steps.

Here's how this can be translated to Orchestrator runbooks:

As Figure 1.9 shows, the overall process is rather short and triggers different runbooks (Resources Available, Create VM-Server, Roles to Deploy, DNS Roles to Deploy, Hyper-V Roles to Deploy, AD Domain Server Roles, Configuration Check) to execute complex technical operations. Those runbooks can be considered as procedures.

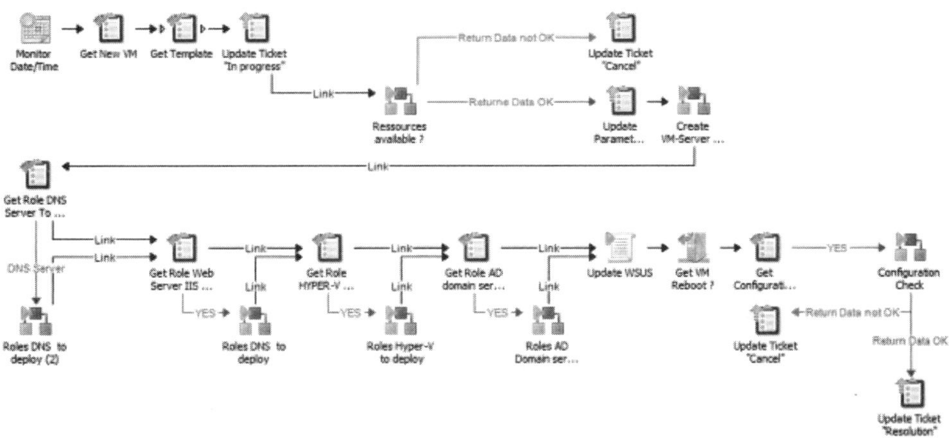

FIGURE 1.9 Runbook showing overall VM delivery process.

The process in Figure 1.10 checks whether enough space is available on any of the virtualization host data stores and returns the correct store to use. If space is insufficient, the return value is zero and the global VM Delivery process stops.

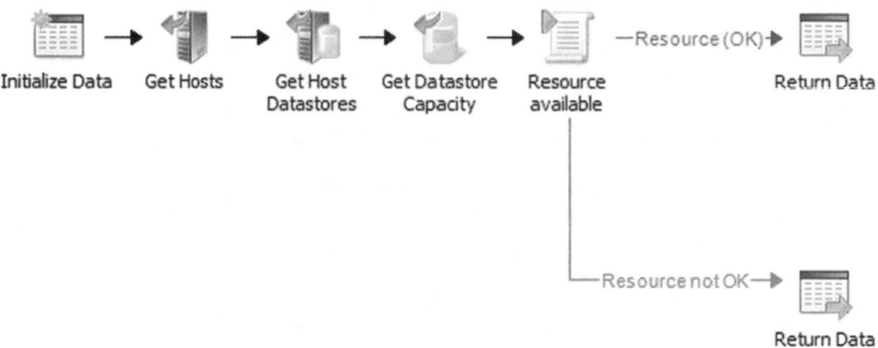

FIGURE 1.10 Check whether enough storage is available.

Figure 1.11 shows the runbook creating a new VM from a template. After this VM is created, it starts and the network configuration is updated. The next step is to join the server on the right domain, which is validated by a system reboot. The system is then updated through WSUS before WinRM is authorized (enabling PowerShell execution remotely).

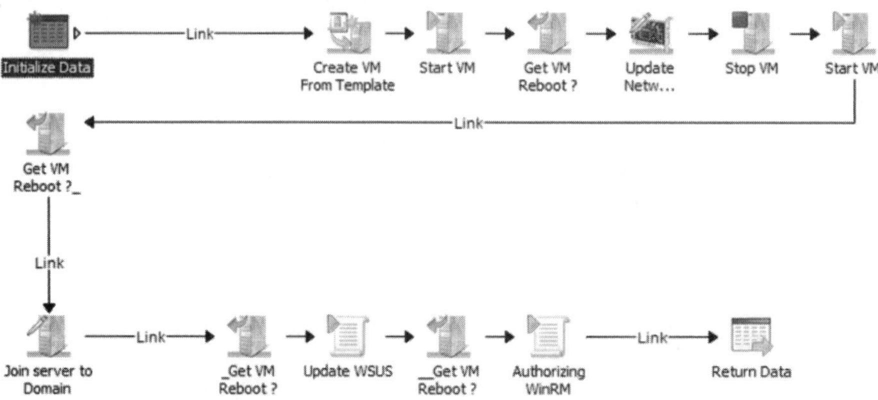

FIGURE 1.11 Create and update the virtual machine.

The VM is now up-to-date, in the correct domain and network, ready to accept PowerShell commands. Deployment of a new role on the server is straightforward, as Figure 1.12 describes. The role to deploy is passed as a parameter to the **Initialize Data** activity. This parameter is used in the PowerShell Deploy Select Role script that actually activates the role. The request ticket is then updated to reflect that the role has been created as requested on the server.

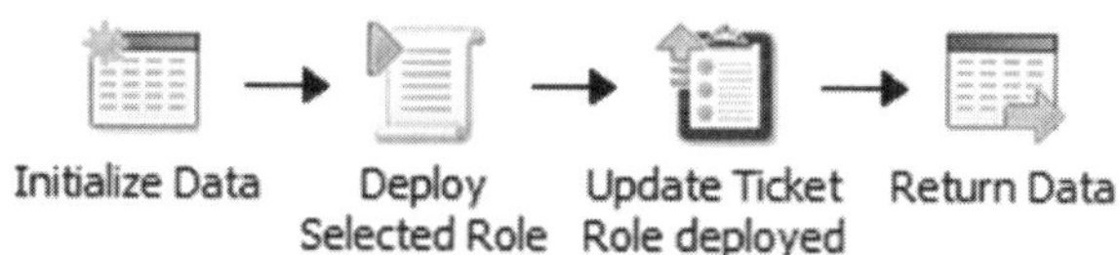

FIGURE 1.12 Roles deployment on the server.

A series of checks is performed on the VM to ensure that the configuration is as expected, as Figure 1.13 shows. This runbook then returns a status to the global process.

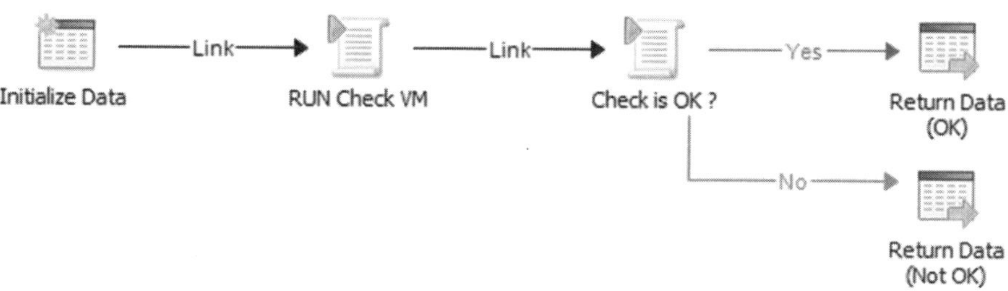

FIGURE 1.13 Check that VM configuration is as expected.

Summary

A System Center Orchestrator project can present great opportunities to improve and stabilize the quality of service of your team and improve responsiveness to user requests.

Here's what you can expect by using Orchestrator:

- Increased stability in your operations, with reduced errors
- Improved productivity through delegated operations to System Center Orchestrator
- Shortened delays for delivery because process are executed without waiting between operations, as with a traditional approach and teams

From an organizational prospective, Orchestrator projects require that you have a global view of IT operations and how different IT teams execute these operations.

This chapter introduced System Center Orchestrator, the integration, automation, and orchestration component of System Center 2012. The next chapter discusses changes in this release.

CHAPTER 2

What's New in System Center 2012 Orchestrator

IN THIS CHAPTER

- The History of Orchestrator
- OIS 6.3 Versus Orchestrator 2012

In its second major release since its acquisition by Microsoft, Orchestrator (previously known as Opalis Integration Server, or OIS) has completed its assimilation into System Center. Chapter 1, "Orchestration, Integration, and Automation," introduced the concepts behind run book automation (RBA), business process automation (BPA), IT process automation (ITPA), and Orchestrator. This chapter focuses on changes to Orchestrator in System Center 2012. If you have an OIS 6.3 background, reading this chapter can provide a smooth transition to understanding this System Center component. The chapter covers technology changes and discusses how Microsoft's rebranding affects Orchestrator's position in System Center. This chapter also provides a brief overview of the history of Orchestrator.

As the first version developed entirely by Microsoft, System Center 2012 Orchestrator has the benefit of the rigorous testing and code standards placed on all Microsoft products. In addition, it has the benefit of several years of experience with customers implementing OIS into their data centers; Microsoft has taken that feedback and fed it into product development. Although the user interfaces for Orchestrator are similar to the previous version, they have received a facelift along the lines of the rest of the System Center components, providing a consistent look and feel across the product.

The underlying theme is that even though Orchestrator appears different and has a new name, the technologies, concepts, and processes underneath essentially remain the same. In fact, this version further emphasizes the features and benefits of OIS 6.3. Integration is still what Orchestrator is about, and it continues to offer the same robust workflow engine. If you used the last release of OIS, System Center 2012 Orchestrator will be a familiar experience. With that said, you will encounter some key terminology changes, new software and hardware prerequisites, several dropped features, and a brand-new Orchestration console.

The History of Orchestrator

Orchestrator has had a relatively short life in the hands of Microsoft, but its predecessors by Opalis Software, Inc., hit the shelves more than a decade ago. Opalis Software enjoyed a successful run, and its history includes a number of milestone developments that helped shape what Orchestrator is today. Even in the first release of the OpalisRobot product, the company approached automation differently from the rest of the world. Simply scheduling jobs was not enough; the real value was in being able to monitor for certain events and use those to trigger an action. By combining low-level task automation with the capability to integrate heterogeneous tools, people, and processes, Opalis enabled much more consistent and reliable automation. This concept came to be known more formally as IT process automation. The following sections look at how Orchestrator came to be and examine the advancements Microsoft has made since the 2009 acquisition.

The Beginnings of Orchestrator: OpalisRobot

Orchestrator started life in 1995 as a program called OpalisRobot; Figure 2.1 shows the Opalis logo. As OpalisRobot evolved over the next decade, it became clear it had an important differentiating feature over its competitors: Whereas other products were essentially task schedulers, OpalisRobot incorporated monitors and triggers. The idea was not only to schedule automated tasks, but also to dynamically identify and respond to specific events in your environment. This enabled administrators to build truly self-healing systems and applications. This concept was a precursor to runbook automation, and it is still very much at the core of Orchestrator today.

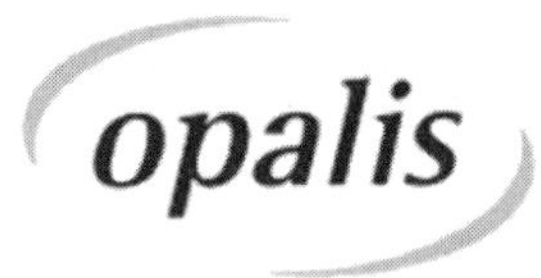

FIGURE 2.1 Opalis logo.

OpalisRendezVous

OpalisRobot was not the only product Opalis Software developed and produced. The company also sold OpalisRendezVous, which provided a graphical user interface (GUI) for transferring files over FTP, file shares, and databases. This product offered a unique "when, what, where" configuration that enabled administrators to control the flow of file distribution, ultimately allowing a company to move quickly from a manual to an automated process. Again, simplicity of use was an underlying principle that made OpalisRendezVous such a useful and popular product. Figure 2.2 shows the OpalisRendezVous interface.

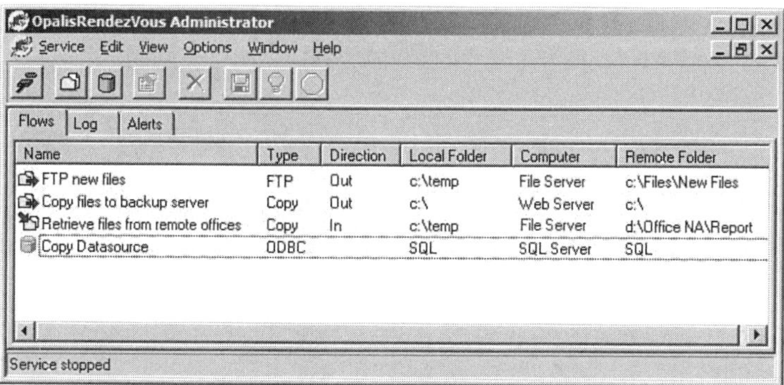

FIGURE 2.2 OpalisRendezVous user interface.

Opalis Innovates

OpalisRobot 3.0 was released in 1997, bringing one of the most important innovations to the product line with the world's first drag-and-drop design interface for workflows. This was an important development because it marked a key concept that exists in current System Center products: simplicity. Ease of operation and administration has been an important theme throughout all System Center components.

A year later, Opalis released a set of add-ons for email and computer telephony integration. These add-ons, today called *integration packs* (IPs), facilitated the addition of activities to the set of out-of-the-box activities shipping with the product. Over the years, Opalis fostered a community of independent developers to create open source IPs that enable the product to automate tasks within many other systems. These IPs changed the perception of OIS from an ITPA tool separate from the rest of the data center to that of a platform resting beneath all the tools and processes in the data center.

This important distinction led to what is now known as the Orchestrator Integration Toolkit. It enables developers to integrate Orchestrator with virtually every other application, regardless of manufacturer, through those other applications' exposed integration surfaces, such as application programming interfaces (APIs), command-line interfaces (CLIs), and databases.

Microsoft currently offers more than a dozen supported IPs for both Microsoft and other vendor applications, such as VMware vSphere and HP Service Manager. Dozens more are available through open source community developers.

OpalisRobot 4.0, released in 2002, was the last release under the OpalisRobot brand. This final release brought a new user interface (see Figure 2.3), some bug fixes, and additional standard automation objects. This release was also the first with support on Linux and Solaris; however, support on non-Microsoft platforms ceased with 4.0 and did not carry forward to later versions of the product.

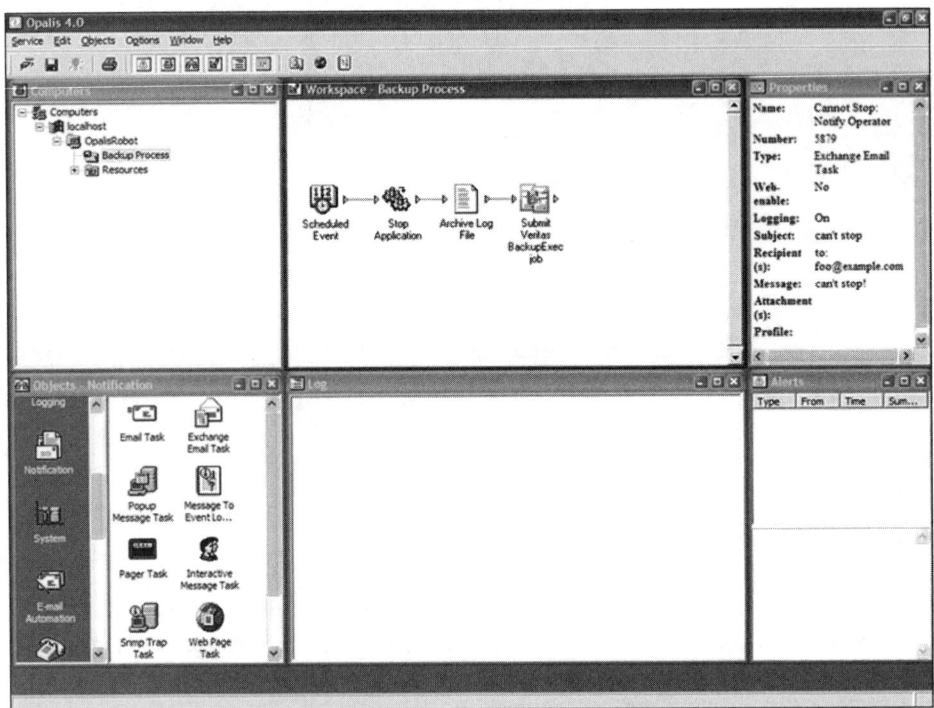

FIGURE 2.3 OpalisRobot 4.0 interface.

Goodbye Robot, Hello OIS

By the early 2000s, it became clear that although Opalis Software clearly understood where it needed to fit into runbook automation and ITPA, OpalisRobot had outgrown its architecture; it was time for a major rewrite of the underlying technology. Opalis retired its RendezVous and Robot product lines and planted its position firmly in the ITPA space. Fundamentally, this was a shift in focus, from developing better runbook activities to providing a better integration platform. New integration packs (then called connector access packs) were released to support this positioning, which included integration into Microsoft Operations Manager.

As part of this new positioning, Opalis rebranded its new automation software as Opalis Integration Server and released OIS 5.0 in 2005. OIS 5.0 brought a round of significant improvements, including the use of an industry-standard relational database management system on the back end, dashboards, improved scalability, and Active Directory integration. The marriage of the administrator-friendly interface, the IP approach, and the new architecture allowed OIS to take its seat as a true ITPA tool, allowing automation of activities to occur across systems and processes.

Issues with the redesigned architecture became evident over the following months, as often occurs with newly released software. Opalis made several incremental improvements to the 5.x release, and those ultimately led to the development of a new workflow engine, called *pipeline mode*. Pipeline mode changed how data was passed between objects, facilitating new capabilities such as embedded looping and the capability to flatten published data. The old workflow engine, referred to as *legacy mode*, remained available until the System Center 2012 Orchestrator release. A final round of minor changes brought about the last major release of OIS with version 6.0.

Microsoft's Acquisition of Opalis Software

Microsoft, having identified a requirement to bolster its line of data center management tools with an ITPA solution, acquired Opalis Software in December 2009. The terms of the acquisition included a final release of OIS for Microsoft that removed any unacceptable features, such as the Java-based prerequisite of the OIS Operator Console displayed in Figure 2.4. For legal reasons, Microsoft would not distribute the open source software required for the Operator Console. However, the console itself was still available and supported until Orchestrator was released as part of System Center 2012 in April 2013.

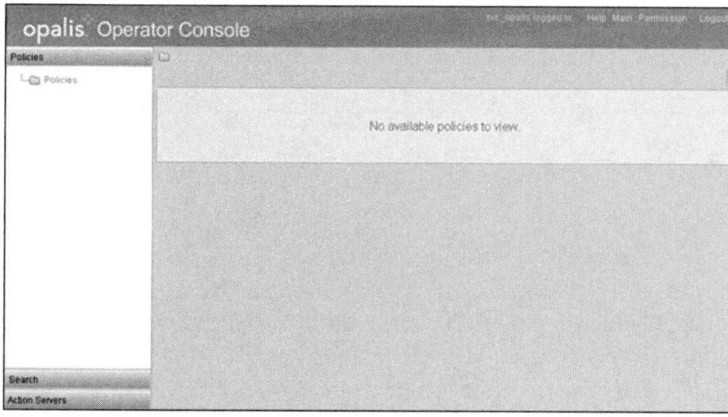

FIGURE 2.4 OIS Operator console.

NOTE: EXISTING CUSTOMER CONSIDERATIONS POST-ACQUISITION

When Microsoft incorporated OIS into its existing System Center licensing, it offered a grant of Server Management Suite Datacenter (SMSD) licenses to existing customers to the monetary equivalent of their lifetime purchases with Opalis Software, as long as they purchased a two-year Software Assurance contract. Opalis Integration Server was the only product Opalis Software offered at the time of the acquisition, so Microsoft continued development of all Opalis software products. The Opalis Dashboard, sold by Opalis Software but developed by Altosoft, was available directly from Altosoft for a period of time, but it has since been discontinued.

Microsoft positioned the Opalis software under System Center. Version 6.3, which was the final update to OIS, included support for OIS on Windows Server 2008 and the OIS Client on Windows 7, and a set of IPs for System Center. Figure 2.5 shows the OIS 6.3 Client.

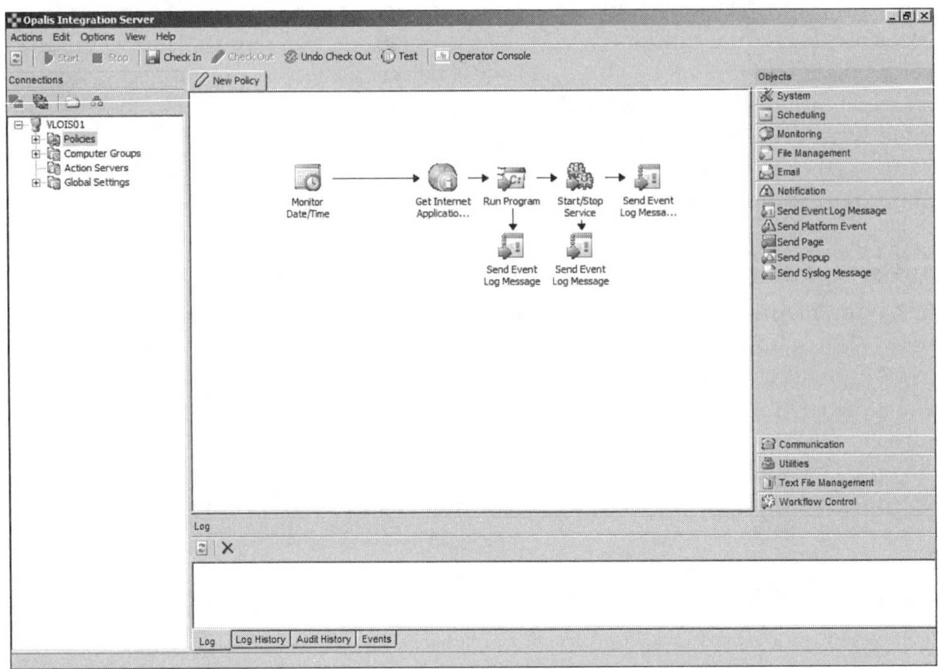

FIGURE 2.5 OIS 6.3 Client.

OIS to Orchestrator

Microsoft announced the rebranding of Orchestrator in March 2011 at the Microsoft Management Summit in Las Vegas. Officially called System Center 2012 Orchestrator, this is the first major release developed wholly by Microsoft. As such, the functionality is migrated into a Microsoft codebase. This means that Orchestrator is now subject to the same rigorous design and testing cycles as the rest of the Microsoft products.

With the System Center 2012 release, OIS 6.3 was no longer available as a standalone download, but Microsoft provided support of the product for an additional 12 months. The company also honored existing support agreements with customers.

Orchestrator brings a series of improvements, including these:

- ▶ Bug fixes
- ▶ Terminology changes
- ▶ A new Orchestration console
- ▶ Updated integration packs
- ▶ A new installer

NOTE: NEW WITH ORCHESTRATOR 2012 SERVICE PACK 1 AND R2

System Center 2012 Service Pack 1 changes to Orchestrator include:

- New integration packs (Exchange Administrator, Exchange Users, FTP, and Representational State Transfer, or REST)
- Updates to the Active Directory, HP Service Manager, VMware vSphere, System Center 2012 Operations Manager, and System Center Virtual Machine Manager 2012 integration packs
- Support for the Windows Server 2012 and SQL Server 2012 platforms

See http://technet.microsoft.com/en-us/library/jj614522.aspx for information.

Changes to Orchestrator in System Center 2012 R2, in pre-release when this book was printed and documented at http://technet.microsoft.com/en-us/library/dn251064.aspx, include:

- Support for Windows Server 2012 R2
- Changes to the installation program to install the Service Management Automation web service and up to three runbook workers
- A SharePoint integration pack
- Updates to the Windows Azure and Virtual Machine Manager 2012 IPs

OIS Migration to Orchestrator

You cannot upgrade OIS to Orchestrator, but you can migrate existing OIS 6.3 policies to Orchestrator 2012. Some of the standard activities have changed, so you might need to adjust your runbooks after migrating them from OIS 6.3. Chapter 5, "Installing System Center 2012 Orchestrator," covers Opalis migration in detail.

Where Orchestrator Fits into System Center

Microsoft has positioned System Center 2012 as a single product with multiple components rather than individual applications, which is representative of the way the tools interact with each other. The components have a high level of integration, and Orchestrator is key to that integration. This integration also reflects the license options: System Center 2012 has a single SKU with an option to purchase either licenses per virtual machine (VM) or an unlimited VM enterprise license. Figure 2.6 illustrates the relationships among the different System Center components.

Microsoft built System Center 2012 to manage on-premise, private cloud, and public cloud data centers. Each component provides a platform; on top is a set of solutions that fulfill those management needs. Here is a description of each component—see http://technet.microsoft.com/en-us/library/hh546785.aspx for additional information:

- **App Controller:** Enables template-based deployment of services and virtual machines to private clouds via Virtual Machine Manager and public clouds using Windows Azure.

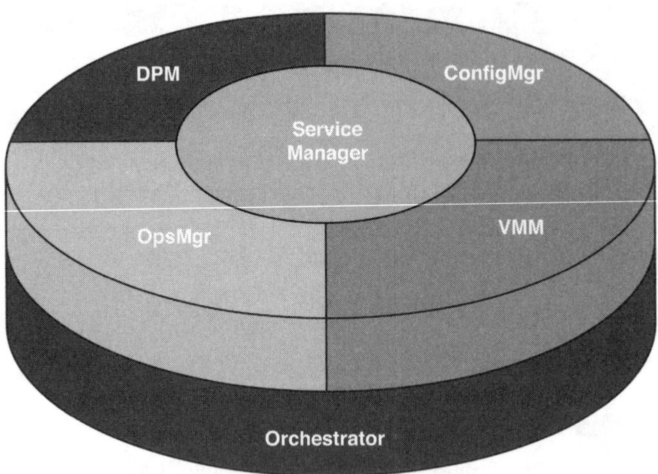

FIGURE 2.6 IT management as a platform.

- **Configuration Manager:** Provides a comprehensive configuration management solution for the Microsoft platform. This component features application delivery, operating system deployment, desktop virtualization, device management, compliance monitoring and remediation, hardware monitoring, and software inventory capability.
- **Endpoint Protection:** Endpoint Protection is built on the Configuration Manager platform and provides antimalware and security solutions. Because it shares its infrastructure with Configuration Manager, you can consolidate endpoint protection and management.
- **Data Protection Manager (DPM):** DPM is a centralized backup solution that features near-continuous backup. It enables rapid and reliable recovery of a Windows environment, including Windows servers and desktops, SQL Server, Exchange Server, and SharePoint.
- **Operations Manager:** Provides an infrastructure management solution that delivers comprehensive health and performance monitoring and alerting to drive performance and availability for data center and cloud-based applications.
- **Orchestrator:** Enables the automated delivery of IT services through a simple user interface that is built for information technology (IT) administrators. Orchestrator enables automation across a heterogeneous datacenter.
- **Service Manager:** Provides a platform for managing Microsoft Operations Framework (MOF) and IT Information Library (ITIL)–based service management processes. These include incident management, request fulfillment, problem management, change management, and release management. Those processes are automated through integration with companion System Center 2012 components.

- **Virtual Machine Manager (VMM):** VMM is a virtual infrastructure management solution for provisioning and centrally managing host, network, and storage resources that support datacenter, private, and public cloud environments.

Orchestrator is unique, in that it does not provide a solution to any problem; it provides a platform and set of activities to enable administrators to generate their own solutions to unlimited problems. Often the question with Orchestrator is not whether you *can* automate something, but whether you *should* automate it. Automation clearly has many benefits, but a certain level of planning must go into the design and creation of runbooks. The good news is that Orchestrator simplifies this process with its user-friendly Runbook Designer.

Orchestrator shines particularly well in the following areas:

- Automation in the data center
- Service delivery and automation
- Creation of self-healing systems

The best way to think of Orchestrator is not as an additional component hanging off the end of the rest of System Center, but one sitting beneath the rest of the components that can read, interact with, and pass data among the various APIs to act as a point of integration. In this way, Orchestrator doesn't necessarily need to action all the automation, but it can act as a puppet master that enables other applications to execute the automation.

OIS 6.3 Versus Orchestrator 2012

On the surface, certain areas of Orchestrator 2012 appear to differ greatly from the OIS 6.3 release, but the underlying concepts and processes remain relatively the same. All user interfaces have had facelifts, and the OIS Operator Console has been completely rebuilt from scratch.

The next sections discuss these changes and include a brief overview of the features that were improved or rebuilt. Additional detail about each of these features and their uses and configuration options is available in Chapter 3, "Looking Inside System Center 2012 Orchestrator," and Chapter 4, "Architectural Design."

Terminology Changes

Thanks to rebranding and the Microsoft acquisition, several terms have changed between OIS 6.3 and Orchestrator, but much parity exists between the legacy and the new Orchestrator features. Some pieces, such as the License Manager, were removed altogether; others, such as the Orchestration console, were rebuilt from the ground up. In general, however, the interfaces and features in Orchestrator should be familiar if you have used OIS 6.3. Table 2.1 lists the terminology changes within the architecture features.

TABLE 2.1 Feature Terminology Changes

OIS 6.3	Orchestrator 2012
SQL Data Store	Orchestrator Database
Opalis Management Server	Orchestrator Management Server
Opalis Action Server	Orchestrator Runbook Server
OIS Client (Authoring Console)	Runbook Designer
Policy Testing Console	Runbook Tester
OIS Operator Console	Orchestration Console
Deployment Manager	Deployment Manager
OIS Web Service (WSDL)	Orchestrator Web Service
Database Configuration Utility	Data Store Configuration
License Manager	—

Orchestrator Database

A Microsoft SQL Server database stores all data and configurations. This database is a critical feature and should be configured for high availability. If the SQL Server goes down, runbook servers cannot execute any runbooks. Orchestrator uses one database with a default name of Orchestrator and a correlation of SQL_Latin1_General_CP1_CI_AS.

NOTE: ORACLE DATABASE SUPPORT

Support for Oracle as the relational database management system (RDBMS) is not included in Orchestrator, as it was in Opalis Integration Server.

Orchestrator Management Server

The management server exists primarily to establish communication between the design features and the SQL database. It is not a critical runtime feature and does not necessarily need to be highly available. This feature fills the same role as the OIS management server in the previous release.

Orchestrator Runbook Server

The Orchestrator runbook server is the feature that actually executes runbooks. You can deploy multiple runbook servers to allow for load balancing. This feature handles the same responsibilities as the action server in the previous release.

Runbook Designer

The Runbook Designer console is used to design, test, and implement all runbooks. This feature is not critical to the operation of existing runbooks and, therefore, does not necessarily need to be highly available. This feature is essentially the same as the OIS 6.3 Client.

Runbook Tester

The Runbook Tester, which is launched within the Runbook Designer, has a similar function and layout to the OIS 6.3 Policy Testing console. This tool is used to test runbooks before deployment and publishes runtime data about each activity as the runbook steps through from beginning to end.

CAUTION: RUNBOOK TESTER COMMITS CHANGES

Several times throughout this book, the authors state that the Runbook Tester actually executes and commits changes when testing a runbook. It does not display "what if" data or scenarios. Keep this in mind, and use a development environment whenever a runbook might affect existing IT services.

Orchestration Console

This console, displayed in Figure 2.7, provides IT operators with a thin-client interface into Orchestrator. The Orchestration console is not critical to the runtime of runbooks, but it enables users to view the state of runbook execution, start and stop jobs, view running and pending instances in real time, and review the execution history of runbook instances. The Orchestration console supersedes the OIS 6.3 Operator Console, and although the underlying technology has changed significantly, it serves the same purpose.

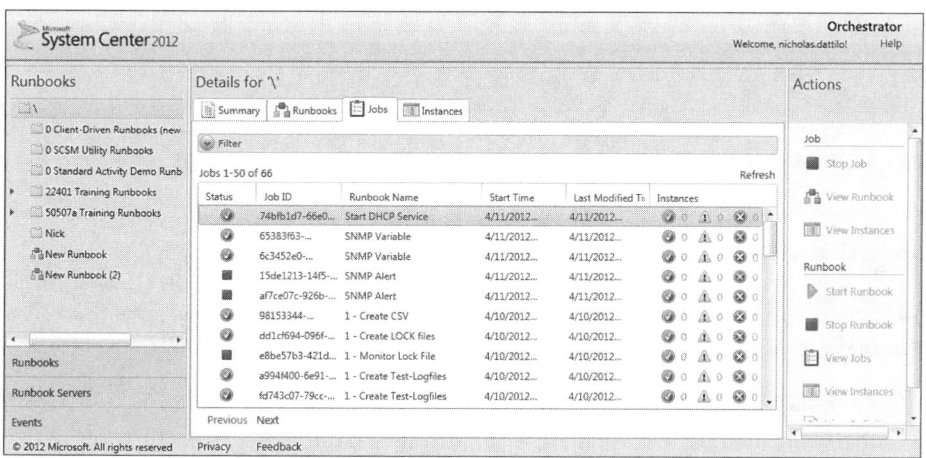

FIGURE 2.7 The Orchestration console.

Deployment Manager

The Deployment Manager is largely unchanged from OIS 6.3 and is used to deploy runbook servers, IPs, and runbook designers. Figure 2.8 shows the Deployment Manager managing integration packs.

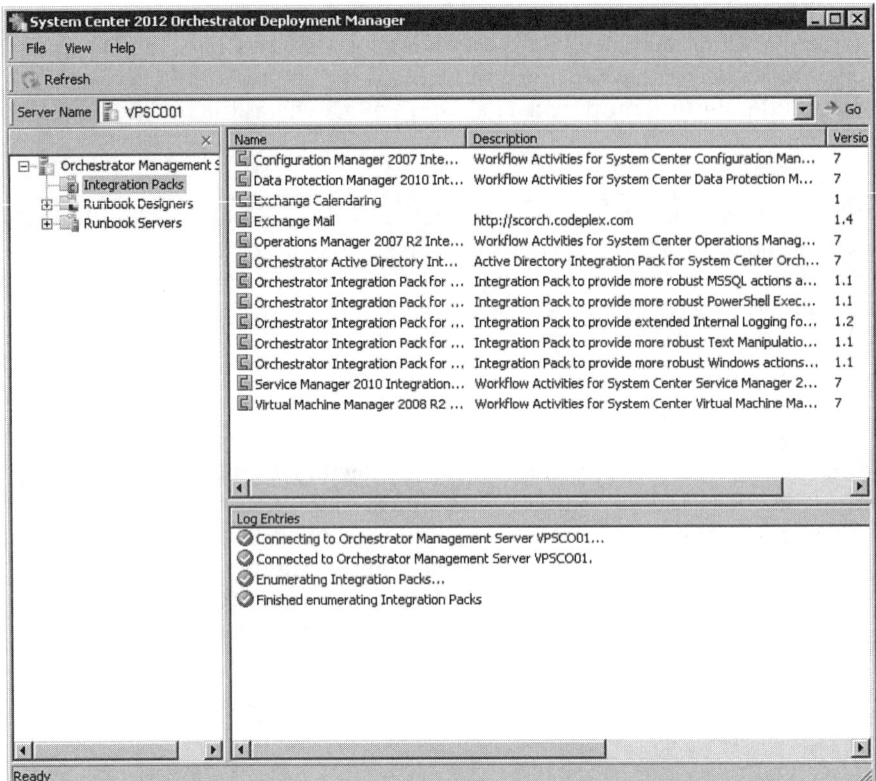

FIGURE 2.8 Orchestrator Deployment Manager.

Orchestrator Web Service

The Orchestrator web service allows for programmatic access to Orchestrator. In addition to providing access for the Orchestration console, this web service uses REST and ODATA standards to make it easier for developers to integrate their programs with Orchestrator.

Data Store Configuration

This utility supersedes the OIS 6.3 Database Configuration Utility and is used to configure the database server and the database itself (see Figure 2.9).

Services

Services have undergone a makeover as well. Table 2.2 lists these changes.

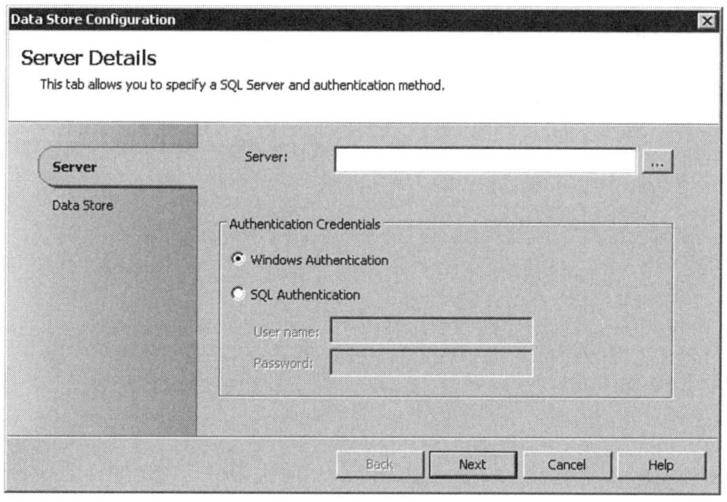

FIGURE 2.9 Orchestrator Data Store Configuration details.

TABLE 2.2 Services Terminology Changes

Opalis 6.3	Orchestrator 2012
Opalis Remote Execution Service	Orchestrator Run Program Service
OpalisActionServerWatchdog	Orchestrator Runbook Server Monitor
OpalisActionService	Orchestrator Runbook Service
Opalis Management Service	Orchestrator Management Service
OpalisRemotingService	Orchestrator Remoting Service

Other Terminology Changes

Other terminology changes relate to the user interface, detailed in Table 2.3. The following sections focus on these.

TABLE 2.3 User Interface Terminology Changes

OIS 6.3	Orchestrator 2012
Custom Start	Initialize Data
Foundation Object	Standard Activity
Object	Activity
Object Palette	Activities Pane
Policy	Runbook
Policy Folder	Runbook Folder

OIS 6.3	Orchestrator 2012
Policy Module	Job Process
Publish Policy Data	Published Data
Request	Job
Trigger Policy	Invoke Runbook
Workflow Control	Runbook Control

Activity

Activity is synonymous with *object* in OIS 6.3: It refers to the tasks dragged and dropped in the Runbook Designer to build runbooks.

Standard Activity

Standard activities are all activities that are available in an out-of-the-box installation; they exclude activities provided by integration packs. These standard activities are sorted into different categories, based on their function. An example of these categories is Runbook Control. Chapter 7, "Runbook Basics," discusses categories for standard activities.

Initialize Data

The **Initialize Data** activity is just a name change from the OIS **Custom Start** object, and operates in a similar way. It allows a runbook to gather user-defined input parameters. This enables runtime values to be gathered via the Orchestration console or through an interface utilizing the web service, such as the Service Manager self-service portal.

Activities Pane

The Activities pane is the pane on the right side of the Runbook Designer that holds all the activities that can be used to build a runbook. Figure 2.10 shows the Activities pane, with some optional integration packs.

Runbook

A runbook is synonymous with a policy in OIS 6.3: It is the collection of activities that orchestrates actions.

Runbook Folder

Runbook Folder replaces the legacy term Policy Folder. These folders contain one or more runbooks and are used to organize runbooks in both the Orchestration console and the Runbook Designer.

Job

A job is a request to run a specific runbook that is waiting to be assigned to a runbook server for processing. These runbooks are assigned first come, first served.

Job Process

A job process is the actual process that executes on the runbook server that executes an instance of a job.

FIGURE 2.10 The Activities pane in the Runbook Designer.

Published Data

When activities run, data is collected. This includes the output of the activity, the time it ran, and whether it was successful. The information is placed in the pipeline data bus. This data can be referenced by another activity farther down the line in the runbook. Referred to as *published data*, this data was known as published policy data in OIS 6.3. Figure 2.11 shows some common published data from the **Compare Values** activity.

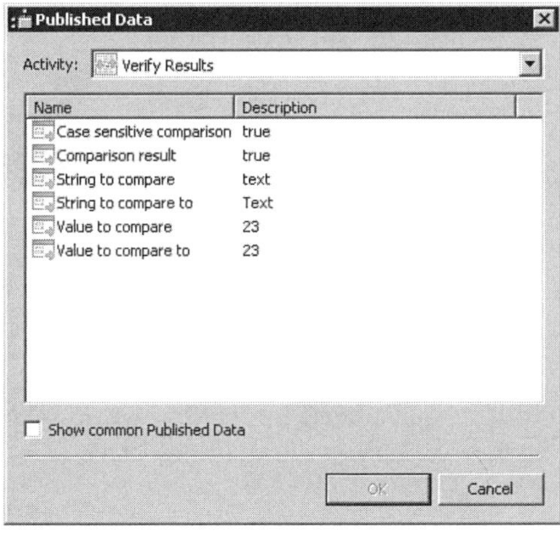

FIGURE 2.11 Viewing published data.

Job

A job is a request to deploy and run a runbook on a runbook server. You can monitor jobs in the Orchestration console, previously shown in Figure 2.7. A job identifies the runbook but does not uniquely identify each specific occurrence of that runbook's execution.

Jobs can deploy a runbook to multiple runbook servers or can run multiple occurrences of the same runbook on a single runbook server. These occurrences, referred to as instances, enable you to uniquely identify each specific occurrence. For example, a System Center Operations Manager alert can trigger an Orchestrator runbook. If Operations Manager sends three alerts that are the same, the job is the request to run a runbook each time that alert is generated. The instance uniquely identifies each execution of that runbook and enables you to view data about that specific occurrence, such as the time it started and what data it generated.

Invoke Runbook

This activity resides in the Runbook Control category and replaces the OIS legacy **Trigger Policy** object. It allows another runbook to be called from within a runbook. A related activity, **Return Data**, enables you to send back the data generated by the invoked runbook to the **Invoke Runbook** activity. This powerful pair of activities plays a big part in more complex multipart runbooks.

CAUTION: INVOKE RUNBOOK SECURITY CREDENTIALS

The **Invoke Runbook** activity can explicitly define security credentials that will be used by the target runbook. This is a seemingly minor change from the old **Trigger Policy** object, but the capability for an entire runbook job to be executed under specific user credentials is a significant new feature.

Runbook Control

This activity category replaces the old Workflow Control category and contains activities that are used to control the behavior of runbooks.

Concept Changes

Conceptually, Orchestrator has not changed much from OIS 6.3. General practices and ideas still apply, and your OIS policies largely still function in Orchestrator as runbooks. If anything, greater emphasis has been placed on the power of Orchestrator's integration with the other System Center components.

Microsoft provides updated IPs for the System Center 2012 components that leverage some of the new features and functionality in those other products. It is also worth noting that the IPs for the legacy System Center products have been updated to work with Orchestrator because the Opalis Integration Server IPs are not compatible with Orchestrator.

Previous versions required that you monitor an application for a certain event to occur in order to trigger a runbook, thus the monitor was a passive monitor. For this passive monitoring system to work reliably, the data being monitored had to be consistent enough to trigger the correct runbooks at the right time. System Center 2012 Orchestrator does not need to monitor events in external applications to trigger runbooks. Runbooks can be triggered via the web service; using integration with other applications or the System Center 2012 Service Manager component can eliminate unnecessary development efforts and issues from data inconsistencies. Chapter 6 explains this integration in more detail.

Architecture and Feature Changes

The architecture for Orchestrator remains largely unchanged from OIS 6.3, aside from some new terminology and prerequisite changes (see Table 2.4). As Figure 2.12 shows and Chapter 3 explores further, the SQL database is still at the heart of Orchestrator. A familiar set of features operates around that SQL database.

Prerequisite/Sizing Changes

As is typical with newly released Microsoft software, hardware and software prerequisites have been updated.

These changes should not necessarily be considered upgrade prerequisites—as stated earlier in the "OIS Migration to Orchestrator" section, no upgrade path from OIS to Orchestrator exists. Chapter 5 discusses this further.

TABLE 2.4 Single Server Prerequisite Changes

Feature	Opalis 6.3	Orchestrator 2012
Processor	2.1 GHz dual-core Xeon 3000 series or equivalent	2.1 GHz dual-core Intel microprocessor or better
Memory	2GB	1GB
Hard Disk	381MB	200MB
Operating System Roles and Features	Windows Server 2003 SP2 or later	Windows Server 2008 R2 or Windows Server 2012 with System Center 2012 Service Pack (SP) 1, IIS, .NET Framework 3.5.1 and .NET Framework 4
Database Server	SQL Server 2005 or 2008	SQL Server 2008 R2 or SQL Server 2012 with System Center 2012 SP 1, using SQL_Latin1_General_CP1_CI_AS collation

Apart from these relatively minor changes, the Orchestration console has been rebuilt and thus has different requirements. The old Operator Console required JavaScript on the accessing browsers and Java parts on the web server hosting the console. The new Orchestration console requires Silverlight on accessing browsers.

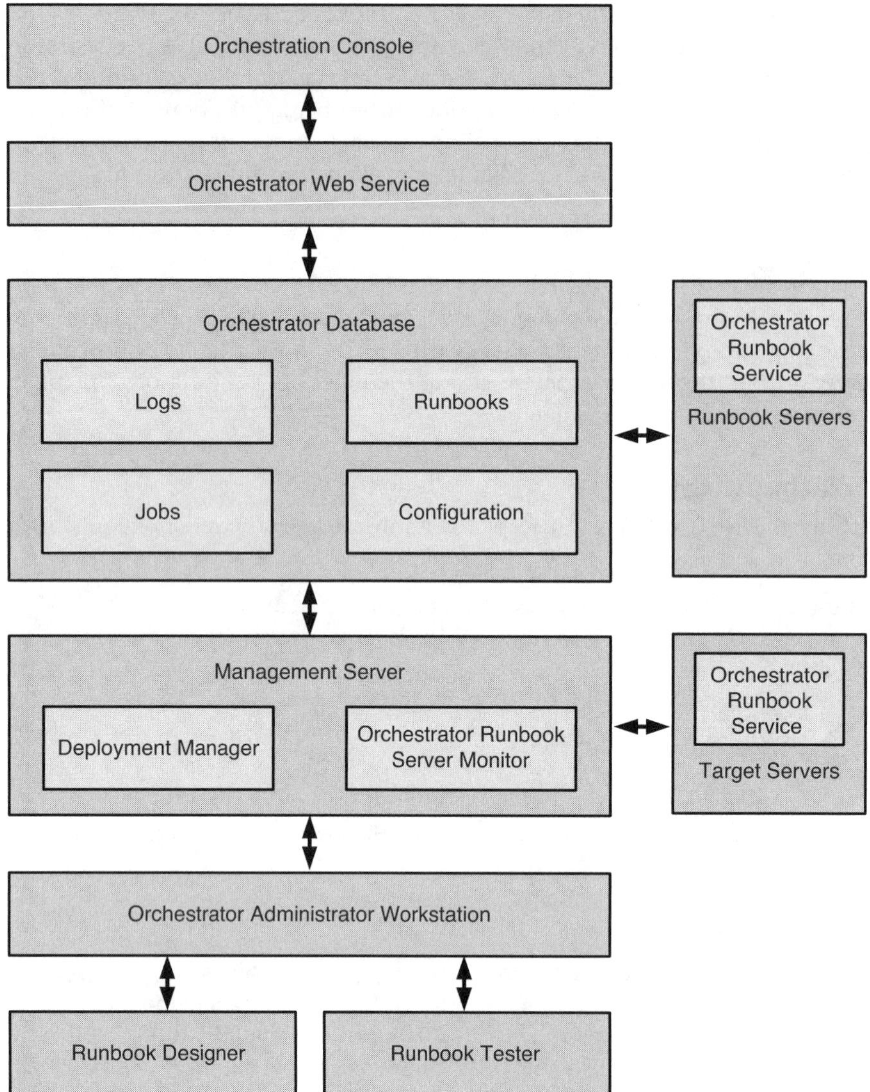

FIGURE 2.12 Architectural diagram.

Sizing and performance guidance has stayed consistent with this new release. The management server is still limited to one per environment, is needed only to connect the Runbook Designer, and does not need to be highly available. The database and runbook servers are the features required for runbooks to execute. Each runbook server is limited by default to 50 runbooks per runbook server. If you are using Service Manager with the Orchestrator connector, you will want the Orchestrator web service to be highly available as well.

Licensing Changes

Microsoft has done a considerable amount of work to simplify the license options for System Center 2012 into an easy-to-understand processor-based licensing model. All the components of System Center 2012 have been consolidated into a single SKU, so purchasing either license offering gives you access to every component. Two editions are available; the only difference between the two is in the number of managed OSEs allowed per license (see Table 2.5).

TABLE 2.5 Licensing Changes

License Offering	Components Included	Managed OSEs
System Center 2012 Datacenter Edition	App Controller	Unlimited on premises, 8 in public cloud
	Configuration Manager	
System Center 2012 Standard Edition	Data Protection Manager	2 per license on premises, 2 in public cloud
	Endpoint Protection	
	Operations Manager	
	Orchestrator	
	Service Manager	
	Virtual Machine Manager	

System Center Advisor, which offers configuration monitoring cloud services for Microsoft server products, is offered at no cost to users of those products. For information on Advisor, see http://blogs.technet.com/b/momteam/archive/2013/03/06/system-center-advisor.aspx and https://www.systemcenteradvisor.com/.

Summary

This chapter examined the evolution from OpalisRobot in 1995 to Microsoft's System Center 2012 Orchestrator. It took a close look at the differences in technology, terminology, and prerequisites. It also discussed where Orchestrator fits into System Center 2012.

The next chapter covers the Orchestrator architecture and deployment scenarios.

CHAPTER 3

Looking Inside System Center 2012 Orchestrator

IN THIS CHAPTER

- Architectural Overview
- Server Components
- Deployment Models
- Windows Services
- Global Settings
- Integration Packs
- Runbooks
- Data Bus
- Connectors
- Consoles
- Communication

System Center 2012 Orchestrator (also referred to as SCOrch) is a new component of Microsoft System Center 2012. Microsoft acquired Opalis Software and Opalis Integration Server (OIS) in December 2009. With the System Center 2012 release, Microsoft renamed OIS to Orchestrator and updated the software to incorporate Microsoft's development standards and integrate with the most recent version of System Center.

Orchestrator enables information technology (IT) organizations to automate IT infrastructure tasks. Automation is achieved through workflows that integrate with both Microsoft and non-Microsoft products. The integration is built using activities that are delivered with integration packs.

The power of Orchestrator lies within the automated procedures and operations (known as *runbooks*) you build, and how you build them. Orchestrator brings the following key components to System Center 2012:

- **Integration:** In a data center, all the different systems need to communicate with each other. With its integration packs—software components designed around tasks targeted to a specific application—Orchestrator makes it possible for services and systems to integrate.
- **Orchestration:** The Orchestrator Runbook Designer makes it easy to drag and drop activities from different integration packs into a runbook. Activities and runbooks are configured in a graphical user interface that does not require coding.

- **Automation:** After the integration is configured and runbooks are created, these runbook can be triggered by a change request, an email, or a number of other ways. Orchestrator carries out the workflow consistently, the same way every time, and in a stable and effective way.

Orchestrator uses a different code base from other System Center components, such as Service Manager and Operations Manager, which share a common architecture and foundation. This is because of its roots from OIS, and might give you a somewhat different initial experience with Orchestrator as you start working with this component.

Architectural Overview

The Orchestrator architecture is designed around its database. The Orchestrator database is the central feature that drives the Orchestrator environment, as all other Orchestrator features depend on data from the database. For example, all configurations are read from the database when a runbook is about to be executed, and all historical data is written to the database as the workflows complete.

Figure 3.1 presents an overview of the System Center 2012 Orchestrator architecture.

The architecture consists of these components:

- **Orchestrator database:** This is the main component and "heart" of Orchestrator; it stores all jobs, runbook, logs, and configuration information.
- **Orchestrator web service:** The Orchestrator web service, shown above the database in Figure 3.1, is a Representational State Transfer (REST)–based service that enables custom applications to connect to Orchestrator. REST defines a set of architectural principles around how to transfer information. Using the web service, other services can start and stop runbooks. The web service can also provide other services with information regarding jobs.
- **Console:** The Orchestration console is a web-based console that uses the web service to interact with Orchestrator in real time. From the console, an operator can start, stop, and view the status of jobs.
- **Runbook server(s):** Runbook servers are shown to the right side of the database in Figure 3.1. These are where an instance of a runbook runs. You can deploy multiple runbook servers in an Orchestrator environment.
- **Management server:** The figure shows only one instance of a management server because you can have only one management server in an Orchestrator environment.

  The primary purpose of the management server, shown below the database in Figure 3.1, is to provide a communications layer between the Runbook Designer and the Orchestrator database. The management server is not required to execute runbooks; these execute as long as runbook servers and the database are online. However, the Runbook Designer requires the management server. When you want to run the Runbook Designer, whether to author runbooks or start runbooks, a management system must be available. This is not the case when using the Orchestration console: Starting, stopping, and monitoring runbooks is possible with the web-based Orchestration console even if the management server is offline.

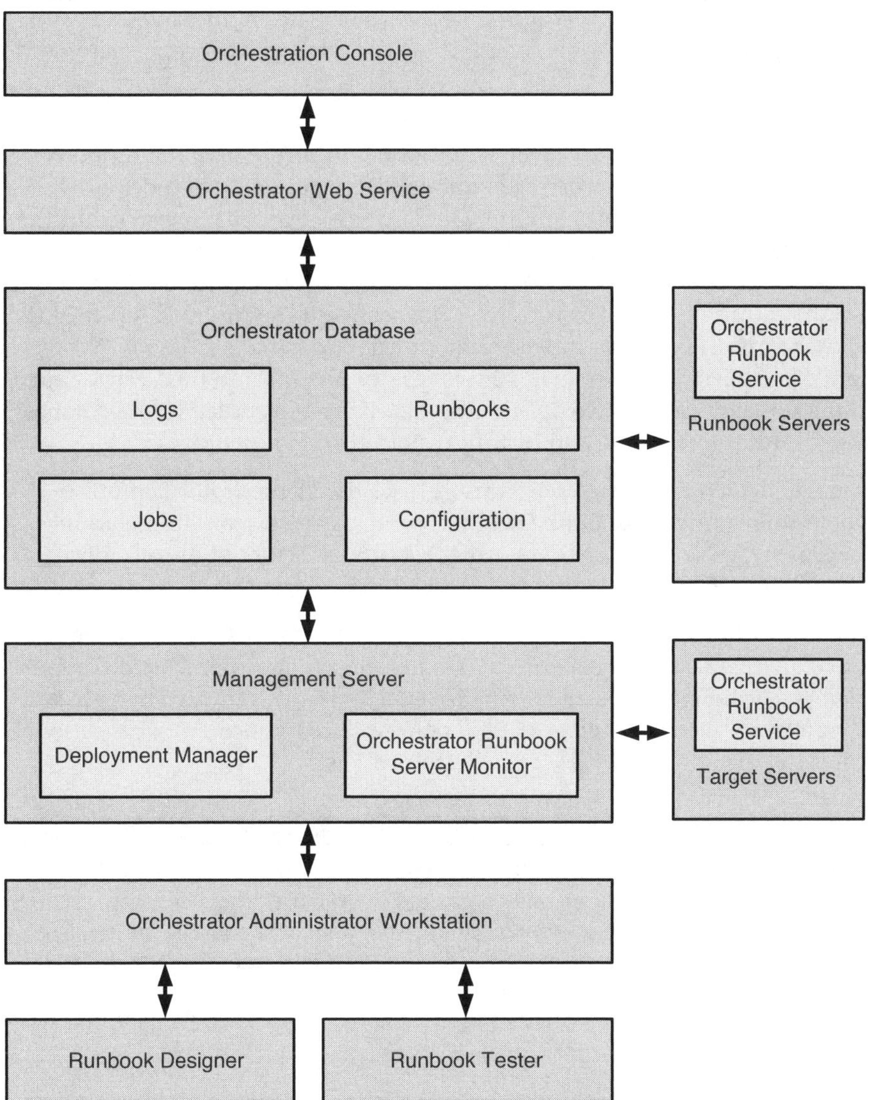

FIGURE 3.1 Architectural overview of System Center 2012 Orchestrator.

- **Runbook Service:** The runbook server uses the Orchestrator Runbook Service to run runbooks. Using this service, each runbook server communicates with the database to send status and results and to receive new jobs.
- **Runbook Designer:** This tool is used to build, modify, deploy, and manage runbooks. The Runbook Designer also contains the Runbook Tester console used for testing runbooks during development. During authoring and design, the runbooks are stored locally on the machine where the designer is running. When a runbook is

ready, you check it in, meaning that it is stored in the Orchestrator database. When you need to modify the runbook, you check it out and store a local copy that you will work with.

When you use the Runbook Designer to check a runbook into the system, the runbook is stored in the database. You can then use the Runbook Designer or Orchestration console to start the runbook. In the background, Orchestrator creates a request to run the runbook; this is referred to as a *job*. On a regular basis (every 2 seconds, by default), each runbook server checks the database for new jobs. If online, the primary runbook server for the runbook gets the job and downloads it to the local cache on the runbook server. If the primary runbook server is offline, a secondary runbook server downloads the job. When a runbook server detects the job, it logs that it is working in the job and then carries out the activities in the runbook. Status, activity results, and data are recorded in the database, enabling you to monitor the real-time and historical status of the runbook.

Deployment Manager, which is a standalone console, uses the Orchestrator Remoting Service to deploy or uninstall the Runbook Designer, runbook servers, and integration packs. The management server hosts the Orchestrator Runbook Server Monitor service, used to monitor runbook servers.

Microsoft supports virtualization of all components of System Center 2012 Orchestrator. However, even when virtualization is supported, it is not always a recommended configuration. As an example, although you could virtualize SQL Server, it is important to have a database that performs well. You often get better performance, particularly disk performance, with a physical machine that uses its own physical disks.

NOTE: KNOW WHERE THE RUNBOOK ACTUALLY RUNS

When you use the Runbook Tester console, the runbook executes on the local machine. This can actually cause tests to fail in some scenarios. For example, when you have installed special software on the runbook server or open firewall ports explicitly for the runbook server, the runbook will not work correctly on the local workstation. For additional information, see Chapter 11, "Security and Administration."

Server Components

System Center 2012 Orchestrator contains six primary features, some required and others optional. In some scenarios, you need multiple instances of some features. Runbook servers are one example.

These are the core features of System Center 2012 Orchestrator:

- Orchestrator management server
- Orchestrator runbook server
- Orchestrator database

- Orchestration console and web service (must be installed on the same machine)
- Orchestrator Runbook Designer

The following sections cover these features.

NOTE: ORCHESTRATOR AND ACTIVE DIRECTORY

The authors recommend that your Orchestrator servers belong to an Active Directory domain, although this it is not a requirement. You can mix components between domains and workgroups; as an example, you can have your management server and database server in one domain, with runbook servers in workgroups or other domains.

Orchestrator can work without any component belonging to a domain, but this requires extra configuration and account administration because you do not have a common account database such as Active Directory. Consider these examples:

- If the runbook servers cannot connect with a domain account to the SQL Server hosting the Orchestrator database, you must configure the SQL Server to use SQL authentication. Microsoft does not recommend SQL authentication because it is less secure than Windows authentication.
- Security roles control who can access and modify runbooks in the Runbook Designer. These roles are more complex to maintain without domain accounts. If you use local (nondomain) accounts, you must administer security settings locally on the Orchestrator management server. If you use Active Directory security groups, you can simply add a user to a security group to grant him or her permissions in Orchestrator.

Management Server

The management server provides a layer between the Runbook Designer and the Orchestrator database. Only one management server can exist in an Orchestrator environment. Orchestrator does not provide the means to have a fault-tolerant management server because this role cannot be clustered.

The management server is not required to execute runbooks. Runbook servers communicate directly with the database to obtain jobs to execute and to report results. The management server is needed only when connecting to the Runbook Designer console or Deployment Manager console. If you need to recover the management server in a disaster scenario, you can reinstall the role and point it to the Orchestrator database.

The Orchestrator Deployment Manager is installed on the management server by default. Deployment Manager is used to deploy new runbook servers, integration packs, and runbook designer consoles. If the management server is offline, you cannot deploy additional runbook designer consoles. However, you can manually install runbook servers and integration packs when Deployment Manager is offline.

TIP: MANUAL INSTALLATIONS

Consider some additional information about manual installations:

- Information on deploying integration packs manually is located on the TechNet Wiki at http://social.technet.microsoft.com/wiki/contents/articles/how-to-install-opalis-integration-server-action-server-without-using-deployment-manager.aspx. (Although this refers to an Opalis action server, the process is very similar to that in Orchestrator.)
- Additional information regarding runbook server deployments is available at http://technet.microsoft.com/en-us/library/hh420386.aspx.
- Information about runbook designer deployments is located at http://technet.microsoft.com/en-us/library/hh420343.aspx.

Runbook Server

Runbooks are executed on runbook servers. A runbook server communicates directly with the Orchestrator database to determine new jobs to execute and to report results. You can deploy multiple runbook servers, depending on constraints such as network requirements and number of runbooks that need to run at the same time.

When a request to start a runbook comes in (manually by an operator or administrator, or through a scheduled activity or other automated mechanism), a job is created in the Orchestrator database. When a runbook server finds the job, it marks it as in progress, copies the runbook locally, and begins executing the runbook. Status, results from activities, and data are inserted into the Orchestrator database. You can view this data in the Orchestrator runbook designer consoles. Results can also be read from the Orchestrator web service. The Orchestration console connects through the Orchestrator web service to the Orchestrator database.

Orchestrator Database

The Orchestrator database is a Microsoft SQL Server database. It is the central component of Orchestrator. The database stores runbooks, configuration, logs, and the status of running runbooks. Without the database, your Orchestrator environment is not functional. The authors recommend that you deploy the Orchestrator database on a well-performing and fault-tolerant SQL Server.

Web Service

Using the Orchestrator web service, custom applications can connect to Orchestrator to start and stop runbooks. They can also get information regarding running runbooks. The Orchestration console uses the web service to connect to the Orchestrator environment. The web service communicates directly with the database.

Orchestration Console

The Orchestration console is a web-based console you can use to start and stop runbooks. An important distinction between the Orchestration console and the Runbook Designer is that when you start a runbook from the Orchestration console, you can input parameters that a runbook needs to run, which you cannot do using the Runbook Designer. Using the Orchestration console, you can also see the status of runbooks and activities within runbooks.

Runbook Designer

The Runbook Designer is the primary tool to author and build runbooks. Using this tool, you can work with runbooks, global settings, computer groups, and connections to external system and services. You can also start the Runbook Tester to test your runbook before deploying it to production. Figure 3.2 shows the layout of the Runbook Designer console, which is divided into five areas:

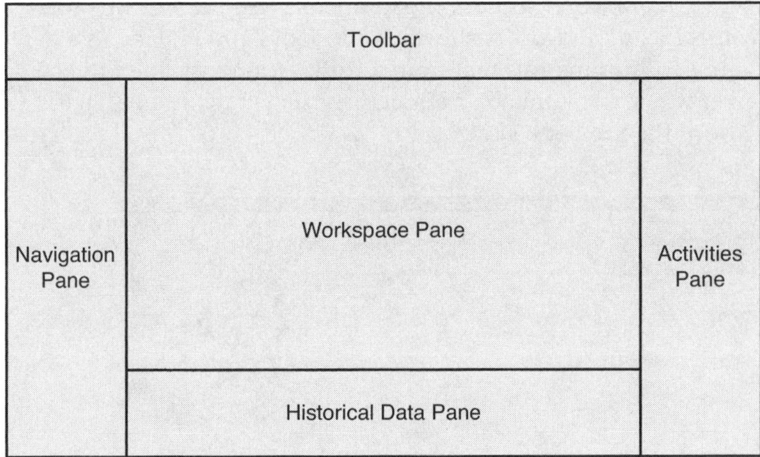

FIGURE 3.2 Layout of the Runbook Designer.

- **Toolbar:** This area contains icons (including Run and Stop runbook) and shortcuts to the Orchestration console and the Runbook Tester.
- **Navigation pane:** Use the navigation tree to navigate through runbooks, global settings, runbook servers, and computer groups. You can control access to objects in the navigation tree using security settings, at either the folder or object level.
- **Workspace pane:** This is where you build your runbook. Use the Workspace pane to drag and drop activities and connect them to each other. Activities are configured in this area.
- **Activities pane:** This pane shows all activities, which are divided into categories. Out of the box, Orchestrator has a number of standard activities that are not connected to a special technology; they can be used in any purpose or any runbook. For example, the Run Program activities are very generic and can be used in a number of scenarios.

- **Historical Data pane:** This pane is divided into four tabs—Log, Log History, Audit History, and Events.
  - The Log tab displays the status of activities when the runbook is being executed.
  - The Log History tab shows the status from when the runbook was executed previously.
  - The Audit History tab displays a log of changes made to the runbook, such as when someone adds an activity.
  - The Events tab shows platform events, such as when a runbook is offline or when a runbook generates a platform event to create a notification.

As mentioned in the "Server Components" section, the Runbook Designer supports role-based security. You can control who can work with which runbooks and folders. As a best practice, the authors recommend running this tool from a workstation instead of directly from the management server where the Runbook Designer is installed by default. Figure 3.3 shows the main window of the Runbook Designer.

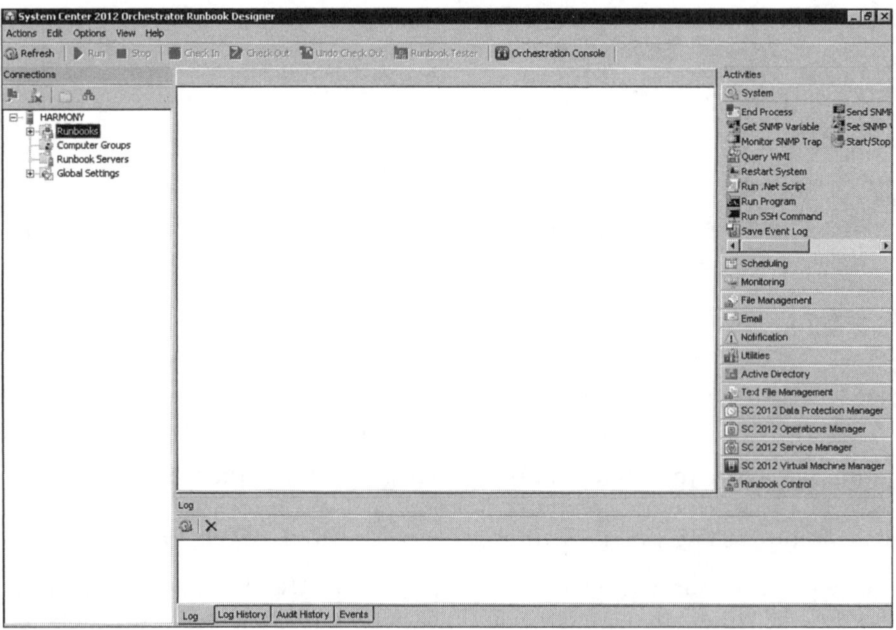

FIGURE 3.3 The Runbook Designer.

For additional detail, Figures 3.4, 3.5, and 3.6 show selected portions of the Runbook Designer console shown in Figure 3.3. Figure 3.4 displays part of the toolbar, the Workspace pane, and the Activities pane. Figure 3.5 shows the Historical Data pane, and Figure 3.6 shows the Navigation pane and a portion of the toolbar.

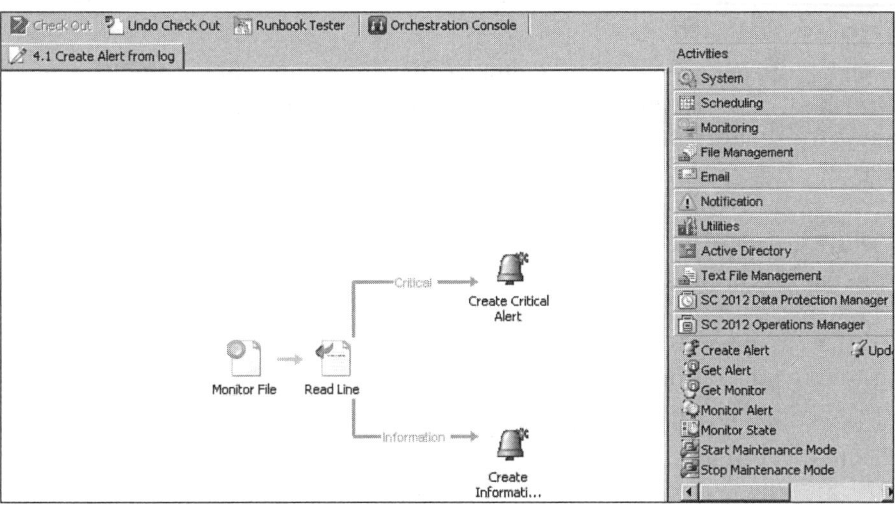

FIGURE 3.4 The Workspace and Activities panes.

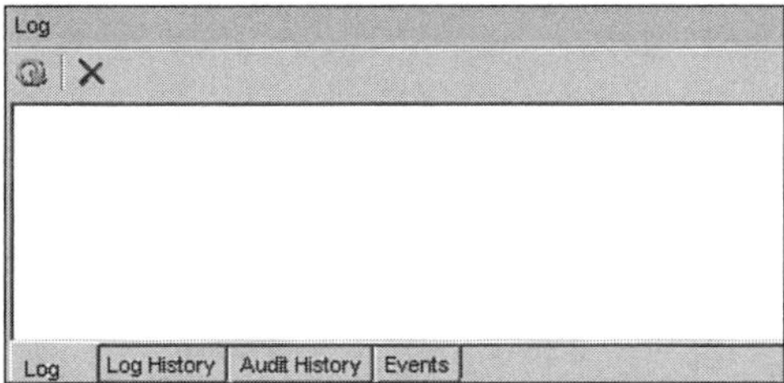

FIGURE 3.5 The Historical Data pane of the Runbook Designer.

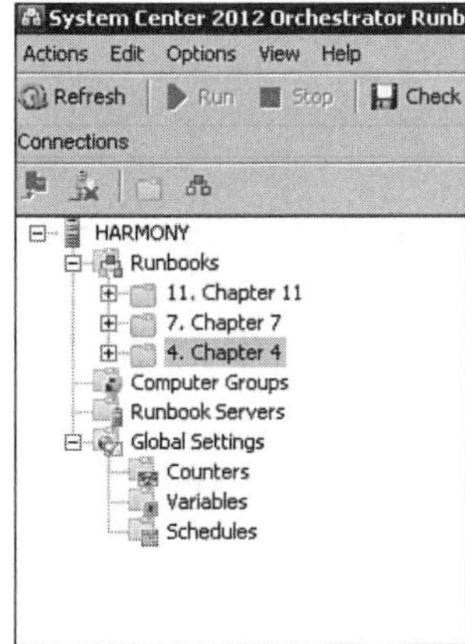

FIGURE 3.6 The Navigation pane.

Deployment Models

Although a number of approaches exist for deploying Orchestrator, most implementations fall within a small set of deployment models. The following sections discuss the most common models for deploying Orchestrator, explain where each model is best suited, and discuss the relative advantages and disadvantages of each model.

Minimum Installation Model

Depending on your organization's requirements, you will deploy Orchestrator on a single server or multiple servers. Two core considerations when determining placement and design are security requirements and the anticipated number of runbooks. You also want to consider how often the runbooks are expected to run and what they execute.

If you have a strict firewall policy that prevents you from placing a runbook server on a central network that can reach all target services, you must deploy multiple runbook servers. Another security-related design challenge arises if you cannot assign a single Runbook Server service account all the permissions it requires on the target machines. Often the Runbook Server service account needs high-level access to execute all tasks. Many organizations have policies regarding high-level access accounts as service accounts. If this is the case, you need to divide runbooks across multiple runbook servers so that each communicates with a limited number of services.

If you have complex runbooks that require a significant amount of CPU time, you might decide to divide execution over multiple runbook servers. Likewise, if you have hundred of runbooks that need to run every 2 minutes, you might need multiple runbook servers.

For additional information on design considerations, see Chapter 4, "Architectural Design."

In the example in Figure 3.7, the database is hosted on the same machine as the management server. Because Orchestrator communicates extensively with the database, you want high-speed communication between these two Orchestrator features and should size and configure the database for optimal performance:

- You might want to host the database on the management server for performance reasons, particularly if the alternative is a shared SQL Server on a remote network with limited hardware resources.
- Orchestrator is database intensive, making it important that the database perform well. With a shared SQL Server, other performance-intensive databases could potentially affect disk and network performance on that system, affecting your Orchestrator database performance.

Figure 3.7 shows a minimum installation of System Center 2012 Orchestrator. The example does not contain the web-based Orchestration console or web service. In some scenarios, you might not need these components. For example, if you have runbooks that do not require input from an operator to run, you could consider eliminating the Orchestration console. The Orchestration console is also used to check the status of runbooks, but you can check runbook status using the Runbook Designer in a small installation.

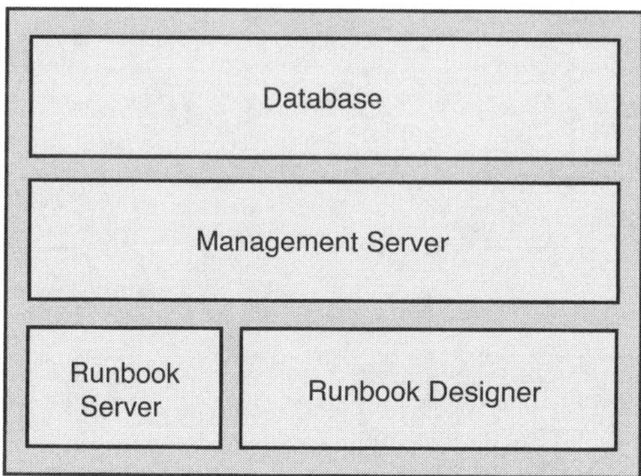

FIGURE 3.7 Minimum installation of Orchestrator on a single server.

Additional Runbooks and Scaling Out

Larger environments need to run many runbooks at once and must provide support for runbooks requiring more than minimal hardware. To meet this requirement, you can deploy multiple runbook servers. You can also deploy the Orchestrator database on a dedicated SQL Server. If your environment contains multiple nontrusted networks and Active Directory forests, you might need to deploy runbook servers to those areas of the network as well. You might also want to consider multiple runbook servers to provide fault tolerance. Figure 3.8 shows an example of an Orchestrator environment with multiple runbook servers and a dedicated database server.

Multiple System Center 2012 Orchestrator Installations

You might want to consider multiple installations of Orchestrator for several reasons. These can include security requirements and permissions, version control, a desire to establish a pre-production and sanitizing environment, and minimized updates to the production Orchestrator database. The next sections discuss these issues.

Security Challenges with Multiple Development Teams

A common challenge in a large environment with multiple teams using System Center 2012 Orchestrator is the permissions required for runbook server service accounts. As an example, if the Hyper-V, Active Directory, and Exchange teams are each developing runbooks, the Runbook Server service account will need access to all three services (in this example, Hyper-V, Active Directory, and Exchange). Depending on the type of work the runbooks will perform, the service account will have different levels of permissions, but most likely these will be high-level permissions.

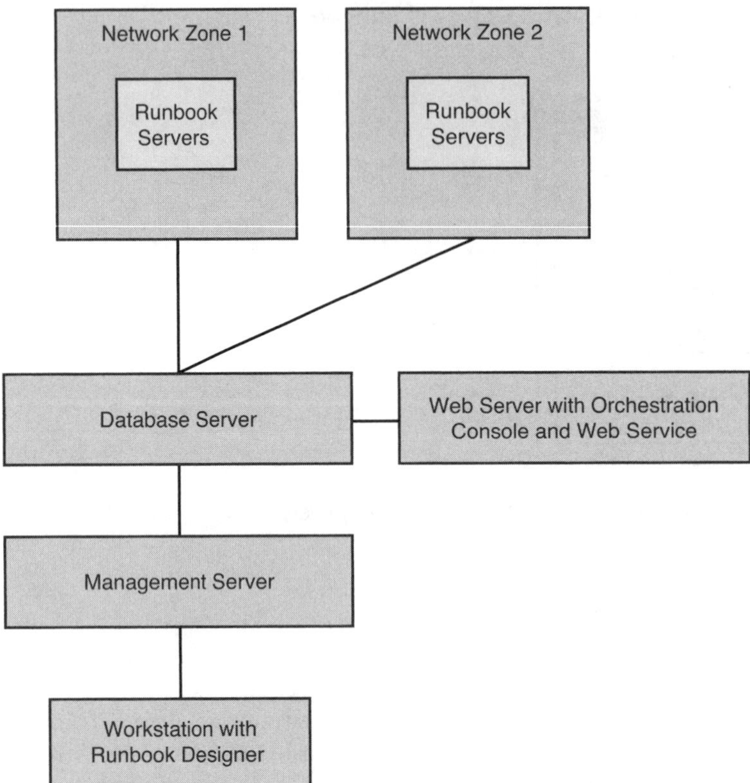

FIGURE 3.8 Large installation of Orchestrator on multiple servers.

Because settings such as the connection to Exchange and Active Directory are global and accessible for everyone using the Runbook Designer, a Hyper-V administrator with access to the Runbook Designer could use the Active Directory service account and modify objects in Active Directory in a negative manner, such as to add an unauthorized user to a security group.

Deploying multiple Orchestrator environments addresses this. An Active Directory domain can contain multiple Orchestrator installations. Orchestrator does not modify Active Directory or add objects to it (other than service accounts that you create manually). This enables you to configure each Orchestrator environment so it can access only what is necessary. For example, only the production Orchestrator environment would have service accounts capable of modifying the IT production environment. You can export and import runbooks between these different environments.

Figure 3.9 shows a scenario with multiple Orchestrator environments:

- Each subject matter expert team has an Orchestrator environment for development and simple testing of runbooks.

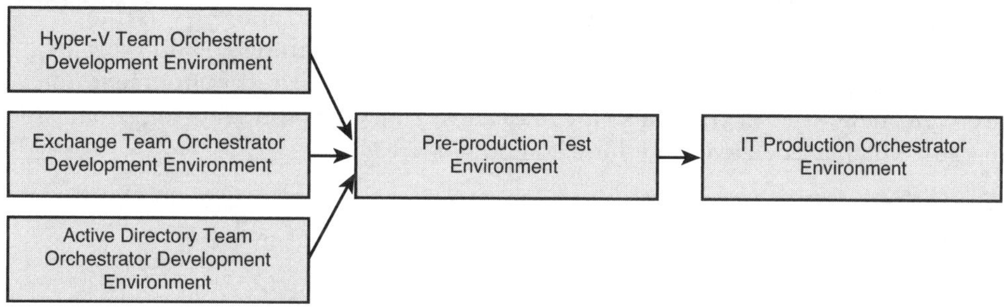

FIGURE 3.9 Implementing multiple Orchestrator environments for improved security.

- In the pre-production environment, runbooks from different teams are merged to be tested against systems and services similar to production.
- Limited access to the production Orchestrator environment is available. Here the only activity occurring is to import runbooks and start them. No runbook authoring or modification occurs in production, and the different subject matter expert team members do not have access to high-level accounts against the IT production environment when developing runbooks.

Establishing Version Control

Runbooks in the production environment should be handled by version control, including change management. Managing all changes to runbooks in production is important. Because System Center 2012 Orchestrator has no rollback or "undo" feature, maintaining earlier versions of runbooks and controlling all modifications to your runbooks is crucial.

Need for a Sanitizing Environment

Multiple environments enhance security, but they bring other challenges. As an example, when you export a runbook, all variables are exported, not just the variables used in the runbook you are exporting. This can be an issue when moving runbooks between environments because you could overwrite a variable with a value used in pre-production and testing when the runbook is imported into the production environment. To avoid this, you can establish a *sanitizing* environment, which is a completely blank Orchestrator environment. This sanitizing environment can be a small virtual machine and does not need to meet Microsoft's hardware requirements. Follow these steps to clean up an export file:

1. Export the runbook you will be implementing into production. In this scenario, you export from the pre-production test environment, meaning that the export includes all variables from your pre-production test environment. For this example, the export file is named export01.export.
2. Import export01.export into your sanitizing environment. This gives you the runbook as well as all variables.

3. The sanitizing environment is a blank Orchestrator environment, so everything it has is from the export01.export file. You can delete everything you don't want to export to production. The new export file from the sanitizing environment (for example, new_export.export) also includes all variables, but this is no longer an issue because you have deleted everything you do not need.

4. The new export file, new_export.export, can be imported into the production Orchestrator environment without risk of overwriting any variables.

Figure 3.10 includes a sanitizing environment to clean up export files.

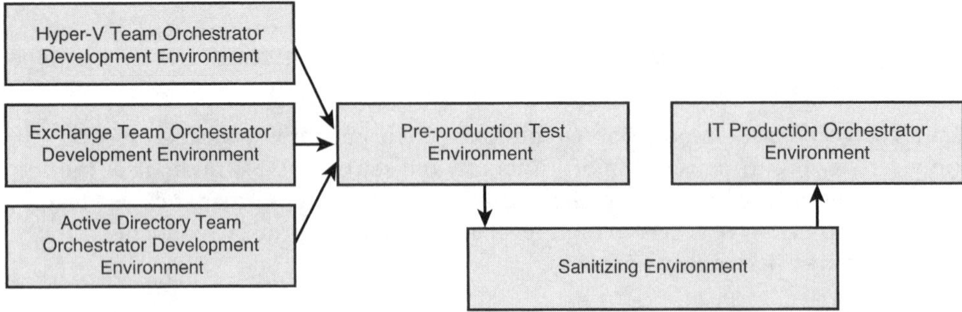

FIGURE 3.10 Multiple Orchestrator environments, including a sanitizing environment.

NOTE: SIZING A SANITIZING ENVIRONMENT

Your sanitizing environment could be an eXtensible Markup Language (XML) editor. The Orchestrator export file is in XML format, which means you can edit it using a tool such as XML Notepad. If you have the knowledge, you can remove the same data from the export file manually as you would in an additional Orchestrator environment. You will not do anything more in the sanitizing environment then delete unnecessary global settings and then generate a new export file.

Managing the Size of the Orchestrator Database

Orchestrator marks objects as deleted when you delete them in the Runbook Designer. Although this can be useful in some scenarios, it can also lead to an unnecessarily large database if you create and delete many objects. The log purge job that is enabled by default in Orchestrator only cleans up runbook historical data. Because deleted objects are not physically deleted, this is another reason to keep test and development separate from your production Orchestrator environment. Because the Orchestrator database performs best when small, you will want to keep the production database as small as possible. Tools such as SanitizeExport can help by removing unnecessary information from runbooks.

NOTE: COMMUNITY RUNBOOK EXPORT TOOL

SanitizeExport.exe is a tool developed by the Orchestrator community to modify the Orchestrator export file. The tool can turn on/off generic login on export runbooks or specific activities in exported runbooks. It also removes all nonreferenced global variables, configurations, computer groups, schedules, and counts from the export file. You can download the tool from http://scorch.codeplex.com/.

Windows Services

Servers running Orchestrator components host a number of Windows services. Different services are installed depending on the Orchestrator server role. If you install all components on one server, that server hosts all services. The next sections describe the services Orchestrator uses.

Orchestrator Management Service (omanagement)

The Orchestrator Management Service (ManagementService.exe) runs on the management server. The service provides an interface between consoles and the database. This service also maintains the Orchestrator database.

Orchestrator Remoting Service (oremoting)

Deployment Manager uses the Orchestrator Remoting Service (OrchestratorRemotingService.exe) to deploy runbook designer, integration packs, and runbook servers.

When deploying a new integration pack to a runbook server, Deployment Manager attempts to open a named pipe to the Orchestrator Remoting Service on the target machine. If Deployment Manager cannot open this pipe, it attempts to deploy the Remoting Service to the ADMIN$ share on the target machine. After that, Deployment Manager tries to install the service by using WMI method `CreateProcess`. If Deployment Manager can create a pipe, the integration pack is copied through the service to the target machine.

On your runbook server, integration packs (OIP files) are stored in the *%Program Files(x86)%*\Microsoft System Center 2012\Orchestrator\Management Server\Components\Packs folder (using default settings). As Figure 3.11 shows, each integration pack is named with a unique ID.

NOTE: WHAT INTEGRATION PACK IS THAT?

To investigate which integration pack a runbook server has locally, you can use a SQL query and the unique ID from the integration pack filename. For example, if the file on the runbook server is {395393EC-6550-45F7-8065-1C8496ACAF95}.OIP, you can use the following SQL query in the Orchestrator database to get the integration pack name:

```
SELECT Name, Description, Version FROM CAPS WHERE UniqueID = '395393EC-
6550-45F7-8065-1C8496ACAF95'
```

Name	Date modified	Type	Size
{0E2EFE13-8612-4093-B4F4-4379BDBC8419}.OIP	10/19/2012 1:34 AM	OIP File	852 KB
{03FAE19D-7FD5-47AA-B7BF-5B25CB7D5009}.OIP	10/19/2012 1:34 AM	OIP File	1,051 KB
{7A17B8D2-D916-4397-B774-26D9EDE3D9F1}.OIP	10/19/2012 1:34 AM	OIP File	758 KB
{12A45CB8-39DE-43a7-8FA2-E90379A5091F}.OIP	11/20/2012 5:13 AM	OIP File	574 KB
{796D217E-1BF5-4C4A-8336-18B5BFD00092}.OIP	11/15/2012 12:24 PM	OIP File	829 KB
{395393EC-6550-45F7-8065-1C8496ACAF95}.OIP	10/19/2012 1:34 AM	OIP File	1,225 KB
{C15C27BB-5A26-44EB-8FF2-4FC12B177CF8}.OIP	10/19/2012 1:34 AM	OIP File	660 KB
{CF73C6E2-308E-4D2E-8968-C19240218E3A}.OIP	11/20/2012 5:54 AM	OIP File	565 KB

FIGURE 3.11 Integration packs stored on a runbook server.

Orchestrator Runbook Server Monitor (omonitor)

The Orchestrator Runbook Server Monitor service (RunbookServerMonitorService.exe) monitors all runbook servers. The service checks the status of each server and reports any failure or errors, such as an Orchestrator platform event. The service actually does not look directly at each runbook server; instead, it reads the heartbeat column of the ACTIONSERVER table in the Orchestrator database. Each runbook server updates the table every 15 seconds. If a runbook server has not updated the heartbeat value for three heartbeat intervals (45 seconds), a platform event is generated. The Runbook Designer console displays platform events.

If a runbook server is shut down properly, the value in the database is updated to `NULL`. The `NULL` value does not generate a platform event. Figure 3.12 shows an example of an Orchestrator platform event when a runbook server is down.

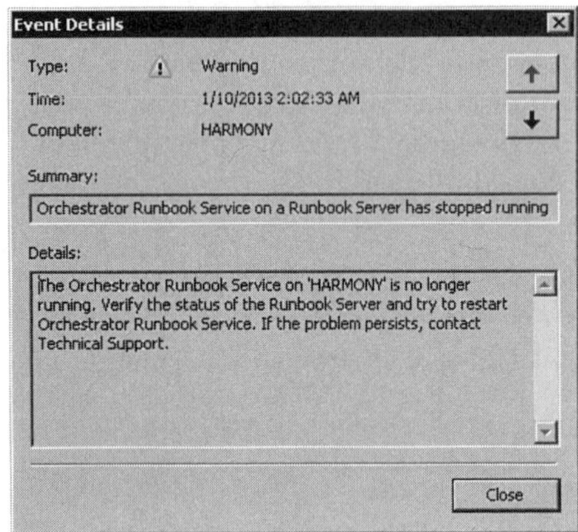

FIGURE 3.12 Example of platform event when runbook server is down.

NOTE: PLATFORM EVENTS

Platform events are displayed in the Runbook Designer console. A platform event can be generated from a runbook or from the Orchestrator platform. A platform event can be a warning that a Runbook Server is not online. You can use the following SQL query to display all platform events from the Orchestrator database:

```
SELECT * FROM EVENTS
```


Orchestrator Runbook Service (orunbook)

The Orchestrator Runbook Service (RunbookService.exe) provides the environment runbooks use to run. This service, which runs on every runbook server, checks the database every 2 seconds to see if there is a new job. If it finds a new job, a new instance of policymodule.exe starts and executes the runbook.

When you start a runbook, you are creating a new job for that runbook instance, meaning that an instance of policymodule.exe is running. When a runbook starts with a nonmonitoring activity, then each time the runbook starts, you will have one job per runbook instance.

Global Settings

Orchestrator has a number of global settings that all runbooks share. These global settings are configured outside the runbook and are requested by one or more runbooks. You can control access to global settings using security permissions on a folder object level. Figure 3.13 shows the Navigation pane of the Runbook Designer, including global settings in the lower part of the navigation tree.

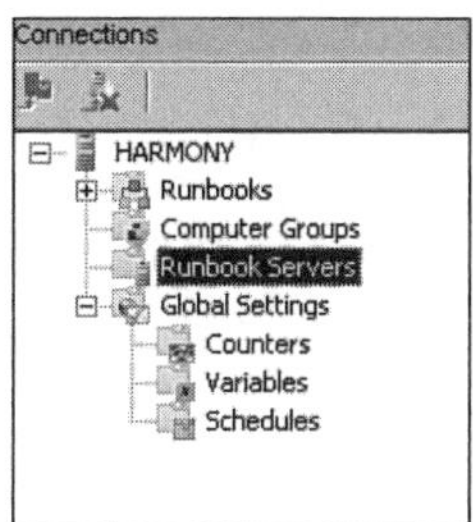

FIGURE 3.13 Global settings in Runbook Designer.

These are the three types of global settings objects:

- **Counters:** Counters are like a "memory stick" where you can store a number. You can store only numbers (numerical values) in a counter. A counter can be read and changed from a runbook. You can use a counter if you need to store a value (number) temporarily when running a runbook. Ensure that you do not use the same counter for multiple runbooks that can run at the same time because this could negatively affect them.

- **Variables:** Variables can be used to input a value into a runbook. A runbook can read a variable during execution but cannot affect the variable—that is, it cannot change the value of the variable. Variables are useful for inputting values into runbooks instead of using hard-coded values. Using variables makes exporting and importing runbooks easier. Updating runbooks is also much easier if you need to only update variables instead of modifying values directly in the runbook. For example, say that you need to change the name of a server that your runbook is using in ten different activities. Instead of updating all ten activities, you can configure each activity to use the variable named *servername* and update that variable only once.
- **Schedules:** If you have a runbook that is triggered every hour but you want it to run only during office hours, you can configure a schedule on the runbook. Using a schedule, you can specify days of the week, days of the month, and hours of the day. As an example, you could configure a schedule to run between 8 a.m. and 5 p.m. the first Monday on each month. Figure 3.14 displays a schedule that runs Monday to Friday between 8 a.m. and 5 p.m.

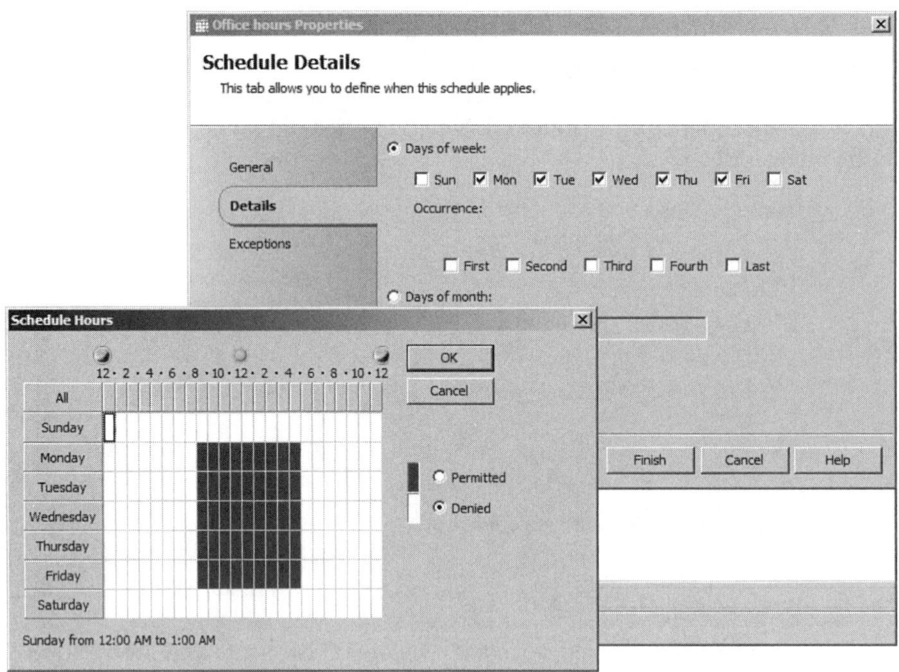

FIGURE 3.14 A schedule that runs Monday through Friday, 8 a.m. to 5 p.m.

Integration Packs

Out of the box, Orchestrator contains approximately 70 built-in standard activities. These are divided into a number of categories, such as System and File Management. You can extend Orchestrator to include more activities by importing integration packs.

An *integration pack* is a collection of custom activities specific to a product or a technology. Integration packs contain activities and, in some cases, connectors or options to configure a connector to an external system. An activity is a task that executes a specific function. For example, the **Run Program** activity runs a program or command. You can configure properties, such as the program to run and parameters. Activities are connected by smart links, which control the flow of the runbook. Each smart link can be configured with include and exclude filters. For example, you can configure smart links to be activated based on the result from an activity. As an example, if the result from activity A is more than 10, the runbook will go from activity A to activity B; otherwise, it will go from activity A to activity C.

You can download integration packs from the Microsoft Download Center at www.microsoft.com/downloads. Each integration pack download includes a guide, instructions on how to use it, and required prerequisites. For example, if you will use the Operations Manager integration pack, you need to install the Operations Manager console on each runbook server because the integration pack uses files from that installation.

In addition to the Microsoft-provided integration packs, Microsoft partners are building and selling integration packs. You also can download community-based integration packs, many of which are available at CodePlex.

If you cannot find an integration pack for your service, or if you have many custom commands and scripts that you will use in multiple runbooks, you can use the Orchestrator Integration Toolkit (previously known as the Quick Integration Kit) to create integration packs. The toolkit is not built into Orchestrator; it is a separate download from the Microsoft website that you install on your workstation. Download the Orchestrator Integration Toolkit at www.microsoft.com/en-us/download/details.aspx?id=34611.

The Orchestrator Integration Toolkit, which Chapter 20, "The Orchestrator Integration Toolkit," discusses in depth, contains three components:

- **Orchestrator Integration Pack Wizard:** This wizard-driven tool helps you create an integration pack from class libraries you have created. You can create your class libraries with the Orchestrator Command-Line Activity Wizard or the Orchestrator SDK.
- **Orchestrator Command-Line Activity Wizard:** This wizard helps you build an assembly file (.DLL) based on PowerShell or the command line. For example, you can build an assembly file with two activities that list files based on PowerShell cmdlets. Figure 3.15 shows a step in the Orchestrator Command-Line Activity Wizard, where you configure the PowerShell cmdlet you want the activity to run. Figure 3.15 also shows that you can use parameters. Parameters are shown as input parameters for your activity.

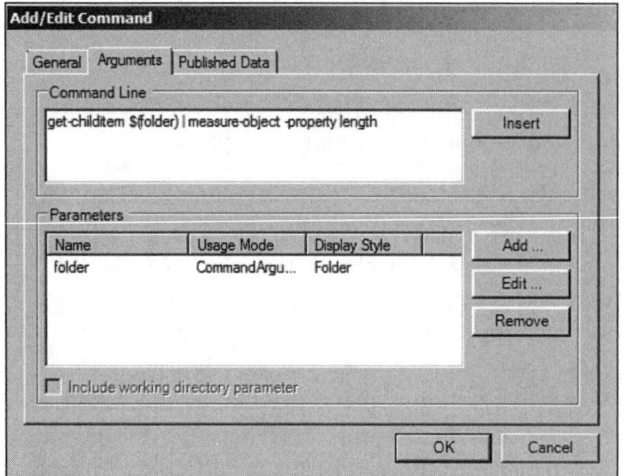

FIGURE 3.15 Configuring a command in the Orchestrator Integration Toolkit.

- **Integration Toolkit integration pack:** This integration pack contains two activities, **Invoke .NET** and **Monitor .NET**. These two activities let you run standard or monitor-type activities from your assembly files. When you create an assembly file with the Orchestrator Command-Line Activity Wizard, you can test it using these activities before including it in an integration pack.

NOTE: COMMUNITY INTEGRATION PACKS

Many integrations packs are available from the community. A good source for community integration packs is the "System Center 2012 Orchestrator Community Releases" page on CodePlex, http://orchestrator.codeplex.com. For additional information on community tools, see Appendix A, "Community Solutions and Tools."

Runbooks

A *runbook* is one or many activities connected with smart links. You can build multiple runbooks in an Orchestrator environment, and these runbooks can invoke each other. Exporting and importing runbooks is possible between Orchestrator environments; Chapter 11 discusses this in detail. The runbook is executed on a runbook server. Figure 3.16 displays a runbook.

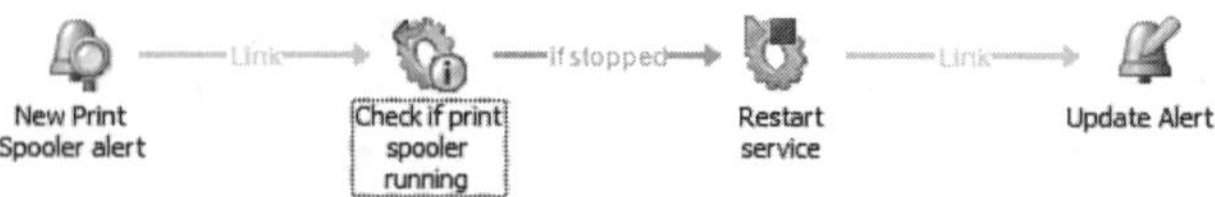

FIGURE 3.16 Example of a runbook.

Data Bus

A key component of runbook execution is the *data bus*. The data bus transfers data between activities within the runbook. The data bus can also transfer data between runbooks if they are invoked by each other. You can access all data on the data bus by right-clicking any text field in Orchestrator. A great benefit of the data bus is that the runbook author does not need to be concerned about the format of output data or about obtaining the correct output from an activity. Instead, the output data from each activity is published on the data bus in a suitable format, ready for use with other activities.

Figure 3.17 shows a runbook with three activities. The first activity reads a file, the second activity reads line 4, and the third activity inserts line 4 in a database. As shown, the third activity can use output data from earlier activities in the runbook; the third activity is subscribing to data on the data bus.

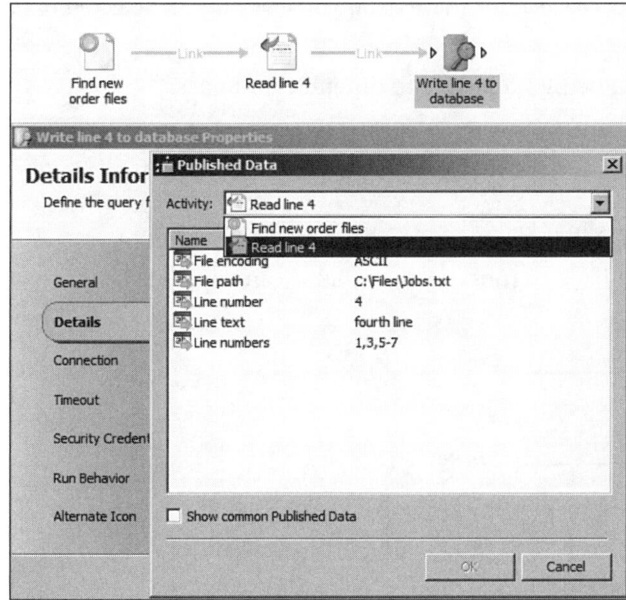

FIGURE 3.17 Published data on the data bus in the Runbook Designer.

Figure 3.18 displays how activities in the runbook publish (output) data to the data bus so that other activities within the same runbook can subscribe to the data and use it as input.

The data bus is stored in the memory of the runbook server executing the runbook. Each runbook is running within a policymodule.exe process. That process also stores the data bus and all data on the data bus. When the runbook completes, the policymodule.exe process for that runbook stops, and all data on the data bus is dropped. If you need access to the data after execution, perhaps to see what was added to the database or a filename, your runbook must include a storage capability. This could be storing the data in a log file or database.

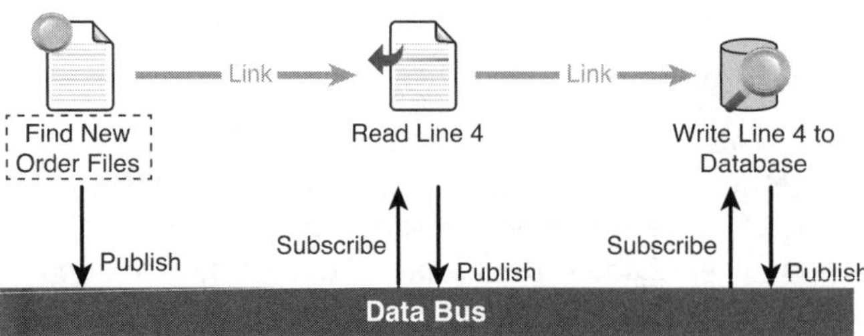

FIGURE 3.18 The Orchestrator data bus.

You cannot share the data bus between runbooks unless the same process is invoking these runbooks. For example, if you start one runbook that starts two other runbooks, you can publish data between runbooks, and you can send data to a runbook when you start it. Although in this scenario the runbooks do not share data, you can publish selected data between the runbooks.

Figure 3.19 shows an example of data being published to different runbooks:

1. Runbook A invokes runbook B.
2. Runbook B executes and publishes data back to runbook A.
3. Later in runbook A, runbook C is invoked.
4. Runbook C publishes the result back to runbook A so that it can continue processing.

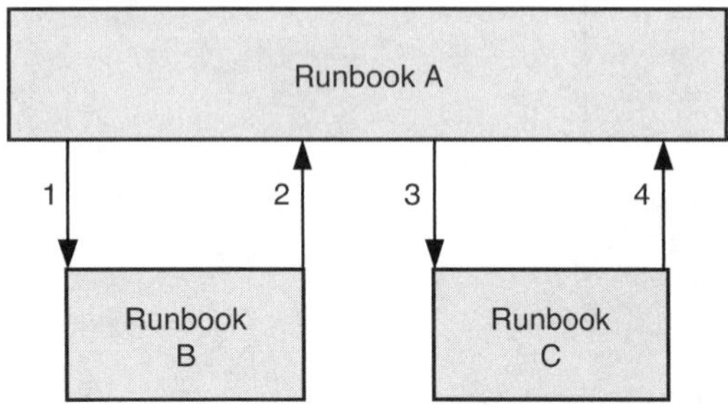

FIGURE 3.19 Data published between runbooks.

Another way to save the data is to trigger the runbook from a tool such as System Center 2012 Service Manager. If you trigger a runbook from a change request in Service Manager, you have most of the data in the change form. If the change request is to create a new account in Active Directory, the change request will include data such as requestor, department, first name, and last name.

Connectors

Some integration packs contain activities that run only locally on the runbook server, such as data manipulation integration packs. However, most integration packs include activities that integrate and connect to external systems, such as the Exchange integration pack that connects to Exchange servers and the Active Directory integration pack that connects to Active Directory environments. Each of these integration pack connections is configured in the Options menu in the Runbook Designer console. The connections are global, meaning that they are accessible to everyone running the Runbook Designer console in the Orchestrator environment. You can configure multiple connections for each integration pack; if you need to work with four Active Directory domains, you must configure four connections.

All integration packs integrate differently, depending on the target system or server, so each has different security requirements for both service accounts and firewall ports. Planning these requirements is an important step in Orchestrator design and planning. As an example, Figure 3.20 shows parameters that the Virtual Machine Manager (VMM) integration pack requires for connecting to System Center 2012 Orchestrator in a VMM environment.

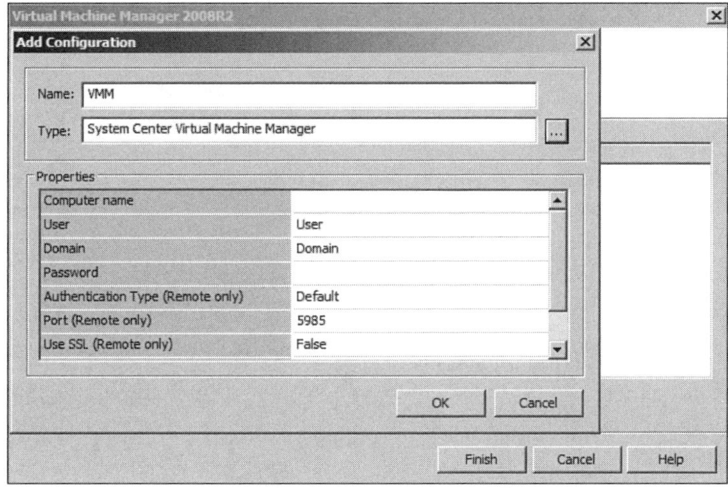

FIGURE 3.20 Virtual Machine Manager connection settings.

Consoles

System Center 2012 Orchestrator includes several different consoles and user interfaces. Some tasks, such as starting a runbook, can be performed from multiple consoles, but one user interface often is preferred. As an example, when starting a runbook, it is best to use the web-based Orchestration console rather than the Runbook Designer console.

The Orchestration console enables you to input parameters when you start the runbook, which is not possible when using the Runbook Designer console.

Using the Orchestration Console

The Orchestration console, new with System Center 2012 Orchestrator, is a web-based console. You can use this console to start and stop runbooks and to retrieve information and status regarding runbooks. You can also use it to input parameter values when starting a runbook. Figure 3.21 displays the web-based Orchestration console. For additional information on using the Orchestration console, see Chapter 6, "Using System Center 2012 Orchestrator."

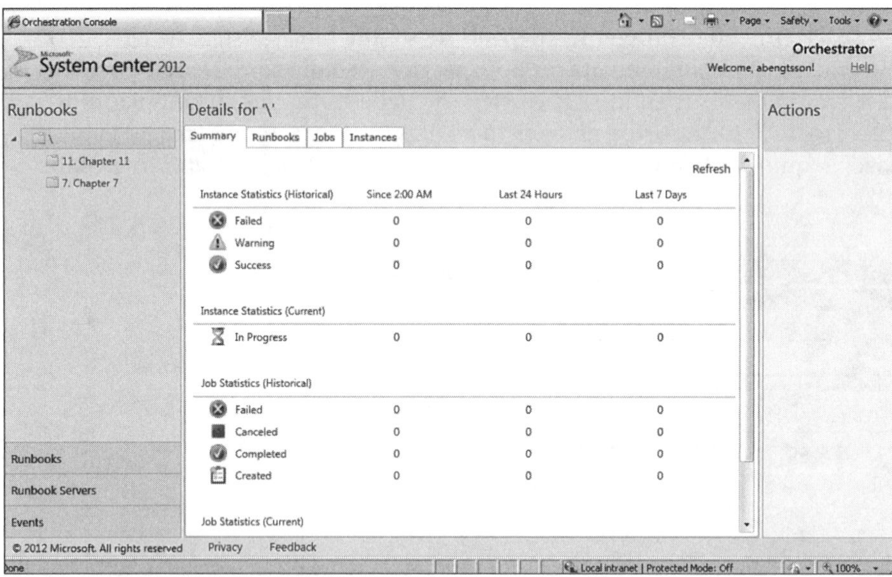

FIGURE 3.21 System Center 2012 Orchestration console.

Using Deployment Manager

Deployment Manager, which is run from the management server, is a tool used to deploy runbook servers, the Runbook Designer, and integration packs. Integration packs are deployed to runbook servers and computers that have the Runbook Designer console installed. Deployment Manager can also be used to uninstall runbook servers, Runbook Designer consoles, and integration packs. Figure 3.22 shows the Deployment Manager console. Chapter 6 provides additional information on using Deployment Manager.

Using Runbook Designer

Runbook Designer is used for designing, modifying, and deploying runbooks. You can run it from a workstation or an Orchestrator server. Figure 3.23 shows the Runbook Designer console displaying a sample runbook.

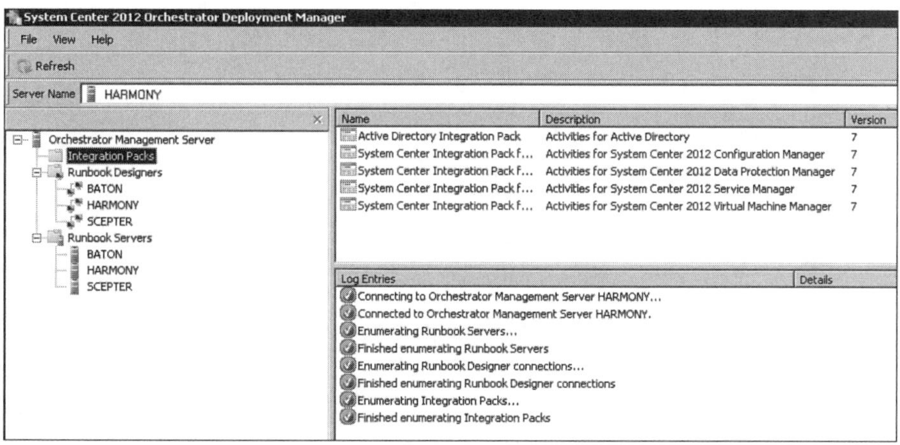

FIGURE 3.22 Deployment Manager console.

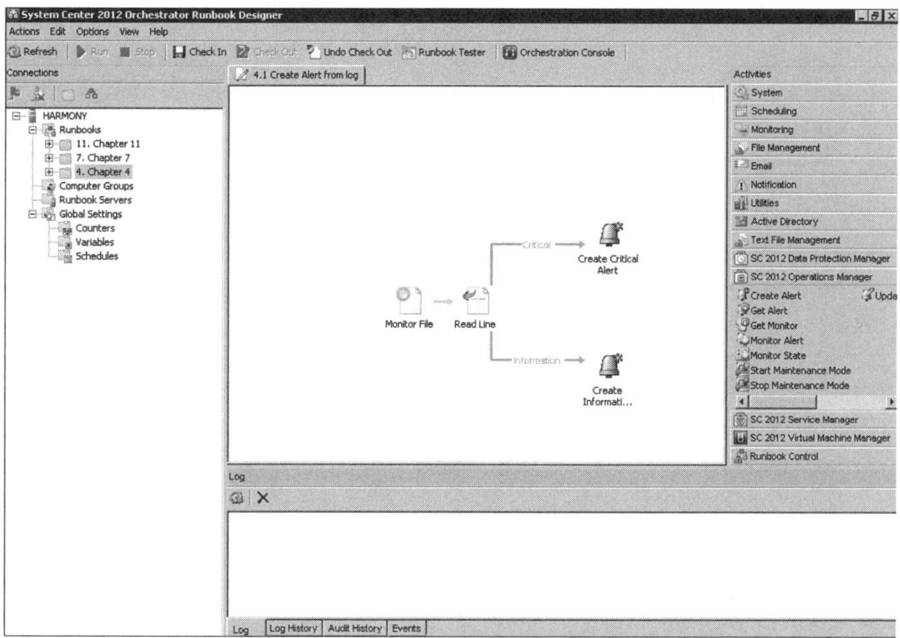

FIGURE 3.23 Runbook Designer.

Using Runbook Tester

The Runbook Tester console, shown in Figure 3.24, is started from the toolbar in the Runbook Designer console. Runbook Tester lets you test and verify runbooks before deploying them to your production environment. Using the Runbook Tester console, you can step through a runbook and review input and output data for each activity.

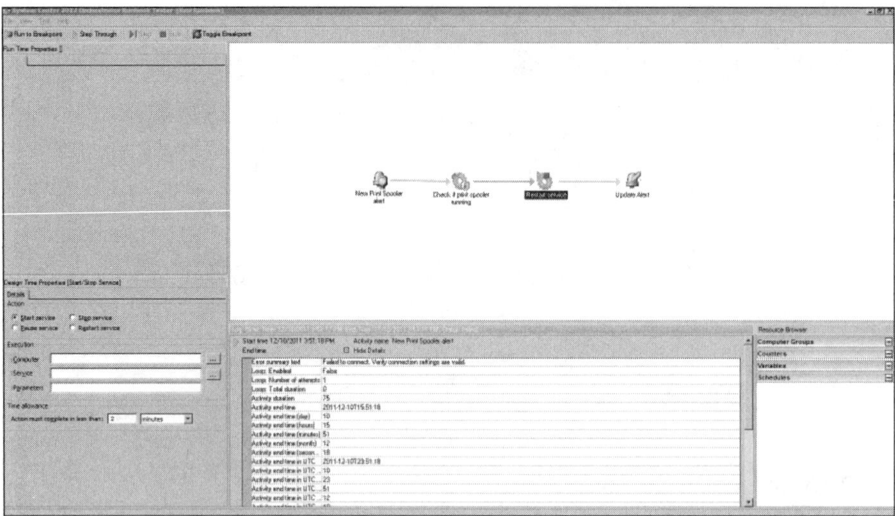

FIGURE 3.24 Runbook Tester.

Figure 3.25 shows the layout of the Runbook Tester console. The Runbook Tester is divided into six areas:

- **Toolbar:** This area contains icons such as Step Through, Run, Stop, and Toggle Breakpoint.
- **Run Time Properties:** This pane shows the configuration of the activity currently running. For example, if you have configured an activity to use a variable, this variable is resolved and shown with its current value.

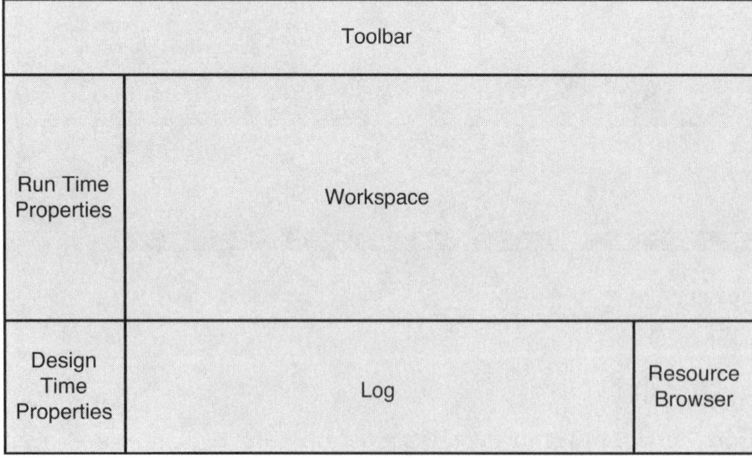

FIGURE 3.25 The areas of the Runbook Tester.

- **Design Time Properties:** This pane shows you the configuration of the currently selected activity. These are the settings you specified during the design. For example, if you configured an activity to use a variable, it is shown as the variable name, not the value.
- **Workspace:** This is where you can see your runbook and select activities.
- **Log:** This is where all published data is shown for each activity.
- **Resource Browser:** In this pane, you can look at computer groups, counters, variables, and schedules. For example, you could look at a variable and the current value.

CAUTION: RUNBOOK TESTER RUNS LOCALLY

When testing runbooks in the Runbook Tester console, the runbook runs locally on the computer. If your runbook requires a special folder structure, you must have the same structure on your local machine. For example, if you open a special firewall port between your runbook server and a target service, the Runbook Tester will not use that port; it will try to connect from the workstation running Runbook Tester directly to the target server.

Data Store Configuration

Figure 3.26 displays the Data Store Configuration tool. You can use this tool to configure which Orchestrator database the local Orchestrator server role will use. If you move the Orchestrator database, you will use the Data Store Configuration tool to update the location of the SQL Server hosting the database and the database name.

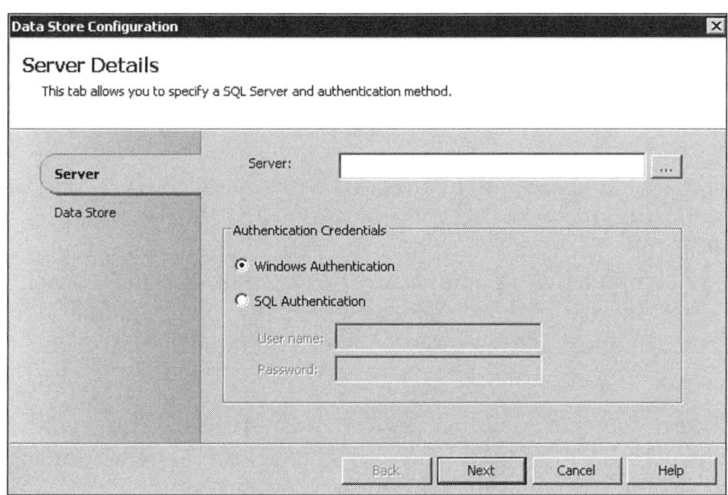

FIGURE 3.26 The Data Store Configuration tool.

Community Tools

Out of the box, Orchestrator does not include a PowerShell provider. However, a PowerShell module is available for download from CodePlex, Microsoft's open source project–hosting web site. The projects at CodePlex are open source and built by the community. Microsoft does not support these projects, so use them in production only after careful testing. The next sections discuss some of the more commonly used community tools. For additional information, see Appendix A.

CodePlex PowerShell Module

The CodePlex PowerShell module provides examples of how to use PowerShell to communicate with the Orchestrator web service. To use this module, perform the following steps:

1. Download the System Center Orchestrator Web Service PowerShell package from http://orchestrator.codeplex.com.
2. Extract the package (for example, to C:\Orchestrator).
3. Start PowerShell and navigate to the folder where the extracted package is located (for example, C:\Orchestrator).
4. Run **import-module .\OrchestratorServiceModule.psm1**.

The CodePlex PowerShell module package includes several sample scripts that show how to use the module.

Orchestrator Remote Tools

Orchestrator Remote Tools is another set of tools that you can download from CodePlex to run runbooks. Orchestrator Remote Tools provides a way to launch runbooks remotely through either a graphical user interface or the command line. You can pass input parameters to the runbook you trigger. Orchestrator Remote Tools uses the Orchestrator web service to communicate with Orchestrator.

Communication

System Center 2012 Orchestrator typically uses standard ports between each server component. As an example, communication between Orchestrator servers and the database uses standard SQL client/server protocols. The communication "hub" in Orchestrator is the database, with which all server components communicate. The Runbook Designer console communicates with the database through the management server. The Orchestration console communicates with the Orchestrator web service, which communicates with the database.

The challenge comes when integrating with multiple services and systems. Each integration pack can require different ports—for example, when integrating with System Center Data Protection Manager, you would use port 5985 with default settings. When planning your Orchestrator deployment, be sure to review network firewall ports requirements.

Table 3.1 lists communication paths and ports. The table shows default ports, which you can change if needed. If you change the default ports, be sure to update your documentation. Using nondefault ports and settings often adds an extra layer of complexity and can make troubleshooting more difficult.

TABLE 3.1 Communication Paths and Ports

Source	Target Server	Port	Note
Runbook Designer	Management server	135, 1024-65535	The Runbook Designer console uses the Distributed Component Object Model (DCOM) to communicate with the management server. You can configure which dynamic ports a server is using.
Management Server Runbook Server Web Service	Orchestrator database	1433	This port is configured during SQL Server installation. You can configure SQL to use another port.
Browser	Orchestration console Orchestrator web service	82 81	This can be configured during Orchestrator installation. Both ports must be accessible for the Orchestration console.
Deployment Manager/ Management Server	Target server	SMB/CIFS. TCP 135, 139, and 445	Ports are used when deploying a runbook server or an integration pack.
Runbook Server with integration pack	Target server		Depending on the activity and integration pack, different ports are used. Review the integration pack guide to see which ports the integration pack requires.

TIP: IF UNABLE TO OPEN ALL FIREWALL PORTS

In some scenarios, you might not be able to open all required firewall ports between the runbook server and target server. An example is in a highly secured environment with multiple locked-down networks. A solution might be to deploy one or multiple runbook servers to each secured network. The runbook server can then connect to target machines within that subnet, and you need to open only one port between the runbook server and Orchestrator database server.

3

Summary

This chapter looked inside System Center 2012 Orchestrator, beginning with an overview and then providing a detailed perspective. The chapter described the Orchestrator architecture, showed a minimum installation, and discussed how to scale out to a large deployment that includes multiple servers. It also discussed components of Orchestrator, such as the data bus, integration packs, and global settings. In addition, the chapter described the different consoles and interfaces that come with Orchestrator out of the box. The last part of this chapter discussed communication, network ports between components, and external services.

CHAPTER 4
Architectural Design

IN THIS CHAPTER

- Planning and Implementing Orchestrator
- Planning for Physical Design
- Planning for Logical Design

System Center 2012 Orchestrator is far from the largest System Center component in terms of its installation footprint, but that doesn't mean planning and design should not be considerations. Design is about capturing your organization's requirements and then building, testing, and stabilizing a solution before deploying it to production. You cannot create a good design if you have not captured your organization's requirements for Orchestrator and its implementation.

This chapter discusses design, the process of planning your Orchestrator environment, and then physical and logical design.

Planning and Implementing Orchestrator

The Microsoft Operations Framework (MOF), introduced in Chapter 1, "Orchestration, Integration, and Automation," consists of documents that provide descriptive (what to do, when, and why) and prescriptive (how to do) guidance for information technology (IT) professionals around the IT service management lifecycle. The goal of MOF is to assist IT organizations in creating, operating, and supporting IT services. It also helps organizations ensure that their investment in IT delivers expected value at an acceptable level of risk.

The IT service lifecycle encompasses the life of an IT service, from the first planning steps through design, implementation, operation, support, and termination at the end of that service. MOF divides the IT service lifecycle into three phases and one layer, as follows:

- **Plan phase:** This phase is for planning and optimizing an IT service strategy based on business goals and objectives.
- **Deliver phase:** The Deliver phase ensures that IT services are developed and deployed effectively and successfully. The phase also verifies that those services are ready for operations.
- **Operate phase:** The Operate phase describes operations, maintenance, and support of the IT service.
- **Manage layer:** The Manage layer works as a foundation providing operating principles and best practices. This layer is about IT governance, risk, compliance, roles and responsibilities, change management, and configuration. This foundation is used during all phases of an IT service lifecycle.

Chapter 1 also introduces the Information Technology Infrastructure Library (ITIL). ITIL is an international standard of best practices on using IT in service management. MOF, which Microsoft created to provide a common management framework for its platform products, is closely related to ITIL; both describe best practices for using IT service management processes.

When planning and delivering an Orchestrator implementation project, you focus on the Deliver phase. MOF divides each phase into service management functions (SMFs). An SMF is a group of activities and processes, each with its own goal and outcome. Here are the SMFs in the Deliver phase:

- **Envision:** The outcome from this SMF is a clear vision and scope for the project. The conceptual design of the solution and project risks is also documented during the Envision SMF, to communicate the project vision, scope, and risks to all project team members. If the vision or scope is incorrect, it will affect the whole project and, ultimately, the Orchestrator environment.
- **Project Planning:** The outcome from this SMF is a project plan document. The project team, customer, and stakeholders should agree that the project plan reflects the organization's needs and that the plan is realistic and achievable.
- **Build:** In the Build SMF, you build a solution that meets all requirements previously identified.
- **Stabilize:** During this SMF, you test the solution and tune it to be stable. The outcome should be a high-quality solution that meets all requirements gathered during the Envision phase.
- **Deploy:** During this SMF, you deploy the solution to production, transferring it from the project team to the operations and support teams.

MORE ABOUT MICROSOFT OPERATIONS FRAMEWORK

Microsoft Operations Framework contains many documents and much guidance. For more information on MOF, see www.microsoft.com/download/en/details.aspx?id=17647. This web page includes, among other guides, the "IT Pro Quick Start Kit."

Capturing all requirements for the proposed solution is important during the Plan phase. When you have a clear scope and vision of the Orchestrator implementation, you can begin your design. Questions to ask stakeholders to define the scope and vision of the project include these:

- Which areas of the organization will be working with Orchestrator?

  The answer to this question affects the security and administration models. As Chapter 3, "Looking Inside System Center 2012 Orchestrator," discussed, global settings, such as account settings for Active Directory (AD) accounts, are accessible by anyone with access to the Runbook Designer console. If two teams that cannot share global settings will use Orchestrator, you must deploy multiple Orchestrator environments in production or have a single production environment with a very limited Administrators group.

- Which security roles will be necessary?

  The required security roles can affect the number of Orchestrator environments because options for building security roles within Orchestrator are limited. Consider a scenario with two highly secured environments that your Orchestrator administrators cannot access. This would lead to deploying an Orchestrator environment in each network with its own administrator group.

  This question also affects the structure of runbooks, as well as permissions to run and start runbooks from the Orchestration console. One of the benefits of Orchestrator is that it can be used as a "proxy" layer. In other words, you can give someone permissions to start a runbook and input parameters that the runbook uses—without giving that person permissions to do everything the runbook does.

  Consider an example: Installing a new Operations Manager agent requires administrator permission in Operations Manager. However, you can let someone without these permissions start a runbook and supply the name of a server to be monitored. System Center Orchestrator then triggers Operations Manager and installs the agent using the Orchestrator Runbook Server service account. This ensures that the task is carried out the same way each time according the runbook design, while enabling you to limit the number of engineers with administrative permissions to the Operations Manager console.

- Which part of the organization will administer and maintain Orchestrator?

  Determining during the Plan phase who will own Orchestrator and administer it is important because this affects the release process of new runbooks. In many organizations, multiple teams author runbooks for Orchestrator. Each expert team owns its runbooks, but a central team administers the Orchestrator environment where these run. Members of this central Orchestrator team often also work as runbook and Orchestrator experts to support the other teams. They verify that best practices are followed and that each runbook is tested properly before moving it into production.

- What is the location of the services and servers with which Orchestrator will integrate?

  The answer to this question affects where you place your runbook servers, and it could affect where you place the Orchestrator database server. If you need to automate a process on a secured and isolated network, you should create an Orchestrator environment on that network as well. If you have an untrusted network where you need to connect to several servers, you might want to place a runbook server on that network, thus limiting the number of firewall ports you must open.

- Do any integration packs (IPs) meet your requirements, or do you need to develop your own?

  Before implementing Orchestrator, verify that it can integrate with the systems you have identified in need of automation. This is most likely accomplished with an integration pack from Microsoft or a Microsoft partner, a community integration pack, or a solution that incorporates standard activities. You can also build your own integration pack with the Orchestrator Integration Toolkit.

- What is the process for approving a new runbook or version of a runbook before it is placed in production?

  Planning the release process of runbooks is an important step, and you should perform it as part of your overall Orchestrator project. The release process can affect the number of Orchestrator environments and security roles.

  If multiple teams use a runbook, or if a runbook includes a mix of activities from different products and expert teams, a process must be in place to test and validate all parts of the runbook and how these parts work together.

  If a central Orchestrator team is administering the Orchestrator production environment, this team must have a process to confirm that the runbooks are ready to place into production. This team cannot validate the logical design of each runbook because team members most likely do not have that knowledge; instead, they must employ a process that includes testing before a production implementation.

- What type of reports do you need to generate?

  What type of follow-up does your organization require for runbooks? For example, must you know the number of service requests Orchestrator has handled or how much time you are saving by using Orchestrator compared to manual tasks? Orchestrator does not come with a report engine or data warehouse, so you must build any reporting capacity yourself. Before you can use data in reports, you must ensure that your runbooks generate this data and store it, perhaps in a common log database. In some organizations, you can store much of this data in System Center Service Manager and use its reporting capabilities. As an example, if you trigger runbooks based on service requests in Service Manager, most of this information is already stored in a Service Manager service request work item. You can then configure Orchestrator to publish data back to Service Manager.

- Where should log data be stored?

  When a runbook completes, all the data on the data bus is dropped. By default, Orchestrator does not log activity, other than that a runbook was executed and the result of that execution. If you want to review specific parameters and results from activities in a runbook, you must build that into your runbook design; the runbook needs to write that information to a log. This log can be multiple log files, a log database, or some other system, such as Service Manager if a Service Manager work item triggered the runbook.

  Another common solution is to create an additional database on the SQL Server hosting the Orchestrator database and use it to log information for all your runbooks.

- Does the Orchestrator environment need to be fault tolerant and highly available?

  Fault tolerance and high availability in Orchestrator affect both your physical and logical design. The physical design is affected primarily by the number of servers and placement of the Orchestrator database.

- What are the biggest pain points today when looking at time-consuming manual work?

  If you do not already have a clear list of scenarios or candidates for automation with Orchestrator, determine where your IT organization is spending most of its time currently. Talk to different teams and role owners to get an overview of where the engineers are devoting their time. You might want to gather different teams for a workshop to collect ideas about existing workflows between teams that can be potential candidates for automation. One of the benefits of Orchestrator is the opportunity to integrate and automate among common IT silos, such as virtualization, AD, and the network.

- What is the purpose or goal of the Orchestrator implementation?

  By summarizing the purpose and goal of the Orchestrator project in several sentences, you can more easily answer questions and stay focused on the goal of the project.

Planning for Physical Design

An Orchestrator design consists of physical design and logical design phases. After the vision and scope have been documented and approved, you can begin concentrating on physical and logical design. Compared to other System Center components, Orchestrator is rather simple in terms of physical design. Orchestrator does not have any complex requirements, uses only one database, and does not require any special hardware (or much hardware). However, depending on what your runbooks will automate, hardware requirements such as database space and hardware for runbook servers could vary.

Hardware Requirements

Chapter 3 discusses the different server features in Orchestrator 2012. Table 4.1 shows the recommended hardware for each feature. The table shows a single-server deployment; this is when you install all the Orchestrator features on the same machine. This implementation is suitable for smaller environments or lab environments, yet it provides flexibility for growth. You can install Orchestrator using a single-server deployment and move features later as necessary, such as placing the database on a dedicated SQL Server or adding additional runbook servers. The other features in Table 4.1 presume a multiserver deployment.

TABLE 4.1 Recommended Hardware for Orchestrator Features

Feature	Memory	CPU	Disk Space
Single-Server Deployment	4GB	Dual Core Intel 2.1GHz+	200MB
Management Server	2GB	Dual Core Intel 2.1GHz+	200MB
Runbook Server	2GB	Dual Core Intel 2.1GHz+	200MB
Database Server	8GB	Dual Core Intel 2.1GHz+	Depends on configuration
Orchestration Console	2GB	Dual Core Intel 2.1GHz+	200MB
Orchestrator Web Service	2GB	Dual Core Intel 2.1GHz+	200MB

Runbook Servers

Hardware requirements for runbook servers vary, depending on the workload the runbooks place on the server. Consider some examples:

- ▶ If you build runbooks that copy large files and temporarily store them in the runbook server, you might need to test the network connection, disk space, and storage hardware, such as a redundant array of independent disks (RAID) configuration, to ensure that read and write operations are optimized.
- ▶ If you have runbooks that use many long-running PowerShell scripts, you must scale your server to support running a large number of PowerShell shells at the same time.

The authors recommend testing all runbooks during the Stabilize phase of the project to determine that they will work on the hardware identified during the design process. Test the runbook servers for the load anticipated during normal operations: If you anticipate that a runbook will run 100 times in a typical day, test that scenario. Running 100 instances instead of a single instance of a runbook changes the hardware workload and logical design of the runbook. The number of runbook servers you need is based on placement requirements, security requirements, and runbook workload.

Orchestrator Database

The size of the Orchestrator database depends on several parameters, listed here:

- ▶ **Number of runbooks:** Orchestrator stores all configuration information for runbooks in the database; a larger number of runbooks can use more space, even if not running, compared with fewer runbooks.

- **How often a runbook runs:** Each time a runbook runs, it writes data to the database. This, together with log settings and the number of activities in the runbook, affects the size of the database.
- **Amount of data runbooks publish:** Say you have a runbook that checks a folder for new files every 5 minutes and then reads each new file and writes the first line of each file to a SQL database. That means there are three activities: **Monitor File, Read Line**, and **Write to Database.**

  For this example, assume that 10 new files are created every 5 minutes, meaning 288 (1,440 minutes ÷ 5) runbook instances per day. The **Write to Database** activity runs 10 instances each time, resulting in 21 object instances each time the runbook runs. (One instance for the **Monitor File** activity, one for each **Read Line**, and 10 new files will result in 10 instances and one **Write to Database** per new file, which will also be 10 instances.) With basic logging, Orchestrator publishes around five data items for an activity. Take a look at the math:

  ```
  24 hours / 5 minutes = 288 policy instances per day
  288 runbook instances x 21 object instances = 6,048 object instances per day
  6,048 object instances x 5 data items = 3,0240 object instance data elements
  per day
  30,240 x 7 = 211,680 object instance data elements per week
  ```

- **Log Purge:** By design, only historical runbook data is groomed from the database. If you create a runbook and later delete it, the runbook remains in the database but is marked as deleted.

  Performing all testing and authoring in a test Orchestrator environment saves space in the production Orchestrator database. Orchestrator retains 500 entries of historical data in the database by default, with a log purge executing daily at 1:00:00 a.m.

  The log purge job purges jobs from the POLICYINSTANCES, OBJECTSINSTANCES, and OBJECTSINSTANCEDATA tables in the Orchestrator database. The Historical Data pane in the Runbook Designer console shows data from these tables:

  - The Log and Log History views show selected data from the POLICYINSTANCES table.
  - When you click on a log entry, the OBJECTSINSTANCES table shows data for the objects in that policy instance.
  - When selecting an object, data for that object is read from the OBJECTSINSTANCEDATA table.

Because the Orchestrator database is the core feature in Orchestrator, it must perform well. Minimizing unnecessary data in the database by purging the logs can improve performance. To configure log purge settings, follow these steps:

1. In Runbook Designer, right-click the top level of the navigation tree, the name of the management server, and then select **Log Purge** from the context menu.

2. In the Log Purge Configuration dialog box, configure suitable settings for your organization. With default settings, the log purge runs every day at 1:00 a.m. It keeps the most recent 500 entries for each runbook in the POLICYINSTANCES table; the POLICYINSTANCES and OBJECTSINSTANCES tables maintain any related data. The database has a maximum limit of 10,000 log entries for all runbooks.

3. In the Log Purge Configuration dialog box, click **Finish** to save your changes.

TIP: DETERMINE WHICH ACTIVITY IS PUBLISHING THE MOST DATA

You can use this SQL query against your Orchestrator database to determine which activity is writing the most object instance data to your database. The query returns the number of instances, the runbook name, and the activity name.

```
SELECT COUNT(OBJECTS.NAME) AS Instances,
   R.Path AS Runbook,
   Objects.NAME
FROM OBJECTINSTANCEDATA
INNER JOIN OBJECTINSTANCES
   ON OBJECTINSTANCEDATA.ObjectInstanceID = OBJECTINSTANCES.UniqueID
INNER JOIN OBJECTS
   ON OBJECTINSTANCES.ObjectID = OBJECTS.UniqueID
INNER JOIN [Microsoft.SystemCenter.Orchestrator.Internal].Resources AS R
   ON OBJECTS.ParentID = R.UniqueID
GROUP BY R.Path,
   Objects.NAME
ORDER BY Instances DESC
```

Trace Logs

You can configure a log level for each process in Orchestrator. The log level controls how much information Orchestrator logs about the process. The log file is written to the local server's hard drive, so if you configure a new log level for a process on a runbook server, the log is written locally on that runbook server and affects only that server. The log level is set to 1 by default. You should change the log level only during troubleshooting and then change it back to 1 when troubleshooting is complete.

CAUTION: IMPACT OF HIGHER LOG LEVELS

Using a higher log level quickly fills up the hard drive. It also incurs a performance overhead; do not change these values without a clear need to do so and without understanding the impact.

Figure 4.1 shows the log level settings in the Windows registry. You can see both the log level setting and the log folder where the log file will be written. The full registry path to the log level setting is `HKEY_LOCAL_MACHINE\SOFTWARE\Wow6432Node\Microsoft\SystemCenter2012\Orchestrator\TraceLogger\PolicyModule.exe`.

Figure 4.2 shows an example of a log for policymodule.exe; the default location is *%ProgramData%*\Microsoft System Center 2012\Orchestrator\PolicyModule.exe\Logs\. Policymodule.exe is the process within an executing runbook. One policymodule.exe instance exists for each runbook.

Figure 4.3 show the runbook that generated the log file when it ran successfully. As the figure shows, this is a simple runbook with only two activities.

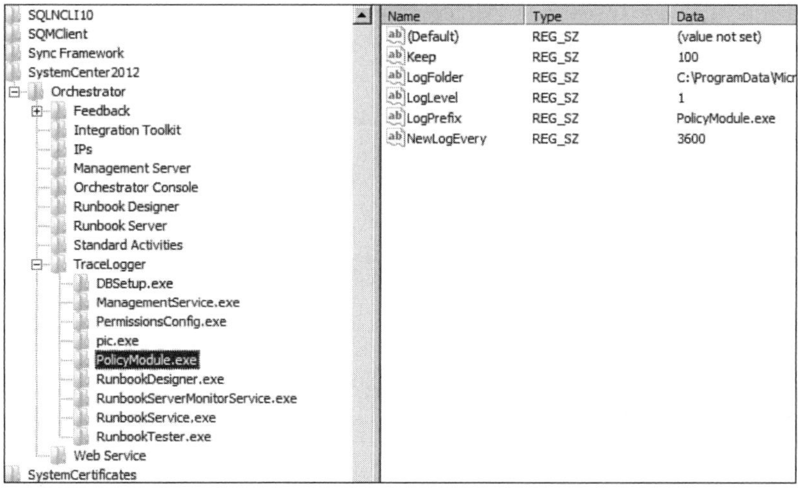

FIGURE 4.1 Log level settings.

```
Process ID: 7388
Version   : 7.0.1154.0
Computer  : HARMONY
User      : .\SCORCHUSER

2012-12-11 22:57:11 [7752] 1 AppendLine: Problem with 'FileOpen': System.IO.IOExceptionThe process
cannot access the file 'C:\TEMP\report.htm' because it is being used by another process.

2012-12-11 22:57:11 [7752] 1 AppendLine:    at System.IO.__Error.WinIOError(Int32 errorCode, String
maybeFullPath)
   at System.IO.FileStream.Init(String path, FileMode mode, FileAccess access, Int32 rights, Boolean
useRights, FileShare share, Int32 bufferSize, FileOptions options, SECURITY_ATTRIBUTES secAttrs,
String msgPath, Boolean bFromProxy)
   at System.IO.FileStream..ctor(String path, FileMode mode, FileAccess access, FileShare share)
   at Opalis.Common.IO.FileCommands.RealFileCommands.Open(String path, FileMode mode, FileAccess
access, FileShare share)
   at Opalis.Common.IO.FileCommands.FilesystemAccess.OpenAppendExclusive(String sFilePath)

2012-12-11 22:57:11 [7752] 1 AppendLine: Problem with 'FileOpen': System.IO.IOExceptionThe process
cannot access the file 'C:\TEMP\report.htm' because it is being used by another process.

2012-12-11 22:57:11 [7752] 1 AppendLine:    at System.IO.__Error.WinIOError(Int32 errorCode, String
maybeFullPath)
   at System.IO.FileStream.Init(String path, FileMode mode, FileAccess access, Int32 rights, Boolean
useRights, FileShare share, Int32 bufferSize, FileOptions options, SECURITY_ATTRIBUTES secAttrs,
String msgPath, Boolean bFromProxy)
   at System.IO.FileStream..ctor(String path, FileMode mode, FileAccess access, FileShare share)
   at Opalis.Common.IO.FileCommands.RealFileCommands.Open(String path, FileMode mode, FileAccess
access, FileShare share)
   at Opalis.Common.IO.FileCommands.FilesystemAccess.OpenAppendExclusive(String sFilePath)

2012-12-11 22:57:11 [7752] 1 AppendLine: Problem with 'FileOpen': System.IO.IOExceptionThe process
cannot access the file 'C:\TEMP\report.htm' because it is being used by another process.
```

FIGURE 4.2 Example log file for policymodule.exe.

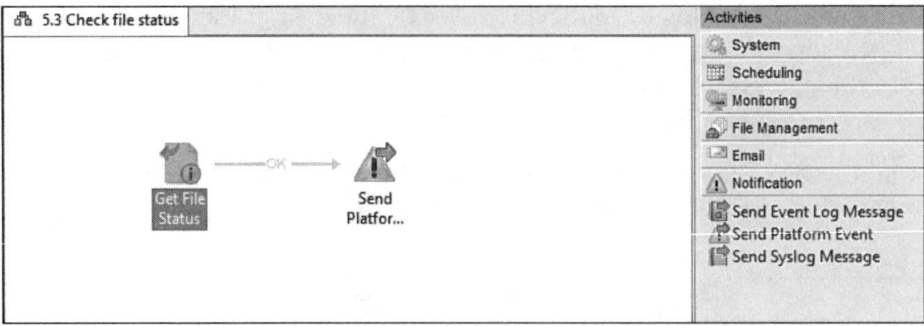

FIGURE 4.3 Simple runbook that generates a log file.

Seven log levels exist:

- **Level 1:** Logs errors only
- **Level 2:** Logs warnings only
- **Level 3:** Logs errors and warnings
- **Level 4:** Logs only informational messages
- **Level 5:** Logs informational and error messages
- **Level 6:** Logs warning and informational messages
- **Level 7:** Logs everything—informational messages, warnings, and errors

Orchestrator Web Service

As Chapter 3 discussed, the Orchestrator web service enables custom applications to connect to Orchestrator. Using the web service, other services can start and stop runbooks. The web service can also provide other services with information regarding jobs.

The Orchestrator web service communicates directly with the database. The Orchestration console, a web-based console, communicates with the web service. The number of requests and clients the web service and the web-based console can handle depends on the server hardware. Using recommended hardware, the console can handle at least six requests per minute. The heftier your hardware, the more requests your web servers and database can handle. The Orchestrator web service can be installed on multiple servers to provide load balancing, high availability, and additional capacity.

SQL Hardware Best Practices

The Orchestrator database is the core component of the Orchestrator environment. An optimally performing SQL Server hosting the Orchestrator database can make a tremendous difference in performance. Disk performance is one of the most common bottlenecks for Microsoft SQL Server. Considerations for the SQL Server system hosting the Orchestrator database include the following:

- **Virtualization:** Although Microsoft supports running the Orchestrator database in a virtual environment, virtualization inherently has a negative impact because of the overhead in the host/guest relationship. If you are considering database virtualization, ensure that adequate resources are available.
- **Separate versus shared instance:** Microsoft supports sharing SQL Server with other databases, but this often affects performance. Inherently, a SQL Server instance hosting multiple databases has a negative impact in performance capabilities as the available resources are shared.

REAL WORLD: ESTABLISH PERFORMANCE BASELINES

If you are considering virtualization or shared SQL instances, establish memory, processor, disk, and network baselines for performance before installing Orchestrator; then check the impact of the virtual or shared environment on Orchestrator performance.

- **Disk configuration:** Configure the SQL Server with one set of disks for the operating system (OS), one set of disks for TempDB, one set of disks for the transaction logs, and one set of disks for the database files. These disks should be different physical disks.
- **Physical database files:** To improve physical I/O, you can split the database over a number of physical files. If you do so, verify that the files have the same size and grow settings. SQL then distributes writes across all database files. If the files are not configured in this manner, SQL Server writes to the file with most free space.
- **Database backups:** Configure regular backups of the Orchestrator database. The transaction logs will grow continuously or crash the database without database backup, which can reduce their size.
- **Autogrow:** Disable autogrow for the Orchestrator database. Autogrow with default settings grows the database only in small pieces, so it can cause performance issues and database fragmentation. The database is locked during autogrow; this can also cause issues. Additional information regarding autogrow is available at http://support.microsoft.com/kb/315512.
- **File sizes:** Configure the TempDB database to be 20%–40% of your Orchestrator database data file size. Configure the transaction log for the Orchestrator database to be 50% of the Orchestrator database data file size. For information on optimizing TempDB performance, see http://msdn.microsoft.com/en-us/library/ms175527(SQL.100).aspx.
- **Disk controllers:** Use physical disk controllers with battery-backed write caching. This improves performance and can prevent data loss during power outages.

Server Placement

Consider three rules when determining physical placement of your Orchestrator servers:

- **Runbook servers:** Each runbook server must have a fast and stabile network connection to the Orchestrator database, with a maximum of 30ms latency, and less than 10ms latency recommended.
- **Runbook Designer:** Runbook Designer connects to the management server, so Runbook Designer users should be connected over a stable network.
- **Access to remote systems:** Runbook servers must be enabled to access remote systems, where you will execute tasks, with a maximum of 100ms latency. Runbook servers must be capable of connecting through firewall ports to these systems. A runbook server uses port 1433 by default to communicate with the SQL Server hosting the Orchestrator database (this is configurable). Depending on the integration pack and specific activities, you might decide to use different ports. Review the specific integration pack guide to see the ports required. Chapter 3 includes a complete list of firewall posts Orchestrator uses.

Network Traffic and Protocols

Standard network traffic rules apply when a runbook server connects and integrates with remote services and servers. A runbook can address network latency and unstable network connections by using another network protocol. As an example, instead of using Simple Message Blocks (SMB) to copy files over the network, consider using File Transfer Protocol (FTP). FTP is a protocol written for file transfer. SMB is more general, written to perform many different tasks.

HyperText Transfer Protocol (HTTP) is used to transfer web pages on the Internet. It is also used for the Orchestration console and Orchestrator web service. Because the HTTP protocol can handle latency and nonoptimized network connections, users of web-based services can be located on a network that is remote from the web servers hosting the Orchestration console and Orchestrator web service.

TIP: ABOUT NETWORK LATENCY

In several scenarios, Orchestrator server features must be placed separate from each other and on different networks. Remember that runbook servers communicate regularly with the Orchestrator database server. Because of the many small queries from the runbook servers to the Orchestrator database, these servers require a stable network connection to the database server, with maximum latency of 20–30ms and a recommended latency of less than 10ms. No more than 100ms latency should occur between the runbook server and the remote servers the tasks are executing on.

Physical High Availability of Orchestrator Components

Table 4.2 lists the different Orchestrator server features and approaches to make them highly available.

TABLE 4.2 Orchestrator Feature High Availability Considerations

Feature	High Availability Approach
Management Server	The management server is not required to execute runbooks. The management server is necessary only when working with the Runbook Designer console. The management server can be highly available if the server is a virtual machine running on a clustered host. Running the management server as a virtual machine on a clustered VM host protects against only hardware failure, not software failure.
Runbook Server	Deploying multiple runbook servers gives this component fault tolerance. If the primary runbook server for a runbook is offline, the runbook is executed on a secondary runbook server.
Database Server	The database can be deployed to a SQL cluster, which provides high availability.
Orchestration Console	You can deploy multiple web servers running the Orchestration console and publish them through a load balancer.
Orchestrator Web Service	You can deploy multiple web servers running the Orchestrator web service and publish them through a load balancer.

4

Even if you configure your physical server components to be highly available, you should design runbooks to handle a failover or interruption. Chapter 10, "Runbook and Configuration Best Practices," discusses additional information about fault tolerance at the runbook level. Figure 4.4 displays a design in which all Orchestrator server features are fault tolerant, based on the information in Table 4.2.

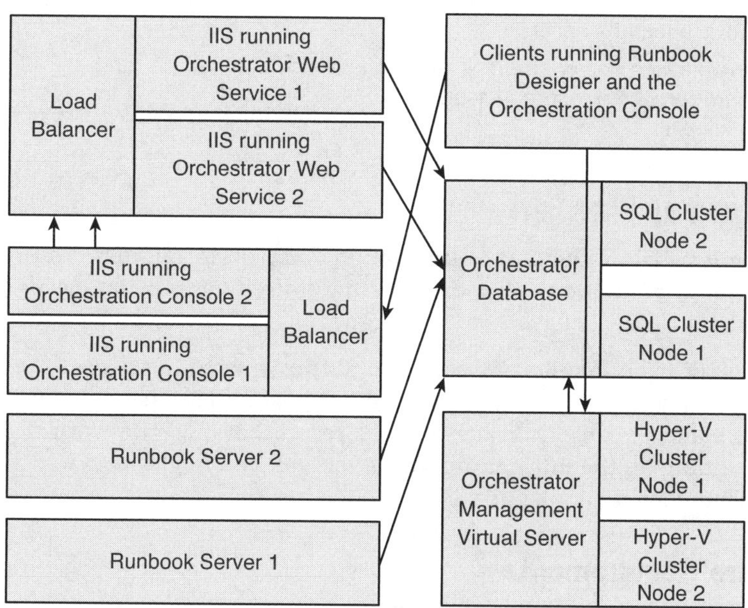

FIGURE 4.4 Fault-tolerant Orchestrator feature deployment.

Scaling Out

After you deploy Orchestrator into production, you might see an increase in the number of runbooks and the workload in each runbook; this could result in a requirement to scale out your Orchestrator environment by adding more servers. Table 4.3 lists how to scale out each Orchestrator feature. Your Orchestrator design should also include planning for scale out. Monitoring performance during operations helps you plan for scaling in the future, and the Orchestrator management pack for System Center Operations Manager gives you a foundation to use for Orchestrator monitoring. (Coauthor Anders Bengtsson has a posting at http://contoso.se/blog/?p=3338 that discusses building an Operations Manager dashboard that can show what is going on in Orchestrator.)

TABLE 4.3 Orchestrator Feature Scale-Out

Feature	High Availability Approach
Management Server	You can have only one management server in an Orchestrator environment. You can move the management server to a more powerful server, if necessary.
Runbook Server	Deploy new runbook servers and configure your runbooks to use the new runbook server as their primary server. You can also configure the new runbook server as the primary runbook server for the Orchestrator environment. Consider an example: If you have multiple secured networks, you could deploy one runbook server to each secured network. You could then configure your runbooks to run on a specific runbook server in a specific network.
Database Server	Move the Orchestrator database to a more powerful SQL Server.
Orchestration Console	Deploy multiple web servers running the Orchestration console, and publish them through a load balancer.
Orchestrator Web Service	Deploy multiple web servers running the Orchestrator web service, and publish them through a load balancer.

Planning for Logical Design

Orchestrator logical design is based on the type of integration you plan to automate and the administration and security model you will use. Orchestrator itself has only one security role out of the box, which is the Orchestrator Users group.

Although Orchestrator itself does not require any special software, integrations packs might; for example, the System Center Operations Manager integration pack requires that you install the Operations Manager console on the runbook server that integrates with Operations Manager. Depending on the integrations packs you use, you might need to install additional software on your runbook servers.

Orchestrator Software Requirements

Chapter 3 discusses the different server features of System Center 2012 Orchestrator. Table 4.4 shows the recommended software for each feature in Orchestrator. Service Pack

(SP) 1 includes support for Windows Server 2012 and SQL Server 2012. These are the software requirements for Orchestrator itself.

TABLE 4.4 Recommended Software for Orchestrator Features

Feature	Operating System	Additional Software
Single-server Deployment	Windows Server 2008 R2 SP 1 or Windows Server 2012	Microsoft SQL Server 2008 R2 SP 1, SP 2 or SQL Server 2012 or SQL Server 2012 SP 1 with the Database Engine Service and SQL_Latin1_General_CP1_CI_AS for collation .NET Framework 3.5 SP 1 Microsoft .NET Framework 4 IIS feature enabled
Management Server	Windows Server 2008 R2 SP 1 or Windows Server 2012	.NET Framework 3.5 SP 1
Runbook Server	Windows Server 2008 R2 SP 1 or Windows Server 2012	.NET Framework 3.5 SP 1
Database Server	Windows Server 2008 R2 SP 1 or Windows Server 2012, depending on SQL version	.NET Framework 3.5 SP 1 Microsoft SQL Server 2008 R2 SP 1, SP 2 or SQL Server 2012 or SQL Server 2012 SP 1 with the Database Engine Service and SQL_Latin1_General_CP1_CI_AS for collation
Orchestration Console	Windows Server 2008 R2 SP 1 or Windows Server 2012	IIS feature enabled Microsoft .NET Framework 4
Orchestrator Web Service	Windows Server 2008 R2 SP 1 or Windows Server 2012	IIS feature enabled Microsoft .NET Framework 4

Microsoft Silverlight 4 is not required on the Orchestrator web service server or the server hosting the Orchestration console, although it is required for any computer running the Orchestration console. The Runbook Designer console is supported on Windows Server 2012, Windows 7, and Windows Server 2008 R2 (both x86 and x64). Microsoft currently does not support the Runbook Designer on Windows 8. Runbook Designer requires Microsoft .NET Framework 3.5 Service Pack 1.

Runbook Design Standards and Best Practices

The authors recommend implementing runbook design standards to maintain a well-working Orchestrator environment, particularly when used by multiple engineering groups. Planning these standards is a key activity during the Design phase. The standards should include guidelines for all components of runbook design and should support a simple way to track information, such as determining which runbook generates a platform event. Your standards also should support exporting and importing runbooks between environments. Consider these recommendations for runbook standards; for a more detailed discussion, see Chapter 10:

- **Folder names:** A recommended naming standard incorporates a number and a short description; these should be unique. Figure 4.5 provides an example.
- **Runbook names:** Similar to folder names, the runbook name should contain a number and short description of the runbook; the convention should correspond to the folder names in Figure 4.5.
- **Global settings:** The structure of global settings should mirror the runbook structure: If there is a runbook in folder 1.1 Dynamic Web Farm that uses variables, these should be in a folder named 1.1 Dynamic Web Farm under global settings. This structure makes it easier to manage exporting and importing runbooks; finding and updating those global settings used in a runbook also becomes straightforward. Figure 4.6 shows a structure for global settings that corresponds to the folder naming standards in Figure 4.5.

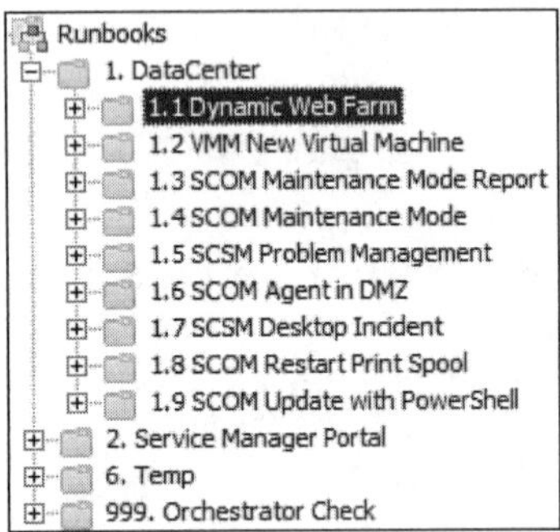

FIGURE 4.5 Example of folder naming standard.

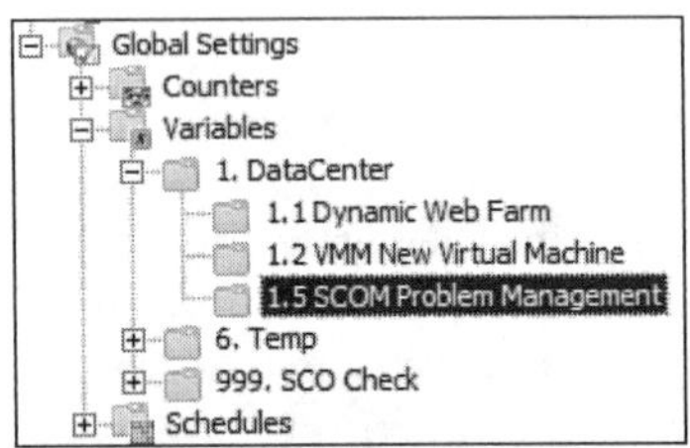

FIGURE 4.6 Example of folder naming standard for global settings.

- **Activity names:** By default, all activities keep their original names when you drag and drop them to your runbook in the Runbook Designer console. It is important to rename these to describe the action they are performing. Each activity includes a description; you can use this to describe both the actions they are executing and additional details. Try using a standard also with your activity names; for example, if you restart a service, prepend the activity name with RESTART; if you monitor for new files in a folder, begin the name of the activity with MONITOR.

- **Link colors:** The smart link color should reflect the different paths the runbook can take. The authors suggest using green to indicate success, red for critical or warning, and orange when there is a logical condition.

Looking at a runbook should provide an engineer with a basic understanding of what the runbook is doing and how it should work; runbooks should be self-documenting.

You can use the Orchestrator Visio and Word Generator, available from CodePlex, as a documentation tool. Figure 4.7 shows an example of using this tool. The tool lets you export an Orchestrator runbook as a Visio diagram, and you can generate a connected Word file. You can download this tool from http://orchestrator.codeplex.com/releases/view/75824.

NOTE: WHY FIGURE 4.7 USES OPALIS INTEGRATION SERVER TERMINOLOGY

You might notice that Figure 4.7 refers to *policies*, an Opalis term, rather than *runbooks*. This is because the Visio CodePlex tool is reading from the Orchestrator database. Microsoft changed the terminology for System Center 2012 Orchestrator, but it has not yet updated the names of the database tables. Because the tool is reading from the database, you will see references to Opalis-like terms such as policies and action servers.

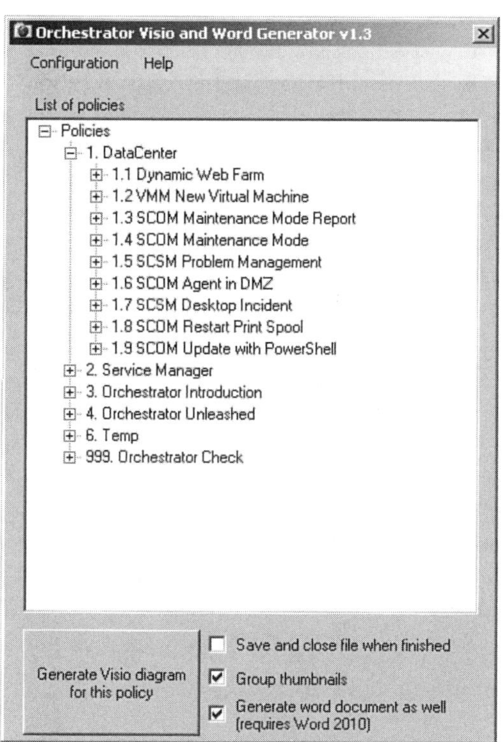

FIGURE 4.7 Example of using runbook standards with the Orchestrator Visio CodePlex tool.

For additional information on runbook design, see Chapter 7, "Runbook Basics"; Chapter 8, "Advanced Runbook Concepts"; and Chapter 10, "Runbook and Configuration Best Practices."

Service Accounts

As part of your Orchestrator installation, you should prepare several service accounts. These service accounts, which the next sections discuss, are used by the different Orchestrator services. Orchestrator requires service accounts for the services in Table 4.5. These accounts must be created before installing Orchestrator. The authors recommend using service accounts from Active Directory when possible, although this is not required. Orchestrator servers can be installed in workgroups and use local user credentials.

TABLE 4.5 Orchestrator Server Features and Services

Server Feature	Service
Management Server	Orchestrator Management Service
	Orchestrator Runbook Server Monitor service
Runbook Server	Orchestrator Runbook Service

Orchestrator Management Service Account

When you install the management server, you must specify a service account for the Orchestrator Management Service. This account is also used for the Orchestrator Runbook Server Monitor service. The service account can be a local account, although the authors recommend using an Active Directory account for the service account. If the SQL Server hosting the Orchestrator database is a remote server, you should use an Active Directory account; otherwise, you must use SQL authentication—which Microsoft does not recommend for security reasons. The service account must have local administrator privileges on the management server. During installation, the Orchestrator setup grants the Management Service account permissions to log on to the management server as a service. The Orchestrator setup also adds the service account to the Microsoft.SystemCenter.Orchestrator.Admins role in the Orchestrator database.

Orchestrator Runbook Service Account

The Orchestrator Runbook Service is installed on each runbook server in your Orchestrator environment:

- When you install a runbook server on your management server when installing the management server feature, the Orchestrator Runbook Service uses the same service account as the Orchestrator Management Service.
- If you explicitly deploy the runbook server feature to a separate server, you can specify a service account for the Orchestrator Runbook Service.

By default, all activities in a runbook run under the Orchestrator Runbook Service account. Because most of the activities and runbooks will access resources on other servers, the authors recommend that the account used for the Orchestrator Runbook Service be an Active Directory account so that it can be granted access to these other servers. The Runbook Server Service account is granted permissions during runbook server setup.

Depending on the activities in your runbooks and the services to which you are connecting, the service account might need high-level permissions. As an example, if a runbook is performing Active Directory administration, Exchange administration, and SharePoint administration, the service account most likely will have administrator permissions on all three systems. Although you could specify different accounts for each activity, it would require additional administration and is not recommended by the authors. You can also invoke a runbook with a specific account; for additional information see Chapter 11, "Security and Administration." Alternatively, you can use different runbook servers, running with different service accounts, for different categories of runbooks.

Determining the Development Process and Security Model

As part of the Plan phase, consider that many different teams will likely be involved in your Orchestrator runbook development environment. This, combined with potentially complex runbooks and the negative result of an incorrectly coded runbook on your production environment, emphasizes the need for processes in place to control access to production. As Chapter 3 discussed, you can export and import runbooks between environments, although you might need to clean up the export file. As part of the process of exporting and importing these runbooks, you should ensure that the runbook was tested and documented; the receiving Orchestrator team might not have any knowledge regarding the technology with which the runbook is integrating. Figure 4.8 shows a suggested development process. The process includes several test phases and an update phase:

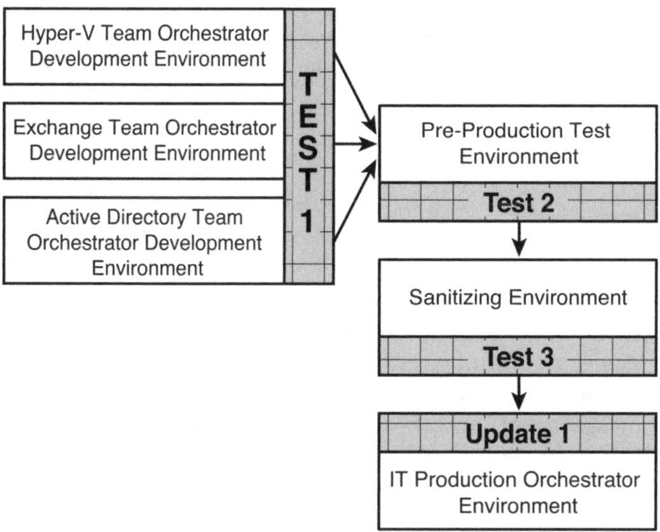

FIGURE 4.8 Example of development phase.

- **Test 1:** Each subject matter expert team carries out this phase. For example, after the Hyper-V team authors a runbook around virtual server provisioning, it tests the core functionality and ensures that the logical design is correct. The logical design considers the runbook's functionality against Hyper-V and verifies that it is following best practices.
- **Test 2:** A different subject matter expert team verifies the Test 2 phase. Say that the Active Directory team and the Exchange team have each built a runbook; this is now merged into a larger runbook, and the teams test the integration of these runbooks with each other. Test 2 also verifies that the runbook can handle interruption, can fail over to another runbook server, fulfills the organization's design standard, and supports the load anticipated in production. An example of load could be 50 instances of a runbook running every hour.
- **Test 3:** This phase verifies that nothing has changed in the runbook design while cleaning up the export file. Because all functions were tested during Test 2, it is important that nothing be changed during this phase.
- **Update 1:** During Update 1, runbook variables are updated to support the production environment, such as using the production Active Directory and production paths for folders and files. It is important that nothing else change when the runbook is deployed into production; only variables are updated according to the documentation created during the development phases.

Runbooks should be administered using version control. This means that, for each version deployed into production, you should create a package that includes the runbook and documentation. The documentation includes justification and rationale for the runbook, including all parameters, global settings, and variables. Releasing a new runbook or version of a runbook should follow a change or release management process.

- Change management is an approach to the efficient and correct handling of all changes to control IT, to minimize downtime and incidents.
- Release management consists of a methodology to plan, schedule, and control the moment of software releases from a sandbox environment to a production environment.

The goal here is to protect the production environment from unintended changes and ensure that the correct version of software is implemented. From an Orchestrator and runbook perspective, testing and review of all runbooks is an important part of these processes. At least two independent resources should perform reviews when moving between environments; having someone other than the runbook developer perform the review can help ensure identification of changes that could cause harm—whether accidental or malicious.

Figure 4.8 displayed multiple Orchestrator environments. The authors recommend multiple environments, to keep development and testing isolated and separate. A separate Orchestrator environment is used for production; this environment is limited to a small group of administrators. The production environment should be the only one with access to production system and services; this is an additional security boundary to ensure that you do not affect production during the test and development cycles.

Figure 4.9 shows different categories of Orchestrator environments. You can use these different types to build your administration model:

- **Category 1:** Category 1 consists of the production Orchestrator environment and the sanitizing environment. Cleanup must be performed correctly, and the runbook must be updated properly for the production environment; therefore, the Orchestrator central expert team should execute this process. Because the Orchestrator production environment includes service accounts with access to many production services and systems, you should limit the membership to the administrator group for this environment.
- **Category 2:** This is a central test environment that the central Orchestrator team owns, although many engineers working in category 3 environments have access to run tests in this environment. The central Orchestrator team ensures that this environment mirrors production, including integration pack versions, patch level, and runbook versions.
- **Category 3:** Category 3 environments are totally isolated and administrated by each expert team. This can consist of multiple environments, such as a number of small sandbox environments on virtual machines. The central Orchestrator group does not administer these environments; each expert team manages the security model.

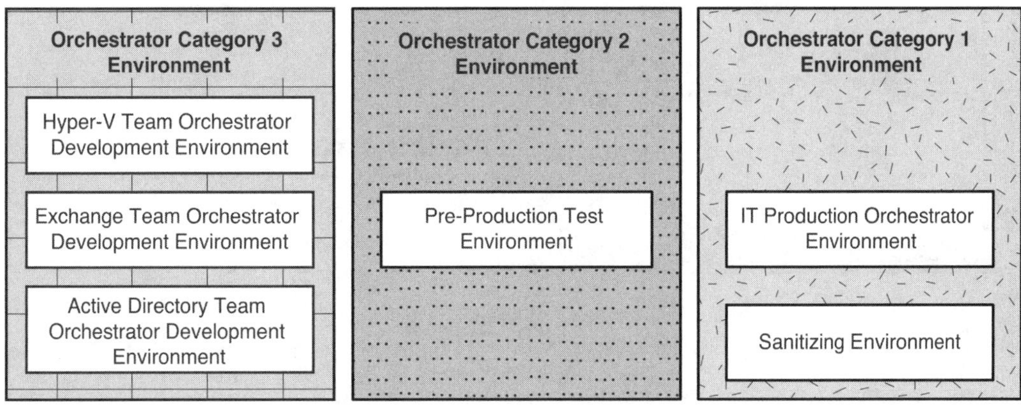

FIGURE 4.9 Examples of administration models.

Consider a scenario in which you need to install the Operations Manager agent on various systems. Possible approaches follow:

- **Allow subject matter experts, such as your Exchange team, to install the Operations Manager agent on new Exchange systems:** Installing the agent requires giving Operations Manager administrator permissions to the Exchange team. They can then start the Operations Manager console and install a new agent.
- **Have the subject matter experts contact the Operations Manager group:** Instead of the Exchange team installing the agent, the team will contact your Operations Manager administrator's team to request installing the agent.
- **Use Orchestrator to build a runbook to install the agent, and then allow your Exchange team to run that runbook from the web-based Orchestration console:** When the runbook starts, the Exchange team members will input the name of the server where they want to install the agent. The runbook can verify that they have permissions on the target server, so the agent is installed only on machines within their role. Here Orchestrator becomes a proxy because engineers can run processes with Orchestrator instead of using standard consoles, and they need access only to runbooks, not the target product. Orchestrator ensures that the task is carried out according to the process every time while limiting access to each product.

Scenarios such as this that include multiple security roles require additional planning. Who gets access to which runbook? Figure 4.10 displays a dialog box of permission settings for a runbook. Figure 4.11 shows a dialog box of permission settings for a runbook folder. This is administered in Runbook Designer and mirrored to the Orchestration console. Chapter 11 discusses the steps to configure security.

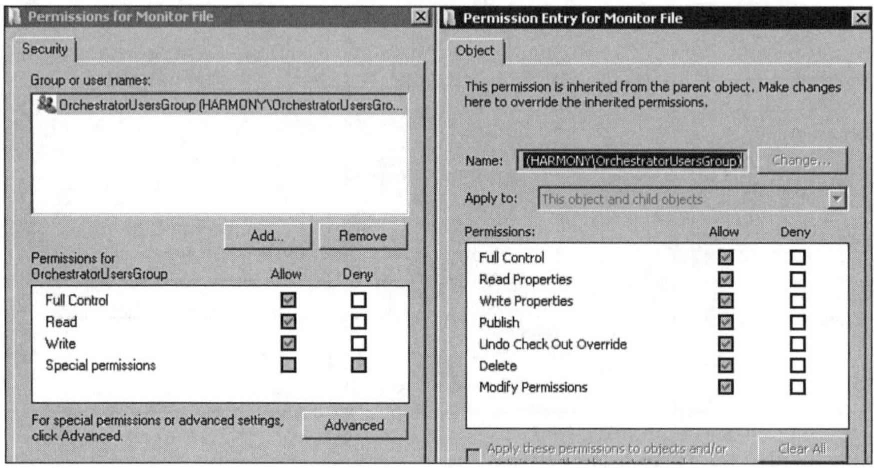

FIGURE 4.10 Security settings of a runbook in Runbook Designer.

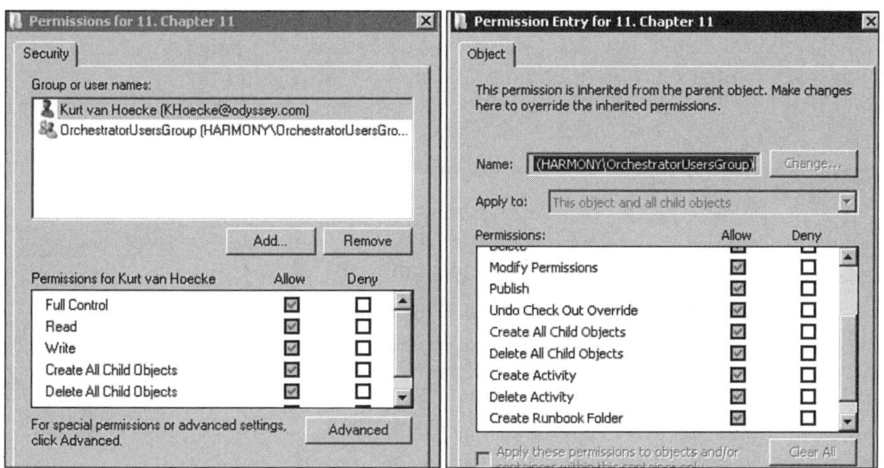

FIGURE 4.11 Security settings of a runbook folder in Runbook Designer.

REAL WORLD: USING RUNBOOKS FOR TROUBLESHOOTING

A common scenario is to use the Orchestration console when troubleshooting runbooks for incidents. Help desk personnel can start runbooks even if they do not have permissions to the target server. Runbooks can also be used for simple daily tasks such as unlocking Active Directory user accounts. Instead of giving engineers direct permissions to Active Directory, they can access a runbook that only unlocks accounts.

Designing Logical Fault Tolerance

The first runbook server installed is your default/primary runbook server. You can install additional runbook servers that will function as standby servers. If the primary runbook server does not write a heartbeat to the Orchestrator database, runbooks will fail over to the secondary runbook server. Each runbook server monitors the other runbook servers, verifying the heartbeat time stamp in the Orchestrator database.

TIP: DETERMINING THE LAST HEARTBEAT OF THE RUNBOOK SERVER

The Orchestrator Runbook Server Monitor service (RunbookServerMonitorService.exe) is installed on the Orchestrator management server by default. This service monitors runbook server status and generates a platform event on failures. The platform event is shown in the Runbook Designer console.

If a runbook server has not updated the Heartbeat column in the ACTIONSERVERS table for 45 seconds, the Orchestrator Runbook Server Monitor service generates an alert, also viewable in the Platform Event pane in the Runbook Designer console. You can use the following SQL query to see heartbeat information for your runbook servers:

```
SELECT Computer, Heartbeat, Account, Role FROM ACTIONSERVERS
```

The Role column represents the order in which the runbook servers will be used. The computer with 0 in the Role column is the primary runbook server. The secondary runbook server is 1, and so on. Table 4.6 shows sample results from the SQL query.

TABLE 4.6 Runbook Server Information

Computer	Heartbeat	Account	Role
SCEPTER	2012-04-11 11:20:36.927	ODYSSEY\OR_SVC	2
BATON	2012-04-11 11:20:36.910	ODYSSEY\OR_SVC	1
HARMONY	2012-04-10 00:21:18.873	ODYSSEY\OR_SVC	0

If your runbook fails over to another runbook server, it will start at the beginning of the workflow when it runs, regardless of how many activities were previously run on the first runbook server. Although adding runbook servers is part of your overall Orchestrator design, you should consider these implications when building runbooks because they should be designed for fault tolerance. Consider some examples:

Figure 4.12 shows a runbook with four activities. The runbook checks a database for new computer object requests and then creates new computer objects. The first activity triggers every 15 minutes, and the second activity queries a database for any new requests for computer objects. If new requests occur, computer objects are created in Active Directory. The request is then updated and marked complete in the database. This runbook will work at least as long as you request different computer objects.

FIGURE 4.12 Example of a runbook without fault tolerance.

However, this runbook will not function properly when you request a new computer object with the same name as a computer object that already exists in Active Directory. The runbook will simply halt and generate an event (see Figure 4.13). The request in the database is still marked as incomplete, and because no logging is occurring in the runbook, investigating why and where the runbook stopped is difficult. If the request is still marked as incomplete, the runbook also might pick up the same request again and continue to try to create the computer object.

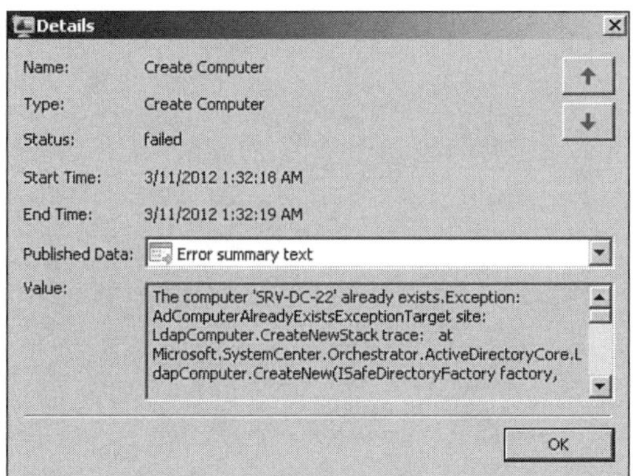

FIGURE 4.13 Runbook halts because the object already exists in Active Directory.

Figure 4.14 shows a newer version of this runbook. A check is added to see whether the computer object already exists in Active Directory. If it does, the runbook updates the request in the database with a note that the computer object already exists. However, if the incorrect server name is input in the request, you will still need a computer object and must resubmit the request with an updated suggestion for the name. This could become a reiterative manual process.

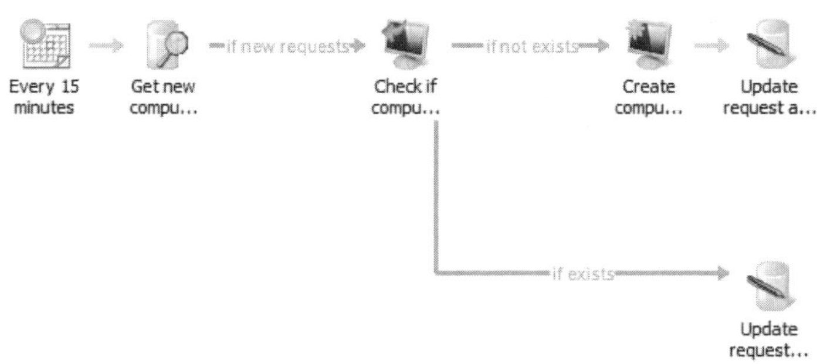

FIGURE 4.14 Runbook fault tolerance example with a check of whether it already exists.

Figure 4.15 shows a third version of the same runbook. This version includes an object to create a computer object in Active Directory even if the requested name is already in use. The second **Create computer object** activity increments the number at the end of the computer name. As an example, if you request a computer object named FILESERVER and a computer in Active Directory is already using that name, the runbook will increment the computer name with a sequence number, such as FILESERVER02.

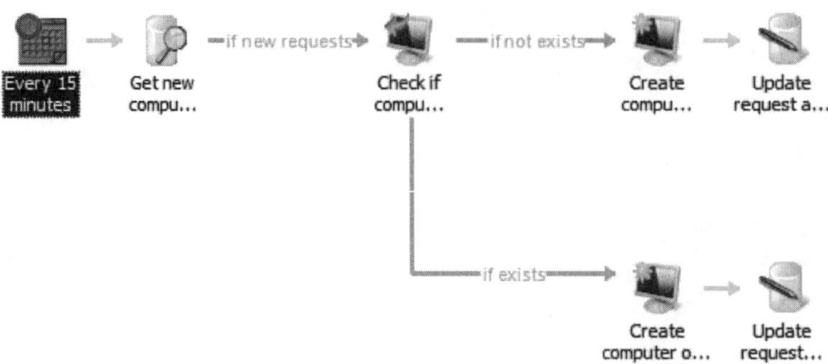

FIGURE 4.15 Runbook fault tolerance example with additional check.

You must consider many scenarios when thinking about what an activity could output or what could trigger the runbook. Poor processes do not get better because you build them inside Orchestrator; you should design stable and good processes that you can then move from Visio or paper to Orchestrator.

REAL WORLD: USING ORCHESTRATOR SHOULD BE ABOUT AUTOMATING PROCESSES

Many runbook authors try to use Orchestrator to create processes instead of using it to automate processes. During runbook design, remember that you are taking a process and automating it. A bad process does not become better by putting it inside Orchestrator.

Chapters 7, 8, 9, and 10 discuss runbook design in greater detail.

Summary

This chapter discussed the steps and phases that comprise designing an Orchestrator environment. The design should start with a clear and documented vision and scope of the project. Why are you implementing Orchestrator, and how will it be used? When you have approval of the scope and vision, you can start with physical and logical design. The decisions made during physical and logical design should be in the vision and scope documentation.

The chapter also discussed hardware and software requirements, which depend on the type of runbooks you will build and run; this is also true for service accounts, security models, and service placement. It covered the importance of processes and standards for a successfully Orchestrator environment, which includes a process for development and for moving runbooks between environments, in addition to standards for naming and structuring runbooks and their components. The chapter also discussed the importance of designing for fault tolerance within runbooks.

PART II

Installation and Implementation

IN THIS PART

CHAPTER 5

Installing System Center 2012 Orchestrator

IN THIS CHAPTER

- ▶ Orchestrator Installation Roadmap
- ▶ Installing Orchestrator
- ▶ Performing Post-Installation Tasks

This chapter discusses how to install System Center Orchestrator. Installing Orchestrator is a relatively straightforward and easy process. The setup wizard is similar to those of other System Center components; you select a bundled or standalone installation, depending on your infrastructure design. This chapter covers both methods of installation and discusses pre-installation prerequisites and post-installation steps, providing a complete roadmap for installing System Center Orchestrator.

By this point in the book, you should have a good understanding of the different Orchestrator components (as discussed in Chapter 3, "Looking Inside System Center 2012 Orchestrator") and be familiar with planning for an Orchestrator environment and the different options for configuration (as discussed in Chapter 4, "Architectural Design").

Following the procedures explained in this chapter enables you to successfully install System Center Orchestrator and extend its infrastructure.

Orchestrator Installation Roadmap

Installing a System Center component is not difficult; each component is primarily wizard driven. However, without proper planning, a "simple" installation could create issues down the road. Similar to other software installations, the authors recommend instituting a planning phase before running the setup wizard.

The following sections include information regarding an Orchestrator installation:

- The "Planning for Installation" section lists information you need to know before starting the installation.
- The "Installing Orchestrator Features" section describes the installation and installation options.
- The "Performing Post-Installation Tasks" section provides an overview of configuration and installation options, such as integration packs after installing the Orchestrator features.

Planning for Installation

Have all required information available when beginning your Orchestrator installation. Decisions to make before installing Orchestrator include determining the placement of the various Orchestrator features and database and web console locations. The following sections present an overview of the information you need before you begin installation and a checklist for installing the different Orchestrator features. This includes design concepts and installation prerequisites.

NOTE: MICROSOFT DOCUMENTATION FOR DEPLOYING SYSTEM CENTER 2012 ORCHESTRATOR

Microsoft's TechNet jumping-off page for deploying Orchestrator is at http://technet.microsoft.com/en-us/library/hh420337.aspx.

Orchestrator Design

As part of the design process, create a System Center 2012 Orchestrator design document that describes the infrastructure elements. The design decisions in the document define what is configured during installation. At a minimum, you should answer the following items while designing your infrastructure. Chapter 4 provides information regarding your design of the Orchestrator environment, including the following:

- Orchestrator server placement in the data center
- Orchestrator features and high availability requirements of these features
- Service account definition and usage for the Orchestrator environment
- Orchestrator database high availability requirements

After addressing these areas and compiling the necessary information, you can evaluate installation prerequisites.

Installation Prerequisites and Feature Assignment

Review prerequisites for the servers in scope of the Orchestrator architecture. Chapter 4 discusses hardware requirements and provides information regarding software prerequisites. A System Center 2012 Orchestrator installation has six primary features, discussed in this chapter:

- Orchestrator management server
- Orchestrator runbook server
- Orchestrator database
- Orchestration console and web service (must be installed on the same machine)
- Orchestrator Runbook Designer

The authors recommend installation in an Active Directory domain, although this is not required. You can deploy Orchestrator in a single-server environment or using multiple servers, depending on security considerations and the number of anticipated runbooks. For additional information, see Chapter 3.

Consider this brief overview of the Orchestrator system requirements:

- Operating system for server features (management, runbook, and web service servers)
  - Windows Server 2008 R2 Service Pack (SP) 1 Standard, Enterprise, or Datacenter editions
  - Windows Server 2012 Standard or Datacenter editions
- Operating system for client features (Orchestrator Runbook Designer)
  - Windows 7 (32- or 64-bit)
  - Windows Server 2008 R2 SP 1
  - Windows Server 2012
- SQL Server supported versions
  - SQL Server 2008 R2 SP 1 Standard, Datacenter
  - SQL Server 2008 SP 1 Standard, Datacenter
  - SQL Server 2012 Standard, Enterprise (64-bit)
  - SQL Server 2012 SP 1 Standard, Enterprise (64-bit); SQL Server 2012 AlwaysOn functionality supported
- Software requirements for Orchestration console
  - Silverlight 4
  - Internet Explorer 8, 9, or 10
- Software requirements for server features
  - .NET Framework 3.5 SP 1 (all server features)
  - .NET Framework 4.0 for Orchestrator web service (or .NET Framework 4.5 on Windows Server 2012)

Figure 5.1 shows the software prerequisites and feature assignments for the Odyssey Orchestrator installation used throughout this book. The installation procedures in this chapter include a complete installation of this Orchestrator environment. Figure 5.1 shows a Windows Server 2008 environment, but you can install Orchestrator in Windows Server 2012 as well if you are using System Center 2012 Service Pack 1.

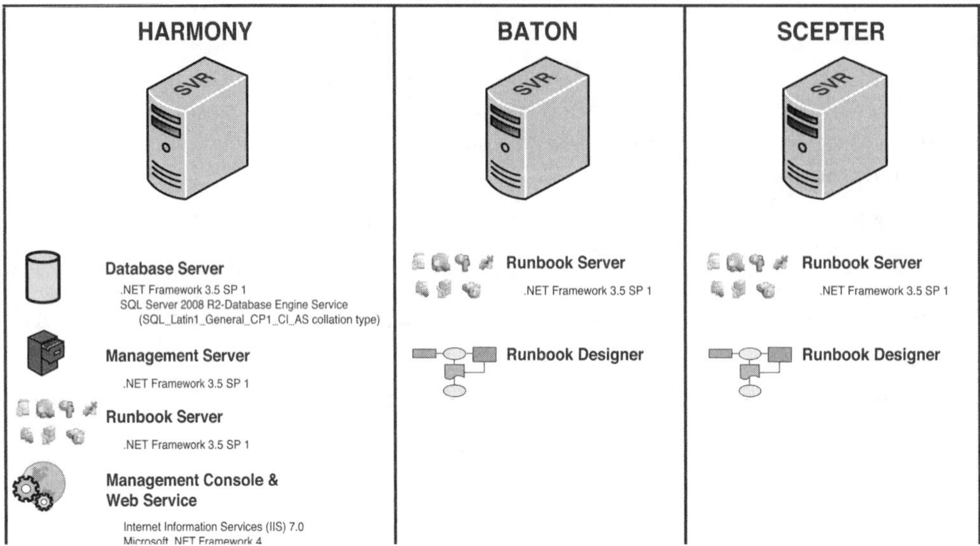

FIGURE 5.1 Orchestrator feature assignment for the Odyssey environment.

Installing Orchestrator Features

You can install System Center Orchestrator using a single-server scenario or install different features on separate servers. The basic Orchestrator infrastructure is a single management server, Orchestrator database, runbook server, and Runbook Designer console. You can also install additional runbook servers and Runbook Designer consoles when requirements change or additional runbooks are placed into production. Primary factors affecting the architecture are high availability and expected load.

TIP: INSTALLATION ACCOUNT SECURITY CONSIDERATIONS

Administrator access on the server is required for installing the Orchestrator features. The authors recommend using a dedicated installation account with adequate rights on the servers used for your Orchestrator deployment. You can use the Management Service account, but administrative rights must be specially assigned for installation because this account does not require local Administrator rights during normal operations.

Performing Post-Installation Tasks

After installing the Orchestrator infrastructure, you must perform some basic configuration before starting to build runbooks. This includes customizing security settings, registering integration packs (IPs), migrating Opalis policies, and establishing backups.

Security settings for your environment must be applied. If different entities can create or execute runbooks, verify that you have designed the appropriate folder and security configuration for the Runbook Designer. This organizes the folder structure in Runbook Designer, and those users who need to initiate runbooks can connect to the Orchestration console to execute the runbook.

The default installation includes a rich set of activities ready for use. These are known as *standard activities*; Chapter 9, "Standard Activities," covers these activities. Registering IPs is a post-installation task to populate your environment with extra activities. Examples of IPs for Orchestrator include the System Center IPs, discussed in Chapter 13, "Integration with System Center Operations Manager," through Chapter 17, "Integration with System Center Date Protection Manager." In an upgrade scenario, post-installation tasks include migrating any existing Opalis policies to Orchestrator runbooks.

Defining a backup strategy for your Orchestrator environment is an important post-installation task. The first task in backing up Orchestrator is to back up the Orchestrator database. The authors also recommend that you regularly export your runbooks to have an offline copy of your automations; this enables you to utilize this runbook export as an additional backup.

The Odyssey Orchestrator environment is built from scratch and focuses on automating System Center. Post-installation, the System Center integration packs must be registered and deployed. Figure 5.2 shows the IPs that will be registered and deployed in the Odyssey Orchestrator environment.

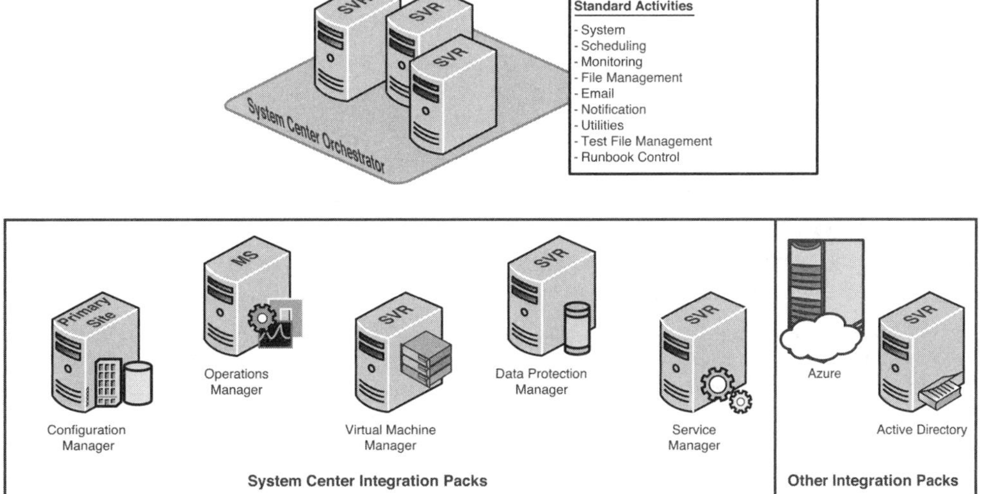

FIGURE 5.2 System Center Orchestrator integration.

Installing Orchestrator

This section discusses the procedures for installing the Orchestrator infrastructure. This design information is used for the installation:

- Orchestrator will be deployed in a data center in a single physical location.
- The Orchestrator features are placed as follows, and Table 5.1 lists an overview of the servers and associated features:
    - Management and runbook server features are installed on a single server.
    - Orchestration console and web service features are installed on the management server.
    - Additional runbook servers are installed on additional servers in the environment.
    - The Runbook Designer is installed on every server in the environment.
    - The SQL Server hosting the Orchestrator database is installed on the management server.

TABLE 5.1 Servers and Orchestrator Feature Assignment for an Odyssey Environment

Server	Orchestrator Feature
Harmony	Orchestrator management server
	Orchestrator runbook server
	Member server
	SQL Server
	Runbook Designer
Baton	Orchestrator runbook server
	Runbook Designer
Scepter	Orchestrator runbook server
	Runbook Designer

- The Odyssey environment used in this book uses the same Active Directory account for the Management Service and Runbook Service accounts. Review the service account information in Chapter 4 to specify the account settings for your environment. The Runbook Service account executes runbooks, unless overridden on a specific runbook configuration.
    - **Orchestrator Management Service account:** Odyssey\OR_SVC
    - **Orchestrator Runbook Service account:** Odyssey\OR_SVC

Installing the Management Server

The first server installed in an Orchestrator environment is the management server. For the Odyssey installation, the Harmony server contains the management server feature together with the other features Table 5.1 summarizes. Perform the following steps to install the Orchestrator management server:

1. To start the System Center 2012 - Orchestrator Setup Wizard on the server where you want to install Orchestrator, navigate to the folder that contains the installation files and double-click **SetupOrchestrator.exe**.
2. On the main setup page, click **Install** (see Figure 5.3).

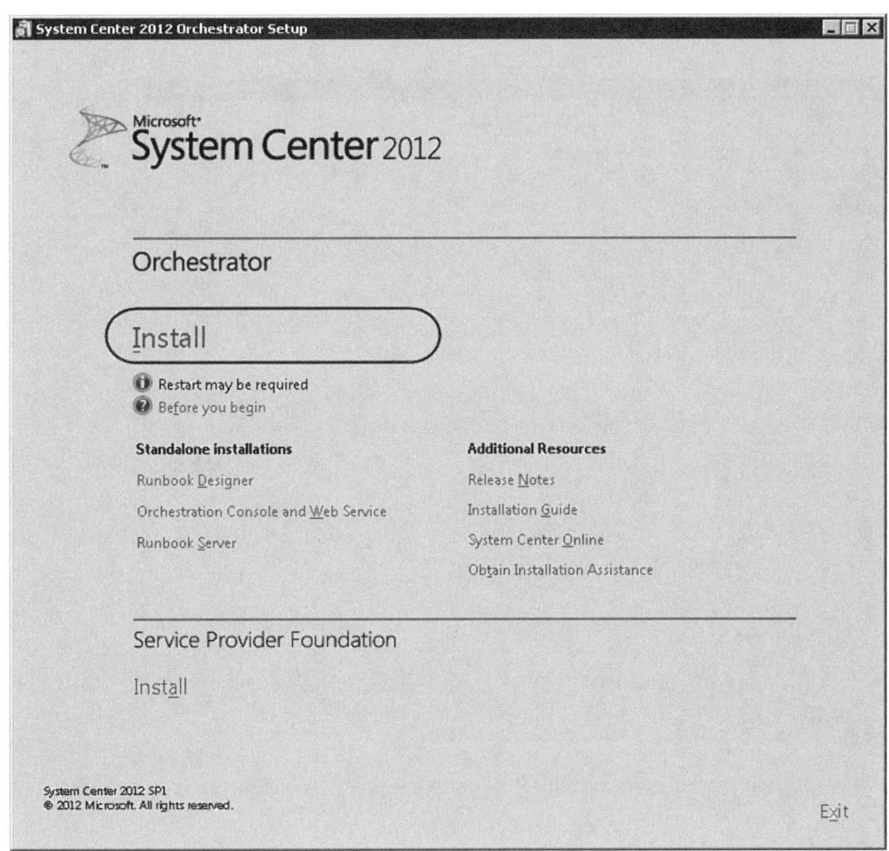

FIGURE 5.3 Splash screen of the System Center 2012 - Orchestrator Setup Wizard.

3. On the Product registration page, enter the name and company for the product registration. If a product key is not provided, an evaluation version of Orchestrator is installed. Click **Next** after specifying all required information.

NOTE: ORCHESTRATOR EVALUATION VERSION EXPIRATION

Full product functionality is available in the evaluation version of Orchestrator. You can enter a valid product key at the expiration date of the evaluation edition (a pop-up warning appears).

4. On the Please read this license agreement page, review and accept the Microsoft Software License Terms. Then click **Next**.
5. On the Select features to install page, select the required features and click **Next**. For the Odyssey environment, the first server to install is the Harmony server, which will host all Orchestrator features. Select all features for the Harmony server installation (see Figure 5.4).

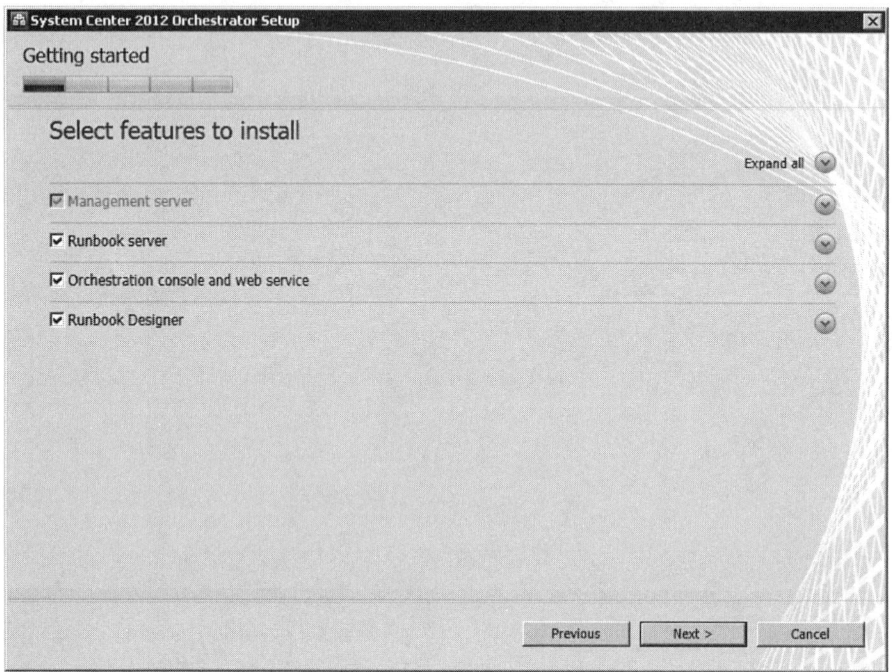

FIGURE 5.4 Selecting the features to install. The management server feature is required.

NOTE: MULTIFEATURE INSTALLATIONS AND SERVICE ACCOUNTS

If you install multiple features at the same time, the same service account is used for each feature. If you need to use different service accounts for each feature, the feature installations must occur as separate installations so that you can specify a specific service account for each feature installation.

6. On the Prerequisites page, the server is checked against the recommended hardware and software system requirements. If the server meets the requirements, the wizard continues to the Service Account selection page.

   If a prerequisite is not met, a warning page displays information about the prerequisite that has not been met and how to resolve the issue. The prerequisite checker can identify three different types of warning levels:

   - A warning for a prerequisites check that did not pass. This type of warning provides information to remediate the condition but does not block you from continuing with the installation. Figure 5.5 displays an example, showing a memory check warning.

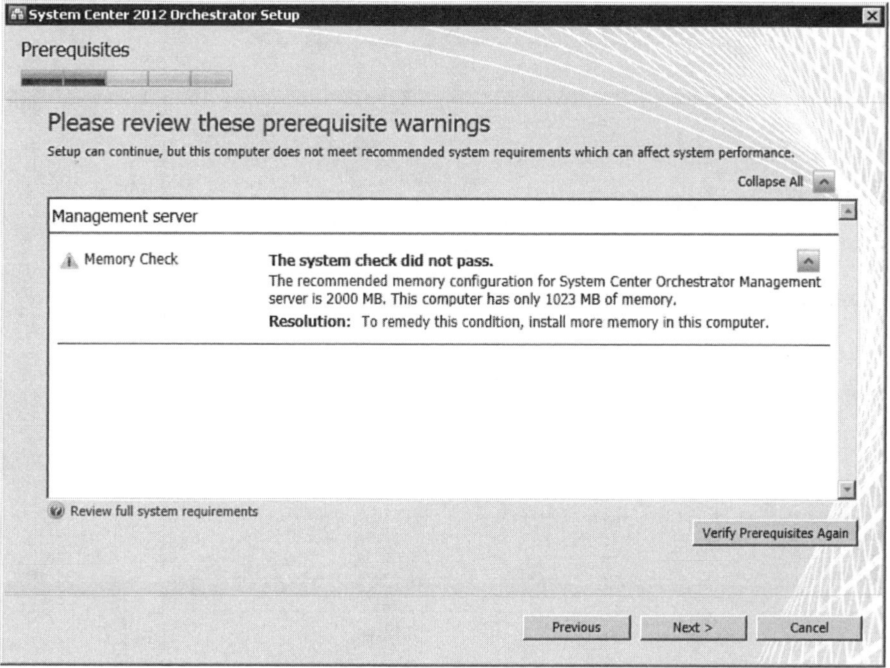

FIGURE 5.5 Example of failed prerequisite check.

   - Installation cannot continue. To fix software warnings preventing installation, the wizard provides a link to install the missing requirement. Figure 5.6 illustrates an example with a warning that Microsoft .Net Framework 4 is missing. .Net Framework 4.5 is checked when installing on Windows Server 2012.

   - Setup will install missing software prerequisites. The wizard can install or configure prerequisites such as Internet Information Services (IIS) (see Figure 5.7).

5

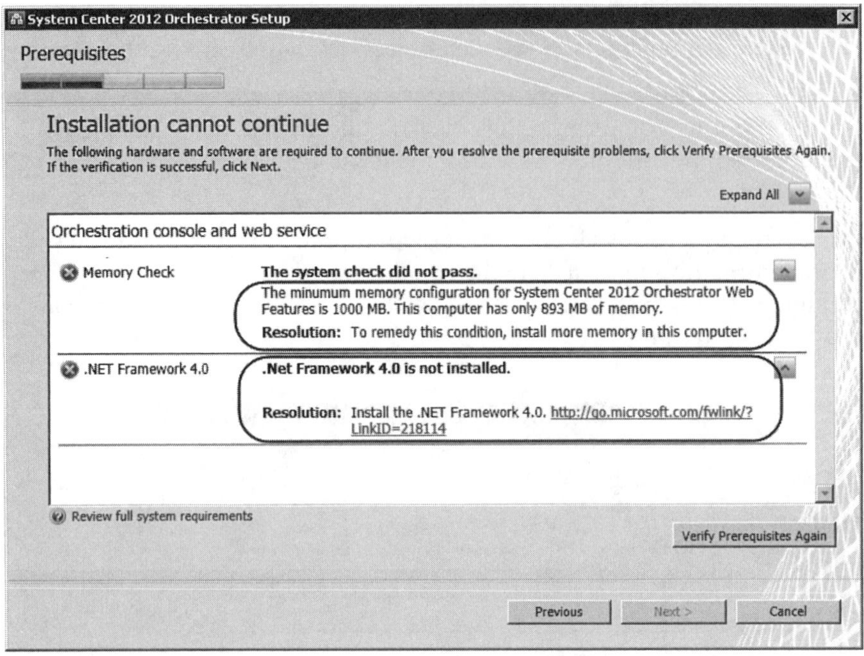

FIGURE 5.6 Example of software prerequisite warnings.

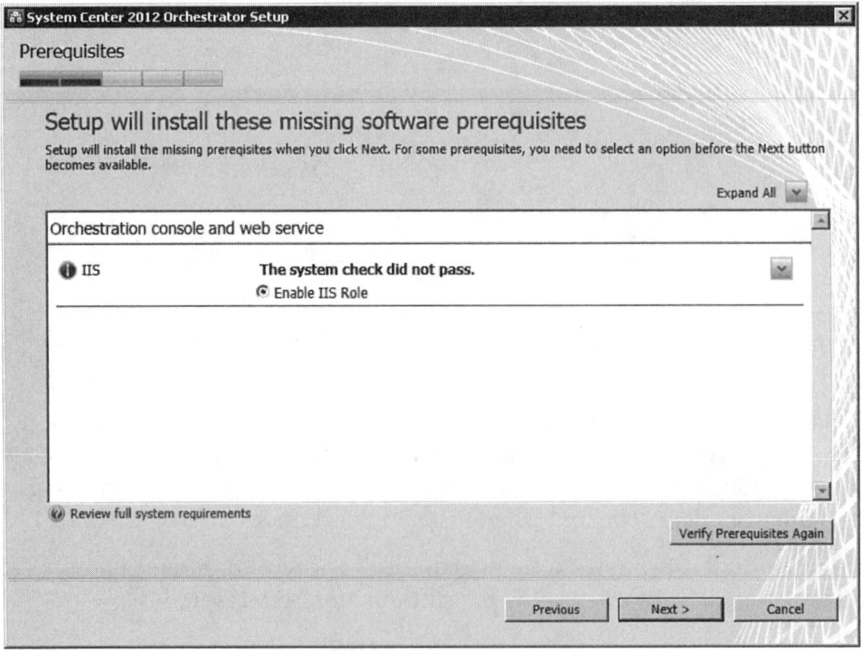

FIGURE 5.7 Windows server feature prerequisite warning.

After resolving any missing prerequisites, click **Verify Prerequisites Again**. After all prerequisites are installed, click **Next**. The All prerequisites are installed page appears. Click **Next** to proceed.

7. On the Configure the service account page, enter the username and password for the Orchestrator Management Service account. Click **Test** to verify the account credentials. If the credentials are accepted, as in Figure 5.8, click **Next**.

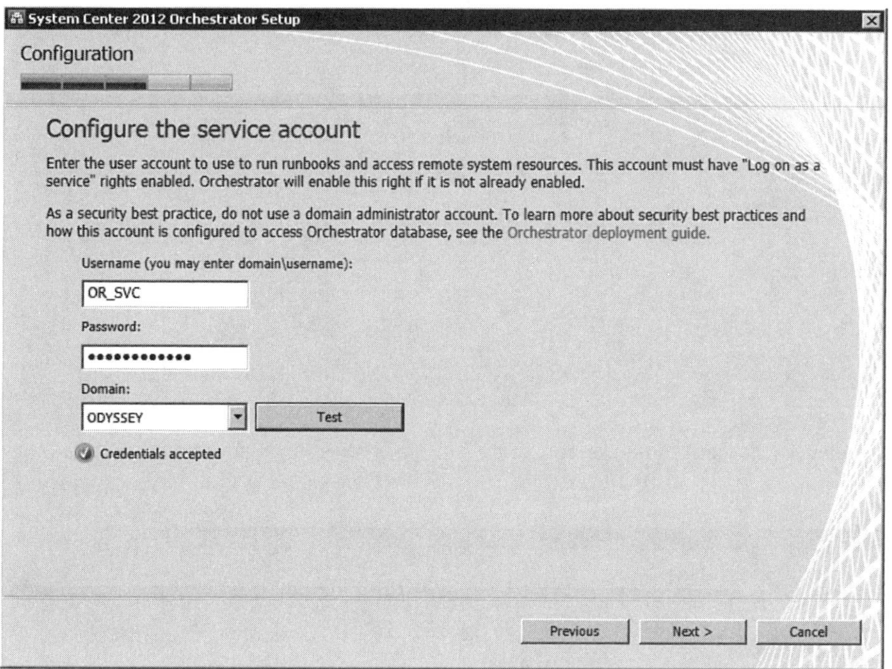

FIGURE 5.8 Configure the service account page of the installation wizard.

8. On the Configure the database server page, enter the name of the server, the instance, and the port number of the Microsoft SQL Server to be used by Orchestrator. You can also specify whether to use Windows Authentication or SQL Server Authentication. Figure 5.9 shows the configuration of the database server on Harmony. Click **Test Database Connection** to verify the account credentials. If the credentials are accepted, click **Next**.

9. On the Configure the database page, specify the name of the new database. For this installation, a new database is created with the default name of Orchestrator, illustrated in Figure 5.10. Click **Next** to continue.

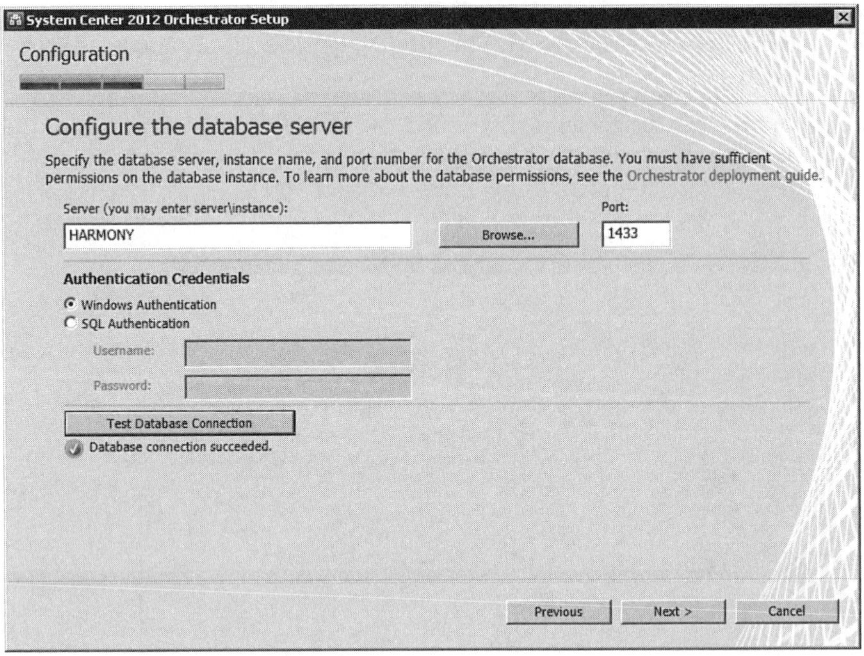

FIGURE 5.9 Specifying the database server, port, and authentication credentials.

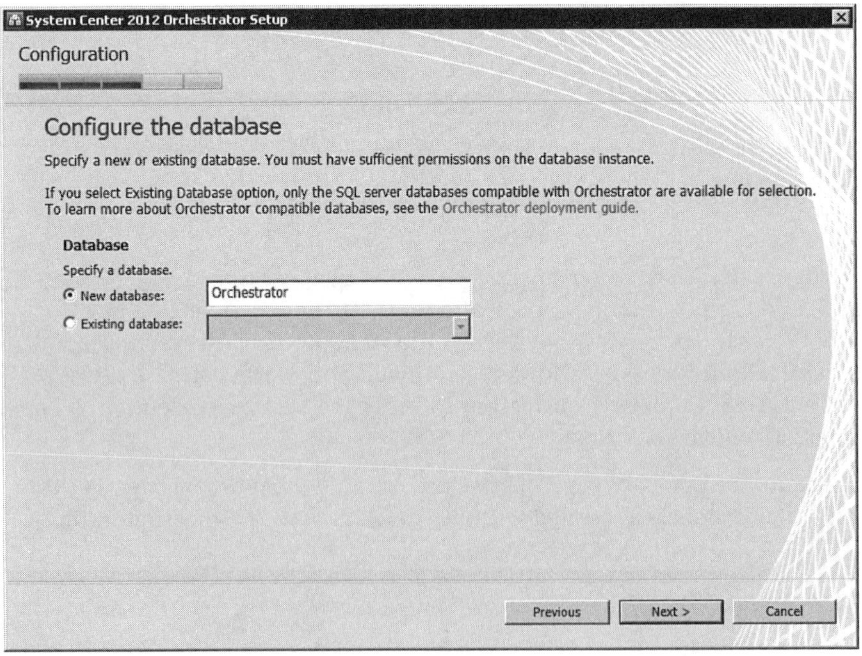

FIGURE 5.10 Configuring the Orchestrator database.

NOTE: RIGHTS FOR CREATING THE ORCHESTRATOR DATABASE

Creating the new Orchestrator database through the installation wizard requires the person running the setup wizard to have sysadmin rights on the SQL Server to create the database.

10. On the Configure Orchestrator users group page, either accept the default or select **Browse** to enter the name of the group that will have administrative access to Orchestrator and can manage Orchestrator permissions. Preferably, this is an Active Directory domain group, but you can also select a local group.

    This page also includes the option to enable remote access for the Runbook Designer. This default-enabled option enables you to install and run the designer on a computer other than the management server.

    Figure 5.11 shows the (default) configuration for this installation. After providing the information, click **Next** to proceed.

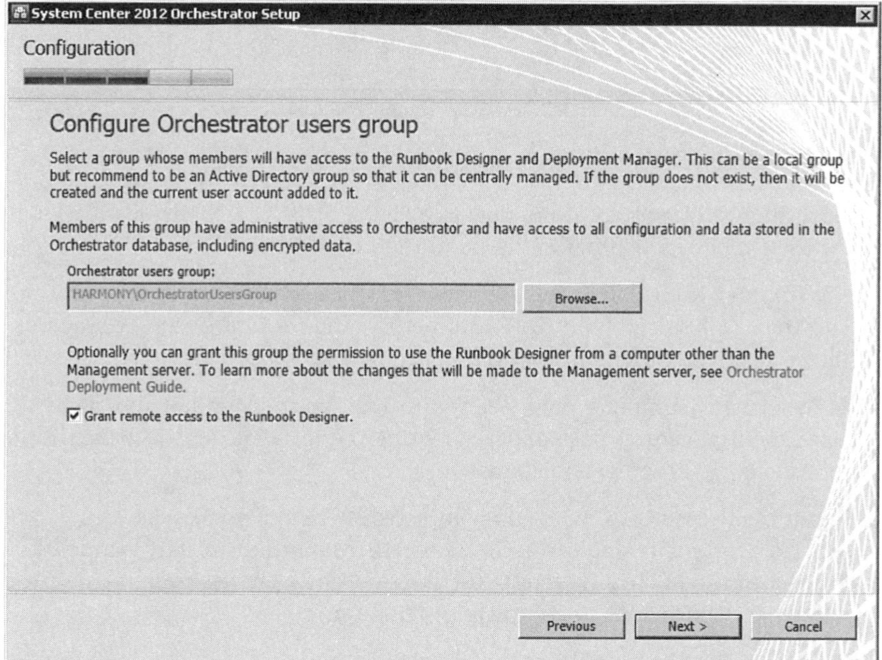

FIGURE 5.11 The Orchestrator user group configuration page.

11. On the Configure the port for the web services page, specify port numbers for the Orchestrator web service and Orchestration console and click **Next**. Figure 5.12 displays the default port numbers selection for Odyssey.

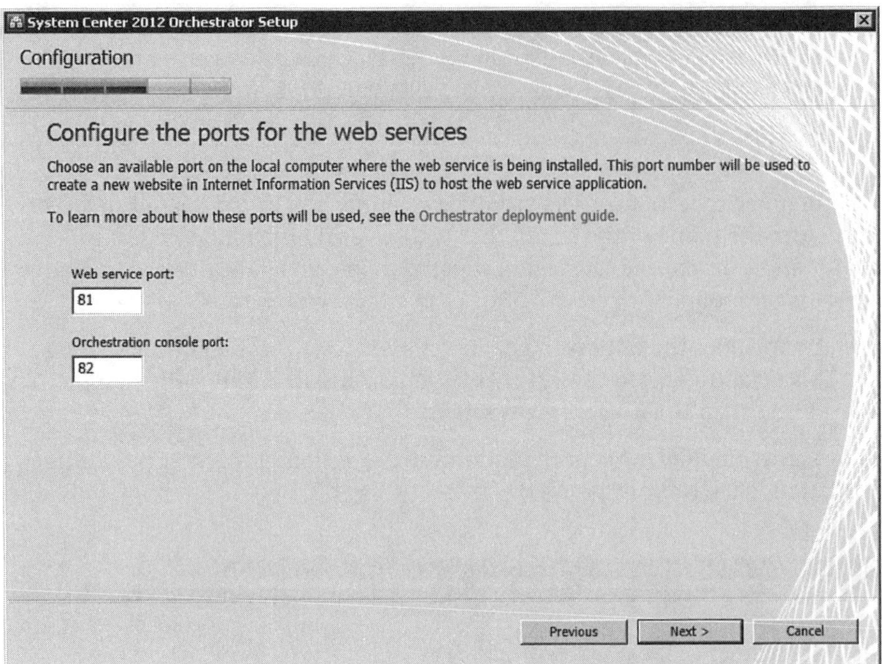

FIGURE 5.12 Web services port configuration page of the installation wizard.

12. On the Select the installation location page (see Figure 5.13), verify the installation location for the Orchestrator program files and then click **Next**.

13. On the Help improve Microsoft System Center Orchestrator page, optionally indicate whether you want to participate in the Customer Experience Improvement Program (CEIP) or Error Reporting; then click **Next**.

14. Review the Installation summary page (see Figure 5.14 for an example) and click **Install**. The Installing features page appears. During the installation, this page shows the feature installation progress and status.

15. When all features are installed, the Setup completed successfully page displays (see Figure 5.15). Optionally you can indicate whether you want to start Windows Update, connect to the Microsoft website for System Center Orchestrator, or start the Runbook Designer. Click **Close** to complete installation.

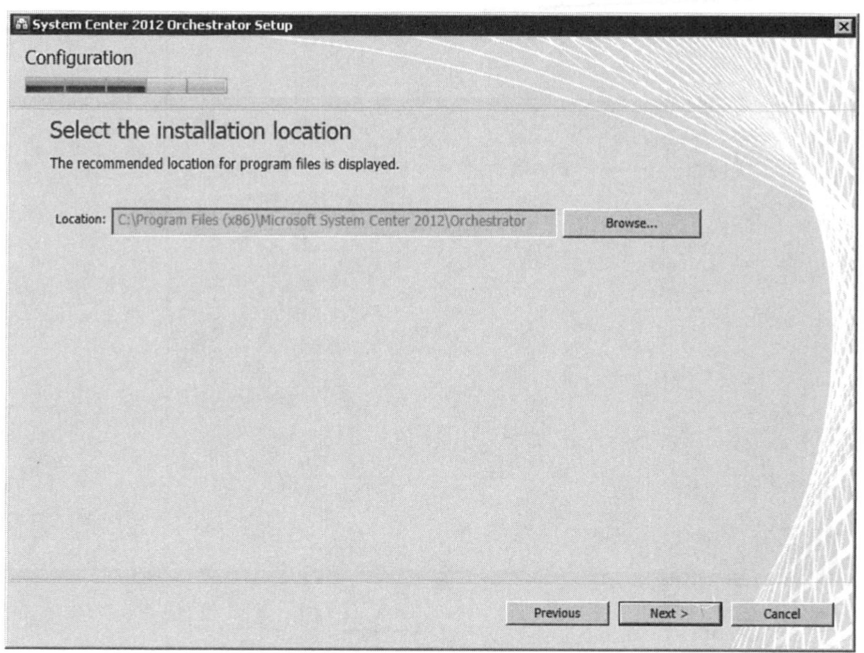

FIGURE 5.13 Specifying the installation location.

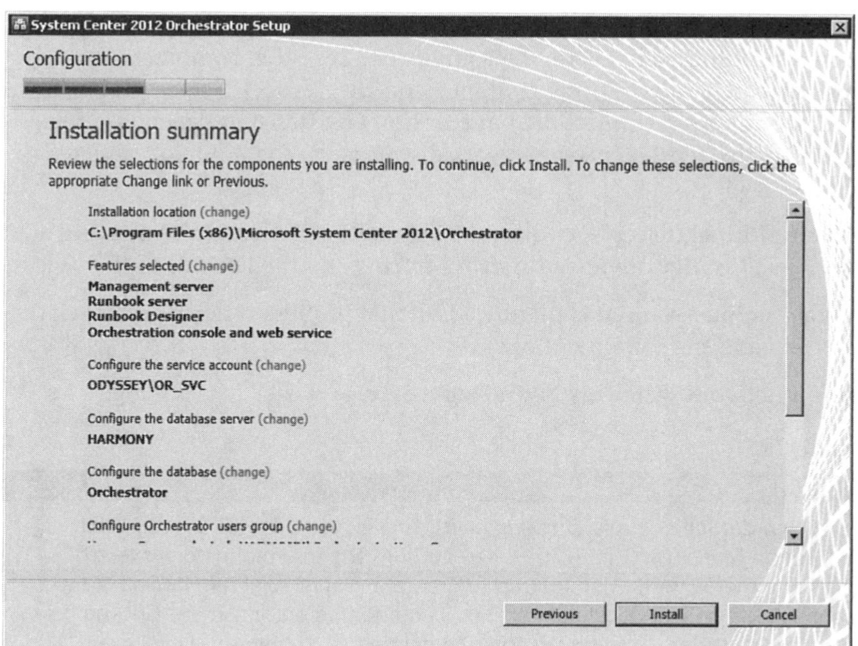

FIGURE 5.14 Installation configuration summary.

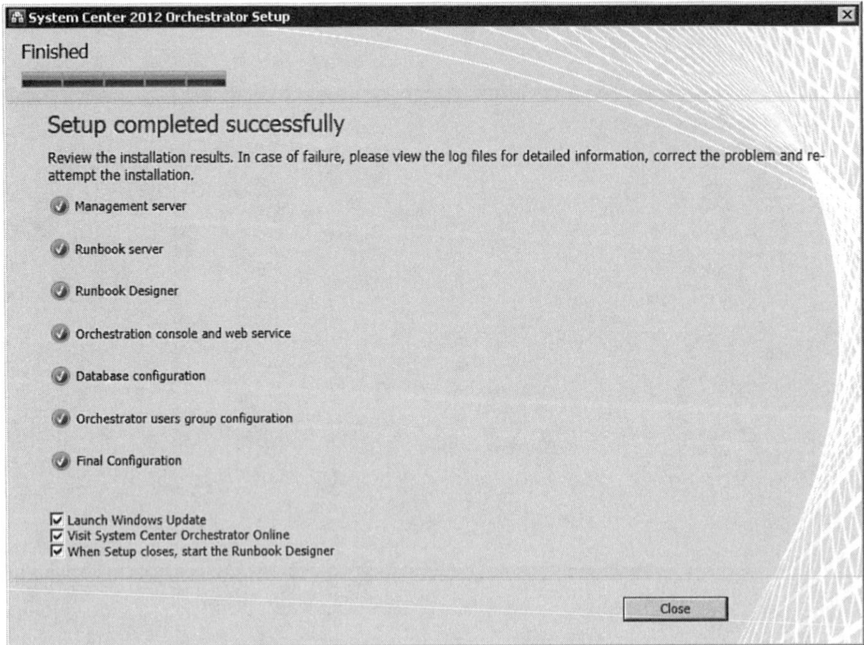

FIGURE 5.15 The Finished page of the Orchestrator Setup Wizard.

Enabling Network Discovery on the Runbook Designer computer is an additional step. Network discovery is a setting that enables the computer to see other computers and allows that computer to be visible to other computers on the network. Server enumerations (the Browse button for server selections) in the Runbook Designer depend on this functionality. Follow these steps to enable network discovery on the Runbook Designer computer:

1. Open the Control Panel, select **Network and Internet** -> **Network and Sharing Center**, and select **Change advanced sharing settings** on the left side of the page.
2. For the Domain profile (you can configure additional profiles, if necessary), click the arrow icon to expand the section options.
3. Select **Turn on network discovery**, as in Figure 5.16, and click **Save changes**.

TIP: ENABLING NETWORK DISCOVERY

No direct group policy setting controls enabling network discovery. The GPO setting you can use is the Turn on Mapper I/O (LLTDIO) driver setting. The information discovered by Mapper I/O allows the Network Map feature to create a graphic diagram depicting the devices and connections on your local subnet. You can find this setting in the GPO editor under **Computer Configuration** -> **Administrative Templates** -> **Network** -> **Link-Layer Topology Discovery**.

Change sharing options for different network profiles
Windows creates a separate network profile for each network you use. You can choose specific options for each profile.
Home or Work
Public
Domain (current profile)
Network discovery
When network discovery is on, this computer can see other network computers and devices and is visible to other network computers. What is network discovery?
Turn on network discovery
Turn off network discovery

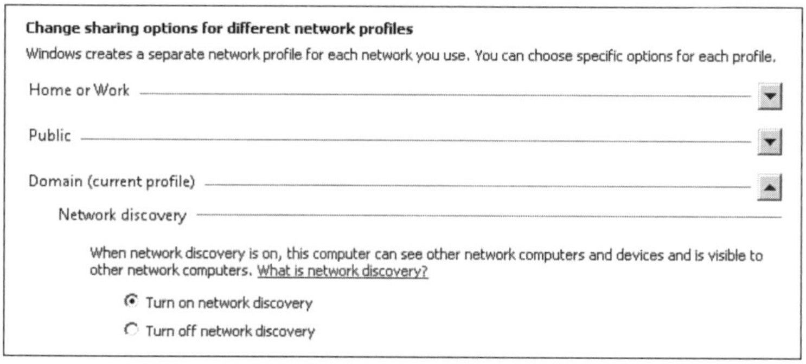

FIGURE 5.16 Enabling network discovery.

Installing the Runbook Server Using Installation Media

Using the **Install** link on the Orchestrator start page, you can install the runbook server with the management server or on a separate server.

Perform the following steps to install the runbook server on a separate computer. For this installation, Baton is an additional runbook server in the Odyssey environment.

1. Start the System Center 2012 - Orchestrator Setup Wizard on the server where you want to install Orchestrator by navigating to the folder that contains the installation files and double-clicking **SetupOrchestrator.exe**.

2. On the main setup page, under Standalone installations, click **Runbook Server** (see Figure 5.17).

3. Provide the required information on the Product Registration page and accept the software license terms on the Please read this license agreement page. Click **Next** on both pages in the wizard to continue.

4. On the Prerequisites page, the server is checked against the recommended hardware and software requirements. If the server meets all the prerequisites, the wizard continues to the Service Account selection page.

5. On the Configure the service account page, enter the username and password for the Runbook Service account. Click **Test** to verify the account credentials. After the credentials are accepted, click **Next**.

6. On the Configure the database server page, enter the name of the server and instance and the port number of the Microsoft SQL Server you want to use for Orchestrator.

   Specify whether to use Windows Authentication or SQL Server Authentication. The Odyssey environment uses the Harmony server and Windows Authentication. Click **Test Database Connection** to verify the account credentials. After the credentials are accepted, click **Next**.

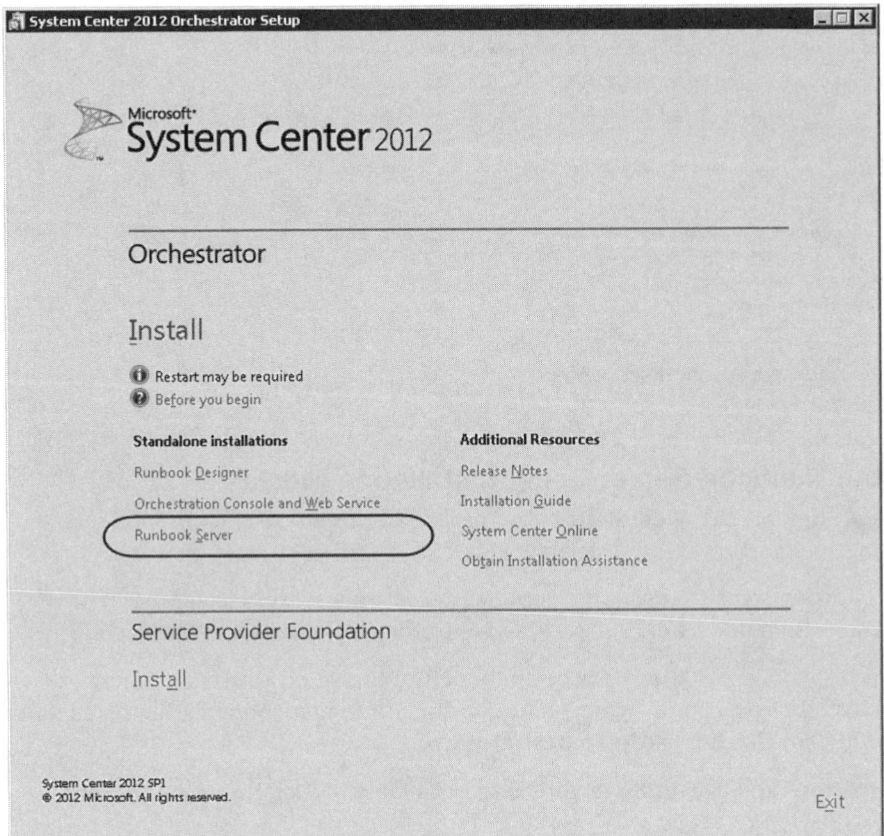

FIGURE 5.17 Opting to install the Runbook Server feature.

7. On the Configure the database page, select an existing database and click **Next**. The Orchestrator database was installed during the management server installation on Harmony, and this database is now selected for this installation (see Figure 5.18). The option to create a new database is grayed out at this point because only the management server installation can create a new database.
8. On the Select the installation location page, verify the installation location for the Orchestrator runbook server installation; then click **Next**.
9. Specify your selection on the Help with System Center 2012 Orchestrator page, and click **Next**.
10. Review the Installation summary page and click **Install**. Figure 5.19 shows an overview of the runbook server configuration on the Baton server. The Installing features page appears and displays the installation progress for each feature.

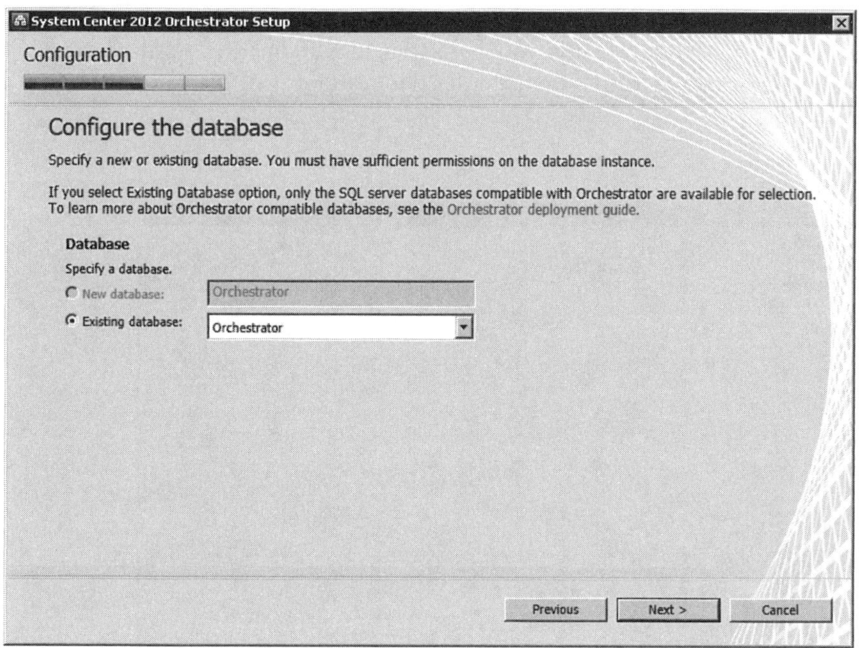

FIGURE 5.18 The Configure the database page when installing the runbook server.

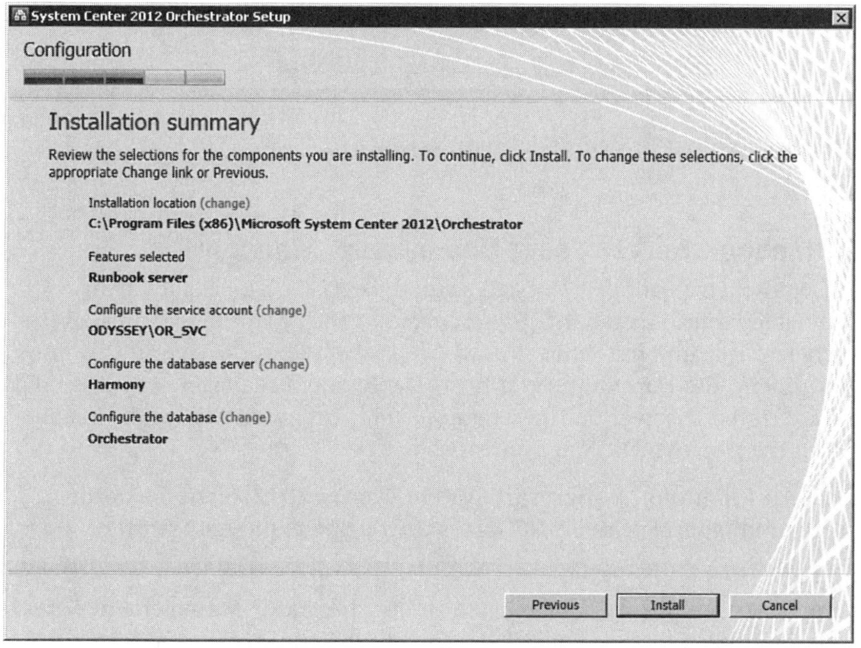

FIGURE 5.19 Configuration summary overview for the runbook server installation.

11. When the runbook server feature is installed, the Setup completed successfully page appears (see Figure 5.20). Optionally, you can indicate whether you want to start Windows Update, or connect to System Center Orchestrator online. Click **Close** to complete the installation.

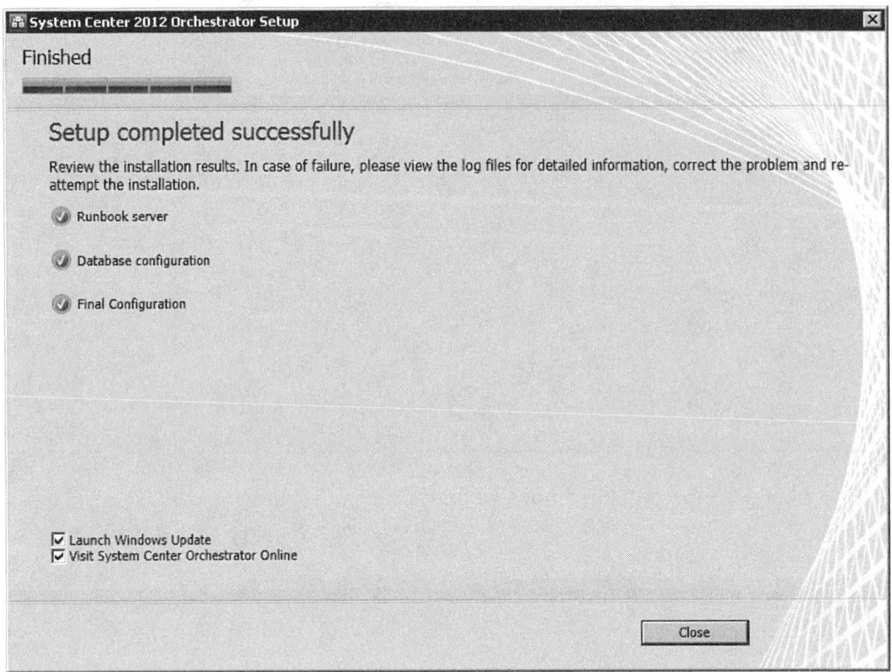

FIGURE 5.20 Runbook server setup completed successfully.

Installing the Runbook Server Using Deployment Manager

You can also use Deployment Manager to install a runbook server. The Deployment Manager method enables you to install integration packs at the same time you install the runbook server, whereas running the Setup Wizard from media does not permit this. In the Odyssey environment, the Harmony server hosts Deployment Manager, which is used here to install a third runbook server on the Scepter system. Follow these steps to install a runbook server from the Deployment Manager console:

1. Select **Start** -> **All Programs** -> **Microsoft System Center 2012** -> **Orchestrator** -> **Deployment Manager**. Figure 5.21 displays the complete program list for Orchestrator.

2. In the Deployment Manager console, expand the **Orchestrator Management Server** and then the **Runbook Servers** folder. Right-click **Runbook Servers** and select **Deploy new Runbook Server** (see Figure 5.22).

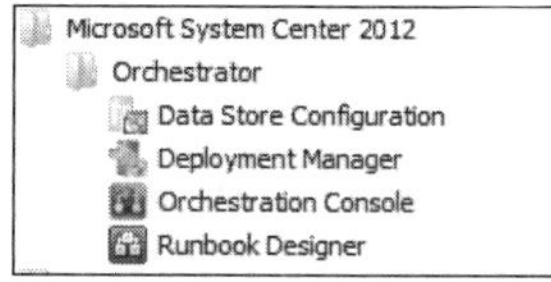

FIGURE 5.21 Orchestrator Start menu items.

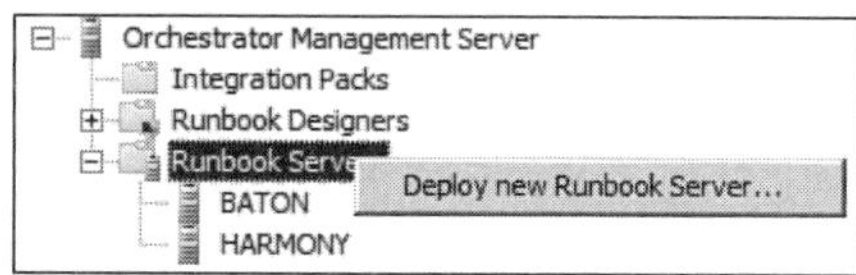

FIGURE 5.22 Deploy New Runbook Server console task.

3. Click **Next** on the Welcome page.
4. On the Runbook Server Selection page, specify the computer where the Orchestrator runbook server feature will be installed. Specify the service account to use.

   For the Odyssey environment, installation of the feature is performed using the OR_SVC service account. Figure 5.23 illustrates the configuration for the additional runbook server installation on Scepter. When all information is specified, click **Next**.

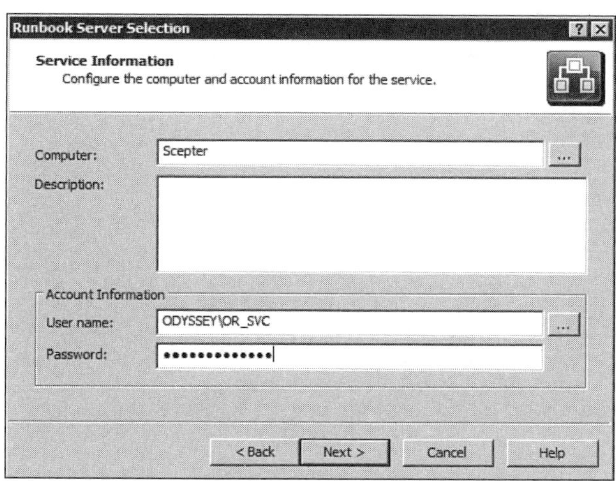

FIGURE 5.23 The Runbook Server Selection page.

5. The Integration Pack or Hotfix deployment page appears (see Figure 5.24). After integration packs or hotfixes are deployed, you can select the individual IPs or hotfixes to be installed together with the Runbook Designer installation. For this installation, IPs are already registered and deployed. Click **Next**.

6. Review the information on the Completing Runbook Server Deployment page and click **Finish**.

7. You can review the runbook server installation in the Log Entries pane of the console, displayed in Figure 5.25.

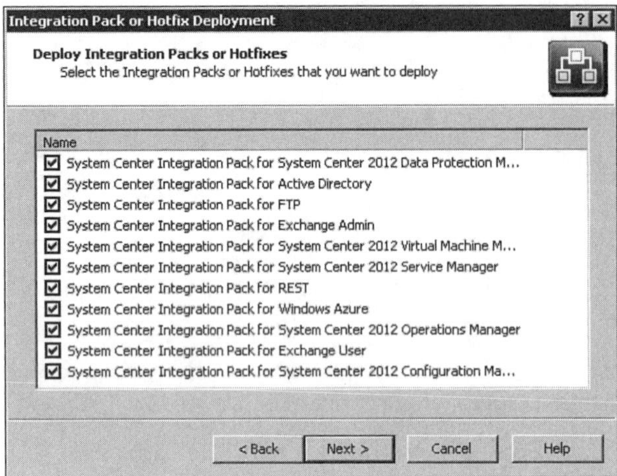

FIGURE 5.24 Runbook server installation, Deploy Integration Pack or Hotfixes selection page.

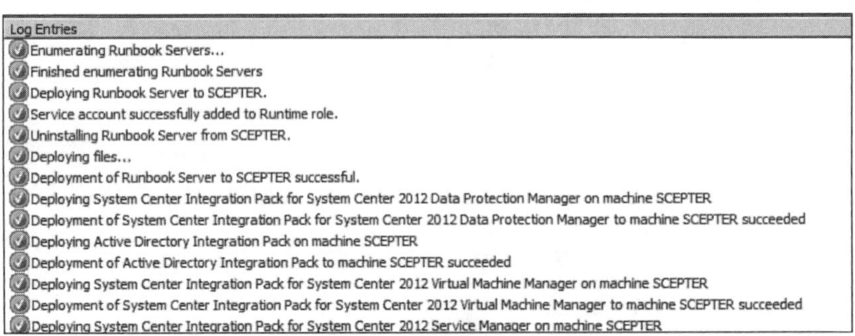

FIGURE 5.25 Runbook server installation review in the Log Entries console pane.

Installing the Web Service

You can install the Orchestrator web service using the **Standalone Installations** section on the Orchestrator installation wizard start page. This can be a single-instance installation, or you can install additional web services to provide high availability of the service. A load balancer, such as Microsoft Windows Network Load Balancing (NLB), can spread the connection load to the console and web service hosted on an IIS server.

To install the Orchestration console and web service on a separate server, follow these steps:

1. To start the setup wizard on the server where you want to install the Orchestrator web service, double-click **SetupOrchestrator.exe**.

2. On the main setup page, under the Standalone Installations section, select **Orchestration Console and Web Service** (see Figure 5.26).

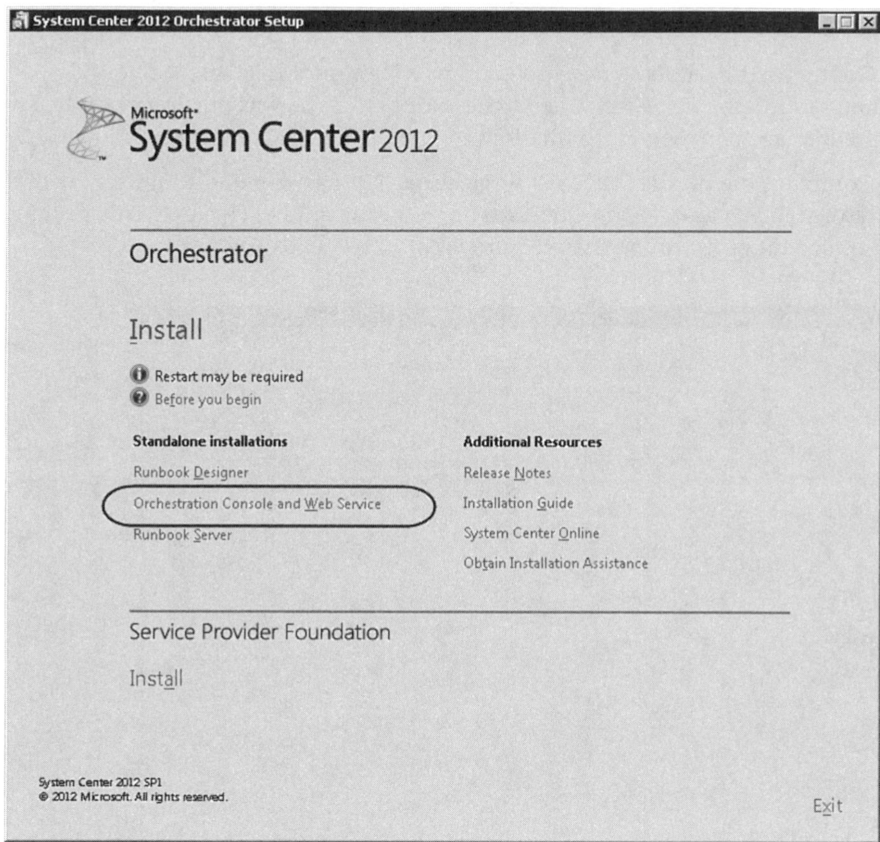

FIGURE 5.26 Selecting the installation method.

3. Provide the required information on the Product registration and Please read this license agreement pages, and click **Next**.

4. The computer is checked for required hardware and software. If your computer meets all the requirements, the All prerequisites are installed page appears. Click **Next** to proceed.

5. On the Configure the service account page, enter the username and password for the service account for the Orchestration console and web service. You can use the same user account as for the management server or specify a different one. Click **Test** to verify the account credentials. If the credentials are accepted, click **Next**.

6. On the Configure the database server page, enter the name of the database server associated with your Orchestrator management server. You can also specify whether to use Windows Authentication or SQL Server Authentication. Configure your settings and click **Test Database Connection** to verify the account credentials. If the credentials are accepted, click **Next**.

7. On the Configure the database page, select the Orchestrator database for your deployment and then click **Next**. The Orchestrator database was previously created during the management server installation.

8. On the Configure the port for the web services page, verify the port numbers for the Orchestrator web service and the Orchestration console, and click **Next**. This installation uses default port numbers (see Figure 5.27).

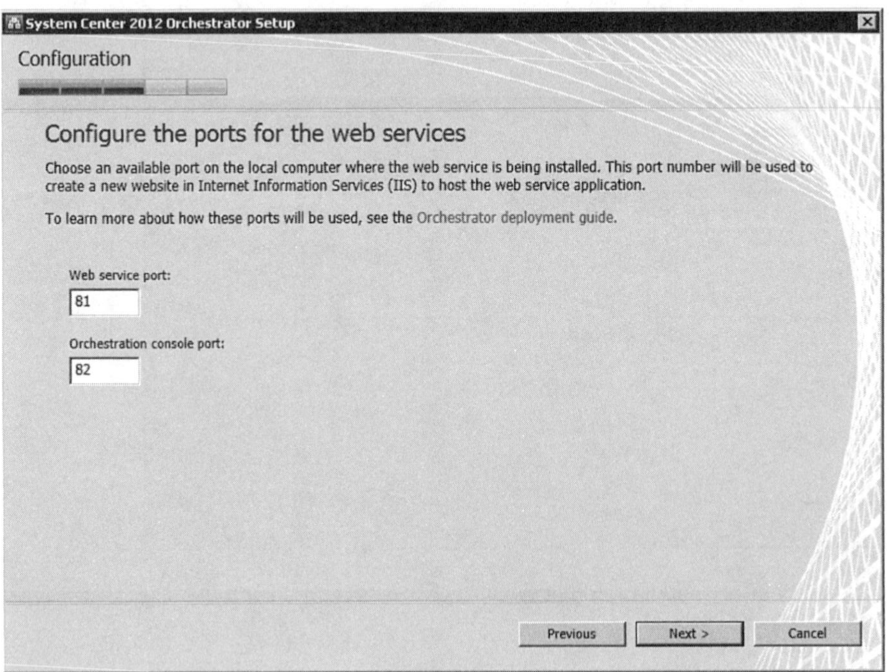

FIGURE 5.27 Orchestration console and web service port configuration page.

9. On the Select the installation location page, verify the installation location and click **Next**.

10. Specify your selection on the Help with System Center 2012 Orchestrator page, and click **Next**.

11. Review the Installation summary page and then click **Install**. The Installing features page appears and displays the installation progress.

12. On the Setup completed successfully page, optionally indicate whether you want to start Runbook Designer; click **Close** to complete the installation.

An additional step in this procedure is configuring the Orchestrator web service to use Secure Sockets Layer (SSL); http://technet.microsoft.com/en-us/library/hh529160.aspx provides information. Here is a high-level overview of the tasks to complete:

1. Request and install a certificate on the computer where you installed the Orchestrator web service. For guidance on requesting and installing a certificate, see the article at http://support.microsoft.com/kb/299875.

2. Configure SSL on the machine that hosts the web service and Orchestration console as follows:

    - **Microsoft System Center 2012 Orchestrator Web Service:** 443

    - **Microsoft System Center 2012 Orchestrator Orchestration Console:** 444

3. You can update the configuration in the IIS Manager. Select the Orchestration console website; then open Application Settings in the ASP.NET pane and change the `ScoServiceUri` value.

4. You can also adjust this configuration in the Orchestration console web.config file:

    - On your Orchestrator web server, locate the web.config file at *%ProgramFiles(x86)%*\Microsoft System Center 2012\Orchestrator\Orchestration Console.

    - Open web.config in a text editor.

    - Locate the service URI key, and update the key to connect to the web service through HTTPS. For example:

Before:

```
<add key="ScoServiceUri" value="http://<domain>:81/Orchestrator2012/Orchestrator.
svc/"/>
```

After edit:

```
<add key="ScoServiceUri" value=" https://<domain>:443/Orchestrator2012/Orchestrator.
svc/"/>
```

Installing the Runbook Designer Using the Installer

Installation of the Runbook Designer using the Orchestrator installer is similar to the other installations. To have a usable Runbook Designer console for your Orchestrator environment, run the installation wizard and then connect the Runbook Designer to your management server. To install the Runbook Designer, follow these steps:

1. To start the System Center 2012 - Orchestrator Setup Wizard on the server where you want to install Orchestrator Runbook Designer, double-click **SetupOrchestrator.exe**.
2. On the main setup page, in the Standalone Installations section, select **Runbook Designer** (see Figure 5.28).

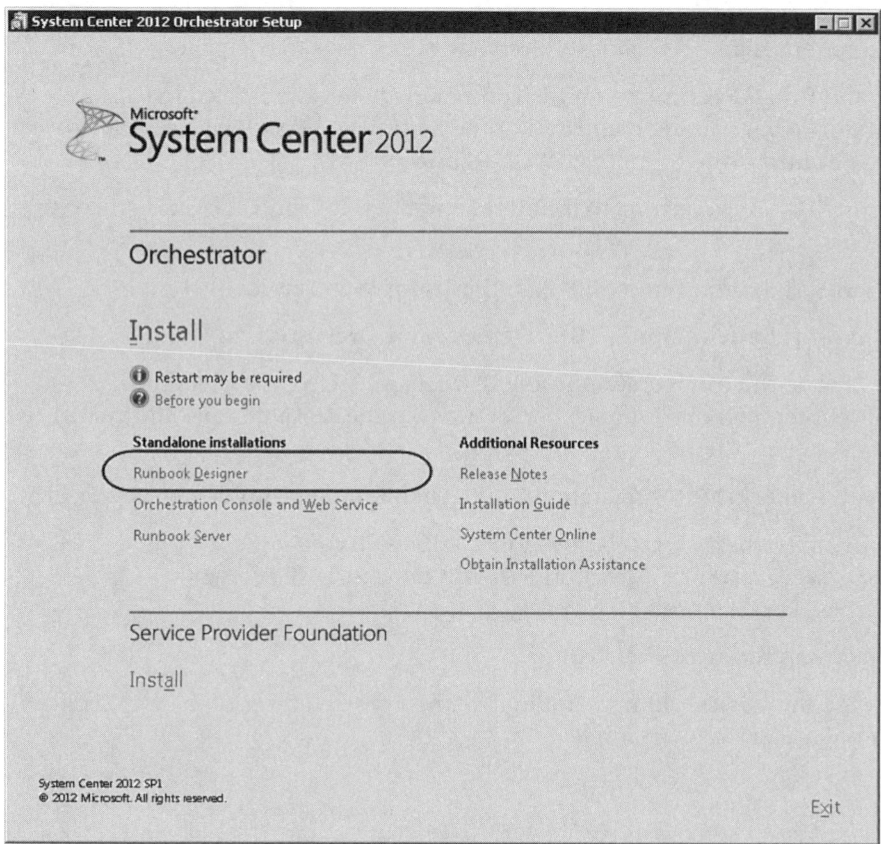

FIGURE 5.28 Selecting Runbook Designer for installation.

3. Provide the required information on the Product Registration page, and accept the software license terms on the Please read this license agreement page. Click **Next**.
4. On the Prerequisites evaluation page, the server is checked against the recommended hardware and software system requirements. If all requirements are met, the wizard continues automatically to the Service Account selection page.

   The "Installing the Management Server" section provides information regarding prerequisites warnings remediation.

5. On the Select the installation location page, verify the installation location for your Runbook Designer installation and click **Next**.
6. Specify your selection on the Help with System Center 2012 Orchestrator page, and click **Next**.
7. Review the Installation summary page and then click **Install**. The Installing features page appears and displays the installation progress.
8. On the Setup completed successfully page, optionally indicate whether you want to start Runbook Designer; click **Close** to complete the installation.

You must connect each Runbook Designer to your management server. This enables the server to be managed using the Deployment Manager. Integration packs, updates, and hotfixes can be centrally deployed to the installed Runbook Designer instances. Perform the following steps to connect Runbook Designer to the management server:

1. Navigate to **Start** -> **All Programs** -> **Microsoft System Center 2012** -> **Orchestrator**. From the Runbook Designer installation program list, click **Runbook Designer**. Figure 5.29 displays the menu items.

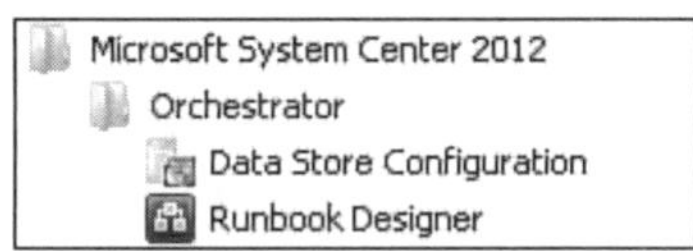

FIGURE 5.29 Runbook Start menu items.

2. In the Runbook Designer console, click the **Actions** menu item and select the **Connect** task. Figure 5.30 shows the Actions list.

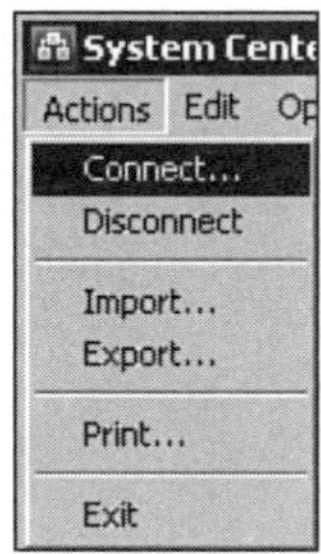

FIGURE 5.30 Connect task selection in the Actions menu.

3. A System Center 2012 Orchestrator Connection pop-up (see Figure 5.31) appears to specify the management server. Enter the server name and press **Connect**.
4. The console connects to the management server; runbooks and other console items are visible in the console. The Runbook Designer is ready for configuring runbooks.

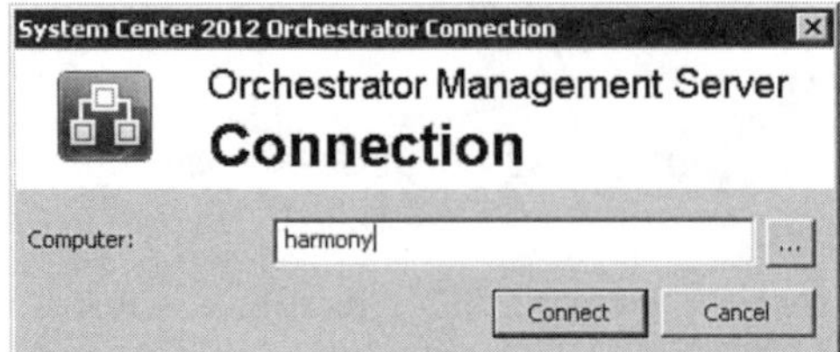

FIGURE 5.31 Orchestrator Connection pop-up.

TIP: ENABLE NETWORK DISCOVERY FOR THE RUNBOOK DESIGNER

Network Discovery enables you to view other computers and lets other computers see your computer. Server selection in the designer depends on this functionality. The "Installing the Management Server" section discusses enabling network discovery.

Installing Runbook Designer Using Deployment Manager

You can install Runbook Designer in two ways: from installation media or using Deployment Manager. Using the Deployment Manager enables you to install the designer and integration packs at the same time. This procedure describes Runbook Designer installation from the Deployment Manager console. Follow these steps:

1. Navigate to **Start** -> **All Programs** -> **Microsoft System Center 2012** -> **Orchestrator** to start Deployment Manager.

2. In the Deployment Manager console, expand the Orchestrator Management Server and Runbook Designers folders. Right-click the Runbook Designers folder and select **Deploy new Runbook Designer** (see Figure 5.32).

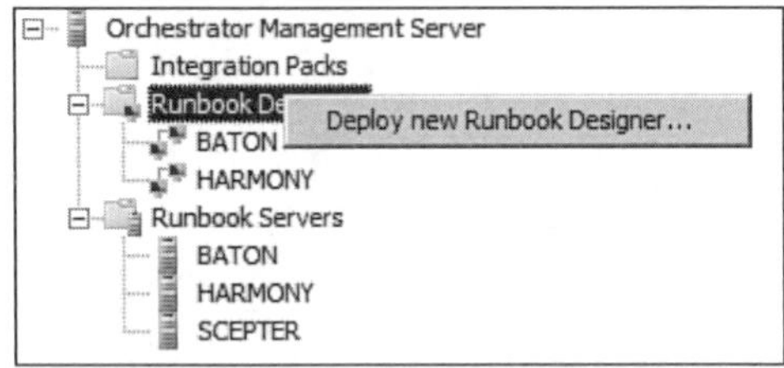

FIGURE 5.32 Deploy new Runbook Designer console task.

3. The Runbook Designer Deployment wizard starts. Click **Next** on the Welcome page (see Figure 5.33).

4. On the Runbook Designer Selection page, specify the computer to which to install this Orchestrator feature. Figure 5.34 illustrates the configuration for an additional Runbook Designer installation on the Scepter server. Click **Next**.

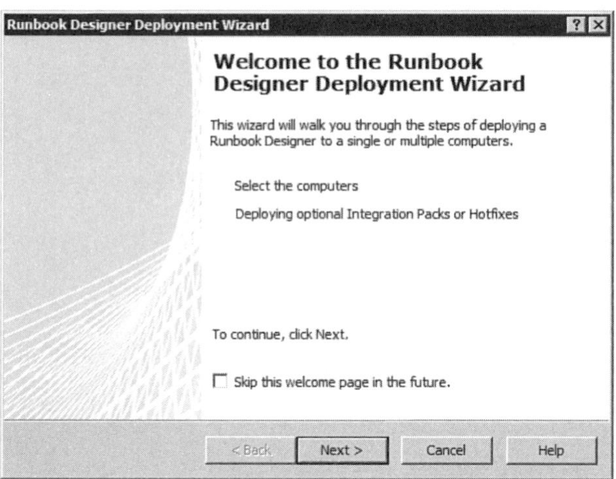

FIGURE 5.33 Welcome page of the Runbook Designer Deployment Wizard.

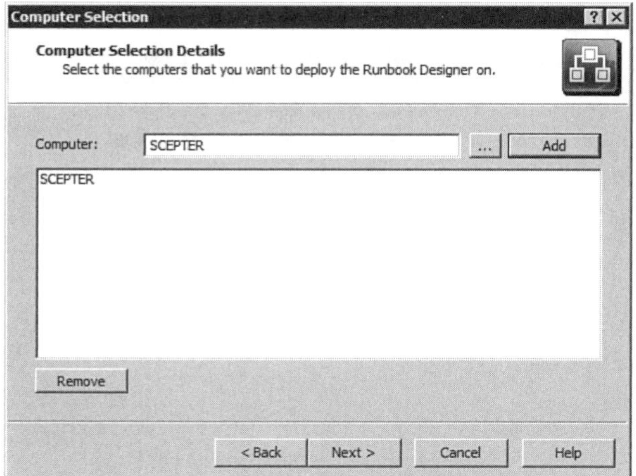

FIGURE 5.34 Computer selection in the Runbook Designer Deployment Wizard.

5. The Integration Pack or Hotfix deployment page appears. After integration packs or hotfixes are deployed, you can select the individual IPs or hotfixes to be installed together with the Runbook Designer installation. For this installation, IPs are already registered and deployed. Click **Next** to proceed with the installation.

6. Review the information on the Completing Runbook Designer Deployment page and click **Finish**.

7. You can review the installation of the Runbook Designer in the Log Entries pane of the console. Figure 5.35 shows the log entries for this installation.

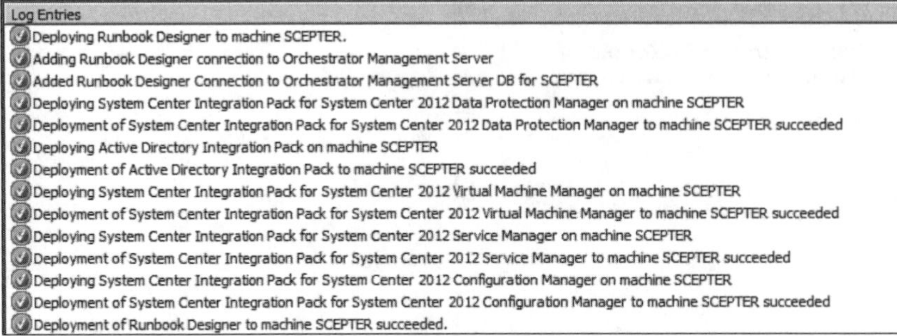

FIGURE 5.35 Runbook Designer Deployment review in the Log Entries console pane.

Using the Command-Line Installation Tool

You can use command-line parameters to automate your Orchestrator feature installation. This lets you easily create a script that installs your entire Orchestrator environment or specific Orchestrator features. This section discusses the setup options for installing various features.

NOTE: SERVER MESSAGE BLOCK (SMB) ACCESS DURING INSTALLATION

If SMB traffic is not supported through firewalls or a specific SMB security configuration is in place that is blocking the installation of integration packs or the runbook server, you can install these features manually via command-line installation.

Listing 5.1 is a script to install the management server.

LISTING 5.1 Command-Line Installation: Management Server

```
SetupOrchestrator.exe
/silent
/Key:[Product Key]
/ServiceUserName:[User Name]
/ServicePassword:[Password]
/Components:[Feature 1, Feature 2,...] (Values: ManagementServer, RunbookServer,
          ➥RunbookDesigner, WebComponents, and All.
/InstallDir:[Path]
/DbServer:[Computer[\Instance]]
/DbUser:[User Name]
/DbPassword:[Password]
/DbNameNew:[Database Name]
/DbNameExisting:[Database Name]
/WebServicePort:[Port]
/WebConsolePort:[Port]
/OrchestratorUsersGroup:[Group SID]
```

```
/OrchestratorRemote
/UseMicrosoftUpdate:[0|1]
/SendCEIPReports:[0|1]
/EnableErrorReporting:[value]
```

Listing 5.2 is a script to install the runbook server (Windows Authentication for SQL access).

LISTING 5.2 Command-Line Installation: Runbook Server

```
SetupOrchestrator.exe
/silent
/Key:[Product Key]
/ServiceUserName:[User Name]
/ServicePassword:[Password]
/Components:[RunbookServer]
/InstallDir:[Path]
/DbServer:[Computer[\Instance]]
/DbNameExisting:[Database Name]
/EnableErrorReporting:[value]
```


Listing 5.3 is a script to install the Runbook Designer.

LISTING 5.3 Command-Line Installation: Runbook Designer

```
SetupOrchestrator.exe
/silent
/Key:[Product Key]
/Components:[RunbookDesigner]
/InstallDir:[Path]
/EnableErrorReporting:[value]
```

Table 5.2 provides an explanation of the installation options for the SetupOrchestrator installer used in Listing 5.1, Listing 5.2, and Listing 5.3. All command options are summarized.

TABLE 5.2 Server Component Requirements and Prerequisites

Command Option	**Description**
Silent	Installation is performed without displaying a dialog box.
/Uninstall	Uninstalls the product. This option is performed silently.
/Key:[*Product Key*]	Specifies the product key. If no product key is specified, Orchestrator is installed as an evaluation edition.

Command Option	Description
/ServiceUserName:[*User Name*]	Specifies the user account for the Orchestrator Management Service. This value is required if you are installing the management server, runbook server, or web services.
/ServicePassword:[*Password*]	Specifies the password for the user account for the Orchestrator Management Service. This value is required if you are installing the management server, runbook server, or web services.
/Components:[*Feature 1, Feature 2,...*]	Specifies the features to install. Possible values are ManagementServer, RunbookServer, RunbookDesigner, WebComponents, and All.
/InstallDir:[*Path*]	Specifies the path to install Orchestrator. If no path is specified, *%ProgramFiles(x86)%*\Microsoft System Center 2012\Orchestrator is used.
/DbServer:[*Computer*[*Instance*]]	Specifies the computer name and instance of the database server. This value is required if you are installing the management server, runbook server, or web services.
/DbUser:[*User Name*]	Specifies the user account to access the database server. This value is required only for SQL Authentication. If Windows Authentication is used, no value should be specified.
/DbPassword:[*Password*]	Specifies the password for the user account to access the database server. This value is required only for SQL Authentication. If you use Windows Authentication, do not specify a value.
/DbNameNew:[*Database Name*]	Specifies the database name if a new database is being created. Cannot be used with DbNameExisting.
/DbNameExisting:[*Database Name*]	Specifies the database name if an existing database is being used. Cannot be used with DbNameNew.
/WebServicePort:[*Port*]	Specifies the port to use for the web service. Required if web services are installed.
/WebConsolePort:[*Port*]	Specifies the port to use for the Orchestration console. Required if web services are installed.
/OrchestratorUsersGroup:[*Group SID*]	Specifies the SID of the domain or local group that will be granted access to the management server. If no value is specified, the default local group is used.
/OrchestratorRemote	Specifies that remote access should be granted to Runbook Designer.
/UseMicrosoftUpdate:[0|1]	Specifies whether to opt in for Microsoft Update. A value of 1 opts in. A value of 0 does not change the current opt-in status.

Command Option	Description
/SendCEIPReports:[0|1]	Specifies that Orchestrator should send CEIP reports to Microsoft. A value of 1 opts in. A value of 0 does not change the current opt-in status.
/EnableErrorReporting:[*value*]	Specifies that Orchestrator should send program error reports to Microsoft. Possible values are always, queued, and never.

Performing Post-Installation Tasks

Post-installation tasks include actions performed after Orchestrator is deployed. This includes tasks such as registering and deploying integration packs and migrating existing Opalis 6.3 policies. The following sections discuss these tasks.

Registering and Deploying Integration Packs

Integration packs contain activities that expand the functionality and capability to interact with Microsoft products and those from other organizations. A set of standard activities is installed automatically. The integration packs you need depend on the different runbooks you want to create and the interactions with other products. Each IP includes a unique set of functions. Integration packs are available from the Microsoft download center at www.microsoft.com/downloads.

Installing an integration pack is a two-step process:

1. Register the integration pack using Deployment Manager.
2. Deploy registered integration packs to runbook servers and runbook designer instances.

The following sections discuss these steps.

Registering Integration Packs in Deployment Manager

After downloading the integration pack and extracting the files to a folder on the server, you can register the IP with the management server. For detailed installation instructions or known issues with the IP, review the guide delivered with the integration pack. Chapter 12, "Orchestrator Integration Packs," and successive chapters provide information on the various integration packs; Chapters 13 through 17 discuss integration with other System Center components. To register integration packs with the management server, follow these steps:

1. On the management server, copy the .OIP file(s) for the integration pack(s) to a local hard drive or network share.

5

2. Start Deployment Manager. In the navigation pane, expand **Orchestrator Management Server**, and right-click **Integration Packs** to select **Register IP with the Orchestrator Management Server** (see Figure 5.36).

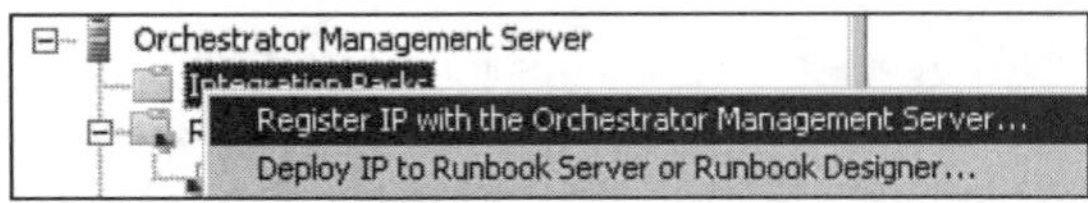

FIGURE 5.36 Register IP with Orchestrator Management Server console task.

3. The Integration Pack Registration Wizard opens (see Figure 5.37). Click **Next** on the Welcome page.

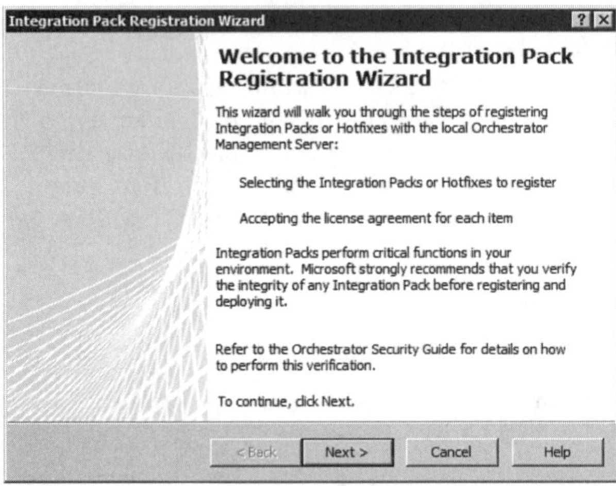

FIGURE 5.37 Welcome page of the registration wizard.

4. On the Integration Pack or Hotfix Selection page, specify the different integration packs and hotfixes. Click the **Add** button to add one or more integration packs. Locate the .OIP file for each integration pack to register (copied locally from step 1) and click **Open**. The System Center 2012 and other integration pack .OIP files are added to the list for the Odyssey environment (see Figure 5.38).

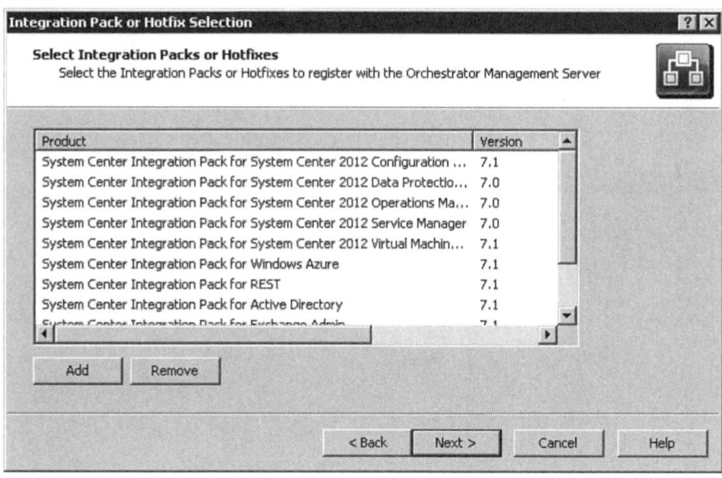

FIGURE 5.38 Integration Pack or Hotfix Selection page of the registration wizard.

5. After adding the different integration packs or hotfixes, the Completing Integration Pack Registration Wizard page appears (see Figure 5.39). Review the information, and click **Finish** to proceed.

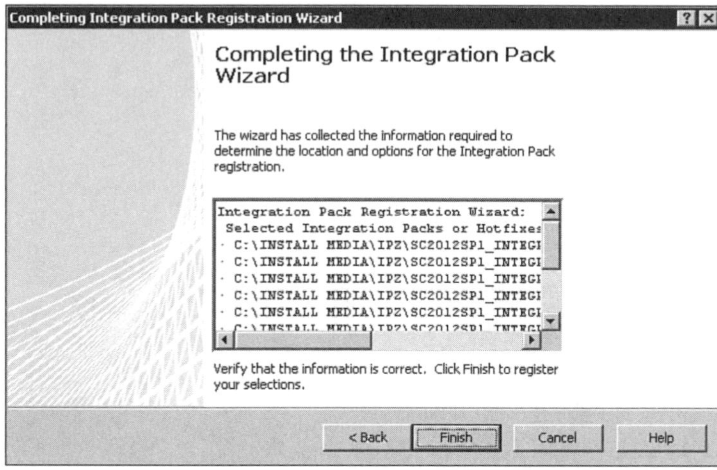

FIGURE 5.39 Completing the registration page of the Integration Pack Wizard.

6. Each (Microsoft) integration pack in the list to register presents an end-user agreement before registration. Figure 5.40 shows a sample end-user agreement. Accept this agreement to start registration of the integration pack.

7. You can follow and confirm registration of the integration packs in the Log Entries pane of the console. Figure 5.41 illustrates a successful registration of the integration packs.

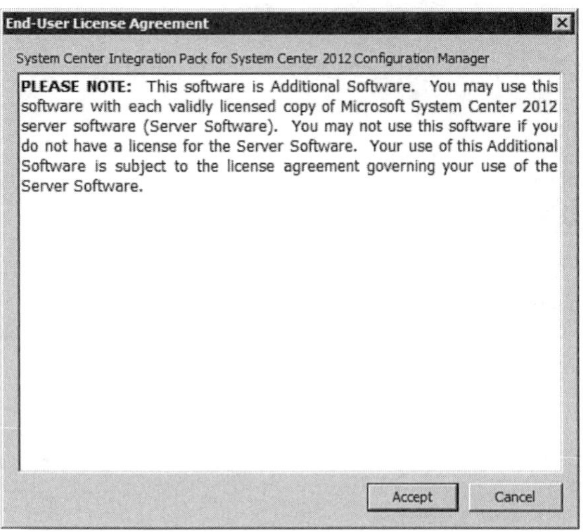

FIGURE 5.40 End-User License Agreement page of the Integration Pack Wizard.

FIGURE 5.41 Successful registration of integration packs.

Deploying an Integration Pack

Next in the integration pack installation process is to deploy IPs to runbook servers and/or runbook designers. To deploy integration packs to runbook servers, follow these steps:

1. You must register the integration packs (.OIP files) before you can deploy them to the runbook servers.

2. Start Deployment Manager. In the navigation pane, expand Orchestrator Management Server and then right-click **Integration Packs** to select **Deploy IP to Runbook Server or Runbook Designer** (see Figure 5.42).

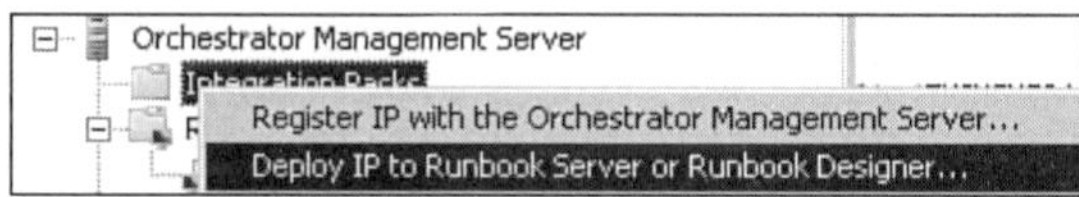

FIGURE 5.42 Deploy IP task in the Deployment Manager console.

3. The Integration Pack Deployment Wizard opens. Click **Next** on the Welcome page.
4. Select the different integration packs or hotfixes on the Integration Pack or Hotfix Deployment page. For the Odyssey environment, the System Center 2012 and Active Directory integration packs are deployed (see Figure 5.43). Click **Next**.

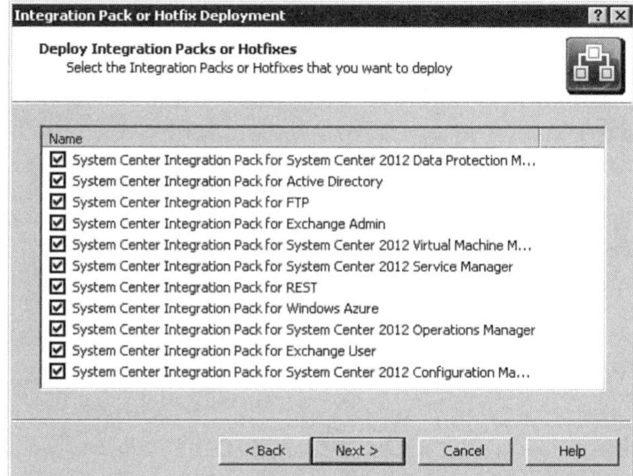

FIGURE 5.43 Integration Pack or Hotfix Deployment page of the installation wizard.

5. On the Computer Selection page, you can add runbook servers to which to deploy integration packs or hotfixes. Click **Add** to specify computers for the deployment. Two servers are selected in this example (see Figure 5.44). Click **Next** to proceed.

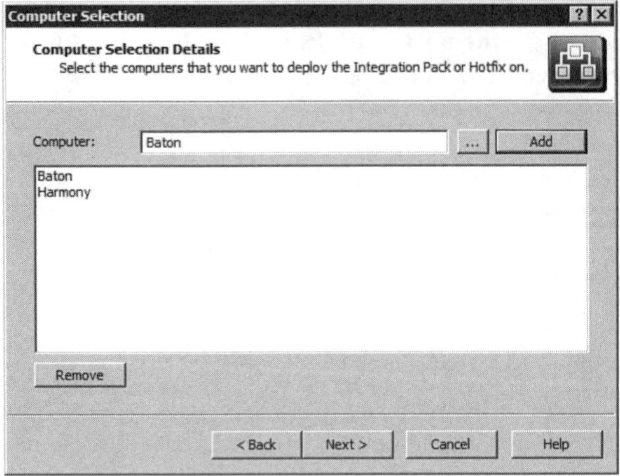

FIGURE 5.44 Computer Selection page of the installation wizard.

6. The Installation Options page lets you start the deployment immediately or schedule the deployment. If a scheduled installation is required, select the **Schedule installation** check box. Select the time and date from the **Perform installation** list to specify when to start the deployment; otherwise, the selected deployment begins immediately.

   The Advanced Option section of the Installations Options lets you control any running runbook during deployment:

   - **Stop all running Runbooks before installing the Integration Packs or Hotfixes:** This stops all running runbooks before deploying the integration pack.
   - **Install the Integration Packs or Hotfixes without stopping the running Runbooks:** Select this option to install the integration pack without stopping any running runbooks.

   Figure 5.45 illustrates the Odyssey IP deployment options.

7. Click **Finish** in the Completing Integration Pack Deployment Wizard dialog box (see Figure 5.46).

NOTE: UPGRADING INTEGRATION PACKS

The process of upgrading an integration pack is actually an uninstall and reinstall of that integration pack. For each computer with a runbook server or Runbook Designer installed, uninstall any earlier version of the integration pack; then follow the post-installation procedure in this section to register and deploy the new version of the integration pack.

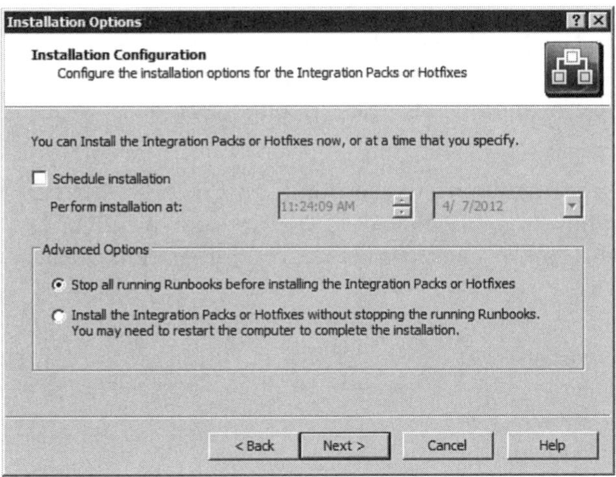

FIGURE 5.45 Installation Options page of the installation wizard.

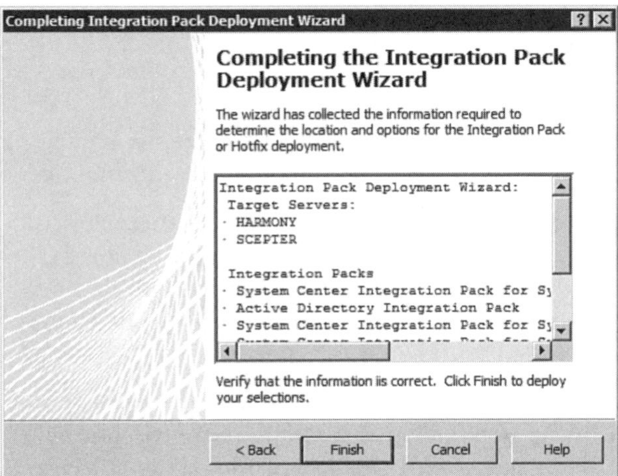

FIGURE 5.46 Successful registration of integration packs.

Migrating Opalis Policies to Orchestrator

When migrating from Opalis Integration Server (OIS) 6.3 to Orchestrator, only policies can be migrated. No upgrade path allows you to upgrade your Opalis servers to Orchestrator. At a high level, here is the path to migrate your Opalis policies to Orchestrator:

1. Review policies in scope for the migration for supportability.
2. Export the OIS 6.3 policies.
3. Use the Orchestrator Runbook Designer to import the policies.
4. Author the imported runbook and test.

Opalis Policy Review

Opalis policies and Orchestrator runbooks do not share all settings or features. System Center Orchestrator is completely new and does not share a common database structure with Opalis. Certain Opalis policies must be modified so the runbook functions correctly in Orchestrator.

Review your Opalis policies before migrating them to Orchestrator. This section discusses the preparation work required before importing OIS policies to Orchestrator as runbooks. Not all Opalis policies can be migrated. Table 5.3 summarizes the valid migration paths of Opalis policies to Orchestrator runbooks.

TABLE 5.3 Opalis Policy Upgrade Path Overview

Product	Upgrade Path
Opalis Robot, all versions	Not supported.
OIS, all versions 5.2 and earlier	Not supported.
OIS 5.3, 5.4, 5.45, 5.5, 5.51, 5.52, 5.6, 5.6.1, 5.6.2, 6.0, or 6.2	Upgrade the earlier version of Opalis to OIS 6.3, and then migrate an OIS 6.3 policy to Orchestrator.
OIS 6.3	Export policies from Opalis 6.3 and import them into Orchestrator as runbooks.

In addition to the supported upgrade path, other items must be reviewed before upgrading your Opalis policies. Consider this information about how to update migrated runbooks:

- **Opalis Policy Mode Setting:** OIS 6.3 provides two modes for policies that defined the behavior of the publish and subscribe data bus. The Policy Mode setting is located on the Run Behavior tab of the properties of the policy. If the Run in pipeline mode box is not selected, the workflow is configured for "legacy" mode. Legacy policies cannot be migrated.

  Orchestrator does not provide a runbook mode setting. The Policy Mode property of an Opalis policy is now the Job Concurrency property in Orchestrator. Orchestrator runbooks use a data model that is compatible with Opalis pipeline mode.

  Although you can import Opalis policies that used legacy mode successfully into Orchestrator, they will not automatically check in. You can identify legacy mode (not compatible) runbooks by looking at the toolbar of the imported runbook:

  - If Checked In, the runbook was an OIS 6.3 pipeline workflow.
  - If Checked Out, the OIS 6.3 workflow was a legacy workflow. You must manually check it in to update the runbook.

- **Unsupported structures:** When a legacy policy is imported with an unsupported structure and you try checking in the migrated runbook, a warning displays. You must first correct any unsupported structures in the workflow before you can check in the runbook. Unsupported structures include the following:

- ▶ **Multiple starting points:** Orchestrator runbooks can have only one activity as the starting point of the runbook.
- ▶ **Cycles:** Runbooks cannot contain smart links that originate with one runbook activity and reference an earlier runbook activity. These cycles are supported on OIS 6.3 legacy mode, but not in Orchestrator.

- ▶ **Opalis ROI setting:** System Center Orchestrator does not support the OIS 6.3 Return On Investment (ROI) settings. Orchestrator ignores these settings during the import process if they are present in the Opalis policies.
- ▶ **Opalis legacy objects:** OIS 6.3 provides legacy objects for backward compatibility with older Opalis versions. Migrated runbooks with these legacy objects appear in Runbook Designer with an activity icon with a question mark. You should update these migrated runbooks to remove legacy objects and replace them with corresponding Orchestrator activities. Table 5.4 provides an overview of OIS 6.3 legacy objects with corresponding Orchestrator activities.

TABLE 5.4 Opalis Legacy Object Mapping to Orchestrator Activity

Opalis Legacy Object	Orchestrator Activity or Resource
File	Orchestrator Text File Management category (Append Line, Delete Line, Find Text, Get Lines, Insert Line, Read Line, and Search and Replace Text activities)
Create Folder	Create Folder
Delete Folder	Delete Folder
Copy File	Copy File
Delete File	Delete File
Move File	Move File
Rename File	Rename File
Get File Status	Get File Status
Monitor File	Monitor File
Monitor Folder	Monitor Folder
Filter Email	Run .NET Script or Orchestrator Integration Toolkit
Process Email	Run .NET Script or Orchestrator Integration Toolkit
Read Email	Run .NET Script or Orchestrator Integration Toolkit
Filter Exchange Email	Integration packs for Exchange Admin and Exchange User
Process Exchange Email	Integration packs for Exchange Admin and Exchange User
Read Exchange Email	Integration packs for Exchange Admin and Exchange User

- ▶ **Opalis policy objects not supported in Orchestrator:** A small number of Opalis policy objects do not have corresponding Orchestrator activities. If a migrated runbook includes unsupported policy objects, they are marked with a question mark. This also occurs with unsupported legacy objects in imported OIS policies in

Runbook Designer. Table 5.5 provides an overview of those OIS 6.3 legacy objects without corresponding Orchestrator activities.

TABLE 5.5 Unsupported OIS Policy Objects

Opalis Policy Object	Description
Send Page	Infrequently used and out-of-date.
Purge Event Log	Infrequently used and out-of-date.
Send Pop-Up	Unsupported.
Monitor Event Log Capacity	Infrequently used and out-of-date. Replaced by functionality in System Center 2012 Operations Manager.
Monitor Performance	Infrequently used and out-of-date. Replaced by functionality in Operations Manager.
Disconnect Dial-Up	Infrequently used and out-of-date.
Get Dial-Up Status	Infrequently used and out-of-date.
Wait	Meaningful only in OIS 6.3 legacy mode runbooks. Junction is the closest Orchestrator activity.

- **Opalis policies using missing objects:** The following SQL query, run against the Opalis data store, identifies Opalis policies that contain objects that Orchestrator no longer supports. This query returns the Opalis policy name and the name of the object in the policy. Update any policy this query identifies after importing it into Orchestrator, to remove the reference to the deprecated object. (For details, see http://technet.microsoft.com/en-us/library/hh420340.aspx.)

```
Select
      policies.[Name] as [Policy Name],
      objects.[Name] as [Object Name]
From
      [Objects] objects join
      [Policies] policies
      on objects.[ParentID]=policies.[UniqueID]
Where
  objects.objecttype = '2081B459-88D2-464A-9F3D-27D2B7A64C5E' or
  objects.objecttype = '6F0FA888-1969-4010-95BC-C0468FA6E8A0' or
  objects.objecttype = '8740DB49-5EE2-4398-9AD1-21315B8D2536' or
  objects.objecttype = '19253CC6-2A14-432A-B4D8-5C3F778B69B0' or
  objects.objecttype = '9AB62470-8541-44BD-BC2A-5C3409C56CAA' or
  objects.objecttype = '292941F8-6BA7-4EC2-9BC0-3B5F96AB9790' or
  objects.objecttype = '98AF4CBD-E30E-4890-9D26-404FE24727D7' or
  objects.objecttype = '2409285A-9F7E-4E04-BFB9-A617C2E5FA61' or
  objects.objecttype = 'B40FDFBD-6E5F-44F0-9AA6-6469B0A35710' or
  objects.objecttype = '9DAF8E78-25EB-425F-A5EF-338C2940B409' or
  objects.objecttype = 'B5381CDD-8498-4603-884D-1800699462AC' or
```

```
objects.objecttype = 'FCA29108-14F3-429A-ADD4-BE24EA5E4A3E' or
objects.objecttype = '7FB85E1D-D3C5-41DA-ACF4-E1A8396A9DA7' or
objects.objecttype = '3CCE9C71-51F0-4595-927F-61D84F2F1B5D' or
objects.objecttype = '96769C11-11F5-4645-B213-9EC7A3F244DB' or
objects.objecttype = '6FED5A55-A652-455B-88E2-9992E7C97E9A' or
objects.objecttype = '9C1DF967-5A50-4C4E-9906-C331208A3801' or
objects.objecttype = 'B40FDFBD-6E5F-44F0-9AA6-6469B0A35710' or
objects.objecttype = '829A951B-AAE9-4FBF-A6FD-92FA697EEA91' or
objects.objecttype = '1728D617-ACA9-4C96-ADD1-0E0B61104A9E' or
objects.objecttype = 'F3D1E70B-D389-49AD-A002-D332604BE87A' or
objects.objecttype = '2D907D60-9C25-4A1C-B950-A31EB9C9DB5F' or
objects.objecttype = '6A083024-C7B3-474F-A53F-075CD2F2AC0F' or
objects.objecttype = '4E6481A1-6233-4C82-879F-D0A0EDCF2802' or
objects.objecttype = 'BC49578F-171B-4776-86E2-664A5377B178'
```

- **Modify Opalis policies containing special characters:** Occasionally, Opalis policies contain special characters. These characters are in objects and links between objects in your policies. The following SQL query, run against the Opalis data store, identifies Opalis policies that contain special characters that Orchestrator does not support. Update the migrated runbooks to remove these special characters and replace them with corresponding Orchestrator-supported characters:

```
SELECT
      Policies.Name,
      Objects.Name,
      Objects.Description
FROM
    Objects join
      Policies
      on Objects.ParentID=Policies.UniqueID
Where
    ASCII(Objects.Name) < 32
    or ASCII(CAST(Objects.Description as nvarchar(max))) < 32 and
    Policies.Deleted is NULL
```

5

Migration of Opalis Policies to Orchestrator Runbooks

The actual migration of Opalis policies to Orchestrator runbooks includes the export from the OIS 6.3 Client and import of the exported Opalis file in the Runbook Designer. When complete, you can start modifying the migrated runbooks as necessary so that they function correctly in Orchestrator. Follow these steps to export the OIS policies:

1. Identify the OIS 6.3 policies you want to migrate to Orchestrator.
2. In the OIS 6.3 Client, select the policies that you want to migrate, click **Actions**, and then click **Export**.

To import Opalis policies, perform the following steps:

1. Navigate to **Start** -> **All Programs** -> **Microsoft System Center 2012** -> **Orchestrator**. From the Runbook Designer installation program list, click **Runbook Designer**.
2. In the Runbook Designer console, click **Actions** and select **Import**.
3. As Figure 5.47 shows, the Import dialog box provides a box file location, password specification, and import behavior for global settings. To import Orchestrator runbooks, specify the necessary information and click **Finish**.

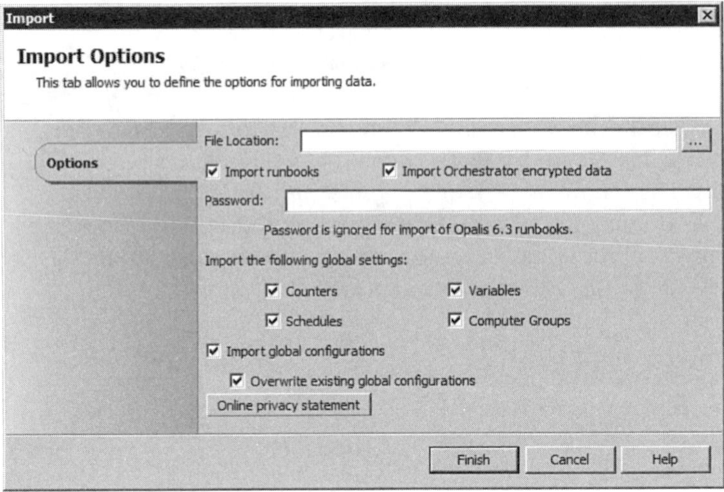

FIGURE 5.47 Importing data options page.

You might see a warning message that you need to update the migrated runbook. For details on migrating Opalis policies and updating the migrated runbooks, refer to the "Opalis Policy Review" section.

Summary

This chapter covered the process required to install System Center Orchestrator in a new environment, including installation of a feature-complete management server and standalone installations of specific Orchestrator features. This included an overview of important information required for the installation. The chapter also discussed post-installation tasks such as installing integration packs and migrating OIS policies. The next chapter provides an overview on how to use Orchestrator 2012.

CHAPTER 6

Using System Center 2012 Orchestrator

IN THIS CHAPTER

- ▶ Framework for Creating Runbooks
- ▶ Analyzing the Desired Automation
- ▶ Translating Actions to Runbook Activities
- ▶ Creating the Runbook in Orchestrator Runbook Designer
- ▶ Validating the Runbook
- ▶ Managing Runbooks Using the Orchestration Console
- ▶ Managing Runbooks with the Orchestrator Web Service

System Center 2012 Orchestrator can be used to create runbooks for automating certain tasks in your environment. These can range from simple operational tasks to scenarios in which the runbook execution is part of an overall process. Automation with Orchestrator means you are standardizing a task by executing activities in a particular order, and these activities will continue to occur as long as the runbook is used.

To guarantee an automation executes correctly, you must understand the scenarios in which the runbook will be used, what it needs to accomplish, and the criteria used to validate the results. During design, you need to ensure that you have all logic available to convert that information into runbook activities. The steps of information gathering, translation into activities, runbook creation, and runbook validation will provide quality assurance for the automation you are implementing. This chapter discusses the process of designing and building runbooks. It describes different approaches for managing the runbooks, such as the Orchestration console and the Orchestrator web service.

Framework for Creating Runbooks

Before initiating an automation project, you should obtain and understand all information applicable to that project. Creating runbooks is not just opening the Runbook Designer and wondering, "What am I going to automate today?" Design requires planning and gathering information. If you are automating your own task, you probably know what the runbook must deliver. If you are creating automation for other teams or something that interacts with other services, you must capture what information is necessary to create the solution.

This section defines a framework for implementing runbooks, from formulating an initial concept to placing the automation into production. This is not all-inclusive, but more an approach of how to capture the required information, translate that into Orchestrator activities, and bring the runbook into production, with each phase evaluated for your specific environment. Defining a runbook implementation framework helps deliver quality automation and prevent later issues because you did not have all the required information during design. Using a framework might not remove all pitfalls from the process, but it gives you an approach to use for implementing quality runbooks. Gathering and using the correct information to build the runbook helps you eliminate considerable debugging time as you implement your solution.

Figure 6.1 provides a graphical overview of a framework for creating a runbook, and the following sections further elaborate these phases.

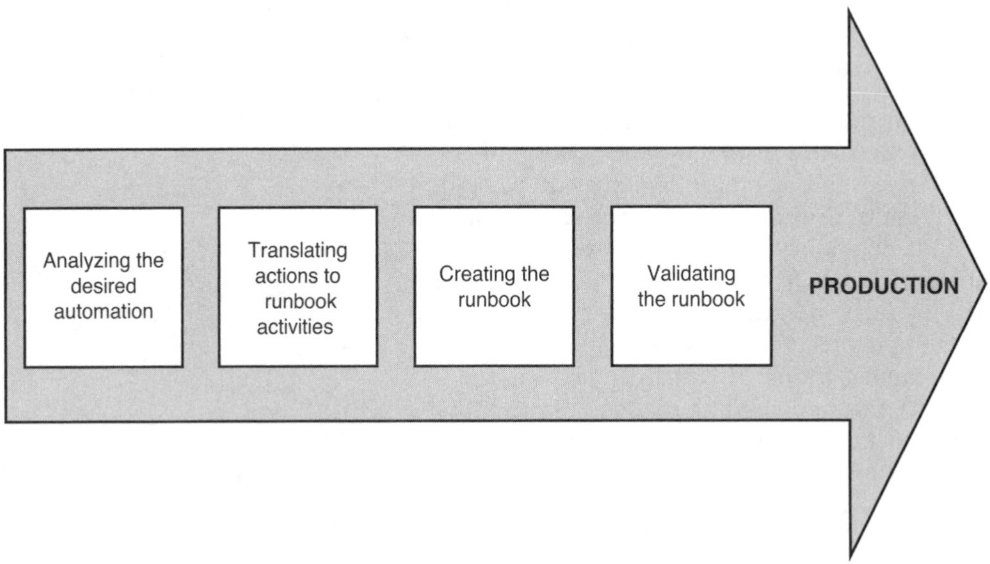

FIGURE 6.1 Runbook creation framework.

Analyzing the Desired Automation

You create a runbook because of a requirement to automate, replace scripts, integrate with service management, or facilitate a required (automated) step in a process. When you create a runbook, you need to identify its usage scenario. This helps you understand who needs access to the runbook and determine any infrastructure-related requirements.

You then must go deeper to discover technical details and translate those into runbook activities. Translating the desired automation into runbook activities provides a high-level breakdown of the workflow, including input and required interactions. You then can start building the runbook in the Runbook Designer. Steps defined during this process become activities in the runbook. Runbooks are then tested and validated in a test environment (where possible). When completed, your automated solutions are implemented into a production environment; this can be scenario specific.

Orchestrator Usage Scenarios

Runbooks can be used in many areas of your computing environment. You can configure runbooks to automate information technology (IT)-related tasks, runbooks that automate certain tasks on the production floor, or runbooks that configure automation for an information worker. To determine requirements, speak with individuals in the areas for which you need to configure runbook automation. Each area has its own requirements; these can be functional or security related. Consider some areas that can differentiate usage scenarios for runbook automation:

- **Request provisioning automation:** In this scenario, the automation is triggered from the Orchestration console or an external tool. In many cases, external information must be provided for the runbook to run successfully.
- **Process automation:** Automation can be process related, with certain tasks in the process flow automated using Orchestrator runbooks. This could be automation interacting with the production floor, or batch processing that helps overall handling of the process.
- **Scheduled tasks automation:** These are recurring tasks, which you can automate and schedule in Orchestrator.

These are common areas; specific automation requirements might dictate defining additional areas to capture those needs. Categorizing automation scenarios at this level enables you to define the high-level requirements for your runbook automation. These include the following:

- **Naming conventions for runbooks:** The authors recommend that you define naming conventions for your runbooks. This makes them recognizable and keeps the Orchestrator consoles organized.
- **High availability requirements:** The runbook might need to run 24x7. This will affect runbook server assignment.
- **Triggers defined for the runbook(s) you are creating:** Different start activities are available with runbooks. Your usage scenario indicates whether the runbook needs to scheduled, needs to monitor something, or is initiated from the console.
- **Security delegation for design and usage:** This includes the security context for where the automation can run and who needs access to the runbooks.

Runbook configuration depends on how the runbook will be used; this must be considered during your analysis. Obtaining requirements helps you describe the tasks and later configure activities in your runbook. In this phase, you need answers for the following questions:

- Who will use the runbook?
- From where will the runbook be used?
- Are there security requirements?

This phase can be illustrated with an example, which is used throughout the chapter:

- You need to develop a runbook that creates an Active Directory user object following company standards.
- The user environment (home folder, remote desktop, and so on) and settings must be specified based on the user role provided with the request. All users are mailbox enabled; mailbox specifications are linked with the role specified at the start of the runbook.
- The organization's primary business application must be configured to provide access for the new user.
- Human Resources (HR) will use this runbook at intake of new hires.
- The IT department needs to be informed so they can prepare hardware for the new user.

A functional analysis of this request provides the following information:

- **Who uses the runbook:** The user group that will use the runbook in this example is HR. You must provide access for the HR department to have the rights to run the runbook. Here are possible tasks:
  - Configure security on the runbook for HR to initiate the runbook.
  - Configure notifications for events or completion of the runbook for the target user group.
  - User training may be required to use runbooks in Orchestrator.
- **From where will the runbook be used:** Although not directly formulated in the example, HR will need to connect to the Orchestration console to run the runbook. A potential task is providing Orchestrator web console access to the target user group.
- **Security requirements:** Not specified, but interviewing the business application administrator determines that a specific account must be used to create the user account in the application.

Addressing these questions captures the high-level requirements. You should document your work; Figure 6.2 provides an example of a documentation starting point.

Discover the runbook usage scenarios	
Who will use the runbook?	HR Department - AD Security group ODYSSEY\HRDepartment
From where will this runbook be triggered?	Orchestrator web console
Security Requirements	Dedicated account needed for application

FIGURE 6.2 Runbook scenarios documentation.

NOTE: INTEGRATION WITH EXTERNAL TOOLS

Integrating with an external tool to initiate runbooks entails discovering the integration requirements. As an example, an automation can be integrated in an overall service request process, as is the case with System Center Service Manager, and access to the runbook (the service request process) would be configured in Service Manager. Individual security configuration on the runbooks would not be required because the runbook is initiated by a connection account.

Analyzing Actions in the Automation

The "Orchestrator Usage Scenarios" section discussed determining how the runbook will be used and by whom; you can now analyze configuring the runbook at the action level. Before diving into the Runbook Designer and building a runbook, you should describe the actions the automation requires.

This analysis breaks down the complete runbook. It includes describing details on the activity inputs (required or optional), how each action must be executed, conditions for execution, and desired output. You also should think about error handling; the runbook might need to capture scenarios such as whether you depend on the output of an activity during execution, or the action to take if the activity output is incorrect.

This analysis is not difficult. As you start working with Orchestrator, you become more familiar with its activity library and activity capabilities. In some cases, you know all details and can directly list the different actions. For other automations, you must obtain the information from the requestor of the automation. This analysis results in a list of actions and specifications on how the action must operate to achieve the desired result.

TIP: DOCUMENTING YOUR ANALYSIS

One approach for documenting the list of actions and specifications is to use an Excel spreadsheet, which you use for input when creating the runbook in the Runbook Designer.

To create the list of actions, componentize the tasks that must be performed. Actions in a workflow might require information before they will execute. The result of executing an action can be an input for another action in the workflow. Using the Runbook Designer, you can define the actions as Orchestrator activities and connect these actions to each other, creating a workflow.

Evaluate how each action is performed manually, verifying that no dependencies exist. This lets you discover the need for additional actions, data manipulation, or specific checks. Consider actions to take if something goes wrong or a required property is not set correctly; this provides input for error handling and lets the runbook behave correctly regardless of the scenario. Here are questions for when you create your runbook:

- **Activity input:** What information is necessary to execute the action? Is a specific format required, or do you need to manipulate the data input for the action?
- **Execution behavior:** Are there specific conditions for the execution, or do properties need to be set during execution of the activity?
- **Activity dependencies:** Are any actions required before you can execute the activity?
- **Activity output:** What is the desired result or output of the activity? The output can be a single string or an array of information that can be further used in the runbook.

Consider the action of creating a user. Analyzing that request delivers a list of activities, which must be further evaluated with the requestor to confirm that the list is complete. The breakdown of the workflow could look like this:

- Define the start parameters for the runbook.
- Apply a naming convention for the user account.
- Create a new user home folder.
- Get the new user's role specifications.
- Create the user in Active Directory and set the required properties on the object.
- Create the user's account in the primary business application.
- Create an Exchange mailbox for the user.
- Apply a mailbox setting based on the specified user role.
- Send notification of the new user's hardware requirements to the IT department.
- Send details of the newly created user to the HR mailbox.

REAL WORLD: USE A FLOWCHART TO DESCRIBE THE FLOW OF THE RUNBOOK

Listing the activities and providing detail for them is the input for your activities; for large runbooks, the authors recommend creating a flowchart drawing of the automation flow. This is the "blueprint" of your runbook.

You now have a list of actions which provides an indication of the Orchestrator activities you need in your runbook and those for which you must find a customized solution. For example, creating a user account in Active Directory is an Orchestrator activity that comes with the Active Directory integration pack (IP); creating the user account in a business application could require performing some scripting or creating custom activities. To make this clearer, let's drill down into this example.

Starting the Runbook Action

This is the first step in the runbook workflow. All information required as input for the runbook execution needs to be specified on this action.

- **Activity input:** This is the information required to create a user account following the company's specifications:
  - First name
  - Last name
  - User role
  - Start date
  - Department
- **Execution behavior:** This is how the runbook will run:
  - The runbook will be started from the Orchestration console by the HR department.
  - The provided input must be evaluated before the runbook continues.
- **Activity dependencies:** No dependencies exist for this action.
- **Activity output:** Information is available for use in other actions of the workflow.

The first action of the workflow describes the information required to run the runbook. This includes evaluating the input to the runbook, which results in additional actions in the runbook to check that the information is provided and that an existing role or department is specified. An email can be sent to the initiator or relevant parties if details are missing or invalid.

Creating the User Account in the Primary Business Application

Creating a user account needs additional information before it can be translated into an Orchestrator activity or activities.

- **Activity Input:** This is the information required to create a user account using the primary business application.
    - **First name:** Specified on start of runbook
    - **Last name:** Specified on start of runbook
    - **Username:** Output of "Apply naming convention for user account" action
    - **Department:** Specified on start of runbook
- **Execution behavior:**
    - The account must be created using the primary business application.
    - After the account is created, you can create a script to configure the user in the primary business application.
- **Activity dependencies:** The business application must be available. If not, the runbook must stop executing any additional actions.
- **Activity output:** The employee number of the new user is created in the business application.

Here information provided at the start of the runbook is used, with other data, such as the username, being an output of another action in the workflow. The logic used to create the username (naming conventions or other logic) must be described on that action.

The runtime behavior specifies that creating and configuring the account is a two-step process. The dependencies include a requirement to check web service availability before creating the account. Here you must go back to the business application owner to evaluate the options for runbook error handling if the web service is unavailable when the runbook executes. This could include calling another runbook to resolve the unavailability of the web service or sending a notification to the application owner. The output is an employee number that can be used in the next actions of the workflow.

The advantage of this analysis is that the information is documented in a readable format for the designer of the runbook. In the "Orchestrator Usage Scenarios" section, an Excel spreadsheet was created to document creating the runbook. This spreadsheet can be extended with the specific automation workflow information gathered during this phase. Figure 6.3 illustrates an Excel spreadsheet that includes information from analyzing the example used in this chapter.

The outcome of this phase is a documented high-level overview of the actions necessary to implement the automation. You now can start configuring the runbooks in the Runbook Designer. Documenting all the steps does not mean you do not need to contact the application or service owner for more detailed information while building the runbook, but it provides the minimal information to begin building the runbook.

Runbook action list

Action		Information	Description
Apply naming convention for user account	*Activity Input*		
		First name	From Start Runbook input
		Last name	From Start Runbook input
	Execution Behavior		
		Apply naming convention activity	
		Create and share folder on home folder server	Server: <ServerX>
	Activity Dependencies		
		First name, last name, role, department is specified	Stop runbook when not OK
	Activity Output		
		Username	string
		Home folder share name	integer
Create user in Active Directory	*Activity Input*		
		First name, last name, role, department, start date	string
		Username	from **Apply naming convention** activity
	Execution Behavior		
		Create user account in department OU	
		Configure group membership based on role	
	Activity Dependencies		
		Username output from **Apply naming convention** activity	Stop runbook when not OK
	Activity Output		
		All user properties - available for next activities	

FIGURE 6.3 Runbook activity documentation.

6

Translating Actions to Runbook Activities

The next phase, consists of mapping each action defined during analysis into Orchestrator activities. An action such as "Create user in Active Directory" from the example used in the "Analyzing the Desired Automation" section can be mapped to the **Create User** activity from the Active Directory IP.

As you translate actions into activities, you might discover gaps in your activity library. You might discover actions that are required but cannot be directly mapped to an Orchestrator activity. You have several options here: PowerShell commands, .NET code, and scripting can be a first approach; you might also investigate a vendor or community IP. An overview of the different options follows:

- Standard activities, available out of the box
    - *Standard activities* are a set of generic activities with a generic execution target, consisting of a series of configuration tabs to control behavior of the activity. Chapter 9, "Standard Activities," discusses these.

- The execution of script or code is an activity that can be used as a *wrapper* around your own development to integrate this in a runbook.
- Registered and deployed integration packs
    - Microsoft creates integration packs for System Center products, Active Directory, Exchange, and other applications. Review the list of available IPs at http://technet.microsoft.com/en-us/library/hh295851.aspx.
    - CodePlex is a good source for community-developed IPs. Orchestrator community contributors create and update these integration packs. To find the list of available integration packs and utilities on www.codeplex.com, execute a search on this website using a keyword of "Orchestrator."
    - Vendor-specific IPs have additional activities that perform actions on their products.
- Extend the activity library using the Orchestrator Integration Toolkit (OIT), which includes different tools to create and test your own integration pack activities. For more information, see Chapter 20, "The Orchestrator Integration Toolkit."
    - The Command-Line Activity Wizard (CLI Wizard) enables you to encapsulate commands, arguments, and parameters into a Microsoft .NET assembly that you can include as an activity in your IP.
    - Use the Integration Pack Wizard to quickly build your own Orchestrator integration packs from existing assemblies.
    - With the Orchestrator SDK, you can build your own custom Orchestrator activities.

Always document your automation. You can add information regarding translation from actions to Orchestrator runbook activities to the Excel spreadsheet that was created during analysis.

For runbooks that do not include many activities, you can translate and create the runbook simultaneously. For complex runbooks, the analysis and translation phases become mandatory. Consider a runbook you are creating that interacts with other services in the company where you do not have control. The analysis and translation exercise provides an opportunity to gather the required connection or configuration details for these activities in your runbook. A good design and translation includes handling failures and warnings of activities, utilizing naming conventions, using link colors wisely, and splitting long and complex runbooks into parent and child tasks that pass data to each other.

Now that you have defined activities, including their sequence and configuration, you can start drag-and-drop activities to create the workflow.

Creating the Runbook in Orchestrator Runbook Designer

You create runbooks using the Runbook Designer. Use the information gathered from previous phases of your analysis as input, and translate each action in the workflow into Orchestrator activities, linking them to each other to create the desired flow.

During analysis, you defined the actions for completing the automation. This list of actions must be translated to a chain of activities in the runbook. Sometimes you can do this directly in the Runbook Designer; for other runbooks, you might need to think about flow as an offline exercise. Use standard activities or activities from a deployed IP as your library of actions for building the runbook. Depending on the level of detail defined for the actions during analysis, one or more activities might be necessary to translate the action into activities in your runbook.

Creating the runbook is a drag-and-drop exercise of activities in the Runbook Designer, linking them to accomplish the desired flow. Configure the behavior of each action in activities or conditions that link the activities. You might be able to accomplish your goal in one runbook, or you might need additional runbooks. Common actions used in different runbooks can be created as separate runbooks, invoked from the automation you are building.

REAL WORLD: PLACING COMMON ACTIONS IN SEPARATE RUNBOOKS

An example of an action that you might want to put in a separate runbook is error handling. You could use a central runbook to report failures of activities that write events or create alerts in your monitoring system, such as System Center Operations Manager. Other runbooks can invoke this error-handling runbook for failed activities, similar to a programmer calling a subroutine.

Use the Runbook Tester to validate the automation or perform an intermediate check of your runbook. This can be started from the toolbar above the central Design workspace in the Runbook Designer. The Runbook Tester lets you test and validate runbooks in a debugging environment. You can run an entire runbook in the Runbook Tester, or you can test one activity at a time, similar to using developer tools. You can add breakpoints to stop the execution at any activity.

The following sections further describe configuring the runbook. Chapter 7, “Runbook Basics,” and Chapter 8, “Advanced Runbook Concepts,” describe runbook creation.

Configuring the Runbook Designer

Before you start building runbooks, you must configure the Runbook Designer environment. This configuration is for all runbooks; you customize it before creating runbooks and can modify it as requirements change. Navigate to the Options menu item and select **Configure** to open the Runbook Designer Configuration dialog box, shown in Figure 6.4. Select the options you will use, and click **Finish** to save your changes.

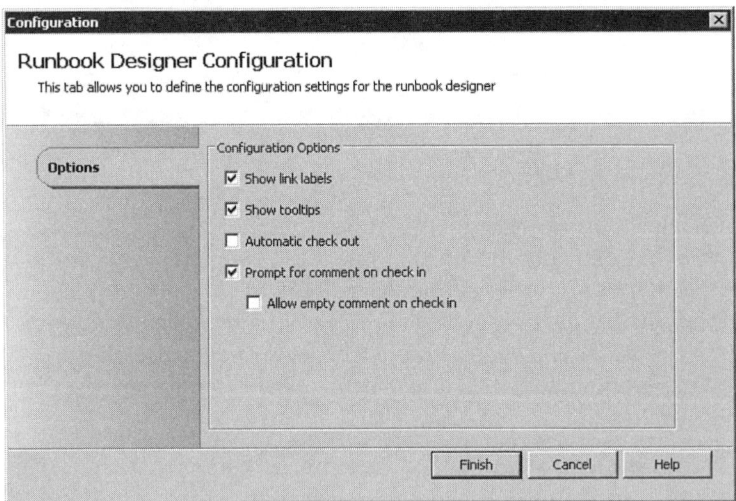

FIGURE 6.4 Runbook Designer settings.

Here are settings you could define for the Runbook Designer:

- **Show link labels:** Display the name of each link. This text comes from the Name field on the General tab of the link's Properties dialog box.
- **Show tooltips:** Display tooltips when you navigate your cursor over an object in a runbook. This text comes from the Description field on the General tab of the activity's Properties dialog box.
- **Automatic checkout:** Automatically check out a runbook when you begin to edit it. If this is not selected, you are asked whether you want to check out the runbook.
- **Prompt for comment on check in:** Display the Comment dialog box when you check in a runbook. Select **Allow empty comment on check in** to leave the comment blank.

Let's start with building the runbook from the example used in the "Analyzing Actions in the Automation" section of this chapter. The goal is to create a workflow that creates a new user and configures the environment for that user.

As in every environment where you change an item in an application, keep things organized. In the Navigation pane of the Runbook Designer, right-click the Runbooks folder and select **New** -> **Folder**.

TIP: USING RUNBOOK FOLDERS IN THE RUNBOOK DESIGNER

You can create folders to keep runbooks organized in the Runbook Designer and for security purposes because permissions can be set at the folder level. This lets you protect your runbooks and create workspaces for other runbook administrators. If you synchronize runbooks with System Center Service Manager, a folder is required as a synchronization root.

Creating a runbook is similar to creating a folder. In the Navigation pane, right-click the folder where you want to store the runbook and select **New -> Runbook**.

Checking In and Checking Out

Multiple individuals can be authorized in Orchestrator to create and update runbooks. To prevent someone else from overriding your changes, only one user at a time can modify a runbook. To edit a runbook, you must check it out. Another user cannot edit that runbook until you commit all changes by checking in the runbook in, or revert all changes by undoing the checkout:

- **Check out:** When a user is editing a runbook, the runbook is checked out; no one else can edit it. If the runbook is already being edited, a pop-up window opens, informing you that someone is editing the runbook.
- **Check in:** When a user editing the runbook performs a check-in operation, all changes made are committed; other runbook administrators can then edit the runbook after they check it out. Check-in comments describe the changes that have been made.
- **Undo check out:** When this occurs, all changes made after the runbook was checked out revert to the original state of the runbook. After the undo check out operation is completed, another runbook administrator can edit the runbook.

Configuring Runbook Properties

Your first task after creating the runbook is configuring its properties. Name the runbook in a manner that documents what it is doing; this eases administration and monitoring of your runbook environment. Chapter 7 describes runbook creation. You can configure these properties:

- **General:** On this tab, you specify the name and description of the runbook and the schedule defining when the runbook can run.
- **Runbook Servers:** The Runbook Servers tab displays the list of runbook servers assigned to run this runbook. If the list is blank, the default primary runbook server runs the runbook.
- **Logging:** This tab enables you to specify what published data is stored for the runbook you are creating. You can publish activity-specific data and/or common activity data.
- **Events:** Specify a value in the Seconds box, indicating that you should be notified if this runbook runs for more than the specified number of seconds. Select the check box to be notified if the runbook fails to run.

- **Job Concurrency:** The value in the Maximum number of simultaneous jobs box configures the maximum number of simultaneous jobs for a runbook.
- **Returned Data:** Specify the data the runbook will return when it completes execution.

TIP: LOGGING CONFIGURATION ON THE RUNBOOK

You can control what published data is stored for the runbook you are building. Enabling the **Store activity specific Published Data** option can help troubleshoot runbook execution. When enabled, activity information is available in the Log History of the runbook.

The environment is now configured for building your runbook. Orchestrator runbooks are visual representations of the automation being built, with building blocks of runbook features such as activities, smart links, and schedules.

Using Activities and Links in Your Runbook

Activities are the intelligence in your runbooks, with smart links defining the runbook's flow. Each activity is represented with an icon and performs a specific task when it runs. To use an activity in a runbook, drag an activity from the Activity pane to the Runbook Designer workspace. Each activity has configuration properties specific to the actions the activity performs. To create the flow, link each activity to other activities. After an activity has run, it invokes any other activities to which it is linked.

Activities used in the runbook are dependent on the action that needs to be executed in the flow. The first activity specified is based on whether the runbook needs to have input before it can start, monitors for an event, or runs at a scheduled time:

- When a runbook needs input before it can execute the workflow, the runbook must start with the **Initialize Data** activity.
    - The administrator executing the runbook can provide input using the Orchestration console.
    - This activity could also be specified when the runbook is invoked by another runbook.
    - When Orchestrator is integrated with other tools (such as System Center Service Manager), the Orchestrator web service provides the input.
- Monitoring for an event can be the trigger for a runbook. If you are monitoring the uptime of an Internet application, you could perform different actions when there is a false response from the monitoring activity.
    - Activities for monitoring services, disk space, Internet applications, processes, and so on are included out of the box as monitoring activities. Chapter 7 provides additional information.

  - The System Center integration packs and other IPs can extend the list of monitoring activities in your library by monitoring product-specific events.
- Runbooks can be configured to run at a specific or reoccurring time. The runbook will be continuously executing, waiting for the event to occur at a specific time or interval period.

If the runbook has a smart link, it invokes the next step in the runbook as soon as the previous task completes. The term *smart* is justifiable; the link you create between activities can be configured with conditions to control flow. By default, successful execution of the current activity is the trigger to invoke the next activity. You can adjust this default behavior with Include or Exclude conditions on the link. Right-click a smart link and select **Properties**; a pop-up appears to configure the link:

- **General:** Name and provide an optional description of the link on the General tab. You can make this visible in the Runbook Designer using the configuration settings of the runbook.
- **Include:** This tab specifies the conditions that enable data to flow to the next activity in the runbook.
  - To change the values that make up the condition, select each underlined portion of the smart link condition.
  - To change the result in the link condition, select the returned result that is underlined. A dialog box opens to specify the string to compare with.
- **Exclude:** The Exclude tab specifies the conditions to cause data to be excluded from the next task. This works in a similar manner to the Include tab.
- **Options:** This tab specifies the optional configuration for the smart link.
  - You can set the link color and width.
  - You can specify the trigger delay on the Options tab. You can specify the number of seconds that you want the smart link to wait before invoking the next activity in the runbook.

TIP: NAME AND USE COLORS FOR SMART LINKS

Give the links in your runbook meaningful names so that you can follow their flow. A name that corresponds with the condition that is set on the link using different colors can improve the visualization of the activity workflow. Show link labels must be enabled in the Runbook Designer to show the name on the link.

Figure 6.5 shows a sample link configuration with an Include filter.

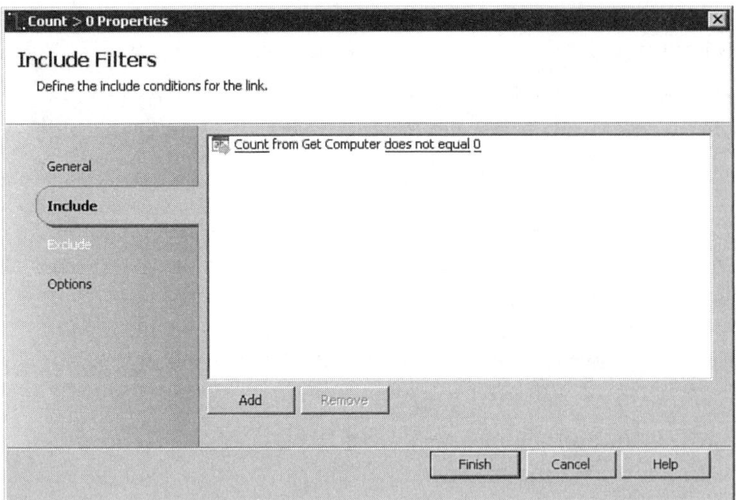

FIGURE 6.5 Configuring a smart link.

NOTE: INCLUDE AND EXCLUDE CONDITIONS ON SMART LINK

Be careful when mixing include and exclude conditions. The conditions on the Exclude tab supersede the rules on the Include tab. In addition, conditions on each tab are joined by using an "or" condition. Only one of the conditions on a tab must be true for the entire tab to be true.

Data Manipulation When Configuring Activities

It is not well known that you can manipulate returned data in the property fields of an activity. With Orchestrator, you can manipulate string data from text files, published data, or other sources. Using the available functions, you can convert this data into a usable form. You can perform data manipulations on text, and you can perform simple arithmetic operations.

You can insert a data-manipulation function into any box that allows you to type text. Data-manipulation functions must be enclosed in square brackets ([and]). Consider some examples:

- Text data manipulation:
  - **Syntax:** [Upper('orchestrator unleashed')]
  - **Returned data:** ORCHESTRATOR UNLEASHED
- Arithmetic manipulation:
  - **Syntax:** [Sum(1,3,5,7,9)]
  - **Returned data:** 25

Data manipulations can be nested into other functions. If you want to use a data-manipulation function within another function, the nested function does not have to be enclosed in square brackets. Consider an example of a nested field function:

- **Syntax:** [Field(Field('username=kmeyler@odyssey.com','=',2),'@',1)]
- **Returned data:** kmeyler

Table 6.1 provides an overview of the data manipulation functions; Chapter 8 includes usage examples.

TABLE 6.1 Data Manipulation Functions

Function	Usage and Parameters
Upper	Returns text in upper case Syntax: **Upper**('Text') Text: The text that is being converted to upper case
Lower	Returns text in lower case Syntax: **Lower**('Text') Text: The text that is being converted to lower case
Field	Returns text in a specific position Syntax: **Field**('Text', 'Delimiter', Field Number) Text: The text that is being searched Delimiter: The character that separates each field Field Number: The position of the field that is being returned (starting at 1)
Sum	Returns the sum of a set of numbers Syntax: **Sum**(firstNumber, secondNumber, thirdNumber, ...) Number: The number that is being added; you can use any set of numbers, each separated by a comma (,)
Diff	Returns the difference of two numbers Syntax: **Diff**(Number1, Number2, <Precision>) Number1: The number that will be divided Number2: The number that will be subtracted from Number1 Precision (optional): The number of decimal places to which the result will be rounded
Mult	Returns the product of a set of numbers Syntax: **Mult**(firstNumber, secondNumber, thirdNumber, ...) Number: The number being multiplied; you can use any set of numbers, each separated by a comma (,).
Div	Returns the quotient of two numbers Syntax: **Div**(Number1, Number2, <Precision>) Number1: The number that will be divided Number2: The number that will divide Number1 Precision (optional): The number of decimal places to which the result will be rounded

Function	Usage and Parameters
Instr	Returns the position of the first occurrence of text within another text Syntax: **Instr** ('SearchText', 'TextToFind') SearchText: The text that is being searched TextToFind: The text that you are searching for
Right	Returns a subset of the text from the right side of the full text Syntax: **Right**('Text', Length) Text: The full text Length: The number of characters from the right side that will be returned
Left	Returns a subset of the text from the left side of the full text Syntax: **Left**('Text', Length) Text: The full text Length: The number of characters from the left side that will be returned
Mid	Returns a subset of the text from the middle of the full text Syntax: **Mid**('Text', Start, Length) Text: The full text Start: The starting position in the text where you want to begin returning characters Length: The number of characters starting from the Start position that will be returned
LTrim	Trims leading spaces from text Syntax: **LTrim**('Text') Text: The text being trimmed of leading spaces
RTrim	Trims the trailing spaces from text Syntax: **RTrim**('Text') Text: The text being trimmed of trailing spaces
Trim	Trims leading and trailing spaces from text Syntax: **Trim**('Text') Text: The text being trimmed
Len	Returns the length of text Syntax: **Len**('Text') Text: The text that is being measured

Using Published Data

During runbook execution, each activity in the runbook publishes data that other activities can use. This is the power of Orchestrator: having this published data available for every activity in the flow.

- Subsequent activities in a runbook can subscribe to published data and provide new published data as output of its execution, which the following activities in the runbook can use.

- Link conditions can also use published data in the condition configuration of the smart link. After the activity is executed, the data becomes available for the next link or flow of activities. The activities must be linked before the published data is available.
- Published data can be accessed from any text box in the properties of the activity. Right-click the text box and select **Subscribe -> Published Data** (see Figure 6.6) to open the Published Data dialog box.

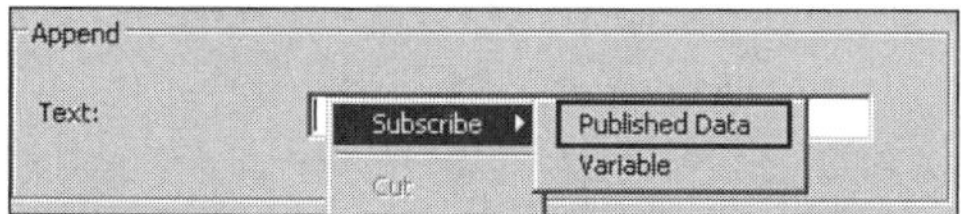

FIGURE 6.6 Accessing published data in an activity.

You have common activity and activity-specific data published after the activity executes:

- **Common published data:** This is information surrounding the activity execution and behavior. Examples are activity start time, runbook name, and looping configuration; this data is always published on the Orchestrator data bus.
- **Activity-specific published data:** This is information that the activity itself returns. Different activities can return data or retrieve information from an outside source. Data output from an activity can be a single string value or might be a list of data found based on the input of the activity.

Activities can return any number of data items. Each data item is passed to the activity that follows, after going through link condition filtering. When the next activity in the runbook runs, it runs once for each item of data produced by the previous activity. As an example, the **Query Database** activity runs and retrieves three rows from the database. These three rows of data make the next activity run three times, once for each row returned. This next activity does not have to subscribe to the data for this to occur.

Using Computer Groups with Runbooks

Orchestrator workflows can be configured to automate all your data center systems. You can target a single computer or a group of computers. When a group is selected, the activity is executed on every computer in the group. Figure 6.7 shows the Computer Group selection.

Any standard activity that requires a computer name in the configuration properties dialog box, such as the **Send Event Log Message** activity in Figure 6.7, can utilize the subscription of a computer group. Other activities can use the computer group when you need to define a remote system or computer. Chapter 8 discusses computer groups in more detail.

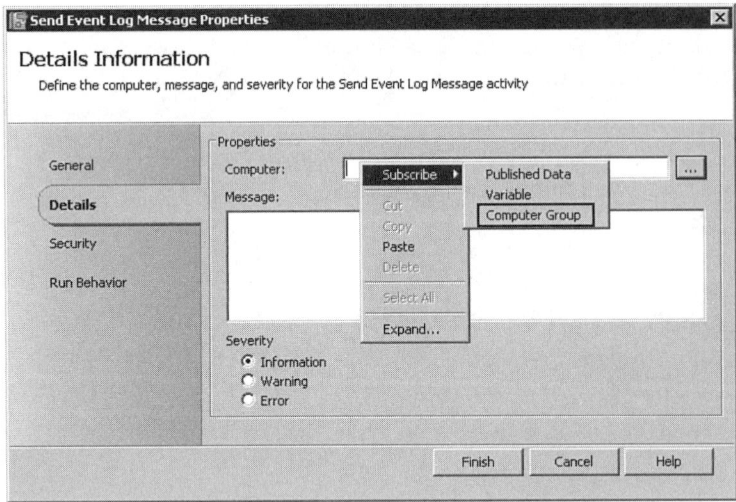

FIGURE 6.7 Selecting a Computer Group.

A computer group can be created in the navigation workspace of the Runbook Designer. As with other global settings and runbooks, you should keep this organized by creating folders to keep similar items together in the console. Follow these steps:

1. Right-click the Computer Group folder, and select **New -> Computer Group** (see Figure 6.8).

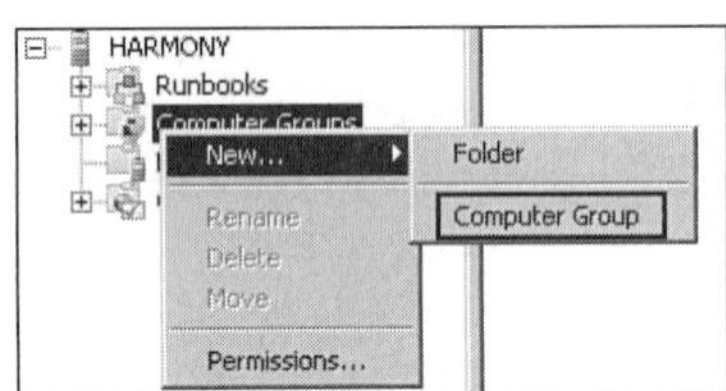

FIGURE 6.8 Menu selection to create a computer group.

2. The New Computer Group dialog box opens (see Figure 6.9). On the General tab, you can specify the name and description of the computer group.
3. On the Contents tab in Figure 6.10, you can add computers to the group. Click **Add**; the Add Computer to Group dialog box opens. You can type or browse for the specific computer to add. Click **Finish** to save your changes and close the wizard.

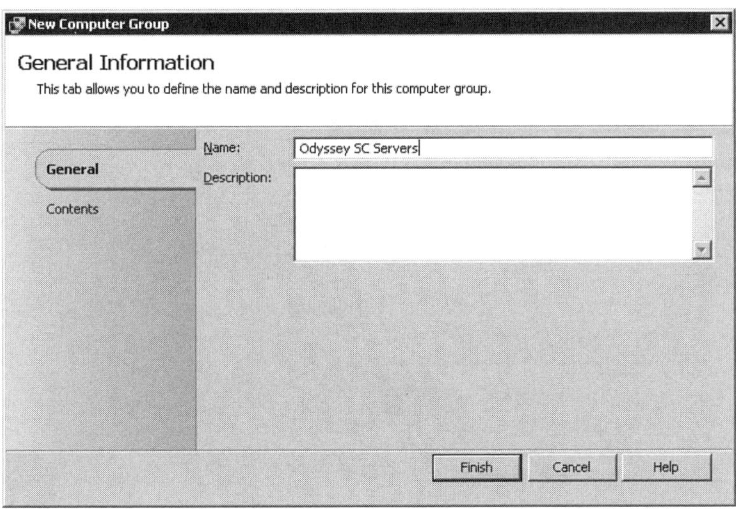

FIGURE 6.9 General tab of the **Create Computer Group** dialog box.

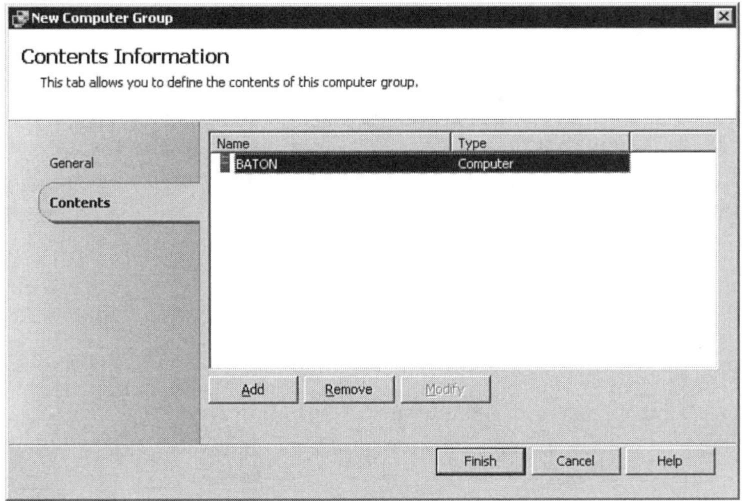

FIGURE 6.10 Contents tab of the **Create Computer Group** dialog box.

6

Using Regular Expressions

Orchestrator lets you use regular expressions to match a string to a pattern. The regular expression can contain different elements that define the pattern. The strength of regular expressions is brought into Orchestrator runbooks, where they can be used for filters or data manipulation. An example of an activity that can utilize regular expressions is the

Find Text activity in the Text File Management set of activities. Figure 6.11 shows an example of when you can use a regular expression in the Search text field.

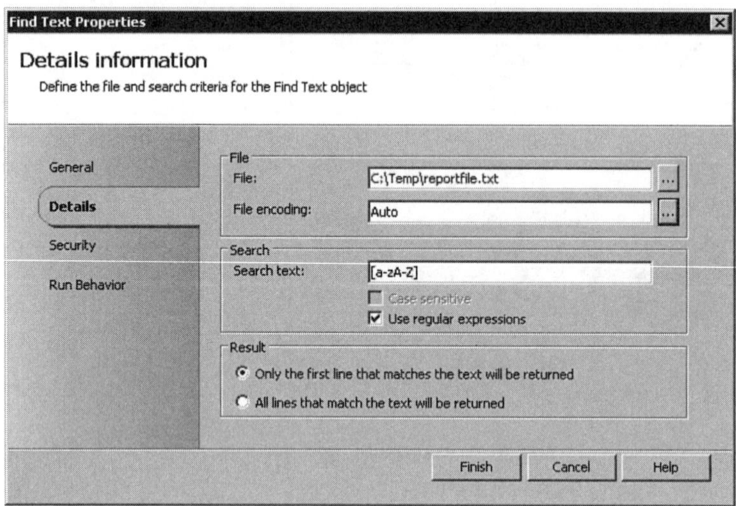

FIGURE 6.11 Using regular expressions in activity configuration.

To build regular expressions, you must create an expression that contains the text you are searching for and special characters that create a pattern describing how the text you are searching for appears. Table 6.2 provides an overview of RegEx characters and some sample patterns; examples of usage are in Chapter 8.

TABLE 6.2 Regular Expression Characters

Character	Description
.	Matches any character except a newline.
*	Matches the preceding item zero or more times. For example, the "x*" pattern matches any string of x's in a row "x", "xxx", "xxxxxxx", and an empty string "".
+	Matches the preceding item one or more times. This is like *, but you must have a least one of the preceding item to make a match. For example, the "ab+" pattern matches "abbbbb", "ab", but does not match "a". To contrast, the "ab*" pattern matches "a".
?	Matches the preceding item zero or one time. For example, the "ab?" pattern matches "a" or "ab" but does not match "abbb".
|	Matches either the preceding expression or the following expression. Logical OR operator.

Character	Description
$	Matches the expression at the end of the input or line. For example, "ab$" matches "I took a cab" or "drab" but does not match "absolutely not".
^	Matches the expression at the beginning of the input or line. For example, "^od" matches "odyssey" or "odd future" but does not match "I work in the odyssey lab".
\	For characters that are usually treated as special. This indicates that the next character is literal and is not to be treated as a special character. For example, "\." means match the "." character and not just any character.
[ ]	A character set. Matches any one of the enclosed characters. You can specify a range of characters by using a hyphen. For example, "[a-zA-Z]" matches any letter of the alphabet.
[^]	An excluded character set. This is the opposite of []. If any of the characters inside the brackets exists, the regular expression match fails. You can specify a range of characters by using a hyphen. For example, "[^a-zA-Z]" makes sure that none of the letters in the alphabet is present.
( )	A group expression. This groups an expression into an item to which you can apply special characters. For example, "a*(ba)+' matches "ba" "aba" or "ababa" but does not match "abbba" or "abaa".

9

NOTE: USING REGULAR EXPRESSIONS

Regular expression matching in Orchestrator is performed based on the Microsoft .NET Framework. If you are familiar with creating regular expressions based on other languages, note that there are differences in how .NET matches regular expressions versus other languages such as Java.

Using Counters

Counters are useful when you need to track values that must be incremented, enabling you to modify and check the status of a value you can use to track important statistics. As an example, you could use counters if you are monitoring a service and want to react only when an event has occurred *x* times.

To create counters in the Runbook Designer, expand the **Global Settings** folder in the Navigation pane, right-click the folder where you want to store the counter configuration, and select **New** -> **Counter** (see Figure 6.12).

In the Counter dialog box in Figure 6.13, you can specify the name, description, and default value of the counter. Click **Finish** to save your changes.

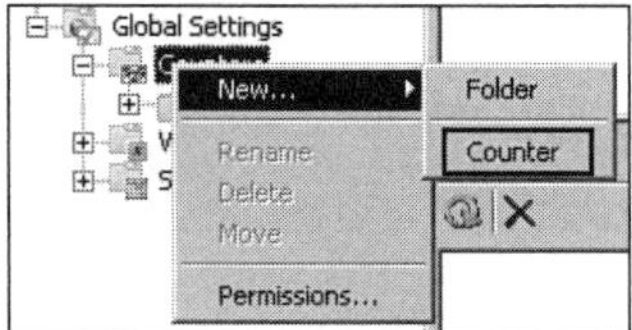

FIGURE 6.12 Creating a new counter.

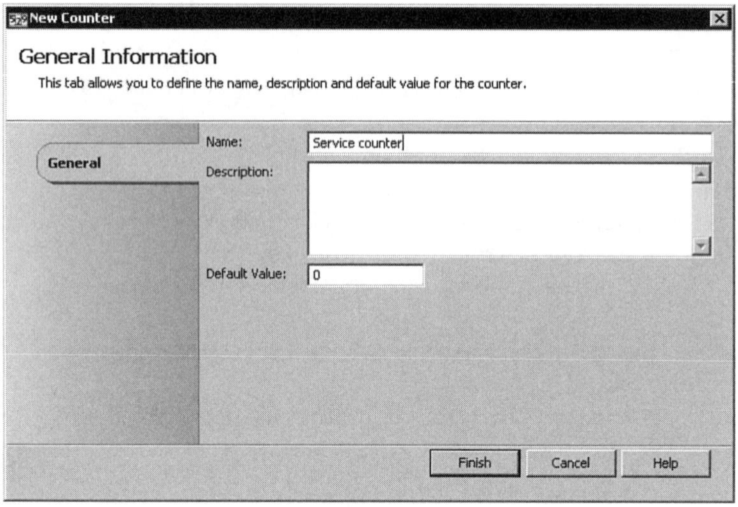

FIGURE 6.13 General tab of the New Counter dialog box.

Setting, resetting, incrementing, or decrementing the counter requires the **Modify Counter** and **Get Counter Value** activities. You can configure multiple runbooks or simultaneous jobs to modify a specific counter, although running simultaneous jobs that change (set, reset, increment, or decrement) a counter can cause the counter value to become unreliable. You can read the value of counters in runbooks that run simultaneously, but you should control modifications on the counter. Chapter 9 has information on the different counter activities.

Using Schedules

You can use schedules with runbooks to define when they can run. Schedules use the system clock of the operating system on the runbook server to verify the runbook's start time. This enables schedules to function in virtual machine environments and to continue running even when the system clock is adjusted by changes with Daylight Saving Time.

Configure saved schedules on the runbook properties, or use these in runbooks to evaluate date/time conditions with the **Check Schedule** activity. The schedule is created in the Navigation workspace of the Runbook Designer in the Global Settings folder.

To create a schedule, expand Global Settings, right-click the folder where you want to store the schedule, and select **New-> Schedule** (see Figure 6.14) to open the New Schedule dialog box. On the General tab, you can specify the name and description of the schedule. On the Details tab, select the days this schedule allows runbooks to run (see Figure 6.15).

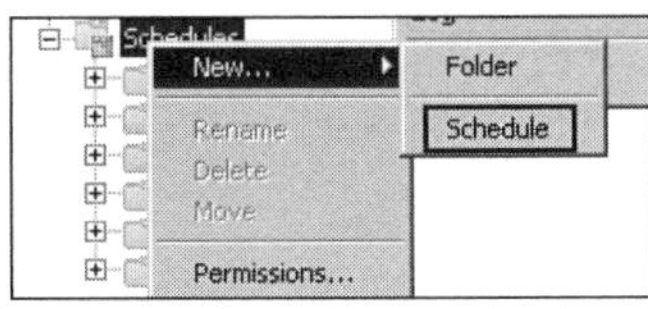

FIGURE 6.14 Creating a new schedule.

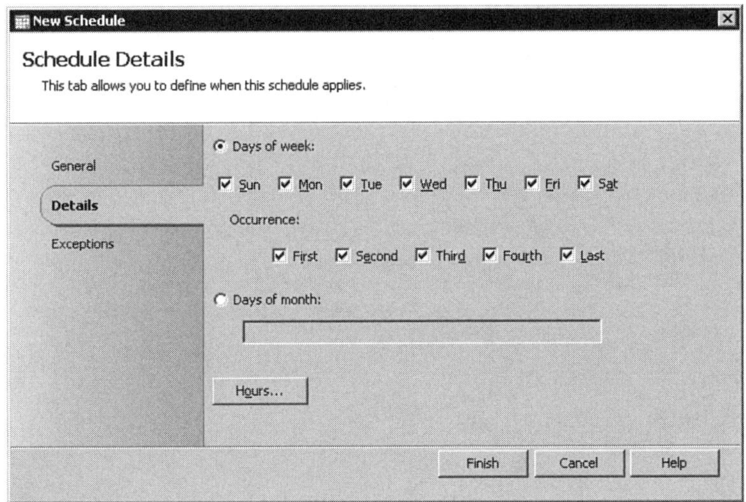

FIGURE 6.15 Details tab of the New Schedule dialog box.

- **Days of week:** You can use this option to select the days of the week when this schedule allows runbooks to run. The occurrence is the weeks of the month when the schedule allows runbooks to run.
- **Days of month:** Select this option and specify the days of the month when this schedule allows runbooks to run.
  - Specify the days of the month by entering the number of the day.
  - Use hyphens to describe ranges and commas to separate entries. For example, typing **1-5** includes the first through the fifth day of the month.
  - You can specify a combination of days and ranges of days to create complex descriptions of the days of the month.

- Select **All** to specify all days of the month.
- Select **Last** to specify the last day of the month.

On the Schedule Exceptions dialog box in Figure 6.16, you can specify dates to allow or deny runbook execution. The overview displays all days that are exceptions to the rules defined on the Details tab. Select the Exceptions tab and click **Add** to open a dialog box where you can both select a date and select Allow or Disallow to allow or not allow the runbook to run on that day.

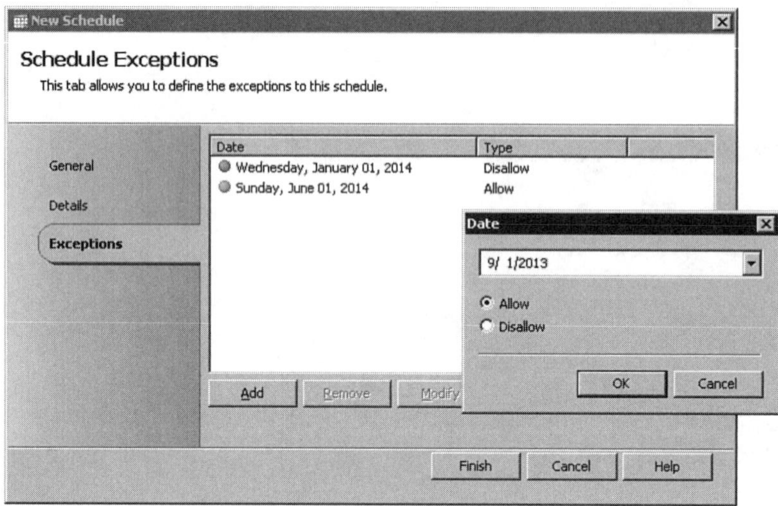

FIGURE 6.16 Configuring schedule exceptions.

Creating and Using Variables

Variables are useful when you have settings used in different activities for different runbooks. If these values require updating, changing each activity individually would be inconvenient. Using variables, you can specify a value in one location and then use that value anywhere else by inserting the variable into the activity settings.

You can configure variables in the Global Settings folder in the Runbook Designer. To create a variable, expand the Global Settings folder, click-right the folder where you want to store the variable, and select **New -> Variable** (see Figure 6.17).

You can specify the Name and Description on the General tab of the dialog box. The value can be any value specified for the variable. You can choose to encrypt the value so that it is not a readable property in the logging of the runbook. Figure 6.18 shows the Variable creation dialog box, where a sample variable with a value of **Odyssey** is created.

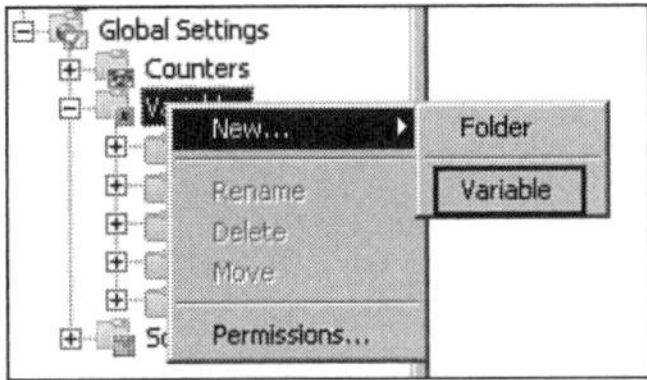

FIGURE 6.17 Creating a new variable.

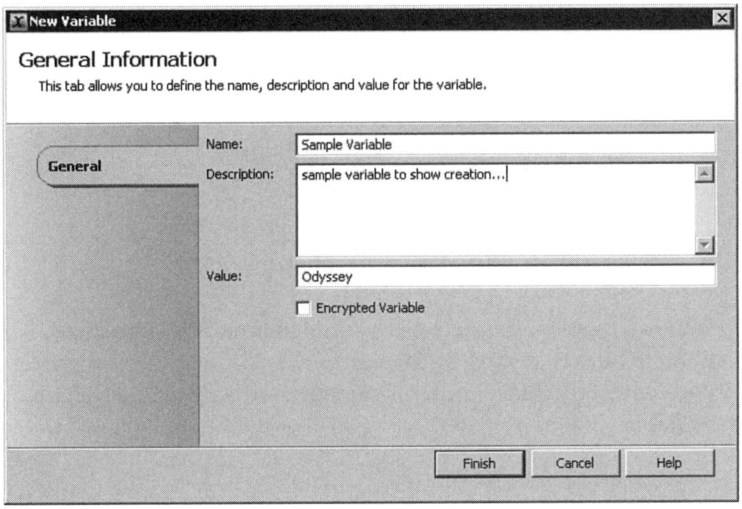

FIGURE 6.18 General tab of the New Variable dialog box.

NOTE: USING ENCRYPTED VARIABLES

Variables that are encrypted can be decrypted only by certain fields in activities such as password fields. If you are using an encrypted variable in other fields, the result will be the encrypted text.

Variables can be used in different runbook activities. Although you can configure permissions on the variable, they are accessible for every runbook administrator. You can subscribe to a variable in any text field of the activity properties. Let's reuse the **Send Event Log** activity introduced in the "Using Computer Groups with Runbooks" section of this chapter. Perform the following steps:

1. In the Properties dialog box of the activity, right-click the Computer box; select **Subscribe** and then select **Variable** to open the Select a Variable dialog box (see Figure 6.19).

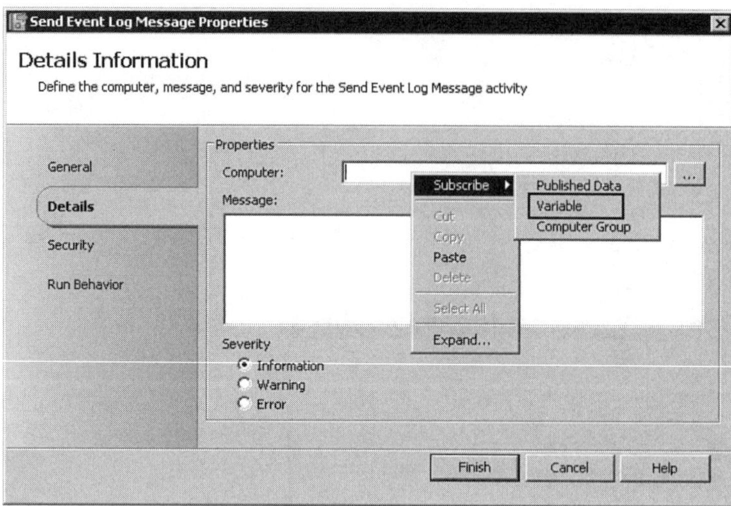

FIGURE 6.19 Specify using a variable.

2. In the Variable dialog box in Figure 6.20, select the variable name and then click **OK**. A placeholder {variable} is inserted next to the computer name in the Computer box. When the activity executes, the placeholder is replaced with the value specified when configuring the variable.

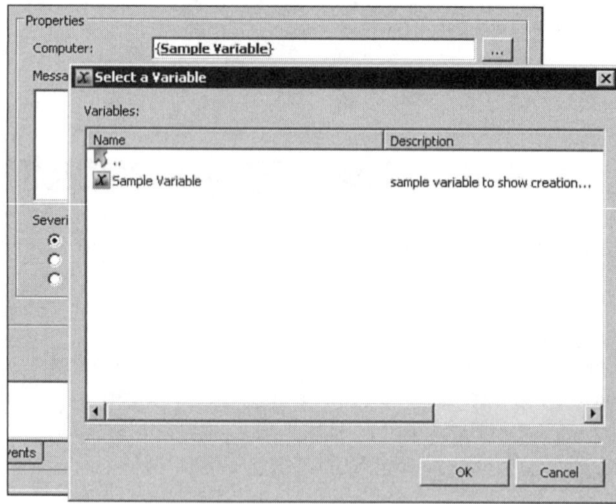

FIGURE 6.20 Selecting a variable.

Chapter 8 discusses the `NOW()` and `%ENVVAR%` variables that are available out of the box.

Validating the Runbook

You can validate and test your runbooks in the Runbook Tester, accessible in the Runbook Designer (see Figure 6.21). Runbooks do not have to be complete to use the Runbook Tester. For larger runbooks, performing some intermediate checks for specific activity results in the workflow is useful. This can help you understand the format used to store the information or to check a result of a chain of activities. Realize that the activities are actually executing the task. The authors recommend testing and validating your runbook against a test environment, and placing runbooks in production only after positive validation in a test environment.

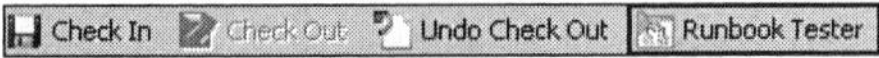

FIGURE 6.21 Runbook Tester link in the Runbook Designer.

When you run your runbook in the Runbook Tester, the tester runs in the currently logged-on user context. This is different than in normal operations, where runbooks are running in the Orchestrator Service account context. Make sure you are running the Runbook Designer with adequate rights to execute the runbook activities.

TIP: SECURITY CONTEXT OF RUNNING RUNBOOK IN TESTER

If you need to use specific credentials for your runbook and you want to test how they will work when the runbook runs, you can launch the Runbook Tester as another user if it is launched automatically from Runbook Designer. Run the Runbook Designer by holding down the Shift key and right-clicking **Runbook Designer**. Select the **Run as different user** option and specify the account to use. Your alternate user must have rights in the Runbook Designer to see the runbook and must be part of the Orchestrator Users group to be able to load the runbook in the Runbook Tester.

Select the **Runbook Tester** option (see Figure 6.21) to launch the Runbook Tester and load the relevant runbook. You can also start the Runbook Tester by right-clicking the checked-out runbook and selecting **Runbook Tester**.

With the Runbook Tester loaded, you can see your runbook in the Runbook Tester workspace. The runbook can be tested with different options (see Figures 6.22 and 6.23):

FIGURE 6.22 Runbook Tester toolbar—Run and Step Through links.

FIGURE 6.23 Runbook Tester toolbar—Step, Stop, and Toggle Breakpoint links.

- **Run:** You can run through the entire runbook, using the Run link on the toolbar. In the Log pane, you can see the completion status of each activity.
- **Step Through:** This starts the runbook, assuming an immediate breakpoint on the first activity.
- **Toggle Breakpoint:** Use a runtime link to set breakpoints on the runbook activities you want to evaluate. This enables you to execute the activity workflow until the breakpoint, where you can review the intermediate state of the properties in the runbook. Breakpoints are marked with a red circle on the activity; the Runbook Tester stops upon these activities.
- **Step:** This runtime link is used to progress to the next activity or the next breakpoint in the runbook. Use the **Stop** link to stop the runbook.

The Run Time Properties pane on the left of the Tester console displays resolved published data items. This is important when you use several published items for activities because you might want to see what data is carried between activities. The best way to see this is with the Runbook Tester. The Design Time Properties pane shows information specified during design for the current selected activity. At runtime, you can compare the published data with the values in the Run Time Properties pane. Figure 6.24 shows the Text property of the **Append Line** activity that is translated during runtime.

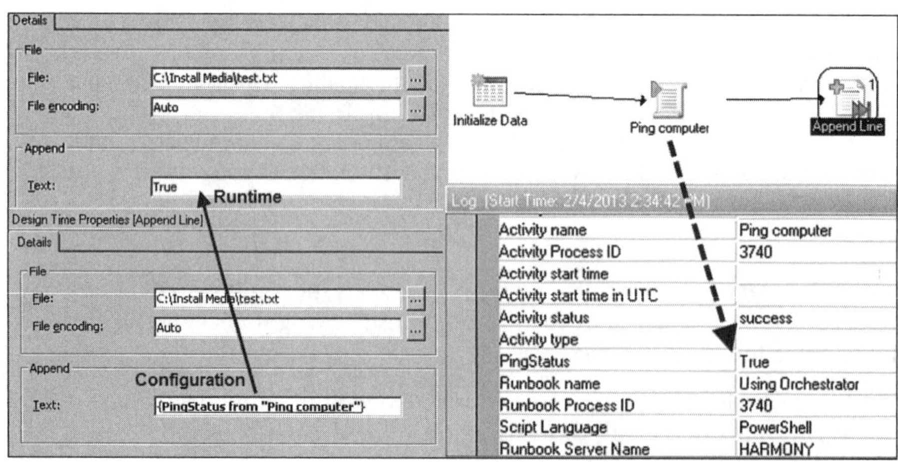

FIGURE 6.24 Runbook Tester runtime properties.

Log information is accessible at the bottom of the Runbook Tester. This pane logs each activity's common and activity published data. Figure 6.24 shows an example in which the published data output from the **Ping Computer** activity is logged together with the common published data.

The Resource pane of the Runbook Tester logs resources used in the runbooks. This includes counters, variables, computer groups, and schedules.

Functional testing and validation occurs in the Runbook Tester. When the runbook is doing what it should, you have created the chain of actions and everything then is working from a technical aspect. If you are targeting systems or services of other departments that you do not administer, you must involve the application or service owner in the runbook validation. While the runbook technically can be running successfully, the result of the execution must be validated on the application or service itself. After the application or service owner has validated the runbook result, you have an end-to-end validation of your automation, and the runbook is ready for production.

Managing Runbooks Using the Orchestration Console

Runbooks can be triggered to run from the Runbook Designer, the Orchestration console, or the Orchestrator web service. After the runbook is checked in, it is ready to run. The user or service account that will be running the runbook must be provided access to trigger the runbook. Runbooks can be triggered with different entries, and each entry requires its own configuration.

Runbook access permissions are set through the Runbook Designer. The Orchestrator Users group has full access to a runbook by default. You can give access to additional users to run, start, stop, view, and change runbooks at either the folder level or the individual runbook level. These permissions must be configured to delegate control of your runbooks to other administrators.

The Orchestration console is the interface to runbooks. This is accessed from the Orchestrator Start Menu shortcut or the link in the Runbook Designer (see Figure 6.25), or you can browse directly to the URL.

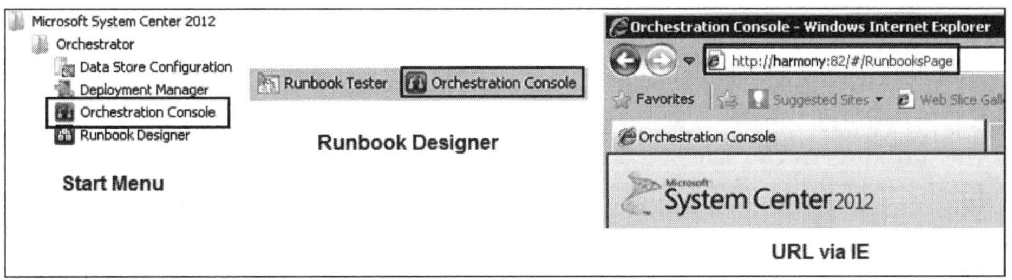

FIGURE 6.25 Accessing the Orchestration console.

You can run the Orchestration console from any computer with a browser, without installing a separate tool. The functions you can perform in the Orchestration console are a subset of the functions in the Runbook Designer. The console is intended for administrators or users who need to manage the operation of runbooks but are not required to modify them. You can modify runbooks only in the Runbook Designer.

In the Navigation pane on the left site of the Orchestration console in Figure 6.26, you can navigate through runbooks, the runbook server, and events.

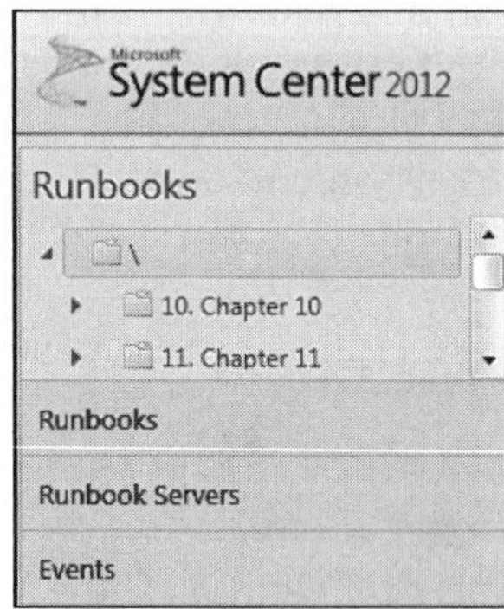

FIGURE 6.26 Navigation pane of the Orchestration console.

The Runbooks tab in the Navigation pane provides access to Orchestrator runbooks. It displays the folder structure from the Runbook Designer, from which you can list the status of running jobs and instances of each runbook. For environments with a large number of runbooks, you can refine the list by specifying a filter. You can review this information in the console:

- **Summary:** This tab provides an overall summary on the folder level and individual runbook execution overview when a runbook is selected.
  - The statistics are displayed and updated every 10 minutes.
  - Each column in the Summary tab displays the number of jobs and instances that finished with a particular status (Succeeded, Warning, or Failed) within the last hour, last day, and last week.
- **Runbooks:** This tab displays when you select a folder in the Runbooks workspace. It lists the runbooks in the selected folder and specifies the status of any running jobs and instances of those runbooks.
- **Jobs:** This tab lists the jobs created for a given runbook and their completion status. For a folder, it lists the jobs created for all runbooks in the folder and their completion status.
- **Instances:** This tab lists the instances that have been created for the runbook and their completion status when a runbook is selected. When a folder is selected, it lists the instances that have been created for all runbooks in the folder and their completion status.

The Runbook Servers tab in the Navigation pane provides a view of the status for jobs and instances for each runbook server. Selecting a runbook server in the Navigation pane provides an overview of running and completed jobs:

- **Jobs:** This tab lists the jobs that have run on the runbook server and their completion status.
- **Instances:** This lists the instances that have been created on the runbook server and their completion status.

The Events tab provides an overview of the log events. These events are a combination of management server and runbook server events. You can use filters to define criteria to limit the events displayed in the workspace of the console. The source name is provided if the event occurred on a specific server; for those events, you can navigate directly to the runbook server using the View Runbook Server action link to review more detailed information.

For many of the selectable items in the Navigation and Workspace pane, you can run one or more actions from the Actions pane of the console. Select an object in the console to see the available actions in the Actions pane. The available functionality follows:

- **Start Runbook:** This action triggers the runbook for execution. When a runbook starts, a job is created and waits for an available runbook server to process the runbook. Monitoring activity jobs run continuously once started, potentially producing multiple instances of a runbook.

  When a runbook server is available, the job provides an instance of the runbook to the runbook server to process. The Start Runbook action opens the Start Runbook page (see Figure 6.27), where you can specify the runbook parameters and select runbook servers.

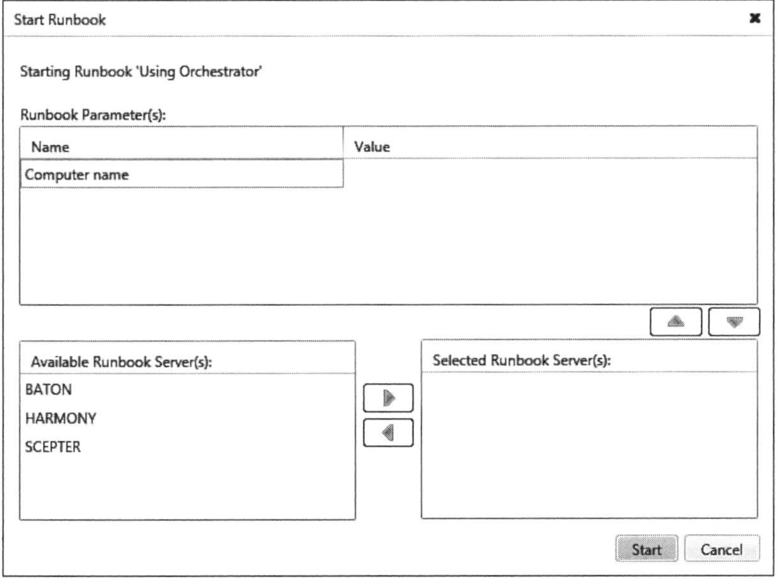

FIGURE 6.27 Start Runbook page in the Orchestration console.

- **Runbook Parameters:** Value(s) must be specified, if any, that are required to execute activities in the runbook. Configuration parameters specified on the **Initialize Data** start activity are listed in this view.
- **Runbook Server(s):** You can select from the available runbook server(s). The primary runbook server runs the runbook if no selection is made on this page.

- **Stopping Jobs and Runbooks:** Job requests can be stopped from the Orchestration console. This cancels the request for a runbook to run. When the runbooks is executing activities, you can stop it from executing. For both actions, a pop-up displays to acknowledge the stop request.
- **View Jobs:** This link opens the Jobs Workspace tab for the selected item in the console, where you can review jobs at the runbook, runbook server, and folder level.
- **View Instances:** This opens the Instances Workspace tab for the selected item in the console, where you can review the running and completed instances of jobs and runbooks.
- **View Definition:** This link brings you to a page (see Figure 6.28) where the runbook is illustrated, as in the Runbook Designer. The overview provides input/output parameters, together with the runbook diagram. The Runbook Summary section can be closed on the right site of the page to return to the Orchestration console.

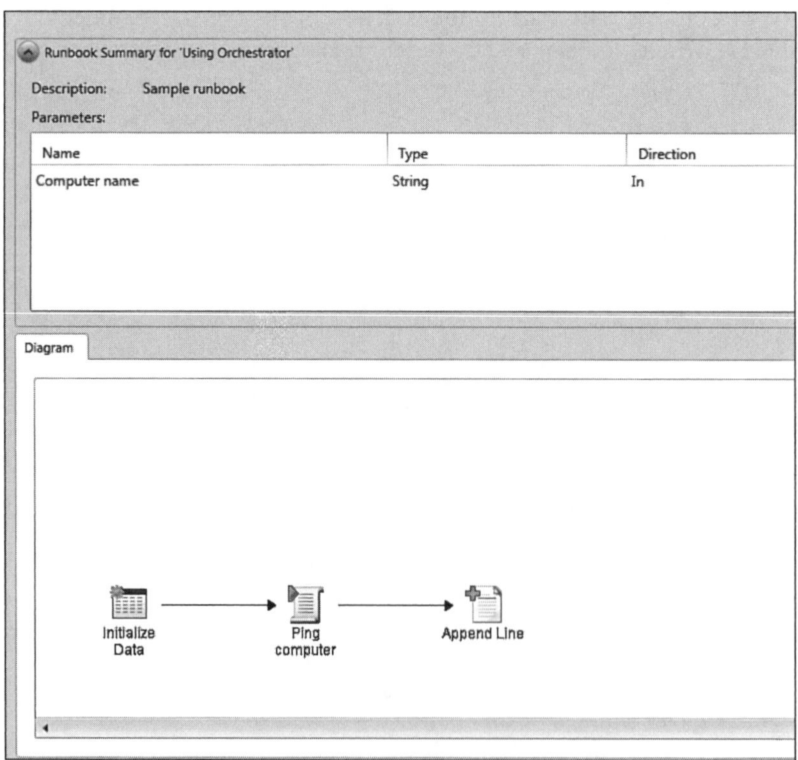

FIGURE 6.28 Runbook Summary page in the Orchestration console.

- **View Runbook:** This action links to the Summary tab in the workspace of the console that is available when a job is selected.
- **View Details:** This link in the Action pane (see Figure 6.29) provides a real-time runbook overview. When the runbook is running, you can follow the activity execution step by step in the Diagram workspace. It provides an overview of the runbook input and output parameters, each with its tab item on the Summary page. A Diagram view with execution results and activity details appears in the lower section of the page. This page is useful for troubleshooting runbooks.

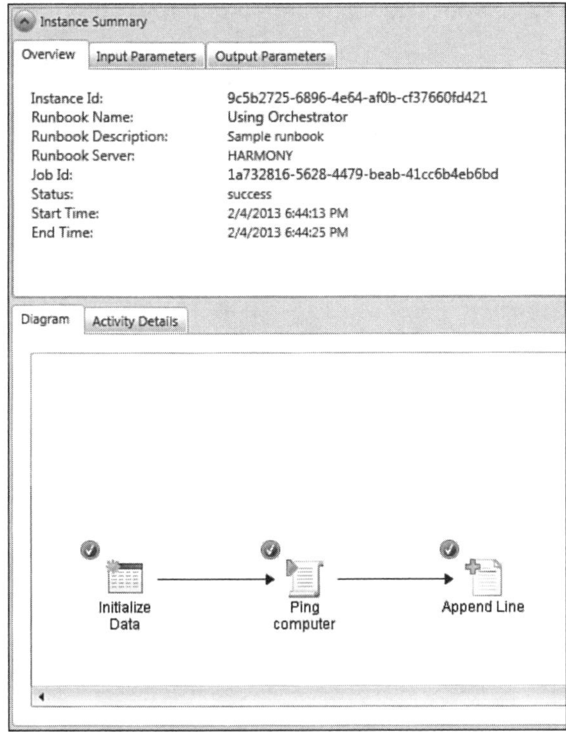

FIGURE 6.29 Instance Summary page in the Orchestration console.

Managing Runbooks with the Orchestrator Web Service

Orchestrator 2012 exposes a REST OData web service that enables programmatic access to Orchestrator runtime resources such as runbooks, jobs, and events, and enables you to start runbooks and stop jobs.

An OData service represents data as resources and relationships between resources. The exposed Orchestrator resources can be queried using Internet Explorer. The syntax of the OData query has three sections:

- **[Service Root URI]:** The connection to the web service in your Orchestrator environment
- **[Resource Path]:** The resource you are trying to query
- **[Query Options]:** The query to filter the returned information

Here is the complete syntax: http(s)://< **Service Root URI>/<Resource Path>?<Query Options>**

A sample URL that connects to the Odyssey Orchestrator service root URI is http://Harmony:81/Orchestrator2012/Orchestrator.svc/. Figure 6.30 shows the Orchestrator resources in the Odyssey environment.


```
  <?xml version="1.0" encoding="utf-8" standalone="yes" ?>
- <service xml:base="http://harmony:81/Orchestrator2012/Orchestrator.svc/" xmlns:atom="htt
  - <workspace>
      <atom:title>Default</atom:title>
    - <collection href="Folders">
        <atom:title>Folders</atom:title>
      </collection>
    - <collection href="Runbooks">
        <atom:title>Runbooks</atom:title>
      </collection>
    - <collection href="RunbookParameters">
        <atom:title>RunbookParameters</atom:title>
      </collection>
    - <collection href="Activities">
        <atom:title>Activities</atom:title>
      </collection>
    - <collection href="Jobs">
        <atom:title>Jobs</atom:title>
      </collection>
    - <collection href="RunbookInstances">
        <atom:title>RunbookInstances</atom:title>
      </collection>
    - <collection href="RunbookInstanceParameters">
        <atom:title>RunbookInstanceParameters</atom:title>
      </collection>
    - <collection href="ActivityInstances">
        <atom:title>ActivityInstances</atom:title>
      </collection>
    - <collection href="ActivityInstanceData">
        <atom:title>ActivityInstanceData</atom:title>
      </collection>
    - <collection href="RunbookServers">
        <atom:title>RunbookServers</atom:title>
      </collection>
    - <collection href="RunbookDiagrams">
        <atom:title>RunbookDiagrams</atom:title>
      </collection>
    - <collection href="Statistics">
        <atom:title>Statistics</atom:title>
      </collection>
    - <collection href="Events">
        <atom:title>Events</atom:title>
      </collection>
    </workspace>
  </service>
```


FIGURE 6.30 Orchestrator web service resources.

Web Service Resource Discovery

For any given resource, relationships to other resources are also exposed. This means that a resource such as a runbook has metadata (URLs) that represent the relationships to other resources such as jobs and activities. This metadata information can be reviewed by simply adding the resource name after the URL to explore the resources. The following list describes the OData resource path specification and the query option to query the resources:

- The *resource path* defines the resource that you want to work with. This can be a single resource, such as a runbook, or it can be a collection of resources, such as all runbooks or a collection of jobs related to a particular runbook. Providing the name of a collection alone in the resource path returns all instances of that resource.
  - http://Harmony:81/Orchestrator2012/Orchestrator.svc/Runbooks is an example of a URL to review the runbook metadata. This query returns all runbooks.
  - A single member of a collection can be queried by specifying its key property enclosed in parentheses: http://Harmony:81/Orchestrator2012/Orchestrator.svc/Runbooks(guid'8a4e40ce-7e9e-4fba-9752-095b3afee1b7').
  - A single property from a single member of a collection can be queried by specifying the name of the property at the end of the URL for the specific member: http://Harmony:81/Orchestrator2012/Orchestrator.svc/Runbooks(guid'8a4e40ce-7e9e-4fba-9752-095b3afee1b7')/Name.
  - Members of one collection related to a single member of another collection can be queried by specifying the name of the related collection at the end of the URL for the specific member: http://Harmony:81/Orchestrator2012/Orchestrator.svc/Runbooks(guid'8a4e40ce-7e9e-4fba-9752-095b3afee1b7')/Jobs.
- *Query options* enable you to refine further which data is returned and how it is ordered. Each option is specified with a dollar sign ($), with multiple options separated with an ampersand (&).
  - **$expand:** The expand query option includes members for one collection that are associated with the members in the collection that you are returning: http://Harmony:81/Orchestrator2012/Orchestrator.svc/Runbooks?$expand=Jobs.
  - **$filter:** The filter query option enables you to limit the results of the query to only entries that match the specified criteria. Common operators can be used to build the criteria for the filter: http://Harmony:81/Orchestrator2012/Orchestrator.svc/Runbooks?$filter=IsMonitoreqtrue.

9

- **$inlinecount:** The inlinecount query option enables you to include a count of the total number of entries in the request response. The following example returns records 151–200 and includes the total number of records in the request response:

  http://Harmony:81/Orchestrator2012/Orchestrator.svc/Jobs?$skip=150&$top=50&$inlinecount=allpages.

- **$orderby:** This query option specifies the property that the returned entries are ordered by—for example: http://Harmony:81/Orchestrator2012/Orchestrator.svc/Jobs?$orderby=Name.
- **$select:** You can return a subset of properties when you add the $select option in the query, such as http://Harmony:81/Orchestrator2012/Orchestrator.svc/Jobs?$select=Id,Name.
- **$skip:** The $skip option enables you to skip the specified number of entries in the query—for example: http://Harmony:81/Orchestrator2012/Orchestrator.svc/Jobs?$orderby=Name&$skip=10.
- **$top:** With the $top option in the query, you can control the number of entries that are returned, such as http://Harmony:81/Orchestrator2012/Orchestrator.svc/Jobs?$orderby=Name&$skip=10&$top=10.

NOTE: CONFIGURE INTERNET EXPLORER TO EXPOSE ALL ODATA DATA

By default, Internet Explorer does not display all data returned from an OData Orchestrator service. To configure Internet Explorer to expose all the available data, navigate to Tools -> Internet Options; on the Content tab, click **Settings** in the Feed and Web Slices section. Deselect **Turn on feed reading view**, and click **OK** twice to save your changes.

For performance reasons, the Orchestrator web service limits the number of entries a single request returns. To retrieve members of a particular collection that exceeds the maximum number for that collection, you must retrieve multiple pages using multiple requests. Use the $skip and $top options to browse your list. The limits are adjustable using Internet Information Services Manager (IIS) under Application Settings. In the IIS Manager console, expand **Sites** -> **Microsoft System Center 2012 Orchestrator Web Service** -> **Orchestrator 2012**, and double-click **Applications Settings**. On the Application Settings page in Figure 6.31, you can change the default values.

Using Visual Studio to Interact with the Web Service

To use the Orchestrator web service, you can use any programming language or scripting language that is capable of sending an HTTP request and receiving its response. In this section, Visual Studio is used to create applications that use the Orchestrator web service with coding examples in the C# programming language.

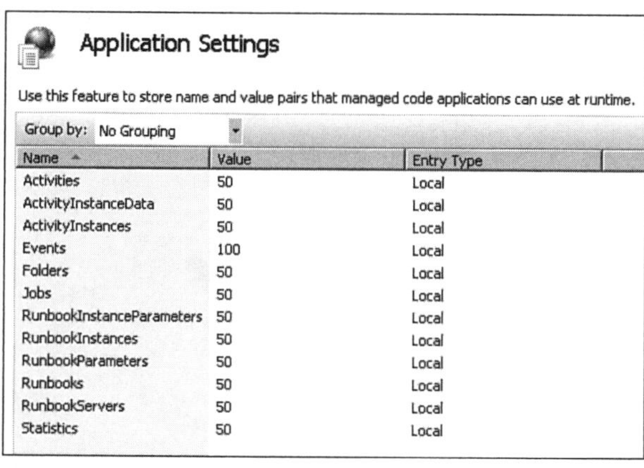

Application Settings
Use this feature to store name and value pairs that managed code applications can use at runtime.
Group by: No Grouping
Name
Value
Entry Type
Activities 50 Local
ActivityInstanceData 50 Local
ActivityInstances 50 Local
Events 100 Local
Folders 50 Local
Jobs 50 Local
RunbookInstanceParameters 50 Local
RunbookInstances 50 Local
RunbookParameters 50 Local
Runbooks 50 Local
RunbookServers 50 Local
Statistics 50 Local

FIGURE 6.31 Orchestrator web service application settings.

The first task after creating your project is adding a service reference to the project you are building; this enables you to work with the web service without the complexities of building HTTP requests. You then start your code by creating an `OrchestratorContext` object. This object gives you access to all the collections and entries the Orchestrator web service provides. This solution requires adding a service reference to the Orchestrator web service in your Visual Studio project. Follow these steps:

1. In the Solution Explorer of your project, right-click **References** and select **Add Service Reference** (see Figure 6.32).

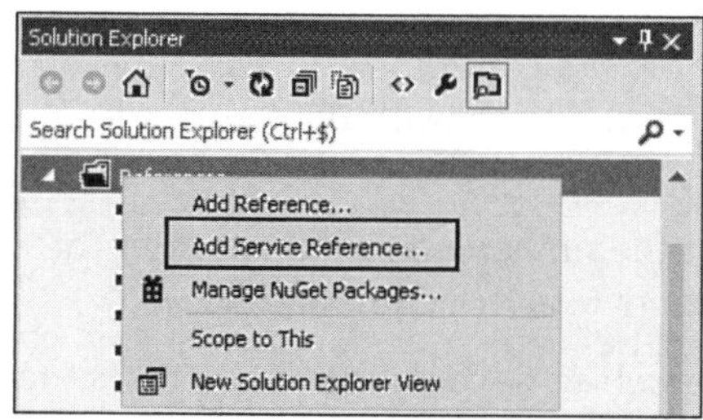

FIGURE 6.32 Selecting Add Service Reference in Visual Studio project.

2. The Add Service Reference page appears. Specify the Orchestrator web service URL and select **Go**. When the discovery is finished, the service and service resources display in the form. Figure 6.33 shows an example for the Odyssey Orchestrator web service. Provide a name for the web service namespace, and click **OK**.

After referencing the namespace in your code, you can start coding against the Orchestrator web service. You can retrieve Orchestrator information and trigger actions.

Create the Orchestrator context in the code; this is the connection to the Orchestrator web service. For the example used in Figure 6.33, this could be:

```
String OrchService = "http://Harmony:81/Orchestrator2012/Orchestrator.svc";
OrchWebService.OrchestratorContext Orchcontext = new OrchWebService.
OrchestratorContext(new Uri(OrchService));
```

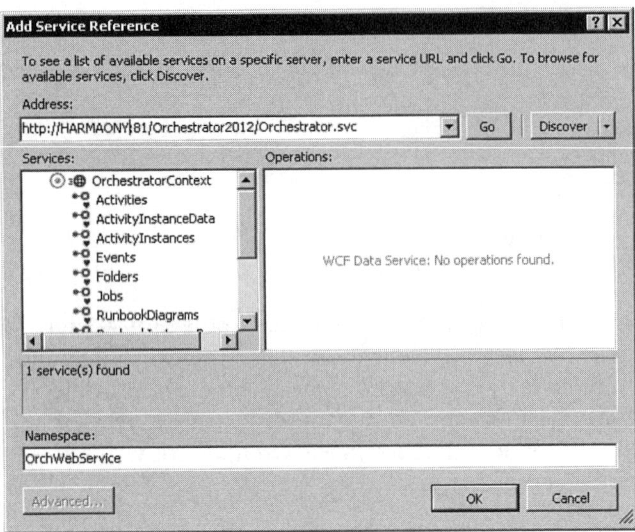

FIGURE 6.33 Configuring a service reference.

Verify that you are working in the correct security context to connect to the web service. The context is created in your code; you then can start interacting with the web service. Consider some sample code:

- **Read information from runbooks:** You can get the runbook information from the web service. Accompanying this explanation, Figure 6.34 displays the code:
    - **serviceRoot:** This is the connection to the web service in your code. This is the URL of the Orchestrator web service.
    - **OrchestratorContext:** This is created to the specified serviceRoot. The credentials to connect to the service can be in the user context (DefaultCredentials) or a named account.
    - **var Runbook = OrchContext.Runbooks.Where(Myrunbook => Myrunbook.Id == <some value>).SingleOrDefault();:** This is how the runbook information is retrieved.

  You now can start interacting with the runbook. In the example in Figure 6.34, the count for jobs is evaluated. If the count of jobs for the runbook is not 0, the Id and name are written to the console.

```
public void GetRunbook()
{
    Guid RunbookId = new Guid("00000000-0000-0000-0000-000000000000");
    string serviceRoot = "http://HARMONY:81/Orchestrator2012/Orchestrator.svc";
    //Create Orchestrator context
    OrchWebService.OrchestratorContext context =
        new OrchWebService.OrchestratorContext(new Uri(serviceRoot));
    context.Credentials = System.Net.CredentialCache.DefaultCredentials;
    // named user account: new System.Net.NetworkCredential("user", "password", "DOMAIN");

    //Get the runbook
    var Runbook = context.Runbooks.Where(Myrunbook => Myrunbook.Id == RunbookId).SingleOrDefault();
    if (Runbook.Jobs.Count > 0)
    {
        // Do something....
        Console.WriteLine("Id: {0}", Runbook.Id);
        Console.WriteLine("Name: {0}", Runbook.Name);
    }

}
```

FIGURE 6.34 Getting runbook information from the web service.

- **Read information from job:** You can retrieve job information from the web service. You can interact with the jobs or retrieve information about a cancelled job (see Figure 6.35). Consider this information:
  - **serviceRoot:** This is the connection to the web service in your code. It is the URL of the Orchestrator web service.
  - **OrchestratorContext:** This is created to the specified serviceRoot. The credentials to connect to the service can be in the user context (DefaultCredentials) or a named account.
  - **var job = context.Jobs.Where(MyJob => MyJob.Id == jobId).SingleOrDefault();:** This is how the runbook information is retrieved.

```
public void GetJob()
{
    Guid jobId = new Guid("00000000-0000-0000-0000-000000000000");
    string serviceRoot = "http://HARMONY:81/Orchestrator2012/Orchestrator.svc";
    //Create Orchestrator context
    OrchWebService.OrchestratorContext context =
        new OrchWebService.OrchestratorContext(new Uri(serviceRoot));
    context.Credentials = System.Net.CredentialCache.DefaultCredentials;
    // named user account: new System.Net.NetworkCredential("user", "password", "DOMAIN");

    //Get the job
    var job = context.Jobs.Where(MyJob => MyJob.Id == jobId).SingleOrDefault();
    if (job.Status != "Canceled")
    {
        // Do something....
    }
}
```

FIGURE 6.35 Getting job information from the web service.

You now can start interacting with the job. You can gather information about a specific job or stop a running job.

- **Trigger start job:**
  - You must know the input parameters for the runbook. This must be coded in an XML stringbuilder to parse the parameters in the job.
  - Runbook triggering is actually creating a job in Orchestrator. The RunbookID and parameters are specified when creating the job in the code. `AddToJobs(<Job>);` is the line to create the job via your C# code (the job is created before with the runbookid and parameters defined).
  - For a detailed example, see Microsoft's MSDN site at http://msdn.microsoft.com/en-us/library/hh921685.aspx.
- **Trigger stop job:**
  - Other actions such as stopping a job can be done in a similar manner: Obtain the job and update the status of the job to "Canceled" with the `UpdateObject(<job>);` method.
  - Doing this is rather simple; let's look at the code in Figure 6.35. In this example, the job context is retrieved and adding the `UpdateObject(<job>);` method to this example makes the job stop. Figure 6.36 illustrates this.

```
public void StopJob()
{
    Guid jobId = new Guid("00000000-0000-0000-0000-000000000000");
    string serviceRoot = "http://HARMONY:81/Orchestrator2012/Orchestrator.svc";
    //Create Orchestrator context
    OrchWebService.OrchestratorContext context
        = new OrchWebService.OrchestratorContext(new Uri(serviceRoot));
    context.Credentials = System.Net.CredentialCache.DefaultCredentials;
    // named user account: new System.Net.NetworkCredential("user", "password", "DOMAIN");

    //Get the job
    var job = context.Jobs.Where(MyJob => MyJob.Id == jobId).SingleOrDefault();
    if (job != null)
    {
        job.Status = "Canceled";
        context.UpdateObject(job);
        context.SaveChanges();
    }

}
```

FIGURE 6.36 Stopping a job using the web service.

  - A detailed example on how to stop a job is documented on MSDN at http://msdn.microsoft.com/en-us/library/hh921668.aspx.

You can interact with Orchestrator using your own custom application. The functionality of the application you build can vary: this could be an interface to run the runbooks, a connector with other services, or an interface to integrate with another application. The information in this section provides a basic overview of how to interact with the web service in your Visual Studio project. Detailed information, sample code, and information around the Orchestrator web service is available at http://msdn.microsoft.com/en-us/library/hh921667.aspx.

Using PowerShell or VBScript to Interact with the Web Service

PowerShell scripts and VBScript cannot use a service reference that simplifies coding, as you can use in your Visual Studio project. You must build the URL to perform the query or action that you want to perform and include it in an HTTP request:

- The `GET` request method retrieves data from the Orchestrator database.
- The `POST` request method must be used to update data. Data is returned in XML according to the Atom Publishing Protocol (AtomPub) standard, and you must provide logic in your script to parse and interpret this information.

This is a different approach to start interacting with the web service via PowerShell. You can initiate the request to get information about a resource with PowerShell using the `System.Net.HttpWebRequest` class. Consider this example to get a job using the web service:

```
$jobID = "<your job GUID>"
$Orchurl = -join ("http://HARMONY:81/Orchestrator2012/Orchestrator.svc/
Jobs(guid'",$jobID,"')")
$jobrequest = [System.Net.HttpWebRequest]::Create($Orchurl)
$jobrequest.Method = "GET"
$jobrequest.UserAgent = "Microsoft ADO.NET Data Services"
# $jobrequest.Credentials = Get-Credential
```

The `System.Net.HttpWebResponse` class captures the response of the request. Take a look at an example:

```
[System.Net.HttpWebResponse] $jobresponse = [System.Net.HttpWebResponse]
$jobrequest.GetResponse()
```

Using `IO.StreamReader` class, you can modify resource properties. When complete, you can start to prepare the connection to `POST` the request. The following is an example of a request:

```
$request = [System.Net.HttpWebRequest]::Create ($Orchurl)
$request.UseDefaultCredentials = $true
# Request header
$request.Method = "POST"
$request.UserAgent = "Microsoft ADO.NET Data Services"
$request.Accept = "application/atom+xml,application/xml"
$request.ContentType = "application/atom+xml"
$request.KeepAlive = $true
$request.Headers.Add("Accept-Encoding","identity")
```

```
$request.Headers.Add("Accept-Language","en-US")
$request.Headers.Add("DataServiceVersion","1.0;NetFx")
$request.Headers.Add("MaxDataServiceVersion","2.0;NetFx")
$request.Headers.Add("Pragma","no-cache")
# Build request stream from the request
$requestStream = new-object System.IO.StreamWriter $request.GetRequestStream()
```

After building the request stream, you can initiate the request to the web service and again capture the result of the request.

To make this more practical, let's illustrate these PowerShell commands with an example. This next example is a PowerShell script to start a runbook. The request body of the request must include the runbook ID and runbook parameter information. You can find the runbook ID and parameter GUID(s) by exploring the web service with Internet Explorer. Here's how you can do this:

- Get the ping runbook ID from http://Harmony:81/Orchestrator2012/Orchestrator.svc/Runbooks.
- Locate the parameters GUID by finding a completed job for this runbook and exploring the job information at http://Harmony:81/Orchestrator2012/Orchestrator.svc/Jobs(guid'05fee26a-379b-45ae-be32-975372a38b25')/Parameters.

After gathering this information, you can build the PowerShell script to start the runbook. Figure 6.37 shows the runbook details and the request header for this example.

```
$creds = Get-Credential("domain\username")
$url = "http://Harmony:81/Orchestrator2012/Orchestrator.svc/Jobs/"
$request = [System.Net.HttpWebRequest]::Create($url)
$request.Credentials = $creds
$request.Timeout = 60000
$request.Accept = "application/atom+xml,application/xml"
$request.Headers.Add("Accept-Charset", "UTF-8")
$request.ContentType = "application/atom+xml"
$request.Method = "POST"
```

FIGURE 6.37 Runbook details and request header.

The second part of the script is creating the request body. In this part of the request, you specify the runbook GUID and the parameters for the runbook. In the ping runbook example, one parameter exists: the name of the computer to ping. Figure 6.38 shows the request body for this example.

```
$requestBody = '<?xml version="1.0" encoding="utf-8" standalone="yes"?>

<entry xmlns:d="http://schemas.microsoft.com/ado/2007/08/dataservices"
xmlns:m="http://schemas.microsoft.com/ado/2007/08/dataservices/metadata"
xmlns="http://www.w3.org/2005/Atom">

<content type="application/xml">

<m:properties>

<d:Parameters>&lt;Data&gt;&lt;Parameter&gt;&lt;Name&gt;Parameter1&lt;/Name&gt;
&lt;ID&gt;{10000000-0000-0000-0000-000000000000}
&lt;/ID&gt;&lt;Value&gt;BALTON&lt;/Value&gt;&lt;/Parameter&gt;
&lt;Parameter&gt;&lt;Name&gt;</d:Parameters>

<d:RunbookId type="Edm.Guid">bb302592-4234-4aaf-9096-244c191ff2b8</d:RunbookId>

</m:properties>

</content>

</entry>
'
```

FIGURE 6.38 Request body in PowerShell script.

TIP: SPECIFYING ADDITIONAL PARAMETERS FOR YOUR RUNBOOK

The example in Figure 6.38 contains one parameter, but you can specify multiple parameters in the data section of the parameter list. The following example shows how to repeat the parameter line for multiple input parameters of your runbook:

For readability when making changes, take this code snippet and find and replace all occurrences of **>** with **>** and all occurrences of **<** with **<**.

```
<d:Parameters>&lt;Data&gt;&lt;Parameter&gt;&lt;Name&gt;Parameter1&lt;/Name&gt;
&lt;ID&gt;{10000000-0000-0000-0000-000000000000}&lt;/
ID&gt;&lt;Value&gt;Value1&lt;/Value&gt;&lt;/Parameter&gt;
&lt;Parameter&gt;&lt;Name&gt;Parameter2&lt;/Name&gt;&lt;ID
&gt;{20000000-0000-0000-0000-
000000000000}&lt;/ID&gt;&lt;Value&gt;Value2&lt;/Value&gt;&lt;/
Parameter&gt;&lt;/Data&gt;</d:Parameters>
```

The code then becomes this:

```
<d:Parameters><Data><Parameter><Name>Parameter1</Name>
<ID>{10000000-0000-0000-0000-000000000000}</ID><Value>Value1</Value>
</Parameter>
<Parameter><Name>Parameter2</Name><ID>{20000000-0000-0000-0000-000000000000}</
ID><Value>Value2</Value></Parameter></Data></d:Parameters>
```

Use the updated snippet as a guideline when updating the values in the first string.

The last part in the script builds the request stream. Figure 6.39 displays code where the request stream from the request is created. The request is sent to the service with the `$requeststream.Write($requestBody)` command. The response of the request is captured via `$response=$request.GetResponse()` and written to the `$Output` string variable. Streams are closed on the end of the script.

```
$requeststream=new-object System.IO.StreamWriter $request.GetRequestStream()
$requeststream.Write($requestBody)
$requeststream.Flush()
$requeststream.Close()
$response=$request.GetResponse()
$requestStream=$response.GetResponseStream()
$readStream=new-object System.IO.StreamReader $requestStream
$Output=$readStream.ReadToEnd()
$readStream.Close()
$response.Close()
```

FIGURE 6.39 Request stream in PowerShell script.

You can execute a PowerShell script to retrieve the execution information after running the code to start the runbook. Figure 6.40 shows code for providing execution information after initiating the script that starts the runbook. When the job is created, the job ID is provided. In case of a failed job creation, the status code of the request is provided.

```
if ($response.StatusCode -eq 'Created')
{
    $xmlDoc = [xml]$responseString
    $jobId = $xmlDoc.entry.content.properties.Id.InnerText
    Write-Host "Job ID: " $jobId
}
else
{
    Write-Host "Start runbook failed - Status: " $response.StatusCode
}
```

FIGURE 6.40 Execution information.

The web service enables easy automation of the Orchestrator runtime from any application. The Orchestration console is one example of an application that uses the web service to connect with Orchestrator. Appendix A, "Community Solutions and Tools," discusses other tools or applications that you can use to connect to the Orchestrator environment.

An example of a System Center component that connects to Orchestrator to trigger runbooks is System Center Service Manager. Using a connector configured in the Service Manager console, runbooks are synchronized and can be integrated in different Service Manager processes. Runbook information is synchronized with Service Manager so that the required input can be provided for triggering the runbooks.

View Orchestrator Data by Using Excel PowerPivot

You can use Microsoft PowerPivot for Microsoft Excel to create reports in Orchestrator. This feature lets you import and analyze available information from the web service. You can use information imported in Excel for reporting, or you can analyze this information with PivotTables.

To use this functionality, you must configure the Orchestrator web service as a data feed on your PowerPivot, create relationships between tables, and then manipulate the data to fit your requirements. PowerPivot for Excel is an add-on developed and published by Microsoft. For Microsoft Excel 2010 or earlier versions, you need to install this add-on; it must be enabled in Excel 2013. The next procedure describes how to connect to the web service and use this information in the Excel PowerPivot worksheet. You can review detailed information and download the installer at www.microsoft.com/en-us/bi/power-pivot.aspx. Perform the following steps:

1. Open Microsoft Excel and use a blank workbook. Select the PowerPivot ribbon tab to open the available options for this functionality (see Figure 6.41).

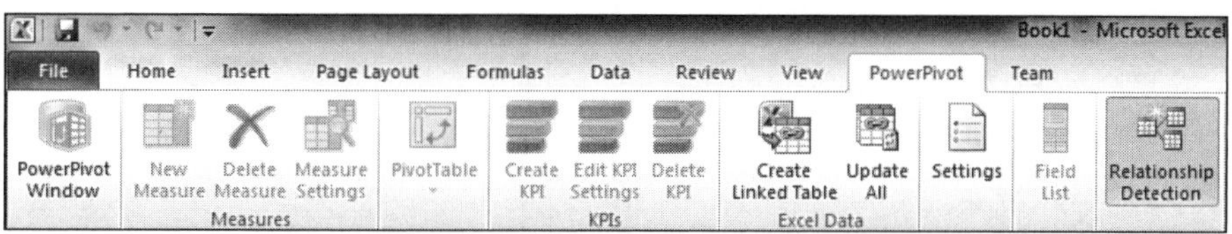

FIGURE 6.41 Excel PowerPivot window.

2. Click **PowerPivot Window** on the ribbon. A PowerPivot window for the Excel book opens (part of the menu in Figure 6.42). Click **From Data Feeds** on the ribbon to open the Table Import Wizard (see Figure 6.43).

FIGURE 6.42 Excel PowerPivot menu.

3. Enter the Orchestrator web service URL in the Data Feed URL drop-down. The web service URL is on port 81 of the Orchestrator SQL Server. For example, http://HARMONY:81/Orchestrator2012/Orchestrator.svc is specified in Figure 6.43. Click **Test Connection** to evaluate your connection to the web service. Click **Next** to proceed to the next step.

TIP: CONNECTION TO THE WEB SERVICE FAILS

If your connection to the Orchestrator web service fails, you can use the Advanced button to specify detailed information. In the Advanced dialog box, you can set the security from Integrated Security to Basic, Change Persist Security Info to True, and specify a username/password to use in the connection.

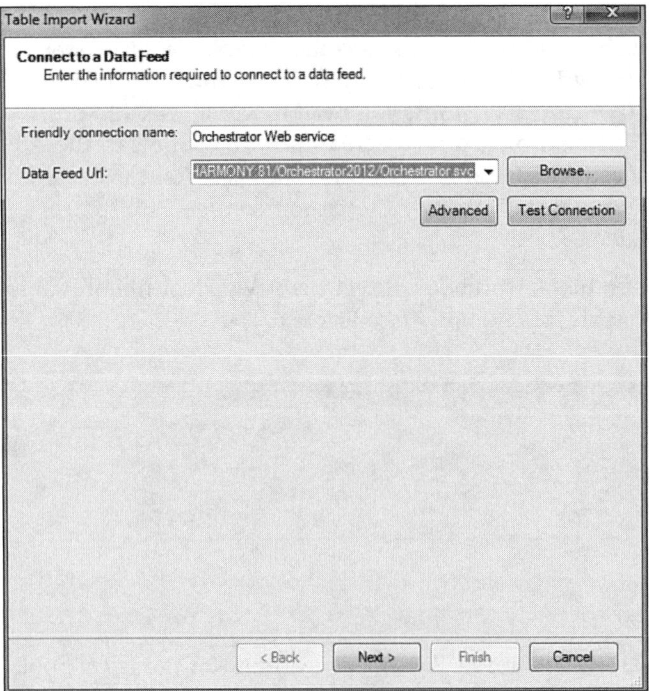

FIGURE 6.43 Table import wizard for PowerPivot.

4. On the Tables and Views selection page, you can select the tables you want to import. For this example, shown in Figure 6.44, the Activities and Runbooks tables are selected. Note that the OData provider in PowerPivot does not support the data contained in the Runbook Diagram box. Attempts to add a RunbookDiagrams table will fail. Click **Finish** to start importing the tables.

5. Figure 6.45 displays the results from importing. Click **Close** to complete the import wizard and start using the data.

6. Tables are imported and available on the Excel sheets. Figure 6.46 shows a sample data sheet from the imported Runbooks table.

Analysis using the PowerPivot functionality requires some additional configuration. Import the needed information by running through steps 1–5 from the previous procedure in this section, and then create the relationships between the columns of the imported tables. Consider the example in which the RunbookServers, Runbooks, and RunbookInstances tables are imported. Follow these steps:

1. Select the RunbookInstances sheet in the PowerPivot for Excel and create the relationships:

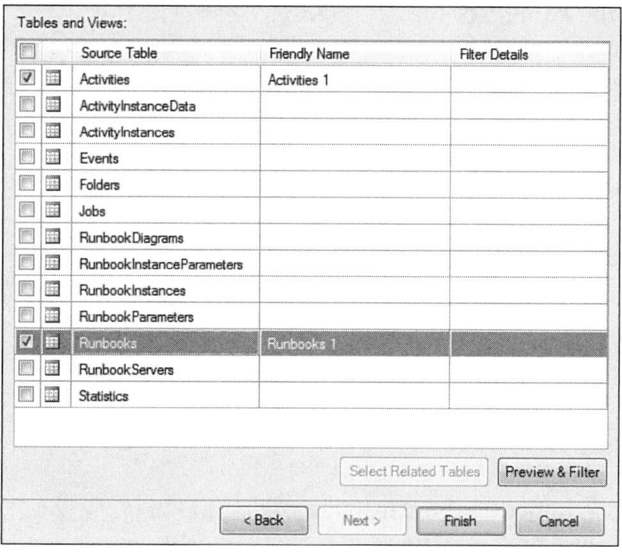

FIGURE 6.44 Table selection for import in PowerPivot.

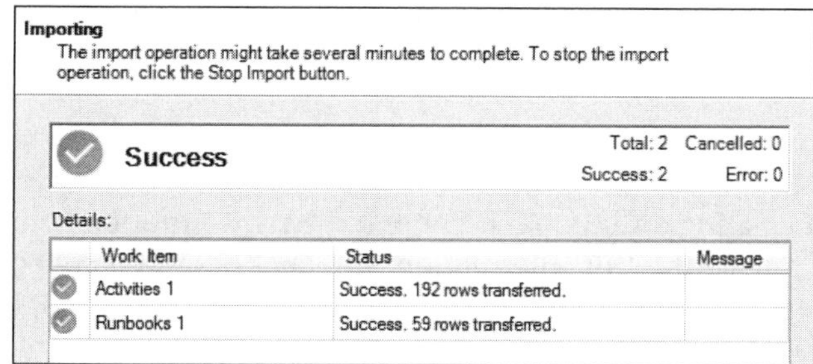

FIGURE 6.45 Importing results.

Id	RunbookId	Name	TypeName	Description	CreationTime	CreatedBy	LastModifiedTime	LastModifiedBy	Enabled
{495...	{AC745EC2-6A...	Start Test...	Trigger Policy		22/02/2013 18:16...		22/02/2013 18:16:27		TRUE
{22F...	{2A1E3B4F-D1...	Start VM ...	Trigger Policy		22/02/2013 18:16...		22/02/2013 18:16:14		TRUE
{707...	{35E517C3-75...	Initiate C...	Custom Start		22/02/2013 18:16...		22/02/2013 18:16:41		TRUE
{70D...	{632CD006-6D...	Update P...	Trigger Policy		22/02/2013 18:16...		22/02/2013 18:16:42		TRUE
{4D3...	{648866D2-28...	Return M...	Publish Policy...		22/02/2013 18:16...		22/02/2013 18:16:28		TRUE
{5CB...	{6FE3DD53-1C...	Invoke H...	Trigger Policy		22/02/2013 18:16...		22/02/2013 18:16:33		TRUE
{74A...	{74DE125B-87...	Stop VM	Run .Net Script		22/02/2013 18:16...		22/02/2013 18:16:45		TRUE
{DA6...	{632CD006-6D...	Update P...	Trigger Policy		22/02/2013 18:17...		22/02/2013 18:17:21		TRUE

FIGURE 6.46 Imported Runbooks table in Excel worksheet.

- Right-click the header of the RunbookId column and select **Create Relationship**. In the Related Lookup Table list, select **Runbooks**; in the Related Lookup Column list, select **Id**; and then click **Create**.

- Right-click the header of the RunbookServerId column to select **Create Relationship**. In the Related Lookup Table list, select **RunbookServers**; in the Related Lookup Column list, select **Id**; and then click **Create**.

2. The pivot table can be created from the imported data by dragging and dropping the properties of the imported tables in the column, row, or sum labels of the PivotTable. On the PivotTable ribbon, select **PivotTable** and, in the Create PivotTable dialog box, select **New Worksheet**. Click **OK** to continue.

   - In the PowerPivot Field List, under RunbookServers, click and drag **Name** to the Row Labels box.
   - In the PowerPivot Field List, under Runbooks, click and drag **Name** to the Row Labels box.
   - In the PowerPivot Field List, under RunbookInstances, click and drag **Status** to the Column Labels box.
   - In the PowerPivot Field List, under RunbookInstances, click and drag **RunbookId** to the Sum Values box.
   - Right-click **RunbookId** to select **Summarize by**, and then click **Count**.

You now have live data in the worksheet to create an overview of the runbook execution. You can create diagrams, create graphics, or even make this information available via SharePoint.

Summary

This chapter discussed the process of creating a runbook. It defined the steps in runbook creation for capturing requirements, translating this information into Orchestrator activities, and building the runbook in the Runbook Designer. Following the process described in the "Framework for Creating Runbooks" section ensures that you have captured the necessary information before you begin building your runbook. The framework also describes creating the runbook in the Runbook Designer and using the Runbook Tester to validate the runbook.

Runbooks that are checked in are available for execution. You can manage this using the Orchestration console or the Orchestrator web service. The "Managing Runbooks Using the Orchestration Console" section discussed the console interface and the tasks you can launch from the different workspaces. The console has limited functionality, but its advantage is that it is accessible from any client with a web browser. The chapter also discussed different ways to interact with the web service, how to start building a Visual Studio application, and how to interact with the web service using PowerShell.

CHAPTER 7

Runbook Basics

IN THIS CHAPTER

- ▶ Anatomy of a Runbook
- ▶ Using Activities
- ▶ Orchestrator Standard Activities
- ▶ Monitoring Activities
- ▶ Orchestrator Custom Activities
- ▶ Orchestrator Workflow Control
- ▶ Drag and Drop
- ▶ Managing Runbooks
- ▶ Runbook Logging
- ▶ Building Your First Runbook

Information technology (IT) terms defines a *runbook* as essentially a series of procedural steps that an operator or administrator follows. Runbooks are generally written to account for contingencies, allowing a branching of decisions based on a specific outcome. As an example, a runbook might tell an operator to contact the on-call support personnel if a specific error arises. A contingency might be to contact the secondary on-call support personnel if the first person is unreachable.

In System Center 2012 Orchestrator (SCOrch), a runbook operates in much the same manner. You provide it with a series of steps (activities) that encapsulate an entire process using branches, loops, and flow control. Runbooks are flexible, allowing modification to account for contingencies that might not have surfaced when you originally created it. Runbooks can be powerful, bridging multiple platforms that often contain an assortment of permissions, thus requiring administrative diligence and version control. Runbooks can be intelligent, using information to decide on various activities to perform.

This chapter discusses the basic concepts of what comprises a runbook. It covers managing a runbook, using version control, establishing and finding logs, and delegating security. The chapter also guides you through the steps of creating your first runbook, beginning with a single activity and then adding complexity. This results in a functional runbook with multiple activities, which you can build further using advanced concepts in Chapter 8, "Advanced Runbook Concepts."

Anatomy of a Runbook

At its core, a runbook is a set of activities that define a process. Various components make up a runbook, including properties that define the runbook, activities within the runbook, and security that controls the access to a runbook. The activities in the runbook are central to the purpose of the runbook:

- Even though a runbook is defined as a set of activities, a runbook without any activity is technically still a runbook, albeit an empty one. Although it holds all the properties of a runbook, it is an empty container.
- Conversely, activities without a runbook provide no value because they must be inside a runbook to execute. For activities to work with each other, they must be linked to pass information downstream until the end of the runbook is reached.

Each runbook has a specific set of properties that define when and where the runbook can run, how many instances of the same runbook can run at the same time, whether to store additional information in logs, and whether the runbook should return any data when called by other runbooks. These properties are defined in runbooks under a series of tabs in the runbook properties. You can access runbook properties by right-clicking the Runbook tab in the Workspace pane of the Runbook Designer and choosing **Properties**.

The following sections discuss the basic properties of a runbook.

General Information

The General tab, in Figure 7.1, includes an option for defining the runbook name. You can also change the runbook name by right-clicking the Runbook tab itself and choosing **Rename**. The more important function of this tab is defining a schedule for the runbook. When a schedule is provided, a runbook runs only as its schedule defines.

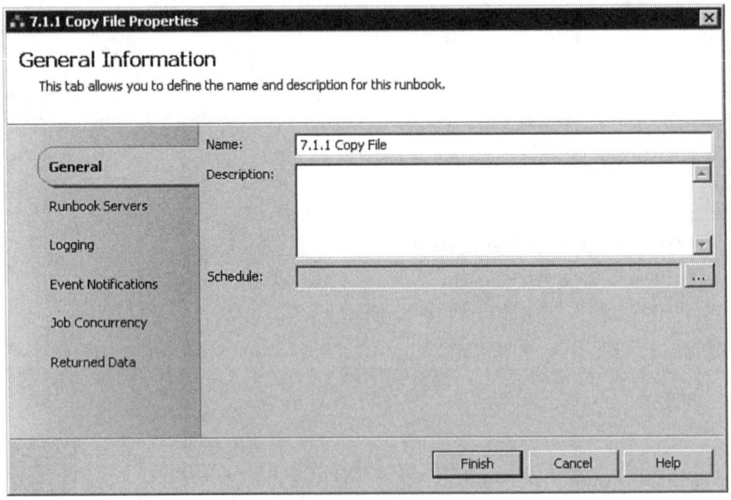

FIGURE 7.1 Runbook General properties.

NOTE: RUNBOOK SCHEDULE GRANULARITY

Be advised that although you can apply a schedule, the granularity of the unit of measure is limited to 1 hour. This defines only the specific hours a runbook is allowed to run, such as Saturday 8 a.m. to 5 p.m. If you need a more advanced schedule, refer to Chapter 8.

Runbook Servers

The Runbook Servers tab, in Figure 7.2, enables you to specify which runbook server is used to execute the runbook. By default, this override is turned off, allowing the default primary runbook server to handle the runbook.

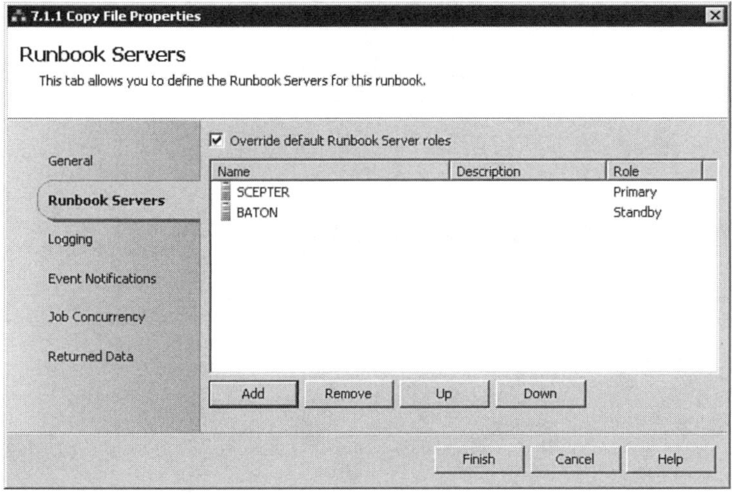

FIGURE 7.2 Runbook Servers properties.

Logging Properties

On the Logging tab in Figure 7.3, specify whether to store activity-specific published data, common published data, or both. Note that enabling logging increases the size of your Orchestrator database.

Event Notifications

Figure 7.4 displays the Event Notifications tab. This tab includes options to inform you if an error condition occurs. Specifically, the runbook can provide an event whenever the runbook runs longer than a specified amount of time (in seconds) or if the runbook fails to run.

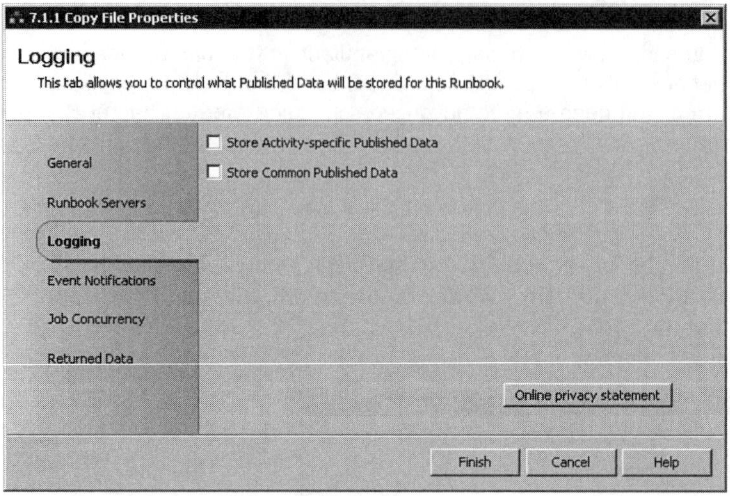

FIGURE 7.3 Runbook Logging properties.

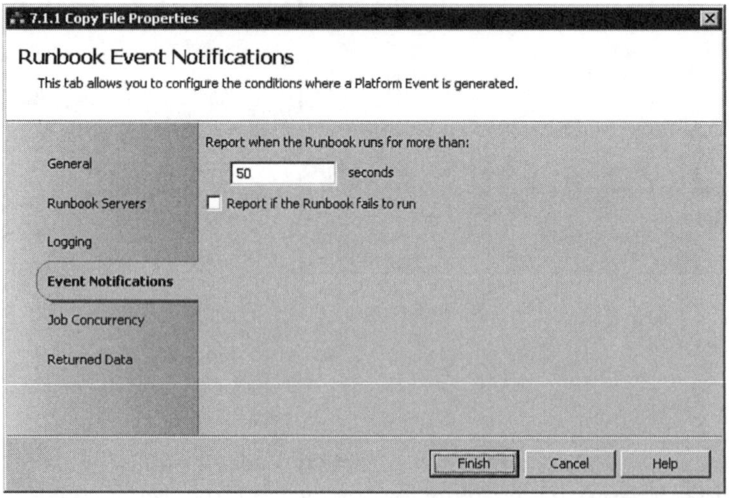

FIGURE 7.4 Runbook Event Notifications properties.

Job Concurrency

The Job Concurrency tab, in Figure 7.5, lets you define how many jobs of the same runbook can run simultaneously. Keep in mind that a runbook using a monitoring activity as its starting point cannot have concurrent jobs.

NOTE: DECIDING WHEN TO USE CONCURRENT JOBS

When deciding whether to use simultaneous jobs, consider whether the activities in the runbook have a chance of operational collision. For example, if you are writing to a log and need it to be in a sequential order, having multiple jobs writing to the same log might cause entries to become out of position.

If the runbook calls any applications, it would be prudent to ensure that they are capable of handling multiple requests at the same time.

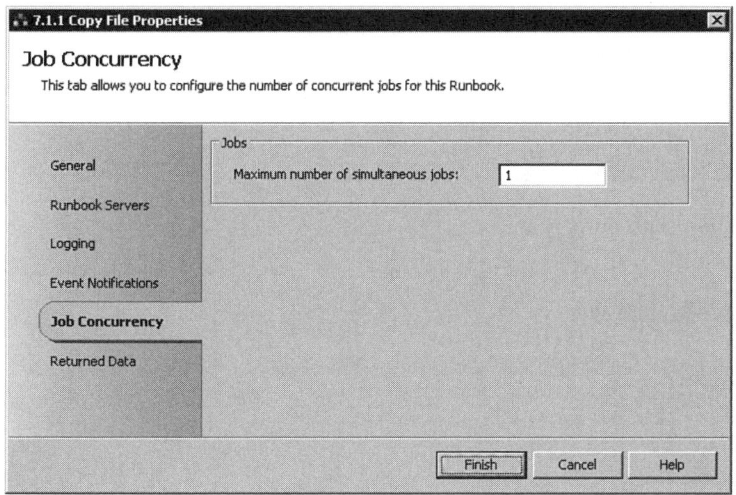

FIGURE 7.5 Runbook Job Concurrency properties.

Returned Data

The Returned Data tab (see Figure 7.6) specifies the schema for information returned to the **Invoke Runbook** activity. Adding values in this tab lets you specify the name and type of data the runbook returns.

Chapter 8 discusses returned data and associated activities in more detail.

Runbook Security

Runbook permissions are assigned through the Runbook Designer console. Viewing the permissions of a runbook should look similar to viewing other Windows security dialog boxes because it follows the same type of access control list (ACL) dialog as any folder (see Figure 7.7).

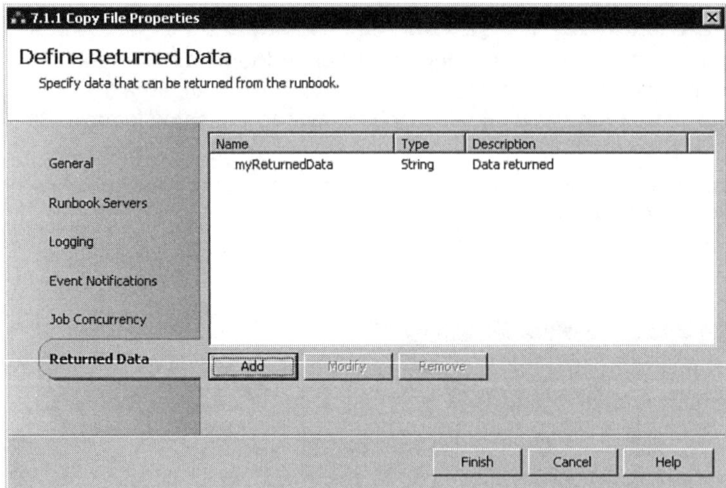

FIGURE 7.6 Runbook Returned Data properties.

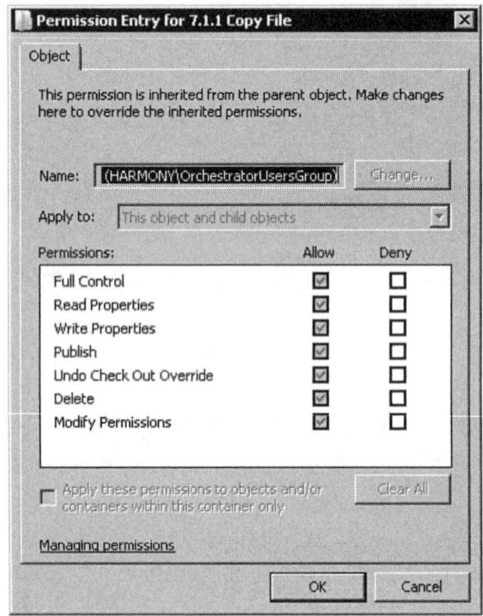

FIGURE 7.7 Runbook Permission Entry properties.

Consider these important concepts of runbook security:

- **OrchestratorUsersGroup:** By default, the local group OrchestratorUsersGroup receives Full Control access to the runbook. These default permissions are inherited from the root folder, unless blocked somewhere on the path. Unchecking **Include inheritable permissions from this object's parent** prevents any permission from the parent object from propagating to the current object. In Figure 7.8, the Orchestrator service account no longer shows because it was removed after turning off permission inheritance.

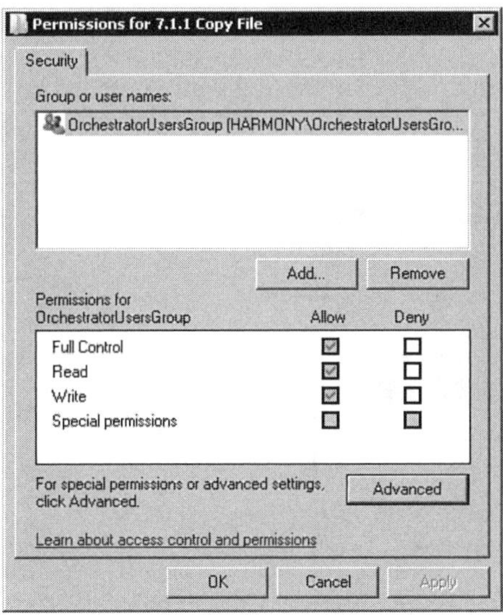

FIGURE 7.8 Runbook Permissions properties.

NOTE: BEHAVIOR OF ORCHESTRATORUSERSGROUP

OrchestratorUsersGroup is referenced here, but it might not exist in your environment if you identified another group during the Orchestrator installation.

- **Permission Inheritance:** If you choose to turn off inheritance, you must decide to either add or remove the inherited permissions. If you add the inherited permissions, they are added as explicit permissions. Removing these removes any object that is inherited from the ACL. Canceling simply aborts the operation. Figure 7.9 shows these options.
- **Runbook Permissions:** Runbooks contain seven distinct permissions that can be assigned to an individual user or a group:
  - **Full Control:** Grants all available permissions to a runbook and all its activities.
  - **Read Properties:** Grants permission to read all properties and permissions of the runbook, as well as activities inside the runbook.

    Without Read Properties permission, all other permissions (except Full Control) are ineffective because the runbook will not be visible.
  - **Write Properties:** Grants permission to write all properties of the runbook, as well as the activities in the runbook.

- **Publish:** Grants permission to start and stop the execution of a runbook.
- **Undo Check Out Override:** Grants permission to undo the checking out of a runbook by another user.
- **Delete:** Grants permission to delete a runbook.
- **Modify Permissions:** Grants permission to change the access control list of a runbook.

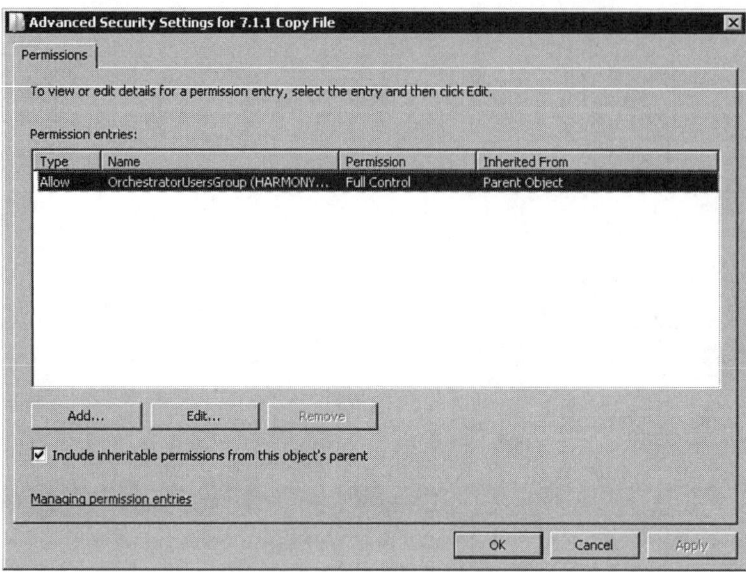

FIGURE 7.9 Runbook Advanced Security properties.

Table 7.1 displays common tasks related to runbooks and the permissions required to perform those tasks.

TABLE 7.1 Security Permissions Required for Tasks

Task	RP	WP	P	UC	D	M
Examine the settings of a runbook	X					
Look at the properties of an activity in a runbook	X					
Export a runbook	X					
Import a runbook with overwrite	X	X				
Import a runbook as new*	X	X				
Commit changes to a runbook	X	X				

Task	RP	WP	P	UC	D	M
Commit changes to an activity in a runbook	X	X				
Undo another user's checking out of a runbook	X			X		
Delete a runbook	X				X	
Allow a user to manage the permissions for a runbook	X					X
Start and stop a runbook			X			

** This is correct as long as the user has Create Activity permissions on the folder where the runbook resides.*

Using Activities

A runbook consists of one or more activities that perform a simple task or a complex procedure. If a runbook is greater than a single activity (and it should be), workflow controls are required to define a starting point and link activities in a defined sequence.

An activity is the most essential element of a runbook. Without an activity, a runbook is simply an empty shell. Even though a runbook can be a single activity—such as copying a file—not much gain results from utilizing a system as powerful as Orchestrator to manage such a trivial event. The real strength of Orchestrator is in sequencing activities to run an entire process, eventually connecting runbooks to orchestrate a series of processes.

Orchestrator comes with out-of-the-box activities to help automate nearly any process. Figure 7.10 displays these activities, known as *standard activities.* Other activities are provided through integration packs, some published by Microsoft and others by third-party developers.

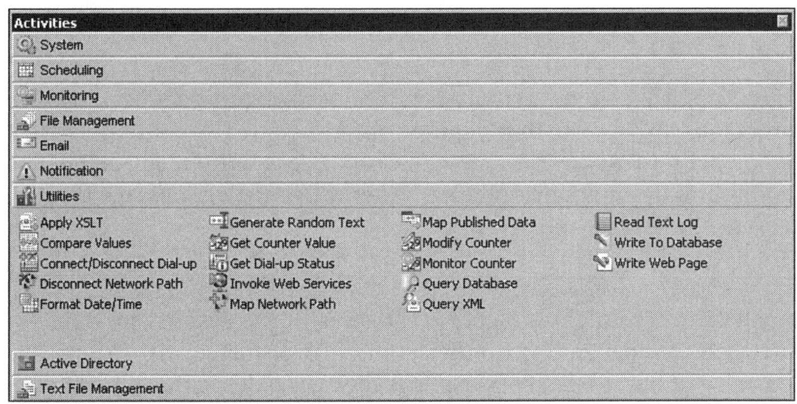

FIGURE 7.10 Orchestrator activities list.

Activity Properties

All activities share a subset of common properties. Activity-specific properties are available that define a configuration specific to the action. You can access properties of an activity by right-clicking the activity and choosing **Properties**. However, activity properties are not available from the Activity pane. You must first move the activity to the Workspace pane.

General Tab

This tab (see Figure 7.11) defines the name of the activity and the description. The authors recommend naming the activity with enough detail to indicate the process that is occurring. The activity becomes self-documenting, making it easier to view an entire runbook and understand what is occurring at each step.

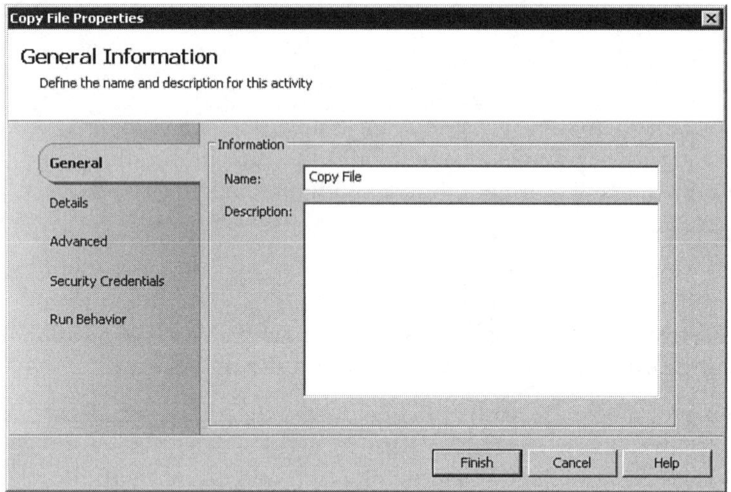

FIGURE 7.11 General tab of an activity.

Details Tab

The Details tab, in Figure 7.12, is where the activity is typically configured. Depending on the activity, additional tabs might exist that require configuration. The content in the Details tab differs based on activity. As an example, the **Copy File** activity requires the configuration of the source and destination, whereas the **Send Event Log Message** activity requires a computer name, message, and severity.

Advanced Tab

Some activities contain an Advanced tab (see Figure 7.13). As with the Details tab, the contents of the Advanced tab vary depending on the activity. For instance, if the **Copy File** activity is provided an age filter, the activity uses the file age to determine whether it should be copied.

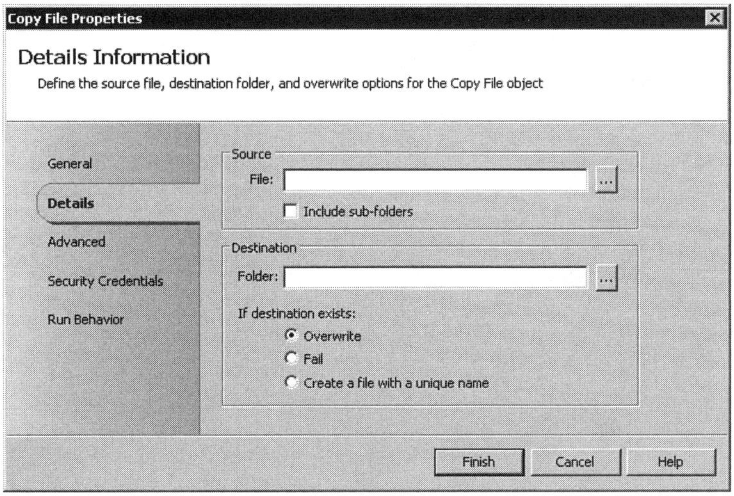

FIGURE 7.12 Details tab of an activity.

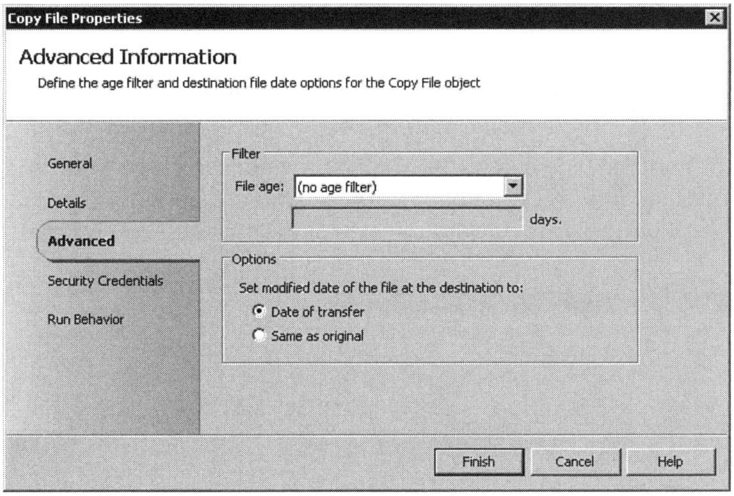

FIGURE 7.13 Advanced tab of an activity.

Security Credentials Tab

If the activity object is designed to allow a different user account to execute the activity, you can use this tab (see Figure 7.14) to modify the security credentials. You might find this useful, for example, when the Orchestrator Runbook Service account might not have access on a remote computer.

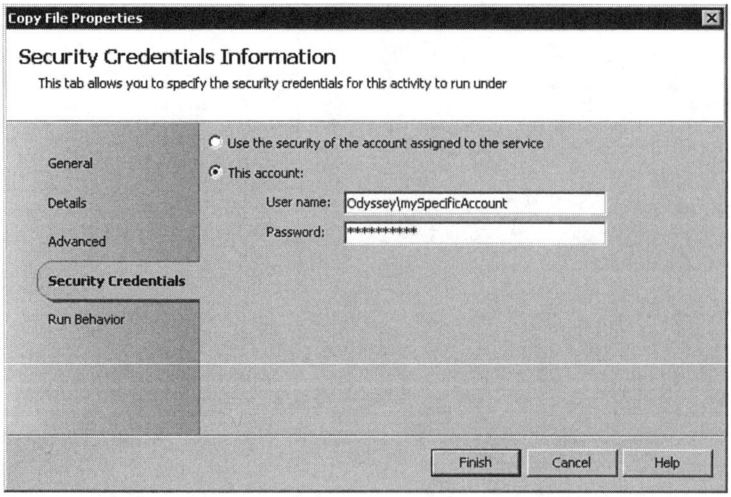

FIGURE 7.14 Security Credentials tab of an activity.

Run Behavior Tab

The available options in the Run Behavior tab, in Figure 7.15, control how the activity publishes data and what should happen if the activity does not operate as expected:

- **Returned Data Behavior:** When an activity publishes data, the data from the activity might come back as multivalued. When this occurs, the published data from the activity is passed as multiple outputs. You might need to flatten the published data so that you are passing an output only once to the next activity.

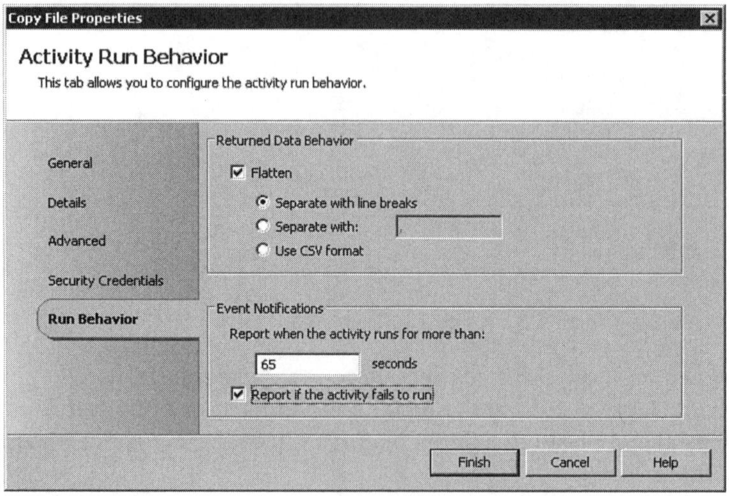

FIGURE 7.15 Run Behavior tab of an activity.

For example, if you are querying for users using the **Get User** activity, specifying **Sam Account Name Starts with A** would return all users whose username begins with the letter A. If you were sending this output to a text file, you would not necessarily need multiple outputs; you would need just a single, flattened output.

When flattening output, Orchestrator supports using line breaks or separating the items with a specified delimiter (defaulting to a comma). You can also specify that the output use comma-separated values (CSV) format.

- **Event Notifications:** Since activities in a runbook are linked, running mostly in sequential order, a stalled activity can cause the entire runbook to stop processing. Specifying the number of seconds an activity should take enables detection of these stalls. When a stall is detected, a platform event is sent. Optionally, you can define whether the event should report when the specific activity fails to run.

Published Data

Published data is the information published to the data bus from an activity, as described in Chapter 2, "What's New in System Center 2012 Orchestrator." All activities publish a certain set of data that is common among all activities, regardless of type. Table 7.2 lists the common published data and their descriptions.

TABLE 7.2 Common Published Data

Name	Description
Error summary text	Detailed error description
Loop: Delay between attempts	Specified value of delay between attempts
Loop: Enabled	Whether looping is enabled
Loop: Loop error message	Error message specifically about the loop
Loop: Number of attempts	Number of attempts made in the loop
Loop: Total duration	Total duration the activity was in the loop
Activity start time	Time when the activity started
Activity start time UTC	Time when the activity started, displayed in UTC format
Activity end time	Time when the activity ended (individual data items exist for day, hours, minutes, month, seconds, weekday, year)
Activity end time in UTC	Time when the activity ended, displayed in UTC format (individual data items exist for day, hours, minutes, month, seconds, weekday, year)
Activity duration	Value of how long the activity ran
Activity ID	ID of the activity
Activity name	Name of the activity
Activity Process ID	Process ID of the activity
Activity status	Status of the activity
Activity type	Type of activity

Name	Description
Runbook name	Name of the runbook
Runbook Process ID	Process ID of the runbook (information can be useful when reviewing logs since the logs often note the runbook process ID)
Runbook Server Name	Server name of where the runbook is running

Orchestrator Standard Activities

Orchestrator 2012 comes with nine sets of standard activities, each themed to support scenarios for designing runbooks, discussed in the next sections. More information is available in Chapter 9, "Standard Activities." The next sections describe each of these sets.

System Activities

Activities in the System set include running system commands. Extensibility objects are also in this collection. These objects can be used to "extend" functionality by running embedded scripts or code. Starting and stopping services, monitoring SNMP traps, and saving event logs are system activities as well.

Scheduling Activities

Activities in this set are specifically for performing actions related to schedules. In addition to checking date and time, the runbook can check schedule templates. This allows for creating complex scheduling scenarios to control the execution period of a runbook (see Chapter 8).

Monitoring Activities

Many activities in the Monitoring set check the status of various components (services, processes, drive space, and so on) to monitor for certain conditions to trigger, such as watching a process or an event log.

NOTE: CONSIDER USING SYSTEM CENTER OPERATIONS MANAGER

Although Orchestrator's monitoring activities can look for various conditions and health, the authors recommend using System Center Operations Manager (OpsMgr) because it is designed to handle monitoring workloads more efficiently and with greater capability. OpsMgr is capable of executing runbooks as a response to a monitoring condition.

File-Management Activities

These activities are based on performing actions that relate to a file or folder. For example, you can move, delete, and encrypt files and folders. Additionally, activities are available to monitor when files in a folder are detected as having changed.

Email Activities

A single activity exists for sending email messages using Simple Message Transport Protocol (SMTP). It supports various formats, can send to multiple recipients, and is capable of sending attachments.

Notification Activities

Activities in this set support actions that provide notifications. Orchestrator can write events to the Application event log, activity events to the Events tab in the Runbook Designer, or messages to a syslog server.

Utilities Activities

This collection includes different activities, including the capability to query eXtended Markup Language (XML) files or databases. Other useful activities include managing counters (incrementing, decrementing, and resetting), mapping drives, and transforming date-time fields into other formats.

Text File Management

Use the activities in this set to read, write, and search text files. Activities in this set are often useful in creating custom logs for runbooks. You can also use these activities to read log files, branching the workflow based on the text file content.

Runbook Control

You can use these activities to manage runbooks. For example, these activities are used to define the starting point of a runbook, manage junctions, return data from other runbooks, and launch other runbooks.

Monitoring Activities

A special type of activity known as a *monitoring activity* watches for a specified event or state before the runbook instance continues. Using a trigger condition, an activity is instructed to watch for events that alert the runbook to continue. Monitoring activities include monitoring for folder changes, pinging a computer until it is available, examining drive space, watching the state of a service, and so on.

Unlike other activities, when a runbook starts with a monitoring activity, the activity loads and waits for the specified trigger condition to occur. When the condition occurs, the current instance continues to execute the remaining activities in the runbook. Meanwhile, a new runbook instance is created that continues to watch for the event to occur again. Because of this behavior, it is important to note that when the runbook instance completes, the runbook itself does not stop; it continues to spawn new instances each time the trigger condition occurs. The runbook can be stopped only from the Orchestration console or the Runbook Designer.

A list of tasks you can accomplish when using monitoring activities is available at http://technet.microsoft.com/en-us/library/hh225052.aspx.

Orchestrator Custom Activities

In most cases, the standard activities, along with integration packs (IP) offered by Microsoft or other companies, are sufficient to handle any process. Orchestrator contains extensibility objects included as standard activities to help address a process that might not have a matching activity object.

Activities such as **Run .Net Script** and **Run Program** are popular ways to use Orchestrator to do more than use the activities it contains. As an example, using **Run .Net Script** allows administrators familiar with PowerShell to populate the activity with a script that runs a simple or complex script. Because the script is running inside Orchestrator, it has the benefit of accessing and writing published data on the data bus. This means you can use output from other objects as variables in your script and write the script output into variables that can be sent downstream to other activities. Having the capability to use published data makes it easier to write smaller, concise scripts that can be sequenced in various ways to perform all kinds of activities.

Although using extensibility objects is convenient because of their flexibility, these objects are not as intuitive or polished as objects that come with Orchestrator. Because the script is exposed, it can also easily be altered. Altering values, such as subscribing to different published data, requires changing the script, which could introduce an inadvertent change. To avoid this, you can create activities using the Orchestrator Integration Toolkit (OIT). The OIT is your means of creating activities specifically designed for your requirements, while offering the same type of flexibility you are accustomed to when using out-of-the-box objects. Chapter 20, "The Orchestrator Integration Toolkit," has more information on the OIT.

Orchestrator Workflow Control

A well-designed runbook has a notable sequence to its path. This includes how it begins, how it ends, and how it flows from the start of all activities to the end. You might require that an activity loop repeatedly until the right result of an activity is produced. Other activities might require moving along a different path based on the result of an activity. The next sections discuss aspects of workflow control.

Starting Point

Much like *The Highlander*, there can be only one! A runbook can have only one starting point. Because a runbook operates in largely sequential order, having more than one starting point would confuse the workflow engine. Figure 7.16 shows two different runbooks, with activities flowing from either top to bottom or left to right.

A starting point activity is usually the leftmost activity of a workflow. Visually, it appears accurate because link handles point to the right. Despite the way it looks, a starting point is not required to start in the leftmost position.

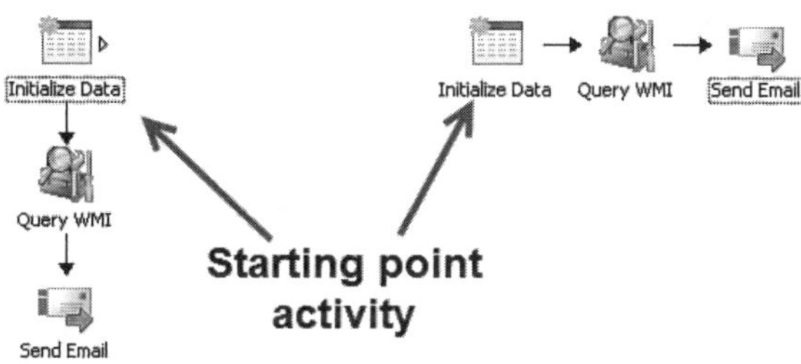

FIGURE 7.16 Starting point of an activity.

Any object without a smart link connected to it is a starting point object. Figure 7.16 shows the **Initialize Data** activity as the starting point activity. Notice that it does not have a smart link pointing to it. All smart links connect from it to another activity. More than one unlinked activity results in a multiple starting point error.

NOTE: WATCH FOR UNLINKED ACTIVITIES

An unlinked object can be in the workspace but not visible. Use the Runbook Tester to identify unlinked objects; it prevents you from running a runbook with an errant object. Figure 7.17 shows an example.

In addition, the Runbook Designer provides a warning message if you attempt to check in a runbook with multiple starting points. Note, however, that although Orchestrator gives you a warning, it does not prevent the runbook from checking in.

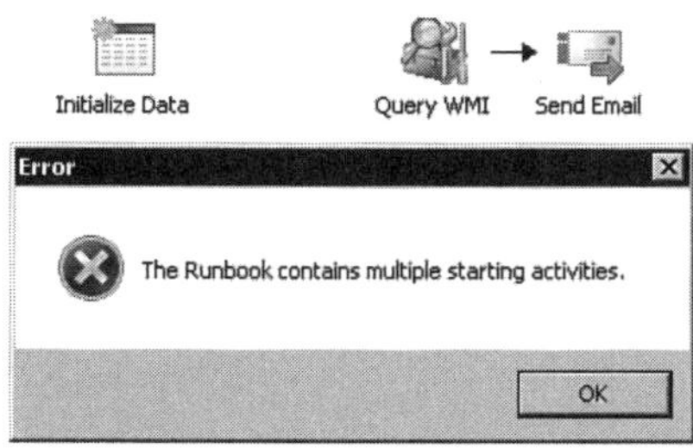

FIGURE 7.17 Error when multiple starting points are present.

When a runbook starts, it begins immediately at the first activity and continues on to each activity until it reaches an ending point or errors out along the way. When the starting point activity is a monitoring activity, the activity waits for a certain condition to occur before continuing to the next activity.

NOTE: SMART LINKS BETWEEN ACTIVITIES

Technically, after the first activity starts, a condition must occur before the activity moves to the smart link. Conditions must also be met in the smart link before the smart link allows the runbook to continue to the next activity. More accurately, the activity waits for a certain event to occur before completing. The link then determines whether to continue to the next activity.

Smart Links

Smart links join one activity to the next in a runbook. In a runbook with more than one activity, smart links must connect all activities. If you leave an orphaned activity, Orchestrator presumes that you have more than one starting point and prevents use of the runbook.

Smart links support decision tree branching with runbooks by providing filtering between activities. Suppose you have an activity that fails and produces an error. After the failure occurs, smart links can direct the flow of the runbook to branch out in order to email an administrator of the failure instead of continuing with the runbook. Figure 7.18 shows an example of a default filter for **Query WMI** to include successes.

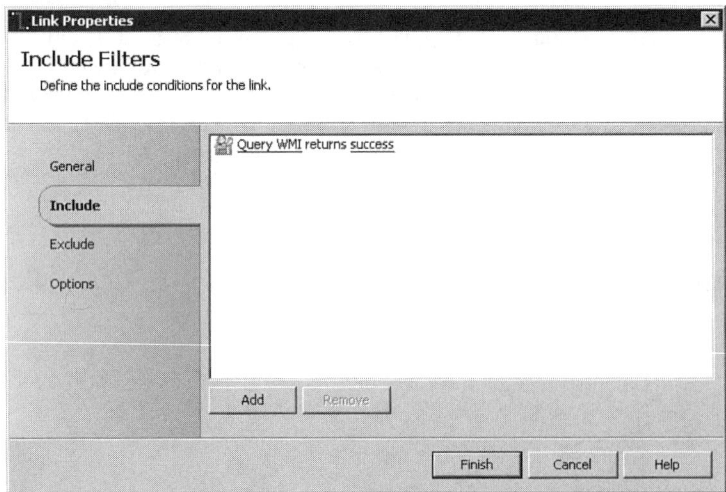

FIGURE 7.18 Smart link property displaying an include filter.

Conditional Filters

Smart links provide different conditions based on the published data selected. For example, selecting published data stored as string values presents a list of conditional filters (see Table 7.3).

TABLE 7.3 Smart Link Conditional Filters

Data Type	Available Filters
String	Contains
	Does not contain
	Starts with
	Ends with
	Matches pattern
	Does not match pattern
	Equals
	Does not equal
Integer	Equals
DateTime	Does not equal
	Is less than
	Is greater than
	Is less than or equal to
	Is greater than or equal to
	Is between
Boolean	Equals
	Does not equal

Linking Activities

Activities in the runbook need to interact with each other. Linking objects creates precedence, providing an order of operation. Additionally, the links provide another valuable facility; they can filter data.

In Orchestrator, links are expressed as lines that connect one activity to the next. You can modify the link color and width to make links more visible. Color-coding links is often useful to indicate different paths that a runbook will take; Chapter 4, "Architectural Design," and Chapter 10, "Runbook and Configuration Best Practices," discuss this.

Each activity contains *link handles* (see Figure 7.19). If an activity produces data, a link handle appears on the right side of the activity. If an activity can receive data, a link appears on the left side of the activity. Most activities contain both handles. Certain activities, such as monitoring activities or the **Initialize Data** activity, contain only right-side handles. This indicates that they are used to start the runbook because they cannot be linked to other activities in a way to receive data.

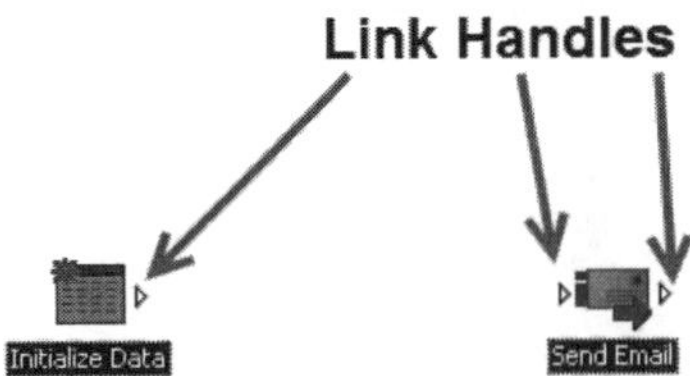

FIGURE 7.19 Link handles.

Embedded Loops

Looping is used to watch for a specific condition before exiting. The activity runs with the same data input during each iteration until the exit condition occurs. For example, if you have a process that is difficult to stop, you might put a loop on the **End Process** activity. This activity then attempts to end the specified process on each cycle. When the status returns as successful, the activity moves to the next activity in the sequence (as long as it is not at the end of the runbook).

Figure 7.20 illustrates an embedded loop on the **Query WMI** activity. Chapter 8 covers embedded loops in greater depth.

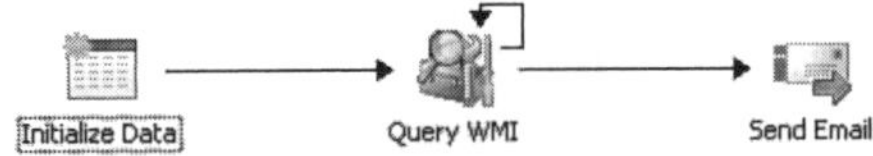

FIGURE 7.20 Embedded loops.

NOTE: EMBEDDED LOOPS CAN BEHAVE LIKE MONITORING OBJECTS

Consider an embedded loop to be similar to a monitoring object. A monitoring object waits until a certain condition is met before moving down the data bus. In actuality, an embedded loop activity can do the same thing, keeping the next downstream activity from occurring until a required exit condition is met.

Drag and Drop

Any Windows user should be familiar with the concept of dragging and dropping. Orchestrator is no exception; this is part of what makes Orchestrator so easy to use. Building a runbook does not look like a script with lines and lines of code. Instead, it is visually represented, which makes understanding the activities that occur much easier to interpret. You can sort and arrange activities by dragging them around the designer workspace. Generally, you should arrange the activities in such a way that the runbook flow makes sense visually. Where the activity is in the runbook does not indicate its sequence order; the order is defined by linking activities (see Figure 7.21).

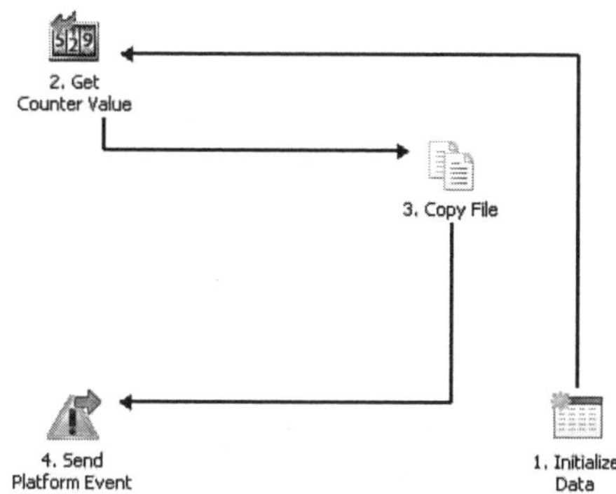

FIGURE 7.21 Drag-and-drop order.

Managing Runbooks

Learning to manage your runbooks properly is critical to the success of your Orchestrator implementation. Imagine if you automated a process only to find out that the runbook wasn't running or, worse, that someone else modified it and broke it. Not only is the process no longer done manually (because it was automated), but the work isn't occurring because the runbook is not working.

Managing runbooks involves more than knowing how to start or stop a runbook. Understanding how version control works in Orchestrator is also important. Creating a system around importing and exporting runbooks can prevent issues where accidental changes are not easily identified or removed.

Take time to understand where logs are located both in the console and outside it, how to enable and disable audit logging, and how to increase log verbosity when the standard logs simply do not provide enough information.

Starting and Stopping Runbooks

When a runbook is checked into Orchestrator, it is available to start. A running runbook runs until stopped. If the runbook's starting point is a monitoring activity, it continually monitors for an event that triggers the rest of the runbook.

If the starting point is not a monitoring activity, the runbook runs to completion and stops. The runbook must be started each time you want it to execute. This is great when running a runbook happens on an ad-hoc basis, such as when periodically moving files to an FTP site.

TIP: RUNNING ON A SCHEDULE

If you want a runbook to run on a schedule, such as every 5 minutes, use the **Monitor Date/Time** activity as the starting point.

Importing and Exporting Runbooks

The capability to import and export runbooks is valuable when transferring runbooks between environments and as a means of quickly recovering a runbook. Orchestrator provides the capability to export a single runbook or all runbooks in a folder. Exported runbooks are saved with an extension of OIS_Export. The next sections discuss the process of importing and exporting runbooks.

Exporting a Single Runbook

Use the Runbook Designer to export runbooks. The export function works only with runbooks that are checked in. To export a runbook, follow these steps:

1. Ensure that the runbook you intend to export is checked in. If not, check in the runbook by right-clicking the runbook and choosing **Check In** or choosing **Check In** from the Runbook Designer toolbar.
2. Right-click the Runbook tab and choose **Export**. Figure 7.22 shows the export options.

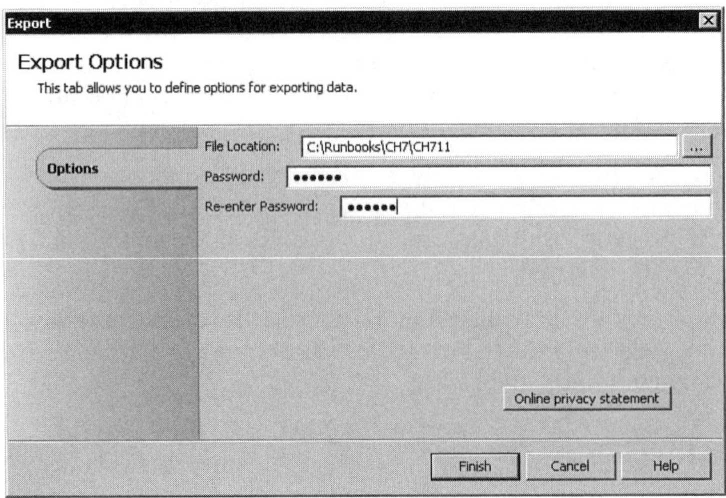

FIGURE 7.22 Export options of a runbook.

3. In the Export Options window, provide a filename and location path for the runbook.

4. Provide a password if the credentials contained in the activities of your runbook require encryption.

5. Click **Finish** to export the runbook.

CAUTION: USING A PASSWORD DOES NOT PROTECT ALL CONTENTS OF THE RUNBOOK

Using the password feature does not protect unencrypted content of the runbook. Only already encrypted fields (credentials and so on) are encrypted upon export.

Essentially, the encrypted data (stored in the data store as part of the runbook) is decrypted and then re-encrypted during export. For more information on security when exporting and importing runbooks, see Chapter 11, "Security and Administration."

If a password was supplied for the export and is later lost, the runbook can still be imported. However, all the encrypted content is imported as blank values and must be re-entered.

NOTE: IMPORTING ENCRYPTED DATA WITHOUT A PASSWORD

If you do lose the password to a runbook and decide to import it without the password, you must deselect the **Import Orchestrator encrypted data** option on the Import dialog box.

Exporting All Runbooks in a Folder

Another export option in Orchestrator is the capability to export all runbooks in a folder. This can be particularly useful when exporting whole sets of runbooks from one environment to another. Additionally, whenever you have multiple runbooks that make up a workflow, organizing them into one folder and exporting the entire folder (or subfolders) makes the process much easier to manage.

To export all runbooks in a folder, bring up the Export dialog box by performing one of the following:

- In the Connections pane, right-click any folder in the Runbooks node and choose **Export**.

  You can save the extra step of telling Orchestrator which runbook folder to export by selecting the export option from the runbook folder itself.

- On the menu bar, click **Actions** and then choose **Export**.

With the Export Options dialog window open (see Figure 7.23), perform the following steps:

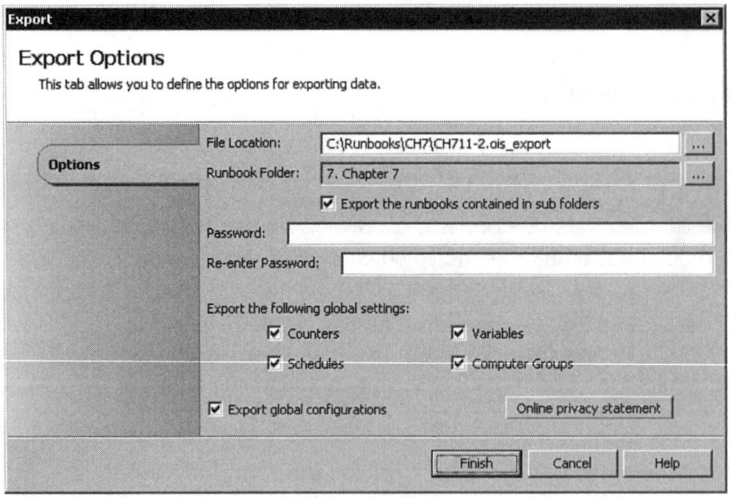

FIGURE 7.23 Options when exporting all runbooks.

1. Provide a filename and location path for the runbook export.
2. If you have runbooks in additional folders under the targeted folder, select the **Export the runbooks contained in sub folders** check box. This option is selected by default.
3. Provide a password if the credentials contained in the activities of your runbook require encryption.

When exporting runbooks in this manner, additional options to export global settings and global configurations are available:

- **Global settings:** These contain counters, schedules, variables, and computer groups. Exporting specific items from these types is not possible. If the type is selected, all the objects for that type are exported.
- **Global configurations:** Global configurations hold all the configuration data for integration packs, as well as configuration data on activities. As with global settings, choosing this option exports all global configurations and cannot be filtered to a specific item.

NOTE: TIME TO EXPORT EQUALS TIME TO IMPORT

Generally, the time it takes to import a runbook is commensurate to the time it takes to export a runbook; therefore, try to keep your runbook exports small. Where possible, do not export from the root of the Runbooks node unless necessary to save time on import.

Importing a Runbook

Regardless of whether the runbook to import is generated from a single runbook export or from a runbook folder export, the import process is the same. The import option is available only from the root of the Runbooks folder on down. This is because, when the Import function is called, the highlighted node is where the import will take place.

To import a runbook, follow these steps:

1. In the Connections pane, navigate to the folder where the import will take place.
2. Right-click the folder and choose **Import**. This opens the Import Options dialog box (see Figure 7.24).

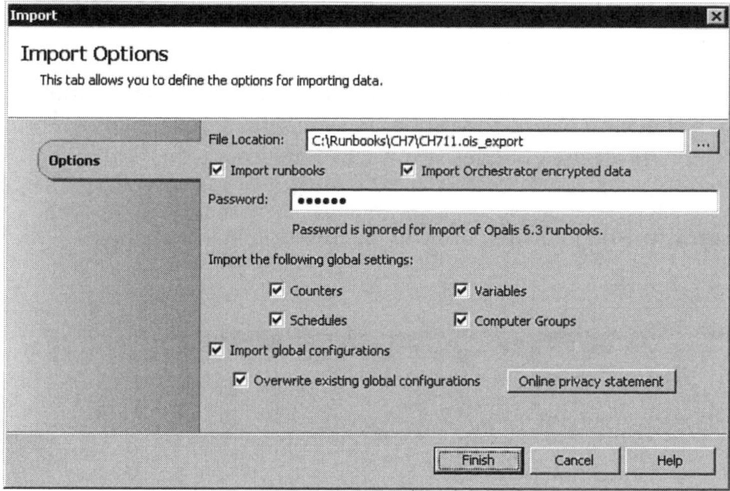

FIGURE 7.24 Runbook import properties.

3. Enter the location of the export file.
4. Provide the password, if one was used during export of the runbook. If a password was used during export and this field is left blank, the encrypted data is imported as blank values. If you do not have the password, deselect the **Import Orchestrator encrypted data** option.
5. Check the appropriate options for importing global settings.
6. Check the option to import global configurations, if required, and overwrite if necessary.

CAUTION: OVERWRITE EXISTING GLOBAL CONFIGURATIONS

Be careful when selecting the option to overwrite existing global configurations. Choosing to overwrite existing global configurations takes the information from the export file and overwrites any existing configurations stored in Orchestrator.

Versioning Runbooks

In most situations, more than one user authors and maintains a runbook. To help prevent unnecessary conflict, Orchestrator offers a rudimentary system of version control, known as *file locking*, which prevents more than one user from authoring a runbook at a time. After a user checks out a runbook, the runbook is not available for modification until that user is finished and checks it back in.

Orchestrator's version control offers three methods of interaction (see Figure 7.25):

- **Check Out:** Before a runbook can be edited, it must be checked out. While a runbook is checked out, no other user may check out the same runbook, blocking any potential editing.

  If an attempt occurs to check out a runbook that is already checked out, the Runbook Designer console provides an error.

- **Undo Check Out:** While editing a runbook, if the changes should not be committed, a user can undo his checking out of the runbook. Be careful not to inadvertently choose this option—it reverts all the changes you might have spent the last several hours performing.

- **Check In:** When a user is finished editing a runbook, checking in the runbook commits all changes.

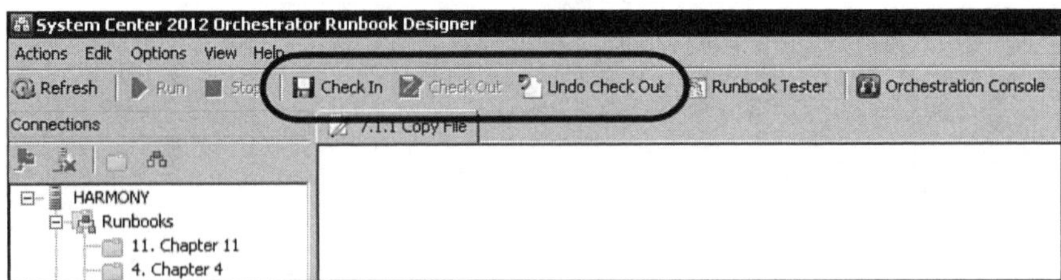

FIGURE 7.25 Versioning toolbar in the Runbook Designer.

NOTE: EXPORT RUNBOOKS FOR RECOVERY CAPABILITY

Because no capability to roll back committed changes exists, the authors strongly recommend that you create a process of exporting runbooks before you make changes. Runbooks should use a naming classification that provides a version number to help track changes.

Auditing Changes

Although committed changes cannot be rolled back, changes to runbooks are captured after a runbook is checked in. This provides some opportunity to understand the changes from one version of a runbook to the next.

Each entry displays the user who made the change, any comments added regarding the change, and the corresponding datetime stamp. Selecting an entry in the audit history (see Figure 7.26) provides additional details, indicating each activity or link where a change was made. Every object shows the attribute that was changed, its previous value, and the current value.

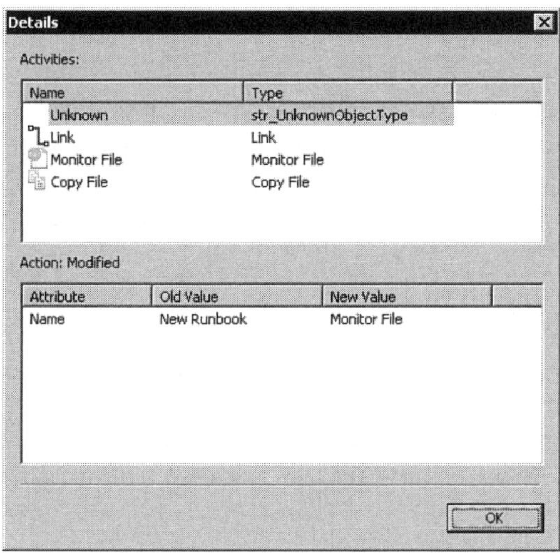

FIGURE 7.26 Viewing audit history.

Having this level of audit capability might seem like a counterpoint to the suggestion in the previous section to create a process of exporting and saving runbooks. However, you cannot use auditing to manage changes, for two valid reasons:

- The activity details in the audit entries often contain attribute names that are foreign or do not match the forms in the activity details. This can lead to confusion regarding the actual attribute that changed.
- Entries cannot be reverted automatically. This means that an administrator must evaluate the entry to understand the changes made and then revert those changes by hand. This can often lead to human error during input or change. If a change to a runbook does not go as planned or does not work as expected, reversing the changes to the same runbook can be an extremely time-consuming process. Imagine this happening during a maintenance window with no way to roll back!

CAUTION: IMPORTING A RUNBOOK DOES NOT CAPTURE CHANGES

Distinguishing the difference between checking in and importing a runbook is important. If you make changes to a runbook and check it in, the audit history shows the activities that were modified.

Say that you have multiple Orchestrator environments—production and development, for example. If you author changes in the development environment and import the runbook to your production environment, the audit history of the overwritten runbook does not display the changes to the activities.

Runbook Logging

Even with a well-designed and planned runbook, at some point, you will need more information to understand why the runbook is not running the way you planned or why an activity ceases to work. The very nature of orchestrating various processes against various platforms means there are many other systems in which something might cease to work. Orchestrator offers myriad logging options: real-time and historic logging, trace logging, and audit logging. The following sections discuss these logging options.

Real-Time and Historic Runbook Logs

Real-time and historic logs provide a high-level view of the overall operation of a runbook. The only difference is that real-time logs display only while the runbook is running. When the runbook completes or stops, the logs are moved to the log history (see Figure 7.27).

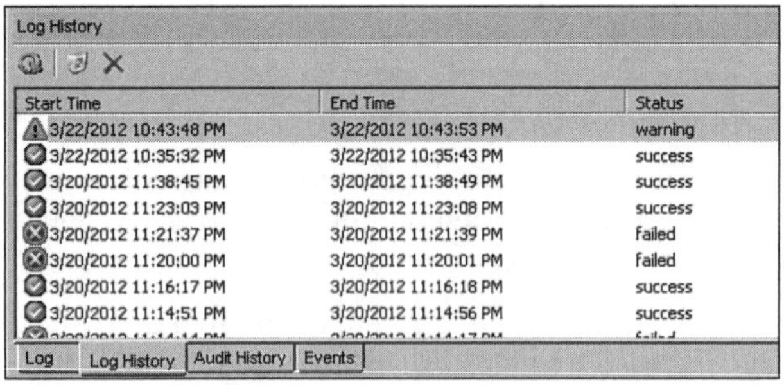

Log History

Start Time	End Time	Status
3/22/2012 10:43:48 PM	3/22/2012 10:43:53 PM	warning
3/22/2012 10:35:32 PM	3/22/2012 10:35:43 PM	success
3/20/2012 11:38:45 PM	3/20/2012 11:38:49 PM	success
3/20/2012 11:23:03 PM	3/20/2012 11:23:08 PM	success
3/20/2012 11:21:37 PM	3/20/2012 11:21:39 PM	failed
3/20/2012 11:20:00 PM	3/20/2012 11:20:01 PM	failed
3/20/2012 11:16:17 PM	3/20/2012 11:16:18 PM	success
3/20/2012 11:14:51 PM	3/20/2012 11:14:56 PM	success

Log | Log History | Audit History | Events

FIGURE 7.27 Log history.

Each log entry displays a start time, stop time, and status. Double-clicking an entry produces a Runbook Details dialog box (see Figure 7.28), which provides each activity processed by the runbook. These entries also provide additional detail when double-clicked. In the details, you can view the start time and stop time of a specific activity. Most of the benefit derived from this view, however, is the published data and associated value. An up and down arrow provides navigation capability to move between activities.

By default, common published data is not captured. You can enable this feature in the Logging tab of the runbook properties by selecting **Store Common Published Data**.

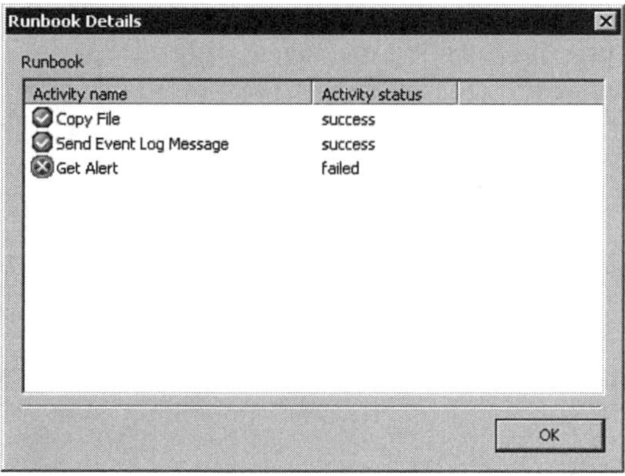

FIGURE 7.28 Log history details.

CAUTION: LOGGING INCREASES THE SIZE OF THE ORCHESTRATOR DATABASE

Enabling additional logging can increase the overall size of the Orchestrator database. The authors recommend that you turn off additional logging when it is no longer required.

Trace Logs

If the console logs are not providing sufficient detail, Orchestrator offers trace logs that provide far more comprehensive information. By default, trace logs capture exception information only; if the problem you are trying to identify or troubleshoot is not an exception, you might need to increase the logging levels.

In the following sections discussing trace logs, all the registry values exist under the following registry key, also displayed in Figure 7.29:

```
HKEY_LOCAL_MACHINE\Software\Wow6432Node\Microsoft\SystemCenter2012\Orchestrator\
TraceLogger\PolicyModule.exe
```

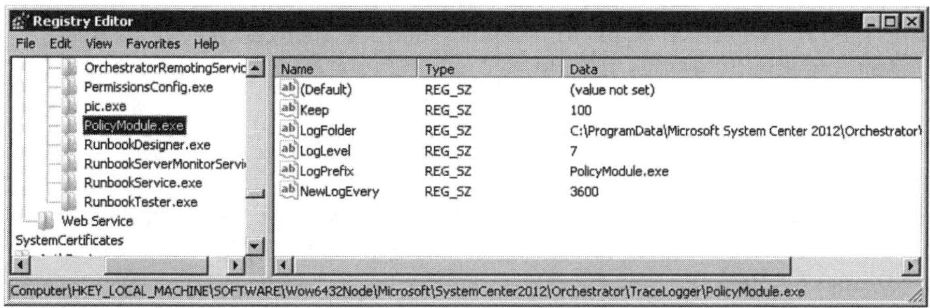

FIGURE 7.29 `PolicyModule.exe` key.

Log Depth

Orchestrator offers three levels of depth for capturing trace log messages. Only exception details are captured by default; you must alter the `LogLevel` registry value to increase logging.

As Chapter 4 described, the `LogLevel` value accepts the following:

- Level 1 logs errors only.
- Level 2 logs warnings only.
- Level 3 logs errors and warnings.
- Level 4 logs only informational messages.
- Level 5 logs informational and error messages.
- Level 6 logs warning and informational messages.
- Level 7 logs everything: informational messages, warnings, and errors.

NOTE: USE LEVEL 7 WITH CAUTION

Increasing the `LogLevel` value to `7` produces an excruciating level of detail. Avoid this level except for very short durations, when it is critical to see every operation in the runbook, even those not related specifically to activities.

Log File Location

Orchestrator stores trace logs in the *%ProgramData%*\Microsoft System Center 2012\Orchestrator\ManagementService.exe\Logs folder. To change this location, modify the `LogFolder` registry value to the path of the new location.

NOTE: THE FOLDER FOR LOGS IS USUALLY HIDDEN

The default log path is usually a hidden folder and thus is not visible when casually browsing the folder path. Make sure you go to the path directly or open Windows Explorer to *%ProgramData%* on the root of the system drive.

Log Prefix

If you are turning up log levels and want to uniquely identify the logs created for this process, you can momentarily modify the `LogPrefix` registry value. The prefix name is followed by a datetime stamp and GUID. This is a typical filename:

```
PolicyModule.exe.20120320231245.{EC4F183E-8E73-4222-99E4-AE69815B8F92}
```

Suppose you need to capture logs at the highest logging possible. You would change the `LogLevel` value to `7` and prepend the prefix with something such as **LL7**, which would generate a log similar to the following:

```
LL7.PolicyModule.exe.20120320233841.{F4D1CE62-37AD-4FE6-B68B-0BB07FFEE908}
```

Having LL7 as a prefix uniquely identifies that this log was captured at LogLevel 7.

Audit Logs

Going deeper, enabling the Orchestrator audit trail provides supplemental information to help trace a runbook's actions when an interaction occurs with an external system or tool. Audit logs are created as CSV files, providing rich, detailed information about the process occurring in these activities.

Unlike trace logs stored in the Orchestrator database, the audit trail is a collection of audit logs that are generated on the management server and runbook server file system. Audit logs grow to a size of 200MB before rolling over to a new log file. A datetime stamp is used in the filename to ensure uniqueness.

Orchestrator does not provide a built-in process for managing these logs through a system of purging or archiving. The authors recommend using a process to keep audit logs from consuming large amounts of space.

Audit logs are stored in the *%ProgramData%*\Microsoft System Center 2012\Orchestrator\Audit folder. Two types of log files exist: runbook publisher and activity runtime information, each with its own set of data. The runbook publisher logs contain information related to the runbook; the activity runtime information logs contain information related to each activity:

- **Runbook publisher:** The computer that ran the runbook, the user who ran the runbook, and the time the runbook ran
- **Activity runtime information:** The time the activity ran, the computer that ran the activity, and XML input the activity received

The utility to enable audit logging is a command-line utility only. To enable audit trail logging, open a command prompt and navigate to the *%Program Files(x86)%*\Microsoft System Center 2012\Orchestrator\Management Server folder (see Figure 7.30); then run the appropriate command:

```
Command Prompt

C:\Program Files (x86)\Microsoft System Center 2012\Orchestrator\Management Serv
er>atlc
Usage:

    To enable Audit Trail logging use:
        atlc /enable
    To disable Audit Trail logging use:
        atlc /disable
    To clear Audit Trail configurations table use:
        atlc /clear
    To display the Audit Trail Scrub List:
        atlc /sl-show
    To clear the Audit Trail Scrub List:
        atlc /sl-clear
    To add an item to the Audit Trail Scrub List:
        atlc /sl-add FieldName

C:\Program Files (x86)\Microsoft System Center 2012\Orchestrator\Management Serv
er>atlc /enable

C:\Program Files (x86)\Microsoft System Center 2012\Orchestrator\Management Serv
er>_
```

FIGURE 7.30 Audit trail enabled.

- **Turn on audit logging:** `atlc /enable`
- **Turn off audit logging:** `atlc /disable`

Building Your First Runbook

Having discussed the components of a runbook and the concept of activities, let's create a set of runbooks that starts simple and increases in complexity. The basic process to automate is a file copy.

TIP: DESIGN THE CONCEPT BEFORE THE RUNBOOK

Consider drawing, mapping, or diagramming a runbook before you start putting together the workflow. Outlining the process to automate can often take much longer than creating the runbook! Having a well-thought-out outline can save you the frustration of unlinking and relinking activities, as well as adjusting subscriptions to published data.

Copying a File

The first runbook consists of a single activity to copy a file. Before creating the runbook, you must set up the environment. Follow these steps:

1. Create two folders on the root of C:\ named **myLogFolder** and **myCollection**. In myLogFolder, create a new file named **myLogFile.txt**. This file will act as a log file that the runbook copies into a new location.
2. In Runbook Designer, create a new folder to store your runbooks. For this example, the folder is named **7. Chapter 7**, to follow the naming guidance described throughout this book.
3. Create a new runbook under the folder, named **7.1 Copy File v1.0**.
4. In the Activities pane, switch to the File Management activities and drag the **Copy File** activity to the workspace.
5. Double-click the **Copy File** activity to define the source and destination in the Details tab:
    - **Source:** C:\myLogFolder\myLogFile.txt
    - **Destination:** C:\myCollection
6. Figure 7.31 shows the completed Copy File Properties window. Click **Finish** to complete the changes to the activity.

Now that the runbook is complete, use the Runbook Tester console to test it. After it runs, a copy of myLogFile will be in the myCollection folder. Running the runbook again overwrites the existing file in the destination folder.

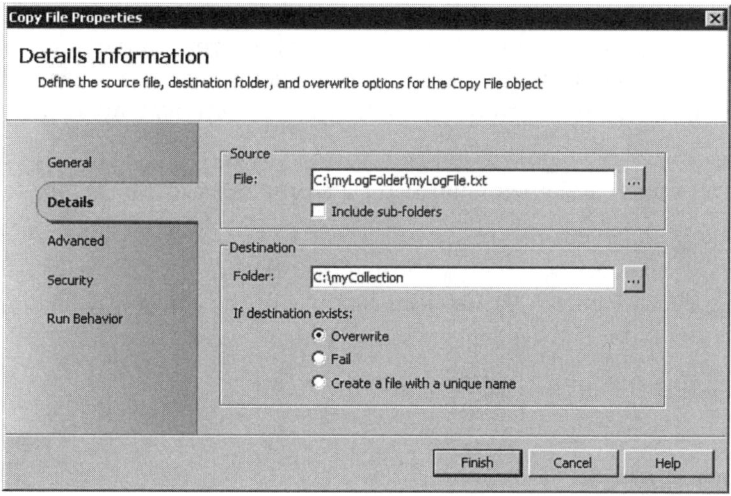

FIGURE 7.31 Completed Copy File properties.

Preserving Copied Files

Suppose you want to preserve the previously copied file instead of overwriting it. You can accomplish this by modifying the settings in the **Copy File** activity to create a file with a unique name. This does not provide any options for how to handle the filename.

The next example uses the **Rename File** activity to change the filename after copying.

To prepare for this runbook, check in the 7.1 Copy File v1.0 runbook and export it. Import the runbook into the same location, and choose not to overwrite it. Do not import any global settings or global configuration. This creates a copy of the runbook with the name 7.1 Copy File v1.0 (1). Now perform the following steps:

1. Rename the runbook titled **7.1 Copy File v1.0 (1)** to **7.1 Copy File v1.1**.
2. Drag the **Rename File** activity to the workspace, and create a link from **Copy File** to **Rename File**.
3. Double-click the **Rename File** activity to open its Properties page. For the source folder, instead of navigating to the folder selected in the **Copy File** activity, use the information from the data bus.

   Right-click in the empty field for Folder, and choose **Subscribe** and then **Published Data**.
4. In the Published Data dialog box, notice that the activity shows **Copy File**. Locate **Destination Folder** in the list and click **OK**.
5. Click **Add**. This opens the Rename Properties dialog box. Open the Published Data properties for the old name (as you did in step 3 for Folder). Locate the filename and click **OK**.

6. Perform the same action for the new name as in step 5. When the published data of {File name from "Copy File"} appears in the New Name field, put your initials and then a hyphen at the beginning of the field; then open the Published Data properties. This time, select **Show Common Published Data**. Choose **Activity End Time (Seconds)**.

   Back in the field, add a hyphen and open Published Data properties again. Choose **Filename**.

   The New name field now reads XYZ-{Activity end time (seconds) from "Copy File"}-{File name from "Copy File"}. Figure 7.32 shows an example of the completed dialog box. Click **OK** and then **Finish**.

7. Change the Copy File properties of If Destination Exists to **Fail**.

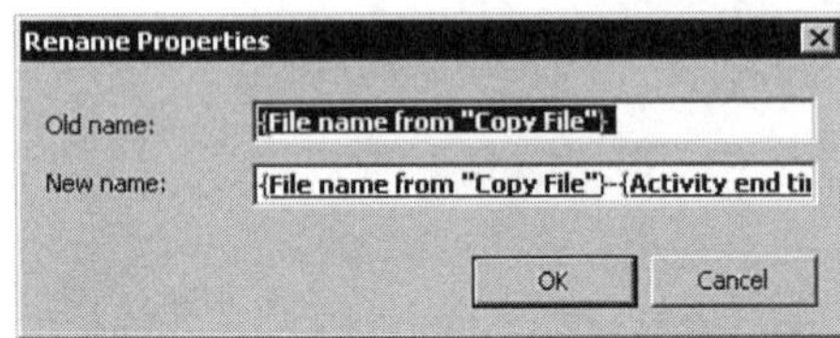

FIGURE 7.32 Rename Properties dialog box configured using published data.

Before testing this runbook, remove any files in the myCollection folder. On the first run of the runbook, myLogFile.txt is copied over and renamed using your initials and the seconds of the end time of the Copy File process.

Running it again creates a second folder that looks nearly identical, with a different time value. In step 7, **Copy File** was modified to fail if an identical filename was detected. Because the file is renamed at the end of the runbook, the **Copy File** activity should never fail unless the **Rename File** activity fails.

Monitoring File Changes

You might decide that copying this file only when a change to the file is detected is more practical. Using a monitoring activity, Orchestrator can detect a file change and then start the rest of the runbook.

Before beginning, check in the previous runbook, export it, and import it using the new name of **7.1 Copy File v1.2**. Remember not to overwrite the runbook or import any global settings or global configuration. Perform the following steps:

1. In your new runbook, drag the **Monitor File** activity from the File Management activities to the left of the **Copy File** activity. Create a link from **Monitor File** to **Copy File**.

2. Open the Properties page for the **Monitor File** activity and add **C:\myLogFolder** for the folder location. Set the filter settings as shown in Figure 7.33.

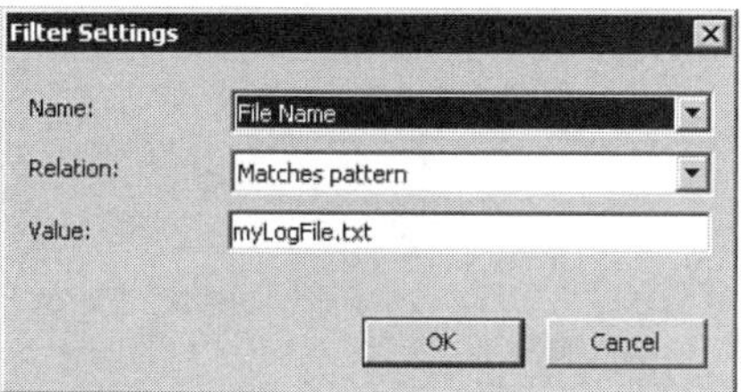

FIGURE 7.33 Configured Filter Settings.

3. Click the Triggers tab and, under the Trigger if one of the files was changed section, select **Changed** and click **Finish**.
4. Because the **Monitor File** activity is providing published data, modify the **Copy File** activity accordingly. Open the **Copy File** activity and change the source to the published data value of {**Name and path of the file from "Monitor File"**}. Click **Finish**.

Your finished runbook now contains three activities. Figure 7.34 shows how your runbook should look.

FIGURE 7.34 Completed runbook to monitor file changes.

To test this runbook, first start the runbook. It waits at the **Monitor File** activity until a change is detected in the file. Open the file; add a comment to it and save it. The runbook continues to the **Copy File** activity and proceeds as it did in the earlier runbook, copying the file and renaming it as illustrated in Figure 7.35.

Using Logic in Links

The previous runbook in the "Monitoring File Changes" section has the **Monitor File** activity looking for a pattern match with filenames that start with "myLog" and end with ".txt". In this example, the runbook in Figure 7.36 copies the file and renames it or overwrites it—based on the filename.

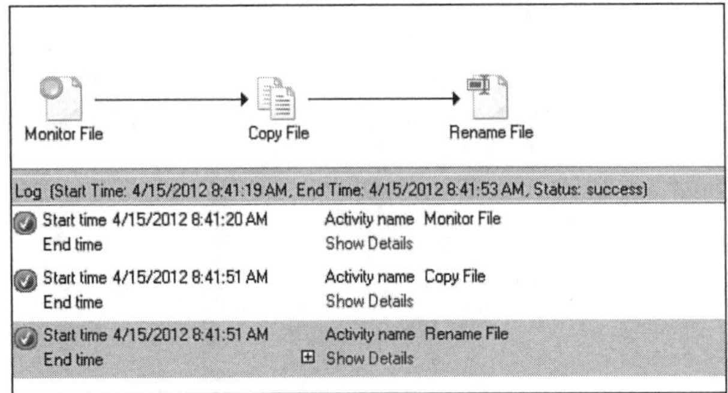

FIGURE 7.35 Testing the runbook.

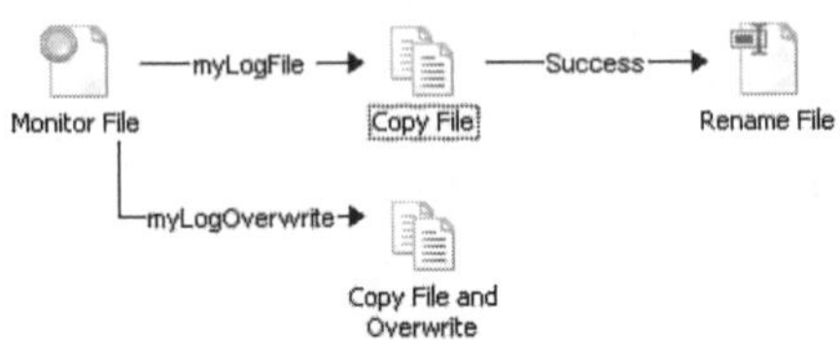

FIGURE 7.36 Using links to add logic to a runbook.

Before beginning, check in the previous runbook, export it, and import it with a new name of **7.1 Copy File v1.3**. Remember not to overwrite the runbook or import any global settings or global configuration. Follow these steps:

1. In your new runbook, drag a second **Copy File** activity to the workspace and rename it to **Copy File and Overwrite**. Drag a link to it from **Monitor File**.
2. Open the properties of **Copy File and Overwrite**. Set it to the same properties as the **Copy File** activity, with the exception of the If Destination Exists property. Set this value to **Overwrite**.
3. Double-click the link from **Monitor File** to **Copy File** to open the Link Properties. The Include tab contains a filter specified as Monitor File Returns Success. Click **Monitor File** and choose **Name of the File**. Set the value to **myLogFile.txt**.

   On the Exclude tab, click **Add**. This populates the filter Monitor File Returns Failed. Click **Finish**.
4. Double-click the link from **Monitor File** to **Copy File and Overwrite**. Perform the same step as in step 3, with the exception of the value of myLogFile.txt. Instead, set it to **myLogOverwrite.txt**.
5. Create a new file in myLogFolder with the name **myLogOverwrite.txt**.

To test this runbook, start the runbook in the Runbook Tester, add a comment to the myLogFolder.txt file, and save it. When the change is detected, the runbook runs through the rename path (see Figure 7.37). When complete, the runbook stops.

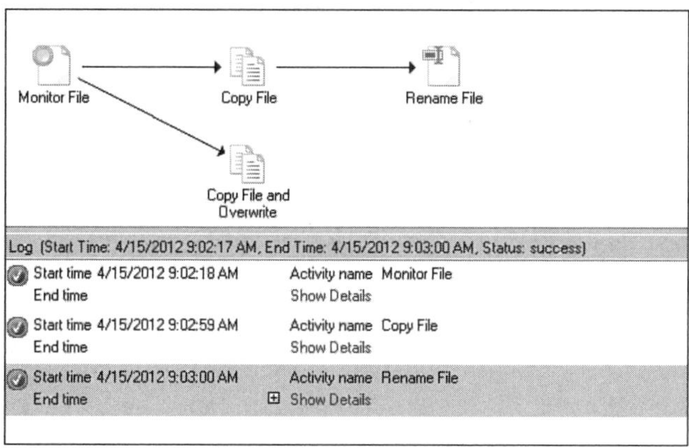

FIGURE 7.37 Observing the Copy File path.

Start the runbook again in the Runbook Tester, and modify the myLogOverwrite.txt file by adding a comment and saving it. When the change is detected, the runbook runs through the overwrite path this time (see Figure 7.38).

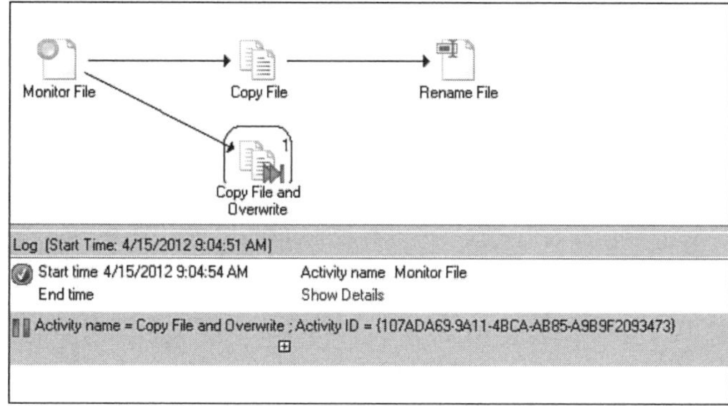

FIGURE 7.38 Observing the Copy File and Overwrite path.

After going through both scenarios, look at the myCollection folder to verify the results.

Summary

This chapter discussed the concepts of runbooks and their properties, such as job concurrency and security. It also discussed activities and their properties, the different types of activities in Orchestrator, the types of standard activities that are included, and the common published data that is available with each activity.

The chapter covered the management of runbooks, including logging and version control. It walked through several scenarios, building up a runbook from a single activity to copy a file, all the way to monitoring file changes, copying the file, and renaming the file to preserve all the previous copies.

Chapter 8 discusses advanced runbook concepts and shows how to use them to build more intelligent runbooks.

CHAPTER 8

Advanced Runbook Concepts

IN THIS CHAPTER

Chapter 7, "Runbook Basics," walked through the steps of building a runbook, beginning with developing a simple, single-activity runbook, to developing a runbook with branching logic. This chapter further explores runbooks by looking at advanced capabilities. Using concepts such as child runbooks, data manipulation functions, pattern matching with regular expressions, and error handling, you can design smarter, more intelligent, production-ready runbooks.

The chapter covers the use of junctions to flatten data (commonly used to reduce the number of data items heading to downstream activities) or synchronize branches in your runbook where logic diverges but needs to come back together. It discusses creating advanced schedules to meet complicated scheduling requirements to handle single or multiple execution periods, each with its own set of restrictions. The chapter describes using looping to control automatic retries of an activity and creating error handling in your runbook to manage problems that arise. It also discusses the purpose of computer groups, counters, and the different types of variables.

Advanced Schedules

Chapter 7 covered the basics of schedules, which should give you some familiarity with how schedules work. To summarize, a simple schedule controls when a runbook runs, typically by indicating either how often to run or when to run. This ensures that a runbook executes on a repeated schedule of some type—every 5 minutes, every 4 hours, once a week, and so on. Other examples of using a simple schedule include checking for file changes on a routine schedule, looking at a process periodically, or reading information in a log or queue.

A schedule might seem like a relatively simple concept, but an Orchestrator schedule has four components. You should understand these so that you can use them effectively:

- **Monitor Date/Time** activity
- **Check Schedule** activity
- Schedule object
- Link filters

The first two components are activities specifically designed for scheduling. The third component holds the schedule defining the hours and days. The last component is a link filter condition set to look at the activity time of execution. Some simpler schedules might not require all these components; some advanced and more complicated schedules might require all of them. The next sections discuss these components.

Using the Monitor/Date Time Activity

The **Monitor/Date Time** activity is specifically designed to offer flexibility in designing recurring schedules. Although Orchestrator provides excellent scheduling capabilities, sometimes a bit more fine-grained logic is necessary. For example, scheduling a runbook to execute every 30 minutes is easy. However, scheduling it to run every 30 minutes but only at the :15 and :45 minute time slices can get a bit tricky.

If you simply set the **Monitor Date/Time** activity to 30-minute time slices, the activity would run at every :00 and :30. You can accomplish advanced scheduling using link filters to specify the time slice that the activity can run. Instead of setting the time slice interval to 30 minutes, you can set the time slice interval to 15 minutes. This instructs **Monitor Date/Time** to run at every :00, :15, :30, and :45.

Setting to this value could cause the activity to execute more often than required. By joining this setting with an appropriate link filter, you can specify the exact time slice interval to :15 and :45. The link filter prevents the rest of the runbook from running if the time slice value does not match.

CAUTION: ACTIVITIES USE LOCAL TIME

The **Monitor/Date Time** activity adheres to the schedule based on the runbook server's system clock; it does not operate under Coordinated Universal Time (UTC). This is important to keep in mind because things such as Daylight Saving Time (DST) could unexpectedly alter the schedule behavior. For example, shifting forward an hour might cause the runbook to skip an execution because the hour when it was scheduled to start was skipped. Likewise, if the time moves back an hour, the runbook might execute twice.

The following steps show how to schedule a runbook (see Figure 8.1) that, at the specified time slice (every 30 minutes at the :15 and :45), invokes another runbook:

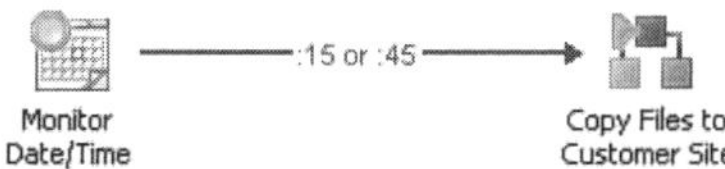

FIGURE 8.1 Sample activity to demonstrate time slices.

1. Under the Details section of Monitor Date/Time properties (see Figure 8.2), set the Interval to **Every 15** minutes and check the value **At time slices within the hour**.

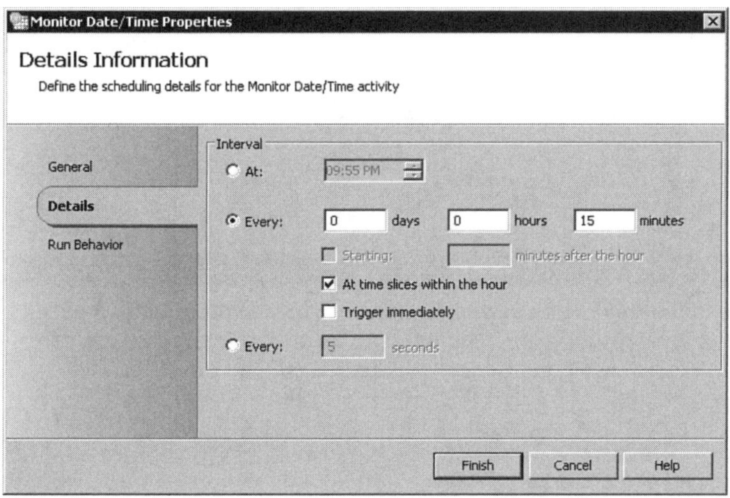

FIGURE 8.2 Details tab of the **Monitor Date/Time** activity.

8

2. In the link properties between the **Monitor Date/Time** activity and the **Invoke Runbook** activity renamed to **Copy Files to Customer Site**, remove the existing include condition **Monitor Date/Time returns success**.
3. Add two new filters for the include condition with the following common published data (see Figure 8.3):
   - **Activity end time (minutes)** from Monitor Date/Time **equals 15**
   - **Activity end time (minutes)** from Monitor Date/Time **equals 45**

   Notice that, when adding more than one filter, the two filters are separated with **or**.

Although the runbook still executes every 15 minutes, it does not proceed further because the conditional filter on the link bars any further action. The completed runbook is similar in appearance to any other runbook using **Monitor Date/Time**. Keep in mind that the logic is in the link filters.

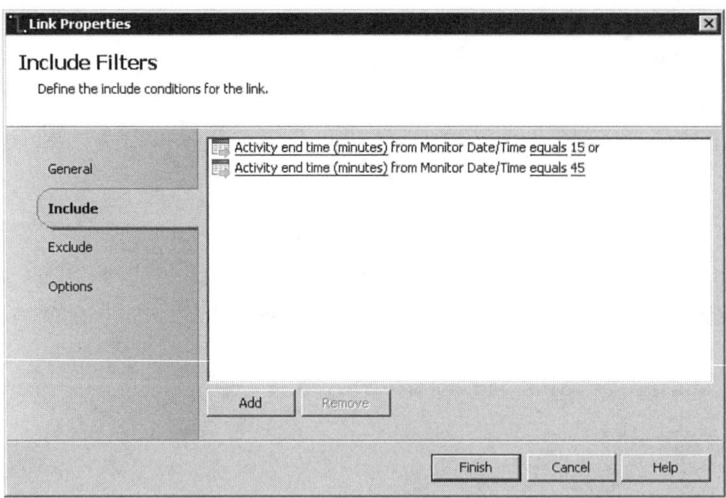

FIGURE 8.3 Adding filters to look at activity end time.

TIP: USE LINKS TO SPLIT PATHS BASED ON INTERVALS

Say that you have a process that runs one set of processes at :15 and :45 and then runs a different set at :30 and :00. By modifying the link filters to each of these paths, you can have the runbook execute completely different operations based on the time slice.

Using the Check Schedule Activity

To complicate matters further with potential real-world scenarios, presume that the runbook under discussion cannot execute except during the hours of 1 a.m. to 6 a.m. This requires configuring the runbook with a **Check Schedule** activity to evaluate the applicability of an assigned schedule. Modify your runbook as the instructions indicate in the next section.

Setting a Defined Schedule to Restrict Hours

To create a defined schedule to restrict hours, follow these steps:

1. Create a new schedule and specify the permitted hours as 1:00 a.m. to 6:00 a.m. (see Figure 8.4).

2. Add a **Check Schedule** activity and specify the schedule template you created in step 1.

3. Modify the link between the **Check Schedule** and **Copy Files to Customer Site** activities, changing the condition Check Schedule returns success to **Conforms to schedule from Check Schedule equals true**.

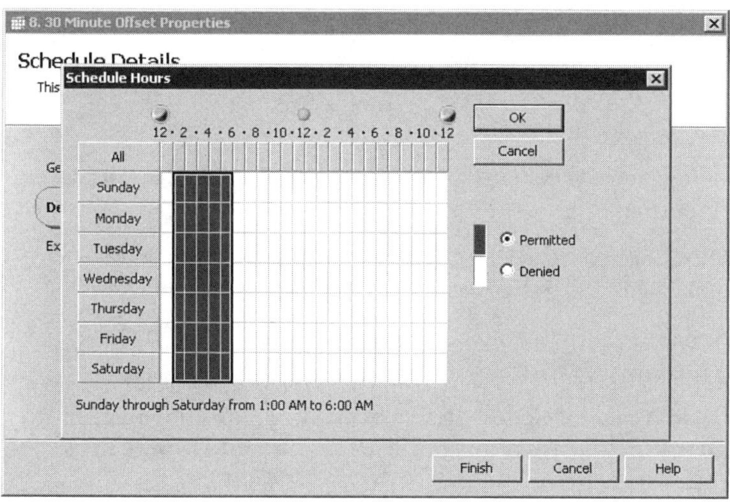

FIGURE 8.4 Specifying the hours in the Schedule object.

Figure 8.5 displays the completed runbook.

FIGURE 8.5 Adding a **Check Schedule** activity to the runbook.

Using Multiple Schedules

To add a layer of scheduling complexity, presume that, during the week, the runbook is allowed to run only during the maintenance window of 1:00 a.m. to 6:00 a.m. However, on the weekend, the runbook can run outside the maintenance window.

You cannot define a single schedule this way, so you must use multiple schedules to achieve the same result. Here is how the runbook might logically operate:

- The runbook checks the system clock and executes every 15 minutes, beginning at :00.
- If the time slice is :15 or :45, the runbook moves forward.
- The runbook checks the weekend schedule—if the time conforms to the schedule, it moves forward to **Invoke Runbook**. If not, it moves forward to the weekday schedule.
- The runbook checks the weekday schedule—if the time conforms to the schedule, it moves forward to **Invoke Runbook**. If not, the runbook ends.

To modify the runbook to account for different weekday and weekend schedules, follow these steps:

1. Create a new schedule named **Weekday**, specifying only Monday through Friday, with 1:00 a.m. to 6:00 a.m. as permitted hours.
2. Create a second schedule named **Weekend**, specifying only Saturday and Sunday, with no restrictions on permitted hours.
3. Modify the original **Check Schedule** activity. Specify the Weekend schedule and name the activity **Check Weekend Schedule**.
4. Create a new **Check Schedule** activity named **Check Weekday Schedule**, and specify the Weekday schedule you created.
5. Create a link from **Check Weekend Schedule** to **Check Weekday Schedule**. In the link properties, change the Include filter to **Conforms to schedule from Check Weekend Schedule equals false**.
6. Create a link from **Check Weekday Schedule** to **Copy Files to Customer Site**. In the link properties, change the Include filter to **Conforms to schedule from Check Weekday Schedule equals true**.

Figure 8.6 shows the completed runbook. Notice that if the time does not match the weekend schedule, **Check Weekday Schedule** is called. Failure to meet the weekday schedule means that the runbook will not progress any further.

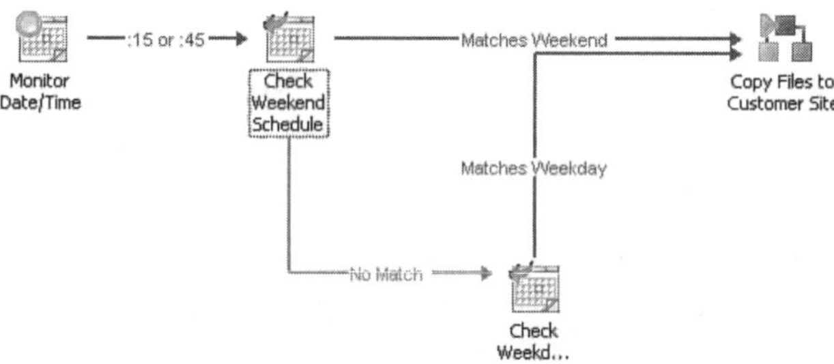

FIGURE 8.6 Runbook with a complex schedule.

TIP: ACHIEVE DEEPER COMPLEXITY BY CHAINING SCHEDULES

For more complexity in your schedule, use the same logic performed in this section and chain together multiple **Check Schedule** activities. You can layer schedules to fit specific complex schedule scenarios you might face.

Invoking Child Runbooks

Breaking out a runbook into multiple runbooks can help keep runbooks modular and shareable. Runbooks designed in a monolithic fashion cannot easily be reused from another runbook.

As an example, a runbook contains a set of activities that renames some files in a folder, copies those that match a certain name filter, and moves others matching a different name filter. To use this same set of activities in another runbook, you would have to copy out the activities into another runbook, move them around, and connect the activities back together. Spending time doing this is inefficient, leaving you with numerous runbooks with the same set of activities in them. Let's presume that, as part of the move operation, the name filter changes, meaning you might have to change the name filter in multiple runbooks.

Instead, if you create that same set of activities as its own runbook, using it elsewhere becomes easier (see Figure 8.7). Anyplace you need to run the activities, you simply call the runbook using the **Invoke Runbook** activity. You can think of this type of activity in programming or scripting terms as a subroutine.

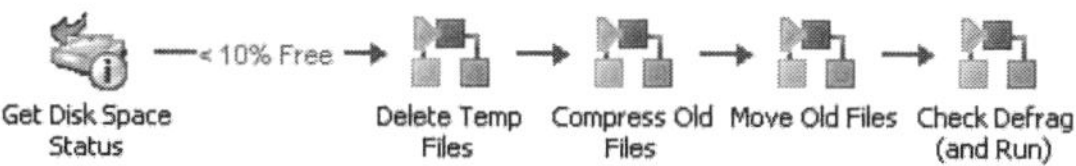

FIGURE 8.7 Invoking child runbooks.

Consider the scenario in which you want to execute a child runbook and return some information from the runbook to the parent runbook. This is accomplished by pairing the **Invoke Runbook** activity with the **Return Data** activity. The concept of returning data elevates invoking a child runbook to operate more like a function.

Returning data is another concept more easily understood when using scripting or programming terms. The concept is that the child runbook executes a set of activities and returns information. A runbook without a **Return Data** activity operates more like a subroutine. It performs some body of work but does not return any data.

For example, you design a runbook that performs a specific set of database queries returning a value or set of values and transforms the output into something usable in another activity. If you create this set of activities as its own runbook, you can call this runbook from other runbooks anytime the database needs to be queried and the output formatted for use. The output can be returned to the parent runbook using the **Return Data** activity. Because the information returned is published to the data bus, any activity or smart link can use this data.

Chapter 9, "Standard Activities," has more information on the **Invoke Runbook** activity.

Looping Considerations

Looping brings powerful capabilities to Orchestrator that all runbook designers should understand. Using looping enables you to incorporate activity level retries, success and failure validations, and monitoring into your runbooks. As an example, Figure 8.8 shows a runbook that looks for a specific process status and kills the process when detected.

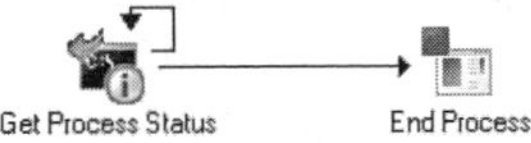

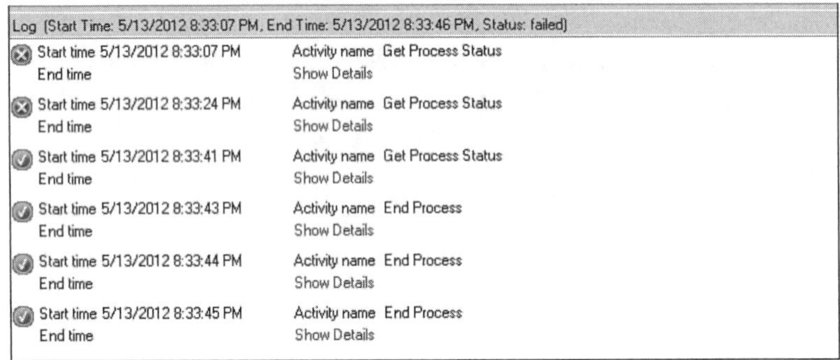

FIGURE 8.8 Looping property set on **Get Process Status**.

Looping enables you to monitor an activity at any location in a runbook. It provides the capability to retry an activity until a condition is met, whether that is success or failure. Activities are useful for building wait conditions—much like a `Do While` or `Do Until` statement in programming or scripting. Essentially, the runbook will wait at an activity until the output of the activity matches a certain condition. Looping can be used to suppress a runbook from continuing until the activity produces a desired result.

Behavior with Multiple Data Items

When information is passed to an activity, it can be passed as a single data item or multiple data items. If an activity receives a set of data items, it executes for each data item received. When a loop is applied to an activity that receives a set of data items, the activity runs for each data item while honoring the conditions set in the looping properties. For example, if you specify a folder in an activity that looks for files, the same folder is used each time the activity loops.

Configuring Looping Properties for an Activity

You can define looping properties on nearly any activity. Certain special activities cannot have looping properties defined. This includes junctions and monitoring activities.

Monitoring activities do not allow looping properties because the monitoring activity behaves like a looping activity by definition.

To define looping properties on an activity, follow these steps:

1. Right-click the activity and choose **Looping**.
2. On the General tab, check the box labeled **Enable** and specify **Delay between attempts**. This is the number of seconds the activity should wait before retrying.
3. On the Exit tab, provide an exit condition. When the condition is met, the activity ceases to loop.

   A condition can be provided on the Do Not Exit tab (instead of or in addition to the Exit condition) that prevents the activity from exiting while the condition is true.

Exit Condition

An exit condition is defined as an expression indicating when the activity should stop looping. For example, say that you are using the **Read Line** activity to look at a log file. If the log file contained a value such as "Processing is complete," the exit condition can be specified to exit when this occurs (see Figure 8.9):

```
Line text from Read Line equals Processing is complete
```

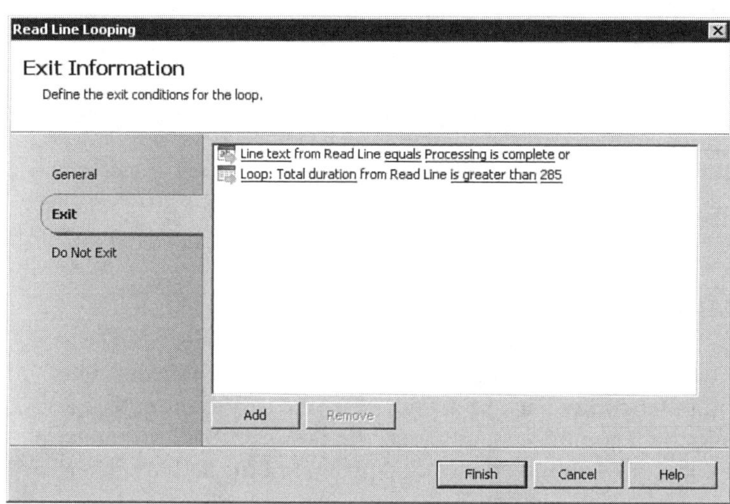

FIGURE 8.9 Exit condition set to end when log file value is found.

When this line is found in the log file, the activity ceases looping and moves to the next activity down the pipeline.

Do Not Exit Condition

A do not exit condition is an expression that indicates not to exit looping. Using the same **Read Line** example as in the previous section, if you knew that specific text in the log file, such as "Processing...", indicated that the process was still active, the Do Not Exit condition (see Figure 8.10) can be set as follows:

```
Line text from Read Line equals Processing...
```

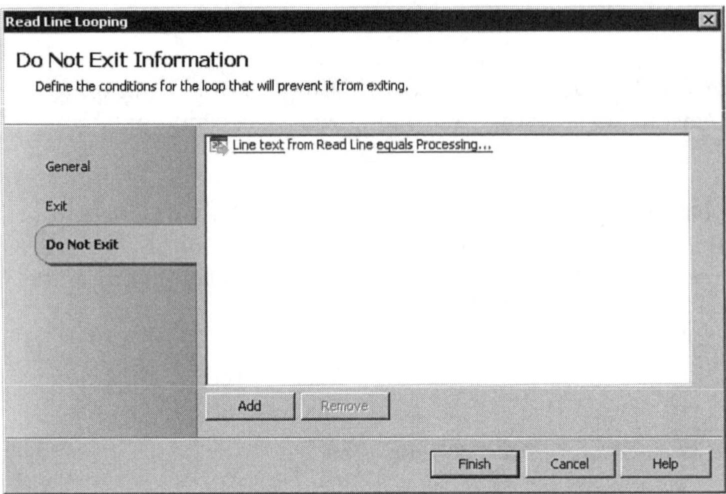

FIGURE 8.10 Do not exit condition showing to continue looping.

This would specify that while the line of text in the log file is "Processing...", the activity should continue to loop.

Preventing Infinite Loops

Realistically, running a loop infinitely until a condition occurs is not always practical. As an example, say that you want to ping a computer (known as the **Get Computer/IP Status** activity) until the computer comes back up from restarting. If the computer hangs during the process, you might want to notify someone of the problem. Unfortunately, if the activity is in an infinite loop, the runbook does not continue to the activity where a notification would occur.

Using time-based or attempt-based values as exit conditions can get around these infinite looping conditions. Essentially, you can configure loops to execute a specific number of times or for a specified duration of time. When a condition is reached, the activity exits the loop. Loops write two specific pieces of published data that can be utilized to prevent infinite looping; these can be used in conjunction with any other exit condition. Imagine if a poorly implemented loop caused the **Read Line** activity to look continuously for a line of text that was never written. Adding a time- or attempt-based condition as described here would solve the problem by instructing the activity to end after a period of time or after a certain number of attempts:

- **Loop: Total duration from Read Line is greater than 60:** This specifies that the total duration during looping should not exceed more than a minute (60 seconds).
- **Loop: Number of attempts from Read Line equals 10:** This example exits the loop whenever the number of attempts reaches 10 tries.

TIP: USING THE DURATION OR ATTEMPTS CONDITIONS

If you are unsure which condition to use to exit a loop, you can use both. Multiple conditions are treated as OR statements. If both conditions are applied, the loop exits when either one of the conditions is met. Figure 8.11 provides an example.

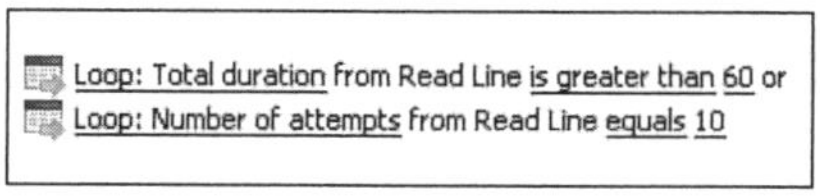

Loop: Total duration from Read Line is greater than 60 or
Loop: Number of attempts from Read Line equals 10

FIGURE 8.11 Setting looping conditions to prevent infinite retries.

Monitoring for Conditions in Activities

An additional benefit of using looping properties is the capability to use an activity for monitoring. Looping lets you monitor for certain conditions and provide a response based on the condition. By using runbooks to look for issues, System Center Orchestrator can add to existing monitoring products by performing actions such as sending SNMP traps or writing information to event logs. By adding looping properties to the activity, the activity continues to check for a condition until it meets the specified exit criteria.

Adding looping properties to an activity enables you to achieve a type of monitoring activity behavior without the monitoring activity. As an example, say that you are monitoring for changes in a log file. However, you want to know only when a specific line of text is added to the log file. When the line of text is detected, an event is written to the event log. No monitoring activity natively performs this function, but using a looping property on the **Read Line** activity gets you close. Figure 8.12 shows an example of this scenario.

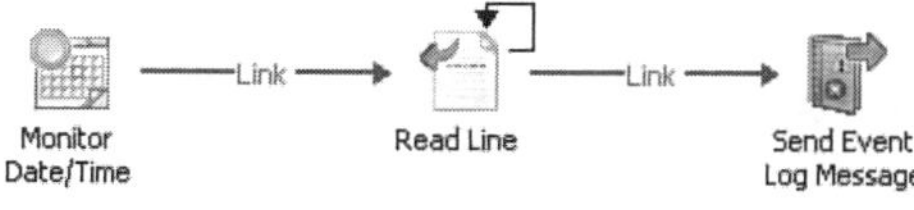

FIGURE 8.12 Looping property used to monitor a log file.

In the figure, the looping property on the **Read Line** activity is set to loop every 5 seconds, reading the last line of the log file. The exit condition looks for the line text or a specified duration of time. If either the line text or the time duration condition is met, the loop completes and the runbook moves to the next activity.

When setting up looping properties to act as a type of monitoring activity, several caveats apply:

- Because this is not a true monitoring activity, the runbook does not return to the monitoring activity after the runbook completes; it simply stops running. This makes it necessary to start the runbook with an actual monitoring activity to achieve the functionality of restarting the runbook from the beginning. You can use the **Monitor Date/Time** activity, shown in Figure 8.13, where it is set to every 300 seconds to accomplish this task.

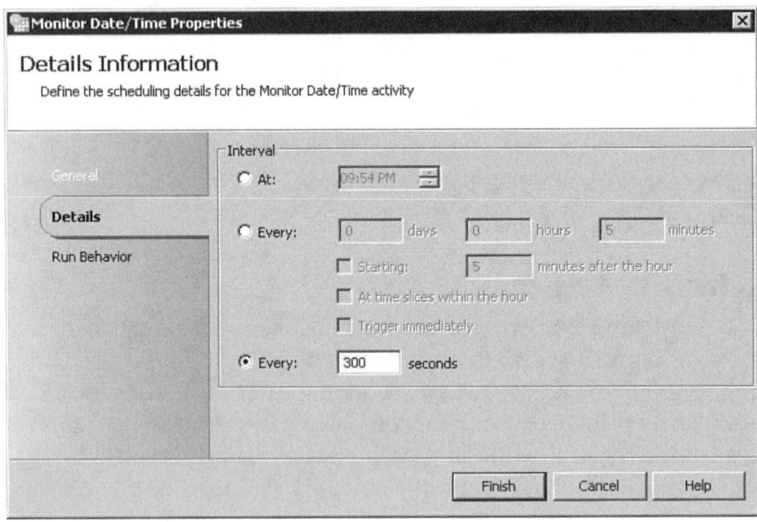

FIGURE 8.13 Adding the **Monitor Date/Time** activity.

- If the looping property causes the activity to loop infinitely until the condition is detected, it is likely the **Monitor Date/Time** activity will spawn multiple instances because it runs every 5 minutes. By setting the exit condition (see Figure 8.14) to also look for **Loop: Total duration from Read Line is greater than 285**, the loop will exit when it has been running for more than 285 seconds (4 minutes and 45 seconds).

  The idea here is that the looping ends, allowing the runbook to run to completion before the **Monitor Date/Time** can spawn another instance of the runbook. Setting up a runbook such as this might require additional testing to ensure that the timing operates as expected.

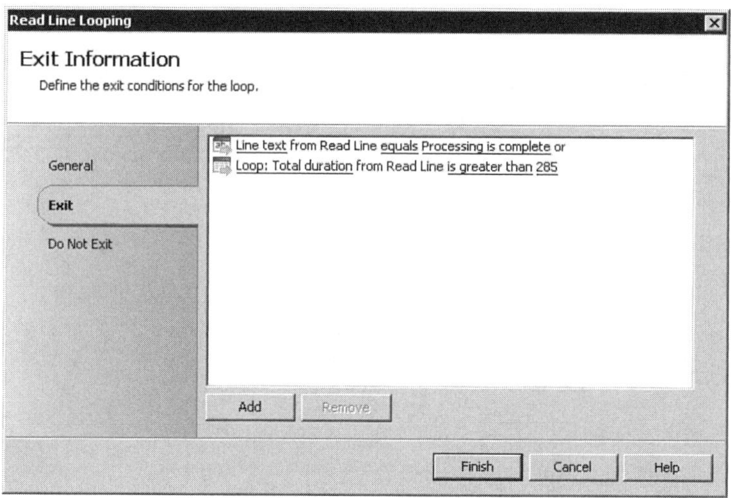

FIGURE 8.14 Exit condition used to prevent multiple instances from spawning.

TIP: SET A RUNBOOK TO INVOKE ITSELF

In the scenario described in this section, you can achieve practically the same effect by having a runbook invoke itself. To do so, set the last step in the runbook as the **Invoke Runbook** activity, configured to point to itself. Be sure that **Wait for completion** is not checked.

Runbook Looping

Looping a runbook is nearly the same process as looping an activity. Because an activity is used to call a runbook, setting looping properties on the **Invoke Runbook** activity follows the same principle as looping any other activity. Looping a runbook properly requires several additional elements:

- Returned data runbook properties
- **Return Data** activity

The next sections discuss these elements.

Configuring the Runbook Properties

As with any runbook that returns data, the Runbook properties must be modified to include a returned data definition. In the following example, a definition named "Verified" as type String holds the resulting end state of the runbook.

Returning Data to the Original Runbook

The looped runbook must use the **Return Data** activity to publish data into the returned data definition that, in this example, indicates the exiting state. The published data is used in the exit condition of the loop to indicate when to exit.

The example runbook publishes either `True` or `False` as the value of the returned data definition "Verified."

In Figure 8.15, the child runbook performs the following activities:

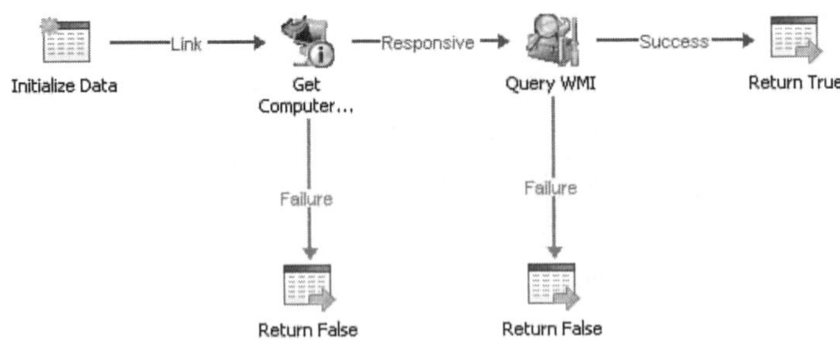

FIGURE 8.15 Child runbook called from parent.

- The computer is checked to see if it responds to a ping. If it does not respond, then "Verified," the returned data definition, is set to `False`.
- If the computer is responsive, a WMI query is performed against the `Win32_QuickFixEngineering` class to determine whether the provided hotfix ID is installed. If it is not installed, "Verified" is set to `False`.
- The value of either `True` or `False` is returned in the definition "Verified."
    - If the value is `True`, a success entry is written to a log file.
    - If the value is `False`, a failure entry is written to a log file.

Looping a Runbook Inside a Runbook

The following example is a simplified illustration of invoking a runbook inside another and continually invoking the runbook until a certain condition is met. These actions occur in Figure 8.16:

- The runbook accepts input as a hotfix ID and computer name.
- The runbook invokes the Patch Verify child runbook, which performs a series of activities and returns a value. The activity loops until either a successful condition is returned or the activity runs 10 times.
- Based on the child runbook, either a success or a failure entry is written to a log file.

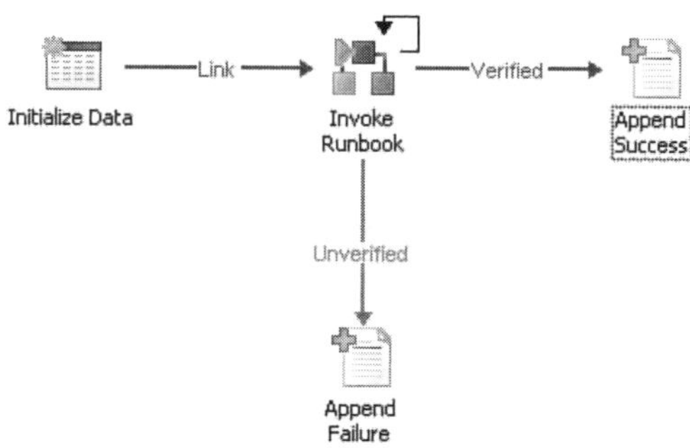

FIGURE 8.16 Runbook looping.

Using Junctions

This section breaks down junctions into two distinct functions: synchronize and republishing data. When a workflow diverts into multiple branches, the branches might need to be synchronized before moving to the next activity in the workflow. When a junction is used, it can return data from a previous activity to make it available to the rest of the workflow or, conversely, return nothing, suppressing data from any previous activity.

Synchronizing Branches

Whenever a workflow branches out, the paths might need to lead back together at some point. Without use of a junction, one path might continue forward inadvertently without waiting for the other branch to complete first. This is where a junction is useful: Terminating branches into a **Junction** activity forces all the branches to complete before continuing forward.

A practical example of using a junction is managing text files properly. If you have multiple branches inserting lines into a text, ending with sending the text file over FTP, you would want to ensure that all lines have been inserted into the text file by all branches before sending the file. By terminating the branches first, you ensure that your text file–management activities have concluded.

Republishing Data

When using a **Junction** activity, you can define whether to republish data from previous activities. If the activity is not set to republish data, activities following the **Junction** cannot access any published data from activities before the **Junction**. Use this feature if there is nothing of value from activities before the **Junction** activity. Ensure that the **Return data from** option is set to <None> to use this feature.

Junctions allow only data from the *selected* path to be available to other downstream activities. As Figure 8.17 shows, by setting the **Junction** activity to use **Get Service Status**, the published data from all the activities preceding the **Junction** activity is available—even the activities before the branching begins.

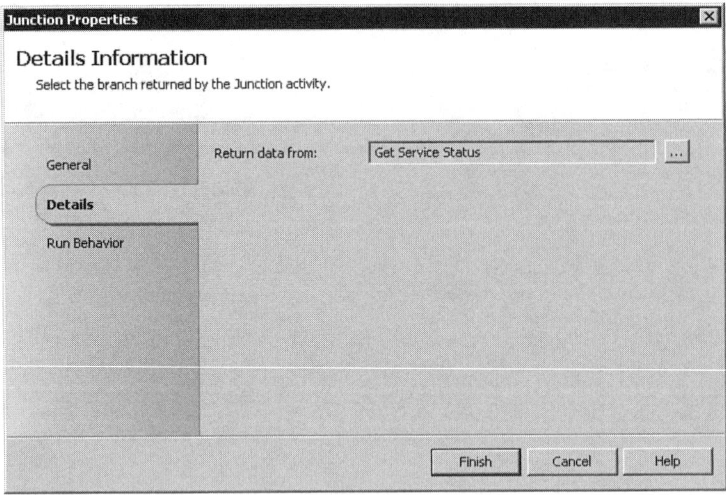

FIGURE 8.17 Republishing data from Get Service Status.

Choosing a Branch

To select a branch in a **Junction** activity, follow these steps, also illustrated in Figure 8.18.

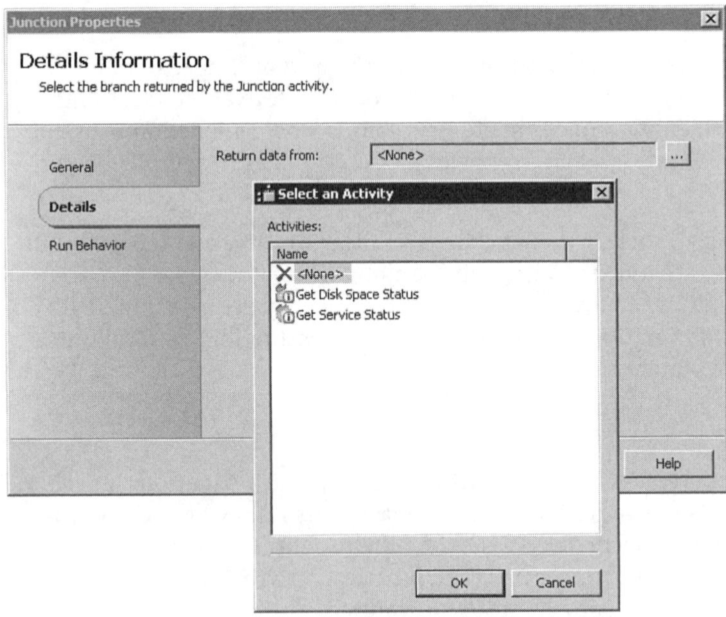

FIGURE 8.18 Setting up a junction property for republishing data.

1. Right-click the **Junction** activity and choose **Properties**, or double-click the **Junction** activity.
2. In the Junction Properties window, click the ellipses (...) button next to **Return data from**.
3. Select the desired branch, represented by the last activity of the branch.

CAUTION: PUBLISHED DATA NOT AVAILABLE AT TIMES WITH JUNCTIONS

When designing a runbook that uses junctions, realize that it is not immediately evident that published data might not be accessible. When a **Junction** activity is not set to republish data, the console does not actually reflect this and allows selection from the data bus regardless.

Data Item Flattening

As mentioned in the "Republishing Data" section, when activities go to a junction that is not set to republish data, all previous information in the data bus is lost. This also includes data items, and because no data items exist in the pipeline, any expected iterations are removed as well. As an example, the runbook in Figure 8.19 performs these actions:

- **Read Line:** Retrieves a list of servers
- **Get Computer/IP Status:** Pings each server in the list
- **Read Line (2):** Reads another text file
- **Append Line:** Writes the text file from **Read Line (2)** into another text file

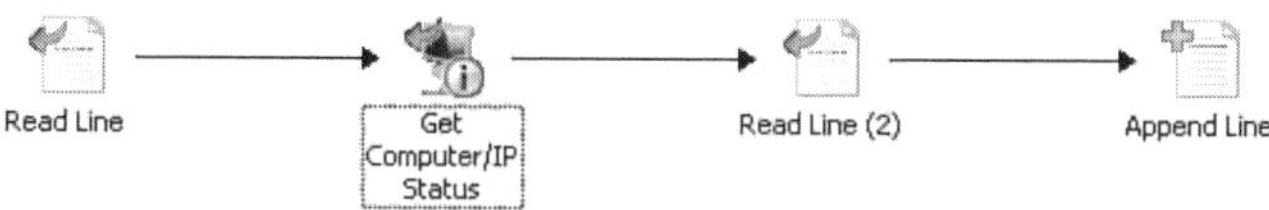

FIGURE 8.19 Data item iterations without flattening.

If the runbook were executed, the **Read Line (2)** activity would read the text file for every successful ping from **Get Computer/IP Status.** Furthermore, each successful activity from reading the file would be sent to **Append Line** to write—once for each successful ping.

A junction can interrupt this activity and cause a forceful separation in the runbook. By inserting a **Junction** activity between **Get Computer/IP Status** and **Read Line (2)**, as Figure 8.20 shows, **Read Line (2)** executes a single time.

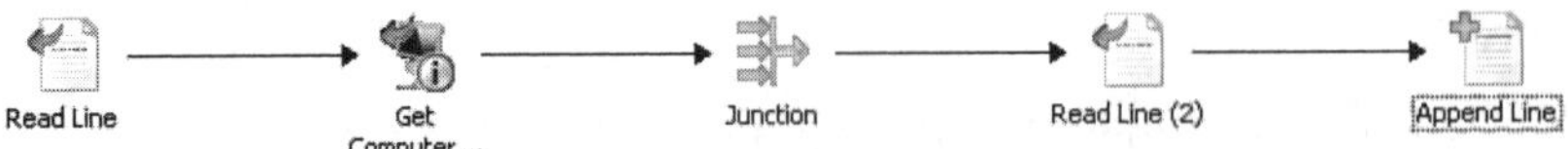

FIGURE 8.20 Iterations flattened with a **Junction** activity.

Junction Examples

To help familiarize you with using **Junction** activities, the next sections look at some examples that illustrate how a runbook might evolve to require using junctions.

In-Line Runbook

The in-line runbook illustrates how a runbook might initially look starting off. This runbook (see Figure 8.21) gets a list of computers from Active Directory, pings each computer, gets the available drive space and then the service status, and writes it to a log file.

FIGURE 8.21 Runbook operating in-line.

Branching Runbook

In the branching runbook in Figure 8.22, the **Get Disk Space Status** and **Get Service Status** activities are split off using a branch. As long as the activities remain in sync, this runbook works perfectly fine.

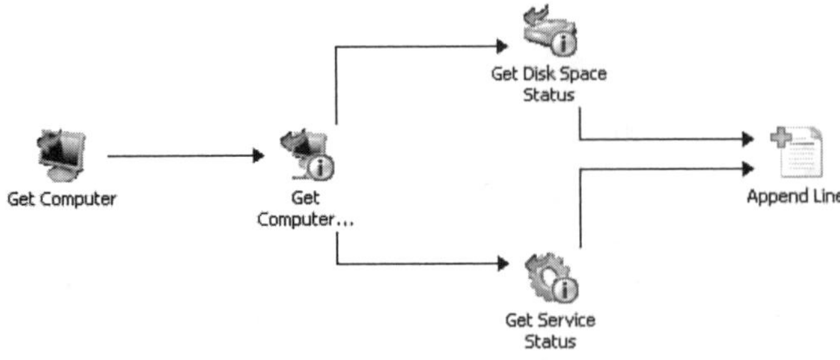

FIGURE 8.22 Branching runbook.

Using a Junction

Introducing a junction provides a means of ensuring that the activities are in sync before moving forward, as the next example shows. Figure 8.23 looks similar to the branching runbook example in the previous section, with the exception of the two **Get Status** activities going to a **Junction** before going to the **Append Line** activity. Both of the **Get Status** activities now must complete before moving to **Append Line**.

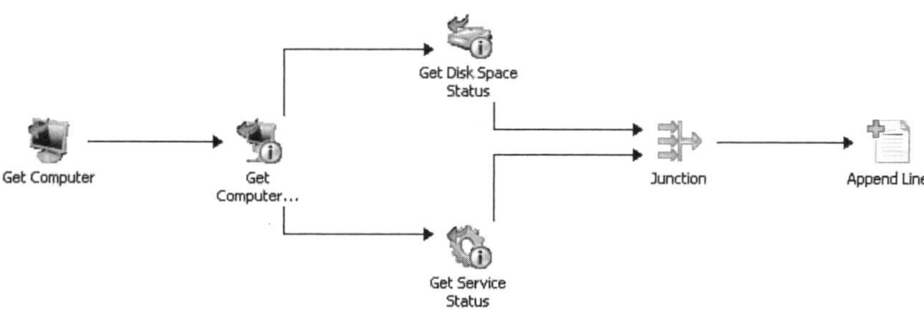

FIGURE 8.23 Simple **Junction** example.

However, after adding the **Junction**, only a single path can be selected to make published data information available to the **Append Line** activity. In this case, you have to select between the disk information and the service information.

Using Multiple Junctions

Figure 8.24 shows a runbook that is somewhat more complicated in the use of junctions. Note that, after the initial branch, the service activity path contains another activity to capture the service status to file. A **Junction** activity synchronizes the branches of activities and then moves to another **Junction**, which suppresses data and reduces the iterations coming down the pipeline to a single iteration. This is so the **Read Line** and **Append Line** activities do not run for each iteration of a computer that responded to a ping earlier in the runbook.

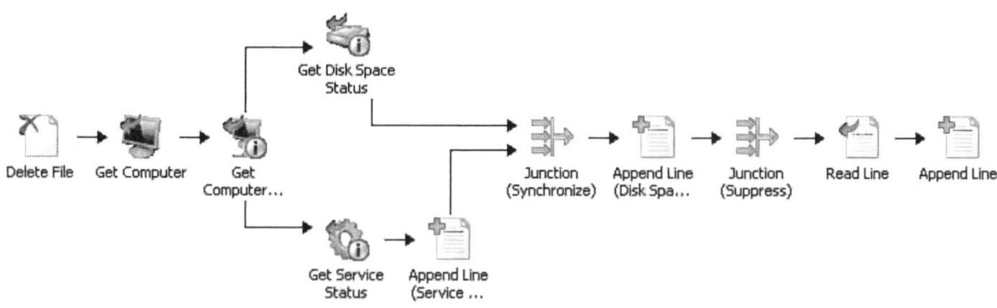

FIGURE 8.24 Runbook with multiple **Junction** activities.

NOTE: USING TEXT FILES NOT RECOMMENDED

Figure 8.24 depicts a way of using a text file to persist data after a **Junction** activity is used. Do this with care—only one process at a time can update a text file. When multiple runbook instances attempt to write to the same text file, this can cause an undesirable behavior in which one instance blocks another instance's access to write to the text file.

Working with Data

System Center Orchestrator includes a wide range of functions to handle the myriad ways data might present itself. Integrating runbooks with more systems undoubtedly presents scenarios in which data requires parsing and manipulating to change values. Often times, changing data is done simply to display it in a way that is pleasing and human friendly. Other times, data has to be changed to make the output of one activity fit the expected input of another activity.

Orchestrator provides three ways of manipulating data, as the next section discusses:

- Using native functionality provided through Orchestrator's data manipulation functions
- Using SQL data manipulation functions through the **Query Database** activity
- Using **Run Program** to issue a command to leverage command shell data manipulation methods
- Using the **Run .Net Script** activity to issue .NET or PowerShell data manipulation functions

Data Manipulation Functions

As introduced in Chapter 6, "Using System Center 2012 Orchestrator," Orchestrator 2012 provides 15 built-in data manipulation functions that allow in-line modification of data or operation using data. This type of manipulation is performed without passing data through an activity and can be handled in any provided text field. As an example, a value such as "Orchestrator" passed through the `Len` function returns a value of 12. Such a function looks like this:

```
[Len('Orchestrator')]
```

Unique to data manipulation, these functions are enclosed in square brackets, as the previous example illustrates.

Available Functions

Table 8.1 displays each available data manipulation function, a usage example, and an output example. All the output examples use the word *Orchestrator*.

TABLE 8.1 Available Data Manipulation Functions in Orchestrator

Function	Usage	Output
Position		
InStr	InStr('Text to Search','Text to Find')	InStr('Orchestrator', 'est') > 5
Len	Len('Text')	Len('Orchestrator') > 12
Return		
Mid	Mid('Text', Starting, Ending)	Mid('Orchestrator',5,8) > estrator
Left	Left('Text', Ending)	Left('Orchestrator',4) > Orch
Right	Right('Text', Starting)	Right('Orchestrator',5) > rator
Field	Field('Text', 'Delimiter', Position)	Field('System;Center; Orchestrator',';',3) > Orchestrator
Trim		
Trim	Trim('Text')	Trim(' Orchestrator ') > Orchestrator
LTrim	LTrim('Text')	LTrim(' Orchestrator') > Orchestrator
RTrim	RTrim('Text')	RTrim('Orchestrator ') > Orchestrator
Convert		
Upper	Upper('Text')	Upper('Orchestrator') > ORCHESTRATOR
Lower	Lower('Text')	Lower('Orchestrator') > orchestrator
Math		
Sum	Sum(Number, Number, ...)	Sum(Len('Orch'),5,5) > 14
Diff	Diff(Number, Number, Decimal Places)	Diff(Len('Orchestra tor'),9) > 3
Mult	Mult(Number, Number...)	Mult(Len('Orch'),2,5) > 40
Div	Div(Number, Number, Decimal Places)	[Div(Len('Orch'),3,2)] > 1.33

Nesting Functions

Data manipulation functions can also be nested inside each other, providing combinations of functions that can handle almost any parsing or manipulation requirement. When you nest a function within a function, closed brackets for inside functions are not required. The following example multiplies the value of 12 (derived from the `Len` function in the previous section) by 8, returning a value of 96:

```
[Mult(Len('Orchestrator'),8)]
```

TIP: CONSOLE LIMITATIONS

Orchestrator does not provide a console rich with secondary notation, such as syntax highlighting in text fields where functions are used. Because of this, the syntax can quickly become confusing when nesting functions. Try to avoid using deeply nested functions because you cannot mark up the text field with any notation to indicate what is occurring. Viewing such a complicated function later might be frustrating to other runbook designers or even the original author.

Regular Expressions

With Orchestrator's filtering capabilities, having a firm understanding of how to perform pattern matching is important so that you can utilize the most precise filter possible to rule out false positives and excessive noise. Regular expressions (also known as *RegEx* and introduced in Chapter 6) are complicated and powerful enough to fill the content of another book (and many have). This section focuses on the available characters you can use, their meaning, and some examples of how to use them.

Regular expressions can be used in places such as link properties (see Figure 8.25) or activity properties (see Figure 8.26) where a filter is created using the "matches pattern" or "does not match pattern" condition. In general, regular expressions are case sensitive. Orchestrator is no exception and does not offer a means to turn off case sensitivity.

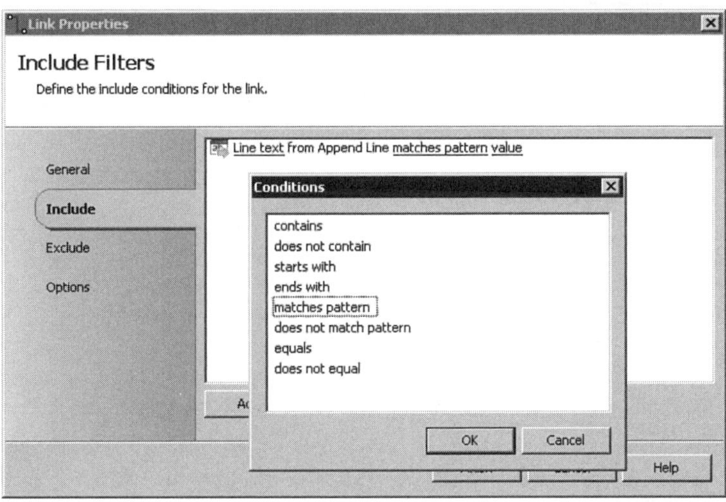

FIGURE 8.25 Regular expression used in a link property.

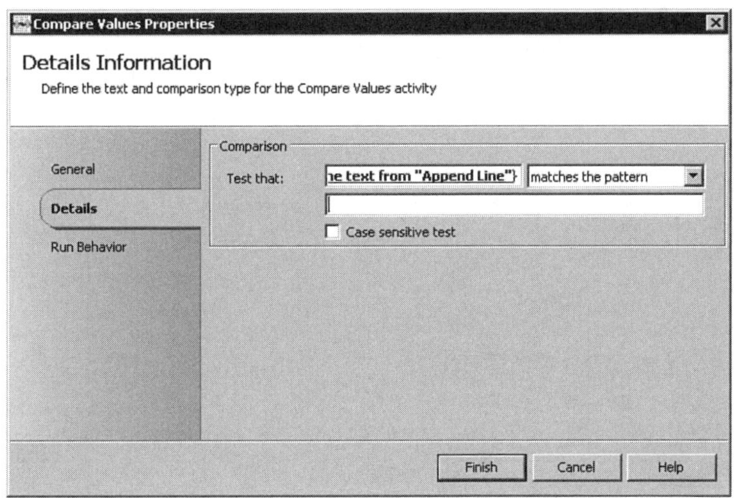

FIGURE 8.26 Regular expression used in the properties of the **Compare Values** activity.

Table 8.2 lists the available characters for use in a regular expression. The examples show the regular expression used, followed by the matching text.

TABLE 8.2 Regular Expressions in Orchestrator

Char	Example
.	Text: Center C.nter > Center Cen.er > Center C.n.er > Center
*	Text: “Center”, “enter” C*enter > Center > enter Text: “Center”, “enter” .*Center.* > Center
?	Text: “Center”, “enter” C?enter > Center > enter
+	Text: “Center”, “enter” C+enter > Center
$	Text: “Center”, “Orchestrator” r$ > Center > Orchestrator Text: “Center”, “center”, “Orchestrator” .*c.*r$ > center > Orchestrator
^	Text: “Center”, “System Center” ^C.*r > Center
\	Text: “Center.”, “+Orchestrator*” Center\. > Center. \+Orchestrator* > +Orchestrator*

Char	Example
[ ]	Text: "Center", "Orchestrator" .*[Cc].*r$ > Center > Orchestrator
[^]	Text: "Orchestrator", "Orchestration" Orchestrat[i].* > Orchestrator
()	
|	Text: "Orchestrator", "System" (Orchestrator|System) > Orchestrator > System
-	Text: "Orchestrator", "Orchestration", "Orchestrate", "Orchestra" Orchestrat[e-o].* > Orchestrator > Orchestration > Orchestrate

Testing Functions and Regular Expressions

Creating several simple test runbooks can be quite useful when testing complex, nested functions or challenging regular expressions. It enables you to test the function or regular expression inside a runbook playground. This offers two benefits:

- If you are working on a runbook that you intend to use in your production environment, the test runbook would not alter any other runbook, providing a safe means to test.
- Having a test runbook speeds up the testing and evaluation phase. Because you can test in a runbook with two activities, you do not have to wait for the runbook to reach the part where the function or regular expression is used.

Function Test

This runbook, which Figure 8.27 displays, contains the following:

- **Initialize Data:** A parameter called myText is created to receive text input upon execution.
- **Append Line:** This writes myText to a text file with the function applied to it.

You would write the data manipulation function with myText into the text field of **Append Line**. The formatted data is written to the text file.

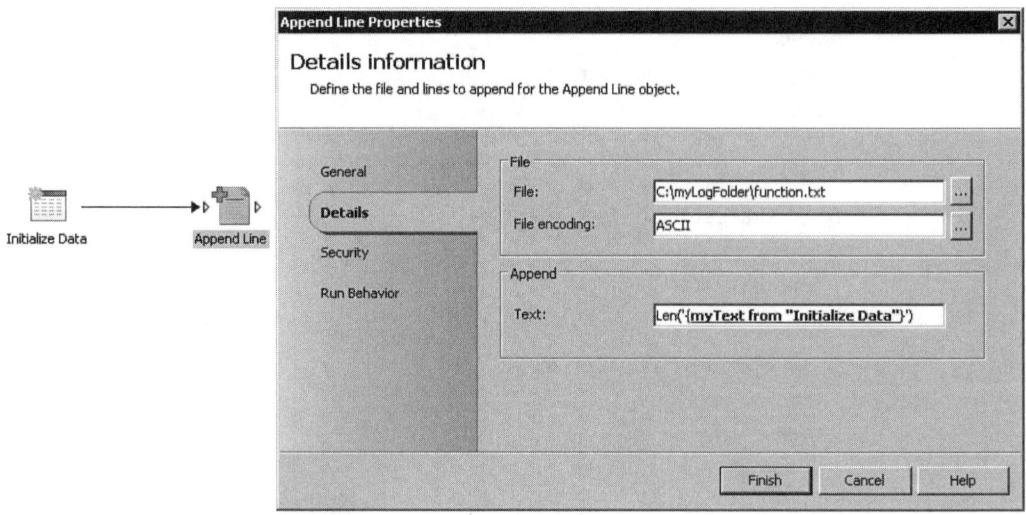

FIGURE 8.27 Testing a data manipulation function.

Regular Expression Test

The runbook in Figure 8.28 provides the following:

- **Initialize Data:** A parameter called **myText** is created to receive text input upon execution.
- **Append Line:** This writes **myText** to a text file if the text matches the regular expression.

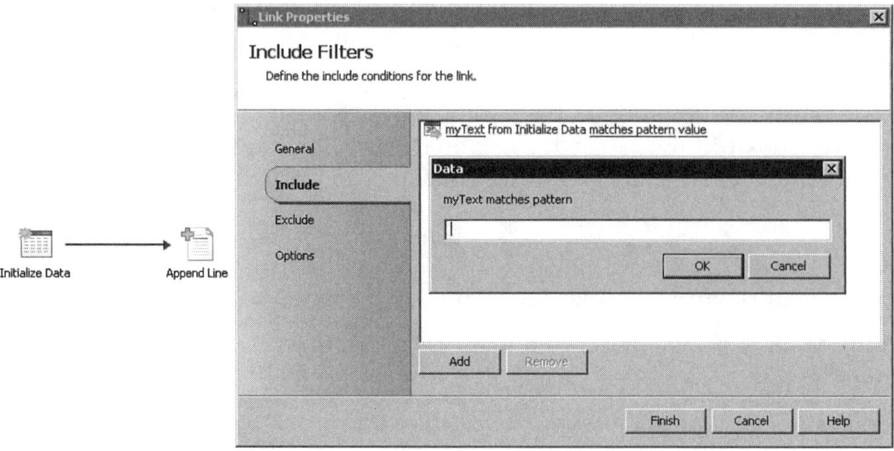

FIGURE 8.28 Testing regular expressions.

Instead of altering the text field, the link between the two activities contains the regular expression. If myText matches the regular expression provided in the link filter, the **Append Line** activity writes the value to the text file.

NOTE: PARAMETERS ARE NOT AVAILABLE IN LINK PROPERTIES

You might be wondering why the Regular Expression Test runbook does not use a parameter for the pattern-matching value. The reason is that parameters are not available as the data part of the link filter.

Error Handling

Most processes, especially when increasing in complexity, are never free of error. Errors can be caused by an activity not working as planned, an input received that does not match the expected format, environmental problems, resource constraints, and so on. An error can come in almost any form. A properly designed runbook should handle most of the common ones.

Error handling in Orchestrator comes in several forms:

- Activities designed to retry a step (looping)
- Activities used to log errors at different points of the runbook
- Link filters that branch the runbook based on output

No one can account for every probability. Trial and error plays a huge part in working through adding error handling, so plan plenty of time to perform an adequate amount of testing. Simply running through the runbook in the Runbook Testing console often helps vet the outcomes the runbook needs to handle.

Overview of a Simple Runbook

As discussed earlier in the "Junction Examples" section, a simple runbook such as the in-line runbook example (shown again in Figure 8.29), without any error handling, is easy to read but could never actually be used in production because it would be prone to failure starting with the very first activity. If the computer cannot be pinged, what is the likelihood that the server is running? If the server is not running, what is the purpose of attempting to check disk space?

FIGURE 8.29 Runbook example with no error handling.

8

Adding Error Handling

How might the runbook in Figure 8.29 look after adding error handling and instrumentation? The following sections examine each step of Figure 8.30 to show how to modify a runbook to include error handling. However, understanding link behavior before that is useful.

FIGURE 8.30 Runbook example with error handling.

Link Behavior Favors Success

By default, links are set with success as the only filter. This means that if the object preceding the link returns a success, the runbook continues to the next activity. Consider, for example, an activity to query an Active Directory object. Say that you queried for all computers that begin with the letter *B*. However, your directory contains no computers that match this criterion. Even though no computers are returned, the query itself ran successfully.

The runbook with no error handling (shown previously in Figure 8.29) does exactly as discussed. If the **Get Computer** activity finds no match, it still returns a successful activity status and moves to the next activity. The **Get Computer/IP Status** activity does the same thing, despite having no computer to ping or a response. Finally, when the **Append Line** activity runs, it writes a statement with nothing in it. This illustrates that, without modifying the default behavior of link filters, the runbook will not execute as you might think. It might be better to say the runbook operates exactly as instructed.

NOTE: A TINY LIMITATION WITH LINKS

When using link filters, keep in mind that a link cannot use published data from any other activity except for the one to which it is anchored. This means that published data from any preceding activity is not available.

When you need to use published data from other activities, use an activity such as **Compare Values** to provide filtering capability using any published data.

Modifying the Runbook for Error Handling

Having discussed the default behavior of link filters and why this is important when dealing with error handling, let's return to the runbook with error handling (see Figure 8.30) and see how it has been modified to handle errors.

Modify Link Filters

To begin, all link filters should be identified and modified to reflect the right condition to indicate a true success. As an example, you might modify the link filters in the runbook as follows:

- **Get Computer to Get Computer/IP Status:** Count from **Get Computer** does not equal 0.
- **Get Service Status to Append Line:** Service Status from **Get Service Status** does not equal. (Though the ending appears missing, this is intended.)

Because **Get Computer/IP Status** and **Get Disk Space** provide a proper success and failure status without modification, the link filter does not need to be modified.

Using Looping Properties to Handle Errors

Though **Get Computer/IP Status** returns the status successfully, a looping property is added to this activity to provide even greater capability to handling issues. For example, say that the targeted computer is not available when the runbook executes starting up after a reboot.

With a looping condition applied, the runbook can attempt to ping the computer multiple times and exit after a period of time if the pings still fail. If the ping is successful, the runbook moves to the next activity. This prevents the runbook from stopping unless the computer has been deemed unreachable. The looping property is configured as Figure 8.31 shows.

NOTE: MANAGING THE NUMBER OF RETRY ATTEMPTS

Be sure to understand this important factor in looping: Looping properties instruct an activity to retry until a certain condition is met. What if the condition is never met? Misconfigured looping properties can cause the activity to retry the same thing endlessly. For example, if the **Get Computer/IP Status** activity is expecting a response to a ping from a working computer, chances are, the condition will be met. However, if the computer is retired, the condition will never be met.

Creating an exit condition using "Loop: Number of attempts" is a great way to limit the number of times the activity should retry. When it equals the specified value (shown earlier in Figure 8.31), the activity exits.

The earlier section "Preventing Infinite Loops" covered this topic.

8

Branch Success and Failure to Separate Paths

When the success path is determined, the failure path becomes a little more obvious. Technically, the runbook in Figure 8.30 handles errors—of course, the errors are handled by simply ignoring them. Although this works, it does not provide much information showing where an activity might have hit a problem unless you are stepping through the runbook in the Runbook Tester.

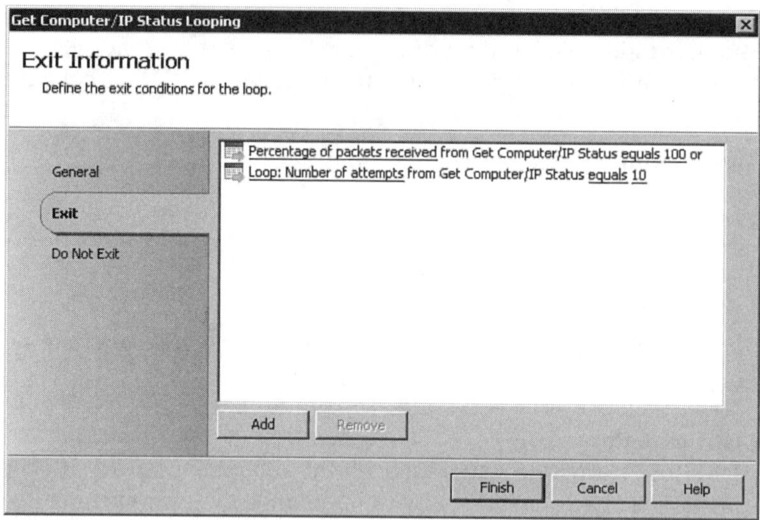

FIGURE 8.31 Looping condition set to attempt to ping a computer multiple times.

Routing failures properly provides a mechanism for detecting problems. As an example, if the **Get Computer** activity does not return any objects, the runbook could write that problem to a log file, send an email, or write an event. Figure 8.32 illustrates redesigning the runbook to provide proper branching to handle a problem scenario. Failures could also be sent to other activities or runbooks that troubleshoot the failure or attempt to resolve it.

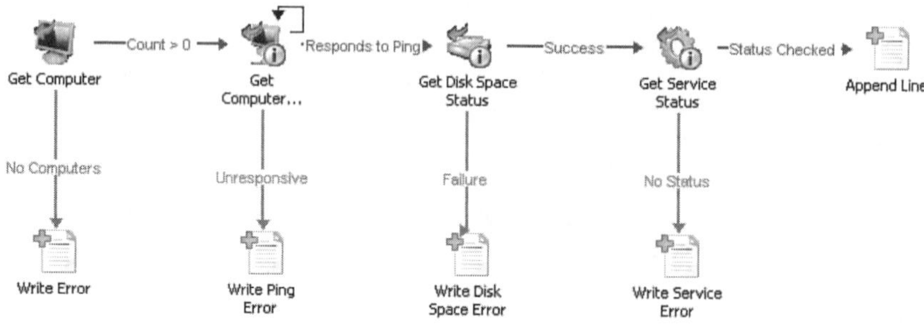

FIGURE 8.32 Runbook example with branching and error handling.

Computer Groups and Alternative Options

If you have ever created a script and wanted to target it to multiple computers, you should be familiar with the concept of computer groups. Using a script, you would provide a list of computers in a text file and then have the script perform an action for each computer.

System Center Orchestrator gives you the capability to create computer groups that activities can target. Instead of having an activity target a single computer, it can target a group of computers. Each computer in the group must be defined, one at a time. Orchestrator supports browsing for computer names, but this is not advised in environments where the browser service is not used or an extensive list of computers names can be returned.

Entry Types

If you are familiar with Opalis Integration Server (OIS) 6.3, you might recall that computer groups had more functionality than in Orchestrator. OIS allowed mixing direct entries with the AD query entry type or the SMS Collection entry type. Orchestrator, however, does not support either of these entry types. Adding computers one at a time is the only entry type available.

The loss of these additional options poses limitations when using computer groups. However, the limitations are easily overcome using functionality that exists in other activities, as indicated here:

- **Active Directory query:** This functionality, which enabled you to specify a query to find computers, can be replicated using the **Get Computer** activity located in the Active Directory Integration Pack.
- **SMS collection:** This functionality, which enabled you to specify a collection of computers, can be replicated by using the **Get Collection Members** activity located in the System Center Integration Pack for System Center Configuration Manager (both versions 2007 and 2012).

NOTE: UNDERSTANDING COMPUTER GROUPS

Computer groups are useful because you do not have to store the information in a text file, database table, or some other retrievable list. Computer groups are also accessible from any activity where the input property has been defined to accept computer groups.

However, the impracticality of creating large computer groups through manual entry probably outweighs the benefit they provide, particularly considering that no scenario exists in which a computer group must be used instead of an activity to send multiple objects down the data bus to the next activity.

Using Computer Groups

A computer group is practical when you are dealing with a small, static set of computers. After you create a computer group, you can use that computer group when a dialog box requests a computer name.

Suppose that you manage a group of computers that are not matched easily by queries. You can use a computer group to group those computers manually. When the computer group exists, you can use them in any runbook where the runbook should execute against the entire set of computers.

Creating a Computer Group

To create a computer group, in the Connections pane of the Runbook Designer, locate the Computer Groups folder under the root. Create a new folder, if necessary, or navigate to the location where you want to create your computer group. Follow these steps:

1. Right-click the folder and choose **New -> Computer Group**.
2. Provide a name and description for your computer group, and then click **Finish**.
3. Double-click the computer group you just created. This opens the Properties window focused on the Contents tab.
4. Click **Add**. Type in the computer name or browse (...) to find the computer to add. Repeat this as many times as necessary.
5. Click **Finish** to complete the computer group.

Adding a Computer Group to an Activity

Any activity that calls for a computer name accepts a computer group. For example, to end a process on multiple computers, you can use a computer group for the target criteria. Perform the following steps to add a computer group to an activity:

1. In the dialog box that requires a computer name, right-click the dialog box and choose **Subscribe**; then click **Computer Group**.
2. In the Select a Computer Group dialog box, navigate through the folders until you find the computer group you want to use, and click **OK**.
3. After selecting a computer group, you return to the dialog box as a placeholder in the same way as published data.

Now when the activity runs, it will run for each computer in the computer group.

Figure 8.33 shows an example of a runbook utilizing a computer group to feed a list of computers into the **Get Computer/IP Status** activity.

Using Variables

If you are new to Orchestrator, the term *variable* might confuse you. Variables in Orchestrator do not behave like traditional variables: A runbook cannot modify them. Variables behave more like constants; they require you to set the value as a static assignment.

Use variables sparingly because they are global in nature. As such, when exporting a runbook, it is easy to export all the variables in an Orchestrator environment. When importing, including the variables can pollute the environment.

The exception to the static behavior in variables is a special class of variables (referred to as special variables) such as `NOW()` and `%ENVVAR%`. These variables have a dynamic behavior.

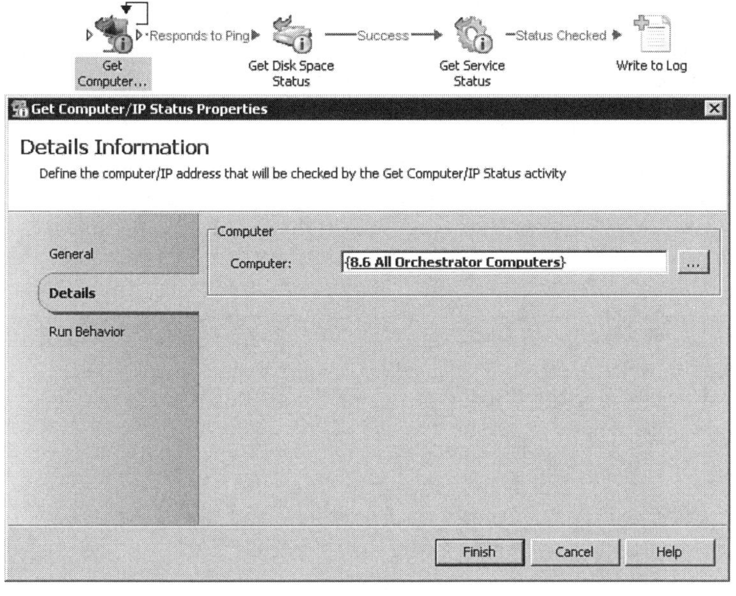

FIGURE 8.33 Providing a list of computers to a runbook with a computer group.

Using NOW() As a Variable

You can use the `NOW()` variable to specify date and time dynamically, providing either the entire current datetime stamp or parts of it. Refer to Table 8.3 to see the functions `NOW()` supports.

TABLE 8.3 NOW Functions

Function	Result
<empty>	7/1/2012 4:28:44 PM
Day	1
Dayofweek	0
Dayofyear	183
Month	7
Year	2012
Hour	16
Minute	28
Second	44
Millisecond	0

When using the `NOW()` variable, the function is placed inside the variable in the format `NOW(Function)`. For example, `NOW(Day)` produces the output "1" in Table 8.3. Leaving `NOW()` with an empty function produces the entire datetime stamp.

Using Environment Variables

Environment variables, expressed as `%ENVVAR%`, return information assigned to the variable called inside the % symbols. As an example, `%SYSTEMDRIVE%` might return "C:".

Keep in mind that environment variables are specific to the computer running the runbook. If you have runbook servers that are configured differently, the environment variable might not match between runbook servers, causing unexpected outcomes. Furthermore, Orchestrator supports the use of both system variables and user variables. User variables are resolved as the service account on the runbook server.

TIP: USING EMPTY VALUES IN A RUNBOOK

You might run into situations in which Runbook Designer rejects the use of a blank value. To get around this, create a variable named **Blank** that has no value. This enables you to insert an empty or null value while designing a runbook.

If an environment variable is not resolved, it simply returns the text of the variable. For example, if `%PUBLIC%` did not resolve, it would return literally "%PUBLIC%".

Using Encrypted Variables

Encrypted variables provide a unique purpose, storing encrypted passwords that can be used in property fields designed to hold encrypted values. If an encrypted variable is used inside a password field, Orchestrator automatically decrypts the value.

This decryption of the variable occurs in all places where text is not displayed, with one exception: the script body of the **Run .NET Script** activity. Whenever the encrypted variable is used inside the script body, the variable is decrypted. To ensure that the decrypted value is not seen, the script body is no longer published to the data bus as it was in earlier versions.

Using Counters

In Orchestrator, counters provide a means of keeping track of a process or activity. Counters have an extraordinary benefit, in that they are globally available. You can check the value of a counter from any activity in any runbook. Figure 8.34 shows a runbook executing the following scenario:

- **Run Every 10 Min:** The runbook executes every 10 minutes.
- **Reset ServerDown:** The ServerDown counter is reset as the first step of the runbook each time the runbook executes, clearing the previous value.
- **Get Computer/IP Status:** A computer group is provided to this activity to ping each computer in the group.
- **Increment ServerDown:** The ServerDown counter is incremented for every computer in the computer group that fails to respond to a ping.

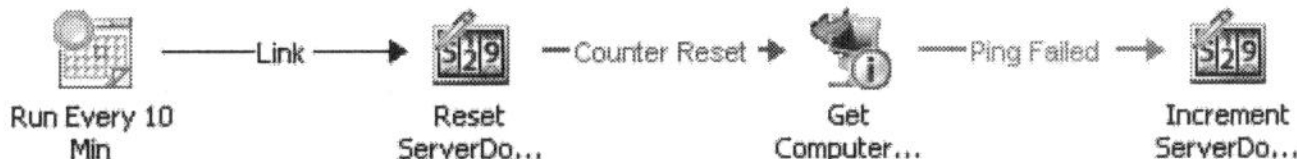

FIGURE 8.34 A runbook checks the members of a computer group for their availability and increments a counter if a member is unavailable.

Meanwhile, Figure 8.35 shows an example of how you can use a separate runbook using the **Get Counter Value** activity to check the current ServerDown counter. If the value is equal to or greater than 2, an event is written. This can be useful, for example, when a count of 2 in a group of three servers might indicate a critical problem because only one node would be left providing service such as web servers in a farm.

FIGURE 8.35 A runbook checks the ServerDown counter and writes an event if it is above a specified threshold.

Of course, the runbook in Figure 8.34 could be designed to write the event as well, but this example uses two runbooks to illustrate how counters are globally available.

NOTE: LIMITATIONS OF COUNTERS

Use counters with care for the same reason they are beneficial: They are globally available.

It is strongly recommended that you not use the **Modify Counter** activity when the same counter might be modified by either multiple executions of a single runbook or across multiple runbooks pointing to the same counter. Counters are not thread-safe and can become unreliable when used in this manner.

Summary

System Center 2012 Orchestrator offers myriad options for creating highly complex runbooks that you can design to meet nearly every scenario. Many native functions are available in runbook design, including data manipulation and regular expressions. Utilizing advanced scheduling capabilities makes it possible to set a runbook to execute at the correct time or interval. Looping properties in an activity provide the capability to monitor an activity and set automatic retry attempts. Finally, using different kinds of variables in your runbook makes it easy to utilize environment variables or datetime to augment capability or reduce the number of times a password must be entered into an activity.

CHAPTER 9
Standard Activities

IN THIS CHAPTER

- Configuring Standard Activities
- Runbook Control Activities
- System Activities Category
- Scheduling Category
- Monitoring Activities
- File Management
- Email Activities
- Notification Activities
- Utilities Category
- Text File Management

System Center Orchestrator is a flexible automation engine that you can use in many scenarios. This engine is powered by Orchestrator activities that you can use to create runbooks to automate data center procedures. As part of installation, a set of activities, known as *standard activities*, is available for use in the Runbook Designer. You can use these generic activities, introduced in Chapter 7, "Runbook Basics," in your runbooks to execute the desired action.

The standard activities made available during installation are also registered automatically when you install additional runbook designers and runbook servers. These 72 standard activities are organized into categories to help you locate the task you want to perform. These activities are not product specific and do not depend on any installed services.

The Orchestrator activities library is not limited to these standard activities; using integration packs (IPs), you can extend the library with product- or vendor-specific activities. Chapter 12, "Orchestrator Integration Packs," through Chapter 18, "Integration with Windows Azure," discuss other integration packs that can extend the Orchestrator activity library.

This chapter discusses the standard activities available with System Center 2012 Orchestrator, showing you the power of these activities available for your use in the Runbook Designer.

Configuring Standard Activities

Each activity has a basic structure, consisting of a series of tabs that contain fields to configure the activity. The General, Details, and Runbook Behavior tabs are available for all activities. Information in the Details, Advanced, and Security tabs is activity specific and contain information used to execute the action. The Advanced and Security tabs are visible depending on the specific activity.

General Tab

The General tab provides a name and description for the activity; the name displays in the Runbook Designer workspace, and the description states the purpose of the activity. The authors recommend naming the activities in your runbook so that the action being executed is recognizable. This improves the readability of your runbook and helps with troubleshooting.

TIP: ENABLING TOOLTIPS

ToolTips can be enabled in the Runbook Designer. These provide field definitions and examples of valid values. When ToolTips are enabled and you hover over the activity in the Designer, the description text appears.

Run Behavior Tab

The Run Behavior tab is available on all activities. This is where you specify how the activity handles multivalue published data; you also can configure event notifications here. Figure 9.1 shows the default settings for the Run Behavior tab. You can specify this information on this tab:

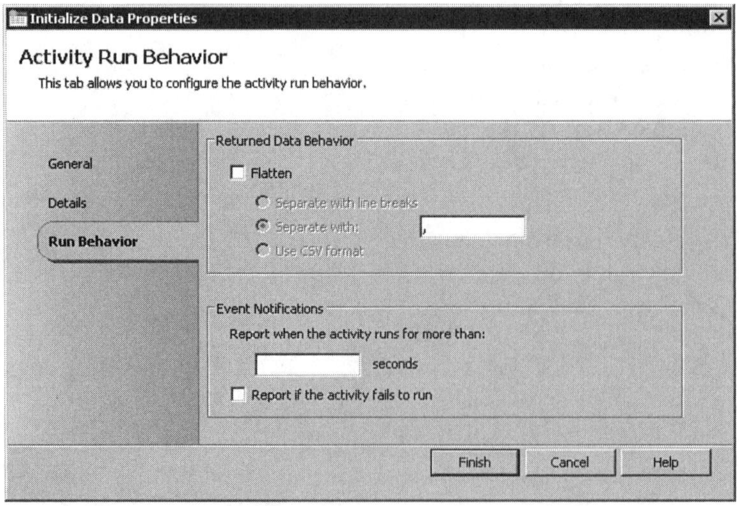

FIGURE 9.1 Run Behavior tab details.

- **Returned Data Behavior:** When your activity has a multivalue output, the published data is passed as multiple individual items on the Orchestrator data bus. Selecting the **Flatten** option flattens all values into a single delimited value. These are the available separators:
  - Use line breaks
  - Specify a character as a separator
  - Use CSV format
- **Event Notifications:** Some activities might be expected to run for a period of time, but for others, this might indicate that the action is failing. You can use the **Event Notifications** setting to send an platform event for delayed activity execution. You can define the number of seconds to wait for completion of the activity; after the specified time is exceeded, a platform event then is sent to report the delay. You can also choose whether to generate a platform event if the activity fails to run.

CAUTION: USING EVENT NOTIFICATIONS

Setting event notifications does not stop the activity from executing after the specified time; it only triggers an event.

Runbook Control Activities

Runbook Control activities are activities used exclusively to control the start and data flow in your runbooks. These include actions to start runbooks, bind runbooks together, and pass data between different runbooks in a workflow. Figure 9.2 shows the activities included in this category, and the following sections describe them.

FIGURE 9.2 Runbook Control category of activities.

9

Initialize Data Activity

The **Initialize Data** activity can be used to start a runbook. This activity can be a simple initiation of the runbook that needs no external information, or you can specify start parameters for the activity (see Figure 9.3). Users are prompted to provide values for these parameters when they start the runbook. You can start runbooks manually, use another runbook to start them, or have the web service trigger them. Consider the characteristics of this activity:

- The activity is placed as the starting point of the runbook.
- The Details tab specifies parameters that the runbook needs.
- This activity enables you to pass data between runbooks.

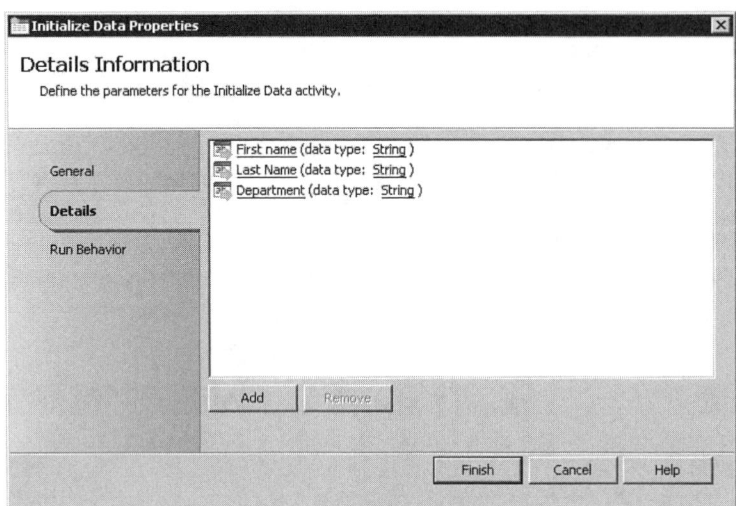

FIGURE 9.3 **Initialize Data** activity details.

Figure 9.3 displays the Details tab of the **Initialize Data** activity. Here you can specify the input parameters for executing the runbook; these can be string or integer values. You can manage the parameters by using the Add and Remove buttons or clicking the underlined text.

Invoke Runbook

The **Invoke Runbook** activity triggers a runbook that was previously specified in the activity's settings. This activity can utilize two other activities in this category: Data can be transferred to the **Initialize Data** activity and returned by the **Return Data** activity of the invoked runbook.

Figure 9.4 displays an example of the Details tab for the **Invoke Runbook** activity. Here a runbook named "Username generator" is specified that contains an **Initialize Data** activity requiring three parameters as input for execution. The following information is useful in configuring the **Invoke Runbook** activity:

- **Runbook:** Use the ellipsis (...) button to browse for the runbook you want to invoke.
- **Invoke by Path:** Select this to force the activity to invoke the runbook by the specific path and name. If you select this, you cannot move the runbook that is invoked to another location without reconfiguring this activity.

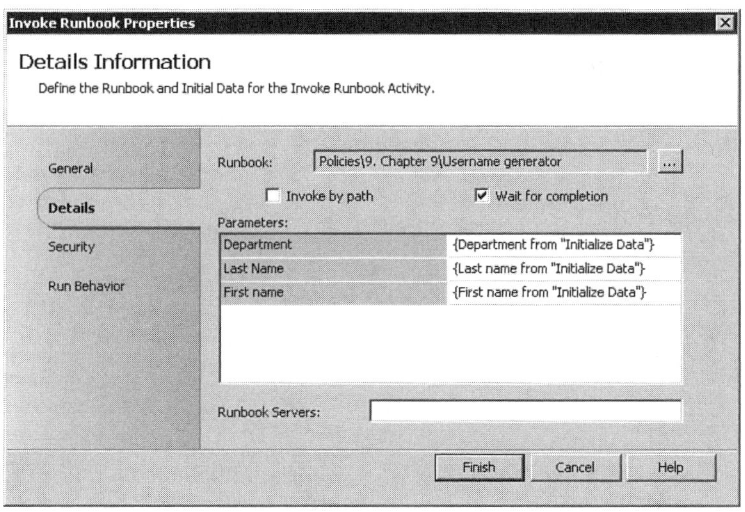

FIGURE 9.4 Sample **Invoke Runbook** Details tab.

- **Wait for completion:** Select this to force the invoking runbook to wait until the invoked runbook is completed. The invoking activity remains in the running state during execution of the invoked runbook.

NOTE: HOW WAIT FOR COMPLETION WORKS

When the Wait for completion option is checked in the **Invoke Runbook** activity, invoked runbooks execute in serial without concurrency.

- **Parameters:** A value can be specified for each parameter when the invoked runbook starts with an **Initialize Data** activity configured with input parameters. You can use subscriptions on published data to assign the values dynamically.
- **Runbook servers:** This property is equivalent in functionality to the Runbook Servers tab in the runbook's properties. It overrides those settings and also global settings. You can specify a list of runbook servers, each separated by a semicolon (;). The order specified in the list is the order used to execute the runbook; only runbook servers identified in this property will be used for execution. As an example, if there are three runbook servers and only "server1;server2" is specified, "server3" is never used even if the specified servers are offline.

You can require an optional security account to invoke the runbook; this is specified on the activity's Security tab. The data that the invoked runbook returns is defined as part of the runbook configuration. The values of this returned data are populated by the **Returned Data** activity in the invoked runbook.

Consider some usage scenarios for the **Invoke Runbook** activity:

- Trigger a related runbook to perform a specific action.
- Use this activity to split large runbook workflows into separate runbooks that each perform a specific action, using all of them together to complete the desired automation.
- Send input to trigger a runbook with variable data that is enumerated in the invoking runbook.

For additional information about the **Invoke Runbook** activity and its usage, refer to Chapter 8, "Advanced Runbook Concepts."

Return Data

The **Return Data** activity enables you to configure nested workflows. Published data of the invoked runbook is published back to the invoking runbook, which subsequent activities in the invoking runbook then can use. Configuration is a two-step procedure. First you configure the runbook to publish the data; then your runbook must use the **Return Data** activity to populate the values for the published data.

Figure 9.5 shows the Returned Data tab in the runbook properties. Here the UserName generator runbook is configured to return UserName when it completes. Figure 9.6 shows the Details tab for the **Return Data** activity to configure a new user account. The UserName value is populated in the invoked runbook by an output of an activity.

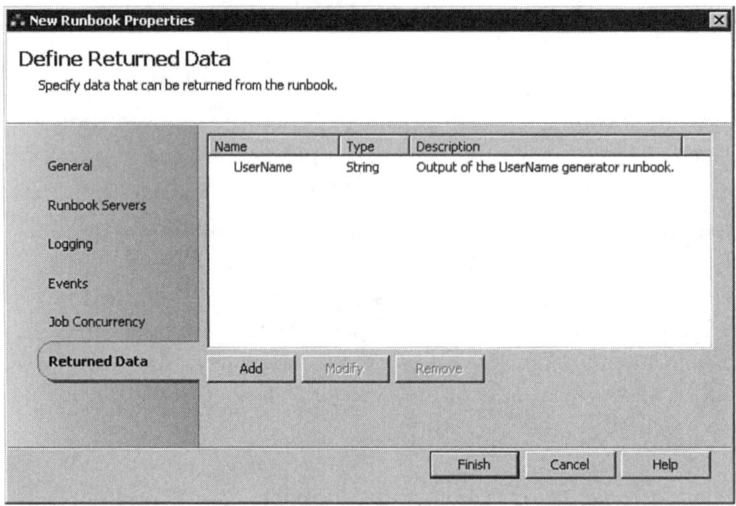

FIGURE 9.5 Returned Data tab for a runbook.

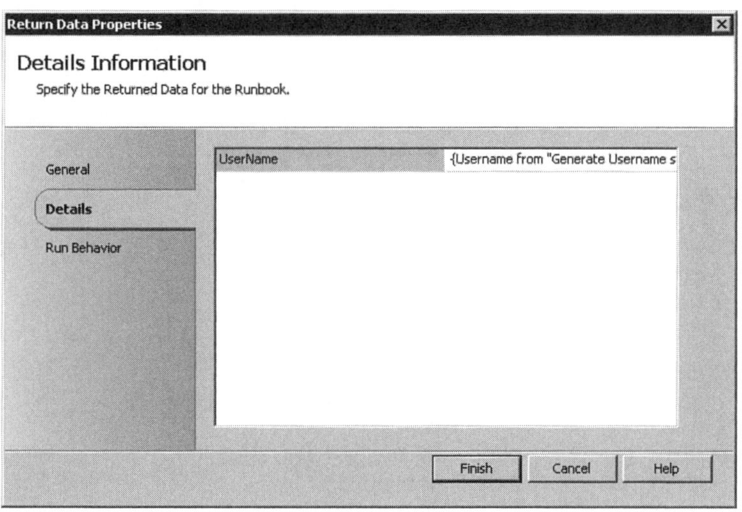

FIGURE 9.6 Return Data Details tab.

NOTE: FRIENDLY DATA PROPERTY NAMING

One of Orchestrator's features is the capability to use friendly names and include descriptions. This example, however, uses "UserName" because it reflects the username Active Directory property that is generated.

Junction Activity

Figure 9.7 shows an example of the Details tab for the **Junction** activity. This activity has the following general uses:

- Place it at various points within a runbook to allow two or more branches to join.
- Determine which of the incoming runbook branches can republish its data to downstream activities.
- Truncate all incoming runbook branch published data (using the <None> option in Figure 9.7).
- The timing mechanism ("wait" functionality) within a runbook allows multiple branches to converge and wait until all branch data has arrived.

For additional information on the **Junction** activity and its usage, refer to Chapter 8.

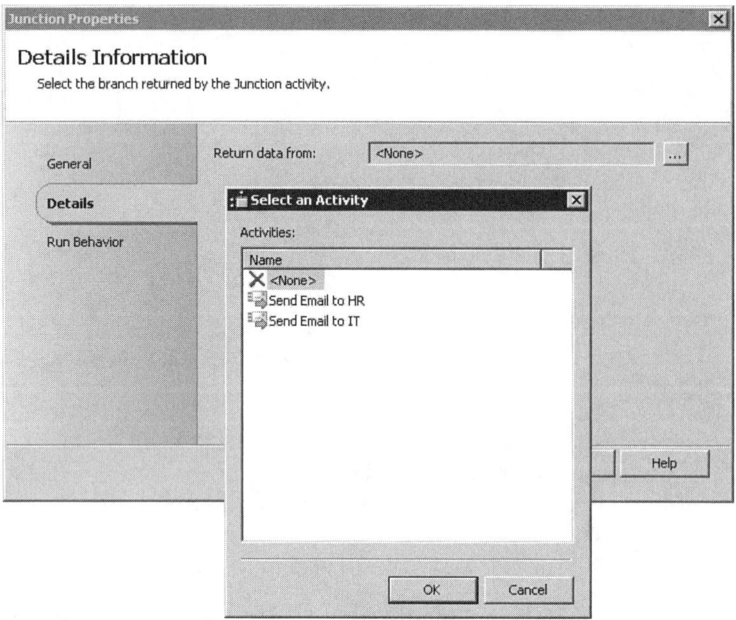

FIGURE 9.7 **Junction** activity Details tab.

System Activities Category

System activities include activities that run system commands and extensibility activities. Actions by System activities include interacting with the system services, monitoring SNMP traps, and saving event logs. The extensible activities allow you to extend functionality by running embedded scripts or code. The capability to run scripts or integrate your own code in the runbook creates opportunities in different scenarios:

- When you need to perform an action in the runbook and no activity fulfills the requirement, you can integrate scripts or code with the extensible activities.
- You can reuse existing scripts or code in your runbooks. You can take advantage of integrating existing work in the runbooks you are creating.

Figure 9.8 shows the activity list included in the System category.

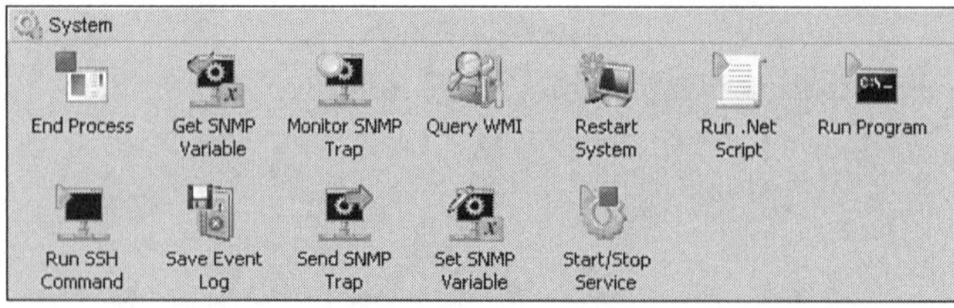

FIGURE 9.8 System category of activities.

Run .Net Script

Run .Net Script is one of the extensible activities in the System category. It offers the capability to execute scripts or code. This is a powerful activity and supports four types of scripts:

- C#
- JScript
- PowerShell
- VB.NET

The **Run .NET script** activity uses the scripting API to execute the scripts against the target specified system. The intelligence of this activity lies in the script specified in the Details tab. The output of the activity is the script output, and it can be published on the data bus for further use by the activities that follow.

Figure 9.9 shows an example of the Details tab for the **Run .Net Script** activity. Here the activity is configured to execute a PowerShell script that counts the running services on the specified system. The services list is generated and filtered by the "Running" status, and the output of the script is the count of running services. This is the script:

```
$RunningServices = Get-Service * |  WHERE{$_.Status -eq "Running"}
$ServicesCount = $RunningServices.Count
$ServicesCount
```

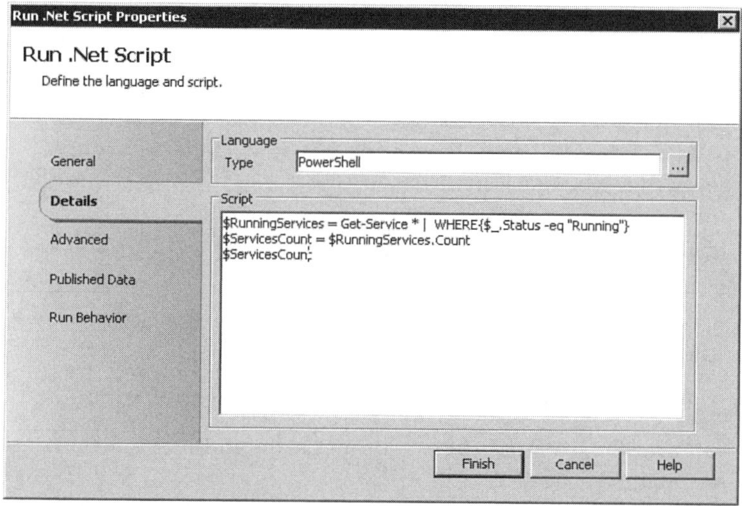

FIGURE 9.9 Details tab of the **Run .Net Script** activity.

The data the script returns is ServicesCount and must be specified on the Published Data tab. A published data variable must be created with the same variable name (without the *$* sign) as used in the script (see Figure 9.10), where a pop-up is used to create the entry.

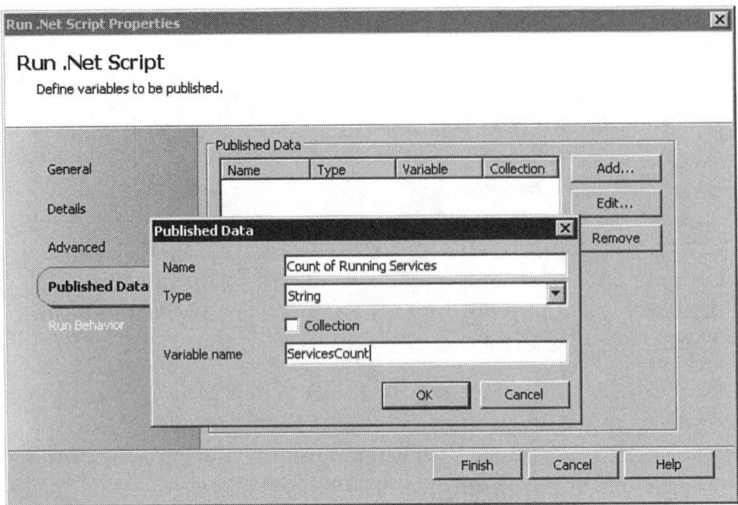

FIGURE 9.10 **Run .Net Script** Published Data tab.

The Details tab for the **Run .Net Script** activity contains these options:

- **Language Type:** This pick list specifies the type of script to be executed. The options are C#, JScript, PowerShell, and VB.NET.
- **Script:** The Script field configures the script that will be executed. The script syntax varies based on the scripting language selection. For C# and VB.NET, declaration of the published data–specific variables is handled on the Published Data tab; other variables need to be declared in the usual manner.

No option exists to specify security credentials on the **Run .Net Script** activity. This activity runs under the service account context, and you must verify that the account has the authority to access resources or perform the actions defined in the script. You can create a specific security context in the script.

The Published Data tab for the **Run .NET Script** activity has these configuration options:

- **Name:** Name of the data the activity publishes. You can create multiple published data items with different names.
- **Type:** Options are Date/Time, String, and Integer. These must be the same as the returned data in the script.

- **Variable name:** Field used to configure the name of the variable from the script to be referenced as published data. In the sample PowerShell script for counting running services, this field is the variable name from the script without the preceding *$* vcharacter, shown in Figures 9.9 and 9.10. If the variable is a collection, it creates List<T>, where T is the Type you select on the form.

Using the Advanced tab of the **Run .Net Script** activity, you can configure namespaces and references. This is possible only when the scripting type is set to C# or VB.NET on the Details tab. You can specify these options on the Advanced tab of this activity:

- **Namespaces:** Add a namespace for each .NET namespace that will be used in your code. This enables you to call the code without using fully qualified names for each class in the script. The authors recommend adding the System namespace to every **Run .Net Script** activity.
- **References:** Assembly Reference(s) that the script requires can be added in this field. Each Assembly (DLL) Reference required by the script (noncommon) must be manually added by selecting the assembly file from the appropriate location on the server. Following the recommendation to add the System namespace, add the System.dll located in the Windows\Microsoft.NET\Framework\<.NET Version> folder to this field.

Figure 9.11 shows an example of the Advanced tab for the **Run .Net Script** activity.

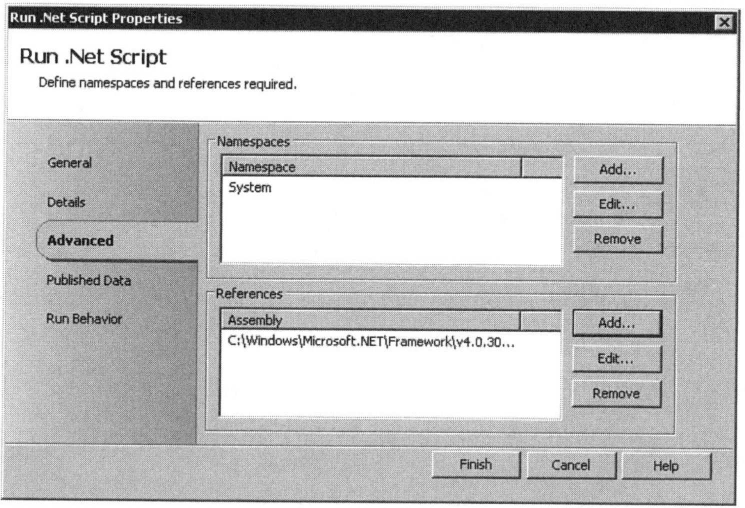

FIGURE 9.11 Advanced tab for the **Run .Net Script** activity.

Using Run Program

The **Run Program** activity executes a program or command on any computer in your environment. You can configure command-line arguments to control the command. **Run Program** can execute any program or command that is locally available on the specified computer; it is based on the PSExec utility (http://technet.microsoft.com/en-us/sysinternals/bb897553.aspx) and executes processes on a remote system. Execution can be interactive for the user or can run in the background. Your configuration of the activity must be the same as when you run the program or command from the Windows Run dialog box or the Windows command prompt. If you plan to use multiple **Run Program** activities in your runbook, it is best to change the icon of the activity on the Alternate Icon tab of the activity's properties, to improve readability.

An example of usage is to initiate a backup on remote systems by running the Windows internal backup application. Figure 9.12 shows an example of executing a program (in this case, the backup application) on the specified computer.

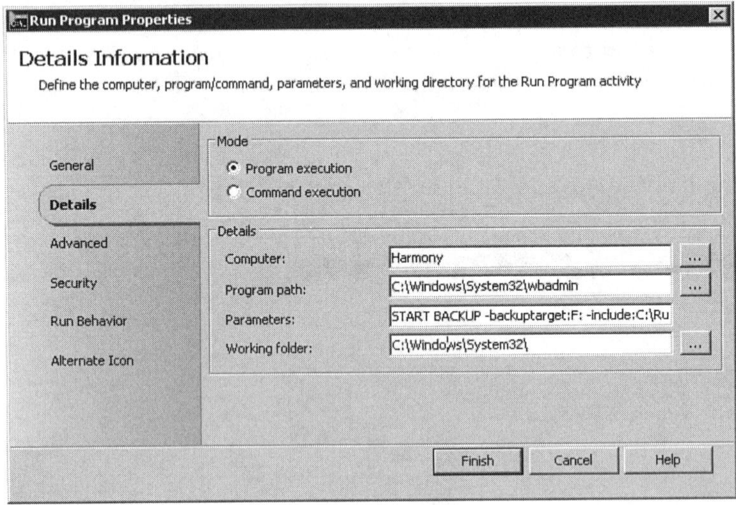

FIGURE 9.12 Details tab for the **Run Program** activity.

The Details tab of the **Run Program** activity has these options:

- **Mode:** Runs a program or command (use the ellipsis buttons to browse and select the program or command details):
  - **Program execution:** Runs a program on the specified computer.
  - **Command execution:** Indicates that a command should be run on the specified computer.
- **Computer:** Specifies the system where the program or command will be executed. You can either specify the value manually or subscribe to published data to specify the value.

- **Program Path/Command:** Gives the full path to the program or command you want to run. The label of this field changes with the Mode selected:
    - When Program execution is selected, the label **Program path** appears. The full path to the location of the program must be specified. Parameters can be added in the Parameters field.
    - When Command execution is selected, the label **Command** appears. You must specify the path to the Command line and command-line arguments on the same line.
- **Parameters:** Configures the parameters to be used during program execution.
- **Working folder:** Specifies the folder where the program or command will be executed on the specified computer. The program or command that the activity executes is behaving as if it is executed from the working folder.

NOTE: PROGRAM VERSUS COMMAND EXECUTION

In Program mode, the application is executed directly. This is different from Command mode, in which the application is executed as an argument to a command prompt (cmd.exe /c *<command>*). The intent of Command mode is to execute commands built into the Windows Command Prompt shell.

The **Run Program** Advanced tab gives you the option to control the execution of the activity and to specify a Run as account for execution. Figure 9.13 shows the default settings for the Advanced tab.

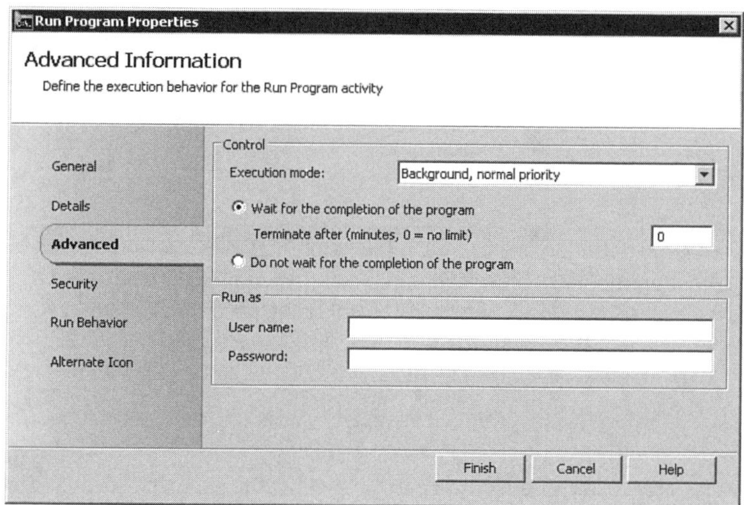

FIGURE 9.13 **Run Program** Advanced tab.

The Advanced tab for the **Run Program** activity has these options:

- **Execution mode:** This drop-down selection enables you to choose from the different execution modes:
    - **Interactive:** Use this option to display the user interface on the computer where the program or command is run.
    - **Background, normal priority:** Select this option to run the program or command in the background without a user interface, with the process priority set to normal.
    - **Background, low priority:** Select this option to run the program or command in the background without a user interface, with the process priority set to low. The authors recommend testing the program execution because some programs might not function correctly using this execution mode.
- **Execution behavior:** Execution behavior is configured by selecting the Wait/Do not Wait radio buttons. Here are the available options:
    - **Wait for the completion of the program:** Select this if you need to wait until the program or command execution finishes before moving to the next activity. If you choose to wait for completion of the program, you can specify an optional termination timeout value. Timeout value is specified in minutes; use the value **0** to indicate that the **Run Program** activity waits indefinitely. If the time expires and the execution is not complete, the activity shuts down the program or command and reports failure.
    - **Do not wait for the completion of the program:** This option causes the activity to just execute the program or command and continue with the next activity in the runbook. Published data will not be available for the next runbook.
- **Run as:** This field configures the Run as credentials to be used for the command. This functionality is similar to choosing Run as administrator or Run as different user in the right-click menu for program execution.

TIP: RUN PROGRAM EXECUTION MODE

In most cases, program execution mode is set to the default of Background, normal priority. Interactive mode is functional on Windows Server 2003 but disabled by default on later versions of Windows Server. When executing a workflow, letting users interact with the runbook is not advisable. This could break the chain of activities or introduce human mistakes.

The **Run Program** activity has a Security Credentials tab to specify the security context for the activity. Do not confuse this tab with the Run as configuration that can be made on the Advanced tab. The **Run Program** activity has two security configurations:

- The Security Credentials tab represents the context under which the activity will execute and interact with the target computer. This account is used for accessing the share and establishing a named pipe connection.
- The Run as fields on the Advanced tab represent the user credentials that will be utilized to execute the program or command on the specified computer.

About Query WMI

The **Query WMI** activity provides the functionality to execute WMI queries against specified computers. The activity specifies the target computer and the WMI query statement. The output is a string; for some scenarios, another activity must translate this string to get the required value. This output is automatically published to the data bus and is available for parsing and/or usage by the next activities in the runbook.

Using the **Query WMI** activity, you can configure the different WMI query options and the security context wherein the query is executed. Figure 9.14 shows an example of the Details tab for the **Query WMI** activity. In this figure, the activity is configured to execute a WMI query call against the `root\cimv2` namespace on the Harmony server. The WMI query is:

```
SELECT State FROM WIN32_Service
```

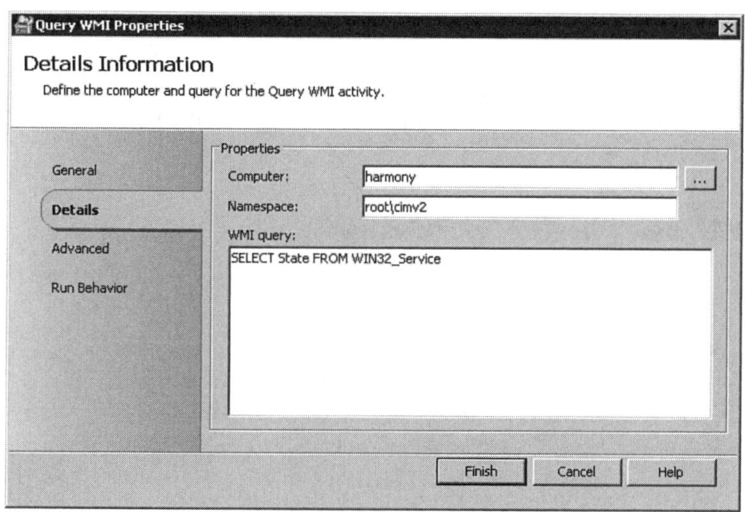

FIGURE 9.14 Details tab for the **Query WMI** activity.

The Details tab for the **Query WMI** activity has three options:

- **Computer:** Use this field to configure the target computer where the WMI query will be executed.

9

- **Namespace:** The Namespace field configures the namespace for the WMI query to be executed. The namespace entered must be available on the target computer.
- **WMI query:** This field configures the WMI query. The WMI query entered in this field must correspond with the namespace entered.

Start/Stop Service

The **Start/Stop Service** activity can start, stop, pause, or restart a Windows service on a specified computer. Indicate the action by selecting one of the available radio buttons. You can specify the execution details on the Details tab of the activity. The Details tab has these available options:

- **Action:** Options are Start service, Stop service, Pause service, and Restart service. If the service is already in the state of the selected action, the action is ignored. A stopped service that receives the restart action from the activity will be started.
- **Computer:** This can be a hard-coded value, a subscription on published data, a variable value, or a computer group.
- **Service:** This is the name of the service on which you need to execute the action.
- **Parameters:** Provide the parameters required to interact with the service.
- **Action must complete in less than:** Specify the maximum amount of time in which the action must complete. The value is specified in minutes or hours.

Figure 9.15 shows the activity configured to restart the World Wide Web Publishing Service on the Harmony computer. Use the Security tab to specify the security account used for executing the activity.

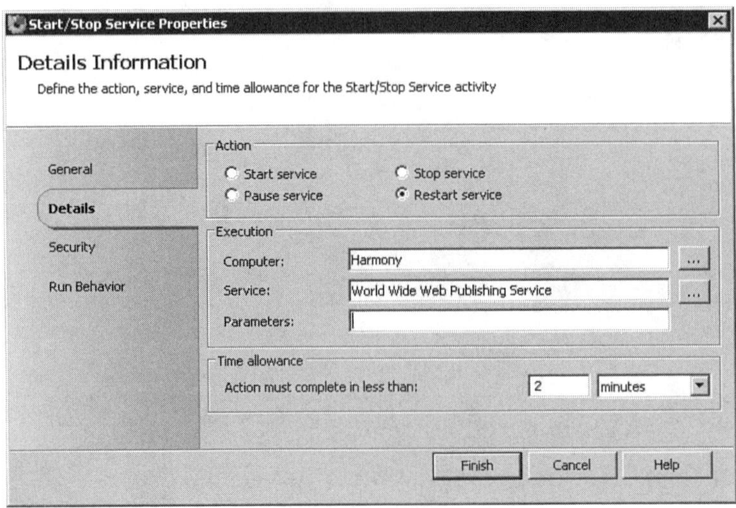

FIGURE 9.15 Details tab for the **Start/Stop Service** activity.

End Process

You can use the **End Process** activity to end processes that are running on the runbook server or on a remote computer. The activity returns a success condition if the specified process ends successfully or the process is not running. The Details tab has these options:

- **Computer:** This can be a hard-coded or generic value. Generic values can be a subscription on published data, a variable value, or a computer group.
- **Process:** Provide the name or process ID of the process that you want to stop with the activity.
- **Options:**
  - **End all instances:** Select this option to end all processes that match the process you specified when multiple instances are found.
  - **Fail if there is more than one instance:** Select this option to fail the activity if it finds more than one process matching the name you specified.
- **Terminate in:** Specify the number of seconds to wait for the process to be shut down. If the time is exceeded, the activity will stop the process.

Figure 9.16 shows an example in which the mmc.exe process is stopped using the **End Process** activity. All instances are ended with the selected option. On the Security tab, you can specify the account used to execute the activity on the specified computer.

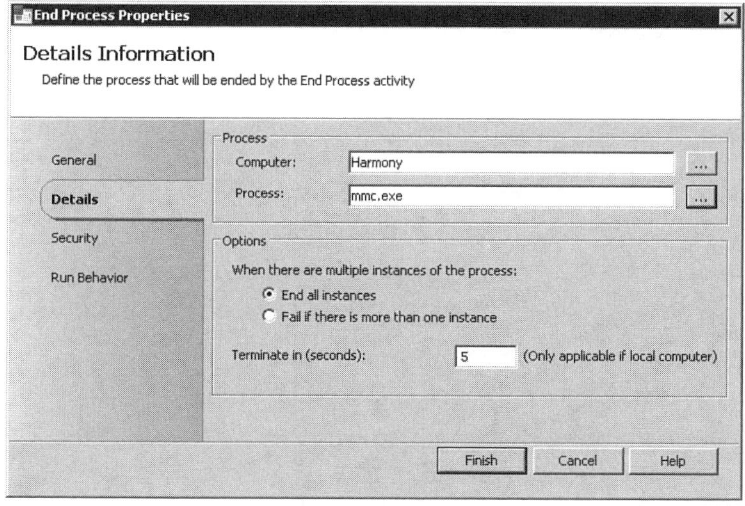

FIGURE 9.16 Details tab for the **End Process** activity.

Restart System

The **Restart System** activity can restart a computer on your network. This activity can wait for the applications to shut down gracefully or can be configured to forcefully shut down any running applications. You can send a message to notify users that the server will be restarting.

You might use the **Restart System** activity, for example, when an application has a high memory consumption that can be remedied only by restarting the system, or in an automated patching deployment that requires a reboot.

Use the Security tab to specify a security account for the activity.

The Details tab (see Figure 9.17) has the following options:

- **Computer:** This can be a hard-coded value. The authors recommend using generic values such as a subscription on published data, a variable value, or a computer group.
- **Message:** This field specifies the message displayed to users of the computer before it is shut down.
- **Wait before rebooting (seconds):** This is the number of seconds after sending the message before the system will shut down.
- **Force applications to close:** Select this option to forcefully shut down any application that is running when the computer is restarted.

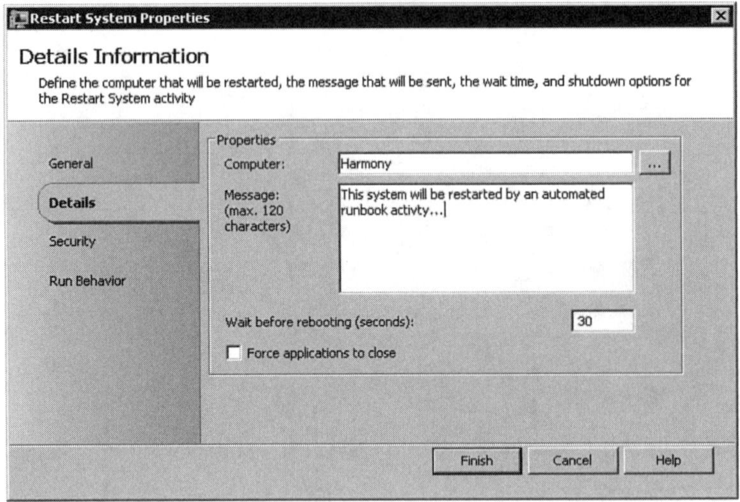

FIGURE 9.17 Details tab for the **Restart System** activity.

Save Event Log

This activity saves event log entries from a system and stores the information in a file. The log information can be used later for troubleshooting or other actions. You can specify the event log, types of events, and a filter. The event log entries are saved to a delimited text file in a format and location you specify.

The **Save Event Log** activity has tabs with the following configuration options:

- On the Details tab in Figure 9.18, you can specify the computer, the event log, and the fields to include in the saved log file. Available fields are Event ID, Source, Category, Description, Type, Computer, and Date/time.

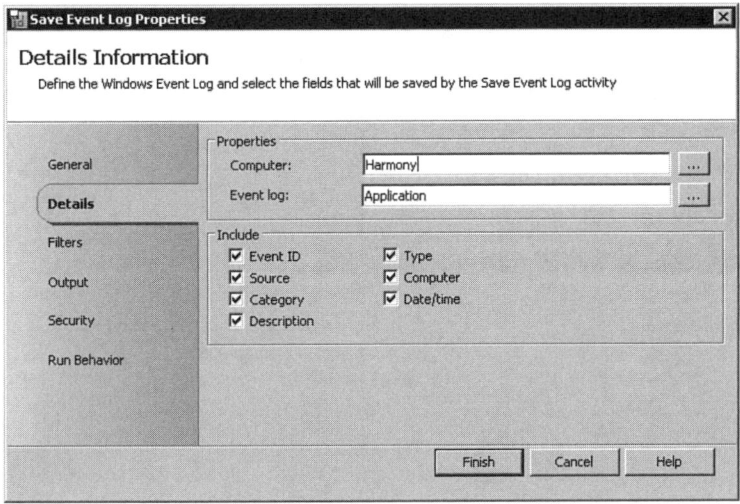

FIGURE 9.18 Details tab for the **Save Event Log** activity.

- The Filters tab (see Figure 9.19) enables you to specify values for the event log fields to query. As an example, if you select to filter on **Type** and select **Error** as the value, only error event log entries are saved in the log file.
- On the Output tab (see Figure 9.20), specify the filename where the entries are saved. You can specify the action to take if a file already exists with that name. This is useful when you automatically generate filenames for this activity because you can specify options to create a new file, append a file, or overwrite the existing file. You can specify Fail if you require specific naming of the output file. The format can be CSV, TAB, or custom delimited (you specify the custom character). Use the Create column headings option to add heading information to the file.

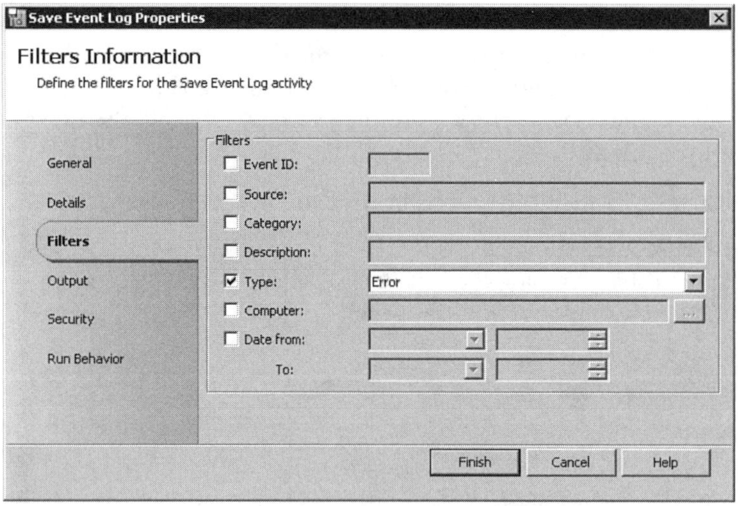

FIGURE 9.19 Filters tab for the **Save Event Log** activity.

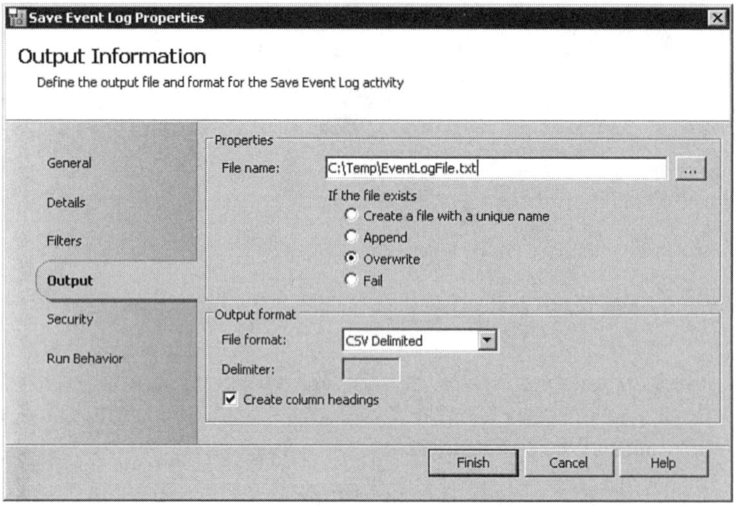

FIGURE 9.20 Output tab for the **Save Event Log** activity.

Run SSH Command

The **Run SSH Command** activity opens an SSH connection to a remote server and runs shell commands on that server. **Run SSH Command** offers the capability to execute programs and commands using specified parameters against non-Windows host computers. The activity is based on PuTTY beta .61 and can run any command in a secure shell. Whether the CLI is called directly from **Run SSH Command** or the activity executes a preconfigured script containing CLI commands, the activity will execute and capture the output. This output is automatically published to the data bus and is available for parsing and/or usage by the next activities.

Figure 9.21 shows an example of the Details tab for this activity. Here the configuration is set to execute an **ls** command against the loopback IP address (**127.0.0.1**) on port **22.** These values are defaults; you can adjust them to specify the computer and port. If the target computer is visible by browsing, you can use the ellipsis to select the computer; otherwise, this value should be retrieved by subscription or be made dynamic by using a variable or computer group.

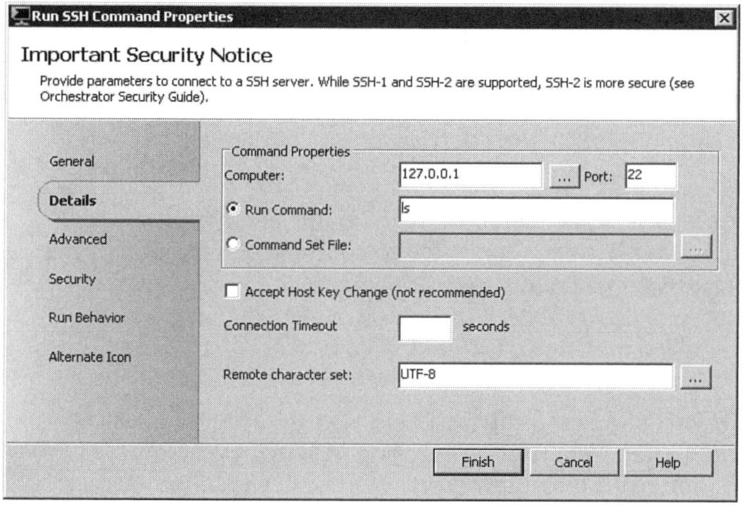

FIGURE 9.21 Details tab for the **Run SSH Command** activity.

You can set the following options on the Details tab for the **Run SSH Command** activity:

- **Computer:** You can configure the target non-Windows host computer where the command or program will be executed. This can be a hard-coded value, a subscription on published data, a variable value, or a computer group.
- **Port:** Configure the connection port for the target computer where the SSH command will be executed.
- **Run Command:** Select this option to configure the command or series of commands (separated by a semicolon [;]) to execute after the connection is established.
- **Command Set File:** Use this option to configure the location for the file that contains the set of commands that will be executed. This file should contain only commands native to the shell scripting language on the target non-Windows host computer.

- **Accept Host Key Change:** Select this check box to accept host key changes. The authors do not recommend using this option in a production environment. This setting instructs the runbook to accept any change in a server, even malicious changes.
- **Connection Timeout:** The timeout threshold can be specified as an integer value (in seconds). If no integer is entered or you enter 0, no timeout occurs and you might need to stop the activity manually.

The Advanced tab specifies the account to authenticate to the target host computer. The tab has these available options:

- **Authentication Username:** This field specifies the username to authenticate against the target computer. You can either use a Username/Password or Username/Key File combination for authentication.
- **Password:** Select this option to configure the password for authentication to the computer.
- **Key File and Passphrase:** Select this option to use a key file and passphrase to authenticate to the computer. Two fields are used to configure the location of the key file and associated passphrase for authentication.

SNMP Activities

The System activity category includes four SNMP activities that you can use to extend the functionality of your Orchestrator runbooks. The group of activities can query, set, monitor, or send SNMP information to allow quick and easy integration of target systems that send or receive SNMP traps. Figure 9.22 highlights the four activities in the Orchestrator Runbook Designer activity library.

FIGURE 9.22 Orchestrator SNMP activities.

Configuration of these activities depends on the target system that sends and receives SNMP traps. The SNMP activities are compatible with SNMP versions SNMPv1, SNMPv2c, and SNMPv3. You can use these SNMP activities in your runbooks:

- **Get SNMP Variable:** Based on a specified management information base (MIB), you can configure this activity to query and return the variable value associated with that MIB.

- **Monitor SNMP Trap:** You can configure this activity to monitor for an event (SNMP trap) on a specified port or use the Microsoft SNMP Trap Service. You can filter the traps by Host, Enterprise Identifier, Generic Identifier, Specific Identifier, and/or Activity Identifiers.
- **Send SNMP Trap:** Use this activity to send SNMP events to available monitoring applications listening for SNMP events. By using an enterprise identifier of a known network device, you can send SNMP traps on behalf of a network device in your environment.
- **Set SNMP Variable:** Configure this activity to update an SNMP variable, specified by its MIB, on a network device.

Scheduling Category

The Scheduling category includes two activities: one to invoke a runbook at a scheduled time and a second to verify that a runbook can run at its scheduled time. The next sections discuss these activities.

Monitor Date/Time Activity

You can specify a time or time interval on the **Monitor Date/Time** activity to invoke your runbook. This activity is useful when you need to regularly run routines that do not rely on events in other systems. On the Details tab, in Figure 9.23, you can set the following options:

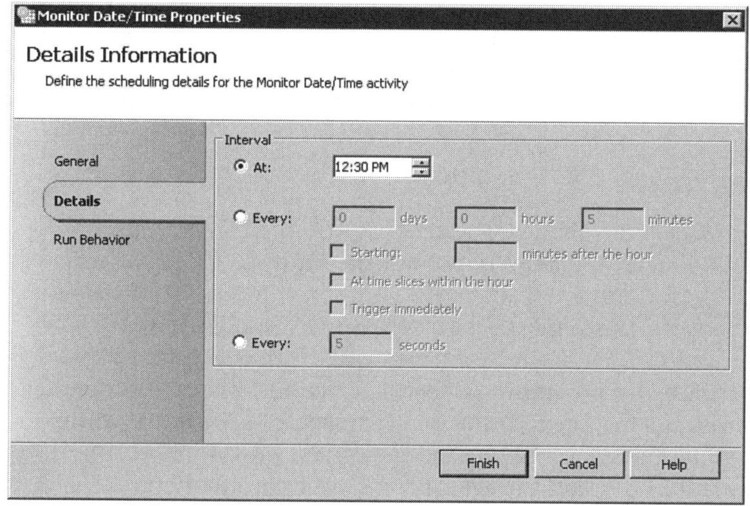

FIGURE 9.23 Details tab for the **Monitor Date/Time** activity.

- **At:** Specify an absolute time to trigger the runbook to execute. The **Monitor Date/Time** activity will be invoked every day at this time.
- **Every:** You can configure an interval on days, hours, and minutes for the runbook to run. This option includes additional options:
    - **Starting:** Configure the minutes after the hour to invoke the runbook. You can set this only when 0 minutes and at least 1 day or hour is specified for the interval.
    - **At time slices within the hour:** Select this option to invoke the runbook at times that are multiples of the minutes specified on the interval. This option is available only when 0 days and hours is specified on the interval. For example, if you specify 10 minutes, the runbook will be invoked at 10, 20, 30, and so on in each hour.
- **Trigger immediately:** The runbook is directly triggered after it is deployed.
- **Every:** On this interval, you can specify the number of seconds between each runbook execution.

Check Schedule

The **Check Schedule** activity is a validation action that checks runbook execution against a specified schedule. If the current time is between the configured intervals, the runbook is executed. The schedule lets you configure days of the week, days of the month, and the hours it is allowed to run the runbook. Chapter 6, "Using System Center 2012 Orchestrator," provides details on configuring schedules.

You can place this activity at the beginning of the runbook and configure it to use a specific schedule. Use the activity details to browse to the schedule template. The activity verifies this template and determines whether the runbook will run.

Monitoring Activities

The Monitoring category includes 12 activities. The actions performed are straightforward: They obtain information about the item or monitor the status of a specific item for the specified computer. These items are IP addresses, disk space, event logs, Internet applications, processes, or services. Customizing the activity is also straightforward: you specify the computer name and select from the available items on that system. Consider a scenario in which you are logging information to a specific drive and want to ensure that the drive is not filling up from the logging information. Here you can use the **Monitor Disk Space Usage** activity to monitor the free space of the drive and perform actions if the drive becomes full. Figure 9.24 displays the available monitoring activities.

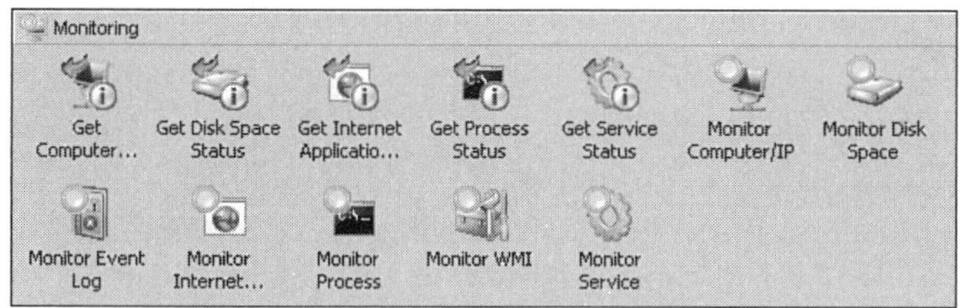

FIGURE 9.24 Monitoring category of activities.

A description of these activities follows:

- **Get Computer/IP Status:** Sends a ping to a remote computer or IP address and waits for a response. If a response arrives, the activity succeeds; if no response comes, the activity fails.
- **Get Disk Space Status:** Queries for disk space information on specified computers. The activity can retrieve the current amount of available disk space on a specified path.
- **Get Internet Application Status:** Queries the connectivity status for specified URLs. The availability check can be configured for a Web (HTTP), Email (SMTP), Email (POP3), FTP, DNS, or custom server.
- **Get Process Status:** Queries the status for a specified process on specified computers. The activity returns a status of failed if the specified process is not running.
- **Get Service Status:** Queries the status of specified services on specified computers. The service status is published after executing this activity.
- **Monitor Computer/IP:** Pings specified computers at a specified polling interval. A trigger condition can be configured based on whether the specified computer is reachable or unreachable.
- **Monitor Disk Space:** Queries the configured computer for disk space information at a specified polling interval. This activity invokes a runbook when the disk space on a computer passes the configured threshold. You can specify the free space threshold for a specific drive and test interval on the Details tab of this activity.
- **Monitor Event Log:** Invokes the runbook when new events match the configured event log filter. Event entries can be filtered from the specified event log, and successive runbooks can perform actions to correct the issue.
- **Monitor Internet Application:** Checks the connectivity status for specified URLs at a specified polling interval. Based on the configuration, a runbook is invoked upon success or failure.
- **Monitor Process:** Queries the status for a specified process on specified computers at a specified polling interval. You can set a trigger runbook condition on the started or stopped status that is returned.

- **Monitor Service:** Queries the status for the specified services on the specified computers at a specified polling interval. A trigger runbook condition can be set on a returned started or stopped/paused status.
- **Monitor WMI:** Invokes a runbook based on the returned result of the WMI event query specified in the activity. Keep in mind that a WMI event query is different from a standard WMI query. Consider this sample syntax for a simple notification query:

```
SELECT * FROM [EventClass] WITHIN [interval] WHERE TargetInstance ISA [object]
```

File Management

The File Management category includes 15 activities to manage files and folders at a specified location. The settings on the Details tab are specific for each activity's action. For example, when you use the **Monitor File** activity, you must specify the file location and define the triggers to execute the runbook. For the **Copy File** activity, on the other hand, you must configure the source and destination together with the copy options. The activities in this category are frequently used together with Text File Management activities. Figure 9.25 shows the File Management activities.

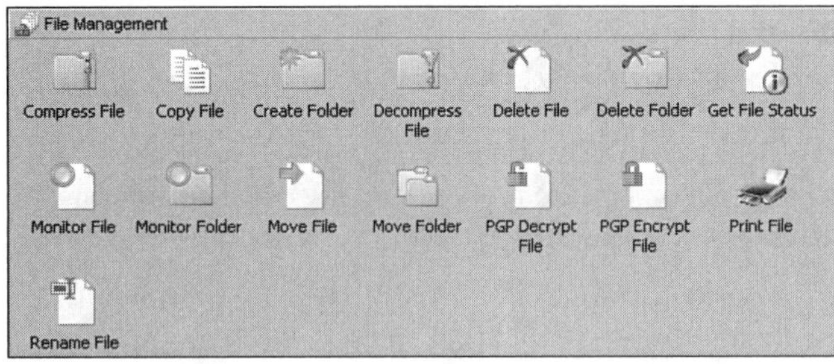

FIGURE 9.25 File Management category of activities.

Customization is simple, and the activity names are self-descriptive, making them easy to integrate into your runbooks. A description of the File Management activities follows:

- **Compress File:** This activity compresses files into zip archives. You specify a path to a file or folder that contains files and the destination location of the ZIP file.
- **Copy File:** You can use this activity to copy file(s) from one directory to another. You must specify a file or files (wildcards such as * and ? are accepted) as well as the destination folder. Optional settings for this activity can include duplicate file handling, file age filtering, and modified date attribute settings.
- **Create Folder:** Use this activity to create a new folder on a local drive or a network location. You must specify the new folder UNC path.

- **Decompress File:** This activity decompresses files contained in a ZIP file. You must specify the original location of the ZIP file and the destination folder. The file overwrite behavior option lets you select the activity to fail, overwrite, or create a new file with a unique name.
- **Delete File:** The **Delete File** activity deletes a file or a selection of files from a specified location. When specifying a file or files, you can use wildcards such as * and ?. File age filtering is optional.
- **Delete Folder:** This activity deletes an existing folder from a specified location. The path to the folder name is the only required information. You can optionally specify whether to delete only empty folders or to delete all files and subfolders at the specified location.
- **Get File Status:** Use this activity to verify the file status at the specified location. You can use wildcards such as * and ? to specify the file(s). Optionally, you can specify file age filtering. The published data from this activity includes much useful file-specific information, including but not limited to existence, extension, flags for read only, archive and hidden, date/times for accessed, modified and created, path and name, encoding type, size, and count.
- **Monitor File:** This activity monitors file changes in the configured folder and/or subfolders and triggers a runbook. You must specify the path to the file(s) you want to monitor. The filename specification can use wildcards such as * and ?.

  Filters can be configured on a number of file attribute filters, such as Accessed date/time, Archive flag, Compressed flag, Created date/time, File Name, Hidden flag, Location, Modified date/time, Owner, Read-only flag, and Size. A number of trigger filters also exist: creation, change, rename, and delete. The change trigger on the Trigger tab can be further filtered by file property changes: attributes, security, creation time, last access time, and last write time. Activity-specific optional configurations for this activity include recursive searching, filter options, and authentication.
- **Monitor Folder:** The **Monitor Folder** activity can invoke runbooks based on the triggers configured on this activity. You can specify the folder UNC path and file filters on the Details tab. You can set the trigger on the number of files or on the total file size of the files in the folder.
- **Move File:** You can use this activity to move file(s) from one folder to another. Specify a file or files (with wildcards such as * and ?) and the destination folder. Optionally, you can specify duplicate file handling, file age filtering, and modified date attribute settings.
- **Move Folder:** You can use this activity to move specified folders. Source and destination UNC paths are required.
- **PGP Decrypt File:** The **PGP Decrypt File** activity decrypts a file or an entire folder tree using a PGP key file and passphrase that you create. When you configure this activity to decrypt an entire folder, the folder tree is preserved.

- **PGP Encrypt File:** The **PGP Encrypt File** activity decrypts a file or an entire folder tree using a PGP key file and passphrase that you create. When you configure this activity to decrypt an entire folder, the folder tree is preserved. The activity supports DSS and RSA4 keys.
- **Print File:** The **Print File** activity prints text files to a printer that you specify.
- **Rename File:** You can use this activity to rename files on the specified location. Specify the UNC path to the source file, together with the destination location where you can specify a new name for the file. You can also include file age filtering, destination date setting, and overwrite actions.

Email Activities

Figure 9.26 shows the **Send Email** activity in the Email folder of the library. You can use this activity to send email messages through a runbook. This is the only activity in this category.

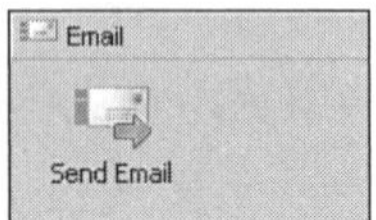

FIGURE 9.26 Email category of activities.

The **Send Email** activity sends an email message using standard SMTP protocol. Use the Details tab to specify the Subject, Recipients, Message, and (optional) attachments. You can configure the sender email address and the SMTP server for sending the email using the Connect tab. Optionally, you can specify priority, mail format, and the SMTP server connection account.

Figure 9.27 displays the Details tab for the activity. An overview of information you can specify follows:

- **Subject:** Specifies the email subject.
- **Recipients:** Configures email recipients. To add a recipient, select Add; this opens a dialog box where you can specify the email addresses of the recipients and the recipient type for each specified email address. You can modify these settings using the buttons by the Recipients field. You can edit the email address by double-clicking the address.
- **Message:** Configures the email message body. You can configure the mail format on the Advanced tab.
- **Attachments:** Specifies email attachments.

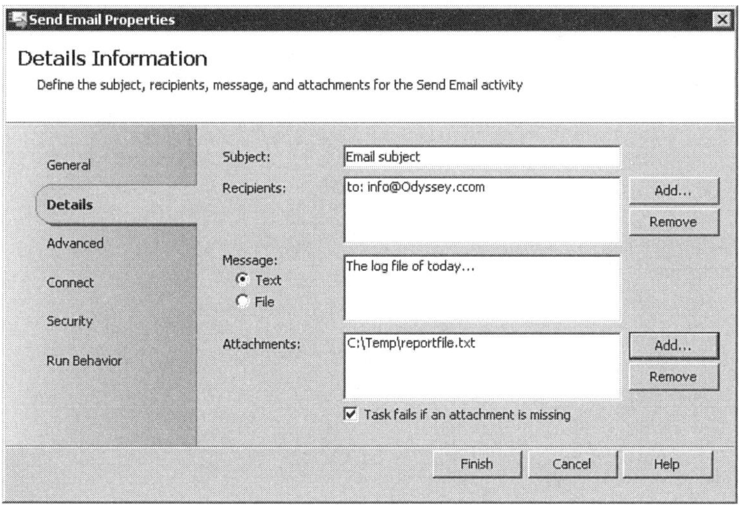

FIGURE 9.27 Details tab for the **Send Email** activity.

NOTE: MESSAGE CONTENT IN THE SEND EMAIL ACTIVITY

The authors do not recommend including more than 1MB of information in the message field. If more than 1MB of text is added in the message body, the activity can fail during initialization. To work around this, you can save the message content in a file and include the content as an attachment to the email.

Optional information such as priority and mail format is configured on the Advanced tab. You might need to use a different account to authenticate against the SMTP server; you can specify the account on the SMTP Authentication section of this tab. You can set the following optional information on the Advanced tab (see Figure 9.28):

- **Priority:** This drop-down configures the email priority; options are Normal, Low, and High.
- **Format:** This drop-down configures the email format; options are Rich Text, ASCII, and HTML.
- **SMTP authentication:** The credential fields (User Id, Password, and Domain) authenticate to the SMTP server (if specified).

The Connect tab has connection parameters for the **Send Email** activity that you can configure You need to specify these options to connect and send emails using this activity; Figure 9.29 shows an example.

- **Email address:** Specify the email account used to send the email via SMTP. This is also the reply-to address.
- **SMTP connection Computer and Port:** These fields configure the SMTP server and port used to send the email via SMTP.

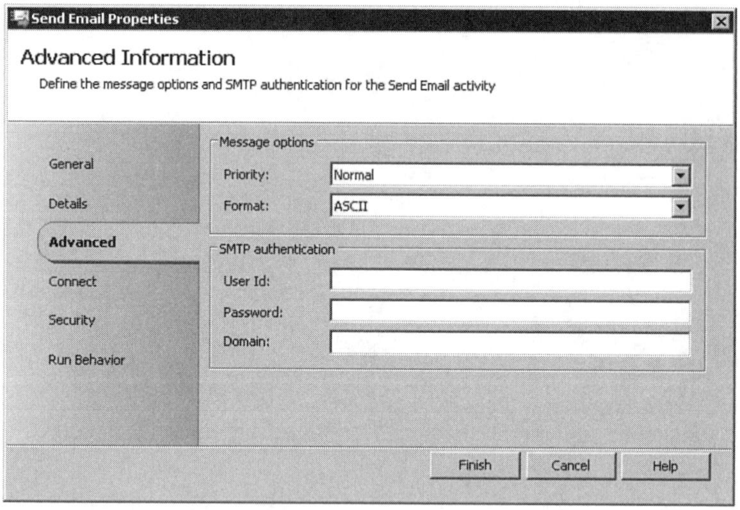

FIGURE 9.28 Advanced tab for the **Send Email** activity.

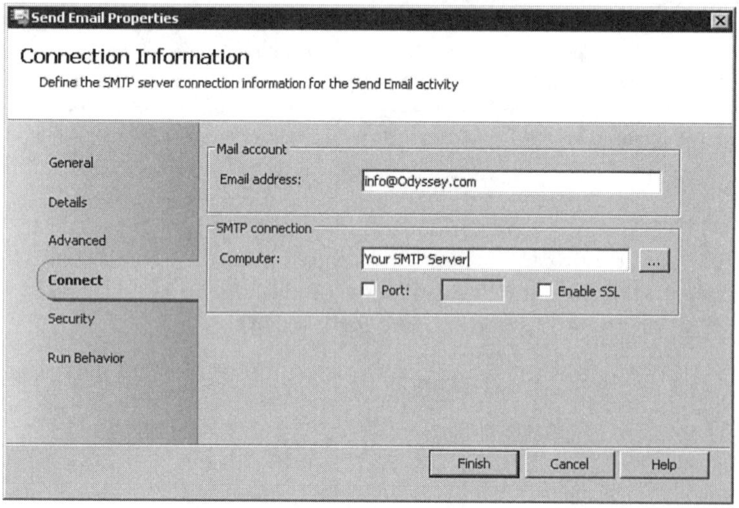

FIGURE 9.29 Connect tab for the **Send Email** activity.

Notification Activities

The Notification category (see Figure 9.30) includes activities that can create an entry in the application event log and post a message on the syslog server.

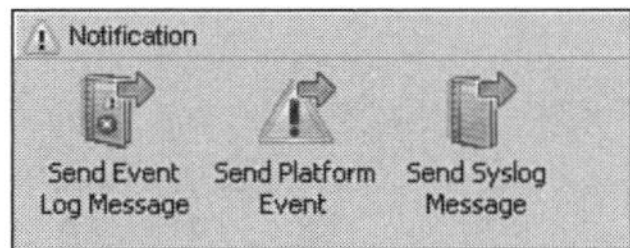

FIGURE 9.30 Notification category of activities.

Send Event Log Message

The **Event Log Message** activity enables you to create a Windows event log message as part of a runbook. You can use this action for error handling or to raise information in the event viewer that another system, such as System Center Operations Manager, can pick up. The **Send Event Log Message** has only one activity-specific tab: Details. The Details tab for the **Send Event Log Message** activity has these options:

- **Computer:** This field specifies the target Windows host computer where the event log message will be created.
- **Message:** This field specifies the Windows event log message details.
- **Severity:** This set of radio buttons configures the Windows event log message severity. Options are Information, Warning, and Error.

Figure 9.31 shows an example of the Details tab for this activity.

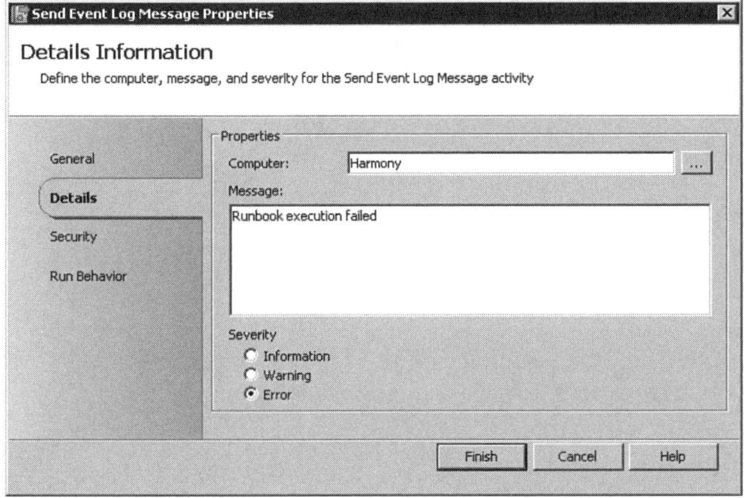

FIGURE 9.31 Details tab for the **Send Event Log Message** activity.

Send Platform Event

The **Send Platform Event** activity is useful during the development and test phases. The Details tab has these available options:

- **Type:** This drop-down specifies the type of platform event to be created. Options are Information, Warning, and Error.
- **Summary:** This field specifies the platform event summary and is limited to 200 characters.
- **Details:** This field specifies the platform event details and is limited to 2,000 characters.

Figure 9.32 shows an example of the Details tab for the **Send Platform Event** activity.

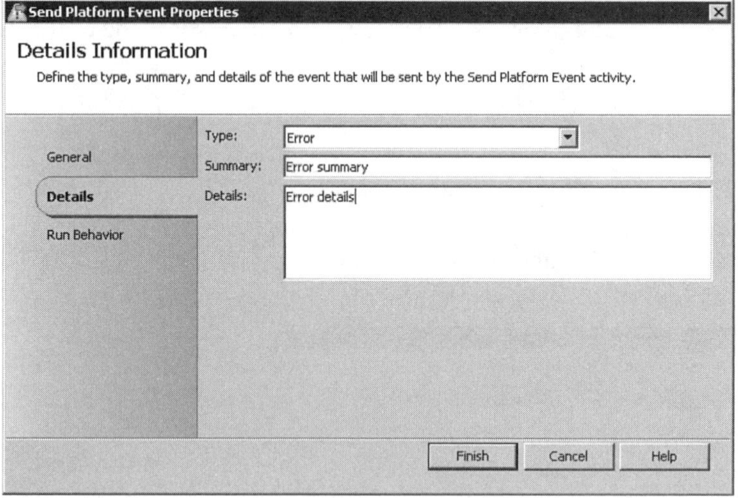

FIGURE 9.32 Details tab for the **Send Platform Event** activity.

Send Syslog Message

The **Send Syslog Message** activity creates a message on the syslog server you specified when configuring the activity. Figure 9.33 shows a sample Details tab.

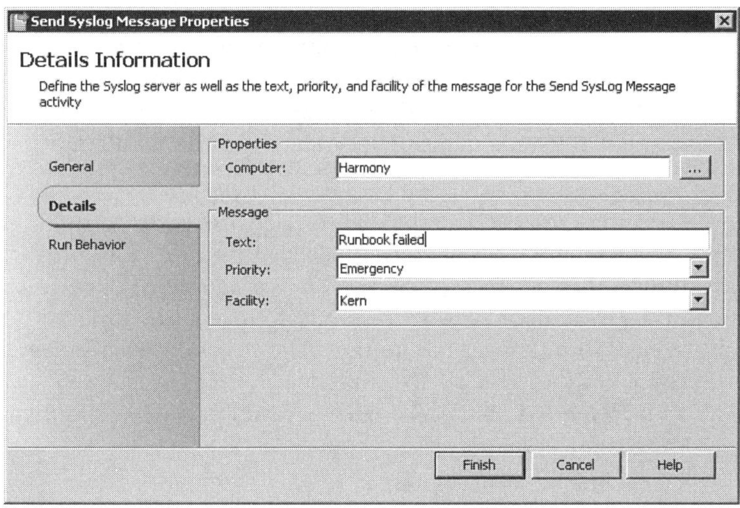

FIGURE 9.33 Details tab for the **Send Syslog Message** activity.

Utilities Category

The Utilities category includes various Orchestrator activities that can run specific actions for data manipulations and retrieval. The activities in this category provide actions to work with published data, manage counters, and create connections to use in your runbooks. Figure 9.34 displays the available activities.

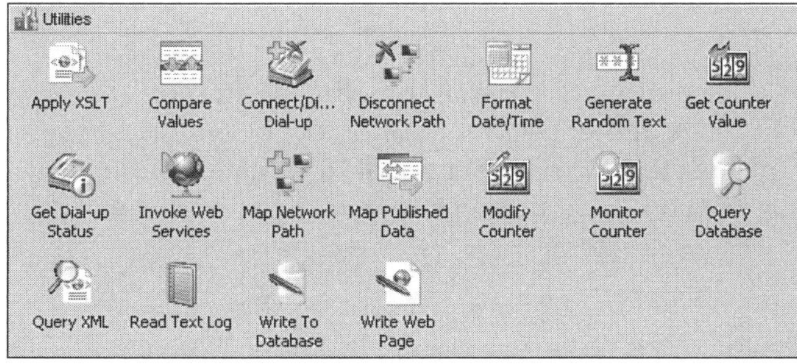

FIGURE 9.34 Utility category of activities.

Counters can keep track of events that the runbook detects. This differs from the counters specified in the Global Settings section of the Runbook Designer, which you can manage only by Orchestrator activities. Counter activities included in this library provide the functionality to get, modify, or monitor the counter value.

You can use the activities in this category to validate, transform, and write specified data to external sources. Keep in mind that out-of-the-box data filtering functionality is available in the parameter fields of these activities. Chapter 6 describes the available functions and regular expressions you can use to configure the correct parameter value. The activities in this category can compare values, format date/time values, and write to different data sources.

To create a connection to a data source, you can use the dial-up, network path, or web service connection activities. These activities enable you to specify the connection information and create the connection to the specific service. The dial-up and network path connections can be integrated in your runbook, and successive activities in the runbook can contact data sources and services through this connection. The **Invoke Web Services** activity connects to the web service and can execute the available methods of the web service. The output is based on the eXtended Markup Language (XML) payload configured on this activity. The **Query XML** activity can query the output.

Using Counters in Orchestrator

Counters are global settings that are available to all runbooks in the Orchestrator environment. The default value is set during initial configuration of a counter; you can manage this value only during runbook execution with the counter activities. You can use counter functionality in different ways: You can use it as an integer variable that is updated in your runbook based on the results of actions, or you can use it as a control value.

The counter value can be used as an integer variable counter value that is incremented or decremented by runbook activities. This functionality could be useful when you need to track the number of times an event occurs. As an example, you could use counters with a monitoring activity in which the counter increments each time an event is detected with that activity. Other activities or runbooks can execute actions if the counter value reaches a specific value.

You can also use the counter value as a control bit. For example, you might want to avoid parallel execution of runbooks. The counter activity is set on the beginning of the runbook to control the execution. It is set to **1** when the runbook is executed and returns to **0** at the end of the runbook. This lets you avoid having a runbook start if another instance or runbook is still busy.

The counters you configure are available for any runbook. This means that different runbooks can update the counters, which can result in undesired counter value modifications. You can avoid this by configuring counters that are dedicated to your runbook workflow and not mixing them with other runbooks that are executing different tasks. This lets you still use the counters in multiple runbooks, but they remain dedicated to the runbooks executing actions for the same purpose. You must control counter usage and you consider what occurs when multiple instances of a runbook are executed simultaneously. Verify that this does not conflict with your overall counter setup.

The following sections describe the Details tab for the different Counter activities.

Get Counter Value

The **Get Counter Value** activity retrieves the value of a counter and returns it as published data on the data bus. The Details tab of the activity specifies the counter you use on this activity. You can use this activity at various points within a runbook to get a counter value. The value of the counter is the output of the activity, and this information is published on the data bus.

Modify Counter

For every counter you want to update in your runbooks, you must use the **Modify Counter** activity. This activity can increment or decrement a counter value and reset it to its default value, or you can specify a value for the counter value. You can specify this configuration on the Details tab:

- **Counter:** Specify the counter in this field. Use the (...) button to navigate in the Counter dialog box for the correct counter.
- **Action:** Use this drop-down box to select the action you want to execute:
  - **Increment** the value of the counter
  - **Decrement** the value of the counter
  - **Set** the value of the counter to a specific value each time the activity is executed
  - **Reset** the value of the counter to the default value each time the activity is executed
- **Value:** You can specify the value for the increment, decrement, or set actions.

Figure 9.35 shows an example of the Details tab for the **Modify Counter** activity. Here the activity is configured to increment the Chapter9 counter by **10** every time the activity is executed.

Monitor Counter

You can use the **Monitor Counter** activity at the beginning of a runbook to monitor one or multiple counter values. After the counter value(s) have complied with the specified criteria, the monitor invokes the execution of the next activity in the runbook.

In the example in Figure 9.36, the **Monitor Counter** activity is set to monitor the Chapter9 counter for a value of **100**. If more conditions are configured on the activity, the AND condition is set between the specified criterion. Configuring the conditions is similar to configuring link filter conditions for your runbook. Click the underlined text to open a dialog box where you can specify or select the value. You can configure operators such as equals, not equal, is less than, is greater than, and others on the monitoring condition. You can adjust the default value of **0** to your needs.

The values found on the counter with this activity are automatically placed on the Orchestrator data bus as published data. This published data can be used in link filtering to determine the flow of the runbook or as input data for the next activities.

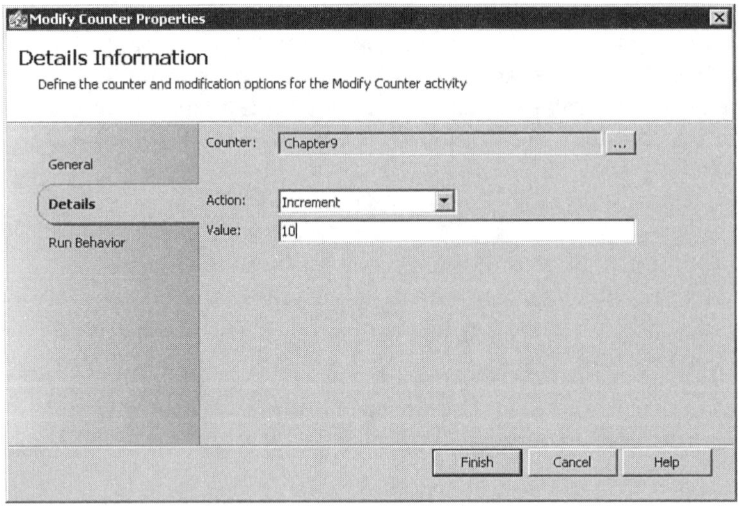

FIGURE 9.35 Details tab for the **Modify Counter** activity.

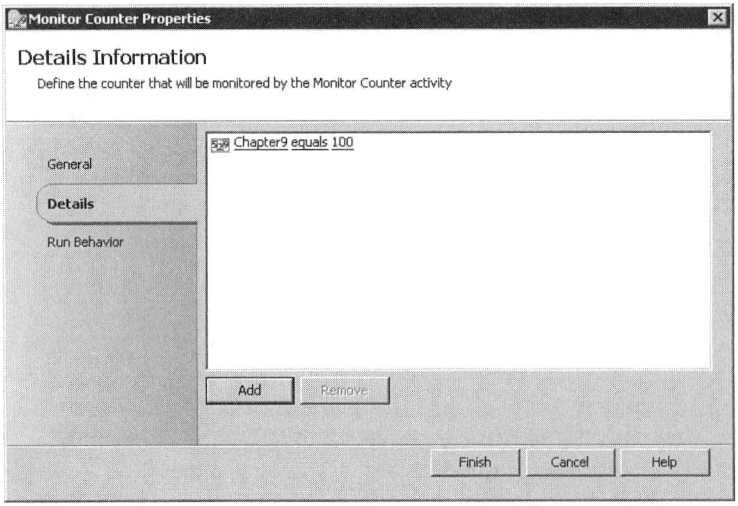

FIGURE 9.36 Details tab for the **Monitor Counter** activity.

Data-Handling Activities

The Utilities category includes a set of activities that handle data from the data bus or another specified location. The next sections describe the configuration and use of the most-used activities. The "Other Utility Activities" section summarizes the remaining activities.

Query Database

This activity offers the functionality to execute database queries against a database source. This activity has power similar to the **Run .NET Script** (because you can integrate query statements) but is dedicated to the database service. The query is executed against the specified database, the output is captured and automatically published on the data bus. This activity supports Access, ODBC, Oracle, and SQL Server database types.

Figure 9.37 shows an example of the Details tab for the **Query Database** activity, which is configured to execute a **SELECT Name, CreationTime FROM POLICIES** query. (The runbooks table in the Orchestrator database is still called POLICIES, as it was with Opalis Integration Server.)

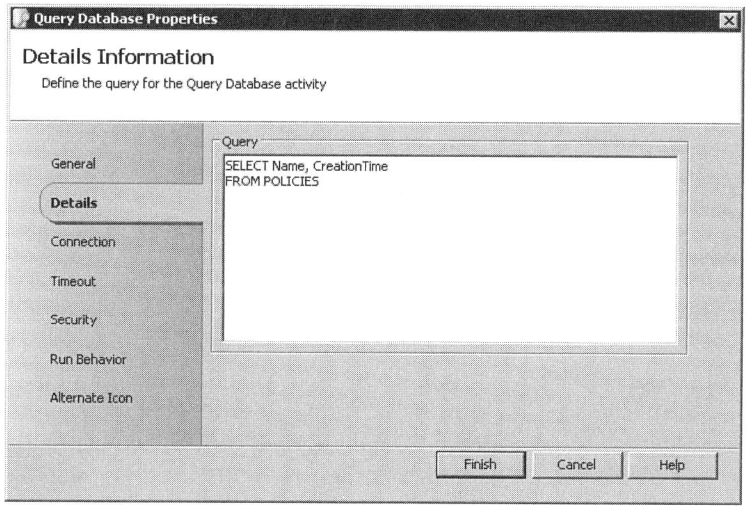

FIGURE 9.37 Details tab for the **Query Database** activity.

You can configure these options for the **Query Database** activity:

- The database query is specified in the Query field in the Details tab.
- You can use the Connection tab to specify the database type and connection parameters for the activity. The following options are configurable:
  - **Database type:** This drop-down list enables you to choose from Microsoft Access (.mdb files only), ODBC, Oracle, and SQL Server (see Figure 9.38). Based on your selection, the dialog box has specific connection information for the selected database engine.
  - **Authentication:** Authentication radio buttons are enabled only when the SQL Server database type is selected. The names of these radio buttons change based on database type, but they are grayed out and not configurable. The radio buttons determine the authentication method used to connect to the target

SQL Server—either Windows Authentication or SQL Server Authentication. If SQL Server Authentication is selected, the User name and Password fields are enabled.

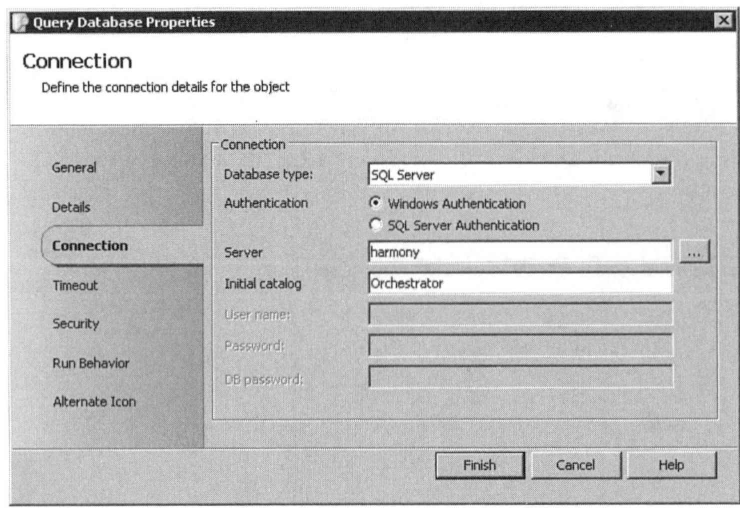

FIGURE 9.38 Connection tab for the **Query Database** activity.

- **Server/Workgroup file/DSN/Service Name:** This field label changes names, depending on the Database type drop-down selection. Regardless of your selection, this field configures the target Server, Database File, DSN, or Service Name where the query will be executed. Selecting SQL Server results in Server, selecting Access results in File, selecting ODBC results in DSN, and selecting Oracle results in Service Name.
- **Initial catalog:** This field label change names and is enabled or disabled depending on your Database type drop-down selection. Selecting SQL Server results in Initial catalog, and selecting Access results in Workgroup file; the two other database engine type selections (ODBC and Oracle) disable this field. Regardless of selection, this field configures the target Database or File where the query will be executed.
- **User name:** When enabled, this field configures the username used in the connection to the target Server, Database File, DSN, or Service Name where the query will be executed.
- **Password:** When enabled, this field configures the password used in the connection to the target Server, Database File, DSN, or Service Name where the query will be executed.
- **DB password:** You can specify this parameter only when you select Access from the database type drop-down selection. It configures the password to open the Microsoft Access database.

- On the Timeout tab, you can specify how long to wait while the database query is executed before the activity generates an error.

Invoke Web Services

The **Invoke Web Services** activity offers the functionality to execute Simple Object Access Protocol (SOAP) calls by sending and receiving simple XML commands. You can use this activity to integrate your own created web services application into your runbook or connect to an external web service. The **Invoke Web Services** activity executes and captures output specific to the executed SOAP calls. This output is automatically published to the data bus and is available for successive activities. The **Query XML** activity (discussed in the "Query XML" section) can execute an XPath query against the **Invoke Web Service** output. In this way, you can capture the needed values from the XML output from this activity.

Figure 9.39 shows an example of the Details tab for the **Invoke Web Services** activity that connects to a public web service. The WSDL for this call is www.webservicex.net/ConvertTemperature.asmx?WSDL. This public web service is available for testing purposes to convert a specified temperature. You can specify the WSDL URL and discover the available methods by clicking the button next to the text field (...). You can discover the XML Request Payload for this method by clicking the Format Hint button. The Format Hint button action partially displays the XML Request Payload field for the selected method. You can specify the values between the XML tags on the payload hint for your needs. Here is what you can specify on the Details tab:

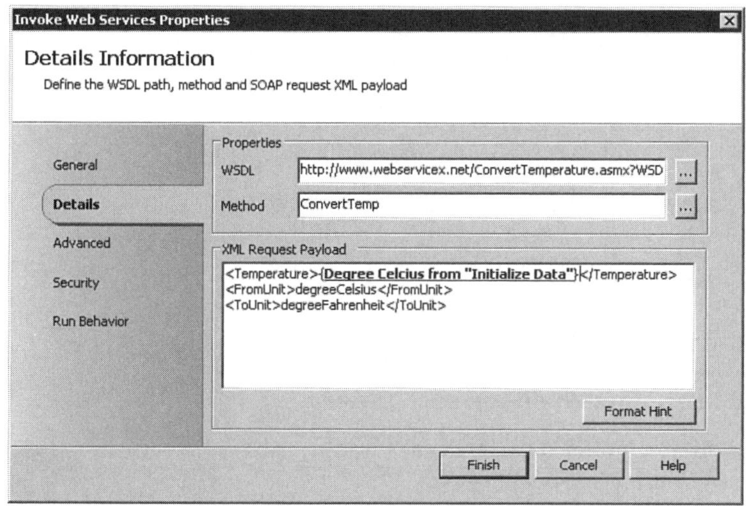

FIGURE 9.39 Details tab for the **Invoke Web Services** activity.

- **WSDL:** The location of the WSDL for the target web service is configured here. The WSDL field can reference either a local file or the URL for the WSDL.

- **Method:** You can specify the name of the method that the activity invokes. Select the available methods by clicking the (...) button next to the parameter field. Available methods are dynamically pulled from the web.
- **XML Request Payload:** Use this field to configure the XML to be sent as the request payload. Clicking the Format Hint button provides the necessary XML syntax for the web service method chosen. You simply have to fill out the string information between the XML tags presented in the hint.

The Advanced tab enables you to specify the location where you can save the output, URL, and protocol for the SOAP call. Figure 9.40 shows the default configuration. The Advanced tab has three options:

- **Response Folder:** To save the XML response files to a specific location, you can enable this option and specify the location to save the file.
- **Address:** Specify the URL location of the web service.
- **Protocol:** Use this drop-down list to configure the protocol that the web service uses during execution. Two options are available: SOAP 1.1 and SOAP 1.2. SOAP 1.1 is the default.

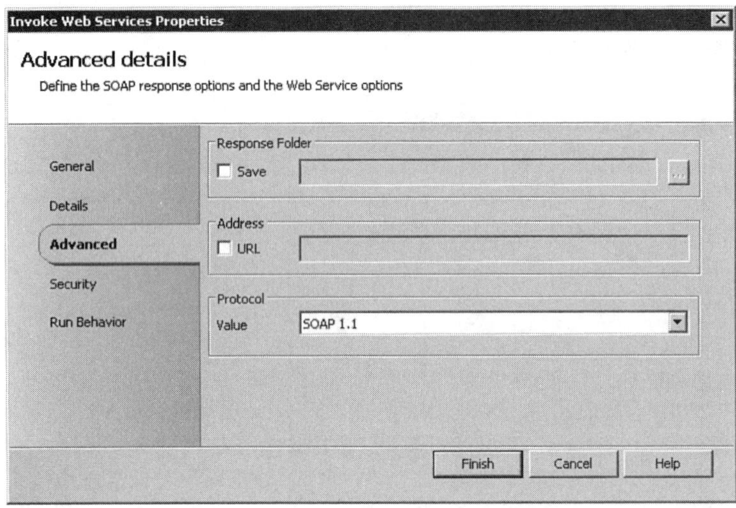

FIGURE 9.40 Advanced tab for the **Invoke Web Services** activity.

The Security tab enables HTTP Authentication when the activity connects to the target web service. This functionality is optional and is disabled by default. To enable HTTP Authentication, select the Enable check box and enter the appropriate credentials for HTTP Authentication into the User name and Password fields on this tab.

Query XML

This activity performs an XPath query on an XML input of the activity. In a typical usage scenario, when the **Invoke Web Services** activity is used, the **Query XML** activity queries the XML output to capture the required value(s).

On the Details tab, you can specify whether to use an XML file or XML text as input for the activity. You can configure the XPath query field with the query to capture the required value. Figure 9.41 shows an example in which the output of an **Invoke Web Service** action is queried for the temperature value.

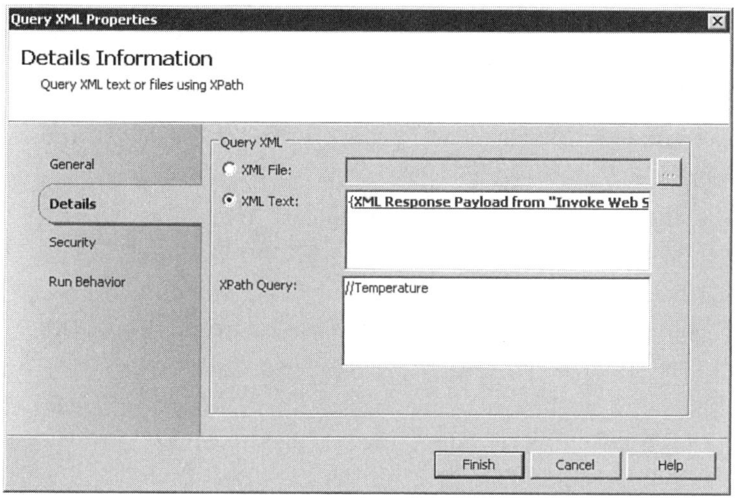

FIGURE 9.41 Details tab for the **Query XML** activity.

Other Utility Activities

This group of activities includes generic activities that are useful in runbook creation. This chapter does not describe these activities in the same level of detail as the other activities because the configuration is simple and the actions are recognizable by the name of the activity. The following list summarizes these activities:

- **Compare Values:** Compares two text values or two numerical values. You select the operator between the two values from the drop-down list.
- **Format Date/Time:** Transforms existing date and time formats into custom formats. You might need to convert the date to or from a specific format when accessing a database or external system. This activity lets you convert the date to your local date format or adjust time differences.
- **Apply XSLT:** Transforms the content of an XML file according to the rules in an XSLT file. This activity would be useful, for example, when you want to convert an XML file to an HTML file.

- **Read Text Log:** Reads lines from a structured text log file. You can specify a specific file or a folder. If you specify a folder, a date filter is applied to get the most recent file in the folder. If you have log files in this folder that change names, you can configure the activity to read from the newest file in the specified folder or read files that match a filename pattern.
- **Generate Random Text:** Creates specified random text values based on specified criteria. You can specify text content to control the output. Upper/lower case, number, or symbols can be selected for length and content. This is useful when you need to generate passwords in a runbook workflow.
- **Write To Database:** Acts similarly to the **Query Database** activity. The activity writes a row into the specified database table. You must specify the server, database type, and database. For additional information, see the "Query Database" section.
- **Write Web Page:** Creates or adds information to a specified HTML file. You can use this activity to append text to an existing web page.
- **Map Published Data:** Transforms the existing published data items or variable values into new values, according to the rules you configure on the activity.
- **Get Dial-up Status:** Retrieves the status of a dial-up or VPN network connection on the runbook server. The line status is published on the Orchestrator data bus. This activity checks the connection before an activity that depends on the connection is executed.
- **Connect/Disconnect Dial-up:** Connects or disconnects a dial-up connection or VPN. With this activity, you can first create the connection in your runbook; successive activities then can make use of this connection.
- **Map Network Path:** Enables you to map a network path using a UNC path.
- **Disconnect Network Path:** Enables you to disconnect a network path.

Text File Management

The Text File Management category includes seven activities to manage text in files. You can perform read, append delete, find, insert, and search actions on the specified text file. Figure 9.42 displays the Text File Management activities in your library.

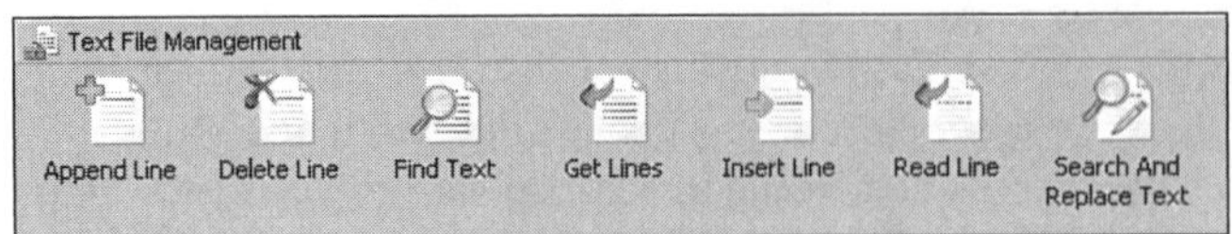

FIGURE 9.42 File Management category of activities.

A description of these activities follows:

- **Append Line:** Appends a line of text to a text file. The file does not need to exist for this activity to function properly, although the folder must exist.
- **Get Lines:** Gets single or multiple lines from the specified text file, according to the criteria you have specified. You can configure criteria on the name property and ranges to select lines in the text file. This activity can retrieve single or multiple lines and automatically publishes them to the data bus.
- **Find Text:** Finds text according to the specified search string. You can use regular expressions to find the correct information, and you can configure the resulting output to return only the first line that matches or all lines that match to the specified criteria.
- **Insert Line:** Inserts lines into an existing file. The activity allows the configured text to be inserted at the specified line number. Other activities in this category can assist in retrieving the line number where the information must be inserted (**Get Lines**, **Read Line**, **Find Text**, and so on).
- **Delete Line:** Deletes lines from an existing file. This activity enables you to delete lines of text based on the specified line number(s). Other activities in this category can assist in retrieving the line number where the information must be inserted (**Get Lines**, **Read Line**, **Find Text**, and so on).
- **Read Line:** Reads lines from the specified file. The activity reads the line of text and passes it to another activity using published data. This range can be from one line to all lines, using "," as a separator for single-line configuration or "-" to indicate ranges.
- **Search And Replace Text:** Searches and replaces text from the specified text file. This activity finds and replaces all instances of the specified search text with the specified replacement text. Case-sensitive and regular expression searches are available.

NOTE: DIFFERENCE BETWEEN GET LINE AND READ LINE ACTIVITIES

When using the **Get Line** activity, a new published data item is created for each item you add in the lines list on the activity dialog of the activity. This differs from the **Read Line** activity, which creates a new published data item for each text line that it reads.

Summary

This chapter provided an overview of the standard activities that are available out of the box in System Center 2012 Orchestrator. It discussed the functionality of these activities using sample configurations. The activities are flexible and can be used for many runbook scenarios. Activities from the Runbook Control, Scheduling, and Monitoring activity categories provide triggers for managing your runbooks. Generic activities such as **Run .Net Script**, **Run Program**, and **Query Database** are powerful and can work as fallbacks when no other standard activity is available for your specific action. The Text File Management and File Management activities are handy for reading or writing log file information in your runbooks or external systems. These are just examples of standard activity usage; many options are available for using these activities.

CHAPTER 10
Runbook and Configuration Best Practices

IN THIS CHAPTER

Chapter 4, "Architectural Design," discussed the importance of processes and standards when working with System Center 2012 Orchestrator. One example is change management—without an effective change management process, you risk losing control over your runbooks. An improperly configured runbook that is not subject to change management could damage your production environment if it deletes the wrong objects in Active Directory. Other important nontechnical areas to consider (which Chapter 4 also discussed) are Orchestrator security and development models.

This chapter focuses on best practices for runbook design and general configuration of the Orchestrator platform. The chapter begins by discussing logical best practices for authoring runbooks. It also covers configuration best practices, including those for SQL Server and the Orchestrator environment.

Runbook Best Practices

System Center Orchestrator is a wide and open platform; you can build a runbook executing any type of workflow, without any logical verification of that workflow. As an example, if you build a runbook that deletes all accounts in Active Directory (AD), Orchestrator executes the runbook without asking, "Do you really want to delete all accounts in Active Directory?" This action could lead to some rather serious issues. Authoring practices and standards thus is extremely important when working with Orchestrator. Most likely, your Orchestrator environment will be shared among a number of engineers—yet another reason to author runbooks using standards—so it is crucial that everyone understand these runbooks and be able to modify them as necessary. Continuing the discussion from Chapter 4, the authors offer these suggestions for runbook best practices:

- **Naming conventions:** Establish naming standards for activities, runbooks, folders, variables, and global settings. Consider why:

    - **Activities:** Each activity has a default name when it is dragged into the Workspace pane. If multiple activities with the same name are added, Orchestrator appends a sequential number to that default name.

      To illustrate, Figure 10.1 shows a runbook with three **Read Line** activities; Orchestrator adds (2) and (3) after the default name for the second and third activities. With default names, no one but the runbook author can sufficiently understand what the runbook does; even the runbook author might face challenges when modifying the runbook. The authors recommend that you always rename your activities to describe their actions. Using short activity names is best; you can use the description field included in each activity to add longer descriptions.

FIGURE 10.1 A runbook with multiple activities, using the default name.

      Figure 10.2 shows an updated version of the first runbook, with new names for each activity. The runbook monitors a folder for new files and then reads the file and creates a user account in Active Directory. The figure shows how using customized activity names make it easier to understand what the runbook is doing.

FIGURE 10.2 The runbook with multiple activities, with descriptive names.

    - **Runbooks:** Naming conventions for runbooks should include a sequence number and short description of what the runbook does. The sequence number is a unique number for the runbook that also describes where it is in the runbook navigation tree; consider these numbers in an outline.

      Figure 10.3 shows part of the navigation pane, with the lower part displaying the runbook tabs. As the figure indicates, you would increment the hierarchy number used in the runbook folder when naming runbooks.

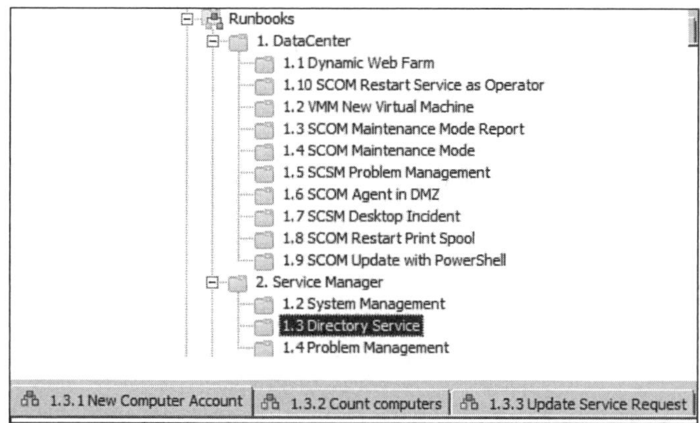

FIGURE 10.3 Naming standards for runbooks and folders.

- **Folders:** The runbook names in Figure 10.3 should also be used for folder names, incorporating a number and a short description. Orchestrator sorts folders alphanumerically, so starting folder names with a number makes them easy to organize. Using a structure built on numbers also makes it easier to track and navigate to a specific runbook.

  The number should be unique, as should the description, when possible. The folder structure is also displayed in the Orchestration console (see Figure 10.4, previously shown in Chapter 4), so make the folder name descriptive and logical.

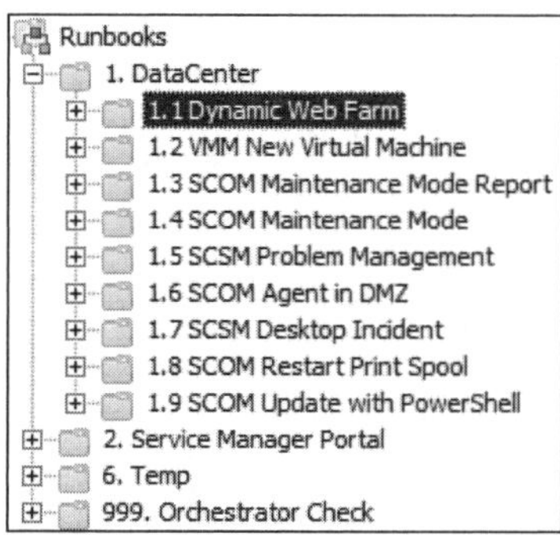

FIGURE 10.4 Example of folder naming standard.

- **Variables:** The name of each variable should reflect where it is used. For example, runbook 1.1.2 uses a variable named *1.1.2 Resolution State*, and that variable contains the value for the resolution state. Include information about how the variable is used and the type of value in the Description field, as in Figure 10.5.

- **Global settings:** Mirror the runbook name and folder structure under global settings. This makes it easy to see which variable belongs to what runbook.

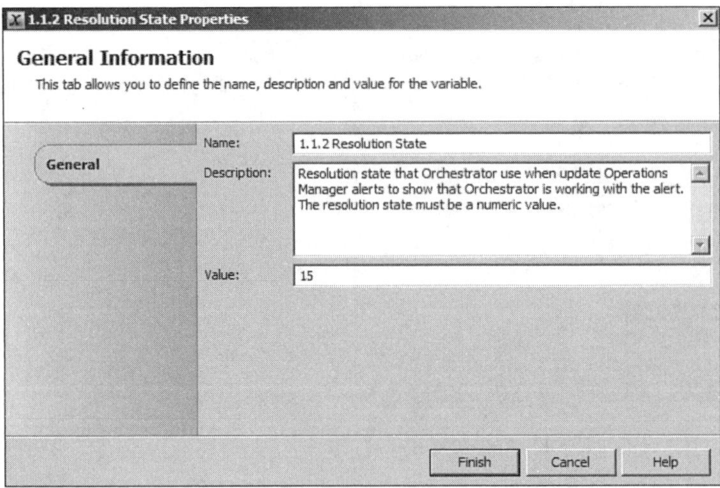

FIGURE 10.5 Example of naming standard for variables.

- **Link colors and labels:** When you look at a runbook, determining the path the runbook should follow should be easy. If the runbook has multiple branches, it should be straightforward to see when the runbook will choose which branch. The authors recommend using a standard set of colors on links and a small description on each link. Figure 10.6 shows an updated version of the runbook previously shown in Figure 10.2, now with two branches:
  - The upper branch (branch 1) creates service accounts.
  - The lower branch (branch 2) creates user accounts.

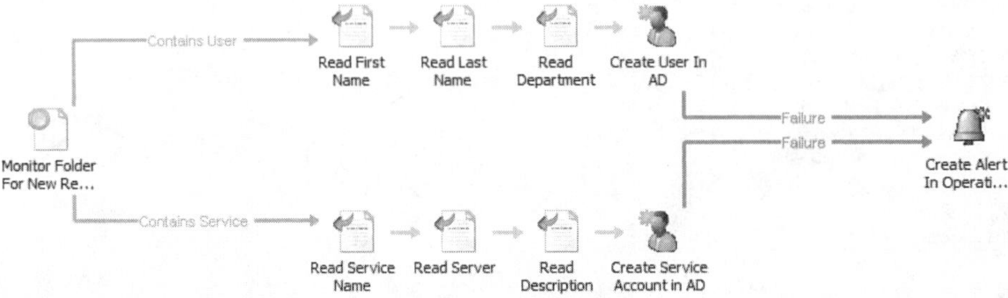

FIGURE 10.6 Using standard link colors to reflect the parameters.

The runbook is monitoring a folder for new files. Depending on the information in the file, the runbook will take different paths. The authors suggest a standard of using orange for links with dependence, green for links that show the normal path, and red to show where the runbook goes in the event of a failure. Each orange link should include a short description of when the runbook goes to which branch. In addition, the green (normal) path is somewhat thicker than the other paths. When looking at a runbook, determining which path the runbook takes should be clear; it is denoted here by a thicker green line.

- **Runbook and activity timeout:** The runbook's Properties page shows the **Report when the Runbook runs for more than** setting. This setting enables you to configure a threshold (in seconds) for how long the runbook runs before it generates an Orchestrator platform event. The runbook does not stop when it exceeds the threshold, but it generates a platform event to inform you that it is running longer than expected. Activity properties have a similar setting, **Report when the activity runs for more than**. This generates a platform event when the activity runs longer than the threshold value. Figure 10.7 shows a platform event for an activity that ran longer than expected. The left side of the figure displays the configuration dialog box for an activity.

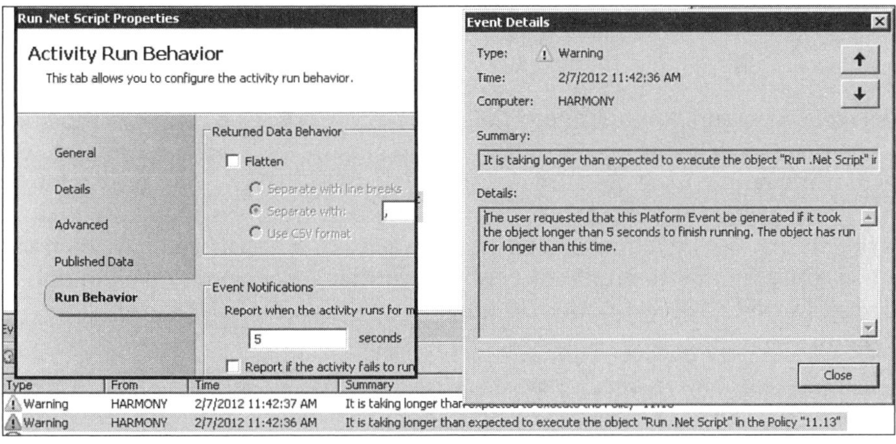

FIGURE 10.7 Run behaviors for an activity.

- **Link condition:** When you create a link, by default, the include condition is success, without an exclude condition. This configuration is acceptable only when everything works as expected. If that is not the case and even a single activity in the runbook fails, the runbook will halt at that activity. This can give results different from those anticipated.

  Consider an example: You have a runbook that creates a new user account and mailbox for new hires. If after creating the user account an activity fails and the runbook stops processing (because there is no subsequent activity in the event of a failure), you have a user account in Active Directory without a mailbox and must clean up the account manually. A better approach is to include a link that addresses a failed attempt to complete an activity.

Figure 10.6 showed failure links from the **Create User in AD** and **Create Service Account in AD** activities. Figure 10.8 displays an updated version of this runbook, adding an activity to create a mailbox for user accounts; if that step fails, it rolls back the user account just created and generates an Operations Manager alert. A well-designed runbook includes links for all possible outcomes from all activities.

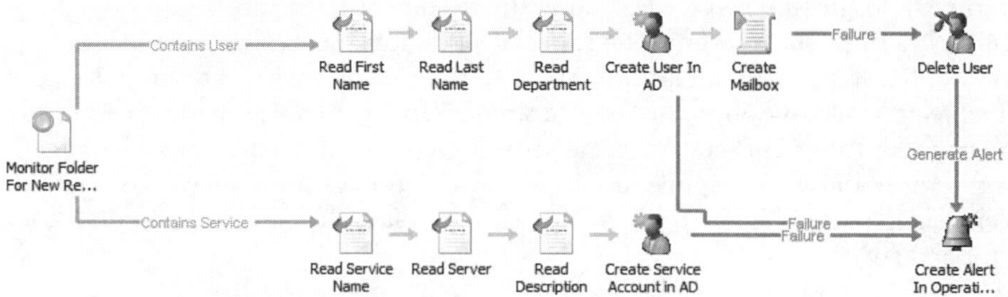

FIGURE 10.8 Failure link handling rollback actions.

- **Link delay:** Your runbooks might need to include a delay or sleep action. Although you can configure a delay on the links between activities, this is not a recommended approach. Consider the issue: Because links are not listed as steps when the runbook is running, you won't see a link as a step in the runbook or see the link delay as a step in the history log. Including a **Wait** or **Sleep** activity is better. These two activities let you easily see that the runbook is waiting at that action so that you do not think that your runbook has stopped running. You can combine a **Wait** activity with the **Run Program** activity or a PowerShell script.

  For more information on building a **Wait** activity, see http://contoso.se/blog/?p=2802.

- **Data validation:** The User Account branch of the runbook in Figure 10.8 shows activities where the runbook reads First Name, Last Name, and Department from a text file, and then creates a user account in Active Directory. Say that the department name is used to determine the organization unit (OU) in Active Directory in which to store the user account. If the department name is incorrect in the input file, the runbook will fail at the **Create User in AD** activity because it cannot find a container with that name.

  You can prevent the runbook from failing at this activity by validating the department name before using it in the runbook. This is accomplished by using a **Map Published Data** activity, which transforms existing published data items into new content. Say that the department value in the text file is HR; this can be translated into an OU distinguished name in AD, such as OU=HR,DC=ODYSSEY,DC=COM. Figure 10.9 updates the runbook to include a **Map Published Data** activity, renamed to **Map Department**, that translates department names into distinguished names. If the department name in the text file is incorrect, the runbook will not try to create a user account.

A best practice is to validate all input data before executing the remaining activities in your runbook. You can perform data validation in a number of ways, such as with the **Map Published Data** activity, but you also can use link conditions or queries against services, such as against AD to validate a user account.

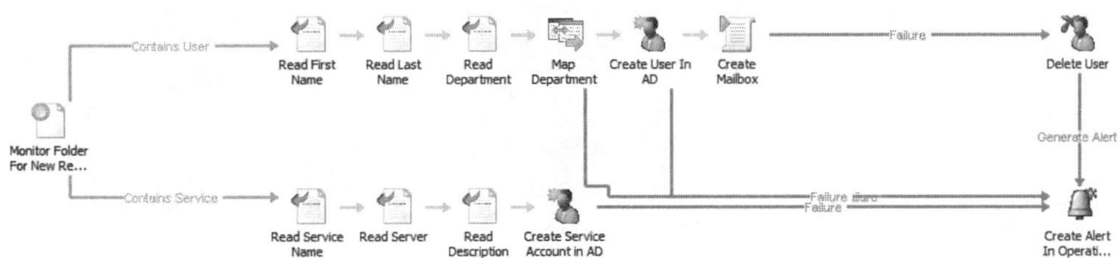

FIGURE 10.9 Validation of input data.

- **Runbook logging:** A runbook's properties include the options to configure logging, store activity-specific published data, and store common published data. These settings provide extended logging, which can be invaluable when troubleshooting and testing runbooks. However, you should turn off logging in production environments to avoid unnecessary overhead in the Orchestrator database. The authors recommend that your runbook write to your own logs, such as a separate database or a log file.

  This can be implemented by building a generic logging runbook that multiple runbooks trigger when they need to write to the log; this approach ensures a common log format for your runbooks and saves time and activities in your runbooks by triggering a log runbook rather than including activities for this in each of your runbooks.

- **Collect and store data:** When authoring a runbook that will query external systems for input parameters, the authors recommend collecting all required data as the first phase of the runbook. A risk exists that external systems will not respond at all or that the data could change while the runbook is executing. By collecting the data at the same time and storing it temporarily, you eliminate the risk that different parts of your runbook use different input data yet you have assumed that it will be the same. This is also useful if you have problems querying external systems for input data, which would result in a potential failure for your runbook. By preventing failure before other activities are performed, you reduce the need for manual cleanup jobs on servers and in services.

  Figure 10.10 shows an updated version of the runbook used to create a user account. An additional activity queries an external telephone system for the phone number of the new employee for whom you are creating the account. The phone number is to be included with the user account in Active Directory. If the query is unsuccessful, the runbook generates an alert in Operations Manager and the user account is not created. This ensures that you do not create the user account unless all input data is validated and correct. To validate the result, you can use a condition on the link to verify that the answer includes specific information, such as 555-, if that is the expected area code in the phone number.

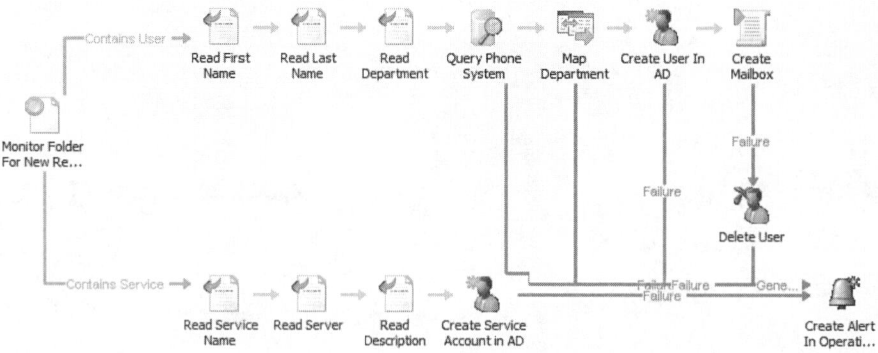

FIGURE 10.10 Collect data before executing your runbook.

- **Variables:** Moving runbooks between Orchestrator environments (such as test, pre-production [sanitizing], staging, and production) might require updating some of the activity-related settings. These settings could be the name of a server or domain. Manually modifying each activity that uses these settings introduces several risks:
  - Updating something incorrectly so that the runbook no longer works as expected
  - Forgetting to update an activity, such as when you have test Active Directory and production Active Directory implementations, and the activity should query the one appropriate for that Orchestrator environment

  You can alleviate this situation by using variables, which you can easily update in Runbook Designer. When you update a variable with a new value, all activities that use the variable are immediately updated with that new value. Using naming standards, discussed at the beginning of this section, helps to easily determine which variables your runbooks are using, indicating the variables to update when moving runbooks between different environments.

Designing Runbooks for Fault Tolerance

Designing runbooks to support failover between different runbook servers and accommodate runbook server restarts requires additional planning. Three common scenarios require designing fault tolerance for a runbook:

- **Runbook server reboot:** When a runbook server that is running a runbook is rebooted, the runbook restarts automatically after the reboot. However, it starts at step 1, the first activity in the runbook.

- **SQL Server reboot:** If the runbook server loses connectivity to the database while running a runbook, the runbook stops. However, when connectivity is restored, the runbook restarts at the first activity in the runbook.
- **Runbook server failure:** If a runbook is configured for multiple runbook servers and the primary runbook server fails, the runbook fails over to a secondary runbook server but restarts at the first activity.

Figure 10.11 shows an updated version of the account-creation runbook that includes logic for restarts. This version has a **Get User** activity named **Check If Account Exists**. The activity checks whether the user account already exists in Active Directory. If it does, the runbook branches directly to **Create Mailbox**; otherwise, the runbook creates the user account.

A large runbook with many different steps and tasks can require a large number of activities to determine whether a step has already run. If you have large runbooks, making them modular by dividing them into smaller runbooks is often preferable.

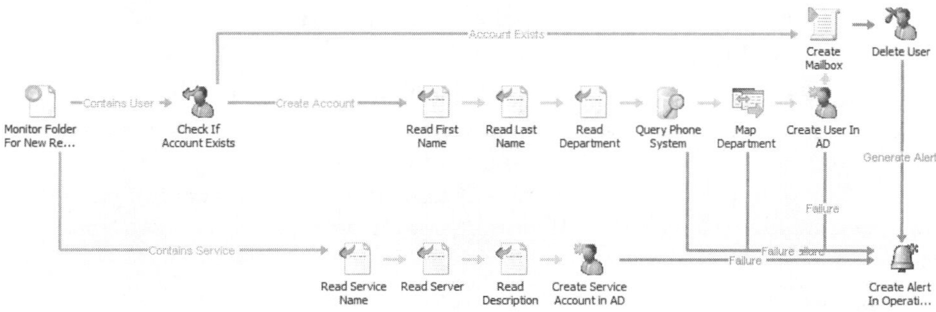

FIGURE 10.11 Runbook supporting restart.

Designing Parent and Child Runbooks

When a runbook is designed to support fault tolerance scenarios or perform many tasks, the number of activities entailed can make it quite complicated. Runbooks containing many activities can be difficult to modify and understand. An alternative approach is to divide your runbooks into smaller, less complicated runbooks and have them triggered from multiple runbooks. This lets you build a library of core runbooks, such as ones to query Active Directory or upload files to a file server, that other runbooks trigger as needed. This gives you a set of generic runbooks that provide features to other runbooks. Although no hard limit governs the number of activities in a runbook, the authors recommend that you divide runbooks with more than 20 activities into smaller parts.

NOTE: TRIGGERING A RUNBOOK CAUSES A SHORT DELAY

When a runbook triggers another runbook, a short delay of several seconds occurs while the new runbook job is written to the database and executed by a runbook server. Be sure to include this in your design. For example, if you trigger 100 instances of a runbook, that activity could take up to 500 seconds to complete, particularly if you configured the second runbook to run only one instance at a time. That could result in a very long runtime for the runbook.

Let's look at an example in which a runbook grows to an unwieldy size. You might have noticed that the runbook used in the examples in this chapter does not accommodate different users with the same name. In addition, the current version (see Figure 10.11) fails on the second attempt because the sAMAccountName attribute of a user account must be unique in an Active Directory domain.

The runbook can be modified to check whether an account with that sAMAccountName already exists and, if so, create the user account using another naming standard. This standard could be the three first letters from the first name and the three first letters from the last name—for example, Anders Bengtström then becomes AndBen. If another user is named Andreas Bengtström, that account could be AndrBen, with the standard of using four letters from the first name and three letters from the last name.

Figure 10.12 shows an updated version of the runbook in Figure 10.11. The runbook now checks whether an account already exists according to the 3×3 standard (three letters in the first name and three letters in the last name). If the account exists, the runbook tests using a 2×2 standard; if this account also exists, it tests using a 4×3 standard. If accounts exist using these standard conventions, the runbook generates an alert in Operations Manager and then stops.

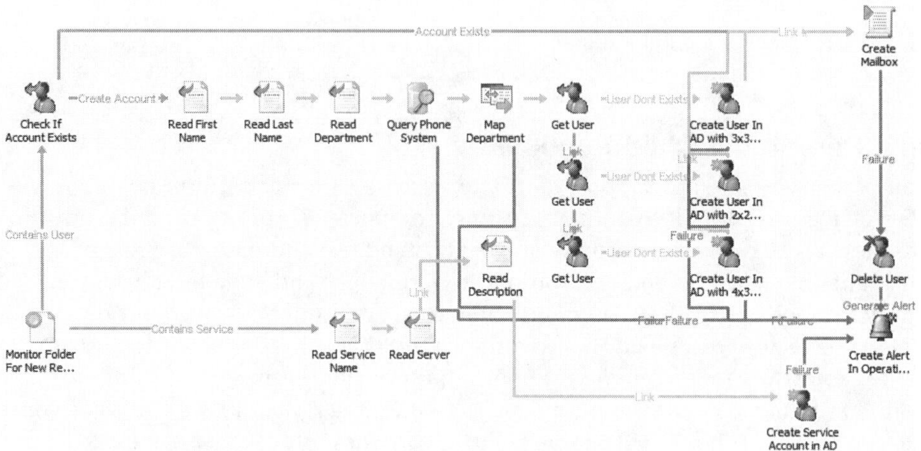

FIGURE 10.12 Runbook supporting different naming standards.

Although the runbook shown here does not yet cover all scenarios and possible outcomes, it is becoming more complex and difficult to view easily. This is a good time to divide the runbook into multiple runbooks to cover all scenarios while making it less complicated and easier to maintain.

Figure 10.13 shows a runbook that the runbook in Figure 10.12 could trigger. This runbook determines a suitable sAMAccountName and creates the account in Active Directory. It then publishes the result back to the runbook that triggered it.

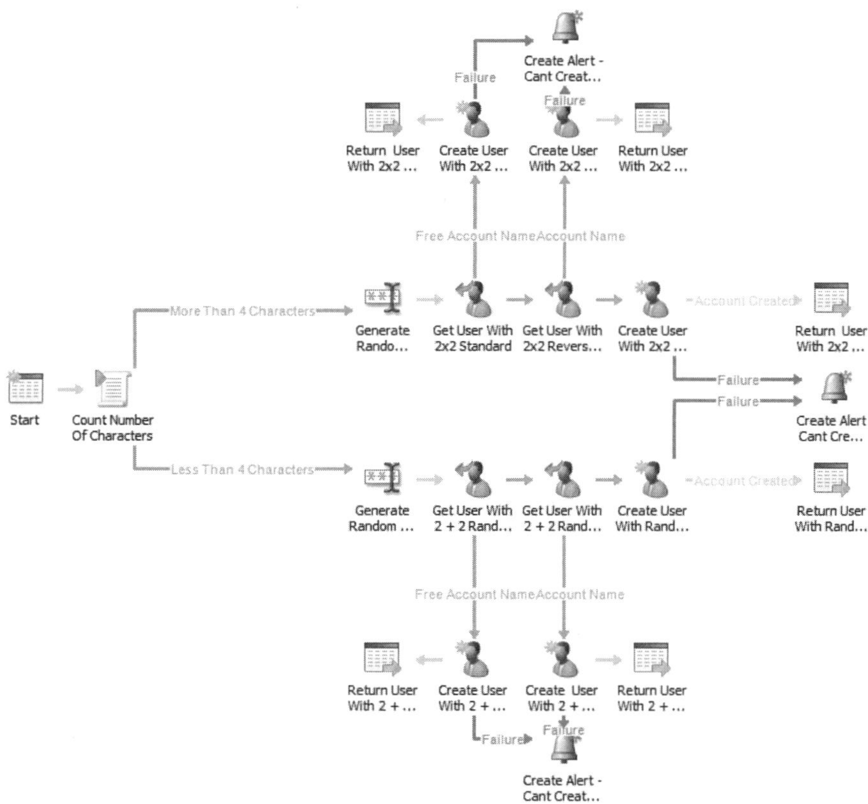

FIGURE 10.13 Runbook handling a sAMAccountName with four branches.

Let's look at the runbook in Figure 10.13 in detail:

1. The runbook begins by counting the number of characters in the first name and the last name. The runbook obtains the first name and last name from the parent runbook that triggered it (the runbook in Figure 10.12). The runbook uses a **Run .NET Script** activity, renamed to **Count Number of Characters**, to count the number of characters. The activity runs a PowerShell script to count the number of characters and publishes this number on the data bus.

2. The runbook then splits into two branches, depending on whether there are four or more characters in the first name together with the last name. In both cases, the runbook generates two random numbers to include in the sAMAccountName, providing a unique sAMAccountName.
3. The runbook tests different combinations of the sAMAccountName. If it finds one not already used in AD, it creates an account. The runbook uses the **Get User** activity from the Active Directory integration pack to check whether an account with the sAMAccountName exists.
4. If **Get User** returns a value of 0, the runbook can create an account with the sAMAccountName; if the account already exists, the activity returns a value of 1.

Some additional information about the runbook in Figure 10.13 includes:

- Filter conditions are used on the links to control the path the runbook will take. If no combination is available, the sAMAccountName is generated using random numbers.
- The runbook uses a **Generate Random Number** activity. This could be modified to generate random numbers only when no other standard can be used; that is the only scenario that requires a random number. This change could reduce the number of activities and process time.
- All branches end with a **Publish Data** activity that publishes the sAMAccountName back to the parent runbook.
- Multiple **Generate Alert** activities generate an Operations Manager alert if an activity fails.
- There are many activities to support different alternatives for usernames. Supporting even more alternatives for usernames requires adding activities. A better solution might be a PowerShell script. PowerShell has many built-in functions, including functions that support text manipulation. The disadvantage of using scripts is that they are more complicated to update.

Figure 10.14 shows a new version of the runbook from Figure 10.12; this is now the parent runbook triggering the runbook in Figure 10.13. The runbook in Figure 10.14 waits for the runbook in Figure 10.13 to finish before it continues. The example uses the **Invoke Runbook** activity to trigger another runbook and **Return Data** for publishing data back to the first runbook. In this example, the runbook in Figure 10.14 triggers the runbook in Figure 10.13. The runbook in Figure 10.13 publishes the account it created; then the runbook in Figure 10.14 can continue.

Note that the runbook in Figure 10.13 uses multiple **Create Alert** and **Return Data** activities. This is because an activity can configure data bus parameters from only one branch. The parameter from the data bus can have a dynamic value depending on the runbook and activities before the current activity, but you can configure an activity to include only specific published data from the data bus.

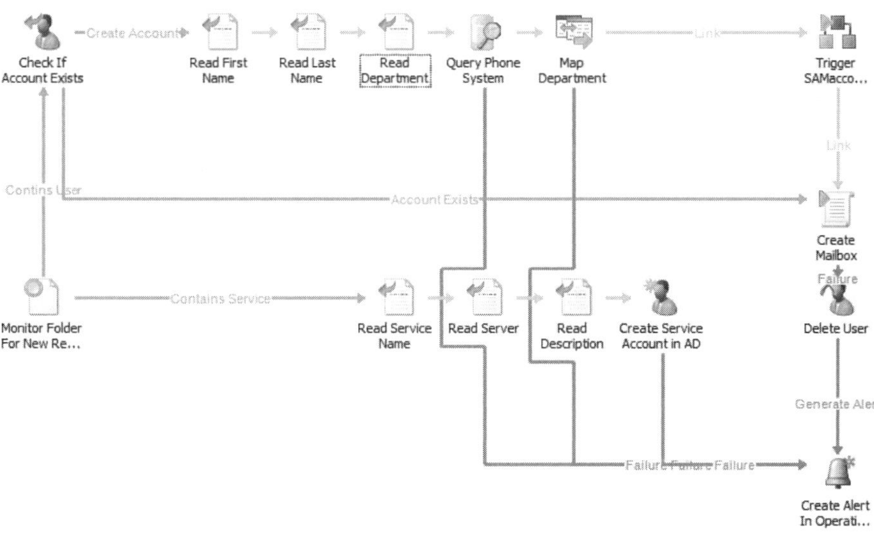

FIGURE 10.14 Runbook triggering another runbook.

In this case, the runbook in Figure 10.13 needs to publish the account name of the account created to the parent runbook; this is the runbook (see Figure 10.14) triggering the runbook in Figure 10.13. The **Publish Data** activity can provide that information; when you configure a **Publish Data** activity, you can select parameters from the data bus that activities earlier in the runbook publish. However, the runbook in Figure 10.13 could choose multiple branches, depending on the outcome of the activity; determining which branch would be used is impossible. You cannot configure the **Publish Data** activity with "publish from *any* Create User activity," and you must always select one specific activity to publish data from, so Figure 10.13 uses a (renamed) **Create User** activity in each branch, with a **Publish Data** in each branch as well.

Having parent and child runbooks makes the logic easier to follow and maintain.

Using the Run Program Activity

Several Orchestrator activities merit some thought before using them. One of these is the **Run Program** activity. The unusual facet of this activity is that it can result in a success value even if the program or command fails to run. As Figure 10.15 shows, **Run Program** reports success, but if you look at the details of the output in this figure, it didn't run the command! In this example, the command was to list files in a folder that did not exist. An approach to ensure that **Run Program** activities are actually working is to add a check after the activity—for example, when you list folders in a folder, you can configure the link to make sure there is no "File Not Found" in the output of the activity.

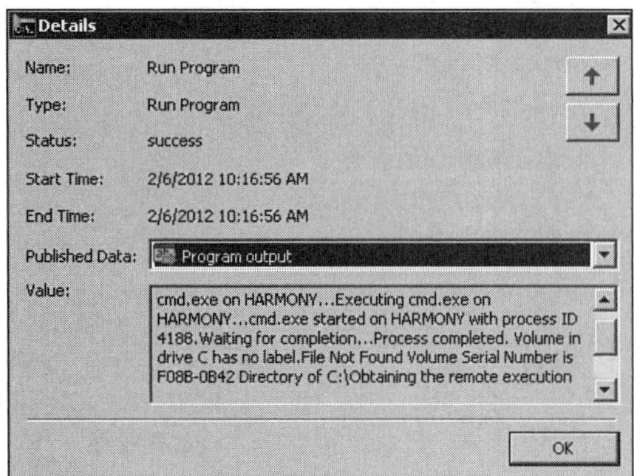

FIGURE 10.15 Validation of input data.

NOTE: OTHER ACTIVITIES THAT MIGHT GIVE A SUCCESS VALUE WHEN THERE IS NO RESULT

Examples of other queries that behave like the **Run Program** activity include query activities such as **Get Computer** and **Get User.** As long as these activities are capable of querying AD, they show a success (green) result. However, the success means that they were able to query AD, not necessarily that they were able to retrieve data.

Looping Within a Runbook

Chapter 8, "Advanced Runbook Concepts," introduced looping. In some scenarios, you need to loop through the same activities multiple times within a runbook. Earlier versions (of Opalis Integration Server) supported legacy mode and let you link activities to go backward in a runbook, but this is no longer possible. To illustrate, Figure 10.16 shows a runbook that counts the number of lines in a text file and generates a random number.

- If the random number is less or equal to a line in the text file, the text from the line in the text file is written in a platform event.
- If the random number is not equal to a line in the text file, the runbook tries to go backward to generate a new random number.

Figure 10.16 also shows a warning dialog box that the runbook contains a cycle; this displays when you check in the runbook. Although you can check in the runbook, when you try to start it, a platform event is generated that says, "The runbook contains a cycle." The runbook will not start. Note that Orchestrator does not check logic until a runbook is checked in.

Instead of including a loop within a runbook, divide your runbook into multiple runbooks and invoke them from each other. Figure 10.17 shows a runbook that counts the number of lines in the text file, generates a random number, and compares the random number with the number of lines in the text file. Here's how it works:

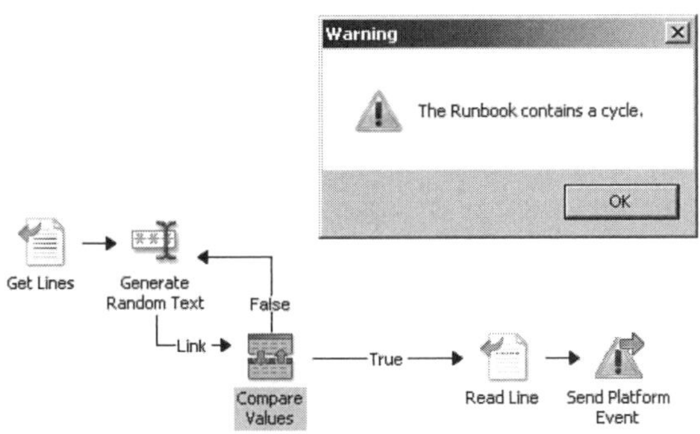

FIGURE 10.16 A cycle (loop) within a runbook.

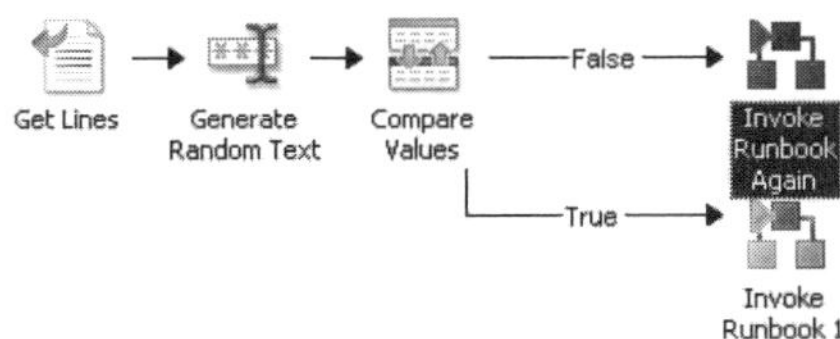

FIGURE 10.17 Runbook invokes itself in a loop.

1. If the random number is equal to a line in the text file, the runbook invokes the runbook in Figure 10.18.

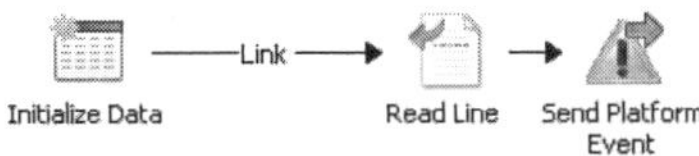

FIGURE 10.18 Runbook triggered by another runbook with start parameters.

2. The runbook in Figure 10.18 reads the line in the text file and writes it to a platform event.
3. If the random number is not equal to a line in the text file, the runbook invokes itself one more time to generate a new random number.

10

The first runbook, in Figure 10.17, forwards the line number to read when invoking the second runbook, in Figure 10.18.

An alternative to the solution in Figure 10.17, where the runbook invokes itself, is to use a parent runbook that invokes a child runbook. In the parent runbook, on the **Invoke**

Runbook activity, you can configure a loop until the child runbook returns an expected result.

Figure 10.19 shows that the first runbook, previously shown in Figure 10.17, is triggered multiple times (in this case, four times) before generating a suitable random number.

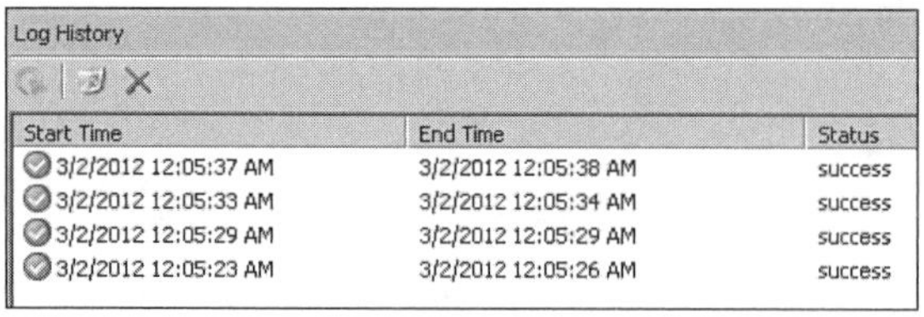

Log History

Start Time	End Time	Status
3/2/2012 12:05:37 AM	3/2/2012 12:05:38 AM	success
3/2/2012 12:05:33 AM	3/2/2012 12:05:34 AM	success
3/2/2012 12:05:29 AM	3/2/2012 12:05:29 AM	success
3/2/2012 12:05:23 AM	3/2/2012 12:05:26 AM	success

FIGURE 10.19 Log history shows the runbook was triggered multiple times.

Configuration Best Practices

Server platform and Orchestrator settings can affect performance. Key to Orchestrator's performance is its SQL database; if it performs poorly, it affects all of Orchestrator. This section discusses runbook server configuration, best practices for the SQL Server hosting the Orchestrator database, and Orchestrator log settings.

Specifying a Runbook Server and Runbook Throttling

Using default settings, each runbook runs on its primary runbook server. If the primary runbook server is offline, the runbook runs on the secondary runbook server. In some scenarios, you want runbooks to run on a secondary runbook server even when the primary runbook server is online—for example, when you have a runbook server on a secured network and this is the only runbook server that accesses some services. To change the default, right-click to open **Properties** of the runbook, override the default runbook server settings, and specify a runbook server to use.

By default, each runbook server can run a maximum of 50 runbooks at the same time. The ASPT tool lets you balance runbooks over a set of runbook servers; if you configure each runbook server to run a maximum of 10 runbooks at the same time, the 11th runbook will start on a secondary runbook server. However, as soon as the primary runbook server has a free slot (meaning that less than 10 runbooks are running), the next runbook will start on the primary runbook server.

By default, ASPT is installed in the management server folder (%*ProgramFiles(x86)*%\Microsoft System Center 2012\Orchestrator\Management Server). The tool enables you to change the maximum number of runbooks that a runbook server can run at once. If you have resource-intensive runbooks, you might want to specify a low number, to distribute the runbook load over multiple runbook servers. Figure 10.20 shows an example of running the ASPT tool. This example configures the HARMONY runbook server to run a maximum of 10 runbooks at the same time. To configure all your runbook servers, run the

ASPT tool with * for the RunbookServerName. The tool will then configure all runbook servers with the new MaxRunningPolicies threshold. Here is the syntax to run ASPT:

```
aspt (<RunbookServerName> or *) (MaxRunningPolicies (1-1000))
```

```
C:\Windows\System32\cmd.exe

C:\Program Files (x86)\Microsoft System Center 2012\Orchestrator\Management Serv
er>aspt
USAGE:
  aspt <RunbookServerName> <MaxRunningPolicies (1-1000)>
OR
  aspt * <MaxRunningPolicies (1-1000)>

C:\Program Files (x86)\Microsoft System Center 2012\Orchestrator\Management Serv
er>aspt HARMONY 10_
```

FIGURE 10.20 Using the ASPT tool to balance runbooks over runbook servers.

Orchestrator does not consider hardware load when determining where a runbook will run; it looks at only the ASPT threshold and the list of runbook servers. If you have multiple secondary runbook servers, Orchestrator starts to fill the first secondary runbook server. When it reaches the ASPT threshold, it sends runbooks to the third runbook server, and so on. To review and configure the order of runbook servers, use the Runbook Servers node in the Runbook Designer.

TIP: ABOUT THE ASP TOOL

More information on the ASPT tool is available at http://technet.microsoft.com/en-us/library/hh420378.aspx.

Configuring SQL Server

The Orchestrator database is a single chokepoint when it comes to performance. All runbook servers query the database frequently, and all configuration information, status, and settings are read from and written to the database. The faster the SQL Server can perform, the better Orchestrator performs. Consider several key areas regarding SQL Server performance:

- **Database files:** Do not place database data files in the same physical drive as the operating system. Place transaction logs and database data files on separate physical drives, and place the TempDB database on its own physical drive. All database files should be placed on physical drives with fault tolerance. Physical drives that together host a logical drive are designed for best performance. For example, a drive built on RAID 10 delivers good write and read performance.
- **Database size:** Keep your Orchestrator database as small as possible. A small database performs faster and increases performance in general.
- **Autogrow:** As Chapter 4 discussed, do not enable autogrow on the Orchestrator database. Autogrow can fragment your database, affecting performance.

In addition, if you host the Orchestrator database on SQL Server Standard edition, autogrow can cause the database to lock out. SQL Server Enterprise does not lock the database during autogrow.

- **Autoclose:** When a database is closed, it takes longer for the next query to execute because SQL Server needs to reopen the database. Using autoclose causes queries to take additional time. By default, autoclose is disabled on the Orchestrator database.
- **Database collation:** On the SQL Server instance used to support Orchestrator, the SQL collation setting must be configured for SQL_Latin1_General_CP1_CI_AS. No other collation is supported.
- **Database recovery model:** To provide the best recovery options, use the default Full Recovery model. This mode makes it possible to recover data up to the last transaction in the database.

  The downside of Full Recovery is that the Orchestrator database transaction logs can quickly become large. You might need to back them up often, to clear the logs and free up disk space.
- **SQL maximum memory:** Make sure the SQL Server leaves adequate memory for the operating system. The SQL Server can be configured to use a maximum threshold of memory (in megabytes). If the SQL Server has access to all memory, the performance and functionally of the operating system could face a negative impact.
- **SQL authentication mode:** The default SQL Server authentication mode is Windows Authentication mode. If the SQL Server is dedicated to Orchestrator, it should be configured to use only Windows Authentication. Enabling mixed authentication adds a layer of accounts that must be administered and secured. This also exposes an extra attack surface to the SQL Server.

Purging the Orchestrator Database

By default, Orchestrator purges runbook logs daily at 1 a.m., keeping the most recent 500 entries in the database. When the purge job runs, Orchestrator deletes runbook instances, activity instances, and activity instance data information from the database. This is the same information you see in the Runbook Designer when looking at log history:

- The list of completed runbooks on the Log History tab in Figure 10.21 is displaying runbook instance information.

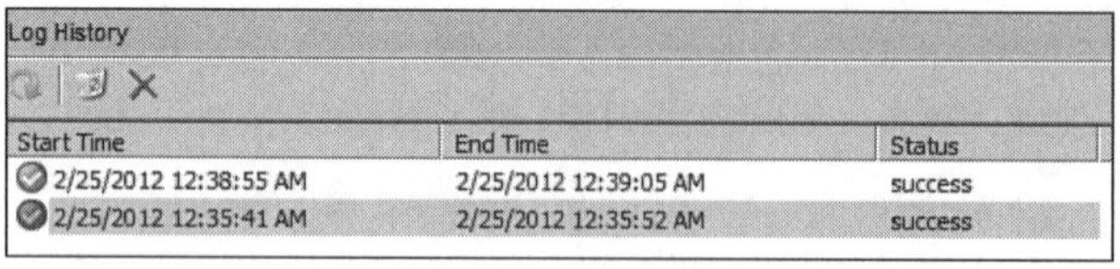

Log History

Start Time	End Time	Status
2/25/2012 12:38:55 AM	2/25/2012 12:39:05 AM	success
2/25/2012 12:35:41 AM	2/25/2012 12:35:52 AM	success

FIGURE 10.21 The Log History tab shows runbook instance data.

- If you open the runbook instance details for one of these runbooks, you are looking at object instance information for that instance (see Figure 10.22).

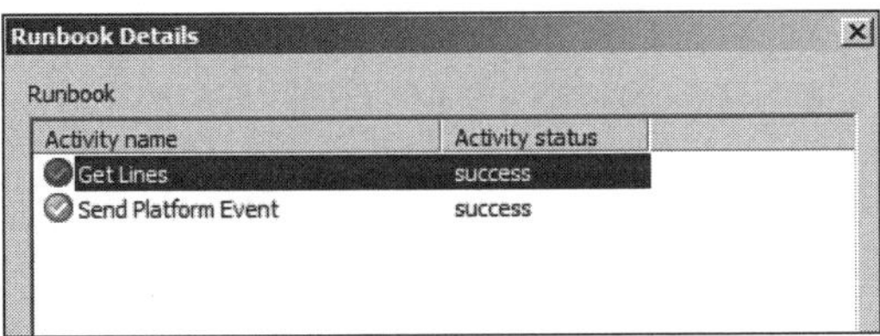

FIGURE 10.22 Runbook information.

- Each object instance includes information about object instance data (see Figure 10.23).

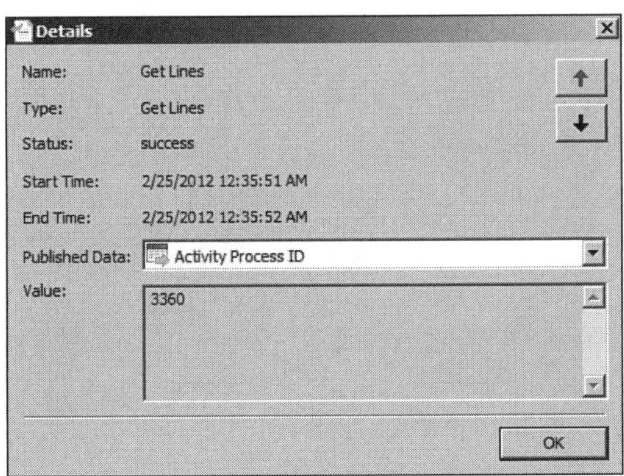

FIGURE 10.23 Object instance details.

The log purge feature affects only runbook historical data; it does not clear deleted data or events from the database. When you delete an activity in a runbook in Orchestrator, the activity is not deleted from the database; it is only marked as deleted (DELETED set to '1' in the OBJECTS table), and the purge job does not clean out objects marked as deleted from the database.

Useful SQL Queries

You can run SQL queries against your Orchestrator database to verify best practices. Remember to verify your database backups before running any queries or performing other activities against the database. Many SQL queries include `DELETED = '0'` as part of the selection criteria; this is because the result should not include objects or activities deleted from runbooks. An activity is not physically deleted when it is deleted in the Runbook Designer; the activity remains in the OBJECTS database table, marked as deleted.

Some of the SQL queries exclude object types. You can run a SQL query against the OBJECTTYPES table to determine what types of objects are being excluded. In this example, the object type listed is `7A65BD17-9532-4D07-A6DA-E0F89FA0203E`, which is a Link object:

```
SELECT * FROM OBJECTTYPES where UniqueID = '7A65BD17-9532-4D07-A6DA-E0F89FA0203E'
```

This next query lists any runbooks with extra logging enabled:

```
SELECT Name from POLICIES WHERE Deleted = '0' AND (LogCommonData = '1' or
LogSpecificData = '1')
```

This query lists any runbook with a blank description field:

```
SELECT Name, Description FROM POLICIES WHERE (Deleted = '0') AND (Description IS
NULL)
```

The following query counts the number of activities in each runbook. This query also includes the runbook timed out setting. Links (object type `7A65BD17-9532-4D07-A6DA-E0F89FA0203E`) are excluded and not counted as activities:

```
SELECT COUNT(POLICIES.Name) AS NOActivities, POLICIES.Name, POLICIES.Version,
POLICIES.PolicyTimeout
FROM OBJECTS INNER JOIN POLICIES ON OBJECTS.ParentID = POLICIES.UniqueID WHERE
(OBJECTS.Deleted = '0') AND (OBJECTS.ObjectType NOT LIKE '7A65BD17-9532-4D07-A6DA-
E0F89FA0203E')
GROUP BY POLICIES.Name, POLICIES.Version, POLICIES.PolicyTimeout
```

The next query lists all activities with default names:

```
SELECT OBJECTS.Name AS ActivityName, POLICIES.Name AS RunbookName
FROM OBJECTS INNER JOIN OBJECTTYPES ON OBJECTS.Name = OBJECTTYPES.Name INNER JOIN
POLICIES ON OBJECTS.ParentID = POLICIES.UniqueID
WHERE (OBJECTS.Deleted = 0)
```

This query lists all **Run Program** activities (Object type is `DD0B3A7B-C7CD-499C-A040-458AD2E94C59`):

```
SELECT OBJECTS.Name AS ActivityName, POLICIES.Name AS RunbookName, TASK_RUNPROGRAM.
Program,
TASK_RUNPROGRAM.WaitTime AS Timeout FROM OBJECTS
INNER JOIN POLICIES ON OBJECTS.ParentID = POLICIES.UniqueID
INNER JOIN TASK_RUNPROGRAM ON OBJECTS.UniqueID = TASK_RUNPROGRAM.UniqueID WHERE
(OBJECTS.ObjectType = 'DD0B3A7B-C7CD-499C-A040-458AD2E94C59') AND (OBJECTS.Deleted = 0)
```

The following query lists all nondeleted objects that are missing a link handling warning result, excluding runbook servers (`3B04C8A0-93DF-4DD0-A88A-D0785A5F217B`), counters (`0BABBCF6-C702-4F02-9BA6-BAB75983A06A`), links (`7A65BD17-9532-4D07-A6DA-E0F89FA0203E`), variables (`2E88BB5A-62F9-482E-84B0-4D963C987231`), and send platform events (`2E88BB5A-62F9-482E-84B0-4D963C987231`):

```
SELECT OBJECTS.Name AS ActivityName, POLICIES.Name AS RunbookName
FROM OBJECTS INNER JOIN
LINKS ON OBJECTS.UniqueID = LINKS.SourceObject INNER JOIN
TRIGGERS ON LINKS.UniqueID = TRIGGERS.ParentID INNER JOIN
POLICIES ON OBJECTS.ParentID = POLICIES.UniqueID WHERE
 (TRIGGERS.Value NOT LIKE '%warning%') AND (OBJECTS.UniqueID IN (SELECT O.UniqueID
FROM
OBJECTS AS O INNER JOIN POLICIES AS POLICIES_1 ON O.ParentID = POLICIES_1.UniqueID
WHERE (O.Deleted = '0')
AND (O.ObjectType <> '3B04C8A0-93DF-4DD0-A88A-D0785A5F217B')
AND (O.ObjectType <> '0BABBCF6-C702-4F02-9BA6-BAB75983A06A')
AND (O.ObjectType <> '2E88BB5A-62F9-482E-84B0-4D963C987231')
AND (O.ObjectType <> '7A65BD17-9532-4D07-A6DA-E0F89FA0203E')
AND (O.ObjectType <> '87E28B20-3E83-45E0-985A-FEEA6CE09084') ))
ORDER BY RunbookName
```

You could change `%warning%` to `%fail%` in the query to list all activities that are missing a link to handle a failed result. The excluded object types are objects that often are not followed by any other activities in a runbook, such as the **Generate Platform Event** activity. The query also excludes infrastructure objects such as runbook servers and variables.

The following SQL query lists all links that have a delay configured:

```
SELECT LINKS.WaitDelay AS LinkDelay, OBJECTS.Name AS LinkName, POLICIES.Name AS
RunbookName, LINKS.Width AS LinkWidth
FROM LINKS INNER JOIN OBJECTS ON LINKS.UniqueID = OBJECTS.UniqueID INNER JOIN
POLICIES ON OBJECTS.ParentID = POLICIES.UniqueID
WHERE (LINKS.WaitDelay <> '0') AND (Objects.Deleted <> '1')
```

Verifying Runbook Design

When different teams author runbooks, ensuring that all runbooks meet the organization's policies for runbook design can become time-consuming. Manually checking all runbooks and verifying their design is possible with a small number of runbooks, but with hundreds of runbooks, reviewing the design and function of each one becomes difficult. A resolution could be to develop a runbook that checks the design of all other runbooks in the Orchestrator database.

The Orchestrator database contains all the runbooks and configuration information for the Orchestrator environment. Querying the database lets you obtain information about runbook design and settings.

The previous section included useful SQL queries to verify runbook design. This section shows how to build a runbook to verify runbook design for runbooks stored in the Orchestrator database. The example runs queries against the database and outputs the results to a report. Begin by performing the following steps:

1. Start Runbook Designer and create a new folder in the navigation tree. In this example, the folder is named **99. Runbook Validator**.

2. In the new folder, create a runbook that will be the master runbook (parent runbook) to trigger the other runbooks. Each child runbook will execute a test. Call the master runbook **99.1 Master**.

3. Create a new subfolder in the Runbook Validator folder. Name the folder **99.1 Links**. In this folder, create a runbook that will execute the first check, which will be to check links with a delay. The runbook is called **99.1.1 Links with Delay**.

4. The runbook will output the results to a text-based report. Because multiple runbooks will use this feature, it will be built as a separate runbook that other runbooks can then invoke.

   In the navigation tree, create a new folder named **99.2 Library**. Figure 10.24 displays the folder structure at this point.

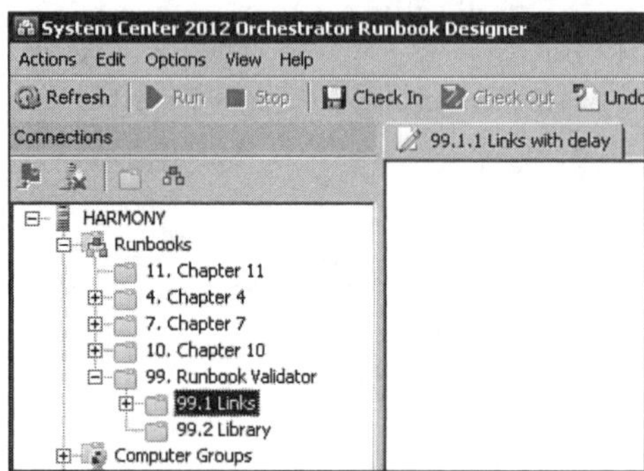

FIGURE 10.24 Folder structure for verifying runbook design.

5. The first check is whether any links are configured with a delay. Navigate to the 99.1.1 Links with Delay runbook and check out the runbook.

6. Add these activities to the 99.1.1 Links with Delay runbook and connect them with links:

   - **Initialize Data**
   - **Query Database**
   - **Invoke Runbook**

7. Create variables for the SQL Server and initial catalog values used by the **Query Database** activity because the same database and server will be used with other queries. Using variables also makes it easier to move these runbooks to another environment; you need only update the variable instead of edit each runbook. Create a subfolder in Variables named **99. Runbook Validator**. In this subfolder, create two variables:

- **Orchestrator SQL Server**
- **Orchestrator database**

Update both variables with settings specific to your Orchestrator environment.

8. Configure the **Query Database** activity Details tab with the following query:

```
SELECT LINKS.WaitDelay AS LinkDelay, OBJECTS.Name AS LinkName, POLICIES.Name
AS RunbookName, LINKS.Width AS LinkWidth FROM LINKS
INNER JOIN OBJECTS ON LINKS.UniqueID = OBJECTS.UniqueID INNER JOIN
POLICIES ON OBJECTS.ParentID = POLICIES.UniqueID
WHERE (LINKS.WaitDelay <> '0') AND (OBJECTS.Deleted <> '1')
```

9. Configure the **Query Database** activity Connection tab with the two variables (see Figure 10.25):
    - **Server**: **{Orchestrator SQL Server}**
    - **Initial catalog**: **{Orchestrator database}**

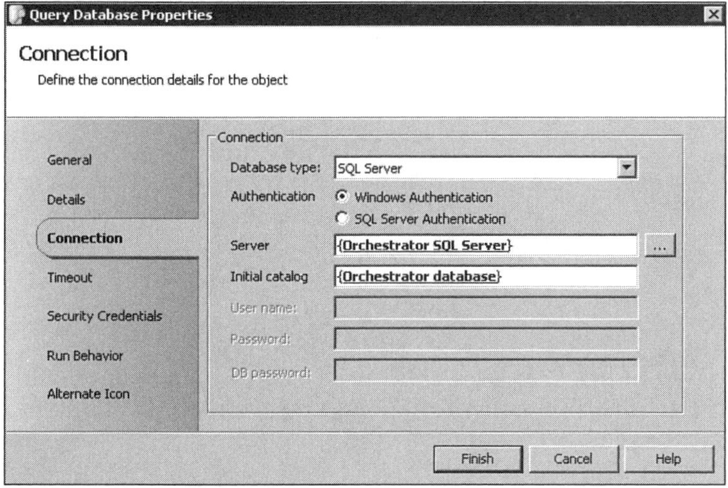

FIGURE 10.25 Query database configuration.

10. Check in the 99.1.1 Links with Delay runbook.

Now create the runbook that will write to the report file. This example creates one report file as a text file, but you can configure your runbooks to create any kind of report file. The report file will create a list with four columns and a header, with each column comma separated. Follow these steps:

1. In the 99.2 Library folder, create a new runbook named **99.2.1 Create Report**.
2. Add an **Initialize Data** activity to the 99.2.1 Create Report runbook.

3. Add an **Append Line** activity to the 99.2.1 Create Report runbook. Connect the two activities with a link.

4. Configure the **Initialize Data** activity with the parameters according to Figure 10.26. These parameters will be input parameters when the runbook is invoked from other runbooks.

5. Create a new variable, **Reportfile**, in the 99.Runbook Validator variables folder. Configure the variable with the path the report file will use, such as C:\TEMP\reportfile.txt.

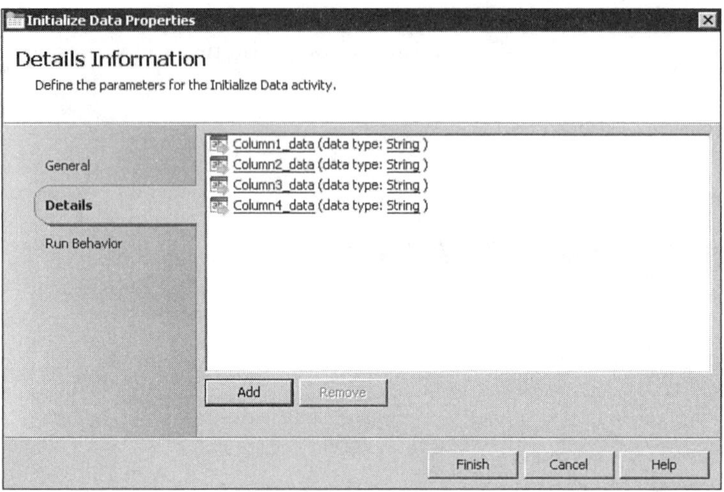

FIGURE 10.26 Initialize Data parameters.

6. In the 99.2.1 Create Report runbook, configure the **Append Line** activity to use the variable for the Report file path. Configure the **Append Line** activity according to Figure 10.27, also shown here:

```
{Column1 data from "Initialize Data"}, {Column2 data from "Initialize Data"},
{Column3 data from "Initialize Data"}, {Column4 data from "Initialize Data"}
```

7. Check in the 99.2.1 Generate Report runbook and navigate to the 99.1.1 Links with Delay runbook. Check out this runbook and open the Properties page of the **Invoke Runbook** activity.

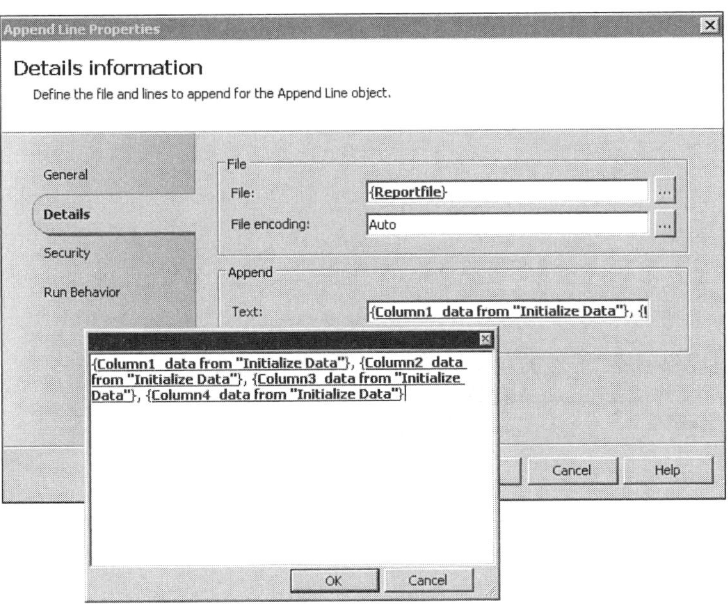

FIGURE 10.27 Append Line configuration.

8. The **Query Database** activity shows the result from the SQL query in one line per row, causing the **Invoke Runbook** activity to be triggered multiple times. Note that this could lead to a performance issue because each **Invoke Runbook** activity takes approximately 5 additional seconds to execute. These examples use a built-in data manipulation feature to split the result line from the **Query Database** activity into strings, each of which is used as an input parameter when the 99.2.1 Generate Report runbook is invoked. Figure 10.28 shows how to configure the **Invoke Runbook** activity, also shown here:

```
[FIELD({Full line as a string with fields separated by ";" from "Query
Database"},';',3)]
```

The FIELD data-manipulation function takes the result line from the **Query Database** activity and splits it into multiple parts based on the comma delimiter. It then takes the third part and uses it as input, so Column1_data will use the first part and Column2_data will use the second part, and so on.

9. Running the runbook now results in a text file that contains all links with a delay. You can add a title and column labels to make the text file more readable.

In the 99.1.1 Links with delay runbook, add an **Append Line** activity between the **Initialize Data** activity and the **Query Database** activity. This is because the **Query Database** activity might produce multiple results, but you don't want to run this activity multiple times, as you do with the **Invoke Runbook** activity.

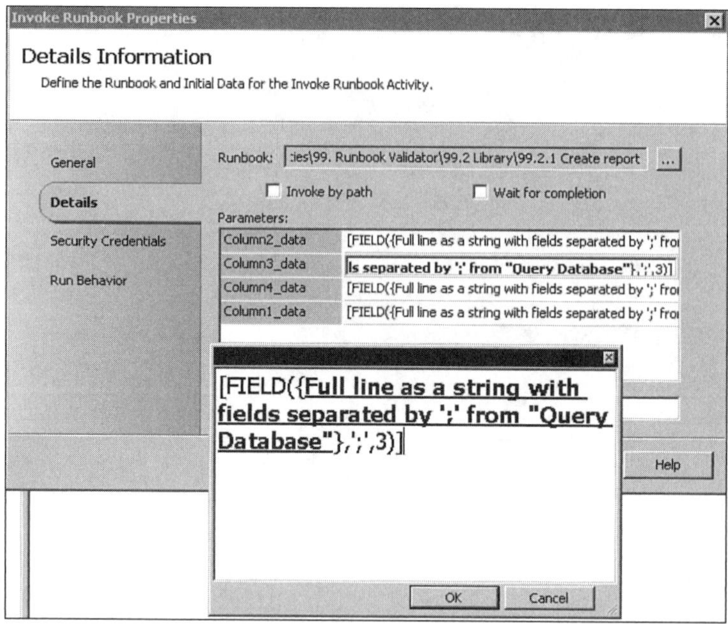

FIGURE 10.28 Data manipulation features to split data from the data bus.

Configure the new **Append Line** activity according to Figure 10.29 or the text shown here:

```
LINKS WITH DELAY
=================
Delay    Link Label     Runbook Name  Link Width
-----------------------------------------------------------------------
```

10. Check in the 99.1.1 Links with Delay runbook.

You have now built one runbook that retrieves input data and writes it to a report file, and another runbook that queries the Orchestrator database for all links configured with a delay. The runbook querying the Orchestrator database invokes the second runbook to write the result of the SQL query to the report file. The last step is to invoke the 99.1.1 Links with Delay runbook from the 99.1 Master runbook. Follow these steps:

1. In the 99.1 Master runbook, add an **Invoke Runbook** activity and configure the activity to invoke the 99.1.1 Links with Delay runbook.
2. Check in the 99.1 Master runbook and run it.
3. When the runbook completes, you can open the report file and review the result.

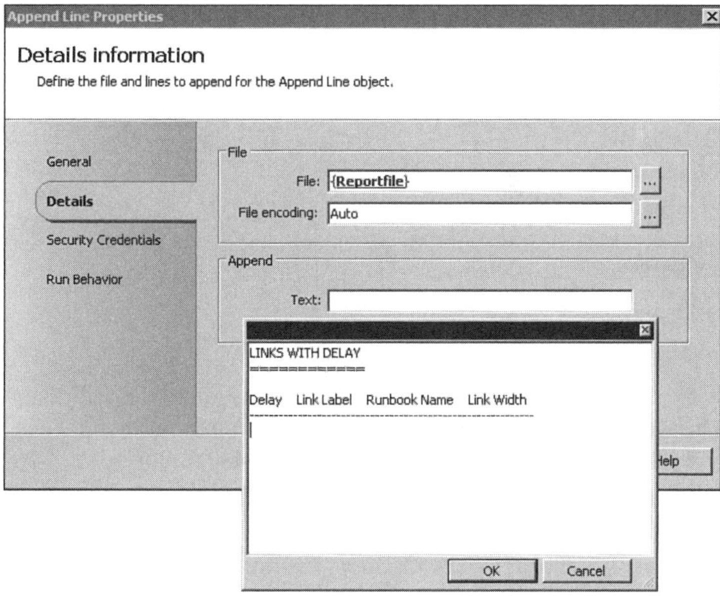

FIGURE 10.29 Append Line writes a topic and column labels.

What if there are no links with delay in your Orchestrator environment? The 99.1.1 Links with Delay runbook triggers the 99.2.1 Generate Report runbook with blank input parameters, which does not provide a good result. To prevent this, update the 99.1.1 Links with Delay runbook to support zero results from the **Query Database** activity. Figure 10.30 shows an updated version of the 99.1.1 Links with Delay runbook.

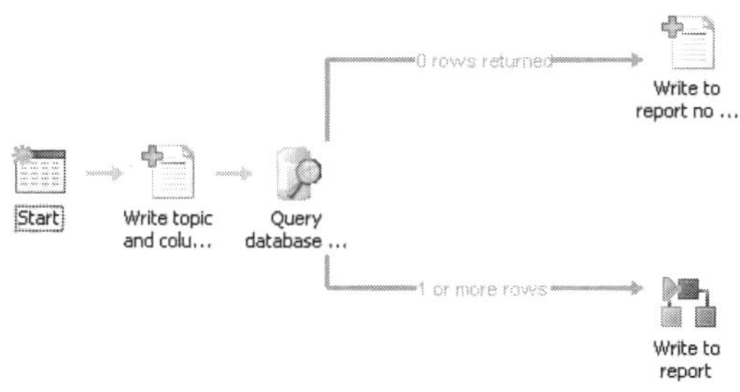

FIGURE 10.30 Updated runbook to handle zero results from SQL.

This updated version has an **Append Line** activity added. This second **Append Line** is configured similarly to the first **Append Line** activity in the runbook; the only difference is that it will write a message "No links with delay found" (see Figure 10.31).

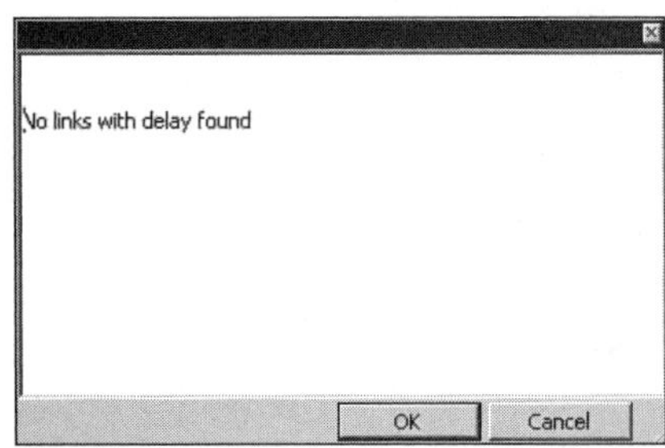

FIGURE 10.31 Report that no links with delay were found.

In the example in Figure 10.30, all the activity names are changed to a name describing what they do. In addition, link colors are changed according to recommendations in the "Runbook Best Practices" section. The two links after the **Query Database** activity use a filter based on the number of results from the query. If there are results, the runbook should branch to the **Invoke Runbook** activity; otherwise, it should execute the **Append Line** activity. Figure 10.32 shows the link settings between the **Query Database** activity and **Invoke Runbook** activity.

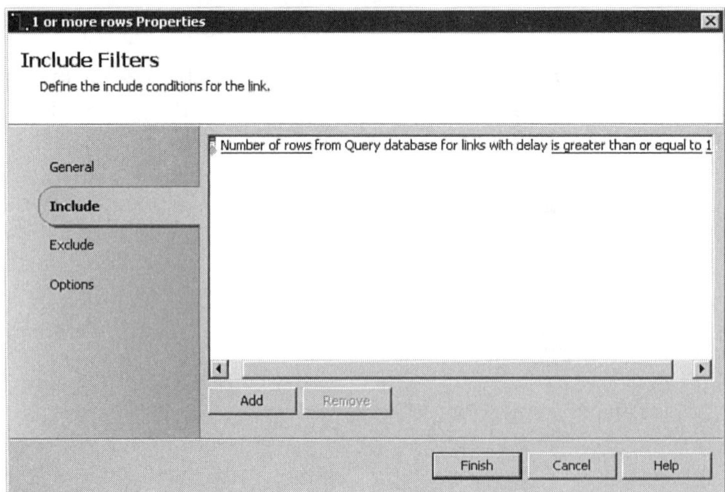

FIGURE 10.32 Configuring the link filter.

To ensure that you always get a current report, add a step in the 99.1 Master runbook to delete old report files. Perform the following steps:

1. Navigate to the 99.1 Master runbook. Check out the runbook and add a **Delete File** activity in front of the **Invoke Runbook** activity.

2. Configure the **Delete File** activity to delete the report file; use the variable to configure the path of the file to delete instead of using hard-coded values.
3. Check in the 99.1 Master runbook and run it.

To add additional runbook design checks, use SQL queries from the "Useful SQL Queries" section or design your own queries based on your organization's requirements. The next example adds a check for activities that use a default name. Follow these steps:

1. Create a new subfolder off the 99 Runbook Validator folder; name this folder **99.3 Naming Convention**.
2. In the 99.3 Naming Convention folder, create a runbook named **99.3.1 Default Name**.
3. Copy the 99.1.1 Links with Delay runbook and use it as a foundation for this runbook. To copy the runbook, navigate to the 99.1.1 Links with Delay runbook, select all activities, right-click, and select **Copy**. Go back to the 99.3.1 Default Name runbook, right-click, and select **Paste**.
4. Update the first **Append Line** activity in the 99.3.1 Default Name runbook, according to Figure 10.33. You should also update the path to the report file.

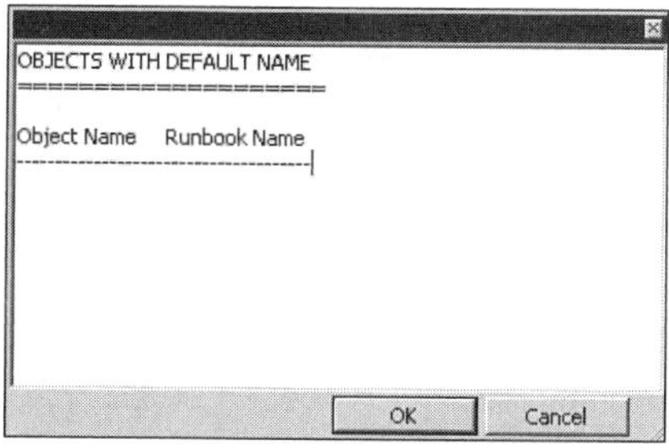

FIGURE 10.33 Updated Append Lines activity.

5. In the 99.3.1 Default Name runbook, update the **Query Database** activity with a new name and new SQL query. Configure this renamed **Query Database** activity with the following SQL query. Note that the query excludes all runbooks with names starting with *99*; this excludes the test runbooks used for the design validation:

```
SELECT OBJECTS.Name AS ActivityName, POLICIES.Name AS RunbookName
FROM OBJECTS INNER JOIN OBJECTTYPES ON OBJECTS.Name = OBJECTTYPES.Name
INNER JOIN POLICIES ON OBJECTS.ParentID = POLICIES.UniqueID
WHERE(OBJECTS.Deleted = 0) AND (POLICIES.Name NOT LIKE '99%')
```

6. In the 99.3.1 Default Name runbook, update the second **Append Line** to write **No objects with default name** to the text file.

10

7. In the runbook, update the **Invoke Runbook** activity with blank values for Column4_data and Column3_data. The SQL query returns two columns with data.
8. Check in the 99.3.1 Default Name runbook and navigate to the 99.1 Master runbook.
9. In the 99.1 Master runbook, add an **Invoke Runbook** activity and configure it to invoke the 99.3.1 Default Name runbook.
10. Configure both **Invoke Runbook** activities in the 99.1 Master runbook to **Wait for completion**. This setting ensures that the second runbook is not invoked until the first runbook reports that it is finished.
11. Check in the 99.1 Master runbook and run it. The 99.1.1 Links with Delay runbook is first invoked and outputs its results to the report file. Next, the 99.3.1 Default Name runbook is invoked and outputs to the same report file.
12. Review your runbooks and update them according to the guidance in this chapter, such as renaming activities to more descriptive names.

This section showed how to build a runbook to validate your other runbooks. In this example, the result was a poorly formatted text file. You can modify this to use a more properly formatted file, such as a HTML report. The example also showed how to automate checking the design of your runbooks.

As with all other runbooks, be sure to test your runbook validator in a sandbox before moving it into production. Many SQL queries and **Invoke Runbook** activities can affect the performance of your runbook servers and the SQL Server hosting the Orchestrator database.

REAL WORLD: COMMUNITY SOLUTION AVAILABLE

Coauthor and former MVP Anders Bengtsson of Microsoft has written a runbook validator package that is available for download. The package includes several runbooks that check runbook design and output to an HTML-based report file. You can download this package from http://contoso.se/blog/?p=3573. This package includes a runbook with all the SQL queries used in this section.

Summary

When you begin working with Orchestrator, you will realize that it is quite easy to build a runbook to execute tasks. However, you will also realize that even the simplest runbook has many "what if" scenarios to consider. After taking into account all the different results and scenarios, you still have to document your runbooks so that your colleagues can understand them as well. This chapter discussed dividing your runbook into multiple runbooks to make them easier to work with and to understand. The chapter also covered how to build runbooks for fault tolerance. It discussed building runbooks as functions and invoking them from other runbooks. The last part of the chapter looked at a solution to automate runbook design validation.

CHAPTER 11

Security and Administration

IN THIS CHAPTER

- ▶ Orchestrator Security Model
- ▶ User Roles and Security

This chapter discusses different aspects of securing System Center 2012 Orchestrator. Orchestrator consists of multiple features, each of which implements security in different ways, depending on the service it provides. Security is multifaceted and involves a number of "if" and "what" considerations. Whereas other System Center components use Run As accounts, Orchestrator can be utilized as a "proxy" layer when running runbooks—that is, an individual with permissions to start a runbook and the input parameters the runbook uses does not require access to the actions the runbook does. This provides additional security and insulates your operators from the operations the runbooks perform.

The chapter includes a discussion of the security model in Orchestrator, including default security settings and approaches for making the Orchestrator environment more secure. The chapter also discusses building customized security groups to control access to different features in the Orchestrator environment.

Orchestrator Security Model

Your security implementation will vary based on how you implement Orchestrator; this could be within a single domain, across multiple domains with cross-domain trusts, across domains with no trust relationship, or outside an Active Directory environment, such as in a workgroup. Microsoft's recommended approach for authentication is using Active Directory, although Orchestrator does not require an Active Directory environment.

If Active Directory is not used or is unavailable, the different features within Orchestrator must use other authentication mechanisms, such as SQL authentication between runbook servers and the Orchestrator database. Authentication and authorization to third-party systems occurs in various ways, depending on the target system. System Center Orchestrator supports encryption; some features are encrypted out of the box, and you can enable encryption for other features as required.

The only data encrypted by default in Orchestrator is specific data in the Orchestrator database, such as passwords, which are encrypted using Advanced Encryption Standard (AES) 128-bit encryption level and SQL Server cell-level encryption. The Orchestrator installer automatically generates an encryption key during database installation, using a random passphrase. Table 11.1 lists information encrypted in Orchestrator.

TABLE 11.1 Encrypted Information in Orchestrator

Component	Description
Activities	All information that is masked (marked with ****) when keyed in the Orchestrator Runbook Designer is also encrypted in the database. This includes passwords but could include other attributes of an activity.
Option menu	The Option menu in the Runbook Designer is used to configure connections to external systems, such as Active Directory. Specifically flagged input fields such as the password in the connection setting are also encrypted in the database.
Variables	When you input a value for a variable, you can check the **Encrypted Variable** check box. This masks the variable value with **** and encrypts the variable in the database.

TIP: SECURING THE DATABASE CONNECTION

For information on encrypting all connections to SQL Server, see http://msdn.microsoft.com/library/ms191192.aspx.

Members of the Orchestrator System or Orchestrator User groups can decrypt passwords. However, SQL Server database administrators and local administrators of the Orchestrator management server can also gain access to encrypted data. In addition, the connection to the Orchestrator database is not secure by default; the exception is when sensitive data is stored or retrieved from the database. Here Orchestrator creates a secured connection to the SQL Server hosting the Orchestrator database using a self-signed certificate. However, this self-signed certificate does not provide strong security and can be subject to man-in-the-middle attacks.

You can use Secure Sockets Layer (SSL) to secure connections to the web-based Orchestration console. SSL can also be used to encrypt the connection from the web service to the database. Traffic is encrypted between an administrator's workstation and the Orchestrator management server by enabling Remote Procedure Call (RPC) encryption. Encryption to third-party systems is dependent on the capabilities of that software.

Figure 11.1 shows an overview of Orchestrator security for the various Orchestrator features. Table 11.2 explains this figure and describes how communication is performed between the Orchestrator features by default.

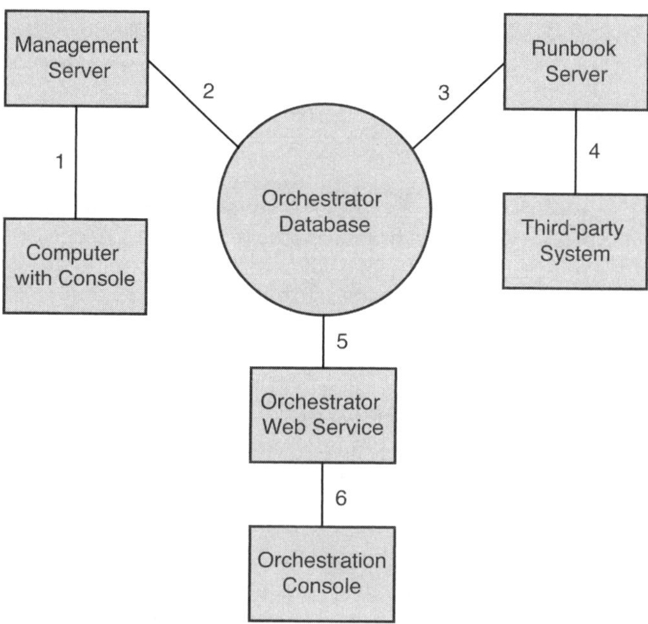

FIGURE 11.1 Orchestrator security by feature.

TABLE 11.2 Orchestrator Security

Link	Feature	Authentication	Channel	Authorization
1	Computer with Orchestrator Runbook Designer and management server	Active Directory	DCOM (RPC encryption, DCOM security settings)	Based on Windows Access Control model; permissions stored in the database
2	Management server and database	Active Directory (password stored in protected file)	SSL	Database permissions
3	Runbook server and database	Active Directory (password stored in protected file) or SQL authentication	SSL	Database permissions
4	Runbook server and third-party system	Depends on integration pack (IP) and target system	Depends on IP and target system	Depends on IP and target system

Link	Feature	Authentication	Channel	Authorization
5	Orchestrator web service and database	Active Directory	SSL	Database permissions
6	Orchestration console and web service	Active Directory	HTTP or HTTPS	Authorization cache stored in the database

TIP: SECURING THE ORCHESTRATOR WEB SERVICE AND CONSOLE

Out of the box, the Orchestrator web service and Orchestration console use HTTP. This is a nonsecure, nonencrypted protocol and should not be used with sensitive data. For information on configuring the Orchestration console and web service to use SSL, see http://msdn.microsoft.com/en-us/library/hh529160.aspx.

An Orchestrator installation creates two security groups, both of which have full administrative access to Orchestrator, including all data in the Orchestrator database and full encryption/decryption rights:

- **Orchestrator Users (OrchestratorUserGroup):** This is the default administrators group in an Orchestrator environment and a member of the Runbook Author user role (for a discussion of user roles and security, see the "User Roles and Security" section). After installation, members of this group can run both the Runbook Designer and Deployment Manager. With default settings, members of this group have the authority to perform the following actions:
    - Create new runbooks; view, change, and run existing runbooks
    - Deploy new runbook servers
    - Deploy new Runbook Designer consoles
    - Register, deploy, and administer IPs
    - View, change, and work with global settings

  If remote access is enabled for the Orchestrator Users group during installation, members of this group can work remotely with Orchestrator. To simplify administration, the authors strongly recommend using an Active Directory security group as the Orchestrator Users group.

- **Orchestrator System (OrchestratorSystemGroup):** This is a local security group created during installation of the Orchestrator management server and Orchestrator runbook server.
    - On the management server, this group includes the service account used for the Orchestrator Runbook Server Monitor service.
    - On runbook servers, it includes the service account for the Orchestrator Runbook Service. Members of this group can execute runbooks.

The account used to install Orchestrator also has full access to the Orchestrator environment. The authors recommend using a service account instead of a personal user account. If you use a personal account and must later remove permissions for that user, it will require a considerable amount of manual work because you must verify security settings on folders and DCOM. Using a domain security group as Orchestrator Users when Orchestrator is installed in an Active Directory environment provides maximum flexibility. Figure 11.2 displays permissions where the installation was performed using the OR_SVC@odyssey.com account and the Orchestrator Users group ODYSSEY\OrchestratorAdmins.

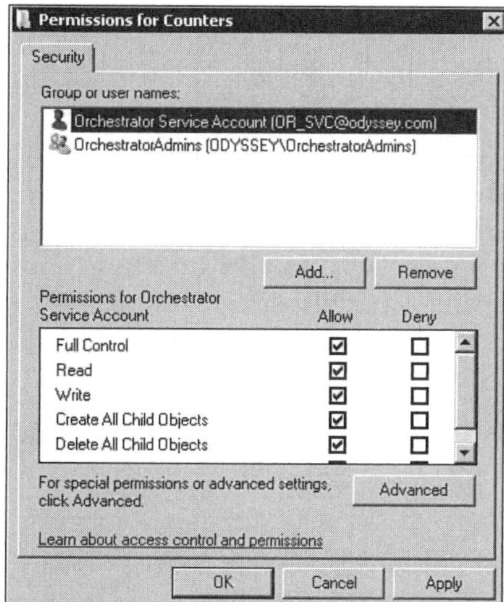

FIGURE 11.2 Default permissions after installing Orchestrator.

TIP: CHANGING THE ORCHESTRATOR USERS GROUP

To change the Orchestrator Users group after installation, use the PermissionsConfig tool. By default, the tool is located in *%ProgramFiles(x86)%*\Microsoft System Center 2012\Orchestrator\Management Server on your Orchestrator management server. For information regarding PermissionsConfig and examples, see http://technet.microsoft.com/en-us/library/hh463588.aspx. The tool enables you to specify the name of the group to use for Orchestrator permissions, a specific user if desired (this user does not have to be a member of the specified group), and whether a system other than the management server can remotely run Runbook Designer.

Running a Runbook Using a Specific Account

The Orchestrator Runbook Service service account is the default account used to execute runbooks. It has permissions to all services and servers with which the Orchestrator environment is integrated. Sometimes you require additional flexibility, such as when you need one runbook to run with a specific account while all other runbooks use the default service account. Several approaches work:

- **Utilizing an additional runbook server that uses a different Runbook Service service account:** All runbooks executing on that runbook server will run under this service account.

  This approach is often used when runbooks are run in multiple network environments, and it is appropriate for reaching into alternate environments such as extranets. An example might be a hoster orchestrating multiple customers that are separated by different Active Directory and network environments.

- **Specifying alternate credentials for many standard activities:** Specifying credentials by activity requires a high level of administration. The authors do not recommend this.

  If you need to specify the same account on multiple activities, the authors recommend using variables because they minimize the risk of incorrect input and make updating runbooks easier. Orchestrator 2012 lets you configure a variable as encrypted, so passwords stored in variables are not displayed or stored in clear text. Even if the variable is encrypted in the database and is not displayed in the Runbook Designer, some activities could publish the encrypted information during runbook execution. Figure 11.3 shows an example of an encrypted variable.

  For additional information about common activity properties such as security credentials, see the TechNet article at http://technet.microsoft.com/en-us/library/hh228165.aspx.

- **Using the Invoke Runbook activity where you can specify an account:** This is good for one-off situations, when using a separate account is on an exception basis.

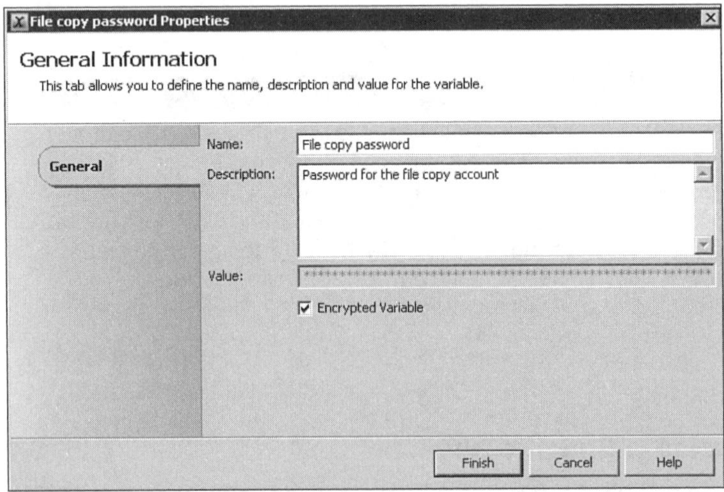

FIGURE 11.3 Encrypt a variable by selecting the Encrypted Variable check box.

This next example illustrates using the **Invoke Runbook** activity to specify a different account when running a child runbook. Here's how it works:

- Figure 11.4 displays a simple runbook that writes the default account name to a text file. The account name is captured by **Run Program**, which runs the WHOAMI command to display the account name. The runbook then is written to a text file using the **Append Line** activity. This runbook invokes the runbook in Figure 11.5.
- The runbook in Figure 11.5 also captures the account name using the **Run Program** activity and writes it to the same file as the first runbook.

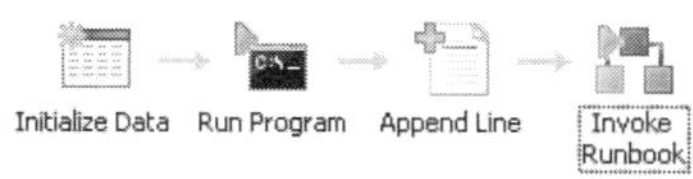

FIGURE 11.4 Parent runbook running with default service account.

FIGURE 11.5 Copy File runbook.

The account used by the second runbook is different from the default. When the runbook in Figure 11.4 invokes the runbook in Figure 11.5 using the **Invoke Runbook** activity, it specifies an account for running the runbook in Figure 11.5. Figure 11.6 shows the account settings.

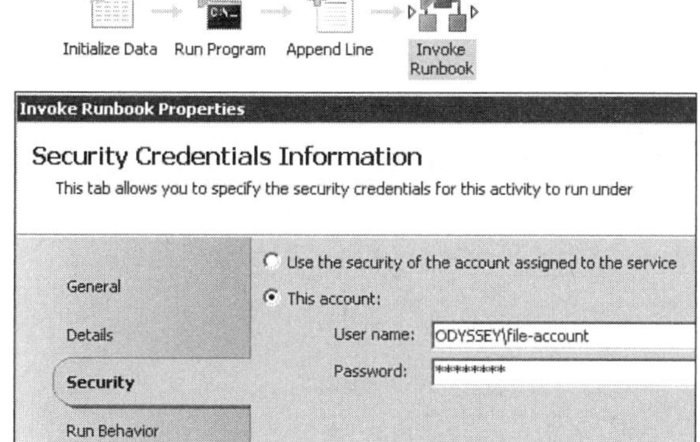

FIGURE 11.6 Specific account configured for the invoked runbook.

The account specified on the Security tab of the **Invoke Runbook** activity must be a member of the OrchestratorSystemGroup; otherwise, an error event will occur (see Figure 11.7). The OrchestratorSystemGroup is a local security group on the Orchestrator management server.

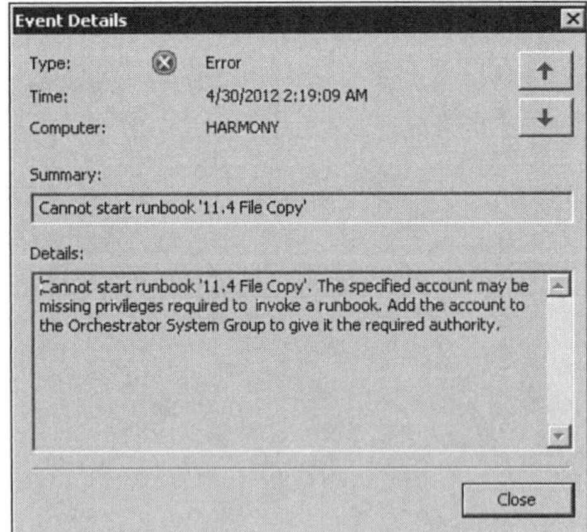

FIGURE 11.7 Error message when an account is missing permissions to invoke a runbook.

Figure 11.8 displays the text file to which both runbooks are writing the account information, displaying the two accounts used to execute the runbooks. The first runbook writes the default Orchestrator Runbook Service service account; the second runbook writes the account specified in the **Invoke Runbook** activity.

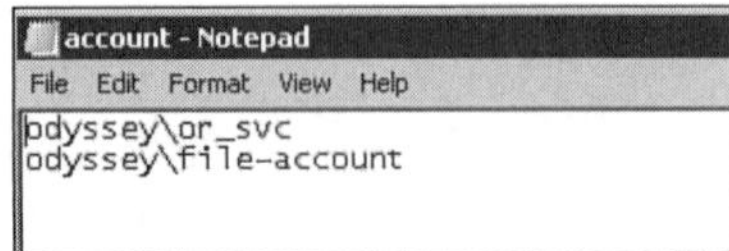

FIGURE 11.8 Different accounts being used in different runbooks.

TIP: DETERMINING THE ACCOUNTS IN USE

You can use a SQL query to determine the accounts being used in your Orchestrator environment. Running the following SQL query against the Orchestrator database lists the activity, username, runbook, and activity type:

```
SELECT OBJECTS.Name AS Activity, OBJECTS.ASC_Username, POLICIES.Name
AS Runbook, OBJECTTYPES.Name AS [Activity Type] FROM OBJECTS
INNER JOIN POLICIES ON OBJECTS.ParentID = POLICIES.UniqueID
INNER JOIN OBJECTTYPES ON OBJECTS.ObjectType = OBJECTTYPES.UniqueID
WHERE (OBJECTS.Deleted <> 1) AND (OBJECTS.ASC_UseServiceSecurity = 0)
```

Auditing in Orchestrator

Orchestrator 2012 supports audit trails. This audit trail consists of several text log files that contain information about the type of integration the runbooks are performing with external systems and activities running on the runbook server. For example, a runbook that includes only a **Send Platform Event** generates log data.

Depending on the actions your runbooks are performing, audit trail log files can grow quite large and consume a significant amount of disk space. If you enable auditing, you should also plan how you will archive and purge these log files. To enable or disable auditing, follow these steps:

1. On the Orchestrator management server, open a command prompt and change directory to the Orchestrator management server folder—by default, *%ProgramFiles(x86)%*\Microsoft System Center 2012\Orchestrator\Management Server.
2. Enable or disable auditing as appropriate using ATLC:
   - To enable auditing, run `ATLC.EXE /enable`.
   - To disable auditing, run `ATLC.EXE /disable`.

Audit trail log files are written to the *%ProgramData%*\Microsoft System Center 2012\Orchestrator\Audit folder. A new log file is created for every 200MB of log data. The Audit folder contains two subfolders used for audit logs:

- **ManagementService:** This folder stores log files that log the date, runbook server, user, and runbook that was started. Figure 11.9 displays an example of the ManagementService log file.

```
2012-May-03 07:20:06,"HARMONY","ODYSSEY\connor","move files"
2012-May-03 07:25:49,"HARMONY","ODYSSEY\john","Clean up grey agents"
```

FIGURE 11.9 Example of the ManagementService log file.

- **PolicyModule:** You will find log files in this folder that log details about each activity in each runbook that is executed. Figure 11.10 shows an example of the PolicyModule log file.

```
2012-May-03 07:20:17,"HARMONY","3896","move files","<Object><UniqueID dataty
2012-May-03 07:20:17,"HARMONY","3896","move files","<Object><UniqueID dataty
2012-May-03 07:25:51,"HARMONY","1440","Clean up grey agents","<Object><Uniqu
```

FIGURE 11.10 PolicyModule log file example.

You can also configure Orchestrator to create trace logs on the management server. By default, log messages are written only when there is an exception in the Orchestrator Management Service; the default folder for the log is *%ProgramData%*\Microsoft System

Center 2012\Orchestrator. The *%ProgramData%* folder is often hidden; access it by typing the path in Windows Explorer. Trace log settings are controlled in the Windows registry under the key `HKEY_LOCAL_MACHINE\SOFTWARE\Wow6432Node\Microsoft\SystemCenter2012\Orchestrator\TraceLogger`. As Figure 11.11 shows, each component of Orchestrator has a set of registry values. Table 11.3 describes which component of Orchestrator each registry key controls.

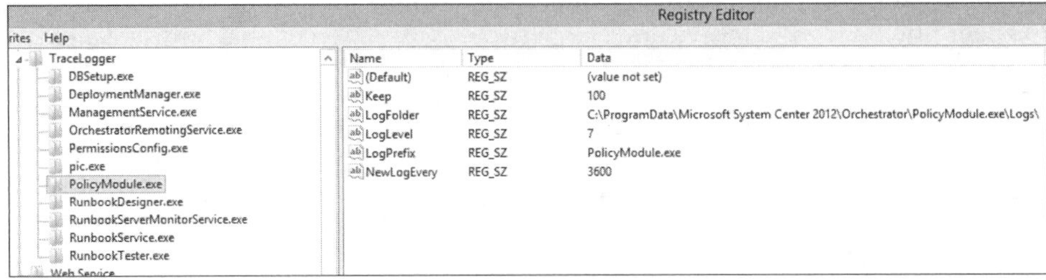

FIGURE 11.11 Trace log settings in the registry.

TABLE 11.3 Trace Log Settings

Component	Registry Key
Audit Trail Tool	Atlc.exe
Data Store Configuration Utility	DBSetup.exe
Management Service	ManagementService.exe
Permissions Configuration tool	PermissionsConfig.exe
Runbook and activities	PolicyModule.exe
Runbook Designer	RunbookDesigner.exe
Runbook Server Monitor	RunbookServerMonitorService.exe
Runbook Service	RunbookService.exe
Runbook Tester	RunbookTester.exe

For each component, you can configure four values:

- **LogFolder:** Location where the trace logs are stored.
- **LogLevel:** Level of details that is logged:
  - **1:** Exception detail only (default)
  - **2:** Warning only
  - **3:** Exception with warning and errors
  - **4:** Only informational messages

- **5:** Informational and error messages
- **6:** Warning and informational messages
- **7:** Full logging

- **LogPrefix:** Log filename prefix. The log filename also includes the date and time the log file is created.
- **NewLogEvery:** Number of seconds until a new log file is created.

The Runbook Designer includes an Audit History tab for each runbook. This tab shows you all changes to a runbook, such as who changed the name of an activity. Figure 11.12 shows Audit History information.

The information the Audit History tab displays is a mix of data from two tables in the Orchestrator database, the OBJECT_AUDIT and CHECK_IN_HISTORY tables. These SQL queries review the audit data:

- Run the following SQL query against your Orchestrator database to retrieve all runbook check-in information, including time stamp, runbook name, and user account:

```
SELECT CHECK_IN_HISTORY.DateTime, POLICIES.Name, SIDS.Account FROM
CHECK_IN_HISTORY INNER JOIN POLICIES ON CHECK_IN_HISTORY.ObjectID =
POLICIES.UniqueID
INNER JOIN SIDS ON CHECK_IN_HISTORY.CheckInUser = SIDS.SID
```

- To review all changes to objects in the Orchestrator database, run this next SQL query. The query shows only objects that are not deleted (`Deleted <> 1`). You can remove the `WHERE` section of the query to see changes to deleted objects:

```
SELECT OBJECT_AUDIT.DateTime, OBJECT_AUDIT.Action, OBJECT_AUDIT.OldValue,
OBJECT_AUDIT.NewValue, OBJECTS.Name AS [Activity Name],
  OBJECTTYPES.Name AS [Activity Type], POLICIES.Name AS [Runbook Name], OBJECTS.
Deleted FROM OBJECT_AUDIT
INNER JOIN OBJECTS ON OBJECT_AUDIT.ObjectID = OBJECTS.UniqueID
INNER JOIN POLICIES ON OBJECTS.ParentID = POLICIES.UniqueID
INNER JOIN OBJECTTYPES ON OBJECT_AUDIT.ObjectType = OBJECTTYPES.UniqueID
WHERE (OBJECTS.Deleted <> 1)
```

You must run both SQL queries to determine who performed a change. The first SQL query shows who checked in the runbook. When the runbook is checked in, it is written to the database; this is when the change that the second query captured is made. Note that the runbook must be checked in to see it using these queries.

Using these two SQL queries and the ATLC audit log, you can monitor any changes made to the Orchestrator environment.

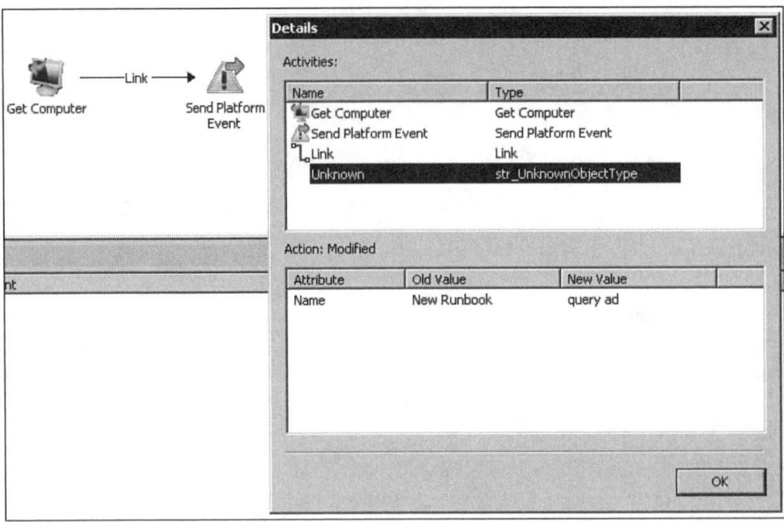

FIGURE 11.12 Example of audit data in the Orchestrator Runbook Designer.

Changing Service Accounts

Orchestrator typically uses three service accounts, although you could use additional service accounts when adding secondary runbook servers:

- Orchestrator Runbook Service account.
- Orchestrator Management Service account.
- System Center 2012 Orchestrator Web Features application pool identity in IIS, used by the Orchestration console and web service. The application pool uses the management server's Orchestrator Management Service account by default.

If all Orchestrator features are installed on the same server, the same account is used for all services. When Orchestrator features are installed on the same server at different times, you can specify different service accounts for each feature.

The Runbook Server Monitor service uses the same account as the Orchestrator Management Service. This service runs on the management server and is responsible for monitoring the health of runbook servers. The Runbook Server Monitor service and Orchestrator Management Service require the same permissions. For additional information regarding Orchestrator service accounts, see http://technet.microsoft.com/en-us/library/hh912319.aspx.

Changing the Orchestrator Runbook Service Account

To change the account used for the Orchestrator Runbook Service, follow these steps:

1. On the SQL Server hosting the Orchestrator database, start SQL Server Management Studio.
2. In SQL Server Management Studio, expand **Security and Logins**.
3. Right-click **Logins** and select **New Login** from the menu.
4. Click **Search** on the Login - New page and select the new service account you will be using. By default, the user or group picker searches the local machine for the account; click **Locations** to change to Active Directory. The authors recommend using a domain account for the service account.
5. On the Login - New page, change the default database to the Orchestrator database. The default name of the Orchestrator database is **Orchestrator**.
6. Click **User Mapping** and select the Orchestrator database. Select **Microsoft. SystemCenter.Orchestrator.Runtime** as the database role. Table 11.4 provides information regarding Orchestrator database security roles. Click **OK**.
7. On the Orchestrator management server, start Server Manager and add the new service account to the local OrchestratorSystemGroup security group.
8. On the Orchestrator runbook server, start the Services management console and update the Orchestrator Runbook Service service to use the new service account. When the service is restarted, the account is granted Log on as a service permissions to the server.

The new service account is now in use on the runbook server. Assign it permissions to the external systems your runbook integrates with, such as file servers. Because all runbooks are executed with this service account, it requires permission to all services with which your runbooks integrate.

Changing the Account Used for the Orchestrator Management Service and Runbook Server Monitor Service

You can change the account used for the Orchestrator Management Service and the Runbook Server Monitor service. Perform the following steps:

1. On the SQL Server hosting the Orchestrator database, start SQL Server Management Studio.
2. In SQL Server Management Studio, expand **Security and Logins**.
3. Right-click **Logins** and select **New Login** from the menu.
4. Click **Search** in the Login - New dialog box and select the new service account. By default, the user or group picker searches the local server for accounts; click **Locations** to change to Active Directory. The authors recommend using a domain account as the service account.

5. Change the default database to the Orchestrator database—**Orchestrator**, by default.
6. Click **User Mapping**, click **User Mapping**, and select the Orchestrator database. Select **Microsoft.SystemCenter.Orchestrator.Admin** as the database role. Click **OK**.
7. On the Orchestrator management server, start Server Manager and add the new service account to the local OrchestratorSystemGroup security group.
8. On the management server, start the Services console and update the Orchestrator Management Service and the Orchestrator Runbook Server Monitor service to use the new account. When the services are restarted, the account is granted Log on as a service permissions to the server.

Changing the Account Used by the Orchestration Console

To update the account that the web-based Orchestration console uses, perform the following steps:

1. On the SQL Server hosting the Orchestrator database, start SQL Server Management Studio.
2. In SQL Server Management Studio, expand **Security and Logins**.
3. Right-click **Logins** and select **New Login** from the menu.
4. Click **Search** on the Login - New page and select the new service account. The user or group picker searches the local server by default for accounts; click **Locations** to change to Active Directory. The authors recommend using a domain account as the service account.
5. Change the default database to the Orchestrator database—**Orchestrator**, by default.
6. Click **User Mapping** on the Login - New page, click **User Mapping**, and select the Orchestrator database. Select **Microsoft.SystemCenter.Orchestrator.Operators** as the database role. Click **OK**.
7. On the server hosting the Orchestration console, open Internet Information Services (IIS) Manager.
8. In IIS Manager, expand Application Pools and select **System Center 2012 Orchestrator Web Features**. Click **Advanced Settings**.
9. Click the **Browse** button next to Identity and select the new service account. Click **OK**.
10. In the IIS Manager, click Application Pools and select **System Center 2012 Orchestrator Web Features**. Then right-click and select **Recycle** from the menu.

Database Roles

Security for the Orchestrator database is implemented through a number of database roles. Table 11.4 describes each role, including the name of the role and its use.

TABLE 11.4 Database Roles

Role	Description
Microsoft.SystemCenter.Orchestrator.Runtime	Gives the services on each runbook server access to information about runbooks. This role is used for the Orchestrator Runbook service account and Runbook Server Monitor service account.
Microsoft.SystemCenter.Orchestrator.Admins	Grants permission to the management server to access tables it requires, to change global settings, and to work with runbooks. The Orchestrator Management Service account uses this role.
Microsoft.SystemCenter.Orchestrator.Operators	This role provides the System Center 2012 Orchestrator Web Service access to the needed permissions to respond to web service requests. Users of the web service obtain their authorization based on the in-application permissions that are defined.

Exporting and Importing Runbooks

Moving a runbook to another Orchestrator environment, such as from test to production, is known as exporting the runbook. During the export process, all encrypted data is decrypted from the database and written to the export file; this file is in eXtended Markup Language (XML) format and has an extension of ois_export.

All sensitive data is encrypted in the Orchestrator database based on an encryption key generated during installation. Sensitive data in the export file is also encrypted, based on the password provided when exporting the runbook. This password is used only to protect sensitive data such as encrypted variables and passwords. All other data can be read and modified in the XML file.

When you an import a runbook, you must supply the password for the export file for the encrypted data to be imported. Otherwise, those data fields are imported as blank and must be reconfigured in the new environment.

Figure 11.13 shows the Import runbook page and the Import Orchestrator encrypted data check box. If you do not check this check box, you are not prompted for a password and no encrypted data is imported. Figure 11.14 displays the error message generated if you provide an incorrect password while importing a runbook.

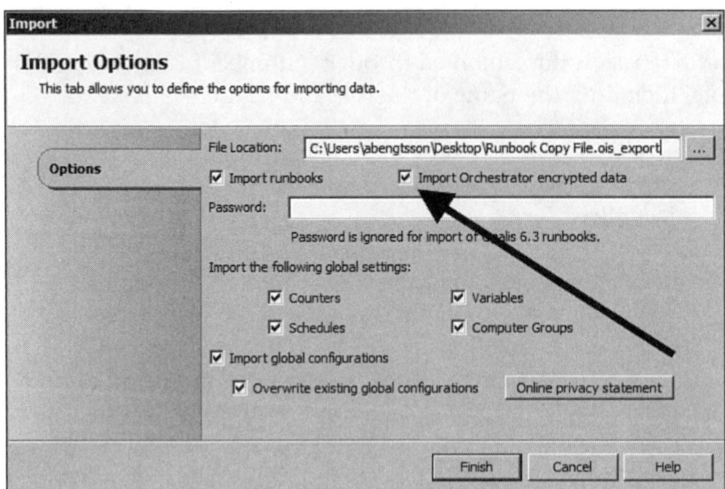

FIGURE 11.13 Import runbook with encrypted data.

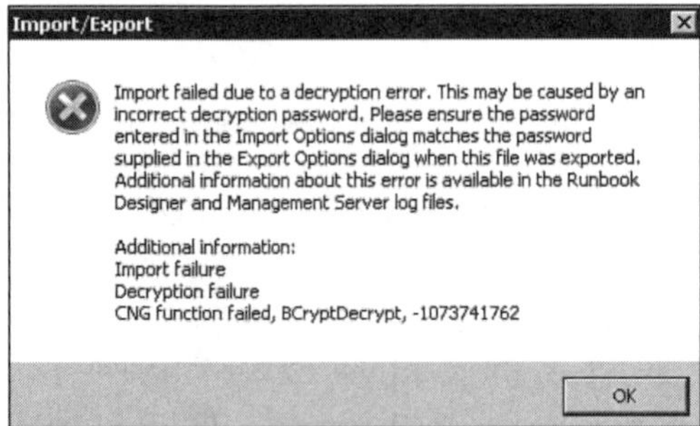

FIGURE 11.14 Message displayed specifying an incorrect encryption password.

Before exporting runbooks, verify that they are not checked out. This is easy to determine when exporting a single runbook. However, if you export a number of folders with subfolders, navigating all of them and verifying the status of each can be difficult. If you export a runbook that is checked out, you are exporting the current version from the database, not the checked-out version; this means that the version being exported might not be current. You can use a SQL query to list all runbooks that are checked out. The following query also shows you the client machine and who checked them out:

```
SELECT POLICIES.Name, POLICIES.CheckOutTime, CLIENTCONNECTIONS.ClientUser,
CLIENTCONNECTIONS.ClientMachine FROM POLICIES
INNER JOIN CLIENTCONNECTIONS ON POLICIES.CheckOutLocation = CLIENTCONNECTIONS.
ClientMachine
WHERE (POLICIES.Deleted <> '1') AND (POLICIES.CheckOutUser IS NOT NULL)
```

Now you are ready to export a runbook. Follow these steps:

1. Start the Runbook Designer.
2. Verify that the runbooks you will export are checked in. Figure 11.15 shows the tabs for three runbooks, illustrating their status:
    - ▶ The Change account runbook on the left showing a lock icon is checked out by another user.
    - ▶ The Default account runbook in the middle has a pencil icon, meaning that it is checked out.
    - ▶ The Password runbook on the right with the runbook icon is checked in.

FIGURE 11.15 Checked out and checked in runbooks.

3. Right-click the tab of the runbook you want to export. Select **Export** from the context menu.
4. Specify an export file location and password. If you do not supply a password, the encrypted data is still exported and is encrypted in the export file. However, the encryption is based on a 0-length string to ensure that sensitive data is not written to the export file in clear text. You also need to use a blank password when importing the runbook. Click **Finish** to begin the export.

You can also export a folder, including all runbooks within that folder. To export a folder and all its runbooks, right-click a folder in the Navigation pane and then select **Export** from the context menu. Figure 11.16 show the Export dialog box when exporting a folder.

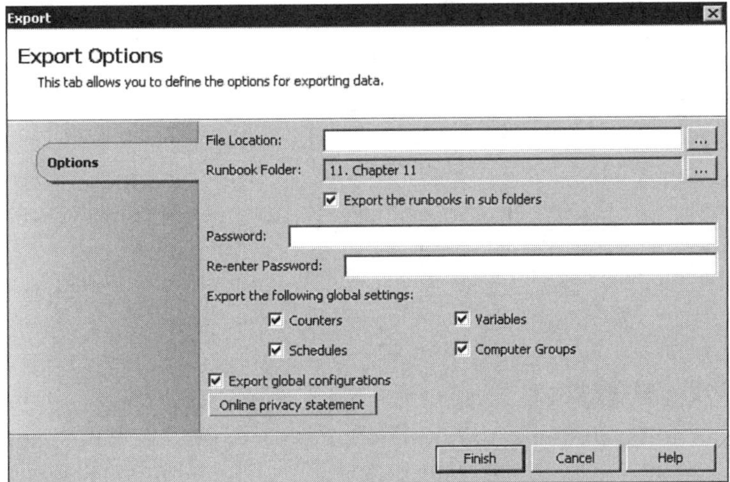

FIGURE 11.16 Export of a folder, including all runbooks.

Notice in Figure 11.16 that you can deselect settings such as counters, variables, and global configurations. This means that if your runbooks do not use computer groups, you can deselect that setting and it will not be included in the export file. Each setting includes all items of that category, so if you export counters, all counters are exported, not just the counters used by the runbooks you export.

To import a runbook or runbooks from an export file, right-click a folder in the navigation pane and select **Import** from the context menu. Figure 11.17 shows the Import dialog box. This page looks similar to the Export dialog box in Figure 11.16.

CAUTION: UPDATING VARIABLE VALUES FROM AN EXPORT FILE

If you import an export file that includes an existing variable, a dialog box appears asking whether you want to override the current variable value or create new variables. If you choose to create new global settings, you must update your runbooks; they are not updated automatically.

For example, if you import a runbook that uses a variable named File Path and, during import, choose not to override existing variables, but to instead create a new variable, this new variable will be named File Path (1), but the runbook you just imported will still use the File Path variable. The mapping between variables in import files and variables already in the Orchestrator environment is based on the variable name.

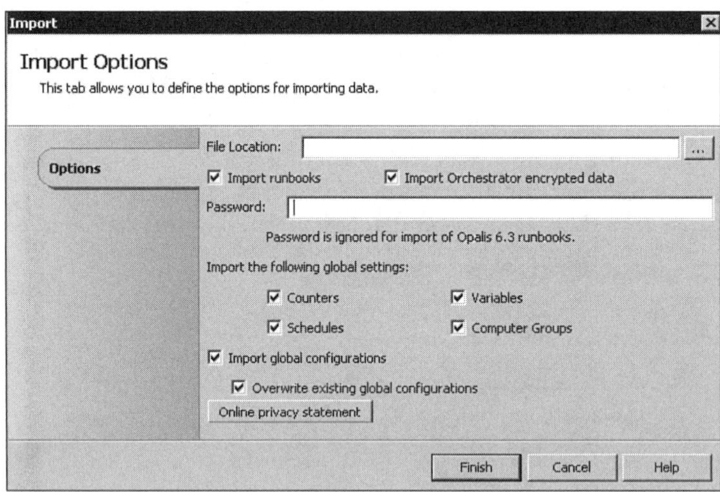

FIGURE 11.17 Import of a folder, including all runbooks.

User Roles and Security

Orchestrator has two core user roles: Runbook Authors and Runbook Operators. Runbook Authors have administrative access to Orchestrator, including the Orchestrator database and configuration. Runbook Operators can access the Orchestration console and web service, based on rights Runbook Authors grant to them. Table 11.5 describes these roles.

TABLE 11.5 Orchestrator User Roles

User Role	How Used	Rights
Runbook Author	Has membership in the Orchestrator Users group. Users placed in this security group are Orchestrator administrators with full access to Orchestrator and the Orchestrator database, including access to encrypt and decrypt data in the database.	Administrators of Orchestrator. Read, write, and update Orchestrator configuration. Full encryption/decryption rights. Access to runbook activities that can interact with external systems using IPs.
Runbook Operator	Grants permission to the management server to access tables it requires, to change global settings, and to work with runbooks. The Orchestrator Management Service account uses this role.	Nonadministrative rights to Orchestrator. Access to the Orchestration console and web service. View and invoke runbooks based on rights granted by Runbook Authors.

Typically, you need to create specialized security groups instead of using the built-in roles because multiple teams will be developing runbooks in Orchestrator, and you might not want the teams to be capable of accessing each other's work.

NOTE: ABOUT ORCHESTRATOR USER ROLES

Orchestrator security works somewhat differently from other System Center components, such as Operations Manager or Service Manager. User roles in those components are mapped to security groups. While Orchestrator has two core user roles, customizing security consists of creating security groups and assigning those groups permissions, but not mapping them to these built-in roles. You might see these then referred to as "roles," but there is no mapping of security groups to roles as with other System Center components.

The next examples use a scenario in which multiple teams are developing runbooks. Three teams are working in the same Orchestrator environment. These three groups, the Active Directory team, the Operations Manager team, and the Orchestrator team, should have different security access to Orchestrator:

- The Active Directory and Operations Manager teams should not see or be enable to modify each other's runbooks or global settings. They should have access only within their own runbook folder(s).
- The Orchestrator team should have all permissions so that it can import and update IPs and edit and import/export all runbooks.

There is also a Help Desk team, which should be able to start runbooks for both the Active Directory and Operations Manager teams.

For ease of administration, the authors recommend utilizing security groups when assigning security permissions instead of adding explicit user accounts to objects in Orchestrator. If the servers hosting Orchestrator components are members of an Active Directory domain, use Active Directory security groups. This example incorporates five groups:

- **OrchestratorUserGroup:** This is the default group configured during installation of Orchestrator.
- **OrchestratorADTeamGroup:** Active Directory engineers are members of this group.
- **OrchestratorOpsMgrTeamGroup:** Operations Manager engineers belong to this group.
- **OrchestratorRemoteConsole:** This group consists of all engineers that will use the Orchestrator Runbook Designer console remotely.
- **OrchestratorSupportTeamGroup:** Help Desk operators are members of this group.

The first task is to install the Orchestrator Runbook Designer to workstations that the different teams use. You should run the Orchestrator Runbook Designer remotely instead of on an Orchestrator server; this can be installed using the Orchestrator Deployment Manager or by performing a manual installation from the Orchestrator installation media. Chapter 5, "Installing System Center 2012 Orchestrator," discusses the steps to deploy the Runbook Designer with Deployment Manager

TIP: INTEGRATION PACKS ARE NOT A SECURITY BOUNDARY

As part of installing the Runbook Designer, you can select IPs to deploy to the target computer. Avoiding deployment of IPs to a workstation does not enhance security: A local user can still add them and connect to the Orchestrator environment.

Notice that if the Runbook Designer is started from a workstation before the appropriate permissions are configured, the connection error dialog box in Figure 11.18 appears. This error is typically due to COM Server application permissions. The error often generates event ID 10016 in the System error log (see Figure 11.19), identifying the application to which the user needs access. To modify the security permissions to the COM Server application, use the Component Services administrative tool (dcomcnfg).

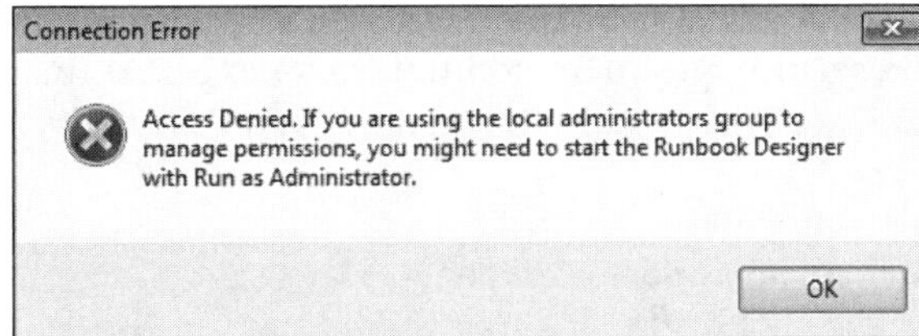

FIGURE 11.18 Connection error when connecting with incorrect permissions.

NOTE: PERFORMING PUSH INSTALL THROUGH FIREWALL

Push installation of the Runbook Designer console is accomplished using SMB/CIFS. TCP ports 135, 139, 445 and TPC dynamic ports must be accessible on the target computer. Ensure that these ports are open if using a firewall. You also need to enable Windows Firewall rules for WMI and DCOM for any activities that use WMI communication, such as monitoring activities. Read more about using the Windows Firewall with Orchestrator at http://technet.microsoft.com/en-us/library/hh912321.aspx.

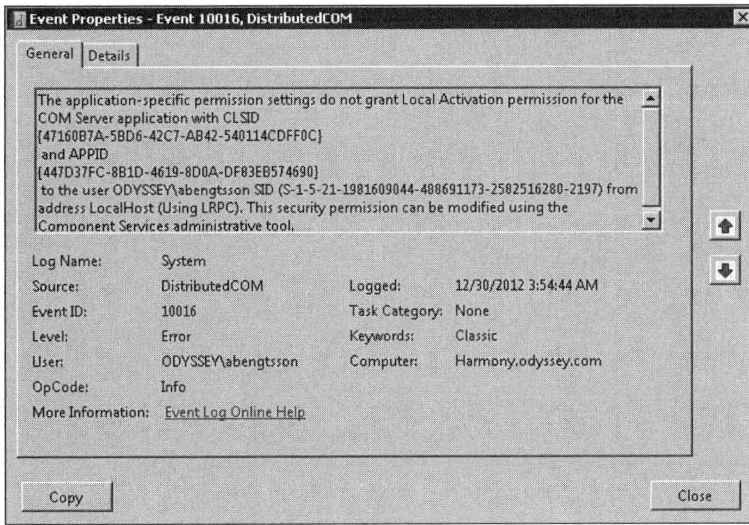

FIGURE 11.19 Missing COM Server application permissions.

Connecting Remotely

This next scenario includes multiple teams that need to run the Orchestrator Runbook Designer remotely. The authors recommend creating a single Active Directory security group that enables all Orchestrator users to connect the Orchestrator management server and then using specific Active Directory security groups for each team's permissions. As an example, an engineer connecting to the Orchestrator environment would need to be a member of the OrchestratorRemoteConsole security group, in addition to an expert team security group, such as the OrchestratorADTeamGroup. The next sections step through configuring the various security groups.

Assigning Permissions to Connect to the Management Server to the OrchestratorRemoteConsole Group

The OrchestratorRemoteConsole Group must be granted access to the Orchestrator management server. Perform the following steps to configure the OrchestratorRemoteConsole group with the necessary permissions:

1. On the Orchestrator management server, open the Component Services console and navigate to **Component Services** -> **Computers** -> **My Computer** -> **DCOM Config.**
2. In the list of DCOM applications, scroll down and select **omanagement.** Right-click and select **Properties** (see Figure 11.20).

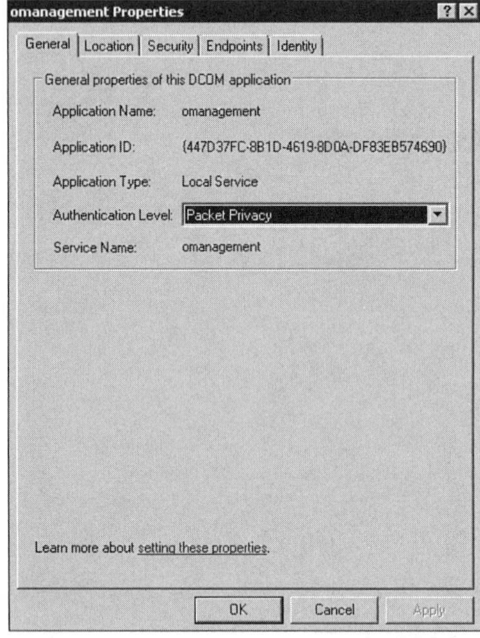

FIGURE 11.20 omanagement DCOM application.

3. In the omanagement Properties window, click the **Security** tab.
4. Click **Edit** in the Launch and Activation Permissions area, click **Add**, and add the **OrchestratorRemoteConsole** security group from Active Directory. Assign the OrchestratorRemoteConsole security group **Remote Launch** and **Remote Activation** permissions (see Figure 11.21). Click **OK**.

5. Click **Edit** in the Access Permissions area, click **Add**, and add the **OrchestratorRemoteConsole** security group from Active Directory. Assign the OrchestratorRemoteConsole security group **Remote Access** and **Local Access** permissions (see Figure 11.22). Click **OK**.
6. In the Component Services console, right-click **My Computer** and select **Properties** from the context menu.
7. In the My Computer Properties box, select the **COM Security** tab.
8. Click **Edit Limits** in the Access Permissions area. Click **Add** and add the **OrchestratorRemoteConsole** security group from Active Directory. Assign the OrchestratorRemoteConsole security group **Remote Access** permissions. Click **OK**.

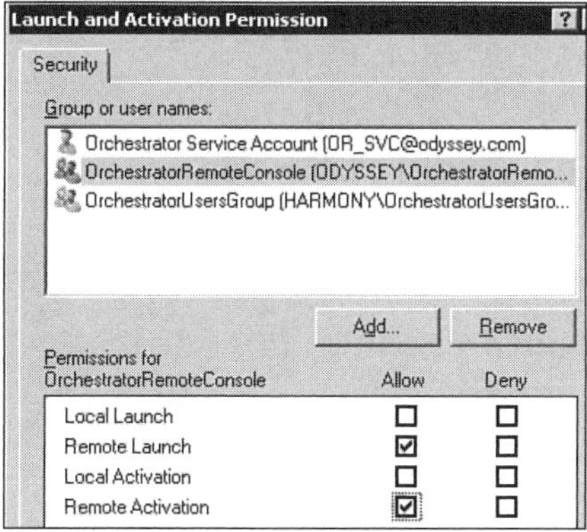

FIGURE 11.21 Remote Launch and Activation permissions.

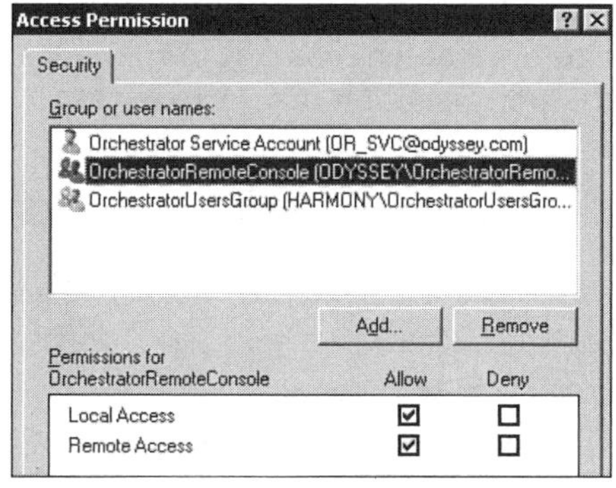

FIGURE 11.22 Remote and Local Access permissions.

9. Click **Edit Limits** in the Launch and Activation Permissions area. Click **Add** and add the **OrchestratorRemoteConsole** security group from Active Directory. Assign the OrchestratorRemoteConsole security group **Remote Launch** and **Remote Activation** permissions. Click **OK**.

10. Close the Component Services console.
11. After configuring all permissions, start the Services console on the Orchestrator management server, and restart the Orchestrator Management Service (ManagementService.exe).

Assigning the OrchestratorRemoteConsole Group Permissions to the Runbooks Folder

All users using the Orchestrator Runbook Designer require Read permissions to the top level of the Runbooks folder. To assign the OrchestratorRemoteConsole security group permissions to the root level, follow these steps:

1. Start the Orchestrator Runbook Designer as an Orchestrator administrator.
2. Right-click the Runbooks folder and select **Permissions** from the context menu.
3. In the Permissions for Runbooks page, click **Add** and add the **OrchestratorRemoteConsole** security group from Active Directory.
4. Deselect everything except Read permissions for the OrchestratorRemoteConsole group.
5. Click **Advanced** in the Permissions for Runbooks dialog box.
6. Select the **OrchestratorRemoteConsole** security group and click **Edit**.
7. In the Permissions Entry for Runbooks page, change the Apply To drop-down menu to **This object only**. Click **OK**.
8. Click **OK** on the Advanced Security Settings for Runbooks page.
9. Click **OK** in the Permissions for Runbooks page.

Assigning Remote Users Group Access to Runbook Servers

Depending on your environment, different teams might need different access to runbook servers. Perform the following steps to assign the OrchestratorRemoteConsole access to all runbook servers:

1. Start the Orchestrator Runbook Designer as an Orchestrator administrator.
2. Right-click the **Runbook Servers** folder; then select **Permissions** from the context menu.
3. In the Permissions for Runbook Servers dialog box, click **Add** and add the **OrchestratorRemoteConsole** security group from Active Directory. Click **OK**.
4. Deselect all permissions for the OrchestratorRemoteConsole except Read. Click **OK**.

Assign OrchestratorRemoteConsole Permission to List Global Settings

Your different teams also need access to global settings. To give the OrchestratorRemoteConsole security group permissions to list global settings, follow these steps:

1. Start the Orchestrator Runbook Designer as an Orchestrator administrator.
2. Expand Global Settings and, one by one, right-click **Counters**, **Variables**, and **Schedules**. Select **Permissions** from the context menu.
3. In the Permissions dialog box, click **Add.** Then add the **OrchestratorRemoteConsole** security group from Active Directory. Click **OK**.
4. Select the **OrchestratorRemoteConsole** group and click **Advanced**.
5. On the Advanced Security Settings page, select the **OrchestratorRemoteConsole** security group and click **Edit**.
6. On the Permission Entry page, select the **Apply To** drop-down list and select **This object only**. Then select only the **List Contents** and **Read Properties** permissions. Click **OK**.
7. In the Advanced Security Settings dialog box, click **OK**.
8. In the Permissions page, click **OK**.

Access Denied Error

You have now configured the OrchestratorRemoteConsole security group with permission to connect remotely to the Orchestrator management server using the Runbook Designer. The security group cannot access anything in the Runbook Designer console other than runbook servers and will receive an error such as the one in Figure 11.23 if they try to access any other area. The next task is to configure permissions for the different teams: the Active Directory team and the Operations Manager team. The next sections discuss this.

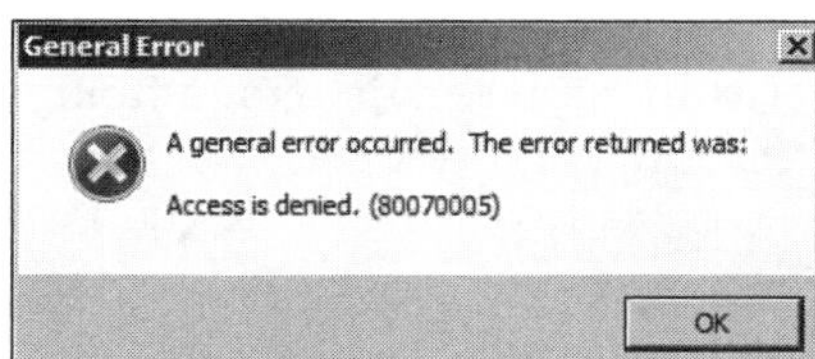

FIGURE 11.23 Missing permissions, access denied.

Creating Runbook Folders

This next example creates two runbook folders under the root Runbooks folder. You create a runbook folder for each team, one folder for the Operations Manager team and one folder for Active Directory team.

When you begin working with Orchestrator security, you will quickly realize the importance of planning. If you realize after some time with Orchestrator in production that you need to reconfigure all permissions in Orchestrator, you might have a massive amount of manual work. It is important to plan your security structure before implementing it.

Perform the following steps to create two runbook folders, one for each team. This procedure also configures permissions on each folder:

1. Start the Orchestrator Runbook Designer as an Orchestrator administrator.
2. Right-click the **Runbooks** folder and select **New Folder**.
3. Name the folder **Active Directory Team**.
4. Create a folder named **Operations Manager Team**.
5. Right-click each folder you created; select **Permissions** from the context menu.
6. For the Active Directory Team folder, click **Add** and add the **OrchestratorADTeamGroup** security group from Active Directory. Click **OK**.
7. For the Operations Manager Team, click **Add** and add the **OrchestratorOpsMgrTeamGroup** security group from Active Directory. Click **OK**.

The Operations Manager and the Active Directory teams also need access to global settings. Follow these steps:

1. Start the Orchestrator Runbook Designer as an Orchestrator administrator. Navigate to **Global Settings**.
2. Under Counters, Variables, and Schedules, create two folders, one named **Active Directory Team** and the other named **Operations Manager Team**.
3. Right-click each new folder and select **Permissions** from the context menu.
    - Click **Add** and add the **OrchestratorADTeamGroup** security group from Active Directory to the Active Directory Team folder. Click **OK**.
    - Click **Add** and add the **OrchestratorOpsMgrTeamGroup** security group from Active Directory to the Operations Manager Team folder. Click **OK**.

    The two teams now have access to global settings.

Assigning Permissions to Runbooks for Help Desk Operators

A common scenario is assigning runbook permissions to individuals that need to start them through the Orchestration console. This could be an engineer in first-level support who requires permissions to start a troubleshooting runbook against a server. Enabling troubleshooting runbooks for first-level support can save considerable time at the second- and third-level support tiers. You can design these troubleshooting runbooks so that even if first-level support has limited knowledge and permissions to the system, it can still start a runbook that performs basic troubleshooting.

This next example uses two Active Directory security groups, OrchestratorWebUsers and OrchestratorFirstLine. Users using the Orchestration console as the only Orchestrator user interface are members of the OrchestratorWebUser security group. First-level support individuals using Orchestrator are also members of the OrchestratorFirstLine security group.

To assign a user permission to connect to the Orchestration console and start a runbook, follow these steps:

1. Start the Runbook Designer as an Orchestrator administrator.
2. Right-click the **Runbooks** folder in the navigation pane and select **Permissions** from the menu.
3. In the Permissions for Runbooks dialog box, click **Add** and add the **OrchestratorWebUsers** security group.
4. Select the **OrchestratorWebUsers** group and click **Advanced**.
5. In the Advanced Security Settings for Runbooks dialog box, select **OrchestratorWebUsers** and click **Edit**.
6. On the Permissions Entry for Runbooks page, change the Apply to drop-down menu to **This object only**.
7. Click **Clear All**.
8. Check **Allow for List Contents** and **Read Properties**, as in Figure 11.24. Click **OK**.
9. In the Advanced Security Settings for Runbooks dialog box, click **OK**.
10. Click **OK** on the Permissions for Runbooks page.

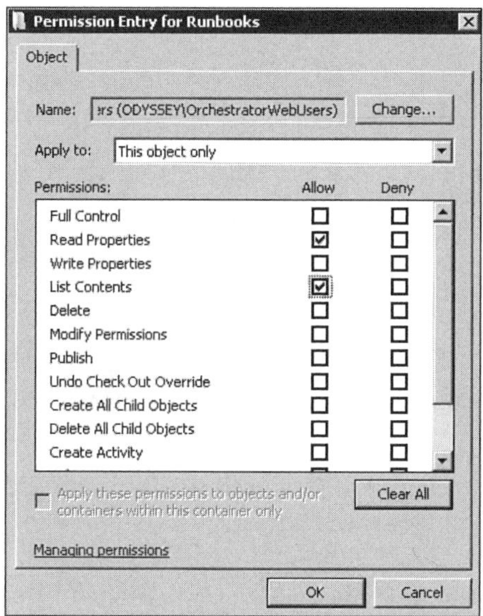

FIGURE 11.24 Permissions for the OrchestratorWebUsers security group.

If a member of the OrchestratorWebUsers security group now navigates to the Orchestration console (default address http://*<servername>*:82), he or she can access the console but not see any Orchestrator data in the console other than the root folder. This example assigned only permissions to see the folder root. By default, all members of the local Users group on the Orchestration console server have permissions to access the Orchestration console folder (by default, *%ProgramFiles(x86)%*\Microsoft System Center 2012\Orchestrator\Orchestration Console). All domain users are members of the Users security group by default. However, without having Orchestrator permissions, they cannot see anything in the Orchestration console.

Figure 11.25 shows the Navigation pane of the Runbook Designer. If you assign permissions to runbooks in the Level 2.1.1 folder, that group or user also requires permission to the Runbooks folder, the Level 2 folder, and the Level 2.1 folder. To give members of the OrchestratorFirstLine security group access to runbooks in the Level 2 folder, follow these steps:

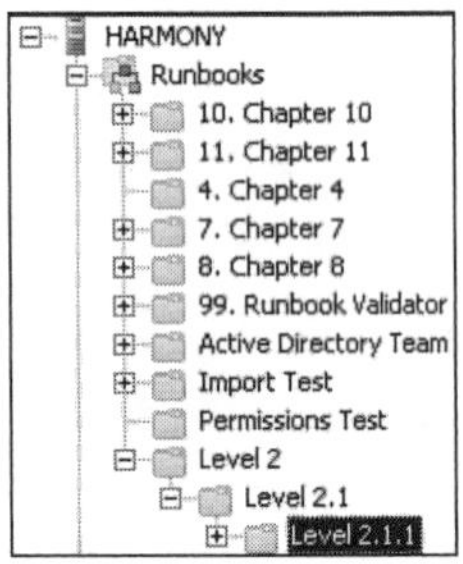

FIGURE 11.25 Example of runbook folder structure.

1. Start the Runbook Designer as an Orchestrator administrator.
2. Right-click the **Level 2** folder in the navigation pane and select **Permissions** from the menu.
3. On the Permissions for Level 2 page, click **Add** and add the **OrchestratorFirstLine** security group.
4. Select the **OrchestratorFirstLine** group and click **Advanced**.
5. On the Advanced Security Settings for Level 2 page, select the **OrchestratorFirstLine** security group and click **Edit**.
6. On the Permissions Entry for Level 2 page, click **Clear All**. Then select **Allow** for **Read Properties**, **List Contents**, and **Publish**. Publish is the permission that gives users access to start and stop the runbook. Figure 11.26 shows an error message that appears if the user tries to start a runbook without Publish permission. Click **OK**.

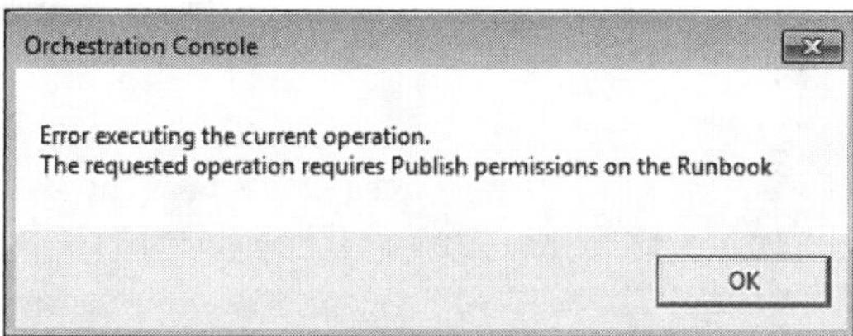

FIGURE 11.26 Error when missing the Publish permission.

7. Click **OK** on the Advanced Security Settings for Level 2 page.
8. Click **OK** on the Permissions for Level 2 page.

Members of the OrchestratorFirstLine security group can now log on to the Orchestration console and start runbooks in the Level 2 folder.

Summary

When you begin integrating your different services and servers in your IT environment, you soon realize that Orchestrator needs a number of permissions to work properly. To automate an IT process, the Orchestrator service account requires the same permissions as the engineers who would be performing that process. Orchestrator can be a powerful tool that saves time for the IT department, but it could be a tool that can cause issues if not used properly.

The chapter looked at the security model in Orchestrator. It also covered how to give permissions to specific components and parts of Orchestrator to different groups of engineers. It discussed how to configure Orchestrator to use multiple service accounts instead of one account with all permissions. The chapter also covered auditing capabilities. Auditing is important in a tool such as Orchestrator because knowing who did what is critical when dealing with security issues.

PART III

Integration Packs and the OIT

IN THIS PART

CHAPTER 12

Orchestrator Integration Packs

IN THIS CHAPTER

- An Integration Overview
- Active Directory Integration Pack
- Exchange Admin Integration Pack
- Exchange User Integration Pack
- FTP Integration Pack
- HP Integration Packs
- IBM Tivoli Netcool/OMNIbus Integration Pack
- Representational State Transfer (REST) Integration Pack
- HP Service Manager Integration Pack
- VMware vSphere Integration Pack
- Community-Developed Integration Packs

System Center Orchestrator (SCOrch) focuses on not only automation, but also integration between disparate systems and platforms. Without integration, Orchestrator would be only a simple automation engine. To deliver integration capabilities with System Center, Microsoft provides the System Center integration packs (IPs). More than a dozen other integration packs are available for download from the Microsoft.com website. Dozens of other IPs are available from the community via CodePlex.com and the TechNet gallery. This means that, without any additional development on your part, you can quickly integrate some of the most popular third-party enterprise monitoring and management platforms into your Orchestrator runbooks. Just as Orchestrator takes advantage of the data bus to transfer information from activity to activity, it can use the same data bus to deliver integration between disparate management and application platforms. This method lets you integrate systems without any coding or scripting.

Although this chapter discusses all the third-party IPs included with Orchestrator 2012 Service Pack (SP) 1 and a number of Microsoft IPs, it does not deal with those specific applications in any detail—that is beyond the scope of this book. The authors include these IPs for your reference and provide examples of how you might use them in your environment. The installation note segments for each integration pack discuss elements related to those systems at a very high level. This chapter is not designed to provide detailed information regarding installation or usage—the following chapters cover the System Center and Windows Azure integration packs and provide that additional level of detail.

An Integration Overview

IPs are software components that plug into the larger Orchestrator framework. An IP consists of a set of activities (a series of tasks) targeted to a specific application. IPs are delivered as a single file with an .oip extension. Integration packs are registered and installed with the Orchestrator Deployment Manager; Chapter 5, "Installing System Center 2012 Orchestrator," describes this process. As each IP is installed, new palettes are added to the Activities window in the Runbook Designer. Each activity has the capability to write its published data to the data bus and subscribe to published data. This enables you to incorporate new systems into your runbooks quickly using the activities available with the IPs.

This chapter briefly discusses a number of IPs that ship with Orchestrator, tells how to configure each IP, and describes the capabilities of the activities in that integration pack. Chapters 13, "Integration with System Center Operations Manager," through 17, "Integration with System Center Data Protection Manager," discuss the five IPs that ship with Orchestrator and are part of System Center. Chapter 18, "Integration with Windows Azure," discusses the Windows Azure IP, available with System Center 2012 SP 1. All the IPs described in this chapter are compatible with the SP 1 update for System Center 2012, and the activities will run on Windows Server 2008 R2, Windows Server 2008 R2 SP 1, and Windows Server 2012 and above.

NOTE: GLOBAL CONNECTION REQUIRED FOR MANY IPS

As you deploy these IPs, you might find that the activities' details are populated only after establishing a global connection to the target. If you do not have a global connection (or an appropriate target), many of the activities appear blank. Selecting the desired connection is required to dynamically populate the properties, filters, and published data elements from the target system.

Active Directory Integration Pack

The IP for Active Directory includes activities that enable automation of a variety of administrative tasks involving users, groups, and computers. The IP includes activities that span the entire account lifecycle, from onboarding to termination, and easily support bulk provisioning tasks.

Active Directory IP Typical Use Case

Consider several examples of how you can use the Active Directory IP in runbooks:

- To provision new user accounts or machine accounts
- To remove user or machine accounts
- To automate user password reset functions via a portal
- To automatically change passwords on service accounts

Active Directory IP Activity List

The IP for Active Directory provides 30 activities, shown in Figure 12.1 and described in Table 12.1. These activities enable you to automate common computer, group, and user administration tasks within your runbooks.

FIGURE 12.1 Activities from the Microsoft Windows Active Directory IP.

TABLE 12.1 Active Directory IP Activities

Activity	Description
Add Computer To Group	Adds a computer to an Active Directory group
Add Group To Group	Adds an Active Directory group to another Active Directory group in Microsoft Active Directory
Add User To Group	Adds a domain user account to an Active Directory security or distribution group
Create Computer	Creates a new computer account in Active Directory
Create Group	Creates a new group account of the specified scope in Active Directory
Create User	Creates a new domain user account in Active Directory
Delete Computer	Deletes a computer account from Active Directory
Delete Group	Deletes a group account from Active Directory

Activity	Description
Delete User	Deletes a domain user from Active Directory
Disable Computer	Disables a computer account in Active Directory
Disable User	Disables a domain user account in Active Directory
Enable Computer	Enables a (currently disabled) computer account in Active Directory
Enable User	Enables a (currently disabled) domain user account in Active Directory
Get Computer	Retrieves a computer account and account properties from Active Directory
Get Group	Retrieves a group account and account properties from Active Directory
Get Organizational Unit	Retrieves an organizational unit (OU) and object properties from Active Directory
Get User	Retrieves a domain user account and account properties from Active Directory
Move Computer	Moves a computer account to the directory location (OU or container) in Active Directory
Move Group	Moves a group account to the directory location (OU or container) in Active Directory
Move User	Moves a domain user account to the directory location (OU or container) in Active Directory
Remove Computer From Group	Removes a computer account from an Active Directory group
Remove Group From Group	Removes an Active Directory group nested with another Active Directory group
Remove User From Group	Removes a domain user from an Active Directory group
Rename Group	Renames an Active Directory domain group
Rename User	Renames a domain user
Reset User Password	Resets the password of a domain user account
Unlock User	Unlocks a (currently unlocked) domain user account
Update Computer	Updates the properties on a computer account
Update Group	Updates the properties of a security or distribution group
Update User	Updates the properties of a domain user account

Active Directory IP Supported Versions

The Active Directory IP supports Windows Server 2012 Active Directory (only when using the System Center 2012 SP 1 version of the integration pack), Windows Server 2008 R2 Active Directory, Windows Server 2008 Active Directory, Windows Server 2003 R2 Active Directory, and Windows Server 2003 Active Directory.

Active Directory IP Configuration Settings

Defining a connection establishes a reusable link between Orchestrator and an Active Directory domain or domain controller (depending on how the settings are configured, as this section describes). You can specify as many connections as you require to create links to multiple Active Directory environments. You can also create multiple connections to the same Active Directory domain to allow for differences in security permissions for different user accounts. The Active Directory IP settings are configured in the Runbook Designer console, under Options -> Active Directory. Figure 12.2 shows details of the Active Directory Configuration Settings options.

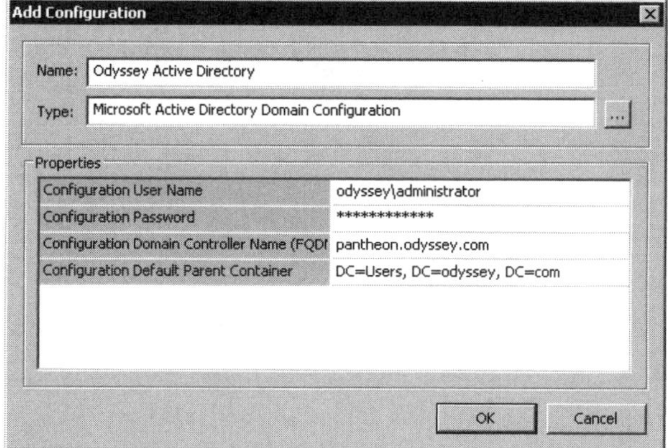

FIGURE 12.2 Configuration menu for the Active Directory IP.

Here is a brief description of the options:

- **Configuration User Name:** The name of a user with administrator rights in Active Directory, using the user or domain\user format. Specifying the domain is required only when the user account being used to perform the actions is from a different domain.
- **Configuration Password:** Password of the specified Active Directory user.
- **Configuration Domain Controller Name:** NetBIOS name or fully qualified domain name (FQDN) of the domain or domain controller with which Orchestrator will communicate. The property says **Configuration Domain Controller Name**, but you can specify just the FQDN of the domain and allow DNS to automatically acquire a domain controller based on the site infrastructure (known as a *serverless bind*). This ensures that the connection will succeed as long as one domain controller is accessible. Specifying a specific domain controller utilizes only the specified domain controller.
- **Configuration Default Parent Container:** Enter the distinguished name (DN) of the default Active Directory container. This is the default Active Directory container that will be used by activities that create or move Active Directory objects.

Exchange Admin Integration Pack

The Exchange Admin IP includes activities that help facilitate the automation of Exchange server administration tasks such as mailbox management for on-premise, remote, or cloud-based environments in Microsoft Exchange and Office 365.

Exchange Admin IP Typical Use Case

Here are several examples of how you can use the Exchange Admin IP in runbooks:

- Automated mailbox provisioning at user onboarding
- Automated removal of a mailbox upon termination
- Automated mailbox migration from on-premise to Office 365-hosted Exchange

Exchange Admin IP Activity List

The Exchange Admin IP contains 17 activities that enable automation of a variety of server administration tasks across on-premise and hosted Exchange. These are shown in Figure 12.3 and explained in Table 12.2.

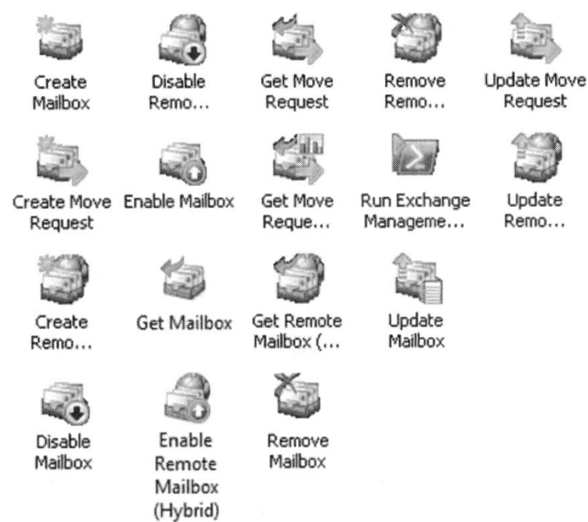

FIGURE 12.3 Activities in the Exchange Admin IP.

TABLE 12.2 Exchange Admin IP Activities

Activity	Description
Create Mailbox	Creates a new Exchange mailbox.
Create Move Request	Creates a new mailbox move request and begins the process of an asynchronous mailbox or personal archive move for an on-premise environment.
Create Remote Mailbox (Hybrid)	Creates a mail-enabled user in on-premise Active Directory and creates an associated mailbox in the cloud-based service (hybrid environment).
Disable Mailbox	Disables the mailbox of an existing user or InetOrgPerson object and removes that object's Exchange attributes from Active Directory. The user account associated with the disabled mailbox remains in Active Directory, but it is no longer associated with a mailbox. The disabled mailbox is not deleted and can be reconnected to a user later.
Disable Remote Mailbox (Hybrid)	Removes a mailbox from the cloud-based service (hybrid environment). When you remove a mailbox with this activity, the associated user object in the on-premise AD is not removed.
Enable Mailbox	Enables a mailbox for an existing AD user or InetOrgPerson object. This activity creates additional mailbox attributes on the user object in AD. When the user logs onto the mailbox or receives email messages, the system creates a mailbox object in the Exchange database.
Enable Remote Mailbox (Hybrid)	Creates a mailbox in the cloud-based service for an existing user in the on-premise Active Directory (hybrid environment).
Get Mailbox	Retrieves the attributes and objects for a mailbox in an on-premise or online environment. This activity enables you to filter against various mailbox attributes to retrieve only mailboxes that match specific criteria.
Get Move Request	Retrieves detailed information for an existing mailbox move request, for an on-premise environment.
Get Move Request Statistics	Retrieves statistical information about existing move requests for an on-premise environment.
Get Remote Mailbox (Hybrid)	Retrieves the mail-related attributes of one or more users in on-premise Active Directory that are associated with mailboxes in the cloud-based service (hybrid environment).
Remove Mailbox	Deletes an existing mailbox and the Active Directory user who is associated with that mailbox, in an on-premise or online Exchange environment. For an environment such as Microsoft Office 365 online, you can use this activity to delete a mailbox.
Remove Remote Mailbox (Hybrid)	Deletes an existing remote mailbox.

Activity	Description
Run Exchange PowerShell Command	Runs Exchange 2010 PowerShell cmdlets.
Update Mailbox	Modifies the settings of an existing mailbox in an on-premise or online environment.
Update Move Request	Changes the attributes of an existing move request, for an on-premise environment.
Update Remote Mailbox (Hybrid)	Modifies the mail-related attributes of an existing user in Active Directory that is associated with a mailbox in the cloud-based service (hybrid environment).

Exchange Admin IP Installation Notes

Several steps are required to prepare your Orchestrator environment for this IP. First, you must register and deploy the Exchange Admin IP to each runbook server and Runbook Designer client where the IP will be used. Before you implement Exchange Admin IP, the following software must be installed on your runbook servers:

- Microsoft .NET Framework 3.5 SP 1
- Microsoft Exchange Management Shell
- Microsoft PowerShell 2.0
- Microsoft WinRM 2.0

For more information about installing and configuring Orchestrator and the Exchange Admin IP, refer to the respective product documentation.

You must also configure PowerShell on the runbook servers to support communication initiated by the activities in this IP. Perform the following steps on the computer where Orchestrator runbooks are executed to ensure that 32-bit PowerShell scripts can be run:

1. Start a Windows PowerShell (x86) command line.
2. To determine whether PowerShell 32-bit scripts can be executed, run `Get-ExecutionPolicy`.
3. If Execution Policy is Restricted, you must change it to RemoteSigned. Run `Set-ExecutionPolicy -ExecutionPolicy RemoteSigned`.

ABOUT THE POWERSHELL EXECUTION POLICY

To protect user data and the integrity of the operating system, Windows PowerShell includes several security features. Among them is the execution policy. The Windows PowerShell execution policy determines whether scripts are allowed to run and, if so, whether they must be digitally signed. It also determines whether configuration files can be loaded.

To see how the execution policy is applied to a specific machine, run Get-executionpolicy -list.

For more information about the PowerShell Execution Policy, get-help about_Execution_Policies provides a comprehensive help file.

Configure Remote PowerShell Rights for the Exchange User

The configured user must be granted remote PowerShell rights on the Exchange Client Access Server (CAS). Perform the following steps to grant the remote rights:

1. On the Exchange server, start the Exchange Management Shell.
2. To determine whether the user has remote PowerShell rights, run Get-User <UserName> and check the value in the RemotePowerShellEnabled field.
3. To grant the user remote PowerShell rights, run the following from a PowerShell prompt:

```
Set-User <UserName> -RemotePowerShellEnabled $true
```

Configure Windows PowerShell to Allow Basic Authentication on the Exchange Server

On the Exchange server, ensure that PowerShell Basic Authentication is enabled. Follow these steps:

1. Start Internet Information Services (IIS) Manager.
2. Navigate to the PowerShell site.
3. Open the Authentication settings.
4. Verify that Basic Authentication is enabled.

Configure WinRM for HTTP Unencrypted Communication

On the machine where Orchestrator runbooks are executed, perform the following steps to configure WinRM trusted hosts and allow unencrypted traffic:

1. Open the Local Group Policy user interface: **Start** -> **Run** -> **gpedit.msc**.
2. In the group policy editor, navigate to **Local Computer Policy** -> **Computer Configuration** -> **Administrative Templates** -> **Windows Components** -> **Windows Remote Management (WinRM)** -> **WinRM Client**.
3. Confirm that Allow unencrypted traffic is Enabled.
4. Add the targeted computer that runs Exchange Server to the Trusted Hosts list.

On the Exchange server, verify that PowerShell does not require SSL:

1. Start Internet Information Services (IIS) Manager.
2. Navigate to the PowerShell site.

3. Open SSL Settings.
4. Confirm that the Require SSL check box is not selected.

Exchange Admin IP Supported Versions

The Exchange Admin IP supports Microsoft Exchange 2010 SP 2, Microsoft Exchange 2012, and Microsoft Exchange Online/Office 365.

Exchange Admin IP Configuration Settings

A connection establishes a reusable link between Orchestrator and an Exchange server. You can specify as many connections as you require to create links to multiple servers. You can also create multiple connections to the same server to allow for differences in security permissions for different user accounts. The Exchange Admin IP settings are configured in the Runbook Designer console under Options -> Exchange Admin. Figure 12.4 shows details of the Exchange Admin options.

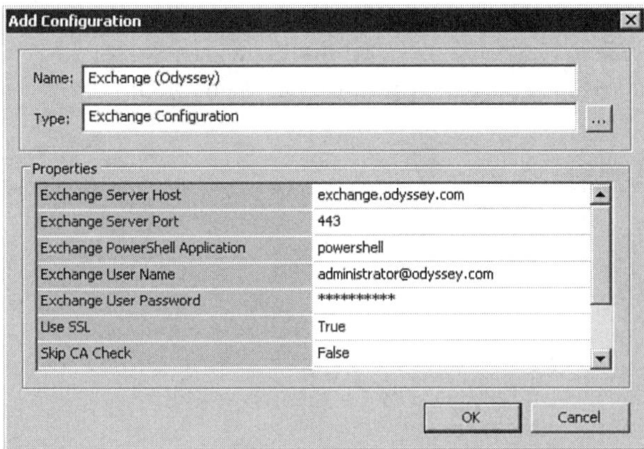

FIGURE 12.4 Configuration menu for the Exchange Admin IP.

The following list briefly describes the options:

- **Exchange Server Host:** This is the user-configurable name for the connection.
- **Exchange Server Port:** This is the listening port of the Exchange web service.
- **Exchange PowerShell Application:** Select either PowerShell or PowerShell-liveid, based on whether the Exchange deployment is on-premise, hosted, or in Office.
- **Exchange User Name:** Enter the name of a user with Exchange Administrator rights.
- **Exchange User Password:** Enter the password of the account specified in the Exchange User Name field.
- **Use SSL:** Set this to True (for SSL) or False (for HTTP).

- **Skip CA Check:** A setting of True causes Orchestrator to skip the step to check that the CA is valid and trusted by the host.
- **Skip CN Check:** A setting of True causes Orchestrator to skip the step to check that the Common Name (CN) on the certificate matches that of the Exchange Server.
- **Skip Revocation Check:** This skips the check of certificate expiration against the certificate revocation list (CRL).
- **Exchange Environment:** Select On-Premise or Online.

Exchange User Integration Pack

The Exchange User IP contains activities that facilitate automated message-level monitoring and automates a variety of email and calendaring tasks. The following sections provide details.

Exchange User IP Typical Use Case

Consider some examples of how you can use the Exchange User IP in Orchestrator runbooks:

- Automated monitoring and response on messages received that meet user-defined criteria
- Automated archival messages or copies of messages that meet user-defined criteria
- Automated meeting generation for any scenarios, such as when scheduling a self-service desktop upgrade
- Message autoreply and meeting updates as part of an email-centric workflow automation

Exchange User IP Activity List

The Exchange User IP contains 11 activities that facilitate workflow automation based on inbound messages to a monitored mailbox, as well as notify desired users at key junctures within a runbook. These activities are described in Table 12.3 and shown in Figure 12.5.

TABLE 12.3 Exchange User IP Activities

Activity	Description
Create and Send E-Mail	Creates and sends a message to one or more recipients.
Create Item	Creates a new appointment, contact group, and email message or task items.
Delete Item	Deletes existing appointments, contact groups, email messages, and task items.
Find Appointment	Retrieves an appointment that meets user-specified criteria.

Activity	Description
Forward Item	Forwards a message or appointment.
Get Item	Retrieves details of an existing appointment, contact group, email message, or task item that satisfies a set of filter criteria.
Monitor Item	Monitors new or modified appointment, contact group, email message, and task items that satisfy a set of filter criteria.
Move or Copy Item	Moves or copies an item to another folder. This activity supports all item types (appointment, contact group, and email messages).
Reply to E-Mail	Autoreplies to email that meets user-specified criteria.
Send E-Mail	Sends an email message from the specified mailbox.
Update Item	Updates an existing item. This activity supports all item types (appointments, contact groups, email messages, and task items).

FIGURE 12.5 Activities in the Exchange User IP.

Exchange User IP Installation Notes

You must register and deploy the Exchange User IP to each runbook server and Runbook Designer client where you will use the IP.

Exchange User IP Supported Versions

The Exchange Admin IP supports Microsoft Exchange 2010 Service Pack 2, Microsoft Exchange 2012, or Microsoft Exchange Online/Office 365.

Exchange User IP Configuration Settings

The Exchange User IP settings are configured in the Runbook Designer console under Options -> Exchange User. Figure 12.6 shows details of the Exchange User options.

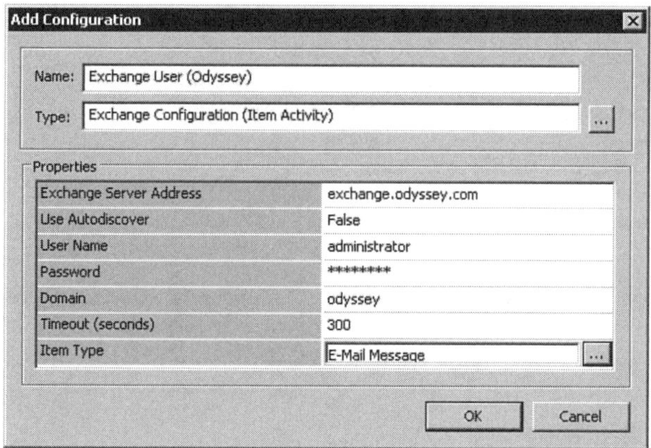

FIGURE 12.6 Configuration menu for the Exchange User IP.

Here are brief descriptions of the options:

- **Name:** Descriptive name for the Exchange environment connected by this configuration.
- **Type:** Options are Exchange Configuration and Exchange Configuration (Item Activity).
- **Exchange Server Address:** FQDN of the Exchange server used for communication. Leave this blank if you enable Autodiscover.
- **Use Autodiscover:** Autodiscovers the Exchange instance based on the email address specified in the runbook. Requires that Exchange Autodiscover be configured.
- **User Name:** Username with permissions to view the items the runbooks will be reading and modifying.
- **Password:** Password for the user specified in the username.
- **Domain:** Active Directory domain of the user account.
- **Timeout:** Password for the user specified in the Active Directory domain.
- **Item Type:** Contains connection information and lets users specify an Exchange item type. The Exchange Item Configuration activity is used by activities that dynamically generate optional and required properties, filter, and publish data, as is the case with the **Create Item** and **Get Item** activities.

NOTE: TYPES OF EXCHANGE CONNECTIONS

Two Exchange connection types exist: Exchange Configuration and Exchange Configuration (Item Activity). Knowing which to use requires some explanation:

- The basic Exchange Configuration contains connection information used by activities in which the item type is either implicit or not required (for example, the **Send E-Mail** and **Delete Item** activities).

- The Exchange Item Type Configuration contains connection information and lets users specify an Exchange item type. The Exchange Item Configuration activity is used by activities that dynamically generate optional and required properties, filter, and publish data (for example, the **Create Item** and **Get Item** activities).

FTP Integration Pack

The FTP IP provides activities that enable automation of common FTP-related file transfer-related tasks. IP also supports multiple configurations of secure FTP for situations when encryption and authentication are required. FTP servers on non-Windows platforms are also supported.

FTP IP Typical Use Case

Consider these examples of how you can use the FTP IP in runbooks:

- Automated and secure Electronic Data Interchange (EDI) file transfers between organizations
- Validation of the transactional availability of FTP sites
- Auditing servers for compliance
- Automated server patching

FTP IP Activity List

The FTP IP contains nine activities to support the automation of common FTP-, FTPS-, and SFTP-related tasks for a variety of FTP configurations and use case scenarios. These are shown in Figure 12.7 and described in Table 12.4.

FIGURE 12.7 Activities in the FTP IP.

TABLE 12.4 FTP IP Activities

Activity	Description
Create Folder	Creates a user-specified folder on a remote FTP server.
Delete File	Deletes a user-specified file on a remote FTP server.
Delete Folder	Deletes a user-specified folder on a remote FTP server.
Download File	Downloads a user-specified file from a remote FTP server.
List Folders/Files	Lists folders and files on a remote FTP server, allowing a search to verify whether a file or folder exists.
Rename File/Folder	Renames a user-specified file or folder on a remote FTP server.
Resume File Download	Resumes a file download. This activity is compatible only with an FTP configuration (not FTPS or SFTP).
Synchronize Folder/File	Performs a one-way synchronization of a folder or file.
Upload File	Publishes all the data from the required and optional properties into published data.

FTP IP Installation Notes

You must register and deploy the FTP IP to each runbook server and Runbook Designer client where you will use the IP.

FTP IP Supported Versions

This IP supports not only standard FTP (on Windows or *NIX platforms), but also FTPS and SFTP.

THE DIFFERENCE BETWEEN FTPS AND SFTP

FTPS (commonly referred to as FTP/SSL) is a name used to encompass a number of ways in which FTP software can perform secure file transfers. Each way involves using a SSL/TLS layer below the standard FTP protocol to encrypt the control and/or data channels.

SSH File Transfer Protocol (SFTP) is a network protocol that provides file transfer and manipulation functionality over any reliable data stream. It is typically used with the SSH-2 protocol (TCP port 22) to provide secure file transfer.

FTP IP Configuration Settings

The FTP IP settings are configured in Runbook Designer under Options –>FTP. Figure 12.8 shows details of the FTP connection options.

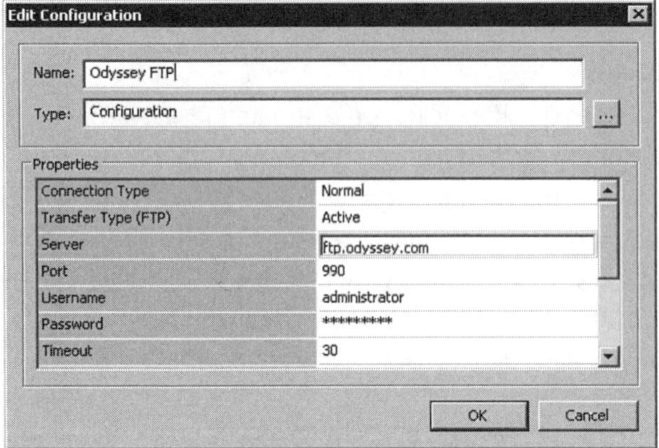

FIGURE 12.8 Configuration menu for FTP IP.

Here is a brief description of the options:

- **Name:** User-configurable name for the connection. This can be the name of the FTP server or a descriptive name to distinguish the type of connection.
- **Type:** FTP transfer type. Can be active or passive.
- **Server:** Name or IP address of the FTP server (NetBIOS name or FQDN).
- **Port:** Port number for the selected connection type.
- **User Name:** Username that will be used to log into the FTP server.
- **Password:** Password for the specified username.
- **Timeout:** Connection timeout (in seconds).
- **Certificate Path (FTP):** The path to a certificate. This configuration property applies to FTP only. This configuration property is optional and can be left blank.
- **Certificate Password (FTP):** The password for the certificate. This configuration property applies to FTP only. This configuration property is optional and can be left blank.
- **HTTP Proxy Server (FTP):** The name or IP address of the HTTP proxy server. If you are using the computer name, you can type the NetBIOS name or the FQDN. This configuration property applies to FTP only. This configuration property is optional and can be left blank.
- **HTTP Proxy Port (FTP):** Port number for the HTTP proxy server. This configuration property applies to FTP only. This configuration property is optional and can be left blank.

- **HTTP Proxy Username (FTP):** The username Orchestrator will use to connect to the HTTP proxy server. This configuration property applies to FTP only. This configuration property is optional and can be left blank.
- **HTTP Proxy Password (FTP):** Password of the specified username.

HP Integration Packs

Multiple integration packs are available for HP management products, including HP Integrated Lights Out (iLO) and Onboard Administrator (OA) in HP Server, as well as the HP Operations Manager and HP Service Manager management components. The next sections discuss these integration packs.

HP iLO and OA

The IP for HP iLO and OA provides two activities that enable you to automate iLO and OA commands in your runbooks for managing HP servers with these components present, enabled, and configured.

HP iLO and OA IP Typical Use Case

Here are some examples of how the HP iLO and OA IP can be used in activities:

- Performing out-of-band commands, such as a graceful reboot when a server is hung
- Performing automated recovery actions when the HP Server management pack generates alerts in System Center 2012 Operations Manager
- Automating server scale-out during periods of high activity, or server shutdown during periods of low activity, as part of a private cloud deployment
- Supporting "green data centers," where servers can be powered down during low usage periods and then powered up on demand

HP iLO and OA IP Activity List

The HP iLO and OA IP has two activities. Figure 12.9 displays the activities in the HP iLO and OA IP, and Table 12.5 lists these activities and describes their functions.

- Run iLO Command
- Run OA Command

FIGURE 12.9 Activities in the HP iLO and OA IP.

TABLE 12.5 HP iLO and OA IP Activities

Activity	Description
Run iLO Command	Runs a command for the targeted Integrated Lights Out connection
Run OA Command	Runs a command for the targeted Onboard Administrator out connection

HP iLO and OA IP Installation Notes

You must register and deploy the HP iLO and OA IP to each runbook server and Runbook Designer client where you will use the IP. The HP iLO and OA IP does require some additional configuration. The integration pack for HP iLO and OA requires the following software to be installed and configured on the servers targeted for management before implementing the integration:

- HP iLO 2
- HP iLO 3
- HP OA firmware 3.31

Detailed steps for installing HP software are outside the scope of this book. For additional information on installing and configuring Orchestrator and HP iLO and OA, refer to the respective product documentation.

HP iLO and OA IP Supported Versions

The IP supports HP iLO 2 and iLO 3 and HP OA firmware 3.31.

HP iLO and OA IP Configuration Settings

The HP iLO and OA IP settings are configured in the Runbook Designer console, under Options -> HP iLO and OA. Figure 12.10 shows details of the HP iLO and OA connection options.

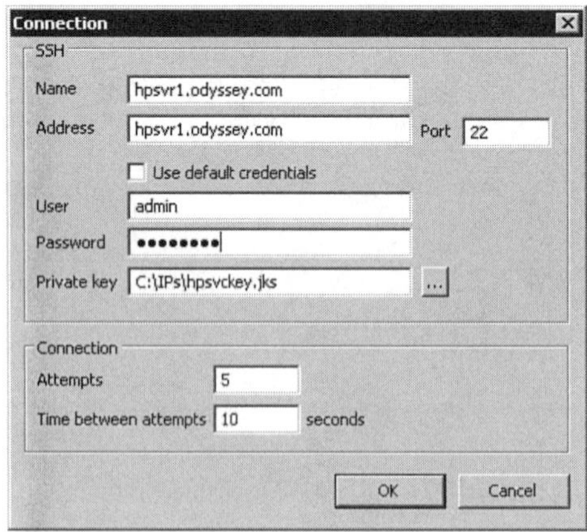

FIGURE 12.10 Configuration menu for the HP iLO and OA IP.

Consider this brief description of the options:

- **Name:** A descriptive name for the connection.
- **Address:** Address of the remote server for the connection.
- **User:** Default username for the connection.
- **Password:** Password of the specified user.
- **Private key:** Enter a default key or click the ellipsis (...) button to browse and select a key.

Here is the connection information:

- **Attempts:** Max number of connection attempts before runbook fails
- **Time between attempts:** Time between failed connection attempts

HP Operations Manager

HP Operations Manager monitors the information technology (IT) infrastructure and consolidates and correlates fault and performance events to help identify the causes of IT incidents. The IP for HP Operations Manager enables you to automate the consolidation and correlation of fault and performance events for monitored components.

HP Operations Manager IP Typical Use Case

Consider these some examples of ways to use the HP Operations Manager IP in runbooks:

- Monitor for new faults and trigger automated remediation.
- Forward events to an upstream monitoring system (manager of managers), such as System Center 2012 Operations Manager.
- Connect the HP Operations Manager ticketing system.
- Dynamically create, delete, and update messages and annotations in HP Operations Manager based on events in external systems.

HP Operations Manager IP Activity List

The HP Operations Manager IP includes 13 activities. Figure 12.11 displays the activities in the HP Operations Manager IP, and Table 12.6 lists these activities and describes their functions.

FIGURE 12.11 Activities in the HP Operations Manager IP.

TABLE 12.6 HP Operations Manager IP Activities

Activity	Description
Acknowledge Message	Acknowledges or unacknowledges a message.
Add Annotation to Message	Adds an annotation to an existing message.
Create Message	Stores a new message on the management server.
Delete Annotation	Deletes an annotation from an existing message.
Delete Custom Attribute	Deletes a custom attribute from an existing message.
Get Annotation	Retrieves annotations for a specified message according to user-specified filter criteria. The activity uses filters to determine which annotations retrieved from the management server should be published.
Get Message	Retrieves messages from a management server according to user-specified filter criteria. The activity uses filters to determine which messages retrieved from the management server should be published.
Launch Tool	Runs a specified command on a specified server.

Activity	Description
Monitor Message	Invokes a runbook when certain HP Operations Manager messages are created, updated, acknowledged, or unacknowledged according to filter criteria that you specify. The activity uses filters to determine which messages should invoke the runbook.
Own/Disown Message	Used in a runbook to take ownership or remove ownership of a message.
Set Custom Attribute	Creates or updates a custom attribute for an existing message.
Update Annotation	Updates an annotation to an existing message.
Update Message	Updates an existing message.

HP Operations Manager IP Installation Notes

You must register and deploy the HP Operations Manager IP to each runbook server and Runbook Designer client where you will use the IP.

HP Operations Manager IP Supported Versions

The IP supports HP Operations Manager 9.x.

HP Operations Manager IP Configuration Settings

The HP Operations Manager IP settings are configured in the Runbook Designer under Options -> HP Operations Manager. See Figure 12.12 for details of the HP Operations Manager options.

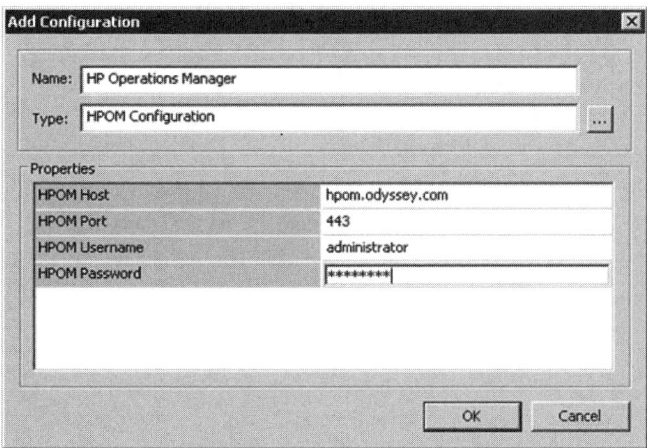

FIGURE 12.12 Configuration menu for the HP Operations Manager IP.

A brief description of the options follows:

- **Name:** User-configurable name for the connection
- **Type:** The ellipsis is used to set to HPOM Configuration
- **HPOM Host:** FQDN of the HP Operations Manager server
- **HPOM Port:** Listening TCP port of the HP Operations Manager server
- **HPOM Username:** Username with administrator rights on the HP Operations Manager server
- **HPOM Password:** Password for the specified user

IBM Tivoli Netcool/OMNIbus Integration Pack

In heterogeneous environments, you can use Orchestrator not only for automated remediation of issues, but also to provide integration between management systems, including disparate monitoring systems and service desk solutions. The IP for IBM Tivoli Netcool/OMNIbus IP includes activities to enable integration between Netcool for automation in a variety of monitoring scenarios. The following sections discuss these scenarios.

IBM Tivoli Netcool/OMNIbus IP Typical Use Case

Here are examples of ways to use the IBM Tivoli Netcool/OMNIbus IP in runbooks:

- Trigger automated alert resolution based on alerts raised in IBM Tivoli.
- Drive automated incident creation from alerts raised in IBM Tivoli.
- Alert forwarding from IBM Tivoli to other monitoring systems, such as System Center 2012 Operations Manager (a manager of managers scenarios).
- Alert correlation to facilitate root cause analysis.

IBM Tivoli Netcool/OMNIbus IP Activity List

The IBM Tivoli Netcool/OMNIbus IP includes five activities. Figure 12.13 displays the activities in the IBM Tivoli Netcool/OMNIbus IP, and Table 12.7 lists the activities and describes their functions.

FIGURE 12.13 Activities in the IBM Tivoli Netcool/OMNIbus IP.

TABLE 12.7 IBM Tivoli Netcool/OMNIbus IP Activities

Activity	Description
Create Alert	Creates a new alert in IBM Tivoli Netcool/OMNIbus
Monitor Alerts	Monitors for alerts that meet user-defined criteria
Delete Alert	Deletes an alert based on an alert identifier
Update Alert	Updates an alert based on an alert identifier
Get Alerts	Retrieves alerts that meet user-defined criteria

IBM Tivoli Netcool/OMNIbus IP Installation Notes

You must register and deploy the IBM Tivoli Netcool/OMNIbus IP to each runbook server and Runbook Designer client where you will use the IP. The IP requires the following software to be installed and configured before implementing any automation:

- IBM Tivoli Netcool/OMNIbus 7.3
- System Center 2012 Orchestrator (required by all Orchestrator 2012 integration packs)
- System Center 2012 SP 1 (System Center 2012 Service Pack 1 integration packs require the System Center service pack to be installed)
- 32-bit Java Standard Edition 7 on each runbook server and Runbook Designer using the integration pack
- Manually added location of the JVM.DLL file to the PATH environment variable
- Installed Sybase JConnect 6 JDBC drivers on each runbook server and Runbook Designer using the integration pack
- Manually copied Jconn3.jar file to *%ProgramFiles(x86)%*\Common Files\Microsoft System Center 2012\Orchestrator\Extensions\Support\NetcoolOMNIbus

IBM Tivoli Netcool/OMNIbus IP Supported Versions

This IP supports IBM Tivoli Netcool/OMNIbus version 7.3.

IBM Tivoli Netcool/OMNIbus IP Configuration Settings

The IBM Tivoli Netcool/OMNIbus IP settings are configured in Runbook Designer under Options -> IBM Tivoli Netcool/OMNIbus System. Figure 12.14 shows the details of the options.

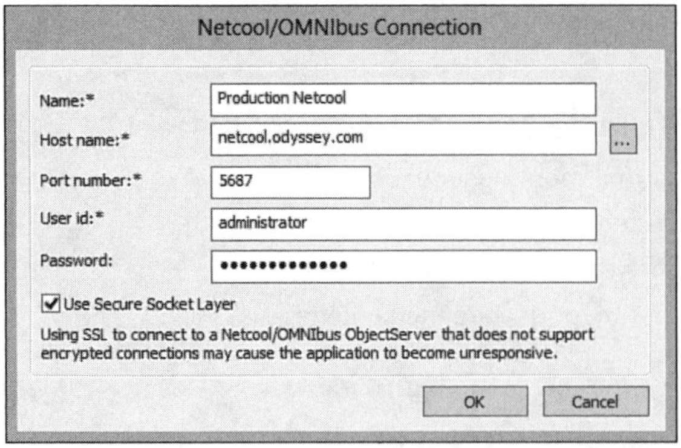

FIGURE 12.14 Configuration menu for the IBM Tivoli Netcool/OMNIbus IP.

A brief description of the options follows:

- **Name:** User-configurable name for the connection
- **Host name:** FQDN of the IBM Netcool host
- **Port number:** Port number if the listening port has been changed from the default
- **User id:** Login with administrative rights in Netcool
- **Password:** Password for the specified user account
- **Use Secure Socket Layer:** Check box to select if SSL should be used when connecting to the IBM Netcool host

Representational State Transfer (REST) Integration Pack

The integration pack for Representational State Transfer (REST) is an add-on for Orchestrator in System Center 2012 SP 1 that enables you to create activities within runbooks that make requests to REST web services to get data or perform functions.

REST IP Typical Use Cases

The REST IP is intended to provide an integration point between Orchestrator and any third-party system or platform with a RESTful API, such as an oData web service. Several typical use cases follow:

- Automating work item creation in a third-party service desk
- Integrating with cloud-based services that provide a RESTful API
- Automating retrieval of geolocation information from publicly available services, such as Bing
- Automating scheduled retrieval of statistical data info from publicly available services, such as Bing

REST IP Activity List

The REST IP includes a single activity, the Invoke REST Service activity, shown in Figure 12.15. This invokes the specified RESTful web service and returns the results.

FIGURE 12.15 Activities from the REST IP.

REST IP Installation Notes

Authentication requirements vary by web service. Contact the specific provider to identify the necessary steps to authenticate and query the vendor web service for data.

REST IP Supported Versions

The integration pack for REST requires that System Center 2012 Orchestrator SP 1 is installed.

REST IP Configuration Settings

The REST IP requires no global configuration settings. Connectivity is configured in the **Invoke REST Service** activity itself, as Figure 12.16 shows. Table 12.8 describes the configurable options.

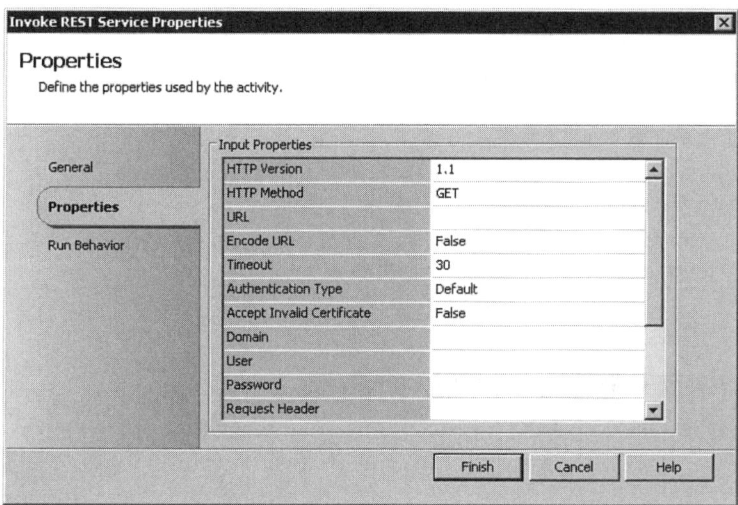

FIGURE 12.16 Activity properties for the REST IP.

TABLE 12.8 REST IP Activity Properties

Element	Description	Valid Values
HTTP Version	The version of HTTP to use.	1.0, 1.1
HTTP Method	The HTTP method to use.	The supported HTTP methods are GET, PUT, POST, and DELETE
URL	The URL to use.	Any valid URL
Encode URL	Whether to encode the URL.	True, False
Timeout	The maximum time to wait for a response.	Positive integer
Authentication Type	The authentication scheme to use when connecting to the REST service.	Default, Basic, Negotiate, Digest
Accept Invalid Certificate	When using HTTPS, set this switch to True to accept an invalid server certificate or False to not accept it.	True or False
Domain	The domain to use for authentication.	String. Can be blank.
User	The username to use for authentication.	String. Can be blank.
Password	The password to use for authentication.	String. Can be encrypted. Can be blank.
Request Header	Special request headers entered in this format: `<Parameter>: <Value>`	Valid HTTP request header parameters and values. Can be blank. Each parameter: value pair must be on a separate line.
Request Body	The request body. If not blank, then Payload File Path must be blank.	String. Can be blank.
Payload File Path	The location of the payload file to use with the request. If not blank, Request Body must be blank.	A valid file location. Can be blank.
PFX File Path	The location of the encrypted client certificate file used for requests.	A valid file location. Can be blank.
PFX File Password	The password to the encrypted file ini .PFX format.	String. Can be encrypted. Can be blank.

HP Service Manager Integration Pack

The IP for HP Service Manager (HPSM) provides five activities that enable you to monitor, create, and manage entries in your HPSM system from your Orchestrator runbooks. The following sections discuss these.

HP Service Manager IP Typical Use Case

Here are some examples of how you can use the HP Service Manager IP in runbooks:

- Monitor for new entries and then triage the source of the event
- Create new entries based on monitoring events that Orchestrator detects or consumes from other systems
- Connect HP Service Manager to a trouble ticketing system
- Use HP Service Manager entry data to forward alerts to a remote system

HP Service Manager IP Activity List

The HP Service Manager IP includes five activities. Figure 12.17 displays the activities in the HP Service Manager IP, and Table 12.9 lists these activities and describes their functions.

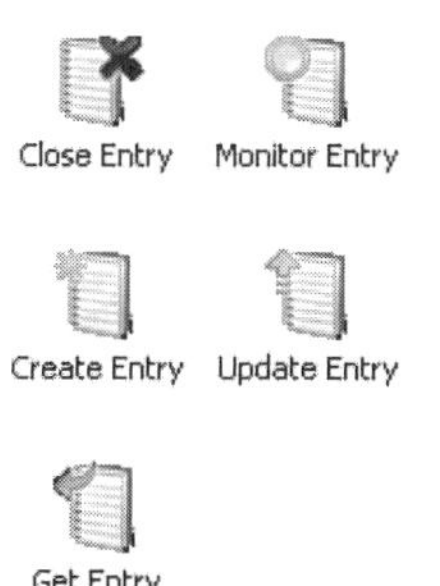

FIGURE 12.17 Activities in the HP Service Manager IP.

TABLE 12.9 HP Service Manager IP Activities

Activity	Description
Close Entry	Closes an existing entry in HPSM
Create Entry	Creates a new entry in HPSM
Get Entry	Retrieves a list of HPSM entries that match a filter
Monitor Entry	Monitors for entries or changes to existing entries that match a filter
Update Entry	Updates an existing entry in HPSM

HP Service Manager IP Installation Notes

To use this IP, you need a separate license to use the web services required for connectivity. You also need the SOAP-API capability word right assigned to the user account associated with the IP.

The HP Service Manager IP requires a connection to the HP Service Manager database when designing runbooks in the Runbook Designer. A valid ODBC connection must be configured before you set up the HP Service Manager connection in the Runbook Designer. For step-by-step configuration of this connection, see the article "Configuring the HP Service Manager Connections" at http://technet.microsoft.com/en-us/library/hh771464.aspx.

This software must be installed on each runbook server and Runbook Designer for the activities in this IP to function:

- Microsoft .NET Framework 3.5 SP 1
- For access to the HP Service Manager database on SQL Server, Microsoft SQL Server Native Client ODBC driver (installed with SQL Server management tools)
- For access to the HP Service Manager database on Oracle:
    - Oracle Client (Net Configuration Assistant)
    - Oracle ODBC driver

HP Service Manager IP Supported Versions

The IP supports HP Service Manager 7.11 or 9.

HP Service Manager IP Configuration Settings

The HP Service Manager IP settings are configured in the Runbook Designer under Options -> HP Service Manager. Figure 12.18 provides details of the HP Service Manager options.

FIGURE 12.18 Configuration menu for the HP Service Manager IP.

A brief description of the options follows:

- **Name:** User-configurable name for the connection.
- **Server Address:** Replace localhost in the URL with the name of the server that hosts the HPSM web service instance. Adjust the port, if necessary.
- **Polling Interval:** If required, alter the polling interval (seconds).
- **ODBC DSN:** DSN of the ODBC connection created previously in the "HP Service Manager IP Installation Notes" section.
- **DB Username:** Username to connect to the HPSM database.
- **DB Password:** Password for the database user account.
- **Username:** Username that will connect to HPSM.
- **Password:** Password for the user account.

VMware vSphere Integration Pack

The IP for VMware vSphere provides activities that enable you to create, modify, and manage VMware virtual machines from your Orchestrator activities. The next sections describe these.

VMware vSphere IP Typical Use Case

Here are some examples of how you can use the VMware vSphere IP in runbooks:

- Provision new virtual machines based on system demand or load.
- Provision new machines based on a change request from another system.
- Alter the locations of running virtual machines in response to events or resource issues.
- Deprovision unused virtual machines to save VMware host resources.

NOTE: USING VMM 2012 FOR VMWARE PROVISIONING

The same functionality achieved with this integration pack and much more is possible through System Center 2012 Virtual Machine Manager (VMM). See Chapter 16, "Integration with System Center Virtual Machine Manager," for more information.

VMware vSphere IP Activity List

The VMware vSphere IP has 32 activities. Figure 12.19 displays the activities in the VMware vSphere IP, and Table 12.10 lists the activities and describes their functions.

FIGURE 12.19 Activities in the VMware vSphere IP.

TABLE 12.10 VMware vSphere IP Activities

Activity	Description
Add Network Adapter	Adds a network adapter to a virtual machine (VM).
Add VM Disk	Adds a disk to a VM.
Clone Linux VM	Clones a Linux VM based on a template, enabling you to configure the VM.
Close Windows VM	Clones a Windows VM based on a template, enabling you to configure the VM.
Create VM	Creates a new VM.
Customize VM	Applies customization to a VM.
Delete Network Adapter Activity (System Center 2012 SP 1)	Deletes a network adapter from a VM.
Delete VM	Deletes a VM.
Delete VM Disk Activity (System Center 2012 SP 1)	Deletes a virtual disk from a VM.
Get Cluster Properties	Retrieves information about a cluster.
Get Datastore Capacity	Retrieves the capacity of a datastore.
Get Host Datastores	Retrieves a list of datastores available for a specified host managed by the VMware vSphere server. This can be used to check capacity of the system when adding a new VM to the managed host.
Get Host Properties	Retrieves a list of properties for a specified host in the VMware vSphere cluster. Properties include Connection Status (powered on, disconnected, and so on) and Maintenance Mode state.

Activity	Description
Get Hosts	Retrieves a list of hosts managed by the VMware vSphere server specified in the connection properties.
Get Resource Pool Properties	Retrieves all the runtime information (and, in System Center 2012 SP 1 only, static configuration information) for a resource pool.
Get Resource Pools	Retrieves a list of resource pools from the VMware vSphere server specified in the connection properties.
Get VM List	Retrieves a list of VMs using filters.
Get VM Properties	Retrieves the virtual hardware information about a virtual machine in the VMware vSphere inventory, based on the VM Path specified in the properties of this activity.
Get VM Status	Retrieves the status of a VM based on the VM Path specified in the properties of this activity.
Maintenance Mode	Used in a runbook to enter and exit maintenance mode for an ESX host controlled by the VMware vSphere vCenter server. Entering maintenance mode prevents VMs from powering up or failing over to the host if it is taking part in a high-availability cluster. This allows the runbook to enable maintenance mode before powering off the host for hardware maintenance.
Migrate VM	Moves a running VM from one host or resource pool to another.
Modify VM Disk Activity (System Center 2012 SP 1)	Modifies virtual disk properties.
Move VM	Moves a stopped VM from one host or resource pool to another.
Reconfigure VM	Changes the configuration settings of a VM.
Reset VM	Resets a running VM.
Revert VM Snapshot	Reverts a VM to a previous state captured by a snapshot.
Set Guest Info Variables	Configures information about the Guest OS.
Set VM CD/DVD to ISO image	Configures a VM's CD/DVD to ISO image information.
Set VM Networks	Specifies which network adapters the VM will use.
Start VM	Starts a VM.
Stop VM	Stops a VM.
Suspend VM	Suspends a VM.
Take VM Snapshot	Takes a snapshot of a VM, capturing state information.

VMware vSphere IP Installation Notes

This IP has no special installation requirements.

VMware vSphere IP Supported Versions

The IP supports VMware vSphere 4.1 or 5.0.

VMware vSphere IP Configuration Settings

Configure the VMware vSphere IP settings in the Runbook Designer under Options -> VMware vSphere. Figure 12.20 shows the VMware vSphere options. A brief description of these options follows:

- **Name:** User-configurable name for the connection.
- **Server:** FQDN of the vSphere system.
- **User:** User who will connect to your vSphere system.
- **Password:** User's password.
- **SSL:** Enter **True** if a secure connection is required to the VMware vSphere server and **False** if this is not required.
- **Port:** Listening port of the VMware vSphere server.
- **Webservice Timeout:** Number of seconds that the activities will wait for a response from the VMware vSphere server before raising an error.

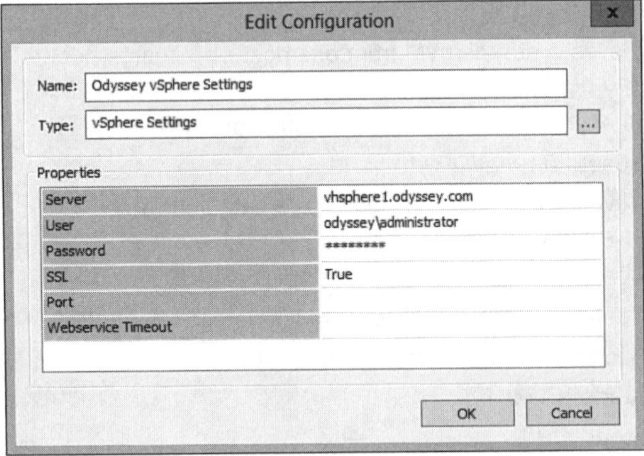

FIGURE 12.20 Configuration menu for the VMware vSphere IP.

Community-Developed Integration Packs

In addition to the Microsoft IPs, members of the System Center community have developed a number of IPs. These IPs are available from two primary sources, both located on CodePlex.com, and briefly described in the next sections. For additional information, see Appendix A, "Community Solutions and Tools."

Orchestrator.codeplex.com

The first location on CodePlex.com is http://orchestrator.codeplex.com/, which is home to a project that current and former Microsoft employees started. IPs on this project include the following:

- Microsoft Team Foundation Server 2010 IP
- Windows PowerShell 2 IP
- Orchestrator Integration Pack for Microsoft SharePoint RC
- IP for Data Manipulation
- IP for Text Manipulation
- IP for MS SQL Tasks
- IP for Windows Tasks
- IP for PowerShell Script Execution
- IP for Standard Logging

Scorch.codeplex.com

The other location is the project at http://scorch.codeplex.com/, which is maintained by Ryan Andorfer and his colleagues. These IPs tend to bridge gaps in existing IPs, provide support for earlier software versions, and provide functionality not included in equivalent Microsoft IPs. IPs on this project include the following:

- 1E Wake On Lan
- System Center Orchestrator Webservice
- Zip
- Port Query
- SQL
- Active Directory
- Configuration Manager 2007
- Exchange Mail
- Exchange Management IP

- Local Security
- Scheduled Tasks
- VMware

MICROSOFT RECOMMENDATIONS ON COMMUNITY-DEVELOPED MANAGEMENT PACKS

Microsoft does not support community-developed runbooks, but it does encourage the use of community-developed resources. New contributions are also encouraged.

Summary

This chapter explored the IPs shipped with the Service Pack 1 release of System Center 2012 Orchestrator. It examined typical use cases for each IP and provided basic information on each activity. It explained any special installation instructions, in addition to providing a clear list of which product versions each IP supports. The chapter also listed target system configuration details for each IP.

The IPs Orchestrator provides make the job of connecting the most common datacenter applications easy—easy enough that it can accomplished without needing to code or script anything. Additionally, by taking advantage of the Orchestrator data bus, these IPs can accept or provide information to any other system involved in your IT process automation.

The next chapters take a much deeper look at the IPs provided with Orchestrator that integrate the System Center 2012 components and Windows Azure.

CHAPTER 13

Integration with System Center Operations Manager

IN THIS CHAPTER

With the release of System Center Orchestrator (SCOrch) 2012, Microsoft provides several important integration packs to tie Orchestrator to the other System Center components. This chapter covers the integration pack (IP) for Microsoft System Center Operations Manager (SCOM). The chapter describes the requirements for using the SCOM integration pack, along with the installation procedure and configuration steps. It explains each activity and provides sample runbooks to show you how to take advantage of this IP.

Integration Pack Requirements

Before getting started, note that the Orchestrator 2012 installation files do not include the SCOM integration pack; you must download it separately. The following sections discuss specific requirements.

System Center 2012 Orchestrator

The SCOM integration pack comes bundled with the other System Center 2007–2012 integration packs in a self-extracting executable. The self-extracting executable extracts the System Center integration packs to the desktop of the current user by default. You can download the integration pack bundle from www.microsoft.com/en-us/download/details.aspx?id=34611.

System Center 2012 Operations Manager

You will be using objects from the integration pack to automate specific components and actions of Operations Manager, so you must have System Center 2012 Operations Manager also installed. The current version of the SCOM IP was written for SCOM 2012 Service Pack (SP) 1. An equivalent integration pack exists for Operations Manager 2007 R2; this has not been tested for earlier versions of Operations Manager 2007 and is supported only by Microsoft for Operations Manager 2007 R2.

Unless indicated otherwise, this chapter focuses on the SCOM 2012 integration pack.

Installing the Integration Pack

For information on the installation steps to register and deploy an IP, see Chapter 5, "Installing System Center 2012 Orchestrator."

Different operations within require different levels of permissions. Some operations require membership in the System Center Operations Manager Operators user role; other operations require administrative access in Operations Manager. You can create multiple accounts with different levels of permissions with Operations Manager for performing different operations. However, not all environments require this level of granularity.

Microsoft recommends using a connection account with membership in the Operations Manager Administrators user role to ensure that the account has the necessary permissions for all Operations Manager–related activities.

Configuring the Integration Pack

All the objects in the SCOM IP use the credentials that the connection account supplies to perform various activities on a management server in the All Management Servers resource pool. Before configuring the connection account in Orchestrator, you should first grant the necessary permissions for the user account in System Center Operations Manager.

Connectivity Requirements

The SCOM IP connects to the Operations Manager management server on port 5724, through the System Center Data Access Service (OMSDK). Before configuring the connection between Operations Manager and Orchestrator, verify that the following are in place:

- The System Center Operations Manager console is installed on each computer where an Orchestrator runbook server or Runbook Designer is installed, if that runbook server or Runbook Designer interacts with Operations Manager.
- Network connectivity on TCP port 5724 is available between the Operations Manager management server and each computer that will interact with Operations Manager.

Detailed information on the required components for communication between System Center Orchestrator and Operations Manager is available at http://technet.microsoft.com/en-us/library/hh830690.aspx.

Granting Access to the Connection Account

Before configuring the connection to Operations Manager, grant access in System Center Operations Manager to the account that Orchestrator will use when connecting to the management server. As mentioned in the "Security Credentials" section, you can configure multiple accounts with varying levels of permissions in Operations Manager. This section discusses the steps to add a user to the Operations Manager Administrators role. Perform the following steps:

1. Launch the System Center Operations Manager Operations console. In the Navigation pane, select the Administration workspace.
2. In the Administration workspace, select the User Roles node.
3. Double-click the Operations Manager Administrators user role, and note the Active Directory groups that have membership in this Operations Manager user role.
4. Open Active Directory Users and Computers, and locate the group that has membership in the Operations Manager Administrators user role.
5. In the Operations console, double-click the group you identified. On the Members tab, click **Add.** Enter the name of the account Orchestrator will use to access this Operations Manager management server.
6. Click **OK** twice to save your changes and exit.

Configuring the Connection Account

For the connection account to perform the actions in the sample runbooks used in this chapter, you must grant rights to this account in Operations Manager. Begin by configuring connectivity to System Center Operations Manager in the Runbook Designer. Perform the following steps to configure connectivity with System Center Operations Manager in the Runbook Designer:

1. In the Runbook Designer, from the top menu, select **Options -> SC 2012 Operations Manager.**
2. In the SC 2012 Operations Manager dialog box, click **Add** and enter the following information:
   - **Name:** User-defined name for this connection.
   - **Server:** Name of the Operations Manager 2012 management server.

- **Domain:** Domain of the Operations Manager 2012 management server.
- **User name:** Active Directory (AD) account with administrator privileges in Operations Manager 2012.
- **Password:** Password for the AD account.
- **Polling:** The desired polling frequency. The default is 10 seconds, but a less frequent polling period is recommended if your runbook automation requirements allow this.
- **Reconnect:** The desired frequency of reconnect attempts. The default is 10 seconds, but as with the Polling setting, a less frequent polling period is recommended to minimize resource consumption on System Center Operations Manager servers.

3. Use the **Test Connection** button (see Figure 13.1) to verify connectivity.

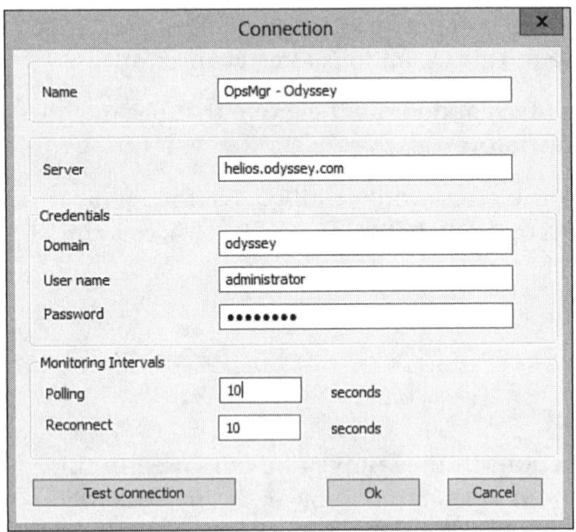

FIGURE 13.1 Configuring and testing the Operations Manager connection account.

4. Click **OK** to create the connection.
5. When complete, the newly created connection in the Microsoft Operations Manager 2012 dialog box should look similar to Figure 13.2.
6. Click **Finish** to save the connection settings.

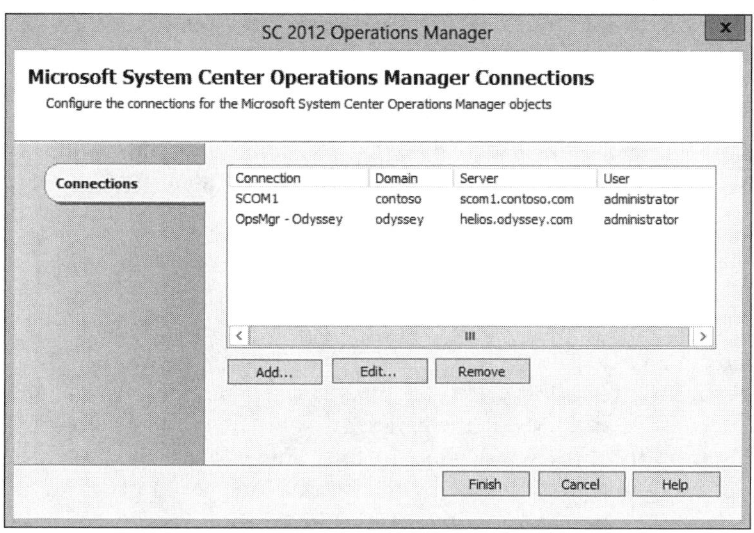

FIGURE 13.2 The Operations Manager connection interface.

Activities at a Glance

For reference, the SCOM IP includes these activities:

- Create Alert
- Get Alert
- Get Monitor
- Monitor Alert
- Monitor State
- Start Maintenance Mode
- Stop Maintenance Mode
- Update Alert

Activities in Depth

If you are already familiar with the integration pack for SCOM 2007 R2, you might notice that the activities in the SCOM 2012 IP are the same as those in the previous version. However, Microsoft has updated the functionality of several of these activities. This part of the chapter examines all the activities that comprise the SCOM IP so that you understand what they do and how to use them. You can use most of the activities on their own, but as with standard activities, combining activities into more detailed sequences of activities is what makes Orchestrator so powerful as a platform for process automation. This section includes a description of the activities in the SCOM IP and some of the more common use case scenarios associated with each.

The SCOM integration pack consists of eight activities:

- **Create Alert:** This activity creates a new alert directly in System Center Operations Manager from Orchestrator, without creating any custom rules or management packs.
    - A common use case for this activity is for CMDB automation between external sources and information technology service management (ITSM) solutions, such as System Center Service Manager. You can create an alert in Operations Manager and create an associated incident in Service Manager or another ITSM solution. Orchestrator integration packs for third-party ITSM solutions, such as HP Service Manager, CA, and BMC Remedy, are available free from Microsoft or commercially from third-party independent software vendors (ISVs), such as Kelverion. For more information about Orchestrator integration packs for third-party systems, see Chapter 12, "Orchestrator Integration Packs."
    - You can also use **Create Alert** as an alert-forwarding mechanism (a product connector of sorts) to consolidate alerts from multiple monitoring systems into a "single pane of glass" in the Operations Manager console.

  The first time this activity is run in a runbook, it installs the Microsoft System Center Orchestrator Integration Library management pack in Operations Manager. The **Create Alert** activity creates an event in Operations Manager, which the Microsoft System Center Orchestrator Integration Library management pack then translates into an Operations Manager alert. More information on this activity is available at http://technet.microsoft.com/en-us/library/hh830722.aspx.

CAUTION: CREATE ALERT OBJECT DOES NOT WORK PROPERLY THE FIRST TIME

Upon the first connection to a new management server where the Microsoft System Center Orchestrator Integration Library management pack is not installed, Operations Manager does not create an alert. The workaround is to run it again. The new alert is created after the activity is run a second time. The failure occurs because the management pack is imported on the first attempt. On the second and subsequent attempts, the workflow functions as designed.

- **Get Alert:** This activity retrieves alerts from Operations Manager that match the criteria you specify. You can use **Get Alert** to retrieve an alert and replicate the information to a ticketing system for troubleshooting.

  Get Alert has been updated for System Center 2012 Operations Manager to include additional published data, including CompanyKnowledge, ManagementPackMonitorName, MonitoringRuleName, ManagementPackName, ManagementPackFriendlyName, ManagementPackDisplayName, ManagementPackId, ManagementPackVersion, and ManagementPackIsSealed.

For information on this activity, see http://technet.microsoft.com/en-us/library/hh830713.aspx.

- **Get Monitor:** This activity retrieves monitoring objects from Operations Manager that match the criteria you specify. You can use the **Get Monitor** activity to retrieve a message and replicate the information to a trouble ticketing system. See http://technet.microsoft.com/en-us/library/hh830695.aspx for additional information.

- **Monitor Alert:** This activity uses filters to determine which properties of an alert will trigger the runbook. Each part of the alert is compared to the values of the filter to determine whether they meet the criteria before triggering the runbook.

  Microsoft has updated the **Monitor Alert** activity for Operations Manager 2012 to include additional published data, including CompanyKnowledge, ManagementPackMonitorName, MonitoringRuleName, ManagementPackName, ManagementPackFriendlyName, ManagementPackDisplayName, ManagementPackId, ManagementPackVersion, and ManagementPackIsSealed.

  You can find additional information at http://technet.microsoft.com/en-us/library/hh830707.aspx.

- **Monitor State:** This activity monitors the state of an Operations Manager activity that you specify. You can use the **Monitor State** activity to trigger a corrective runbook when an object with a Warning state is detected.

  The **Monitor State** activity can be useful in specific monitoring scenarios to trigger corrective actions or maintenance mode operations. More information on this activity is available at http://technet.microsoft.com/en-us/library/hh830738.aspx.

- **Start Maintenance Mode:** This activity puts a monitor in Operations Manager into maintenance mode. All alerts generated by computers the monitor watches while in maintenance mode are ignored. You can use the **Start Maintenance Mode** activity at the start of maintenance procedures to prevent the generation of false alerts.

  Start Maintenance Mode is intended only for placing a server into maintenance mode (Microsoft.Windows.Computer or Microsoft.Unix.Computer); it will not work for group maintenance mode. When you attempt to start maintenance mode for a group, only the group object itself enters maintenance mode; the contained objects do not. Group maintenance mode for Operations Manager in Orchestrator is best performed using the **Run .Net Script** activity with a PowerShell script leveraging cmdlets from the Operations Manager Shell. This is demonstrated in the start Branch Office Maintenance Mode runbook discussed in the "Use Case Scenarios" section.

  See http://technet.microsoft.com/en-us/library/hh830730.aspx for more information on this activity in the OpsMgr 2012 IP.

- **Stop Maintenance Mode:** This activity takes a computer (Microsoft.Windows.Computer or Microsoft.Unix.Computer) out of maintenance mode. If you put a computer into maintenance mode using the **Start Maintenance Mode** activity, you can use the **Stop Maintenance Mode** activity to end maintenance mode before the configured duration has elapsed.

In the case of connectivity problems with a branch office, you would not use **Start Maintenance Mode** and **Stop Maintenance Mode** to put branch office servers into maintenance mode to prevent an alert storm. Using the **Run .Net Script** activity with a PowerShell script leveraging cmdlets from the Operations Manager Shell would be a more effective solution.

For additional information on this activity, refer to http://technet.microsoft.com/en-us/library/hh830743.aspx.

- **Update Alert:** This activity updates the information in an Operations Manager alert. You can use this activity in a runbook to update an alert based on the results from automated diagnostic or recovery actions performed by that runbook.

  The activity is commonly used in runbooks that perform automated remediation of an error condition to update the alert with information regarding the results of the attempt to correct the error. More information on the **Update Alert** activity is available at http://technet.microsoft.com/en-us/library/hh830692.aspx.

TIP: INDICATING THAT ORCHESTRATOR UPDATED THE ALERT

Even though the Last Modified By property of the alert reflects the name of the Operations Manager connection account, you might want to leave a clear indicator that the alert was updated from Orchestrator. You can easily do this by updating the Owner field or one of the ten custom properties present upon an alert with a value such as Updated by Orchestrator at {Object Start Time from "Update Alert"}.

Use Case Scenarios

Each runbook illustrated in the next sections uses activities from the SCOM IP to demonstrate automation of a common Operations Manager–related activity. Using the information from the data bus, you can create workflows that respond to the state components at runtime, such as when the health of activity transitions to an error state in Operations Manager. This practice makes Orchestrator an incredibly flexible platform for bringing in information, even as that information changes, and using runtime values as you would variables in a script.

The following five scenarios demonstrate how to effectively utilize activities from the SCOM IP:

- Incident remediation
- Server maintenance mode (new and improved from *System Center Opalis Integration Server 6.3 Unleashed* [Sams, 2011])
- Group maintenance mode (starting and ending)
- Branch office maintenance mode (preventing alert floods)
- Processing alerts in bulk, including:

- Updating alert resolution state in bulk
- Resolving aging alerts in bulk

Incident Remediation

The Incident Remediation runbook, in Figure 13.3, illustrates how to use Orchestrator with the SCOM IP to automate remediation of common server and application failures.

FIGURE 13.3 Incident Remediation.

Orchestrator features such as looping make it easy to double-check the state of an object (for example, whether a service is started or a website is online), so Orchestrator is an excellent tool for automating even complex recovery tasks in a more reliable manner than is possible with script- or command-based remediation alone.

This runbook performs the following activities:

1. **Monitor Alert:** This activity, in Figure 13.4, is configured to monitor for alerts named **DNS Service Stopped**.
2. **Start DNS Service:** When an alert matching the configured criteria is detected, this renamed **Start/Stop Windows Service** activity is triggered to restart the service.

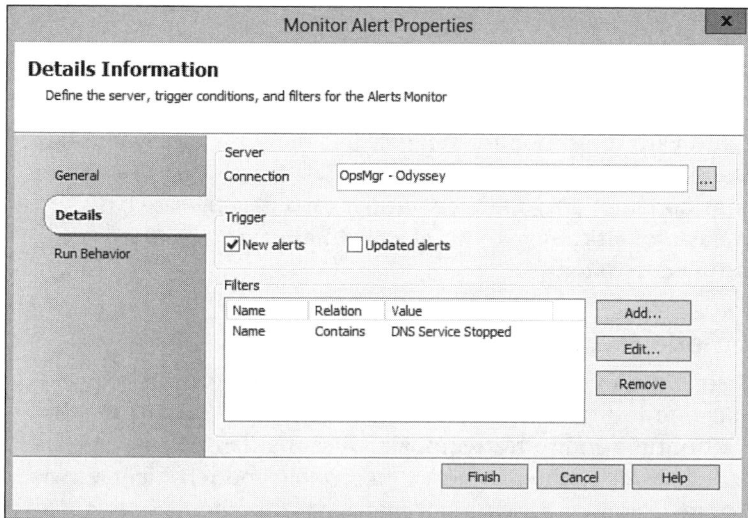

FIGURE 13.4 **Monitor Alert** Properties page.

- **Action:** Start Service
- **Service:** DNS Client

3. **Update Alert:** When the service restarts successfully, the **Update Alert** activity is triggered to update the alert with the values shown here and in Figure 13.5.

- **Alert ID:** {Id from "Monitor Alert"}
- **CustomField10:** Updated by Orchestrator

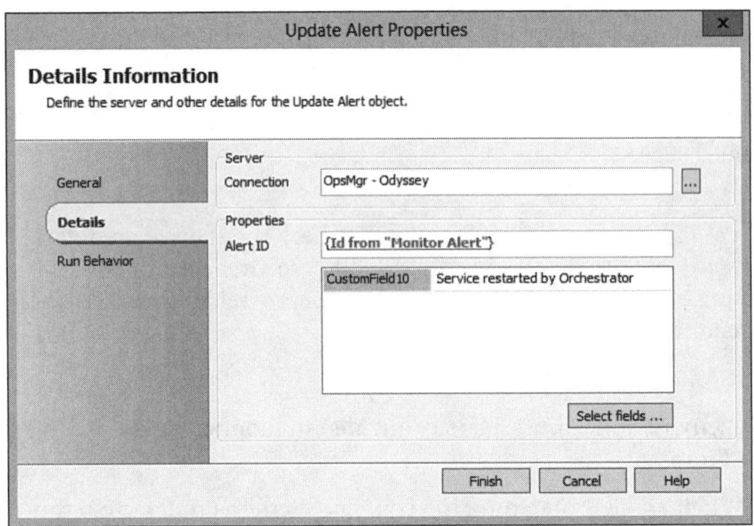

FIGURE 13.5 **Update Alert** Properties page.

Operations Manager automatically closes the alert.

Although this is true here and with most monitor-generated alerts, some other monitor-generated alerts might not automatically close. In that case, updating the alert resolution state to Closed would be appropriate. Verify monitor settings on a case-by-case basis to ensure that the alert is closed automatically without needing manual intervention or a resolution state update from Orchestrator.

Server Maintenance Mode (Windows or *NIX)

Maintenance mode in System Center Operations Manager prevents alerts from being sent when a server or application is offline for planned activities. With the capability to easily pause for fixed periods of time and to reattempt activities that fail, Orchestrator is an excellent tool for executing server maintenance in a predictable and reliable manner. Starting and stopping maintenance mode for an agent-managed computer is simple. The runbook in Figure 13.6 will start or stop Operations Manager maintenance mode for any agent-managed computer; it is intended to be called externally from another runbook as part of a larger maintenance workflow.

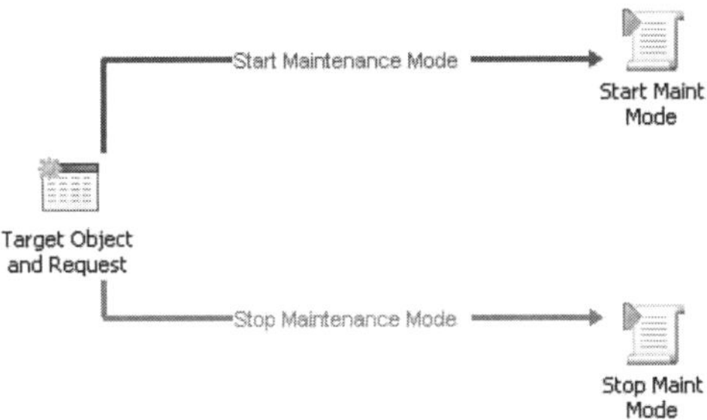

FIGURE 13.6 Start and Stop Maintenance Mode runbook.

Let's begin with a server maintenance mode runbook for Windows computers and then look at how you can quickly and easily modify this runbook to support Linux and UNIX systems as well.

Server Maintenance Mode Configuration

To complete a request to start server maintenance mode, six pieces of information are collected (stopping maintenance mode requires less information). This runbook performs the following activities (covered along with their configuration settings):

1. **Target Object and Request:** This renamed **Initialize Data** activity presents four input parameters to collect the information necessary to carry out the appropriate action.

   The parameters configured on the Details tab (see Figure 13.7) contain the following information:

   - **Comment:** This is a free text comment attached to the maintenance mode event in Operations Manager.
   - **Reason:** The expected value is a string that contains any one of the accepted reason codes (predefined in Operations Manager):

     PlannedOther, UnplannedOther, PlannedHardwareMaintenance, UnplannedHardwareMaintenance, PlannedHardwareInstallation, UnplannedHardwareInstallation, PlannedOperatingSystemReconfiguration, UnplannedOperatingSystemReconfiguration, PlannedApplicationMaintenance, ApplicationInstallation, ApplicationUnresponsive, ApplicationUnstable, SecurityIssue, and LossOfNetworkConnectivity
   - **StartOrStop:** The expected values for this parameter are Start and Stop (not case sensitive). This is used in the branching logic to determine whether the **Start Maint Mode** or **Stop Maint Mode** activity should be initiated.

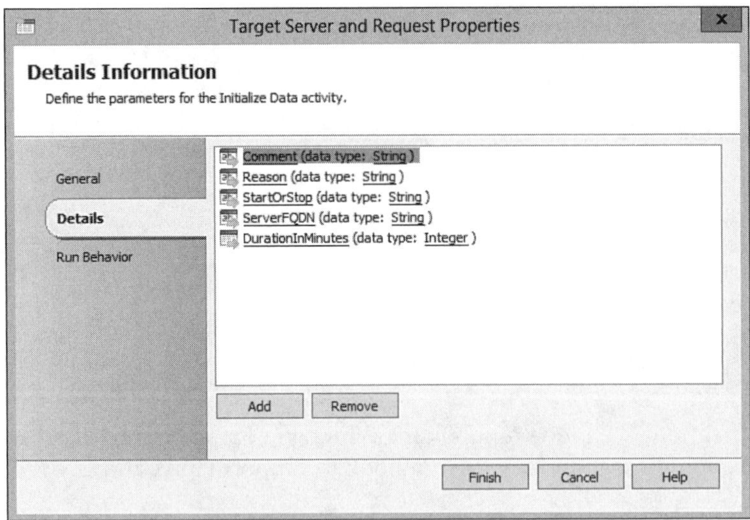

FIGURE 13.7 **Target Server and Request** Properties page.

- **ServerFQDN:** This is the display name of the object or group. The objects that this object hosts or contains are automatically placed in maintenance mode.
- **DurationInMinutes:** The expected value is an integer that presents the desired length of maintenance mode in minutes.

2. **Start Maint Mode:** This activity starts maintenance mode for the specified monitored object (instance) specified in the Monitor field in the activity properties.

   Configure this information on the Details tab (see Figure 13.8):

   - **Connection:** This is the connection for the target Operations Manager environment configured in global configuration (SC 2012 Operations Manager menu item on the Options menu in Runbook Designer).
   - **Monitor: {ServerFQDN from "Target Server and Request"}: Microsoft. Windows.Computer:{ServerFQDN from "Target Server and Request"}**
   - **Reason: {Reason from "Target Server and Request"}**
   - **Duration: {Duration from "Target Server and Request"}**
   - **Comment: {Comment from "Target Server and Request"}**

3. **Stop Maint Mode:** This activity stops maintenance mode for the specified monitored object (instance) in the Monitor field in the activity properties.

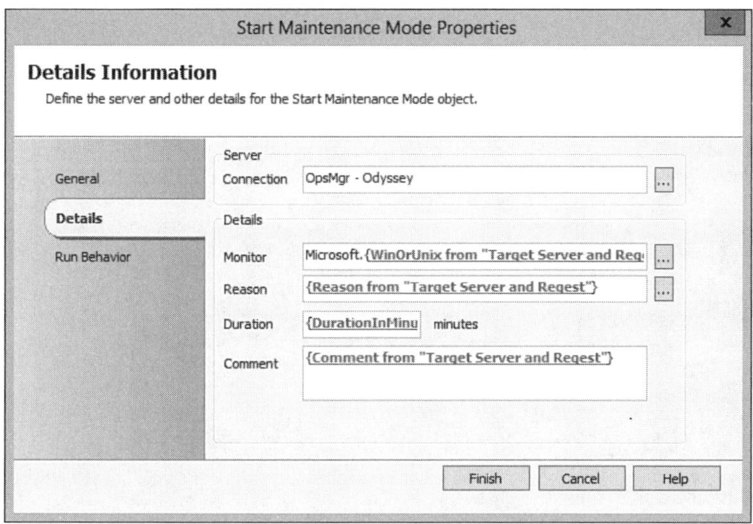

FIGURE 13.8 **Start Maintenance Mode** properties.

Configure this information on the Details tab:

- **Connection:** This is the connection for the target Operations Manager environment configured in global configuration (SC 2012 Operations Manager menu item on the Options menu in Runbook Designer).
- **{ServerFQDN from "Target Server and Request"}:Microsoft.Windows.Computer:{ServerFQDN from "Target Server and Request"}**

TIP: USING THE ELLIPSIS IN ACTIVITY PROPERTIES

To ensure that you get the string for the monitored server right, use the ellipsis to select a monitored computer from the list; then replace each occurrence of the computers FQDN with the published data **{ServerFQDN from "Target Server and Request"}**.

Creating a *NIX Server Maintenance Mode Runbook

Because the **Start Maintenance Mode** and **Stop Maintenance Mode** activities are intended for use with both Windows computers (Microsoft.Windows.Computer) and UNIX/Linux computers (Microsoft.Unix.Computer), creating a server maintenance mode runbook for UNIX/Linux computers based on the Windows example takes only a minute.

Changing the prepopulated string in the Monitor field of both the renamed **Start Maintenance Mode** and **Stop Maintenance Mode** activities (see Figure 13.9) from Microsoft.Windows.Computer to Microsoft.Unix.Computer gets the runbook ready to initiate server maintenance mode for UNIX and Linux computers.

13

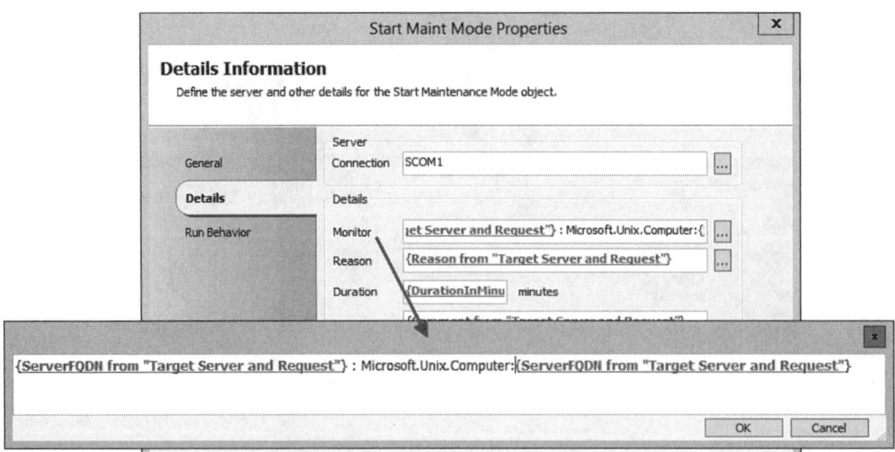

FIGURE 13.9 Updating **Start Maint Mode** for *NIX.

Testing the Runbook

You can test this runbook using the Runbook Tester. Because input is required, you actually cannot test this runbook simply by checking in the runbook and clicking **Run** in the Runbook Designer.

To start maintenance mode, you must specify values for all parameters in the **Target Object and Request** activity (see Figure 13.10).

FIGURE 13.10 Inputs for **Start Maint Mode**.

To stop maintenance mode, you need only provide values for the ServerFQDN and StartOrStop parameters in the **Target Object and Request** activity in Figure 13.11. (Server1 is a "sample" server for purposes of this discussion.)

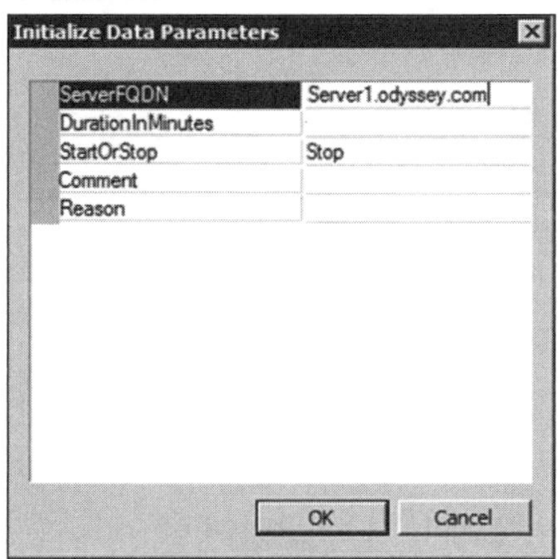

FIGURE 13.11 Inputs for **Stop Maint Mode**.

Server maintenance is the easiest of the maintenance mode options to address in an Orchestrator runbook. When you want to send a group of managed objects (servers, websites, and so on) into maintenance mode, a bit more effort is involved. The following sections explore the steps for creating flexible group maintenance mode runbooks for System Center Operations Manager.

Group Maintenance Mode

This runbook addresses a common Operations Manager scenario by using some activities that the SCOM 2012 IP does not include. (Hey, this is about solving real-world problems, right?)

However, because the Orchestrator runbook server role requires Windows 2008 R2 or Windows Server 2012, this theoretical solution presents a challenge. The problem stems from the fact that Orchestrator is still a 32-bit application. (Microsoft did not have time to convert to 64-bit in the System Center 2012 release.) Before delving into creating a runbook for group maintenance mode, let's examine the blocking issue and decide how to work around it.

64-Bit and 32-Bit Versions PowerShell ISE Challenges

If you are running Orchestrator on a 64-bit operating system (OS) such as Windows Server 2008 R2 and above, and you install the Windows PowerShell ISE, you will notice two versions: a 64-bit version and a 32-bit (x86) version. Always test your PowerShell scripts by running them on your Orchestrator server using the x86 version of the PowerShell console or ISE. This puts you in the same environment Orchestrator will use to run the script and reveals any issues that Orchestrator will face in running 32-bit mode against 64-bit snap-ins. The most obvious side effect of the 32-bit/64-bit problem is trying to load a PowerShell module or snap-in that fails to load. Reattempting with the 64-bit Windows PowerShell ISE and checking which snap-ins or modules are loaded (using `Get-Module` or `Get-PSSnapIn`) shows the module or snap-in loading to confirm the issue. Fortunately, the

Operations Manager PowerShell module will load in the 32-bit PowerShell instance, so enabling script execution resolves this issue.

Possible Workarounds in Other Scenarios

If you are using a System Center component with a PowerShell module that will not load in an x86 PowerShell instance, or if you don't want to (or cannot) allow script execution in the x86 PowerShell instance, you have several possible workarounds:

- **Use PowerShell remoting to loop back to the runbook server and use the 64-bit environment:** This is possible by using `Invoke-Command $env:computername`. It adds a bit of complexity and increases the effort required in writing PowerShell scripts to run in Orchestrator.
- **Use the integration pack for PowerShell Script Execution 1.1 (available on CodePlex):** This IP provides extended PowerShell Script Execution capabilities for the Orchestrator from and against both 32-bit and 64-bit operating systems by implementing PowerShell remoting for you. As with PowerShell remoting, this approach assumes that WinRM is installed and running on the target system, which, in this case, is the Operations Manager root management server (RMS) emulator. It includes two activities:
  - **Execute PS Script:** This activity enables you to specify the remote server, credentials, and WinRM listening port in the activity properties.
  - **Execute PS Script – Global:** This activity uses connection criteria (remote server, credentials, and WinRM listening port) specified in a global configuration (**Execute PowerShell Script** on the Options menu in Runbook Designer).

NOTE: OBTAINING THE IP FOR POWERSHELL SCRIPT EXECUTION 1.1

You can download the Integration Pack for PowerShell Script Execution 1.1 from CodePlex at http://orchestrator.codeplex.com/releases/view/76101.

Creating a Runbook for Group Maintenance Mode in Operations Manager 2012

The next runbook contains three activities (see Figure 13.12) and can be initiated from outside Orchestrator using the Orchestrator web service (such as with System Center Service Manager). Let's step through the configuration to better understand how this runbook works:

1. **Target Object and Request:** This renamed **Initialize Data** activity presents five input parameters to collect the information necessary to carry out the appropriate action.

   The parameters configured on the Details tab (see Figure 13.13) contain the following information:

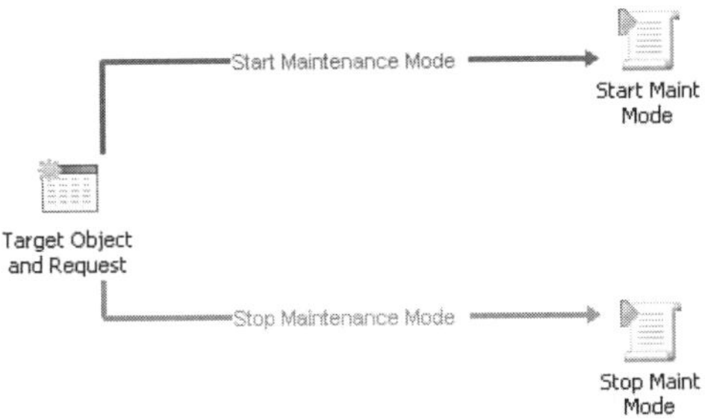

FIGURE 13.12 Group Maintenance Mode runbook.

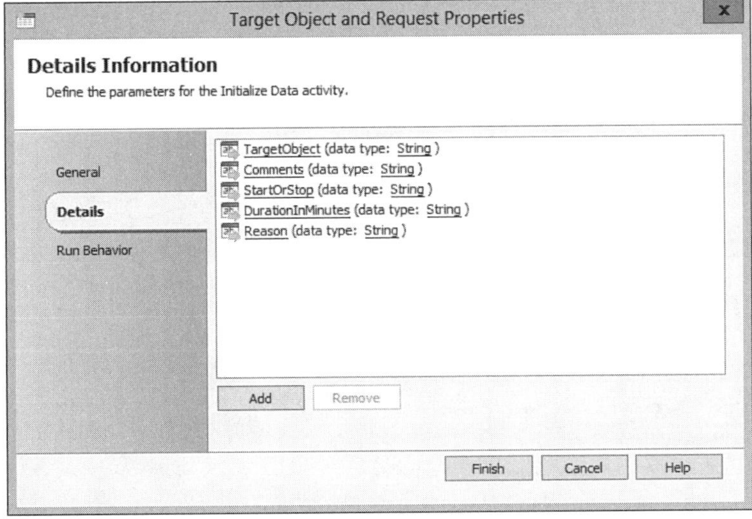

FIGURE 13.13 Runbook inputs in **Target Object and Request** activity.

- **TargetObject:** This is the display name of the object or group. The object that this object hosts or contains is automatically placed in maintenance mode.
- **Comment:** This is an optional field in which the user can enter a comment related to why maintenance mode is being started or stopped.
- **StartOrStop:** The expected values for this parameter are Start or Stop (not case sensitive). This is used in the branching logic to determine whether to initiate the **Start Maint Mode** or **Stop Maint Mode** activity.
- **DurationInMinutes:** The expected value is an integer that presents the desired length of maintenance mode in minutes.
- **Reason:** The expected value is a string containing any one of the accepted reason codes (predefined in Operations Manager, which are:

PlannedOther, UnplannedOther, PlannedHardwareMaintenance, UnplannedHardwareMaintenance, PlannedHardwareInstallation, UnplannedHardwareInstallation, PlannedOperatingSystemReconfiguration, UnplannedOperatingSystemReconfiguration, PlannedApplicationMaintenance, ApplicationInstallation, ApplicationUnresponsive, ApplicationUnstable, SecurityIssue, and LossOfNetworkConnectivity

2. **Start Maint Mode:** This renamed **Run .Net Script** activity (see Figure 13.14) executes a PowerShell script (leveraging the native Operations Manager PowerShell cmdlets) to start maintenance mode for the specified group object and all objects that it hosts or contains for the number of minutes specified in the DurationInMinutes parameter of the renamed **Initialize Data** activity. The script runs on the runbook server where the runbook is configured to run. Figure 13.15 shows the PowerShell script for the **Start Maint Mode** activity, and the script is included with the download material available for this book. Appendix C, "Available Online," provides additional information.

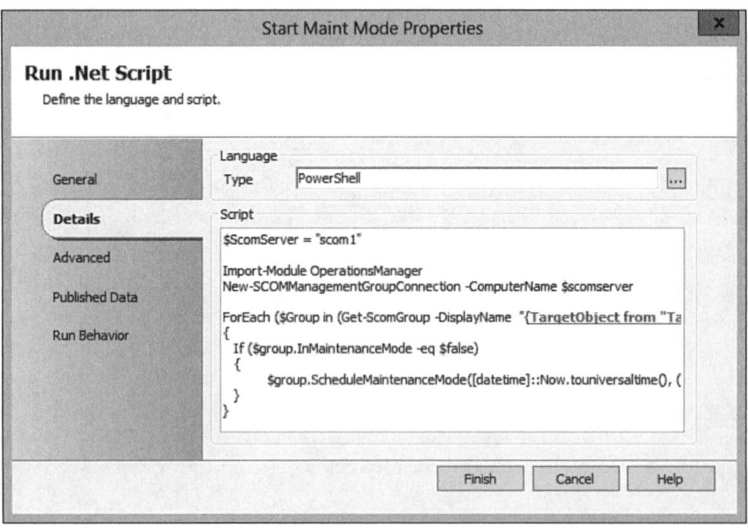

FIGURE 13.14 **Start Maint Mode** properties.

```
$ScomServer = "scom1"

Import-Module OperationsManager
New-SCOMManagementGroupConnection -ComputerName $scomserver

ForEach ($Group in (Get-ScomGroup -DisplayName "{TargetObject from "Target Object and Request"}"))
{
  If ($group.InMaintenanceMode -eq $false)
  {
        $group.ScheduleMaintenanceMode([datetime]::Now.touniversaltime(), `
        ([datetime]::Now).addminutes({DurationInMinutes from "Target Object and Request"}).touniversaltime(), `
        "{Reason from "Target Object and Request"}", "{Comments from "Target Object and Request"}" , `
        "Recursive")
  }
}
```

OK Cancel

FIGURE 13.15 Script for the **Start Maint Mode** activity.

3. **Stop Maint Mode:** This renamed **Run .Net Script** activity executes a PowerShell script (leveraging the native Operations Manager PowerShell cmdlets) to stop maintenance mode for the specified group object and all objects that it hosts or contains. The script runs on the runbook server where the runbook is configured to run. Figure 13.16 shows the PowerShell script for the **Stop Maint Mode** activity, which is included with the download material available with this book.

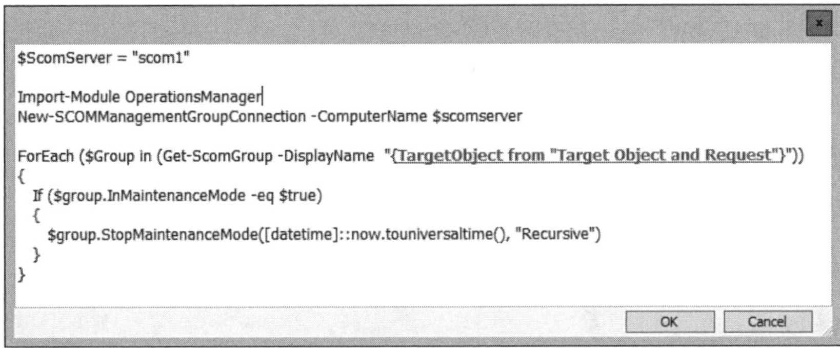

```
$ScomServer = "scom1"

Import-Module OperationsManager
New-SCOMManagementGroupConnection -ComputerName $scomserver

ForEach ($Group in (Get-ScomGroup -DisplayName "{TargetObject from "Target Object and Request"}"))
{
  If ($group.InMaintenanceMode -eq $true)
  {
    $group.StopMaintenanceMode([datetime]::now.touniversaltime(), "Recursive")
  }
}
```

OK Cancel

FIGURE 13.16 Script for the **Stop Maint Mode** activity.

4. **Branching Logic:** The branch logic uses the value that the StartOrStop parameter of the **Target Object and Request** activity provides to trigger either the **Start Maint Mode** or **Stop Maint Mode** activity. Figure 13.17 shows the configuration of the branch logic for the Start Maintenance Mode branch.

13

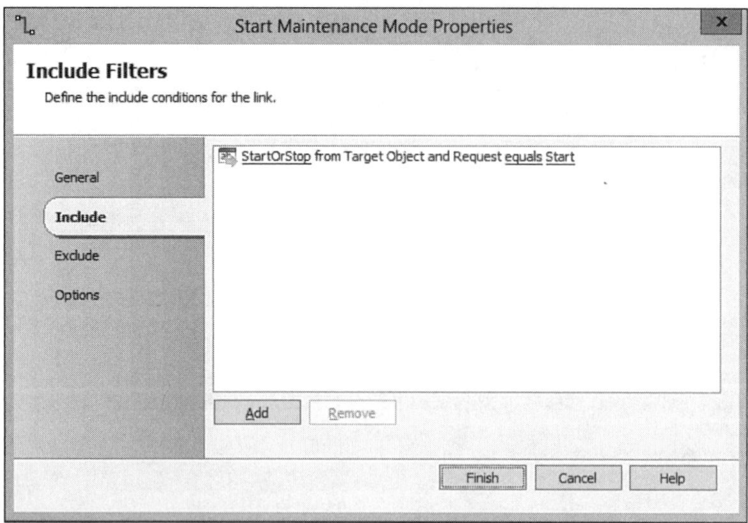

FIGURE 13.17 Branch logic in the Group Maintenance Mode runbook.

TIP: DOING MORE WITH THE GROUP MAINTENANCE MODE RUNBOOK

You can use the Group Maintenance Mode runbook for starting or stopping maintenance mode for any monitored activity in SCOM. The **Initialize Data** activity used to accept input data makes it perfect for use in request offerings in Service Manager 2012. For more information on how to leverage Orchestrator runbooks from Service Manager, see Chapter 19, "Runbook Automation in the Data Center and the Cloud."

You can test this runbook using the Runbook Tester. Because input is required, you cannot test this runbook simply by checking in the runbook and clicking **Run** in Runbook Designer.

To start maintenance mode, you must specify values for all parameters in the **Target Activity and Request** activity (see Figure 13.18).

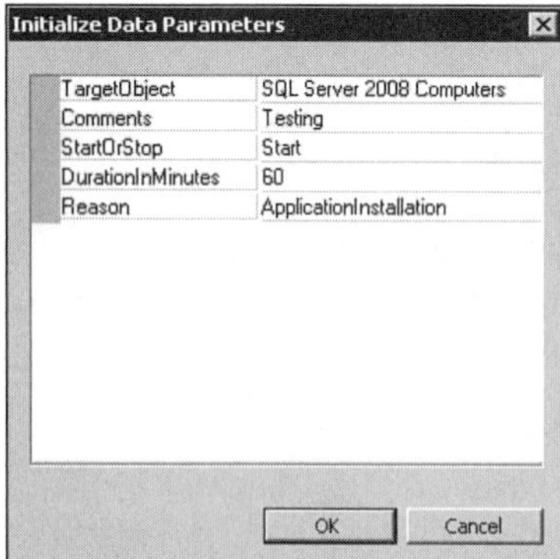

FIGURE 13.18 User inputs to start maintenance mode with the Group Maintenance Mode runbook.

To stop maintenance mode, you need only provide values for the TargetObject and StartOrStop parameters in the **Target Activity and Request** activity (see Figure 13.19). The script does not use the Reason and DurationInMinutes values in the **Stop Maint Mode** activity.

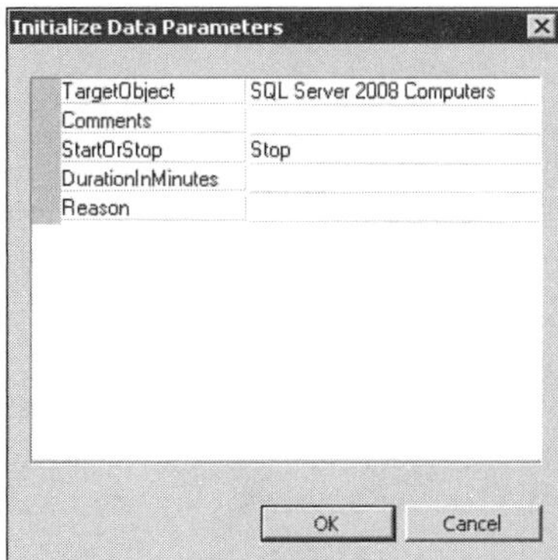

FIGURE 13.19 User inputs to stop maintenance mode with the Group Maintenance Mode runbook.

This group maintenance mode runbook solves a common real-world challenge for Operations Manager administrators, but more good news arises. This runbook can be modified slightly to solve another common headache—stopping the flood of alerts from heartbeat failures when network connectivity to a remote office is lost. The next section discusses this.

Branch Office Maintenance Mode

A common concern in distributed enterprises that utilize Operations Manager for monitoring are the alert floods that result from failures in branch office connectivity. System Center 2012 Operations Manager includes new network monitoring capabilities, including visualization of monitored computers relative to network devices (for example, which computers are connected to a particular network device). However, even the latest version of Operations Manager does not have an alert suppression mechanism to prevent the alert storms associated with failures in network connectivity. Therefore, when a branch office router is unreachable, Operations Manager not only raises an alert for the router itself—about 3 minutes later, it raises heartbeat failure alerts for all servers and other monitored devices hosted at that affected branch office, resulting in an alert storm.

This next pair of runbooks is two halves of a complete solution (see Figures 13.20 and 13.21). They provide a workaround for this alert storm. They first monitor the health state of a network device in Operations Manager and trigger a group maintenance mode script to put all the servers in the affected branch into maintenance mode before the alert flood begins. Then they stop maintenance mode when the condition improves. The Start Branch Office Maintenance Mode runbook runs a PowerShell maintenance mode script when the selected Operations Manager monitor transitions into a critical (error) state. The

Stop Branch Office Maintenance Mode runbook runs a PowerShell maintenance mode script when the selected Operations Manager monitor transitions back to a healthy state.

You could handle this entirely with Orchestrator activities, but the runbook would be substantially more complex. With that in mind, this runbook leverages simple PowerShell maintenance mode scripts to begin or end maintenance mode for a group of servers, based on the health state of the branch office router.

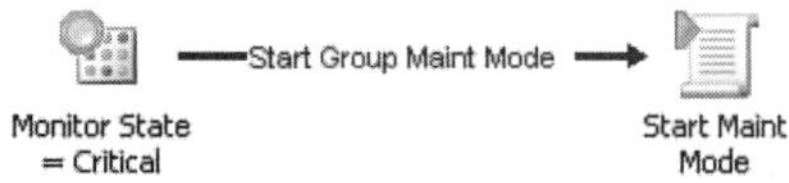

FIGURE 13.20 Start Branch Office Maintenance Mode runbook.

The Start Branch Office Maintenance Mode runbook performs these activities:

1. **Monitor State:** This activity is configured to watch for changes in the state of an availability monitor for a network device. By default, Operations Manager monitors the availability of network routers and switches through ICMP and SNMP. However, you can substitute a custom availability monitor of your own design if you want.
    - **Activity:** <Target network device or other monitored activity>
    - **State:** Critical
2. **Start Maint Mode:** If the unit monitor that monitors the availability of the branch router goes into a critical state, this renamed **Run .Net Script** activity is triggered and runs a simple group maintenance mode script to remove the group that contains branch office servers from maintenance mode.
    - **Language:** PowerShell
    - **Script:** <paste contents of StartMaint.ps1>, available as online content for this book

FIGURE 13.21 Stop Branch Office Maintenance Mode.

The Stop Branch Office Maintenance Mode runbook performs these activities:

1. **Monitor State:** This activity is configured to watch for changes in the state of an availability monitor for a network device. By default, Operations Manager monitors the availability of network routers and switches through ICMP and SNMP. However, you can substitute a custom availability monitor of your own design if you want.

- **Activity:** <Target network device or other monitored activity>
- **State:** Critical

2. **Stop Maint Mode:** If the unit monitor that monitors the availability of the branch router goes back to a healthy state, this renamed **Run .Net Script** activity is triggered. That activity runs a simple group maintenance mode script to remove the group that contains branch office servers from maintenance mode. The Stop Maintenance Mode script (see Figure 13.21) is included in the code download available for this book. (See Appendix C for details.)
   - **Language:** PowerShell
   - **Script:** <paste contents of StoptMaint.ps1>, available with the online content for this book

WHY THE START AND STOP MAINTENANCE MODE ACTIVITIES FROM THE SCOM IP ARE NOT USED

With the RTM release of Orchestrator 2012, when you use the **Start Maintenance Mode** activity to put an Operations Manager group into maintenance mode, only the group activity itself enters maintenance mode. On the other hand, when you use the Operations Manager Shell to put a group into maintenance mode (which makes the request through the SDK), all the activities contained in the group enter maintenance mode as well (because a method called `recursive` is implemented).

In the SP 1 update to Orchestrator 2012, the **Start Maintenance Mode** and **Stop Maintenance Mode** activities are updated to support group maintenance mode recursively. However, the input format that the Monitor property of these activities requires make it challenging to programmatically format the input to this field easily and reliably. Using a script as shown in this example is the most pragmatic approach.

EXTENDING ORCHESTRATOR INTEGRATION WITH OPERATIONS MANAGER

The Orchestrator Extensibility Kit for SC Operations Manager, released as open source on the TechNet Gallery, provides functionality beyond that of the SCOM IP. This Orchestrator Extensibility Kit provides a .DLL that adds the following activity capabilities to Orchestrator:

- Create SCOM Notification Subscription
- Delete SCOM Notification Subscription
- List Pending Agent Installs
- Approve Pending Agent Installs

You can test this functionality using **Invoke .Net** activity from the Orchestrator Integration Kit (OIT). You can use this DLL (and appropriate dependencies) to create an Orchestrator integration pack by using the OIT Wizard.

Download the Orchestrator Extensibility Kit at http://gallery.technet.microsoft.com/Orchestrator-Example-14ed7e36. For additional information regarding the OIT, see Chapter 20, "The Orchestrator Integration Toolkit."

Processing Alerts in Bulk

A common recurring administrative task in System Center 2012 Operations Manager that cannot be completed easily in the Operations console is bulk processing of alert (closing old alerts, changing the resolution state of active alerts, and so on). Although you can automate in PowerShell, filtering down to only the subset of alerts you want to update can be challenging. The Internet has several examples using both PowerShell and Orchestrator, but most (or all) of them involve hard-coded alert names, severities, and priorities, thus requiring multiple runbooks for PowerShell scripts to address all updates scenarios.

The examples for this use case are written with extensibility in mind. Using the **Initialize Data** activity to accept user input for key parameters, these runbooks can be initialized from the Orchestration console, PowerShell, or an external ticketing system such as System Center 2012 Service Manager. Adding **Initialize Data** with parameters allows a single runbook to be leveraged for any number of alerts for which bulk processing is required, minimizing authoring effort.

Sample Runbook: Update Alert Resolution State in Bulk

Begin with the runbook designed to update the resolution states of alerts that meet specific criteria specified by the user initiating the runbook (see Figure 13.22). These are the activities and settings of this runbook:

FIGURE 13.22 Update Alert Resolution State in Bulk.

1. **Get Alert Criteria:** This renamed **Initialize Data** activity is configured to collect information about the alerts that should be closed.
    - **AlertName (string):** This is the full or partial name of an alert in Operations Manager 2012.
    - **Priority (string):** Acceptable values are Low, Medium, and High.
    - **Severity (string):** Acceptable values are Informational, Warning, and Critical.
    - **ResolutionState (string):** Acceptable values are Closed and any custom resolution state available in your Operations Manager deployment.
2. **Get Alert:** This activity builds on the same activity in the previous example, with the addition of the LastModified alert property, which determines alert age.
    - **Connection:** The connection for the target Operations Manager environment configured in global configuration
    - **Name:** Matches pattern {Alert Name from "Get Alert Criteria"}

- **Priority:** Matches pattern {Priority from "Get Alert Criteria"}
- **Severity:** Equals {Severity from "Get Alert Criteria"}

3. **Conditional Link: Alert Count > 0:** The link logic incorporates logic to ensure that the **Update Alert** activity is not triggered when no alerts remain to be processed and that alerts with a resolution state of Closed are excluded.
    - **Include:** Alert Count from **Get Alert** is greater than 0
    - **Exclude:** ResolutionState from the **Get Alert** activity equals "Closed"
4. **Update Alert:** The resolution state specified in the **Get Alert Criteria** activity can be any resolution state (other than New) present in your Operations Manager 2012 deployment.
    - **Connection:** The connection for the target Operations Manager environment configured in global configuration
    - **Alert ID:** {ID from "Get Alert"}
    - **ResolutionState:** {ResolutionState from "Get Alert Criteria"}

NOTE: CUSTOMIZING THESE EXAMPLES TO MEET YOUR NEEDS

Remember that virtually all alert properties are accessible through the filtering in the **Get Alert** and **Update Alert** activities. Thus, you can easily customize the example shown here and made available in the download accompanying this book.

As with all runbooks, completing a trial run in a nonproduction environment is an excellent idea, to avoid mistakes in your live environment.

Sample Runbook: Resolve Aging Alerts in Bulk

The runbook in this section (see Figure 13.23) builds on the Update Alert Resolution State in Bulk runbook example by incorporating an activity to update alert resolution state based on the age of the alert. In this case, the **Format/Date Time** activity calculates a user-defined date *X* days in the past, based on user input to the **Get Alert Criteria** activity at the beginning of the runbook. In this case, the age of the alert is based on the LastModified property of the alert. All alerts that meet the alert criteria (including age) will have their ResolutionState property updated by the **Update Alert** activity.

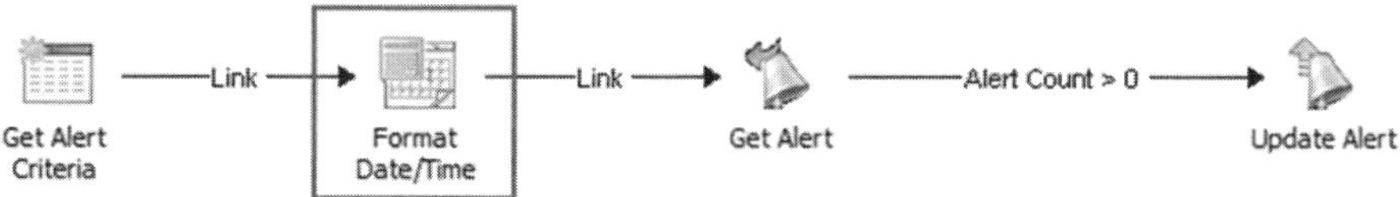

FIGURE 13.23 Resolve Stale (Old) Alerts in Bulk.

Consider the detailed settings of this runbook:

1. **Get Alert Criteria:** This renamed **Initialize Data** activity looks much like the one in the Update Alert Resolution State in Bulk runbook example, but it adds a MinAgeInDays input to capture from the user the desired minimum age of the alerts that should be closed.

    - **AlertName (string):** This is the full or partial name of an alert in Operations Manager 2012.
    - **Priority (string):** Acceptable values are Low, Medium, and High.
    - **Severity (string):** Acceptable values are Informational, Warning, and Critical.
    - **ResolutionState (string):** Acceptable values are Closed and any custom resolution state available in your Operations Manager deployment.
    - **MinAgeInDays (integer):** This is the minimum age of the LastModified property in the alert before it is closed.

2. **Format Date/Time:** Note that the time captured in the **Format/Date Time** activity is UTC time. This is important because it matches time stamps as logged in the OperationsManager database. Input these values:

    - **Date/Time:** {Activity start time in UTC from "Get Alert Criteria"}
    - **Format:** yyyy-MM-ddThh:mm:ss
      Output is Format: yyyy-MM-ddThh:mm:ss
    - **Output Adjustments:** This setting subtracts the user-specified number of days from the current date to calculate the desired minimum age of alerts to be resolved.

    Days: {MinAgeInDays from "Get Alert Criteria"}

3. **Get Alert:** This activity (see Figure 13.24) builds on the same activity in the previous example, with the addition of the LastModified alert property, which determines alert age.

    - **Connection:** This is the connection for the target Operations Manager environment configured in global configuration
    - **Name:** Matches pattern {Alert Name from "Get Alert Criteria"}
    - **Priority:** Matches pattern {Priority from "Get Alert Criteria"}
    - **Severity:** Equals {Severity from "Get Alert Criteria"}
    - **LastModified:** {Date/Time from "Format Date/Time"}

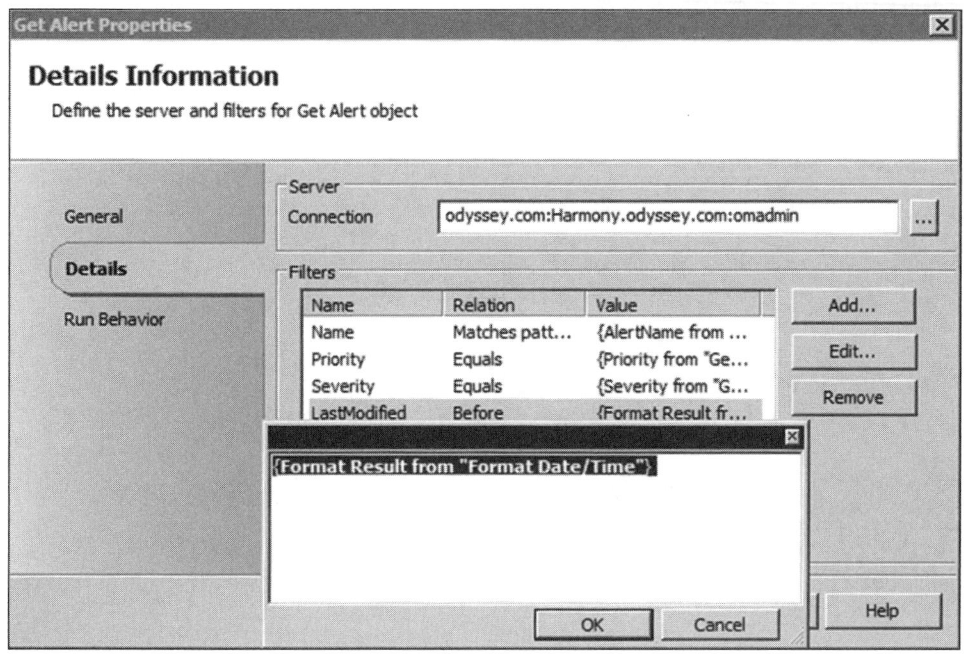

FIGURE 13.24 Filtering based on Alert LastModified property.

4. **Conditional Link:** Alert Count > 0
   - **Include:** Alert Count from Get Alert is greater than 0
   - **Exclude:** ResolutionState from Get Alert equals “Closed”
5. **Update Alert:** Although this particular example is designed to resolve alerts, the ResolutionState specified in the **Get Alert Criteria** activity could be any resolution state (other than New) present in your Operations Manager deployment.
   - **Connection:** The connection for the target Operations Manager environment configured in global configuration
   - **Alert ID:** {ID from “Get Alert”}
   - **ResolutionState:** {ResolutionState from “Get Alert Criteria”}

Testing the Runbook

Because these two examples for bulk alert processing require input, they are most easily tested using the Runbook Tester or the Orchestration console. As mentioned in the “Creating a Runbook for Group Maintenance Mode in Operations Manager 2012” section, runbooks that require user input cannot be tested in the Runbook Designer because the prompt for input cannot be launched from the Runbook Designer interface. Figures 13.25 and 13.26 show examples of acceptable input for **Get Alert Criteria** in each runbook.

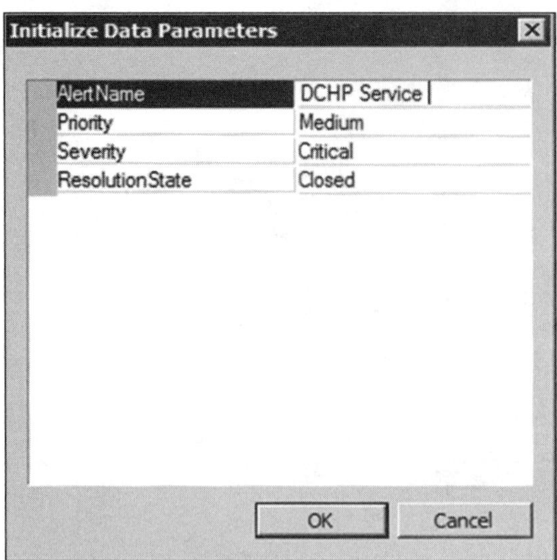

FIGURE 13.25 **Get Alert Criteria** input for Update Alert Resolution State in Bulk sample runbook.

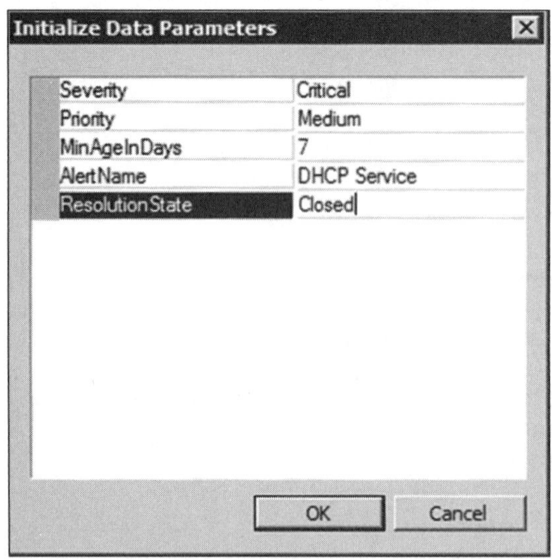

FIGURE 13.26 **Get Alert Criteria** input for Resolve Aging Alerts in Bulk sample runbook.

You might notice that the order of the parameters in Figure 13.22 differs compared to Figure 13.21. This occurs seemingly at random in the **Initialize Data** activity and cannot be controlled by the runbook author.

TIP: EXTENDING ORCHESTRATOR INTEGRATION WITH OPERATIONS MANAGER

The SCOM Extensibility Kit 2.0, released as open source on CodePlex, provides functionality that the SCOM IP does not include. This Extensibility Kit provides a .DLL that adds the following activity capabilities to Orchestrator:

- Create SCOM Notification Subscription
- Delete SCOM Notification Subscription
- List Pending Agent Installs
- Approve Pending Agent Installs

You can test this functionality using the **Invoke .Net Object** from the Orchestrator IP. Use this DLL (and appropriate dependencies) to create an Orchestrator IP by using the OIK Wizard.

Download the SCOM Extensibility Kit 2.0 from CodePlex at http://opalis.codeplex.com/releases/view/50751.

At the time of writing, the release available on CodePlex will not function in Orchestrator without first updating the source code using the PowerShell script referenced in "Migrating QIK API Custom Activities," at http://orchestrator.codeplex.com/wikipage?title=Migrating%20QIK%20API%20Custom%20Activities.

Summary

This chapter covered the configuration requirements of the SCOM IP and provided information on each of the eight objects it contains. It also discussed several use case scenarios demonstrating how many of these objects can be used in runbooks to automate incident remediation and maintenance-related tasks. The next chapter delves into the IP for another System Center component—Service Manager.

Chapter 19 discusses how to initiate these runbooks from PowerShell. Chapter 14, "Integration with System Center Service Manager," discusses integrating runbooks into the Service Manager 2012 self-service portal.

CHAPTER 14

Integration with System Center Service Manager

IN THIS CHAPTER

As one of the System Center integration packs (IPs), Microsoft's System Center Service Manager (SCSM) IP enables administrators to automate Service Manager and integrate with applications such as monitoring solutions and inventory systems. You can use this IP to automate many tasks in Service Manager to deliver services faster and more reliably. This chapter discusses the functionality of the System Center Service Manager integration pack.

The chapter describes the requirements for using the SCSM IP. It covers communication with Service Manager, the installation procedure and configuration steps, how each activity functions, and common use case scenarios. The chapter also presents several sample runbooks to show you how to leverage the SCSM IP fully to automate your organization's processes.

Communication Requirements

Connectivity to the Service Manager environment is leveraged through the SCSM .NET application programming interface (API) that is installed with the SCSM IP. The communication occurs via Windows Communication Foundation (WCF), between the Service Manager .NET API (Microsoft.EnterpriseManagement.Core.dll) on the Orchestrator server and the System Center Data Access Service (OMSDK) on the Service Manager management server.

The Service Manager SDK service on the management server listens on port 5724 for Orchestrator communications. Communication with the SDK service occurs in the Runbook Designer as well as the runbook server because the design is a dynamic experience that updates properties, filters, and published data elements based on the class information selected in the various activities.

Authentication to Service Manager is performed by providing credentials through the Service Manager software development kit (SDK) connection, which the Service Manager server validates using Windows standard security providers. The credentials provided for the IP for SCSM must have membership in SCSM user roles. You can create as many connections as you need to specify links to multiple Service Manager servers. You can also create multiple connections to the same server to allow for differences in security permissions for the different Service Manager user roles.

Integration Pack Requirements

The SCSM IP is not included in the Orchestrator 2012 installation files; you can download the Service Pack (SP) 1 version from the Microsoft download website (www.microsoft.com/en-us/download/details.aspx?id=34611). The following sections discuss specific requirements.

System Center 2012 Orchestrator

The System Center integration packs were among the first integration packs that Microsoft released after acquiring Opalis in late 2009. Opalis Integration Server 6.3 offers an integration pack for Service Manager 2010. With Orchestrator 2012, Microsoft provides new Service Manager integration packs, with different versions depending on the target Service Manager environment. Table 14.1 provides a matrix showing the appropriate Orchestrator integration pack versions to use.

TABLE 14.1 Service Manager Version and Integration Pack Support

Service Manager Release	Orchestrator 2012 RTM	Orchestrator 2012 SP 1
SCSM 2010 RTM	Orchestrator SCSM 2010 IP	Orchestrator SCSM 2010 IP
SCSM 2012 RTM	Orchestrator SCSM 2012 IP	Orchestrator SCSM 2012 IP
SCSM 2012 SP 1	Not supported	Orchestrator SCSM 2012 SP 1 IP

Locale Settings

The activities in the SCSM IP are supported only for use on computers using the ENU locale and U.S. English date format. The U.S. English date format is month/day/year.

Installing the Integration Pack

Installing the IP for Service Manager is similar to the process for other integration packs. Follow these steps:

1. Download the IP from Microsoft's download center. The filename is System_Center_2012_SP1_ Integration_Packs.EXE.

2. Run the EXE file and extract all the files (for example, to C:\TEMP\IP). This folder will contain multiple integration packs for different System Center components.
3. Use Orchestrator Deployment Manager to register and deploy the Service Manager IP, as described in Chapter 5, "Installing System Center 2012 Orchestrator."

Configuring the Integration Pack

All activities in the SCSM IP use the connection details specified for the SC 2012 Service Manager connection to execute functions on the Service Manager management server. If there is more than one Service Manager implementation, you can create connections for each Service Manager server. Additionally, you can create multiple connections for each Service Manager server to allow for differing permissions in the accounts used to access Service Manager.

SC 2012 Service Manager connections are critical for using the Service Manager IP. Perform the following steps to configure an SC 2012 Service Manager connection:

1. In the top menu of the Orchestrator Runbook Designer, select **Options** -> **SC 2012 Service Manager**.
2. In the SC 2012 Service Manager dialog box that opens, click **Add** and supply the relevant connection details. The following information is required (see Figure 14.1):
   - **Name:** Name you are giving the connection
   - **Server:** Name of the Service Manager management server
   - **Domain:** Domain of the Active Directory (AD) user account to use
   - **User Name:** Active Directory account used to connect to Service Manager
   - **Password:** Password for the Active Directory account
   - **Polling:** Interval at which the SCSM connection will be polled by any **Monitor Object** activities that use the connection
   - **Reconnect:** Interval at which the SCSM connection will be retried when disconnected

   The Connection dialog box also provides a Test Connection button for you to test the configuration.
3. Click **OK** to create the connection.

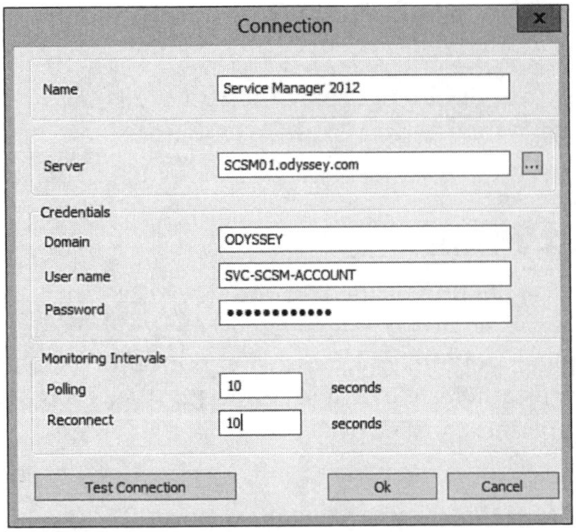

FIGURE 14.1 Configuring the SCSM connection.

Additional information on creating a connection is available on TechNet at http://technet.microsoft.com/en-us/library/hh832008.aspx.

Activities at a Glance

For reference, the SCSM IP includes these activities:

- Create Change with Template
- Create Incident with Template
- Create Object
- Create Related Object
- Create Relationship
- Delete Relationship
- Get Activity
- Get Object
- Get Relationship
- Monitor Object
- Update Object
- Update Activity
- Upload Attachment

Activities in Depth

This section describes each of the activities contained in this IP to provide an understanding of what each does. Each description includes a link to its corresponding TechNet article, which supplies additional information on the activity and lists tables with the properties and published data:

- **Create Change with Template:** This activity uses an existing template to create a new change record. Information on the elements in the activity is available at http://technet.microsoft.com/en-us/library/hh832003.aspx.
- **Create Incident with Template:** Within Service Manager, creating templates for new incident records is common. This activity creates a new incident from one of these templates. Although a template is used, the values provided by the template for the incident can be overwritten. See http://technet.microsoft.com/en-us/library/hh832019.aspx for information on the elements in the activity.

NOTE: MANDATORY FIELDS WITH CREATE CHANGE WITH TEMPLATE ACTIVITY

Mandatory fields in child objects that the **Create Incident with Template** activity creates are not supported. If any mandatory fields exist in child objects that are being created, the activity will fail in Service Manager because there is no way a user can provide the required properties.

- **Create Object:** Use this activity to create any new objects against any class that exists in Service Manager. As an example, you would use this activity to create a new incident. Information on the elements in the activity is available at http://technet.microsoft.com/en-us/library/hh832013.aspx.
- **Create Related Object:** This activity creates a new object in Service Manager that is related to another object that already exists. For information on the elements in this activity, see http://technet.microsoft.com/en-us/library/hh832007.aspx.
- **Create Relationship:** You can use this activity to create a relationship when a relationship does not exist between two entities. As an example, this activity could be included when a configuration management database (CMDB) is automatically updated with configuration items that will belong to a parent configuration item. See http://technet.microsoft.com/en-us/library/hh832012.aspx for information on the elements in this activity.
- **Delete Relationship:** Use this activity to delete a relationship between two activities. For example, in a CMDB where configuration item data is changing frequently, relationships between certain configuration items might no longer be required and, therefore, can be removed. Information on the elements in the activity is available at http://technet.microsoft.com/en-us/library/hh832015.aspx.
- **Get Activity:** This activity returns an activity object for a selected activity class. This activity works only with SCSM activities; however, you could use the Orchestrator

Get Object activity to achieve the same result because it is more generic. Information on the elements in the activity is available at http://technet.microsoft.com/en-us/library/hh832014.aspx.

- **Get Object:** This activity uses filter criteria to return objects for any class that exists in Service Manager. See http://technet.microsoft.com/en-us/library/hh832002.aspx for additional information on the elements in the activity.
- **Get Relationship:** Use this activity to find all related objects in one class from a parent object in another. As an example, you could use this activity to discover all the activities related to an incident. For more information on the elements in the activity, refer to http://technet.microsoft.com/en-us/library/hh832006.aspx.
- **Monitor Object:** This activity monitors for new or updated objects in Service Manager that match a specified criteria. Any object from any class can be monitored, which makes this a useful activity to trigger the start of a runbook. Information on the elements in the activity is available at http://technet.microsoft.com/en-us/library/hh832009.aspx.
- **Update Object:** The **Update Object** activity updates a single property or multiple properties on a Service Manager object. You can use this activity after any object has been created to update the object to reflect its appropriate status or to add information. Further information on the elements in the activity is available at http://technet.microsoft.com/en-us/library/hh832004.aspx.
- **Update Activity:** This activity makes changes to activity records for a selected activity class. For additional information on the elements in the activity, see http://technet.microsoft.com/en-us/library/hh832005.aspx.
- **Upload Attachment:** The **Upload Attachment** activity uploads file attachments to File Attachment objects. To use this activity, the **Create Related Object** activity is first required to create a File Attachment object that is related to the object that encompasses the attached file. After the File Attachment object is created, the **Upload Attachment** activity uploads the file. Information on the elements in the activity is available at http://technet.microsoft.com/en-us/library/hh832011.aspx.

Use Case Scenarios

The next sections present some typical use cases for the SCSM IP. Each example runbook uses at least one activity from the IP and demonstrates a common use. The runbooks are explained in depth to demonstrate how activities can be used to automate common Service Manager processes.

Whereas Orchestrator provides an easy way to build runbooks and solutions to automate Service Manager, internal workflows should be built as part of Service Manager management packs. An example is a workflow that adds an incident template to all incidents with a specific category. Relying on Orchestrator brings an extra layer of complexity to Service Manager.

The following three scenarios are presented to demonstrate how to effectively utilize activities from the SCSM IP:

- Close resolved incidents
- Use change calendar
- Automate service request

Closing Resolved Incidents

A common request in many businesses is to automatically close incidents after they have been in a resolved state for a predefined amount of time. As a manual process, this can consume a significant amount of time.

The runbook in Figure 14.2 will run once per day and close all incidents that have been in a resolved state for five days. Four activities achieve this:

- The **Monitor Date/Time** activity triggers the runbook on a daily basis.
- The **Format Date/Time** activity publishes the date minus five days.
- The **Get Object** activity gets all incidents in the resolved state that have been in the resolved state since the date from the **Format Date/Time** activity.
- The **Update Object** activity closes the incidents and updates the description.

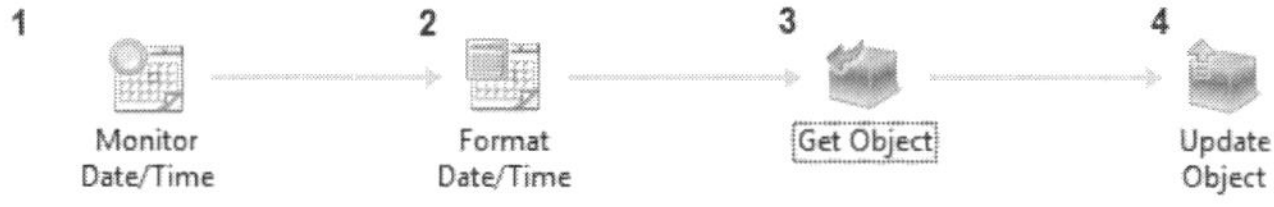

FIGURE 14.2 Close resolved incidents.

The following steps are required to create this runbook:

1. **Monitor Date/Time:** To ensure that this runbook is run automatically every day, the process starts with the **Monitor Date/Time** activity. Using this activity lets you control how often the runbook is run, whether on a minute, hourly, or daily basis.
2. **Format Date/Time:** This activity is required to format the date/time so that a date/time is returned that matches the requirements. As an example, this runbook is closing incidents after they have been in the resolved state for five days, so a date/time is required that is five days earlier than the current date/time.

   Figure 14.3 shows how to configure the **Format Date/Time** activity to adjust the output date by five days. For this activity to work, the current Date/Time is required; this is achieved by creating and using a new variable with the value `Now()`. You can use `Now()` to get the current date and time in a variable.

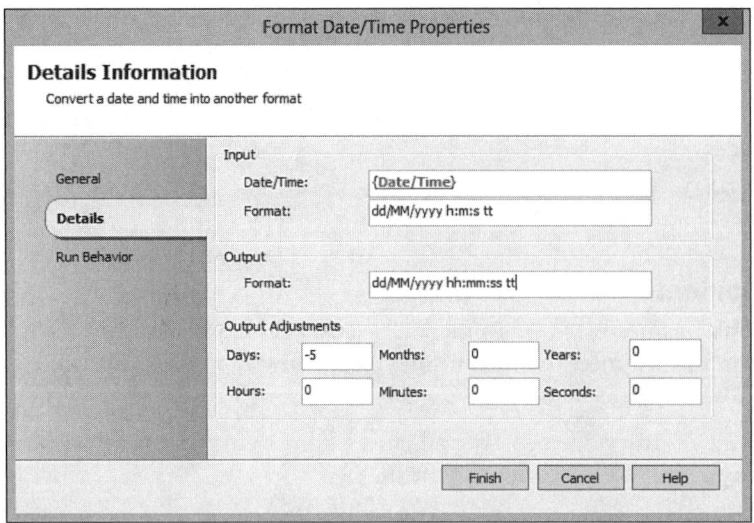

FIGURE 14.3 **Format Date/Time** activity details.

3. **Get Object:** This activity retrieves the globally unique identifier (GUID) of an object that has been in a resolved state for a period longer than the date and time provided by the **Format Date/Time** activity. Figure 14.4 shows how the activity is configured.

    - The properties required for this activity provide the Service Manager connection and the class of the object that needs to be retrieved. In this scenario, there is a connection to the Service Manager management server and the class is set to **Incident**.

    - Filters are specified, as with only the connection and class information, all incidents from Service Manager would be returned. The filters ensure that only the incidents that are required are returned.

    The Resolved date filter in Figure 14.4 has a relation of Before, and the value is the published Format Result data from the **Format Date/Time** activity. There is also a filter in Figure 14.4 based on Status because only incidents in Resolved status are to be included.

    By using these settings and adjusting the output date, only those incident objects that have been in a resolved state for more than five days are returned.

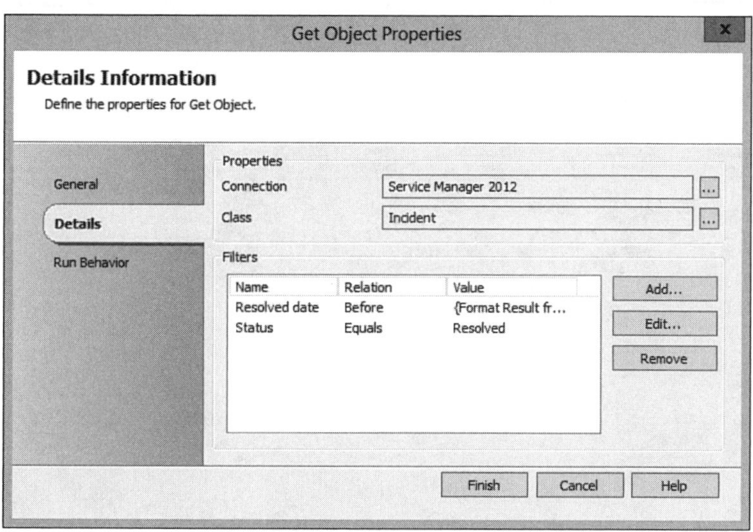

FIGURE 14.4 Get resolved incident objects.

4. **Update Object:** This activity subscribes to the GUID published by the **Get Object** activity and updates the object properties as required. The three properties required for this activity are connection, class, and object GUID. The same connection and class are used as for the **Get Object** activity. Because the object GUID has been published by **Get Object**, the published data can be subscribed to as the value for the property.

   After providing the property data, you can select the fields that require updating. Using the **Select optional fields** button, all available fields for the object are returned and can be selected. This runbook requires incidents to be closed after five days, so the **Status** field is selected and the value is updated to **Closed**. Figure 14.5 displays the configuration of this **Update Object** activity. Figure 14.5 also illustrates that the runbook updates the Description, showing that Orchestrator has closed the incident, and adds the current Description.

14

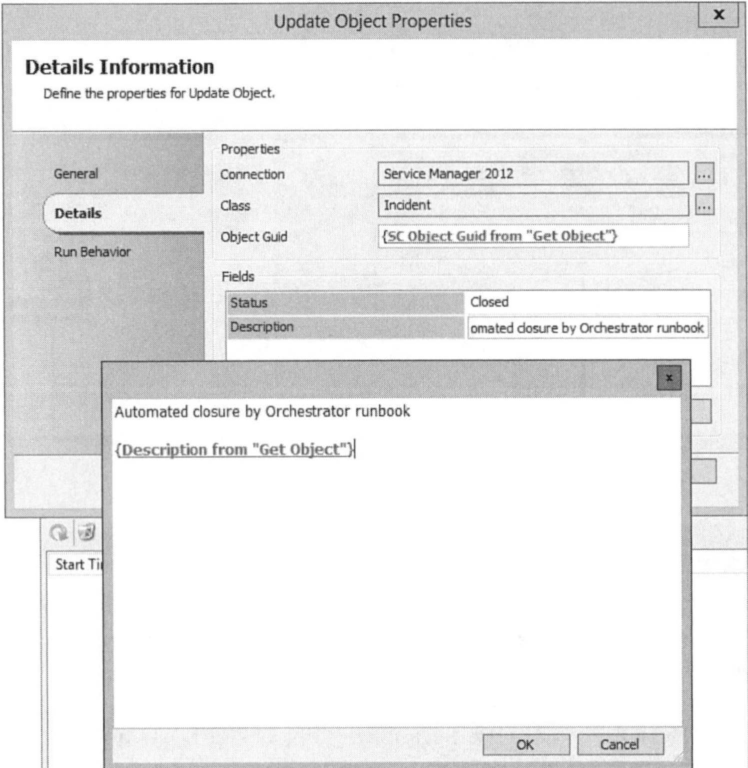

FIGURE 14.5 Close resolved incidents.

Creating a Change Calendar

A change calendar keeps everyone informed about when changes will be performed and provides an overview of planned changes in the environment. System Center 2012 Service Manager handles change requests as work items but does not include change calendar functionality out of the box. This example shows an example of how to resolve this using Orchestrator, the SCSM IP, and the Exchange User IP.

The runbook in Figure 14.6 runs when a new change request is created in Service Manager and creates an appointment in a shared Exchange calendar. The calendar can be published on SharePoint. If an appointment cannot be created, an Operations Manager alert is generated. Three activities achieve this:

- The **Monitor Object** activity triggers the runbook when a new change request is created in Service Manager.
- The **Create Item** activity creates an appointment in an Exchange calendar based on the information in the change request.

- The **Create Alert** activity generates an alert in Operations Manager if the **Create Item** activity fails.

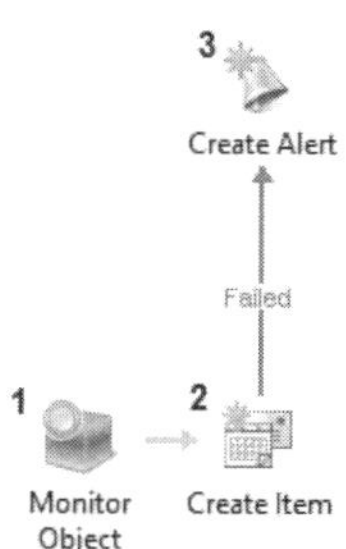

FIGURE 14.6 The Change Calendar runbook.

Follow these steps to create the runbook:

1. **Monitor Object:** This activity monitors Service Manager for new change requests. When a new change request is generated, this activity triggers a new instance of the runbook that will run the **Create Item** activity and the **Create Alert** activity, if needed.

   Figure 14.7 displays how to configure the **Monitor Object** activity. In this example, the activity monitors all new change requests. Because it is possible to create a new change requests in a status other than New, this activity includes a filter for a new change request with New as the status. Using the SCSM IP, you can configure a more detailed filter, if needed, such as specific categories or change requests only when all approval steps are approved.

2. **Create Item:** This activity is from the Exchange User IP. The IP for Exchange Users is an IP that enables you to automate user-centric tasks, such as sending email messages, and work with appointments and tasks. Figure 14.8 displays configuring the **Create Item** activity. All properties except Location are populated dynamically based on the change request found by the **Monitor Object** activity.

3. **Create Alert:** This activity creates an alert in Operations Manager if the **Create Item** activity fails. Figure 14.9 displays how to configure this activity. You can see in Figure 14.9 that the alert description generated in Operations Manager includes the change request ID. Including unique data, such as a unique ID, assists in troubleshooting.

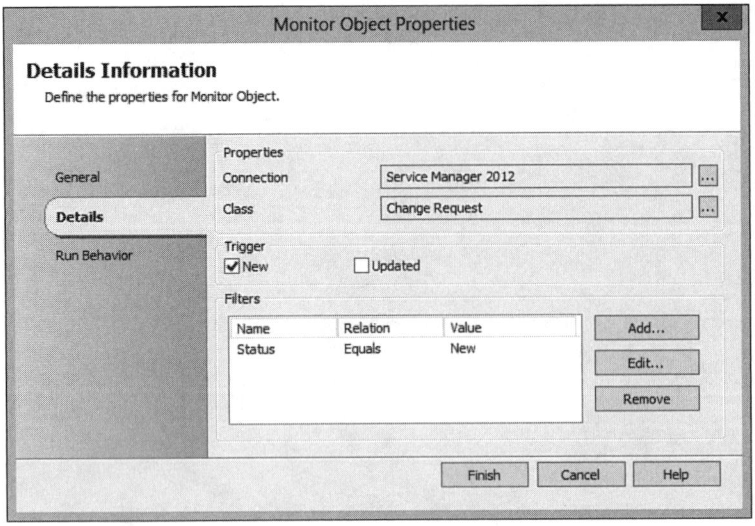

FIGURE 14.7 Configuring the **Monitor Object** activity.

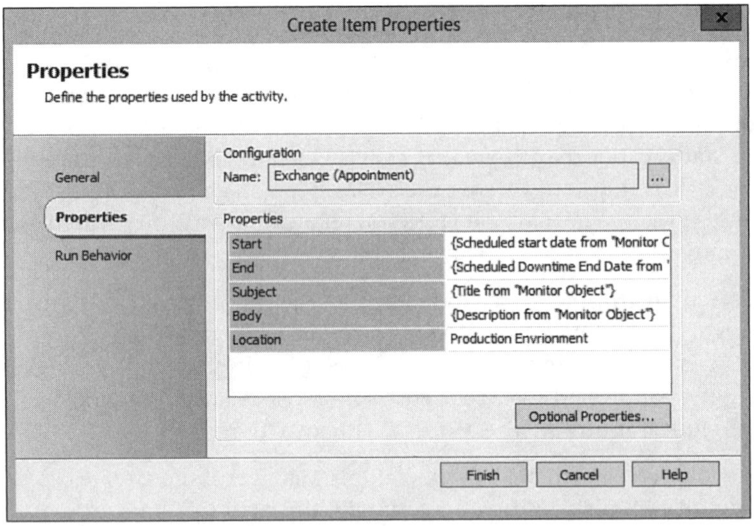

FIGURE 14.8 The **Create Item** activity.

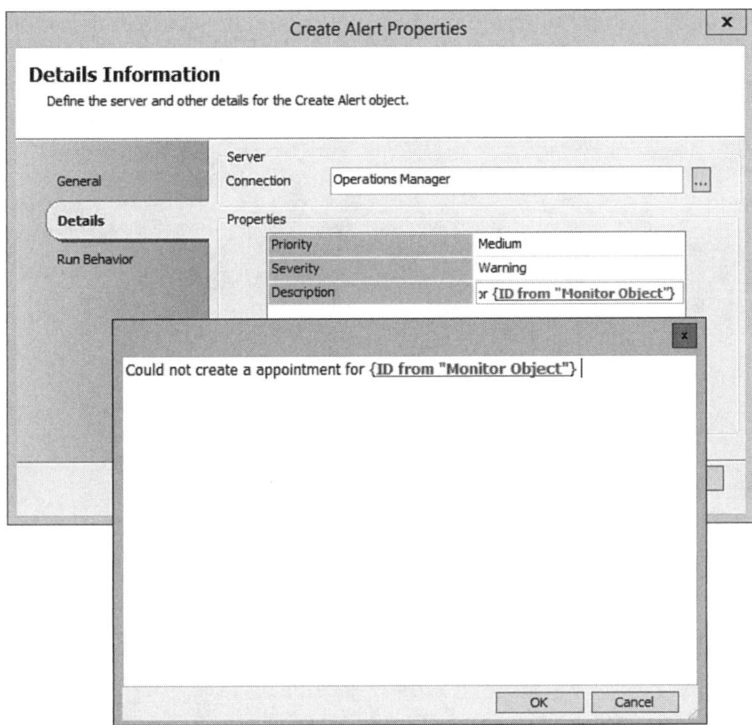

FIGURE 14.9 Creating an Operations Manager alert.

Automating Service Requests

The release of System Center 2012 provides new capabilities for integration between Service Manager and Orchestrator. Service Manager 2010 lets you create templates including activities, such as manual activities and approval activities. As an example, using a change request template, you could first include an approval step and then a manual step. After manager approval, an engineer could execute the manual step. With System Center 2012, you can use runbooks as activities in Service Manager. Runbook activities can be used in incident templates, change request templates, and service request templates. Instead of having an engineer perform a manual step, Orchestrator can now execute a runbook.

The following high-level steps are necessary to use a runbook as an activity in Service Manager, such as in a service request:

1. Create the runbook in Orchestrator.
2. Use the Orchestrator connector in Service Manager to synchronize the runbook to the Service Manager database.
3. In Service Manager, create a runbook automation activity based on the runbook.
4. Create a template that includes the runbook. This could be a change request template or a service request template.

If you use the runbook automation activity in a service request template and you want to publish the service as a service offering in the self-service portal, you also must create a request offering and a service offering. Depending on your organization, you might also need to configure a security role for the new service offering. These steps are described in the Library workspace of the Service Manager console, shown on the right side of Figure 14.10.

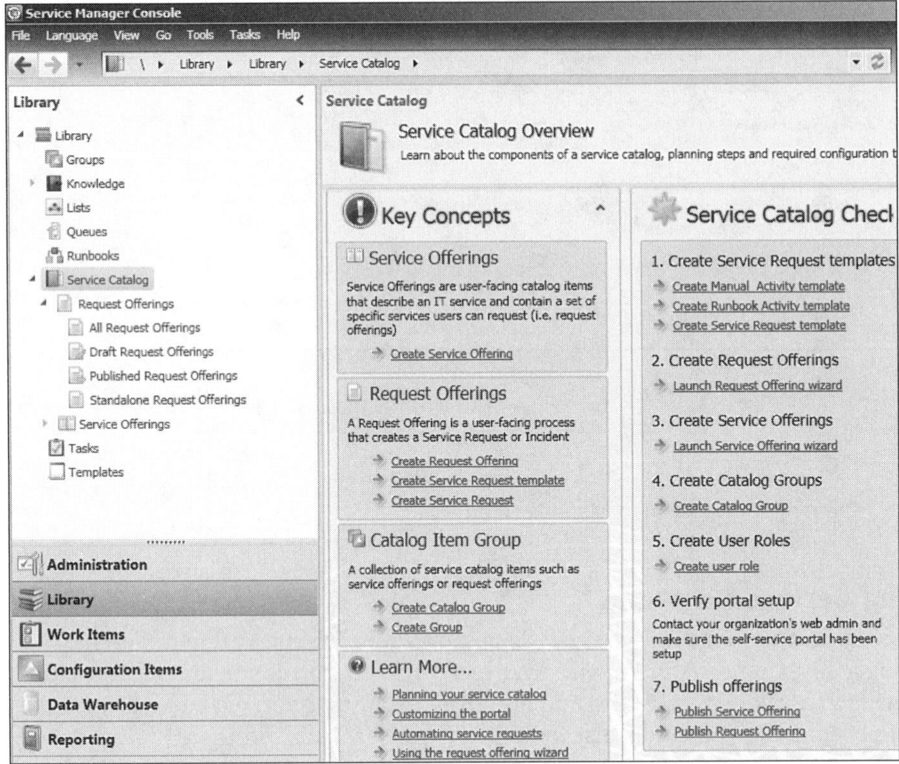

FIGURE 14.10 The Service Manager console shows all required steps on the right side of the Library workspace.

Service Manager invokes the runbook shown in Figure 14.11 when a new service account is requested in a service request. The service request work item can be generated from the Service Manager self-service portal. The runbook generates a new service account and publishes the result back to the service request work item in Service Manager. Six Orchestrator activities achieve this.

FIGURE 14.11 Runbook that creates service account runbook.

Creating this runbook involves the following steps:

1. **Initialize Data:** This activity is the starting point of the runbook and collects required input parameters for the runbook. In this scenario, the runbook requires System, ShortName, and ActivityID as input (see Figure 14.12). All required input parameters are passed from Service Manager. Using Service Manager to front-end Orchestrator is a good approach to have data validated for all input parameters before invoking the runbook.

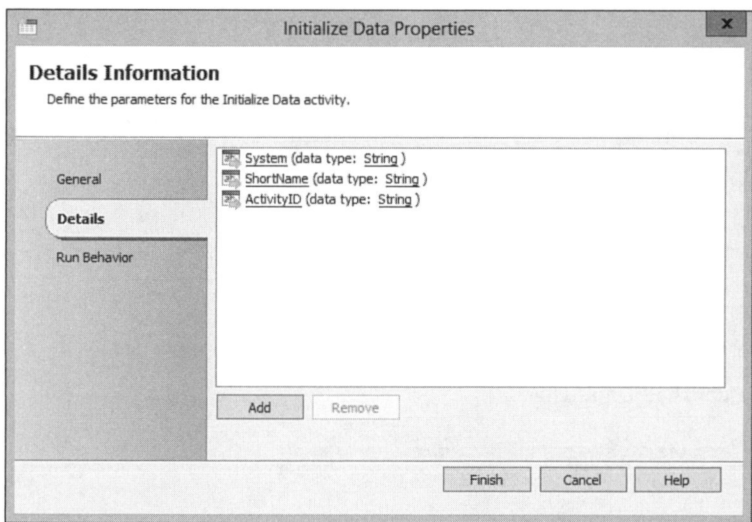

FIGURE 14.12 Using the **Initialize Data** activity.

2. **Map Published Data:** This activity translates the System input parameter in Figure 14.12 to a part of the service account name, according to the organization account naming convention. The **Map Published Data** activity translates existing published data into new values according to the rules that you specify. Figure 14.13 shows the configuration of the **Map Published Data** activity, translating a product name to a short system name that can be used in the service account name. As an example, if a user inputs **Operations Manager** in the self-service portal, it will be translated to SCOM, which will later be used in the account name.

3. **Generate Random Text:** This activity generates a random text with a mix of symbols, numbers, and characters. The result of this activity is used as a password for the new service account.

4. **Create User:** This activity connects to Active Directory and creates the new service account. The format of the new service account name is SVC-ShortSystem-ShortName (for example, SVC-SCOM-SDK). Figure 14.14 shows the configuration of the **Create User** activity. A benefit of creating accounts with Orchestrator is that accounts use a standard format.

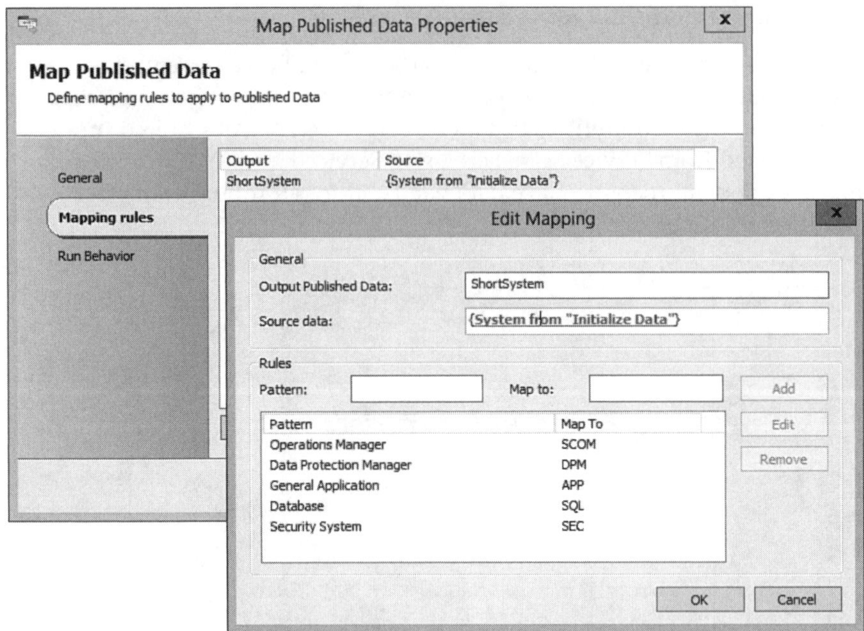

FIGURE 14.13 The **Map Published** Data activity.

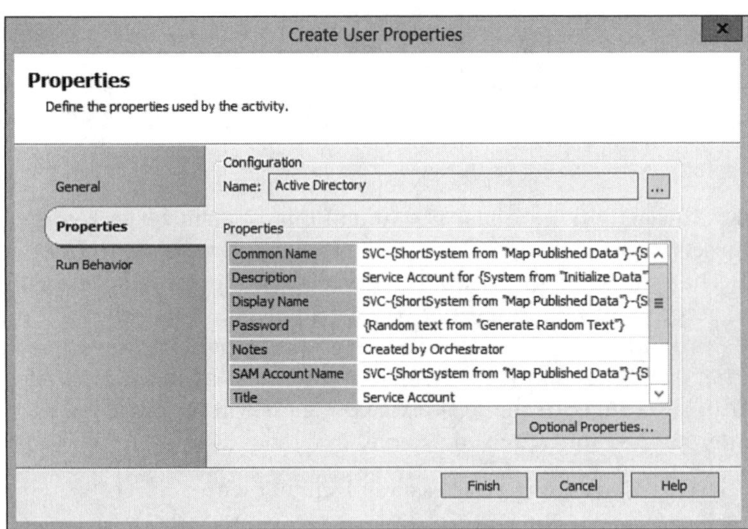

FIGURE 14.14 Configuring the **Create User** activity.

5. **Get Relationship:** The **Initialize Data** activity retrieves the runbook automation activity instance ID from Service Manager. The runbook automation activity instance is related to the service request work item. With the **Get Relationship** activity, the runbook gets the related service request from the runbook automation activity. Figure 14.15 shows the configuration of the **Get Relationship** activity.

Get Relationship Properties

Details Information

Define the properties for Get Relationship.

General

Details

Run Behavior

Properties

Connection: Service Manager 2012

Object Class: Runbook Automation Activity

Object Guid: {ActivityID from "Initialize Data"}

Related Class: Service Request

Finish | Cancel | Help

FIGURE 14.15 Configuring the **Get Relationship** activity.

6. **Update Object:** This activity updates the description field of the service request. The runbook writes the account name and password to the description field. Figure 14.16 show the configuration of the **Update Object** activity.

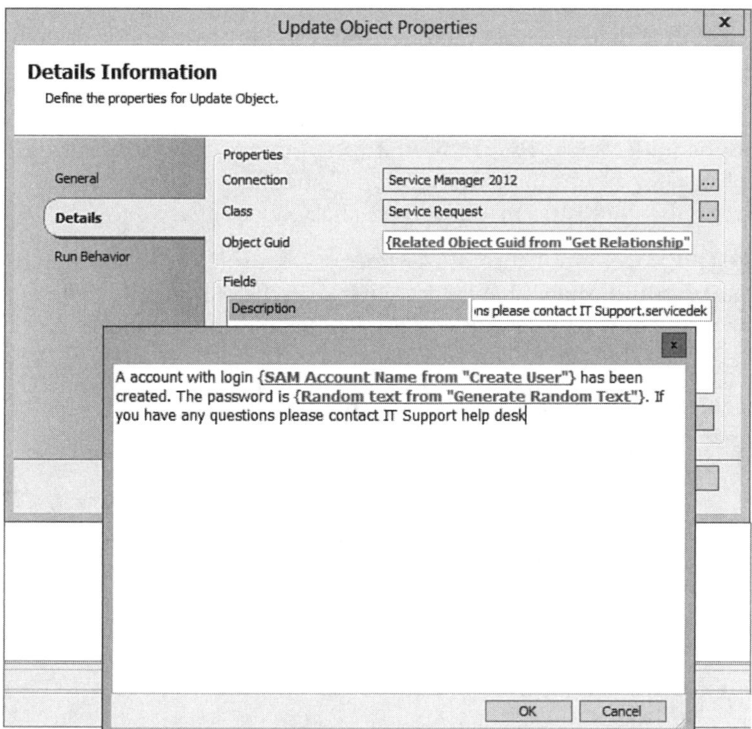

FIGURE 14.16 **Update Object** properties.

The following steps are required to synchronize this runbook to Service Manager and create a runbook automation activity:

1. Start the Service Manager console, navigate to the Administration, workspace and click **Connectors**. In the Tasks pane, click **Create connector** and select **Orchestrator connector**.
2. Click **Next** on the Orchestrator connector wizard – Before You Begin page.
3. On the General page of the wizard, input a name for the Orchestrator connector. For example, you can use the Orchestrator web service server name as the connector name. Click **Next**.
4. On the Connection page, input the URL for the Orchestrator web service. With default settings, the URL could be http://Orchestrator01:81/Orchestrator2012/Orchestrator.svc, where Orchestrator01 is the name of the server hosting Orchestrator web service.

   Select a Run As account to use. This account needs Read and List permissions on the top-level folder (Runbooks) in Orchestrator and Read and List permissions on all runbooks and folders the connector will synchronize. The connector account also publishes permission on the runbooks that Service Manager needs to trigger. When a runbook invokes other runbooks, you need to assign permissions to only the parent runbook because Orchestrator will use its Runbook Server service account to invoke the other runbook.

   Click **Next** to continue. You then are prompted to input the Run As account password. Service Manager uses this information to connect to the Orchestrator web service URL and verify the connection.
5. You are now at the Sync folder page. The Orchestrator connector can synchronize all runbooks in the Orchestrator environment or specific runbooks. To synchronize all runbooks, verify that Sync folder is set to \ and then click **Next**.
6. On the Web Console URL page, input the URL for the web console. As an example, if you are using default settings, the URL would be http://Orchestrator01:82, where Orchestrator01 is the name of the server hosting the Orchestrator web console. Click **Next**.
7. On the Summary page, review all settings and click **Create**.
8. At the Completion page, verify that the connector was created successfully and click **Close**.

You have now created a connector from Service Manager to Orchestrator. Service Manager can use this connector to synchronize runbooks from Orchestrator to the Service Manager database. The connector can also be used to trigger runbooks from Service Manager.

The following steps are required to create a runbook automation activity based on the runbook in Figure 14.11, which creates new service accounts in Active Directory:

1. Start the Service Manager console, navigate to the Library workspace, and select **Runbooks**. In the list of runbooks synchronized from Orchestrator, select the runbook you want to use; in the Tasks pane, click **Create Runbook Automation Activity Template**. In this example, the runbook name is **Scenario 3**. If no runbooks are displayed, verify that the Orchestrator connector has run.

2. On the Create template page, input a name such as **Odyssey.RunbookActivity.Scenario3** and create a new management pack in which to store the activity, using a name such as **Odyssey.ServiceRequestAutomation**. Click **OK**.

NOTE: MANAGEMENT PACK NAMING CONVENTIONS

Naming conventions for management packs, classes, and objects are part of a larger discussion for which you can find a number of opinions in the System Center community. You can read about management pack guidelines and best practices on Microsoft TechNet at http://technet.microsoft.com/en-us/library/hh519659.aspx, with considerations when authoring or modifying management packs at http://technet.microsoft.com/en-us/library/hh519659.aspx. Both pages include information on naming conventions for management packs and discuss when to create a new management pack.

3. For the runbook activity, enter a title, such as **Odyssey.RunbookActivity.Scenario3**. Check the **Is Ready For Automation** check box, allowing Service Manager to trigger the runbook when the runbook automation activity has a status of In Progress. Alternatively, someone would have to initiate the activity manually in the Work Item workspace of the Service Manager console. Click **OK**.

Now that you have created a runbook automation activity, you can create a service request template. Follow these steps:

1. In the Service Manager console, navigate to the Library workspace and select **Templates**. In the Tasks pane, click **Create Template**.

2. On the Create Template page, input a name such as **Odyssey.ServiceRequestTemplate.NewServiceAccount**, select **Service Request** as the class, and select the **Odyssey Service Request Automation** management pack. Click **OK**.

3. On the Service Request Template page, provide a name. This title will be the default name for all service requests using this template. For this example, **Odyssey – New Service Account** is the title. Specify Urgency, Priority, Source, and Area (see Figure 14.17).

4. Click the Activities tab, and then click the green plus (+) icon to add the **Odyssey. RunbookActivity.Scenario3** activity.

5. Click the Runbook tab. Click **Edit Mapping** next to ActivityID. Select the Runbook Automation Activity and Object ID, and click **Close**.

   Figure 14.18 displays where mapping settings are defined. Mapping is used to send data from Service Manager to the Orchestrator runbook. With mapping data, you can connect properties from the service request to the runbook. This example forwards the Runbook Automation instance ID to the ActivityID parameter in the runbook. You can also forward the Service Request ID to the runbook.

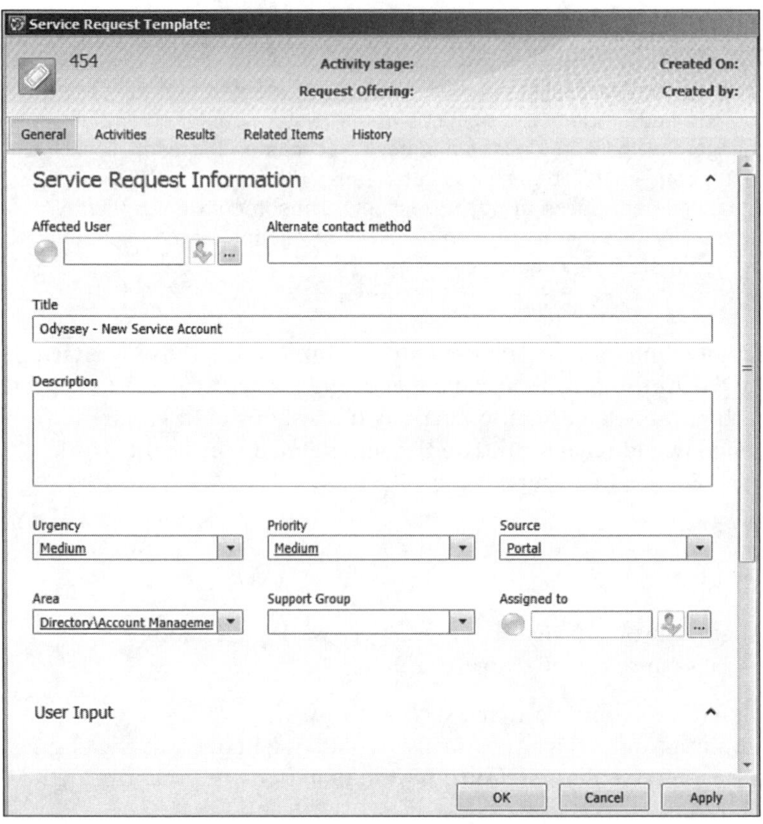

FIGURE 14.17 Configure Service Request template.

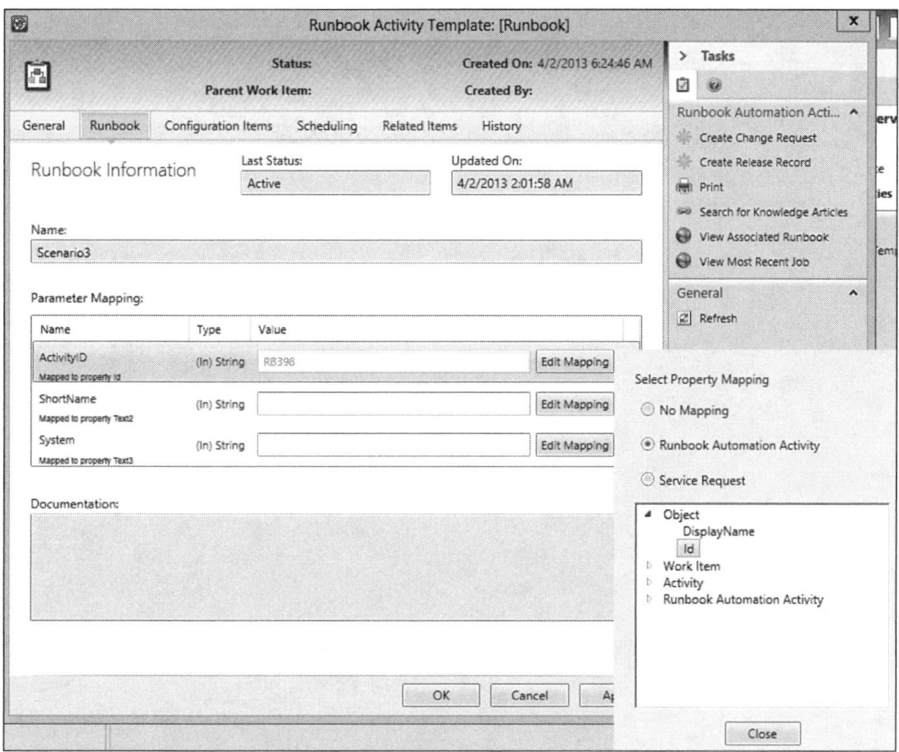

FIGURE 14.18 Specify mapping between service request and runbook.

6. Click **OK** at the Runbook Activity Template: [Runbook] page.
7. Figure 14.19 shows the Service Request template with one activity: the runbook automation activity. You can add more activities, such as an approval activity, or additional runbook activities. Each time this template is used, these activities will be in the service request. Click **OK**.

14

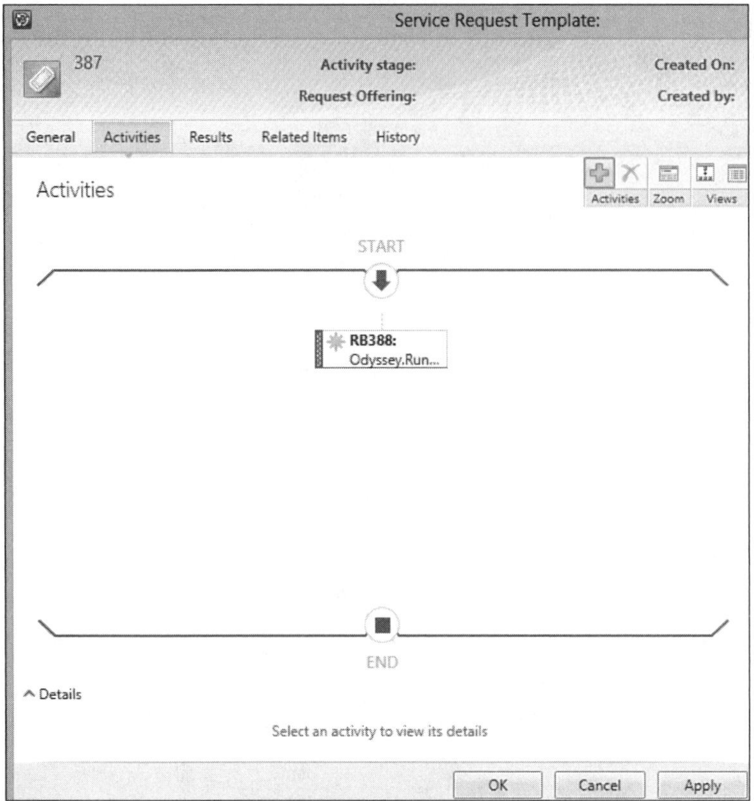

FIGURE 14.19 An activity in the Service Request template.

You can use the template from the Service Manager console, but you then must fill in all required parameters manually, directly into the runbook activity. This also requires permissions to the Service Manager console and knowledge of how to enter the parameters. Using the self-service portal is a better experience, particularly when publishing service offerings for end users and customers.

Request offerings are catalog items; these are for assistance or actions that are available to the user using the self-service portal. Request offerings are placed in logical groups of service offerings. An example of a request offering is requesting a new service account in Active Directory; this request offering is placed in a service offering named Active Directory that includes all request offerings around Active Directory.

To publish the service request to the self-service portal in Service Manager, perform the following steps:

1. In the Service Manager console, navigate to the Library workspace and expand the Service Catalog node. Select **Request Offering** and click **Create Request Offering** in the Tasks pane.

2. Click **Next** at the Create Request Offering page.

3. On the General page, input a title, such as **New Service Account**. Click **Select template** and select the service request template created in the previous procedure, **Odyssey.ServiceRequestTemplate.NewServiceAccount**. Click **Next**.

4. You are now at the User Prompts page. User Prompts are information that is required to be input before submitting an instance of a service request. This information is passed to the runbook as input parameters. In this example, the runbook requires System and ShortName. The service account created by this runbook will be named **SVC-SCOM-SDK**, where SCOM is the system name and SDK indicates the account's purpose. Configure this page as shown Figure 14.20, and click **Next**.

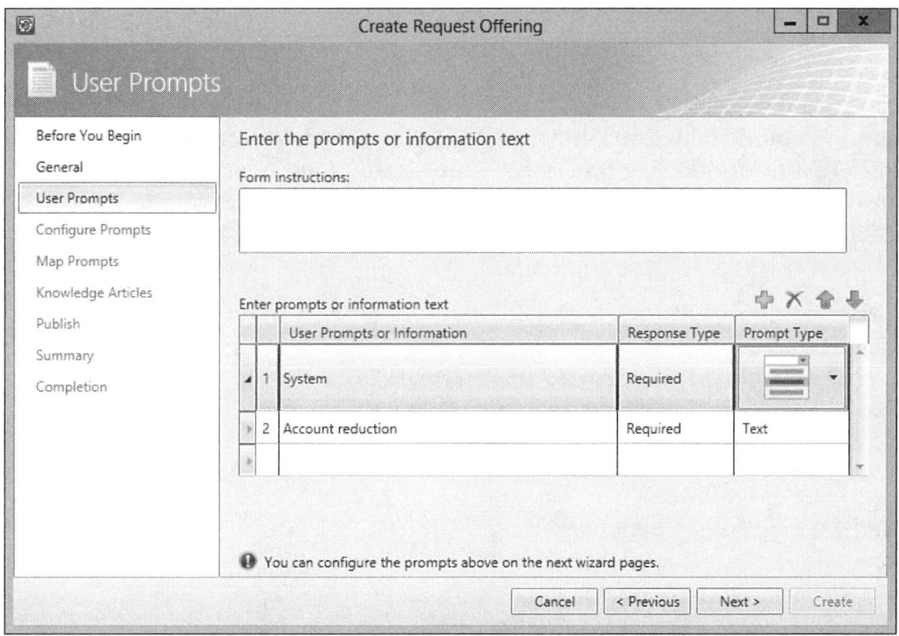

FIGURE 14.20 Configuring user prompts.

5. At the Configure Prompts page, select **System** and click **Configure**. Use the green plus (+) icon to add all options shown on the right in Figure 14.21. These options will be displayed in a drop-down menu in the portal when users request a new service account. In Figure 14.21, you can see the parameters in the runbook on the left and the simple list options in Service Manager on the right. The runbook uses a **Map Published Data** activity to translate the user input to a suitable account name. Click **OK** to return to the Configure Prompts page.

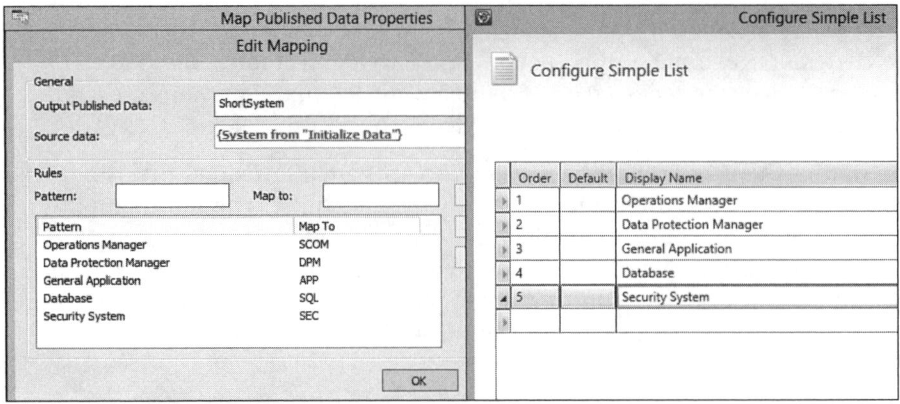

FIGURE 14.21 Configuring drop-down menu options.

6. Now select **Account reduction** (shown in Figure 14.20) and select **Configure**. In the Configure Text Control dialog box, check **Limit string length**. Configure the string length to a minimum and maximum of 3 characters. This requires user to input three characters for the account name, which fulfills the naming convention in Active Directory. Click **OK** and then **Next**.

7. At the Map Prompts page, map runbook input properties with user prompts according to Figure 14.22. Click **Next**.

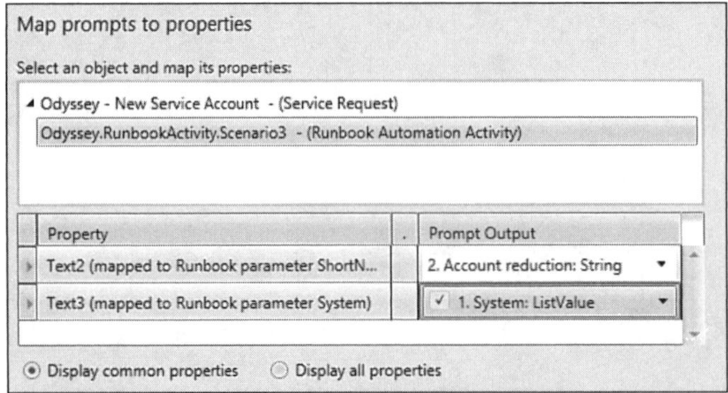

FIGURE 14.22 Map input between runbook and service request.

8. At the Knowledge Articles page, you can connect knowledge articles to this request offering. These knowledge articles will be visible in the self-service portal when using this request offering. Click **Next**.

9. At the Publish page, change the Offering status to **Published**. If the offering status is not Published, the request offering will not be visible in the self-service portal. Click **Next**.

10. On the Summary page, review the settings and click **Create**.
11. At the Completion page, verify that the new offering was successfully created. Click **Close**.

Now you can create a service offering. Follow these steps:

1. In the Service Manager console, navigate to the Library workspace and expand the Service Catalog node. Select **Service Offerings** and click **Create Service Offering** in the Tasks pane.
2. Click **Next** on the Create Service Offering page.
3. On the General page, input a title, such as **Active Directory**. Click **Next**.
4. On the Detailed Information page, complete the service level agreement and cost information. Click **Next**.
5. On the Related Service page, add related business services associated with the service offering. Click **Next**.
6. At the Knowledge Articles page, add related knowledge articles associated with the service offering. Click **Next**.
7. On the Request Offering page, click **Add** and add the New Service Account request offering. Verify that the status is Published. Click **Next**.
8. On the Publish page, change the Offering status to **Published** for the service offering to be visible in the self-service portal. If the service offering is not published, the related request offerings will not be visible as well. Click **Next**.
9. At the Summary page, review the settings and click **Create**.
10. On the Completion page, verify that the new offering was successfully created. Click **Close**.

Figure 14.23 shows the Service Manager self-service portal, including the Active Directory service offering. The default Service Manager self-service portal URL is http://ServiceManager01:82/SMPortal, where ServiceManager01 is the server hosting the portal. Figure 14.24 shows the request form for the service offering, including the two user prompt fields configured in the Create Request Offering Wizard.

When a service request is submitted, a service request work item is created. In the Work Items workspace of the Service Manager console, you can see all open service requests. In Orchestrator, you can also see that the runbook starts within several minutes. Figure 14.25 shows the updated description field of a service request in the self-service portal. The last activity in the runbook updates the service request description with information about the service account that was created. The person requesting the service account can find the result of the request in the self-service portal.

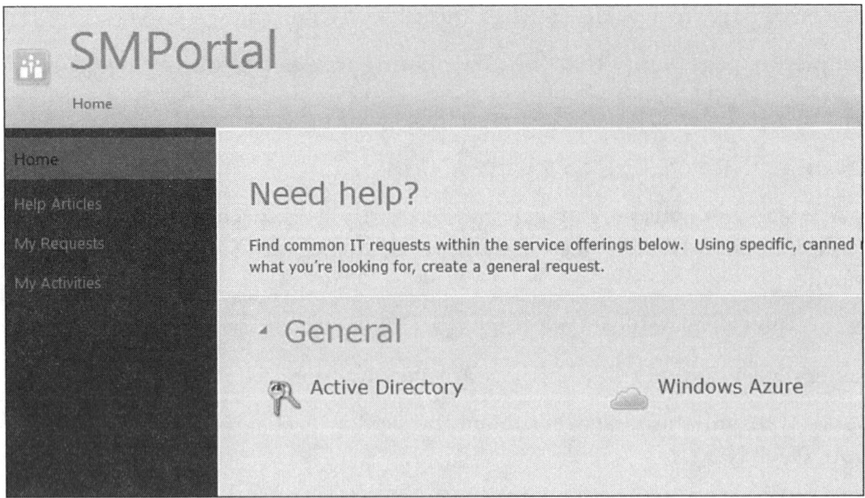

FIGURE 14.23 Service offerings in the self-service portal.

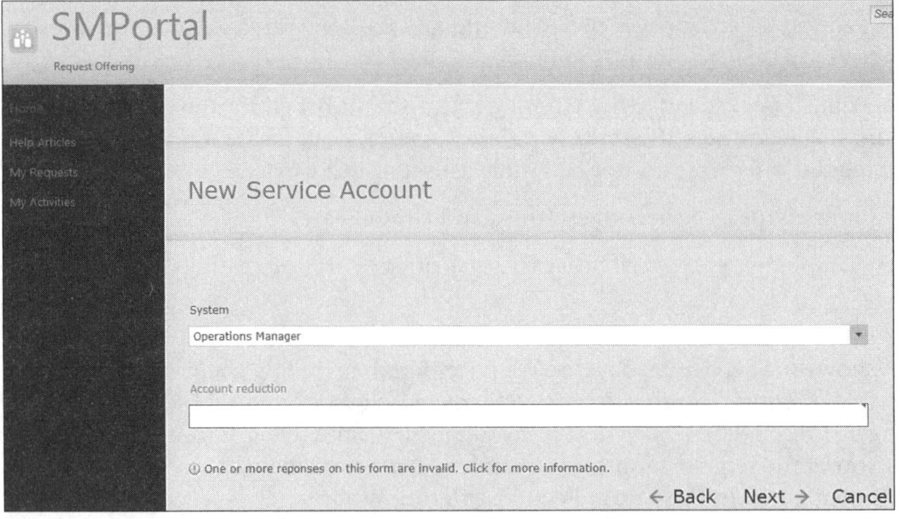

FIGURE 14.24 Service request form in the self-service portal.

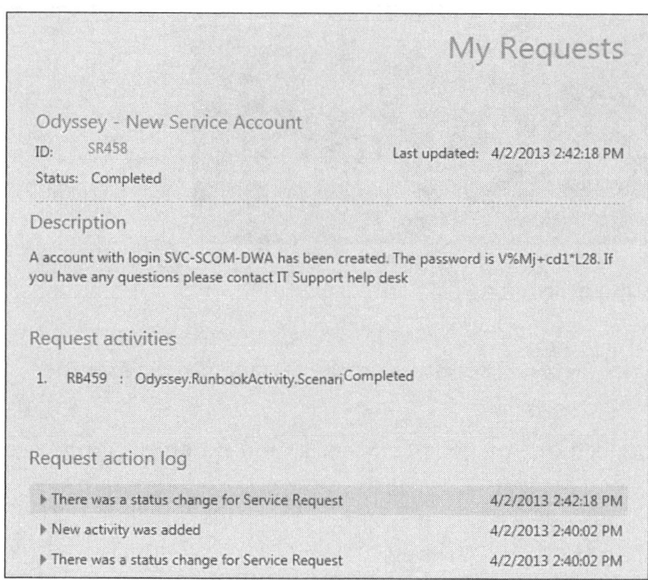

FIGURE 14.25 Service request result shown in the self-service portal.

If you build a runbook solution that generates new accounts, you should design for errors and fault tolerance. As an example, if the account already exists in Active Directory, your runbook should check for this and use another account name for the new account. For additional information, see Chapter 10, "Runbook and Configuration Best Practices."

Troubleshooting the SCSM IP

This section introduces methodologies for troubleshooting the Service Manager IP. The integration pack relies on a number of settings to work properly. When troubleshooting the integration pack, it is important to verify each setting. In general, troubleshooting the Service Manager IP can include the following tasks:

- **Communication:** Verify that the Orchestrator runbook server can connect to port 5724 on the Service Manager management server. To validate that the Orchestrator runbook server can connect to port 5724 on the Service Manager management server, you can use the telnet client—run **telnet ServiceManagerServer 5724**. If the connection is established successfully, a black/blank telnet window appears. If the connection fails to start, investigate whether a firewall is blocking the traffic and confirm that the System Center Data Access Service (OMSDK) is running on the Service Manager management server. You can verify that the System Center Data Access Service is running and listening to port 5724 using the following commands (also see Figure 14.26):

```
Netstat -ano | find "0.0.0.0:5724"
Tasklist /fi "PID eq 2456"
```

```
C:\Windows\system32>netstat -ano | find "0.0.0.0:5724"
  TCP    0.0.0.0:5724           0.0.0.0:0              LISTENING       2456

C:\Windows\system32>tasklist /fi "PID eq 2456"

Image Name                     PID Session Name        Session#    Mem Usage
========================= ======== ================ =========== ============
Microsoft.Mom.Sdk.Service     2456 Services                   0    354,172 K

C:\Windows\system32>
```

FIGURE 14.26 Verify that the OMSDK service is running.

- **Connection Account:** Verify the account specified on the Service Manager connector, previously shown in Figure 14.1.
- **Log:** Enable trace logs, as described in Chapter 11, "Security and Administration."

Summary

This chapter covered installation and configuration requirements of the SCSM IP and information on each of the activities it includes. The chapter also discussed practical application of the SCSM IP, with some common use scenarios. You can use the activities within this IP in many ways to automate business processes. When used together with the other IPs available in Orchestrator, a large percentage of common activities can be automated to provide many business efficiencies.

CHAPTER 15

Integration with System Center Configuration Manager

IN THIS CHAPTER

As one of the System Center 2012 components, System Center Orchestrator (SCOrch) is capable of automating the Microsoft System Center Configuration Manager (ConfigMgr) environment through the System Center Configuration Manager integration packs (IPs). The ConfigMgr IPs can manage ConfigMgr 2007 and ConfigMgr 2012 sites, performing actions such as creating collections, deploying programs, deploying applications, and triggering various client actions. Microsoft provides the System Center IPs as a bundled download.

This chapter describes the requirements for using the ConfigMgr integration pack, along with the installation procedure and configuration steps. It explains each activity and provides some sample policies and use case scenarios to show you how to take advantage of this integration pack.

Integration Pack Requirements

Before getting started, note that the Orchestrator 2012 installation files do not include the ConfigMgr IP; it is available only as a part of a separate download. Specific requirements are discussed in the following sections.

System Center 2012 Orchestrator

This integration pack comes bundled together as System Center 2012 Service Pack 1—Orchestrator Component Addons and Extensions with other System Center 2012 Service Pack (SP) 1 integration packs in a self-extracting executable. This self-extracting executable extracts the System Center integration packs to a specified directory. The integration pack bundle is available at www.microsoft.com/en-us/download/details.aspx?id=34611.

System Center 2012 Configuration Manager

Because you will be using activities from the integration pack to automate specific components of ConfigMgr, it only makes sense that one of the requirements of using this IP is ConfigMgr itself. The current version of the ConfigMgr IP was written for ConfigMgr 2012 SP 1. An equivalent integration pack exists for ConfigMgr 2007 and ConfigMgr 2012 RTM. Earlier versions of ConfigMgr are not supported.

Unless indicated otherwise, this chapter focuses on the ConfigMgr 2012 SP 1 integration pack.

Installing the Integration Pack

For information on the installation steps to register and deploy an IP, see Chapter 5, "Installing System Center 2012 Orchestrator."

ConfigMgr 2012 offers an incredible amount of flexibility in permissions and can be designed to exacting specifications. You will find that different activities in the integration pack require different levels of permissions for performing operational tasks in ConfigMgr. Regardless of what permission you grant the connection account, it requires membership in the local SMS Admins group, either directly or through a nested membership.

Configuring the Integration Pack

All activities in the ConfigMgr IP use the credentials supplied by the connection account to execute various functions on the ConfigMgr site server. If you are managing multiple site servers, you can utilize additional connection accounts for each site server.

Whether you use a single common account to provide Orchestrator management for your entire ConfigMgr environment or you use a different account for each site server depends on the security requirements of your organization, your ConfigMgr topology, and the team(s) responsible for managing ConfigMgr. Another reason for using multiple connections is to leverage accounts with varying sets of permissions. This can be useful if requirements specify the type of security permissions granted. As an example, you might have one set of credentials for workstations and another for servers.

Creating the Connection Account

You must install the integration pack before creating the connection. After the IP is installed, open the Runbook Designer and navigate to **Options -> SC 2012 Configuration Manager** in the menu bar. In the Connections window, add a new connection and supply the following information (see Figure 15.1):

- **Name:** A name for the connection. This is simply the name of the connection. It should be descriptive enough that runbook authors understand how the connection is used. In Figure 15.1, **SCCM Server** is entered.
- **Server:** Name of the Configuration Manager server.

- **Username:** Active Directory (AD) account of a user with privileges to the ConfigMgr environment. Ensure that this name is specified in domain\username format.
- **Password:** Password for the account.

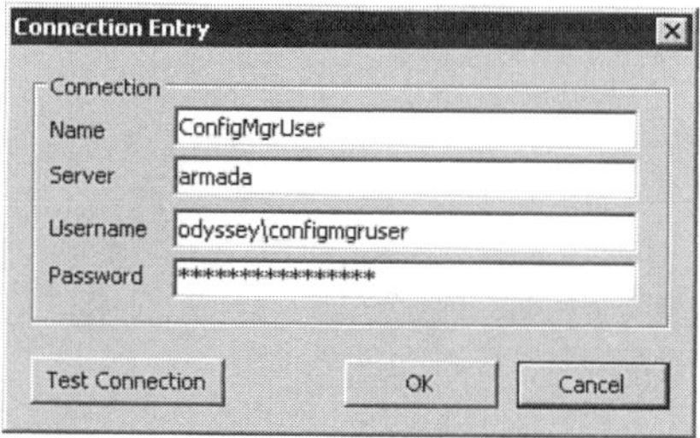

FIGURE 15.1 Connection Entry properties.

Use the Test Connection button in Figure 15.1 to verify that the account has the appropriate privileges to connect to the Configuration Manager server. If you will be assigning the privileges later, you can always come back to the Connection Entry dialog box and verify that the connection succeeds.

CAUTION: TEST CONNECTION DOES NOT VERIFY IN-DEPTH PERMISSION

Performing the Test Connection action does not verify the permissions required to use all the activities in the IP. Test Connection verifies that the connection account can access the Configuration Manager server. This is the equivalent of getting access to a building but not to every office or floor. Specifically, if Test Connection works, the account can access the Configuration Manager Windows Management Instrumentation (WMI) namespace correctly. This permission is assigned through membership in the SMS Admins group.

Granting Access to the Connection Account

You must manage the permissions for the accounts in the Configuration Manager console. Although not recommended, the easiest way to provide access to the connection account is to grant the account the Full Administrator role to the ConfigMgr server. To grant full ConfigMgr access, perform the following steps:

1. Launch the Configuration Manager console.
2. In the Administration workspace, expand the Security node and choose **Administrative Users**.
3. Choose **Add User or Group** on the ribbon bar.
4. In the Add User or Group dialog box, click **Browse** and locate the user that will receive the security role.

5. After selecting the user, click **Add**, select the Full Administrator security role in the Add Security Role dialog box, and click **OK**.
6. Under the Assigned security scopes and collections section, select an appropriate scope or choose **All instances of the objects that are related to the assigned security roles**.
7. Click **OK** to complete the security change.

The completed dialog box should look like Figure 15.2.

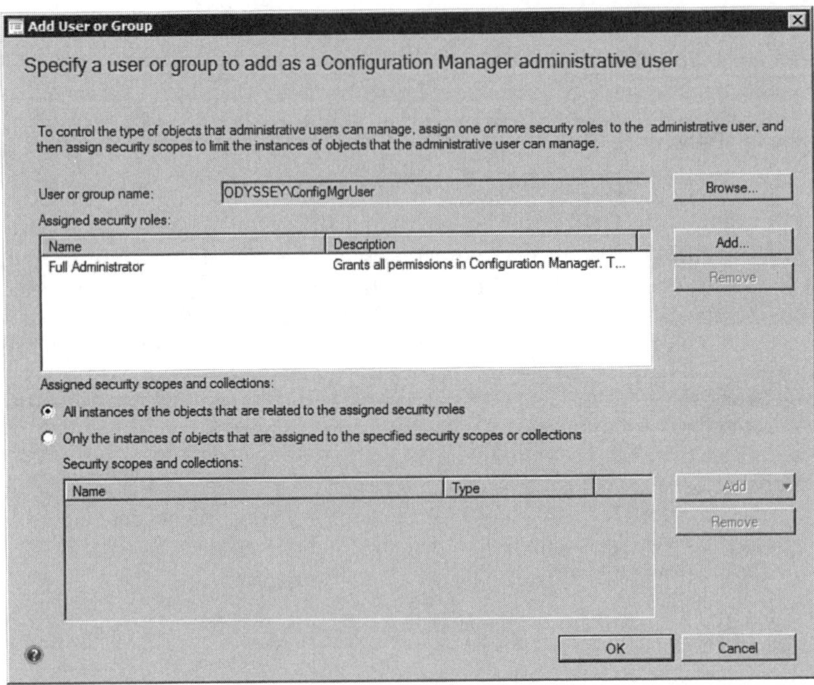

FIGURE 15.2 Configuration Manager permissions.

NOTE: WMI AND DCOM PERMISSIONS

When granting access to Configuration Manager, as outlined in this section, the connection account is added to the local group (SMS Admins) on the Configuration Manager site server. Inclusion in this group automatically provides access to the Distributed Component Object Model (DCOM) and the Configuration Manager namespace in WMI. These permissions are established initially during the Configuration Manager installation. In fact, the Configuration Manager console connects to the site server through WMI as well.

For additional information on configuring DCOM and WMI, read the article on securing a remote WMI connection at http://msdn.microsoft.com/en-us/library/aa393266.aspx.

If your organization requires specific delegation, Configuration Manager supports that. Tables 15.1 and 15.2 list all the activities in the IP and the related permissions required in Configuration Manager to help you plan and assign the right level of permissions.

Note that the activities in these tables are sorted as they are shown in Runbook Designer.

TABLE 15.1 Configuration Manager Permissions and Activities Matrix

	Add Collection Rule	**Create Collection**	**Delete Collection**	**Delete Collection Rule**	**Deploy Application**
Application Admin	X			X	
Application Author					
Application Deployment Mgr					
Asset Mgr					
Compliance Settings Mgr					
Endpoint Protection Mgr					
Full Admin	X			X	X
Infrastructure Admin	X	X	X	X	
OS Deployment Mgr					
Operations Admins	X			X	
Read Only Analyst					
Remote Tools Operator					
Security Admin	X			X	
SW Update Mgr					

TABLE 15.2 Configuration Manager Permissions and Activities Matrix (continued)

	Deploy Program	**Deploy SW Update**	**Deploy Task Sequence**	**Get Collection Members**	**Get Deployment Status**	**Update Collection Membership**
Application Admin				X	X	X
Application Author				X	X	X
Application Deployment Mgr				X	X	X

	Deploy Program	Deploy SW Update	Deploy Task Sequence	Get Collection Members	Get Deployment Status	Update Collection Membership
Asset Mgr				X	X	X
Compliance Settings Mgr				X	X	X
Endpoint Protection Mgr				X	X	X
Full Admin	X	X	X	X	X	X
Infrastructure Admin				X	X	X
OS Deployment Mgr			X	X	X	X
Operations Admins				X	X	X
Read Only Analyst				X	X	X
Remote Tools Operator				X	X	X
Security Admin				X	X	X
SW Update Mgr		X		X	X	X

NOTE: PERFORM CLIENT ACTION

You might have noticed that **Perform Client Action** activity is missing from the permissions tables. This is because this activity is a process that actually executes on the Configuration Manager client and does not require permissions to the ConfigMgr server.

Keep in mind that **Perform Client Action** does not use the ConfigMgr connection account. Instead, it uses the Orchestrator Runbook Server service account.

Connectivity Requirements

Many production environments use firewalls between systems. In situations where Orchestrator might be positioned on the other end of a firewall, making use of certain activities such as the ones in this integration pack can be rather difficult. All the activities use a remote WMI connection to access the Configuration Manager server. It is important to understand that, when a WMI connection is established, the computer is connecting through DCOM.

Consider these port requirements:

- DCOM uses TCP 135 as the Distributed Computing Environment (DCE) endpoint resolution.
- DCOM dynamically assigns TCP ports in the range of 1024 to 65535.

Activities at a Glance

The following activities (see Figure 15.3) are included in the System Center Configuration Manager IP:

- Add Collection Rule
- Creation Collection
- Delete Collection
- Delete Collection Rule
- Deploy Application
- Deploy Configuration Baseline
- Deploy Program
- Deploy Software Update
- Deploy Task Sequence
- Get Collection Member
- Get Deployment Status
- Perform Client Action
- Query ConfigMgr
- Update Collection Membership

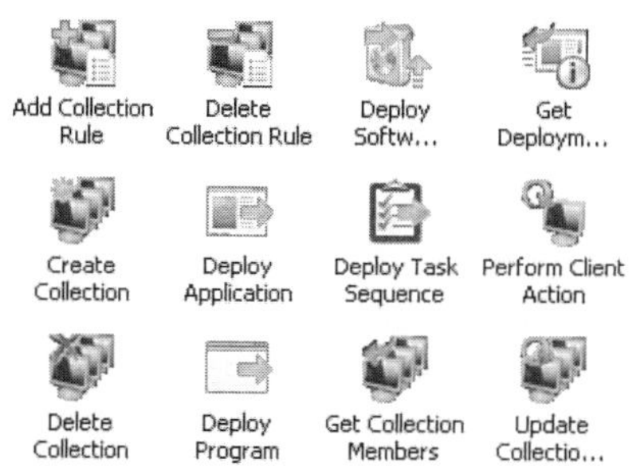

FIGURE 15.3 Configuration Manager integration pack activities.

Activities in Depth

Although you can use many of the activities listed in "Activities at a Glance" on their own, their power lies in how you can combine them to automate even complex provisioning, migration, and maintenance tasks related to ConfigMgr. This section describes the activities in the ConfigMgr IP in detail to clarify their intended function, the other activities with which they are commonly used, and common use case scenarios, where appropriate.

The ConfigMgr integration pack consists of 12 activities:

- **Add Collection Rule:** Adds collection membership rules to a collection. Direct rule, query rule, include collection, and exclude collection rule types are supported. More information about the **Add Collection Rule** activity is available at http://technet.microsoft.com/en-us/library/hh967533.
- **Delete Collection Rule:** Removes collection membership rules from an existing collection. Because modifying collection rules typically is done to redefine the collection membership, it is useful to use this in conjunction with **Update Collection Membership** to refresh the collection membership. Find more detail about this activity at http://technet.microsoft.com/en-us/library/hh967536.
- **Create Collection:** Creates an empty collection in Configuration Manager. At first glance, this activity might not seem to have much substance, but using it in conjunction with an activity such as **Add Collection Rule** exposes just how powerful this activity can be. More detail about **Create Collection** is available at http://technet.microsoft.com/en-us/library/hh967526.
- **Delete Collection:** Removes an existing collection from Configuration Manager. This activity also deletes all information associated with the collection, such as deployments, collection variables, maintenance windows, power saver settings, and anything else that pertains to collection properties.

  A number of safeguards are included with this activity to prevent the accidental deletion of an active collection. The default behavior is to ignore a request to delete a collection when these safeguards are applied, but you can change this behavior by overriding the advanced properties. Additional details about this activity are available at http://technet.microsoft.com/en-us/library/hh967528.
- **Deploy Application:** Creates a new application and assigns it to a collection. This activity supports the ConfigMgr application model, providing all the properties to deploy an application. Find out more information at http://technet.microsoft.com/en-us/library/hh967531.
- **Deploy Configuration Baseline:** Applies an existing baseline to a collection. Optionally, the activity can enable remediation, establish a recurrence pattern, and specify alert criteria. More information is available at http://technet.microsoft.com/en-us/library/jj874389.aspx.

- **Deploy Program:** Deploys legacy applications to computers in a target collection. Legacy applications use the traditional packages and programs concept. Find more information at http://technet.microsoft.com/en-us/library/hh967529.
- **Deploy Software Update:** Works similarly to the **Advertise Task Sequence** and **Create Advertisement** activities from the ConfigMgr 2007 IP. However, this activity specifically controls the delivery and installation of software updates. To use this activity, ensure that at least one update list, deployment template, and deployment package is available. Find out more information at http://technet.microsoft.com/en-us/library/hh967530.
- **Deploy Task Sequence:** Deploys task sequences to collections. The activity can control settings such as rerun behavior and progress bar display, and manage the available, mandatory, and expiration schedules. See http://technet.microsoft.com/en-us/library/hh967540 for more information.
- **Get Collection Member:** Retrieves the membership of a ConfigMgr collection. The membership is captured in the data bus, making it available to other activities later in the runbook. Additional details about this activity are available at http://technet.microsoft.com/en-us/library/hh967539.
- **Get Deployment Status:** Checks the status, regardless of the type of deployment (application, program, software update, or task sequence). Additional details about this activity are available at http://technet.microsoft.com/en-us/library/hh967532.
- **Perform Client Action:** Initiates a number of different cycles, such as Machine Policy Retrieval & Evaluation and Hardware Inventory Cycle. The function of this activity should not be uncommon to ConfigMgr administrators. More information is available at http://technet.microsoft.com/en-us/library/hh967538.

  This action occurs on the ConfigMgr client by connecting remotely to the computer and triggering the selected policy cycle. Be sure that the Orchestrator Runbook Service account has administrative privileges to the computer, or define the username and password of an account with the proper permissions in the Connection tab of the activity.

NOTE: USE CAUTION WHEN USING WITH MANY COMPUTERS

Be careful when using **Perform Client Action** to initiate Configuration Manager policy retrieval on a large number of clients because the runbook server will instruct the clients to retrieve their policies all at once. When triggered this way, the ConfigMgr client will not respect its interval settings and will retrieve the policy immediately. This is effectively the same as initiating the Policy Retrieval action in the Configuration Manager control panel applet.

- **Query ConfigMgr:** Orchestrator runbooks can issue existing ConfigMgr queries through this activity. The results are returned as a collection of items that downstream activities can use. However, some queries (mostly those designed to retrieve status messages) will fail when issued through this activity. More information is available at http://technet.microsoft.com/en-us/library/jj721959.aspx.

15

- **Update Collection Membership:** Another common task for Configuration Manager administrators is to refresh collections. By using the **Update Collection Membership** activity, an administrator can trigger the process that reevaluates and updates the membership of a collection.

  Because collections are refreshed on a schedule (typically once a day), the collection membership could be stale. Consider using this activity before any action—such as **Create Advertisement**—to ensure that all eligible computers are targeted. Additional information about the **Update Collection Membership** activity is available at http://technet.microsoft.com/en-us/library/hh967527.

Use Case Scenarios

This section explores using the ConfigMgr activities to automate real-world scenarios. These scenarios operate independently but are designed to operate together, as the last scenario illustrates. The core scenarios shown here demonstrate how to effectively tie together the activities:

- Create and Populate Collection
- Refresh Computer Policy
- Apply Software Updates

The first two runbooks are created as a means of demonstrating some concepts used to build the third runbook.

Creating and Populating a Collection

The Create and Populate Collection runbook, in Figure 15.4, accepts a collection name and search wildcard to create a Configuration Manager collection and fill it with computers matching the criteria. When the collection is populated with the appropriate collection rule(s), the runbook refreshes the collection to update the membership.

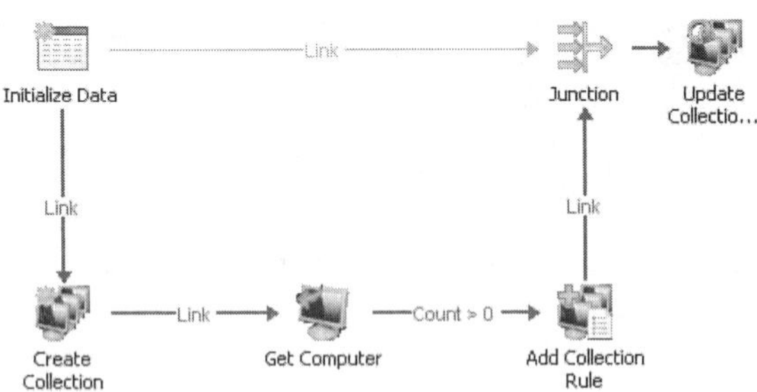

FIGURE 15.4 Create and Populate Collection runbook.

Collections are one of the fundamental elements for doing many things (advertisements, task sequences, software updates, and so on) in Configuration Manager, so this might end up being a nested runbook in many of your runbooks.

You can populate the new collection in many ways. The method used in this runbook is to query AD for computers that match a specified filter. Of course, this does not have to be AD; it could be a text file, a list of machines from System Center Operations Manager, or the name of a machine provided by System Center Service Manager.

CAUTION: IMPORTANCE OF ACTIVITY ORDER

When using Orchestrator, be careful about the order of activities in a runbook. Whenever an activity passes multiple items (such as a list of computers), the next activity will execute for each item it receives.

To illustrate this, if **Get Computer** comes before **Create Collection**, more than one computer might be retrieved. If **Get Computer** finds 10 computers, the next activity (**Create Collection**) tries to create a collection for every computer. This means that Orchestrator would run the **Create Collection** activity 10 times!

This runbook performs the following activities:

1. **Initialize Data:** This activity (see Figure 15.5) is configured with two parameters, CollName and ComputerFilter. This would be supplied as a parameter in an **Invoke Runbook** activity, as an external call to trigger this policy or manually while testing with the Runbook Tester.

   The value supplied for the CollName parameter should be the name of the new collection to create and populate. The **Get Computer** activity uses ComputerFilter to specify a name used with a wildcard expression for retrieving computers.

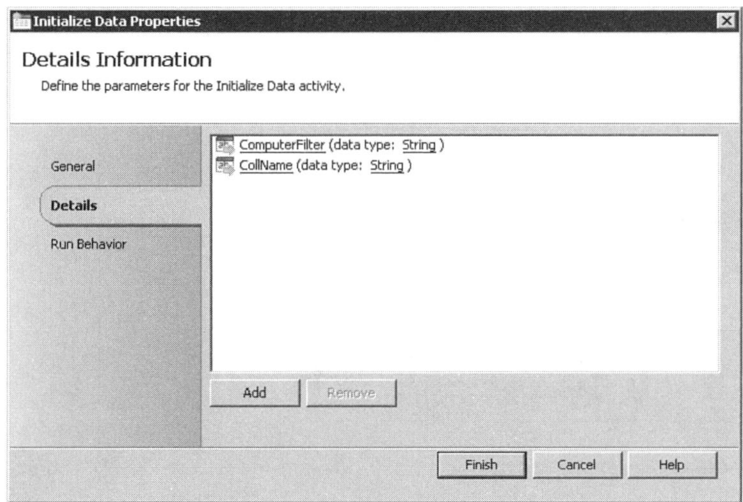

FIGURE 15.5 **Initialize Data** properties.

NOTE: USING FULLY DESCRIPTIVE PARAMETER NAMES

You might notice the use of shortened parameter names in this section. This is not a requirement for Orchestrator's data bus, which is capable of reading fully descriptive parameter names. For example, the parameter named "ComputerFilter" could be named "Computer Name Filter," and "CollName" could be named "Collection Name." This is a matter of preference for the runbook designer. Lengthy, descriptive parameters are useful for describing the values the runbook operator needs to supply when starting a runbook, but they might make it difficult to read the entire parameter when designing a runbook and calling the parameter from the data bus.

2. **Create Collection:** The **Create Collection** activity generates a new collection using the CollName variable from the **Initialize Data** activity as the name. A value for Limiting Collection is required. When modifying the Limiting Collection value, it is possible to introduce errors. For this reason, it is preferable to use the ellipsis button to retrieve a list from the Configuration Manager server to remove the possibility of a typing error when specifying a collection. In this example, the Limiting Collection value is set to **All Systems** (see Figure 15.6).

    - **Collection Name:** {CollName from "Initialize Data"}
    - **Collection Type:** Device
    - **Limiting Collection:** All Systems
    - **Limiting Collection Value Type:** Name
    - **Use Incremental Updates:** True

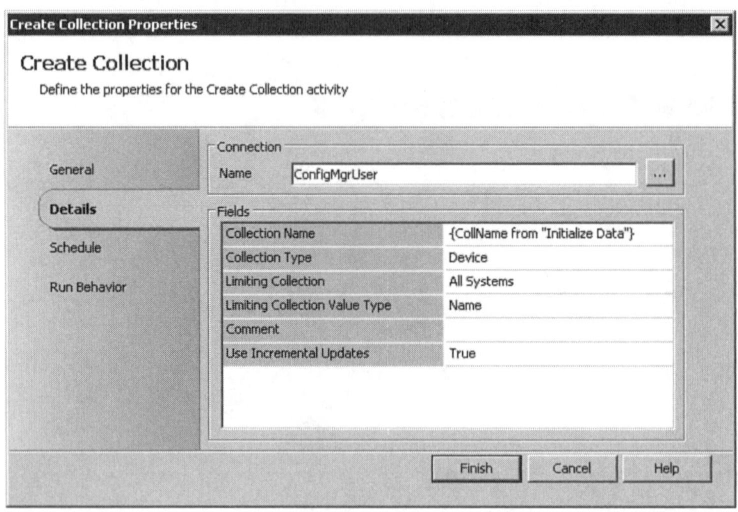

FIGURE 15.6 **Create Collection** properties configured to use published data for the collection name.

NOTE: SET LIMITING COLLECTION VALUE TYPE APPROPRIATELY

In most cases, the Limiting Collection value is specified as the name of the collection. When using the ellipsis to select the Limiting Collection, the values applied are the value type of Name. Be sure the Limiting Collection Value Type is set to Name.

3. **Get Computer:** In the **Get Computer** activity, a connection is made to Active Directory and a query is performed to retrieve a list of computers that match a specified criteria. This activity is not from the ConfigMgr IP, but rather comes from the Active Directory IP.

   - Disabled Equals False
   - Common Name Starts with {ComputerFilter from "Initialize Data"}

   Figure 15.7 shows the configured **Get Computer** activity.

   Smart Link (Count > 0): As long as the filter specified in the **Get Computer** activity is valid, the status returned is success regardless of the number of objects returned. For this reason, the link between **Get Computer** and **Add Collection Rule** must be modified to continue with the runbook only if the count returned is not 0. To do this, modify the Include filter, removing line **Get Computer returns success.** Add **Count from Get Computer does not equal 0**, as in Figure 15.8.

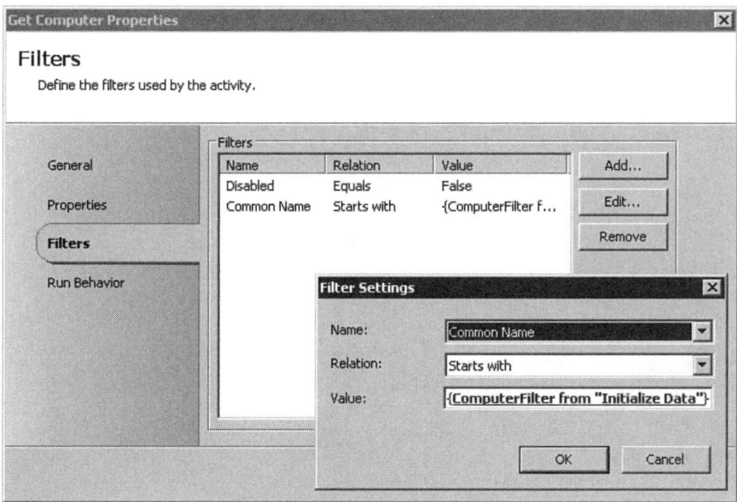

FIGURE 15.7 **Get Computer** properties.

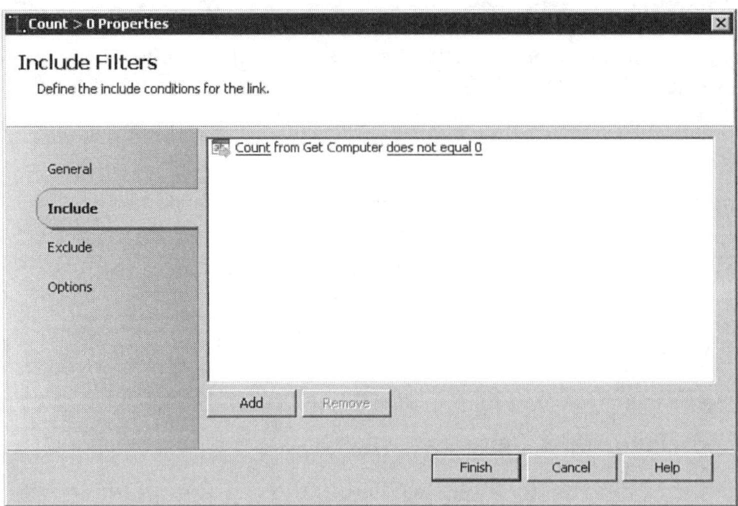

FIGURE 15.8 Link properties (Count > 0).

4. **Add Collection Rule:** The **Add Collection Rule** activity retrieves values from the data bus and uses them to create the direct membership rules that will populate the collection properties. The number of computers passed to this activity dictates the number of iterations this activity will execute. Figure 15.9 shows the configured activity.

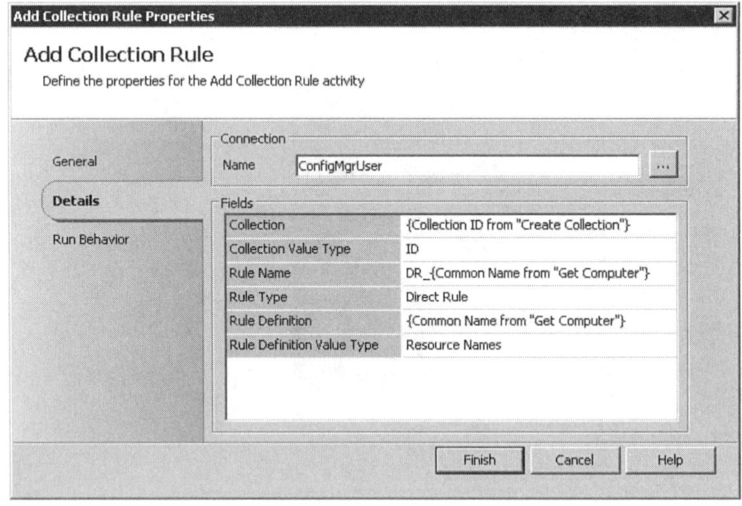

FIGURE 15.9 **Add Collection Rule** properties.

- **Collection:** {Collection ID from "Create Collection"}
- **Collection Value Type:** ID
- **Rule Name:** DR_{Common Name from "Get Computer"}
- **Rule Type:** Direct Rule
- **Rule Definition:** {Common Name from "Get Computer"}
- **Rule Definition Value Type:** Resource Names

TIP: PREPENDING COLLECTION RULE NAMES

Note that, for the Rule Name field in step 4, "DR_" is prepended to the Common Name published data. Using DR for "direct rule" helps easily identify the rule type.

5. **Junction:** When the ComputerFilter is specified loosely enough to return multiple objects from **Get Computer**, multiple iterations of **Update Collection Membership** will execute. Because you need to update the collection membership only once, a junction is used to drop the iterations to one. **Initialize Data** has only one iteration, so this successfully prevents the **Update Collection Membership** activity from executing multiple times.

   Link the **Initialize Data** activity (see Figure 15.10) to the **Junction** activity and set the property of the **Junction** as "Return Data from Initialize Data."

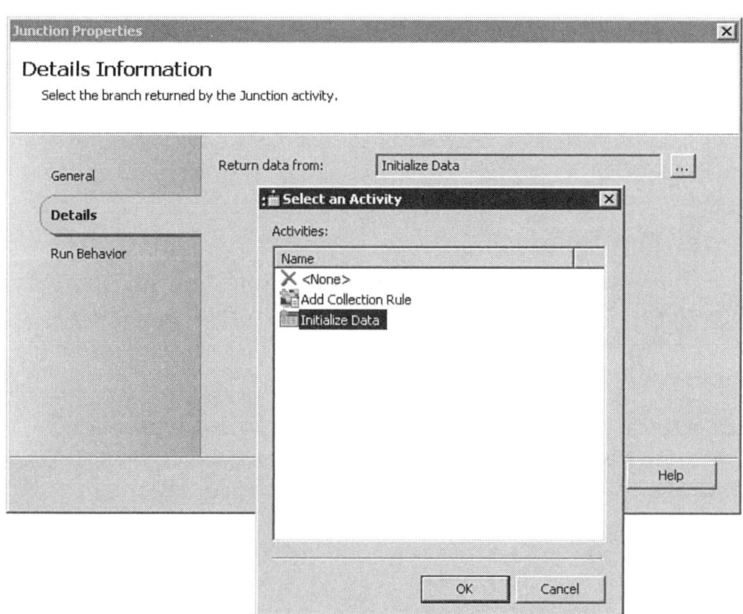

FIGURE 15.10 **Junction** properties.

6. **Update Collection Membership:** After the collection rules are added, the **Update Collection Membership** activity (see Figure 15.11) refreshes the collection membership, which populates the collection with objects that match the newly assigned rules.

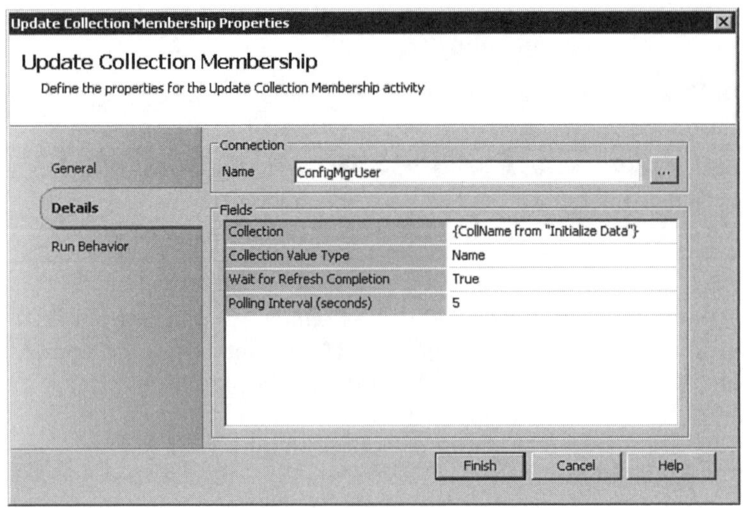

FIGURE 15.11 **Update Collection Membership** properties.

- **Collection:** {Collection ID from "Initialize Data"}
- **Collection Value Type:** Name
- **Wait for Refresh Completion:** True
- **Polling Interval (seconds):** 5

Applying Endpoint Protection Policy

In this example, Orchestrator manages a System Center Endpoint Protection (SCEP) policy for a specified client (see Figure 15.12). The SCEP policy used in this runbook is specifically for a server. You might find yourself in a situation in which a process, service, or any other kind of indicator cannot easily identify a set of application servers.

By using the **Get Computer** activity from the Active Directory IP, you can retrieve only computers that match a given criteria. Because the SCEP policy is for a server, workstations are filtered out, to prevent any workstations from going into the collection.

Orchestrator begins by querying Active Directory for a provided computer name, looking for a computer object with an exact Common Name match. An additional filter checks the operating system, returning a value only if the operating system contains the word "Server."

If an object is found, the next activity adds a new direct rule to an existing collection that has the corresponding SCEP policy deployed to it. Upon refresh of the collection, the device shows. Finally, to complete the runbook, a policy refresh is issued against the specified server. The steps for this runbook follow:

FIGURE 15.12 Apply Endpoint Protection Policy runbook.

1. **Initialize Data:** This activity is configured with a single parameter, ComputerName. It is supplied as a parameter after starting the runbook in the Orchestration console, supplied in an **Invoke Runbook** activity from another runbook, or supplied manually during testing with the Runbook Tester. The value supplied for the ComputerName parameter should be the name of the server to add to the SCEP policy collection.

2. **Get Computer: Get Computer** is provided the name of the server from the ComputerName variable in the **Initialize Data** activity. Additionally, the filter in Figure 15.13 looks for any computer that is not disabled whose name matches the ComputerName variable and in which the operating system value contains the word "Server":

   - **Disabled Equals False**
   - **Common Name Equals {ComputerName from "Initialize Data"}**
   - **Operating System Contains Server**

   Smart Link (Count > 0): As long as the filter is defined properly, the **Get Computer** activity returns a status of success. To ensure that the activity has an object to work with, set the Include filter to **Count from Get Computer does not equal 0**.

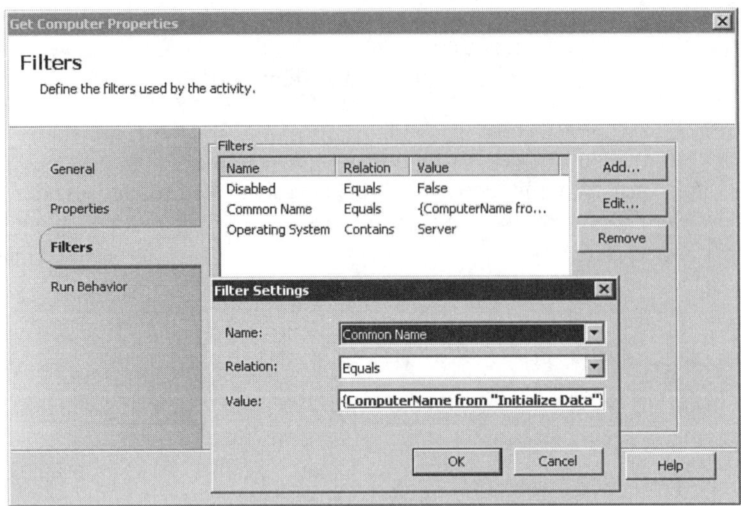

FIGURE 15.13 **Get Computer** filter properties configured to return only servers.

3. **Add Collection Rule:** By using the ComputerName variable as the rule definition, this activity adds a collection rule defining the provided server as a member of the SCEP policy collection. This activity (see Figure 15.14) has the collection value set to **SCEP Policy**, which is a collection that was previously defined, with a SCEP policy applied to it.

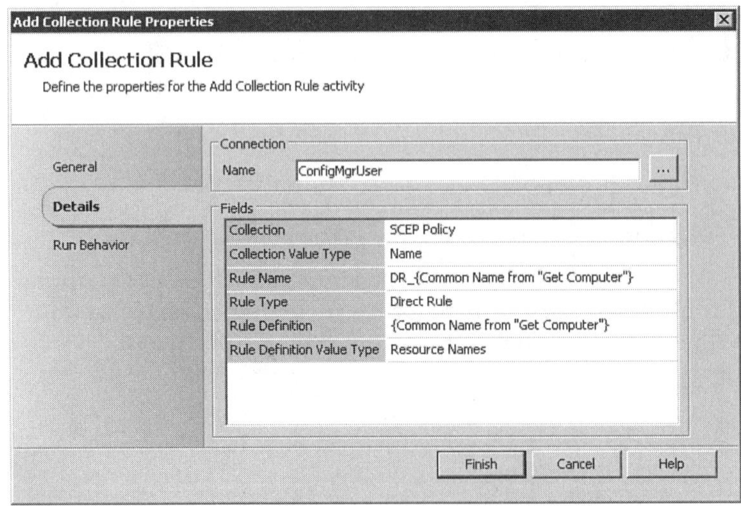

FIGURE 15.14 **Add Collection Rule** properties.

- **Collection:** SCEP Policy
- **Collection Value Type:** Name
- **Rule Name:** DR_{Common Name from "Get Computer"}
- **Rule Type:** Direct Rule
- **Rule Name:** {Common Name from "Get Computer"}
- **Rule Definition Value Type:** Resource Names

4. **Update Collection Membership:** After the collection rule is added to the SCEP policy collection, the collection must be updated so that the new collection rule is evaluated. This happens by default if the collection has a refresh schedule applied. However, you can speed that up by using this activity (see Figure 15.15).
    - **Collection:** {Collection from "Add Collection Rule"}
    - **Collection Value Type:** {Collection Value Type from "Add Collection"}
    - **Wait for Refresh Completion:** True
    - **Polling Interval (seconds):** 5

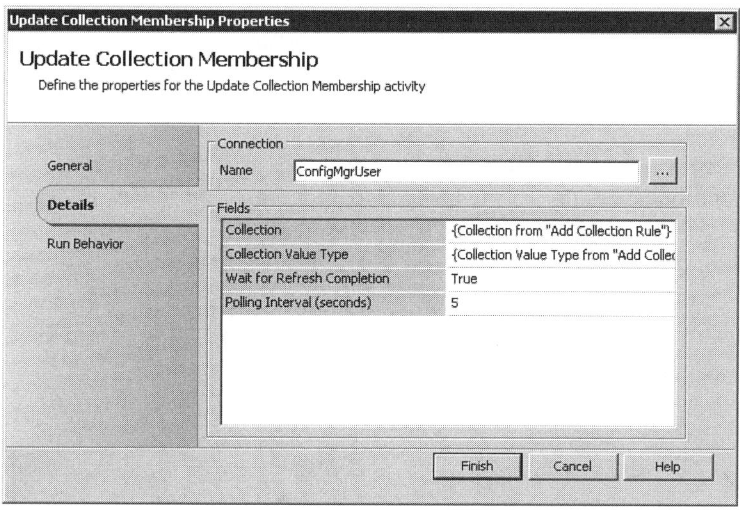

FIGURE 15.15 **Update Collection Membership** properties.

5. **Perform Client Action:** After the collection is updated, the client must check in with the ConfigMgr server to receive the new policy. To accelerate this process, the **Perform Client Action** activity in Figure 15.16 instructs the ConfigMgr client to execute a specified action.

- **Computer:** {Common Name from "Get Computer"}
- **Action:** Machine Policy Retrieval & Evaluation Cycle

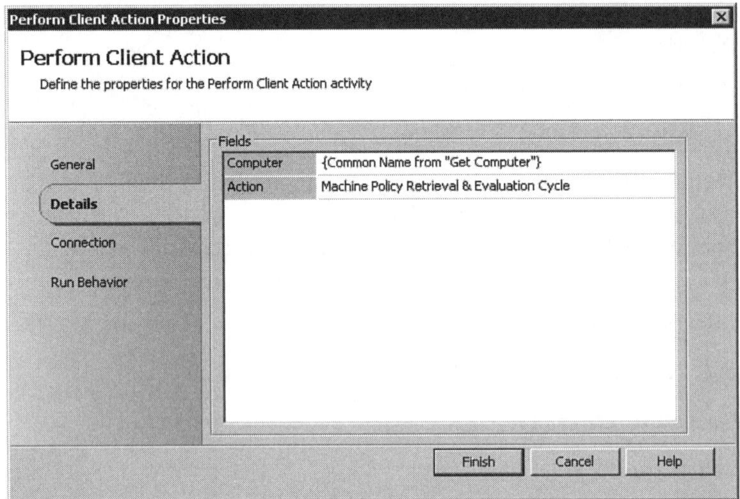

FIGURE 15.16 **Perform Client Action** properties.

Applying Software Updates

In Figure 15.17, the sample runbook Apply Software Updates creates a software update deployment and adds a specified computer to the associated collection. After the computer is added to the collection, Orchestrator initiates ConfigMgr client actions to speed up the software update process.

Adding to the concepts learned in earlier runbooks, this runbook consists of three runbooks that handle different activities. The main runbook calls a child runbook to prepare a collection and another runbook to deploy updates.

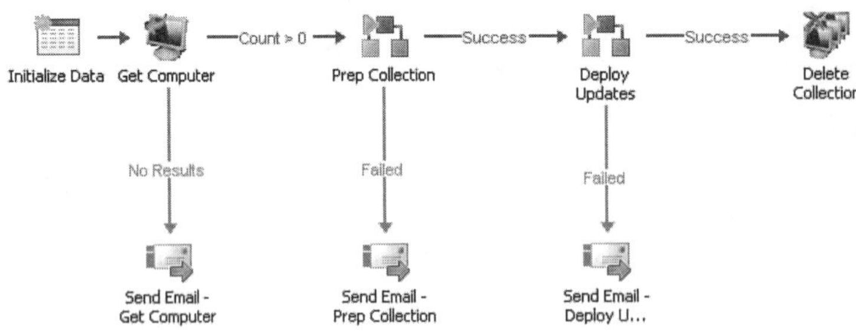

FIGURE 15.17 Apply Software Updates runbook.

Examining Activities in the Main Runbook

The Apply Software Updates runbook is comprised of the following activities:

1. **Initialize Data:** This activity is configured with two parameters: ComputerName and Collection.

   The value supplied for the ComputerName should be the name of the computer for which you want to apply software updates. The value supplied for the Collection parameter should be the name of the new collection to create and populate, used for the purposes of targeting the software update deployment.

2. **Get Computer:** To ensure that the provided name is legitimate, the **Get Computer** activity checks the computer name before allowing the runbook to continue.

   - **Disabled Equals False**
   - **Common Name Equals {ComputerName from "Initialize Data"}**

NOTE: VALIDATING COMPUTERS WORKS FOR DOMAIN MEMBERS

Using the **Get Computer** activity assumes that the computer that requires software updates is a domain member. When it is not a domain member, other considerations should be taken to validate the computer, such as using the **Get Computer/IP Status** activity.

2.1 **Smart Link (Count > 0):** If the Result Count value from **Get Computer** is not 0, it is presumed that at least one value is present. This is an easy way to determine whether a successful query was issued. Set the Include filter to **Count from Get Computer does not equal 0.**

2.2 **Smart Link (No Results > 0):** If the Result Count value from **Get Computer** is zero, no matches occurred; the computer presumably does not exist in Active Directory. The runbook then moves to the **Send Email** activity. Set the Include filter to **Count from Get Computer equals 0.**

3. **Send Email:** This activity (see Figure 15.18) is called only if the **Get Computer** activity returns no matches. It sends the computer name in an email to the administrator, and the runbook performs no further processing.

4. **Prep Collection:** This **Invoke Runbook** activity (see Figure 15.19) calls the Prep Collection runbook, which is responsible for preparing the collection and ConfigMgr policy necessary to deploy the software updates. Two parameters are configured for this activity:

   - **Collection:** {Collection from "Initialize Data"}
   - **ComputerName:** {ComputerName from "Initialize Data"}

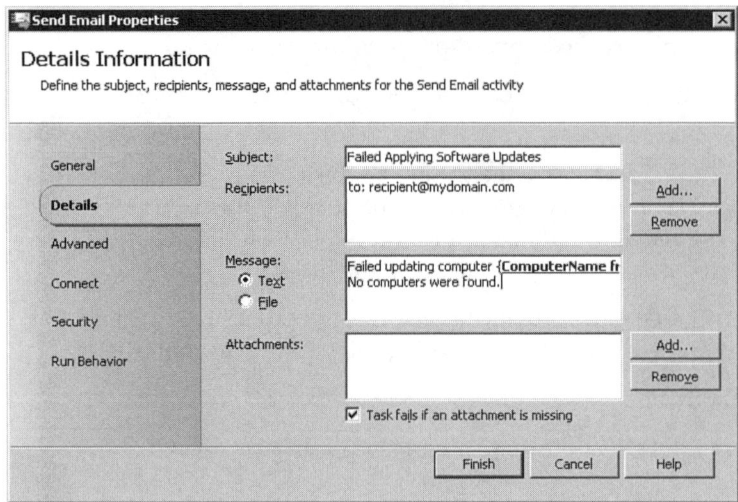

FIGURE 15.18 **Send Email** properties.

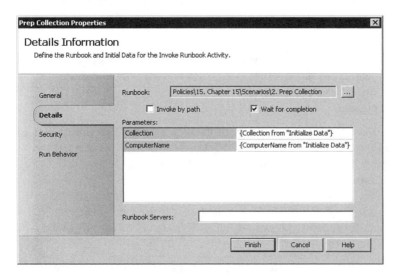

FIGURE 15.19 Prep Collection child runbook properties.

5. **Deploy Updates:** This next **Invoke Runbook** activity calls the Deploy Updates child runbook, which is responsible for executing the necessary activities on the ConfigMgr client to expedite the software update process. One parameter, ComputerName, is configured for this activity (see Figure 15.20).

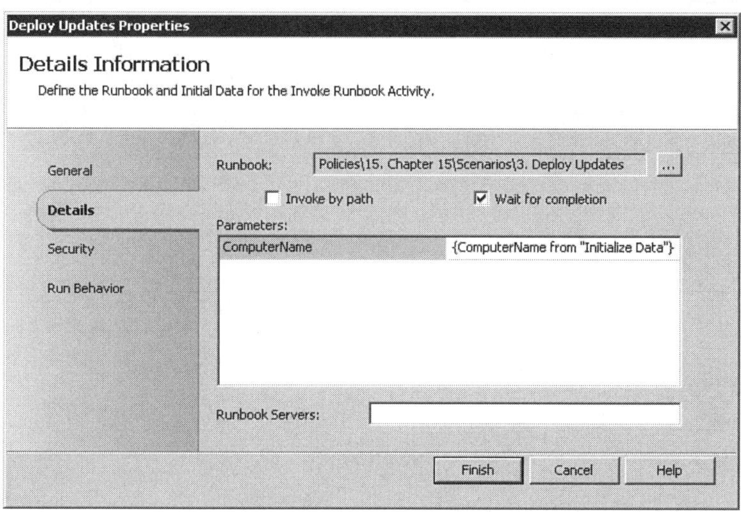

FIGURE 15.20 Deploy Updates child runbook properties.

6. **Delete Collection:** When everything is complete, the **Delete Collection** activity (see Figure 15.21) is called to clean up the collection used during the deployment. It is provided three parameters:

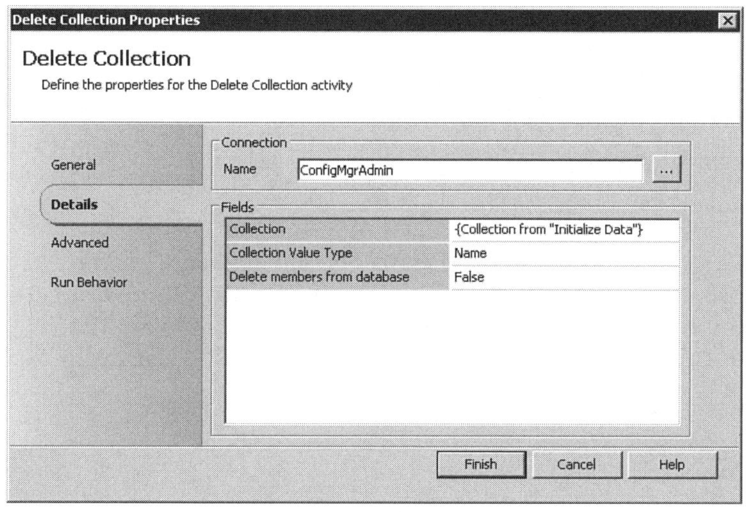

FIGURE 15.21 **Delete Collection** properties.

- **Collection:** {Collection from "Initialize Data"}
- **Collection Value Type:** Name
- **Delete members from database:** False

Preparing the Collection for Deployment

The Prep Collection child runbook takes the Collection and ComputerName variables, creates a collection, applies a software update deployment to it, and adds the collection rule necessary to add the computer to the new collection. Figure 15.22 shows the Prep Collection child runbook.

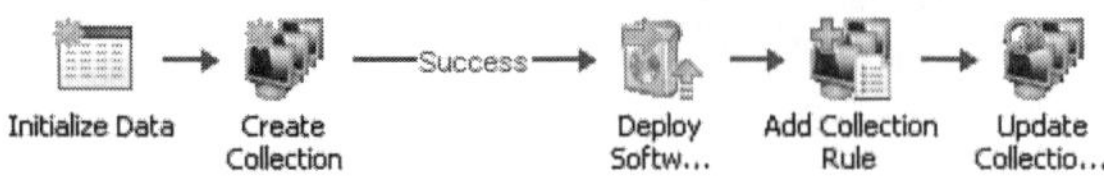

FIGURE 15.22 Prep Collection child runbook.

A description of the Prep Collection runbook activities follows:

1. **Initialize Data:** This activity is configured with two parameters, ComputerName and Collection. When the runbook is called, the **Invoke Runbook** activity supplies the variables from the parent runbook (Apply Software Updates).
2. **Create Collection:** The **Create Collection** activity generates a new collection for deploying software updates. The activity is configured as Figure 15.23 shows and as this list indicates:
    - **Collection Name:** {Collection from "Initialize Data"}
    - **Collection Type:** Device
    - **Limiting Collection:** All Systems
    - **Limiting Collection Value Type:** Name
    - **Comment:** Software Update Example
    - **Use Incremental Updates:** False

    Smart Link (Success): If the collection already exists, the runbook fails, and it does not continue past attempting to create the collection. In reality, if the collection already exists, you can still use it by modifying the smart link going to **Get Computer** so that the Include filter looks for one of the following (see Figure 15.24):

    - Error summary text from **Create Collection** contains already exists
    - **Create Collection** returns success

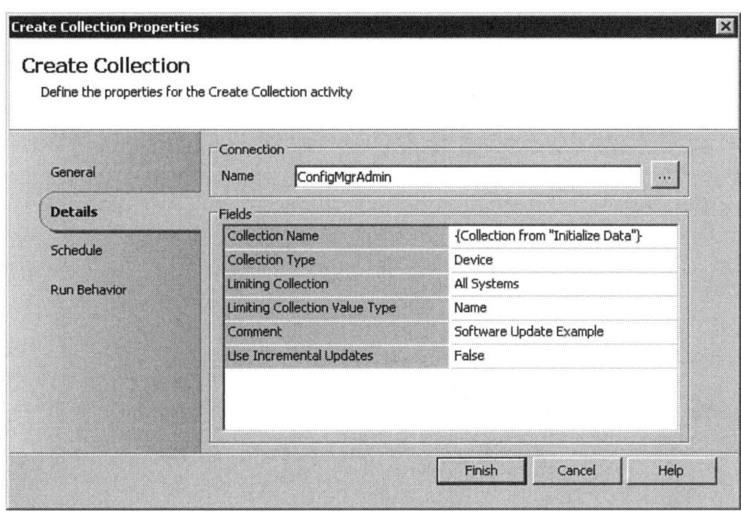

FIGURE 15.23 **Create Collection** properties.

3. **Deploy Software Update:** By providing the template and update values for this activity, the software updates can be applied to a collection. When a device becomes a member of the collection, it receives the software updates policy. Note that the Deployment Name is prepended with **SU_** and followed with the Collection variable. The activity should be configured as follows (also see Figure 15.25):

   - **Deployment Name:** SU_{Collection from "Initialize Data"}
   - **Deployment Description:** Software Update Example
   - **Deployment Template:** Deployment Template
   - **Deployment Template Value Type:** Name
   - **Update/Update Group:** Software Update Group
   - **Update Value Type:** Upgrade Group Name
   - **Purpose:** Required
   - **User Notification:** Show all notifications
   - **Collection:** {Collection from "Initialize Data"}
   - **Collection Value Type:** Name

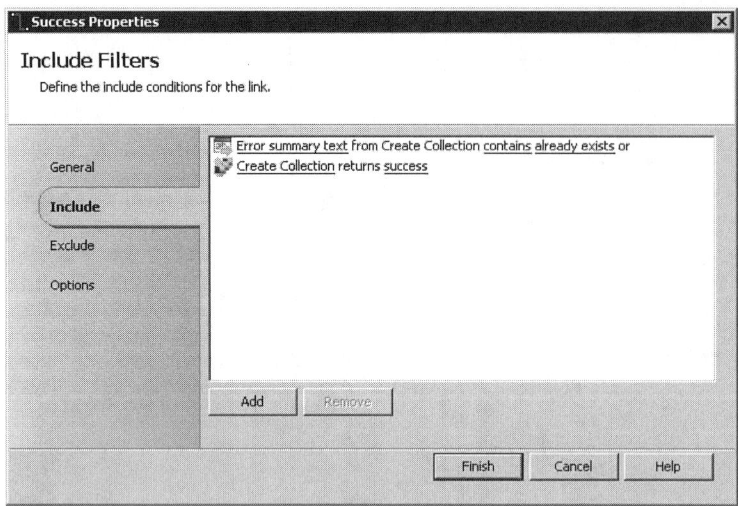

FIGURE 15.24 Smart link properties checking for multiple conditions.

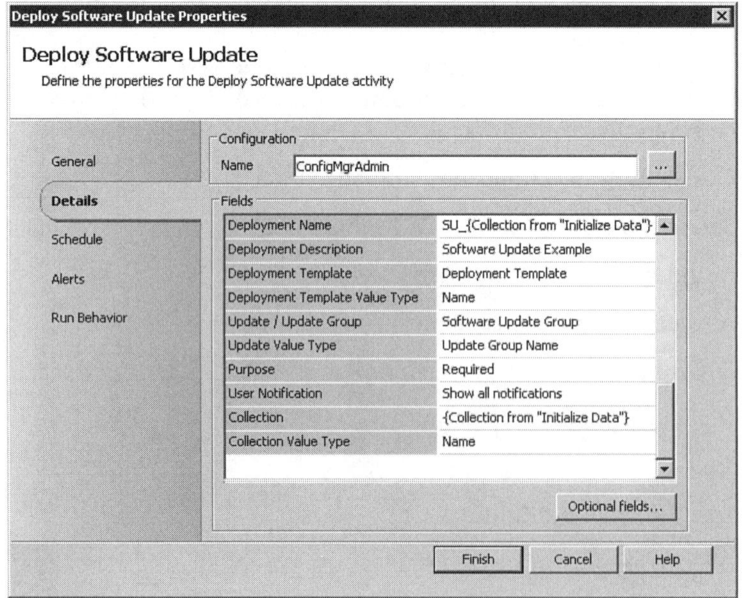

FIGURE 15.25 **Deploy Software Update** properties.

4. **Add Collection Rule:** Using the ComputerName variable as the rule definition, this activity (see Figure 15.26) adds the collection rule to make the provided server a member of the SCEP policy collection.

   - **Collection:** {Collection from "Initialize Data"}
   - **Collection Value Type:** Name
   - **Rule Name:** DR_{ComputerName from "Initialize Data"}
   - **Rule Type:** Direct Rule
   - **Rule Definition:** {ComputerName from "Initialize Data"}
   - **Rule Definition Value Type:** Resource Names

5. **Update Collection Membership:** After the collection rule is added to the collection, the collection should be updated, forcing the collection rule to be evaluated. Figure 15.27 displays the configured activity.

   - **Collection:** {Collection from "Initialize Data"}
   - **Collection Value Type:** Name
   - **Wait for Refresh Completion:** True
   - **Polling Interval (seconds): 5**

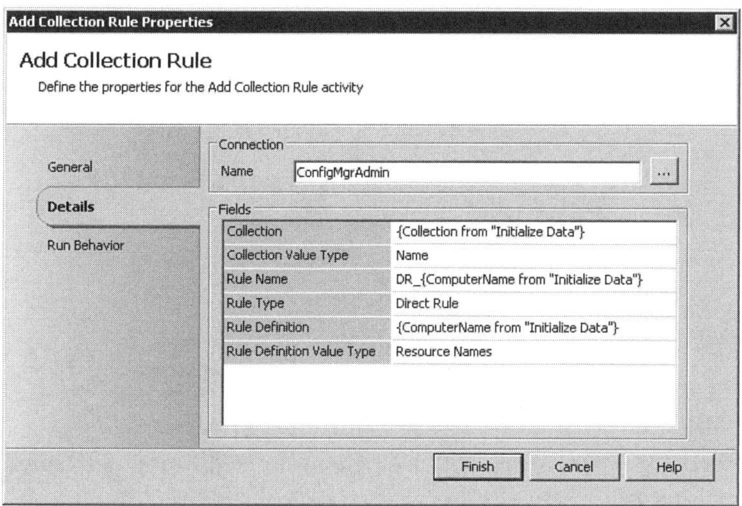

FIGURE 15.26 **Add Collection Rule** properties to add a server to a SCEP policy collection.

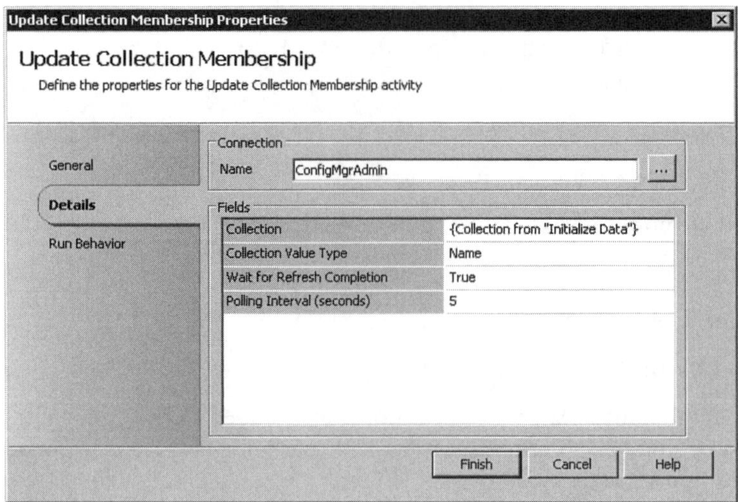

FIGURE 15.27 **Update Collection Membership** properties.

After the Prep Collection child runbook is successfully invoked, processing returns to the Apply Software Updates parent runbook.

Deploying Updates to the Collection

The parent runbook invokes the Deploy Updates child runbook. This runbook is responsible for managing the activities on the targeted client. Figure 15.28 displays the activities of the runbook.

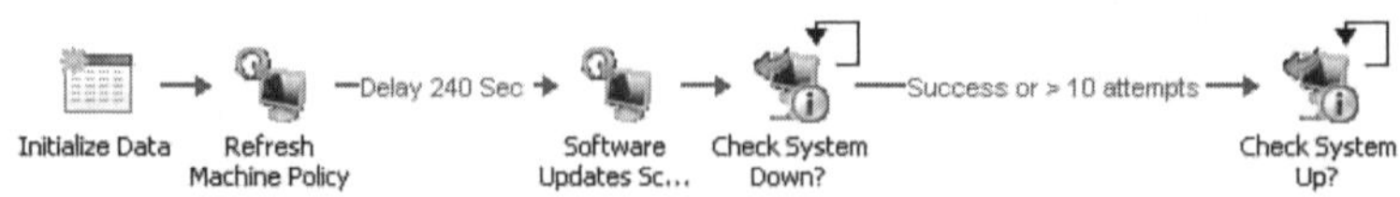

FIGURE 15.28 Deploy Updates child runbook.

A description of the Deploy Updates runbook activities follows:

1. **Initialize Data:** This activity is configured with a single parameter, ComputerName. ComputerName is used in this runbook to specify the targeted computer in each activity that follows.
2. **Refresh Machine Policy:** The **Perform Client Action** activity (see Figure 15.29) is renamed **Refresh Machine Policy** to help identify the step. This activity instructs the computer to refresh machine policies, pulling down any newly assigned policies.

- **Computer:** {ComputerName from "Initialize Data"}
- **Action:** Machine Policy Retrieval & Evaluation Cycle

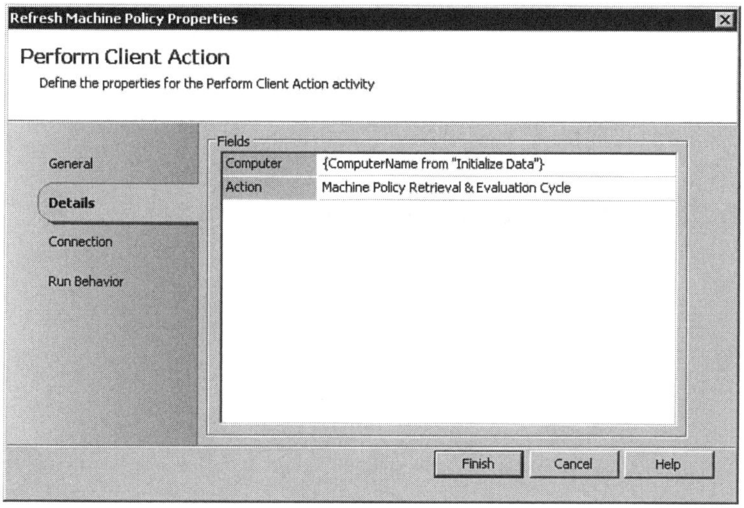

FIGURE 15.29 **Refresh Machine Policy** properties.

Smart Link (Delay 240 Sec): To give the Refresh Machine Policy activity enough time to execute, set the trigger delay to 240 seconds (see Figure 15.30).

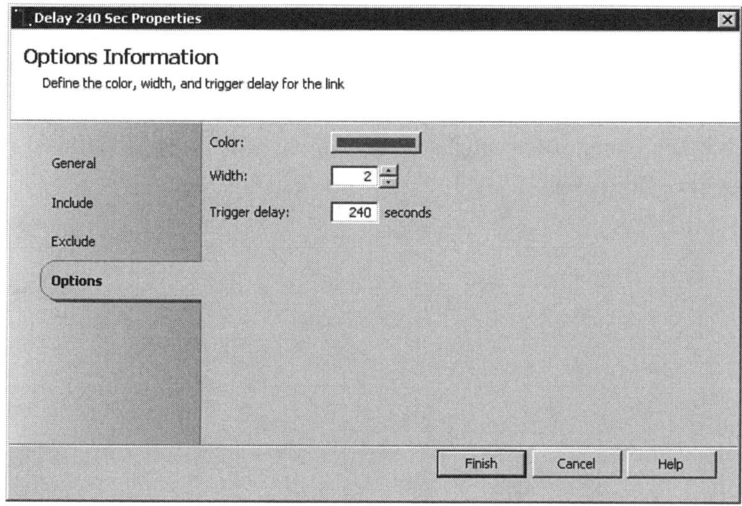

FIGURE 15.30 Smart link trigger delay properties.

3. **Software Updates Scan and Deployment Re-evaluation:** This **Perform Client Action** activity is renamed to help identify this step. The activity in Figure 15.31 is configured to execute the Software Updates Scan and Deployment Re-evaluation action, instructing the computer to initialize the Software Update Scan and Software Updates Deployment Evaluation cycles.

    - **Computer:** {ComputerName from "Refresh Machine Policy"}
    - **Action:** Software Updates Scan and Deployment Re-evaluation

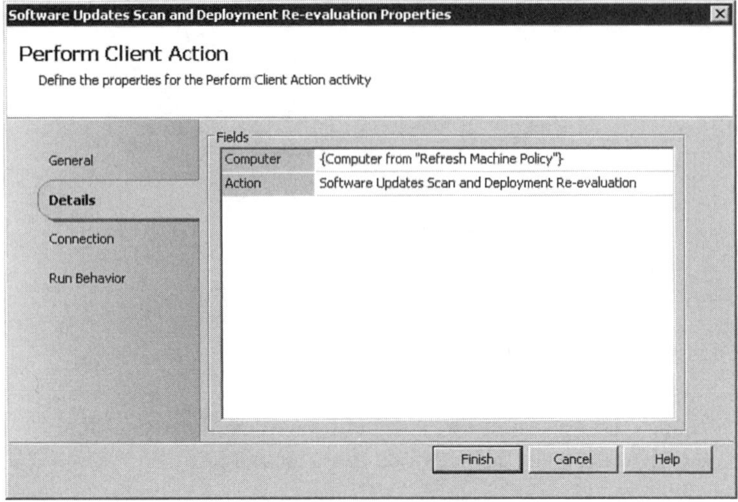

FIGURE 15.31 **Software Updates Scan and Deployment Re-evaluation** properties.

4. **Check System Down?:** The **Get Computer/IP Status** activity, renamed **Check System Down?** for clarity, checks to see if the specified computer stops responding to pings. Assuming that the computer applied software updates, it is often followed by a reboot. Figure 15.32 displays the configured activity.

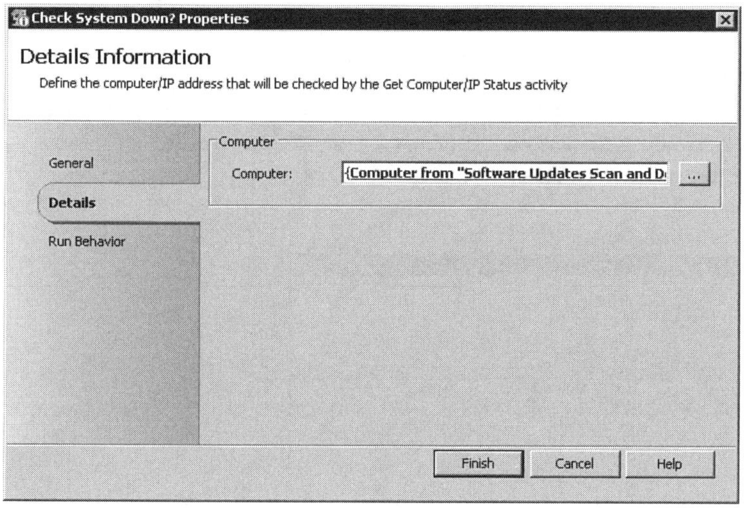

FIGURE 15.32 **Check System Down?** properties.

This activity is configured with a looping property set to check every 30 seconds. The activity exits when the status returns as something other than success or when the number of attempts is greater than 10. This prevents the runbook from being stuck in an endless loop, waiting for the computer to reboot, if no reboot was actually required. The exit condition is expressed as follows (also see Figure 15.33):

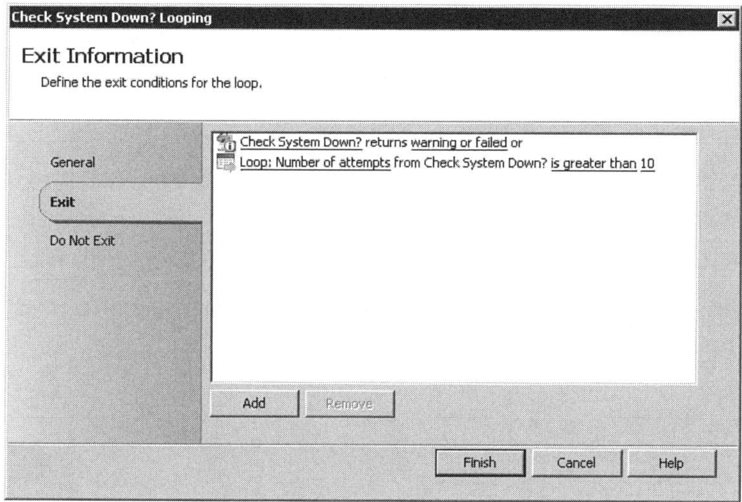

FIGURE 15.33 **Check System Down?** looping properties.

- **Check System Down?:** Returns warning or failed
- **Loop:** Number of attempts from **Check System Down?** is greater than 10

Smart Link (Success or > 10 attempts): To honor the conditions of the previous loop, the smart link between **Check System Down?** and **Check System Up?** must be configured to use the same condition as in Figure 15.34.

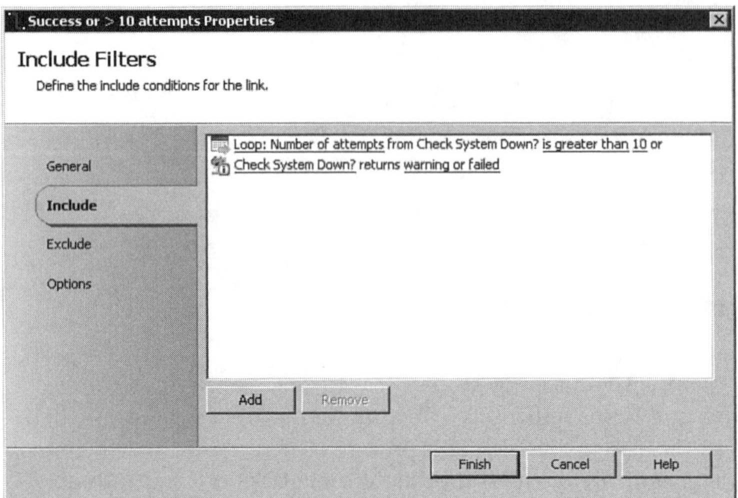

FIGURE 15.34 Smart link properties.

5. **Check System Up?:** The **Get Computer/IP Status,** renamed as **Check System Up?,** checks the inverse condition of step 4. This makes sure the targeted computer is running after the policy cycles are initiated. Figure 15.35 shows the configured activity.

   This activity is configured with a looping property set to check every 30 seconds to see if the computer responds to a ping. If so, the runbook continues.

   If not, the activity continues to check the computer every 30 seconds, up to 10 tries.

When completed, processing returns to the parent runbook, where the **Delete Collection** activity proceeds to clean up the collection used in the deployment.

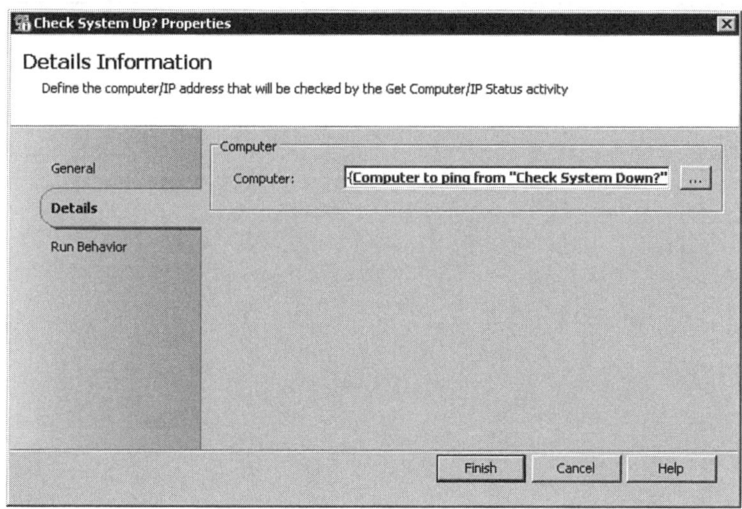

FIGURE 15.35 **Check System Up?** properties.

Summary

This chapter discussed the installation and configuration of the System Center Configuration Manager IP, additional requirements for using the integration pack, and activities included with the integration pack. With ConfigMgr, delegation of permissions can be granular; tables illustrated the rights required to execute the activities in this integration pack. The chapter also illustrated some common use cases for ConfigMgr administrators with activity-specific instructions.

CHAPTER 16

Integration with System Center Virtual Machine Manager

IN THIS CHAPTER

System Center 2012 Virtual Machine Manager (VMM) includes a significant amount of new functionality beyond deployment and management of virtual machines (VMs), including visibility into storage, virtual networking, and role-based security to support delegated administrators and self-service users. As one of the System Center 2012 integration packs (IPs) for Microsoft System Center 2012 Orchestrator (SCOrch), the VMM IP enables administrators to automate Hyper-V and VMware virtualization activities from Orchestrator via Virtual Machine Manager 2012. This chapter discusses the functionality of the Microsoft System Center Virtual Manager integration pack.

The chapter also describes the requirements for using the VMM integration pack. It covers the installation procedure and configuration steps. It also explains how each activity functions, along with common use case scenarios. In addition, it presents several sample runbooks to show you how to leverage the VMM IP fully to automate your organization's server virtualization and private cloud management processes.

Integration Pack Requirements

Before getting started, note that the Orchestrator installation media does not include the VMM integration pack; the IP is a separate download from the Microsoft website, as part of a bundle that includes all System Center 2012 IPs. The following sections provide information on how to obtain the IP, as well as discuss specific installation and configuration requirements to get yourself up and running quickly with automation of VMM 2012 provisioning and management processes.

System Center 2012 Orchestrator

This integration pack comes bundled with the other System Center 2007–2012 integration packs in a self-extracting executable. It extracts the System Center integration packs to the desktop of the current user by default. You can download the System Center 2012 Service Pack (SP) 1 Orchestrator add-ons and extensions, which include the System Center 2012 SP 1 integration packs, from www.microsoft.com/en-us/download/details.aspx?id=34611. The RTM package is available at www.microsoft.com/en-us/download/details.aspx?displaylang=en&id=28725. Microsoft has announced an updated IP for the 2012 R2 release.

System Center 2012 Virtual Machine Manager

You will be using activities from the integration pack to automate specific components of Virtual Machine Manager, so you must also install Virtual Machine Manager. Specifically, this IP requires Virtual Machine Manager 2012. Current versions of the VMM IP are available for both VMM 2012 RTM and VMM 2012 SP 1.

If your organization is still using VMM 2008 R2, Microsoft provides an integration pack for that release, although this book does not discuss that IP in detail. For detailed guidance on how to use the VMM 2008 R2 IP and sample use cases, see *System Center Opalis Integration Server 6.3 Unleashed* (Sams, 2011).

Installing the Integration Pack

For information on the installation steps to register and deploy an IP, see Chapter 5, "Installing System Center 2012 Orchestrator."

Different operations within require different levels of permissions. You can create multiple accounts with different levels of permissions with Virtual Machine Manager for performing different operations. However, not all environments require this level of granularity.

Microsoft recommends using a connection account with membership in the Virtual Machine Manager Administrators user role to ensure that the account has the necessary permissions for all Virtual Machine Manager–related activities.

Configuring the Integration Pack

All activities in the VMM IP use the credentials that the connection account supplies to execute various functions on the VMM server. If you have multiple VMM servers to manage, you can use additional connection accounts for each VMM server. Whether you use a single common account to provide Orchestrator permissions in multiple VMM deployments or you use a separate account for each deployment depends on the security requirements of your organization and the team responsible for managing the virtual infrastructure.

Configuration steps include verifying connectivity requirements, granting access to the connection account, and then configuring that account. The next sections cover these steps.

Connectivity Requirements

The Orchestrator runbook server requires connectivity to a computer with the VMM Administrator console installed. The connection properties enable you to specify a computer where the console is installed, alleviating the need to place this component on each runbook server and Runbook Designer computer.

The computer with the VMM Administrator console installed does need to have Windows Remote Management enabled and configured to accept connections. This requirement is specific to the VMM server.

Security Credentials

To implement the VMM integration pack, grant administrator access in VMM to the Orchestrator Runbook Service account; this account ultimately will be used to contact the server to initiate VMM-related activities.

Granting Access to the Connection Account

Before configuring the connection to VMM, grant administrator access in VMM to the account that Orchestrator will use when connecting to the VMM server. Perform the following steps:

1. Launch the VMM Administrator console. In the Navigation pane, navigate to **Settings -> User Roles**.
2. Double-click the Administrator user role and then click **Add**.
3. Enter the name of the account Orchestrator will use to access this VMM server.
4. Click **OK** twice to save your changes, and exit.

Configuring the Connection Account

For the account to perform the actions configured in the sample runbooks, you must grant rights to the connection account in Virtual Machine Manager. Begin by configuring connectivity to Virtual Machine Manager in the Runbook Designer. Follow these steps to configure the connection:

1. In the top menu of the Runbook Designer, select **Options -> System Center Virtual Machine Manager**.
2. In the System Center Virtual Machine Manager dialog box, click **Add** and then supply the following information (also see Figure 16.1):
   - **Name:** Supply a name for the connection; this is **SVCMM** in Figure 16.1.
   - **Type:** Select **System Center Virtual Machine Manager Connection**.
   - **Computer name:** Enter the name of a computer with the VMM Administrator console installed. This may be (but is not required to be) the VMM server.

- **User:** This is the Active Directory (AD) account of a user with administrator privileges in System Center Virtual Machine Manager.
- **Domain:** This is the AD domain where the System Center Virtual Machine Manager server resides.
- **Password:** This is the password for the AD user account.
- **Authentication Type:** Leave this as Default.
- **Port (Remote Only):** Leave this as the default of 5985.
- **Use SSL (Remote Only):** Leave this as the default of False.
- **Cache Session Timeout (Min.):** Leave this as the default of 10.
- **VMM Server:** This is the name of the VMM server in relation to the computer provided by the Computer name property. As an example, if the Computer name property is set to the VMM server, this value could be set to **localhost**.

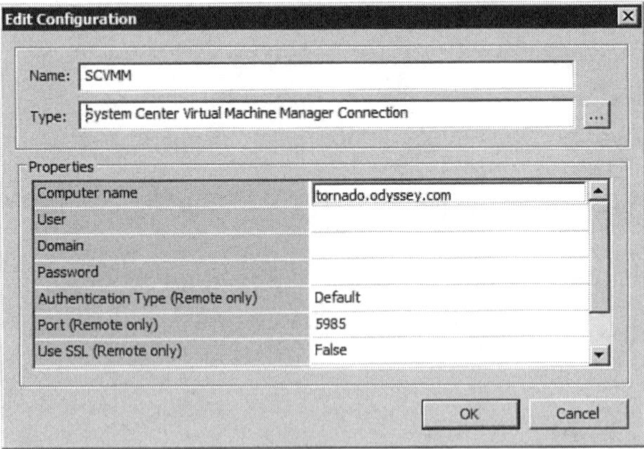

FIGURE 16.1 Configuring the VMM connection.

3. Click **OK** to create the connection.

   When complete, the newly created connection in the System Center Virtual Machine Manager dialog box should appear similar to Figure 16.2.

4. Click **Finish** to save the connection settings.

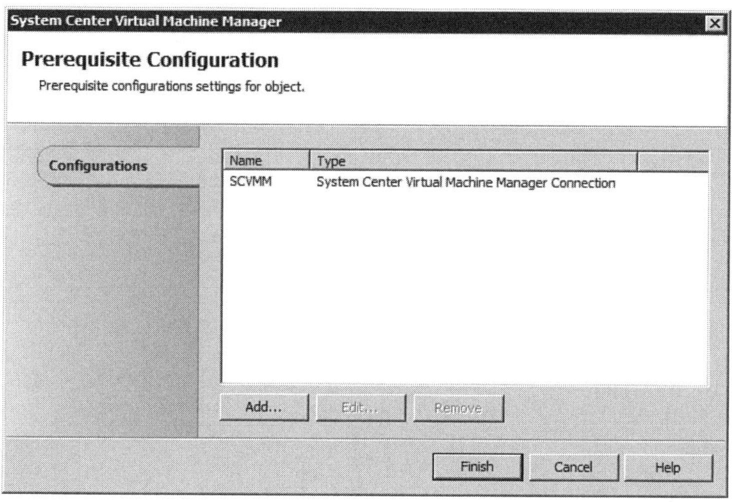

FIGURE 16.2 Configured available VMM connection(s).

Activities at a Glance

For reference, the RTM version of the VMM IP includes these activities:

- Create Checkpoint
- Create New Disk from VHD
- Create Network Adapter
- Create New Disk
- Create User Role
- Create VM from Template
- Create VM from VHD
- Create VM from VM
- Get Checkpoint
- Get Disk
- Get Network Adapter
- Get User Role
- Get User Role Quota
- Get VM
- Manage Checkpoint
- Move VM

- Remove VM
- Repair VM
- Resume VM
- Run VMM PowerShell Script
- Shut Down VM
- Start VM
- Stop VM
- Suspend VM
- Update Disk
- Update Network Adapter
- Update User Role Property
- Update User Role Quota
- Update VM

The following activities were added to the VMM IP in SP 1:

- Apply Pending Service Update
- Configure Service Deployment
- Deploy Service
- Get Cloud
- Get Service
- Get Service Configuration
- Get Service Template
- Get Tier
- Get User Role Quota
- Get VM Host
- Get VM Network
- Get VM Subnet
- Monitor VMM Job
- Scale Tier In
- Scale Tier Out
- Set Pending Service Update
- Stop Service

Activities in Depth

Although you can use many of the activities listed in "Activities at a Glance" on their own, their power lies in how you can combine them to automate even complex provisioning, migration, and maintenance tasks related to VMM. This section describes the activities in the VMM IP in detail to clarify their intended function, the other activities with which they are commonly used, and common use case scenarios, where appropriate.

The RTM version of the VMM IP consists of 23 activities, which are described here:

- **Create Checkpoint:** Saves the state of a virtual hard disk that is attached to a VM and all the disk content, including application data. This also saves the hardware configuration information for VMs on Hyper-V and VMware hosts.

  This activity is commonly used as a part of workflows involving software updates or upgrades to provide a known good point for rollback in case issues result from the update. More details on the properties and published data of this activity are available at http://technet.microsoft.com/en-us/library/hh830696.aspx.

- **Create New Disk from VHD:** Creates a new disk from VHD and then adds the disk to an existing VM.

  Any time you intend to add a new disk to a VM, this activity will likely be involved. For additional information on this activity, see http://technet.microsoft.com/en-us/library/hh830714.aspx.

- **Create Network Adapter:** Creates a new network adapter and attaches it to a specific VM.

  This activity is often used in runbooks involving the **Create VM from VM** and **Get Network Adapter** activities to facilitate creating a network adapter in the new VM that mirrors settings found in an existing VM. Additional information about the **Create Network Adapter** activity is available at http://technet.microsoft.com/en-us/library/hh830693.aspx.

- **Create New Disk:** Creates a new disk and adds it to a VM. Properties of this activity enable you to control disk size, filename, disk type (SCSI or IDE, Boot or System volume), and the VM ID to which the disk will be attached. Additional details about this activity are available at http://technet.microsoft.com/en-us/library/hh830735.aspx.

- **Create User Role:** This activity creates a user role within a designated cloud. For detailed information on the **Create User Role** activity, see http://technet.microsoft.com/en-us/library/hh830710.aspx.

- **Create VM from Template:** Creates a new VM from an existing VM template in VMM. In addition to the default activity properties (Host, Path, VM Name, Source Template Name), this activity includes nearly 30 optional properties corresponding to template properties in VMM, such as hardware and software profile, virtual network settings, answer file, and administrator password.

The **Create VM from Template** activity makes easy work of deploying a VM and configuring basic operating system (OS) properties so that it is ready for software deployment. More information on the properties and published data of this activity is available at http://technet.microsoft.com/en-us/library/hh830737.aspx.

- **Create VM from VHD:** Creates a new VM from an existing VHD in the VMM library.

  Similar to the **Create VM from Template** activity, **Create VM from VHD** includes several optional properties for configuring VM hardware, network, and startup settings. For more information on this activity, refer to http://technet.microsoft.com/en-us/library/hh830698.aspx.

- **Create VM from VM:** Creates a virtual machine from an existing virtual machine. This activity essentially creates a clone from the source VM.

  Take into consideration that, when using **Create VM from VM,** the source VM must be stopped before initiating the cloning operation. You will see the **Create VM from VM** activity preceded by a **Stop VM** or **Shut Down VM** activity to power down the source VM if it is not already stopped. Additional detail about **Create VM from VM** is available at http://technet.microsoft.com/en-us/library/hh830719.aspx.

- **Get Checkpoint:** Retrieves an existing checkpoint associated to a VM to take action.

  This activity is typically used as part of a maintenance or recovery sequence to retrieve a specific checkpoint so that it can then be applied or deleted. It is typically placed before the **Manage Checkpoint** activity in a runbook. Additional information about this activity is available at http://technet.microsoft.com/en-us/library/hh830709.aspx.

- **Get Disk:** Retrieves the properties of a VHD in the VMM library or existing VM. More details on the properties and published data of this activity are available at http://technet.microsoft.com/en-us/library/hh830717.aspx.

- **Get Network Adapter:** Retrieves network adapters and adapter properties from an existing virtual machine.

  The **Get Network Adapter** activity is often used in VM provisioning runbooks (using **Create VM from VM**) to retrieve the settings of a network adapter on an existing VM so that the settings can be matched on the newly provisioned VM. More information on this activity is at http://technet.microsoft.com/en-us/library/hh830725.aspx.

- **Get User Role:** Returns data on all the user roles within the VMM server. A detailed description of the **Get User Role** activity is available at http://technet.microsoft.com/en-us/library/hh830734.aspx.

- **Get VM:** Attempts to retrieve one or more VMs that match the values provided in the available filters. This includes a lengthy list of VM properties available accessible in VMM.

You do not want to create virtual machines with duplicate names; this activity is useful to verify that a virtual machine with a specific name does not already exist, making this activity a necessary element of any VM provisioning runbook. Additional information about **Get VM** is available at http://technet.microsoft.com/en-us/library/gg440691.aspx.

- **Manage Checkpoint:** Either applies (restores) or removes an existing checkpoint.

  You can use this activity in runbooks that involve update management or software deployment to roll back a VM to a previous state when update or deployment activities fail. It is typically placed after the **Get Checkpoint** activity. Additional details about this activity are available at http://technet.microsoft.com/en-us/library/hh830711.aspx.

- **Move VM:** Moves the selected VM from one network location to another. More information on the properties and published data of this activity are available at http://technet.microsoft.com/en-us/library/hh830701.aspx.

- **Remove User Role:** Deletes a user role from the VMM server. Detailed information about this activity is available at http://technet.microsoft.com/en-us/library/hh830715.aspx.

- **Remove VM:** Automating the deprovisioning process is often desirable, whether you want to remove and redeploy a problematic web server or to retire a VM that is no longer needed.

  Removing a VM requires first stopping the VM, which can be accomplished with the **Stop VM** or **Shut Down VM** activities. For additional information on this activity, see http://technet.microsoft.com/en-us/library/hh830732.aspx.

- **Repair VM:** Runs a retry, undo, or dismiss action on a VM that is not functioning correctly. More detail on **Repair VM** is available at http://technet.microsoft.com/en-us/library/hh830729.aspx.

- **Resume VM:** Starts a VM that is currently in the paused state. Additional information about this activity and its properties is available at http://technet.microsoft.com/en-us/library/hh830718.aspx.

- **Run VMM PowerShell Script:** Calls any PowerShell script, including VMM cmdlets. For detailed information on the **Run VMM PowerShell Script** activity, see http://technet.microsoft.com/en-us/library/hh830716.aspx.

- **Shut Down VM:** Shuts down a stopped VM. This activity takes the VM offline, which is required before VM cloning or removal. More details on the properties and published data of this activity are available at http://technet.microsoft.com/en-us/library/hh830724.aspx.

- **Start VM:** Starts a VM that has been paused, shut down, or stopped. More information on this activity is available at http://technet.microsoft.com/en-us/library/hh830742.aspx.

- **Stop VM:** Stops a VM that is in a paused or running state. More information about **Stop VM** is available at http://technet.microsoft.com/en-us/library/hh830687.aspx.
- **Suspend VM:** Pauses a virtual machine that is currently running. You can resume, stop, or start a virtual machine in a paused state. More details on the properties and published data of this activity are available at http://technet.microsoft.com/en-us/library/hh830705.aspx.
- **Update Disk:** Increases the size of an existing VHD or updates disk properties, such as bus or bus type.

  This activity can be useful in incident remediation runbooks to increase the size of virtual disks that are running out of space when Operations Manager raises an alert. See http://technet.microsoft.com/en-us/library/hh830731.aspx for additional information on the **Update Disk** activity.
- **Update Network Adapter:** Makes changes to an existing network adapter.

  This activity is often used after **Get Network Adapter** to configure adapter settings on a new VM to match those of the existing VM. Additional information about this activity and its properties is available at http://technet.microsoft.com/en-us/library/hh830740.aspx.
- **Update User Role Property:** Updates the user-specified role property (such as Actions Permitted or Member Names). More details on the properties and published data of this activity is at http://technet.microsoft.com/en-us/library/hh830708.aspx.
- **Update User Role Quota:** Updates the quotas for a certain user role and cloud. See http://technet.microsoft.com/en-us/library/hh830691.aspx for additional information on **Update User Role Quota**.
- **Update VM:** Changes a variety of properties of an existing VM, such as Performance Resource Optimization (PRO) settings, installs Virtualization Guest Services, or changes VM quota points used in self-service quota calculations.

  This activity can be used after initial VM provisioning to update VM settings specific to its intended service role. More details on the properties and published data of this activity are available at http://technet.microsoft.com/en-us/library/hh830697.aspx.

The SP 1 version of the VMM integration pack incorporates 17 additional activities, described here:

- **Apply Pending Service Update:** Applies the pending service update to a specified service. More details on the properties and published data of this activity are available at http://technet.microsoft.com/en-us/library/jj614552.aspx.
- **Configure Service Deployment:** Configures a VMM service for deployment. Additional information about this activity and its properties is available at http://technet.microsoft.com/en-us/library/jj656639.aspx.

- **Deploy Service:** Creates a service using a specified service template. See http://technet.microsoft.com/en-us/library/jj614533.aspx for additional information on this activity.
- **Get Cloud:** Returns all clouds on the VMM server that meet the filtering criteria. More details on the properties and published data of this activity are available at http://technet.microsoft.com/en-us/library/jj656642.aspx.
- **Get Service:** Returns data on all the services within the VMM server. For more information on the **Get Service** activity, see http://technet.microsoft.com/en-us/library/jj614556.aspx.
- **Get Service Configuration:** Returns all service configurations on the VMM server that meet the filtering criteria. See http://technet.microsoft.com/en-us/library/jj656641.aspx for detailed information on the **Get Service Configuration** activity.
- **Get Service Template:** Returns a list of all service templates. More details on the properties and published data of this activity are available at http://technet.microsoft.com/en-us/library/jj614550.aspx.
- **Get Tier:** Returns data on all tiers within the VMM server. For more information on the **Get Tier** activity, see http://technet.microsoft.com/en-us/library/jj614577.aspx.
- **Get User Role Quota:** Returns information about all user role quotas in a VMM server. See http://technet.microsoft.com/en-us/library/jj614534.aspx for details on the **Get User Role Quota** activity.
- **Get VM Host:** Returns all virtualization hosts on the VMM server that meets the filter criteria. More details on the properties and published data of this activity are available at http://technet.microsoft.com/en-us/library/jj656637.aspx.
- **Get VM Network:** Returns all virtual networks on the VMM server that meet the filtering criteria. For more information on **Get VM Network** and its properties, see http://technet.microsoft.com/en-us/library/jj656640.aspx.
- **Get VM Subnet:** Returns all virtual subnets on the VMM server that meet the filtering criteria. For more information on this activity, see http://technet.microsoft.com/en-us/library/jj656638.aspx.
- **Monitor VMM Job:** Monitors a VMM job. More details on the properties and published data of this activity are available at http://technet.microsoft.com/en-us/library/jj614526.aspx.
- **Scale Tier In:** Removes one virtual machine instance from a specified service tier. See http://technet.microsoft.com/en-us/library/jj614571.aspx for details on the **Scale Tier In** activity.
- **Scale Tier Out:** Adds one virtual machine instance to a specified service tier. More details on the properties and published data of this activity are available at http://technet.microsoft.com/en-us/library/jj614557.aspx.

- **Set Pending Service Update:** Sets a specific service template as the pending service update. More details on the properties and published data of this activity are available at http://technet.microsoft.com/en-us/library/jj614525.aspx.
- **Stop Service:** Stops a VMM service. For more information on this activity, see http://technet.microsoft.com/en-us/library/jj614568.aspx.

Advanced Deployment Capabilities in VMM 2012

As with orchestration and runbook concepts, let's take a quick look at the fundamentals of some of the advanced virtualization deployment capabilities in VMM. Specifically, this discussion moves beyond VM templates to a new template model in the latest release of VMM, called a *service template*.

WHY A SECTION ON VMM 2012 DEPLOYMENT IS IN AN ORCHESTRATOR BOOK

With all the new deployment capabilities in VMM 2012, you will derive much less value from this chapter if you do not understand the basics of this new functionality. With that in mind, this section was written to bring you up to speed on the new VMM functionality that factors into the VMM 2012 IP. If you are not familiar with service templates in VMM 2012 and how they work, the authors recommend that you read this section before proceeding.

VM templates offer some great benefits. The most important is the capability to deploy multiple VMs with consistent configurations. At the same time, VM templates have some limitations, including these:

- You can deploy only a single virtual machine at a time. After deployment, the VMs do not contain a reference back to the virtual machine template from which they were deployed.
- No mechanism exists for tracking the configuration of a deployed VM against the template from which it was deployed.
- You cannot update a VM template and then easily apply those changes against deployed VMs.

To address these shortcomings, Microsoft added a new template type in System Center 2012 Virtual Machine Manager, called a service template, as well as a number of new profile types. A service template can contain definitions for one or more virtual machines, including multiple machine tiers. VMs within a service template can be of different types—an example is a multitier web application. A service template can define the front-end web tier, the middle-tier business logic server, and the back-end database tier. Each tier can define different configurations—hardware configuration, operating system (OS) configuration, and application configuration.

A service template is a source for service deployment and a configuration baseline for deployed services. Deployed instances of services maintain a reference back to the service template from which they were deployed, enabling a basis for comparing current settings to those of the original template from which the VMs were deployed. With the many new application and networking features in VMM and Hyper-V, this can be handy when you want to check VMs for any drift from the expected configuration.

This also opens up the capability to update a deployed service by updating the service template from which it originated and then applying those changes to the deployed service instances, often without affecting application availability.

You can configure machine tiers as scale-out tiers where appropriate, which enables dynamically deploying additional VMs in the tier, up to your specified maximum. Service templates also introduce application deployment; current support is for three "first class" application deployment technologies:

- **WebDeploy:** For IIS applications
- **Server App-V:** For virtualized server applications
- **SQL DAC:** Abstract data tier in SQL Server 2008 R2 or SQL Server 2012

TIP: DEFINITION OF A "FIRST CLASS" APPLICATION

In describing application deployment technologies, *first class* refers to the fact that the metadata for deployment of these technologies is fully understood—that is, configurations of these technologies can be customized.

For automated actions that cannot be completed with service template settings, VMM service templates support *generic command execution* (GCE). GCEs can be written in PowerShell, VBScript, JScript, or at the command line (such as MSI). You can configure a service template to runs GCEs at four points in service deployment: before the first application installation, after the last application installation, and before and after each application.

For application settings that cannot be controlled through any UI setting, service templates allow for execution of scripts (PowerShell, VB, batch, or SQL) before and after significant deployment steps within the service template, such as deployment of a virtual machine or an application. These CGE scripts are defined in the service template and executed as part of the service deployment.

For additional reading on the advanced capabilities of service templates in VMM, see the topics under "Creating Profiles and Templates in VMM" at http://technet.microsoft.com/en-us/library/hh368987.aspx.

Figure 16.3 depicts a running service instance encompassing an n-tier application containing web, application, and database servers with WebDeploy and Server App-V applications, and a SQL data tier deployed entirely from a service template in VMM 2012. Notice that each logical component (service, machine tier, VM, and application) has unique icons so the object type is easy to identify.

REAL WORLD: VM DEPLOYMENT IN HYPER-V AND SYSTEM CENTER 2012

The Microsoft best practice for VM deployment (to Hyper-V or any hypervisor supported by System Center 2012) is to wrap all virtual machine templates in service templates, whether these will be single virtual machines or multitier, multivirtual machines, and then deploy virtual machines from the service template. This allows them to take advantage of all service template features in any deployed virtual machine. Virtual machines deployed from standalone virtual machine templates *cannot* be retrofitted to service templates.

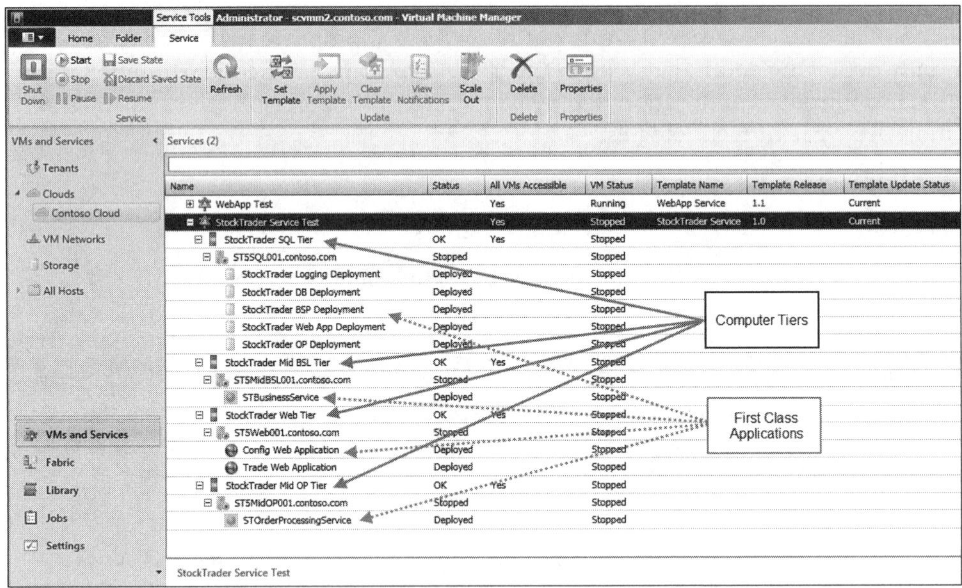

FIGURE 16.3 Service instance deployed using a VMM service template.

Configuring Service Templates

Service templates are authored in the new Service Designer within VMM. Within the designer, the virtual machines are defined with settings such as tiers, applications, OS settings, networking requirements, and load balancers, which today include BigIP F5, NetScaler, and Windows Server NLB. Service templates are not fire-and-forget objects; they are always linked with the deployed service, and the template can be used to update deployed services.

Typically, when you are creating a service template, deployment-specific information such as hosts and load balancers is not available—you just know that you need a host for the VM or a load balancer for the service. Although a full discussion is outside the scope of this book, it is worth noting that service templates in VMM 2012 SP 1 can be configured to deploy the service instance to not only Hyper-V on Windows Server 2012, but also many of the most recent versions of VMware, including vSphere 5.0 and 5.1.

The VMM Service Designer

The Service Designer presents a simple drag-and-drop interface. When a service is first created, the author selects a basic framework (how many tiers, whether a load balancer is required, and so on) for the service. The template is then filled in using objects from the library palette:

- ▶ The ribbon at the top of the designer provides the list of actions that can be performed in the designer.
- ▶ In the Designer Canvas, you are looking at the service template for a StockTrader service that has four tiers—web tier, business logic middle tiers, and SQL tier. All the tiers are connected to a logical network called Redmond.
- ▶ The Details pane at the bottom provides the property settings for the selected object in the canvas (see Figure 16.4).

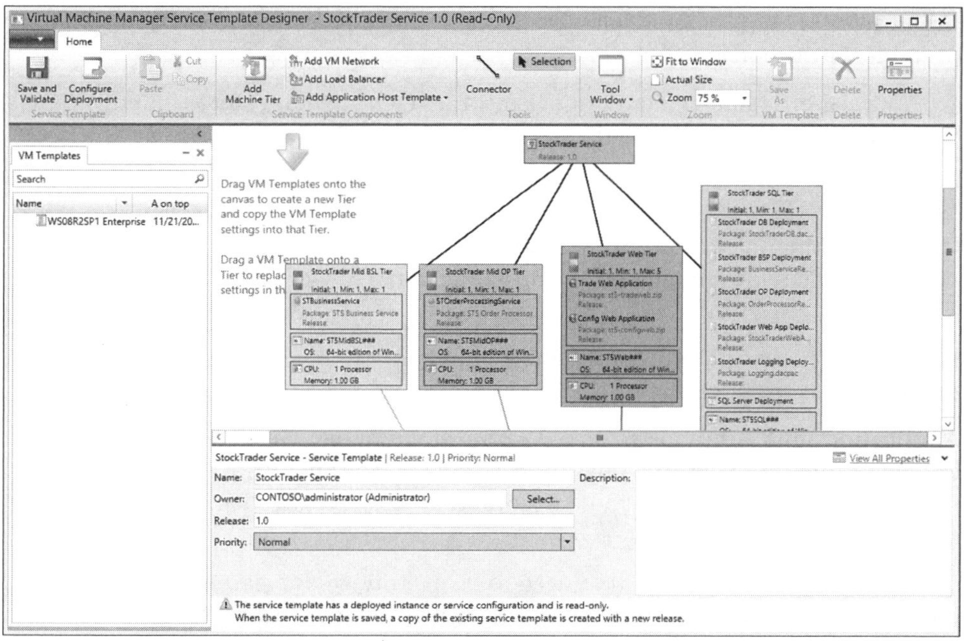

FIGURE 16.4 VMM 2012 Service Designer interface.

Service Template Components

The VMM 2012 service template provides a new way to model a service. Service templates contain the definitions for virtual machines, their connectivity, and application definitions; this is the starting point for a virtual machine or a service. Service templates include the following components:

- **Service template:** The service template consists of one or more computer tiers. You can configure additional settings, such as deployment order and servicing order (if the template contains multiple computer tiers), to control the order of operations during deployment and VM servicing after deployment.
- **Computer tier:** A computer tier (also called a machine tier) consists of exactly one virtual machine template. One or more computer tiers can be used. Computer tiers can also be configured with minimum, maximum, and default scale-out settings. These determine the minimum, maximum, and default number of VMs hosted in the tier for use in deployment and capacity-related scale-out and scale-in operations.
- **VM templates:** These contain a hardware profile, guest OS profile, and reference to a VHD in the library.
  - In the guest OS profile, you can define what roles/features need to be installed.
  - Virtual machine templates have one application profile, which, in turn, has one or more application deployments—WebDeploy, SQL DAC, or Server App-V packages. Application deployments always have references to the application bits in the library.
  - Virtual machine templates can also contain a SQL profile, for installing a SQL server instance in a VHD that contains a Sysprep instance of SQL 2008 R2 or SQL Server 2012. This consists of one or more SQL deployments that can have SQL scripts and library resources for the SQL scripts.
- **Generic command executions:** You can have your custom EXEs run during application deployment. Examples might be installing an MSI package or enabling firewall rules.
- **Load balancer templates:** Load balancer templates can be set up for each computer tier that needs to be scaled out.
- **Application host template:** In an enterprise environment, SQL databases typically are deployed to existing physical SQL servers. To support this scenario, service templates can contain one or more host profiles for deploying SQL DAC packages to existing physical servers.
- **Global settings:** Any settings that need to be overridden as a part of service deployment are available at the Service template level as Service settings.

Additional Service Template Properties

For services that include multiple machine tiers, you should configure three additional and very important settings: deployment order, servicing order, and upgrade domains. Each setting is configured in the settings of each machine tier within the service template. The following sections discuss these settings.

Deployment Order

Deployment order determines the order in which machine tiers are deployed during service deployment. For example, if the database must be running to install the front-end application components, you would first configure the data tier containing the SQL instances to be deployed. This setting should be configured in the properties of each machine tier. Figure 16.5 shows the deployment order setting in the Service Designer interface.

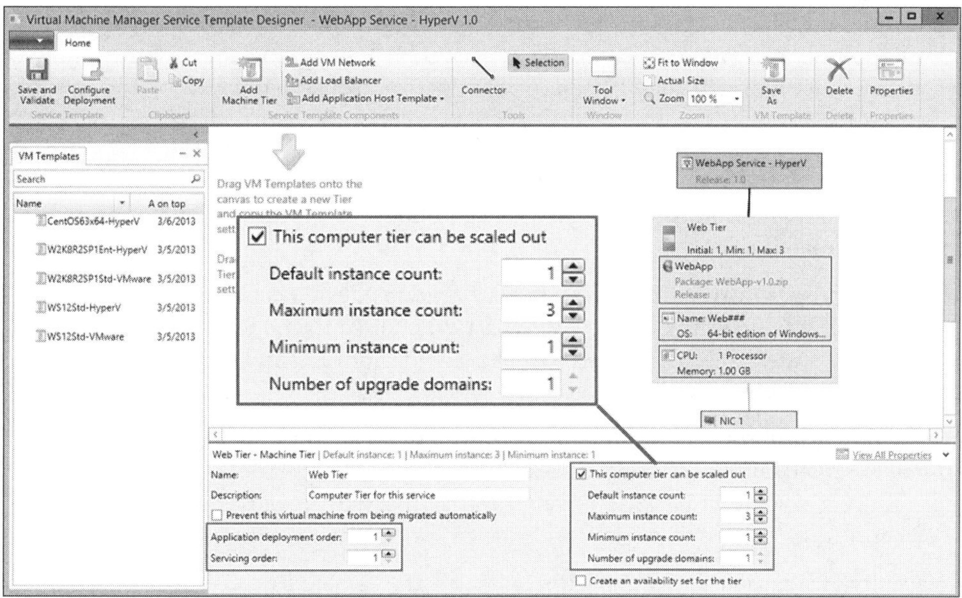

FIGURE 16.5 Machine tier settings within a VMM service template.

Servicing Order

Servicing order determines in-place servicing, as described in the upcoming "Updating Running Service Instances" section. This setting should be configured in the properties of each machine tier. Figure 16.5 shows the servicing order setting in the Service Designer interface.

Scale-Out

For machine tiers that contain a role in which multiple instances can provide high availability and/or greater capacity, you can configure the tier and enable it for scale-out. The minimum, maximum, and default number of virtual machines (instances) per tier can be configured on the computer tier template for that tier. A service is initially deployed using the default instance count for each tier. Figure 16.5 shows scale-out settings in the Service Designer interface.

Upgrade Domains

Upgrade domains specify how scale-out tiers in a service are upgraded. The number of scale-out instances in a service is divided by the number of defined upgrade domains; this sets the maximum number of virtual machines in that tier that can be upgraded at any point in time. This setting should be configured in the properties of each machine tier. Figure 16.5 shows the upgrade domain setting in the Service Designer interface.

As an example, a service instance has four web tier virtual machines running and has specified two upgrade domains. The number of tier instances is divided by the number of upgrade domains. Two of the web tier virtual machines will be taken out of the load balancer (if applicable), updated, and then added back to the load balancer. The other two web tier virtual machines will then be removed, updated, and added back.

Updating Running Service Instances

When a service template is updated, it can result in one of two types of updates: in-place updates or image-based updates.

- **In-place updates (also called *conventional updates*):** The OS image is not replaced. This type of update occurs with a configuration change to the template (more resources allocated to one or more virtual machines, for example) or when the application itself has been updated.
- **Image-based updates:** This is used with applications where state can be maintained in place (Server App-V) or saved and restored. This update model often results when the OS needs updating; because the applications were deployed using Server App-V, they can just be lifted and transferred to the new updated OS instance.

For in-place updating, the following occurs to enable the update to take place:

1. Select the tier to update based on the servicing order.
2. Select virtual machines based on upgrade domain.
3. Remove the selected virtual machines from the load balancer configuration.
4. Execute the pre-service GCE.
5. Apply application-level changes.
6. Execute the post-service GCE.
7. Repeat steps 1–6 for each updated application.
8. When updates are completed, virtual machines are added back to the load balancer configuration.

The process then repeats for this tier, if applicable, based on the upgrade domain setting and the number of instances in the tier. When a tier is completed, the process moves on to the next tier, if applicable

Image-based updating follows the same pattern as in-place updating, with one exception: If save-state or restore-state GCEs are in place, or if Server App-V is used, a data disk is added to the virtual machine. The data disk is attached on the fly, and the state of the application is saved to the data disk. The new OS VHD is swapped out for the old OS VHD, the new OS is customized, the applications are reinstalled, and the state of the application is restored.

Each runbook illustrated in this section uses two or more activities from the VMM IP.

For additional information on in-place servicing in VMM 2012, see the article on updating a service in VMM, at http://technet.microsoft.com/en-us/library/gg675089.aspx.

Use Case Scenarios

Using the information from the data bus is generally advantageous because the information is not a static value. This practice makes Orchestrator an incredibly flexible platform for consuming information as it exists at runtime, and using it as you would variables in a script.

The scenarios in the next sections are explained at length to demonstrate how to effectively tie together the activities to automate common processes related to virtualization management in VMM 2012 with Orchestrator:

- Enabling self-service (provisioning cloud capacity and role-based security)
- Virtual machine provisioning
- VM checkpoint and recovery
- VM lifecycle management
- Service provisioning
- Capacity management (scale-out and scale-in of machine tier)
- In-place servicing (of service deployed from service template)

Enabling Self-Service

Several factors differentiate the Microsoft private cloud from traditional virtualization in a private cloud:

- Shared across multiple customers (business units) within an organization
- Provides self-service provisioning and management
- Delivers elasticity (the capability to scale rapidly when demand necessitates)
- Provides metered/measured usage (for potential chargeback)

To support self-service, VMM 2012 provides role-based security with a self-service user profile. You can use this profile to configure custom self-service user roles to enable users to provision and manage their own virtual machines deployed to a private cloud infrastructure. The first steps in providing self-service through VMM 2012 follow:

1. Provision a cloud, which sets limits on resource consumption for one or more host groups.
2. Create a self-service user role and associate the role to the newly provisioned cloud.
3. Update the properties of the user role, including assigning role quota, assigning membership (one or more AD user groups), adding role actions (those activities users are allowed to perform), and assigning resources (VMs, service templates, and Run As accounts).

Figure 16.6 shows a sample runbook that executes these steps. The following list describes the activities in this runbook.

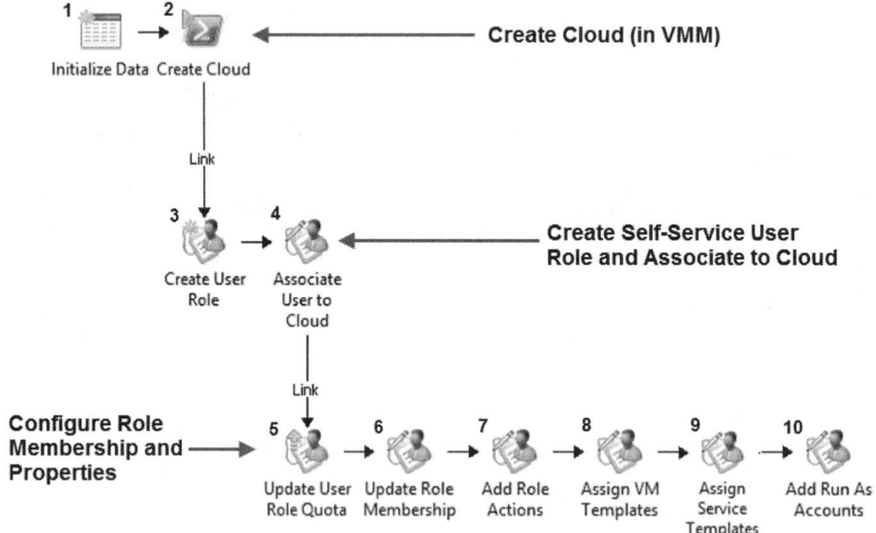

FIGURE 16.6 Provisioning and configuring a cloud and self-service user role in VMM.

1. **Initialize Data:** The runbook begins with an **Initialize Data** activity, to collect necessary input to provision and configure a cloud and self-service user role. Figure 16.7 shows the necessary inputs for provisioning; an explanation of their purpose follows:
   - **CostCenter:** The accounting code for chargeback
   - **ServicePackage:** An optional parameter intended to capture class-of-service (such as Gold, Silver, or Bronze)
   - **Status:** An optional parameter intended to indicate the production status of the cloud (such as Production, Stage, Test, or Development)

- **BusinessUnit:** The project or business unit to which the cloud will be assigned
- **Company:** Intended to capture the company name (in a parent/child company scenario)
- **RoleGroup:** Active Directory security group that will be granted membership in the new self-service user role

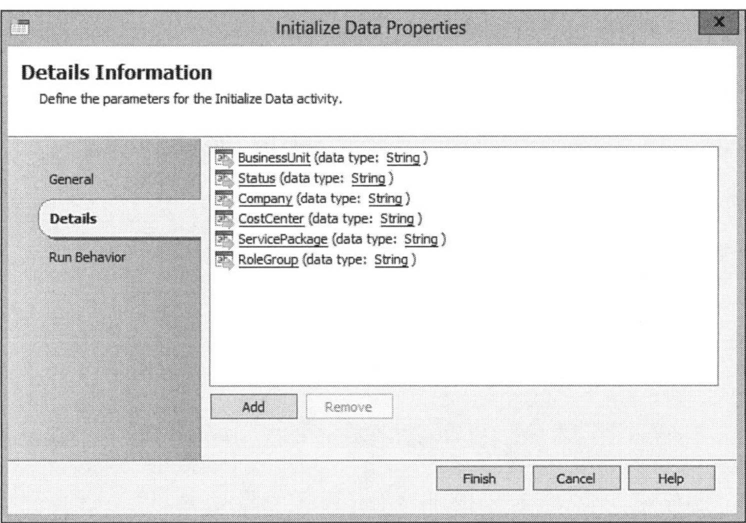

FIGURE 16.7 **Initialize Data** parameters.

2. **Create Cloud:** No native activity exists to create a cloud in VMM, so you must use a PowerShell script to provision new clouds. In this case, **Create Cloud** is a renamed **Run VMM PowerShell Script** activity. This activity accepts input from the **Initialize Data** activity to create a cloud with the appropriate name, based on the company name, business unit, status (Production, Stage, Test, or Development), or service package (such as class of service—for example, Bronze, Silver, or Gold).

    - **PowerShell Script:** Copy and paste the sample script into the field provided, inserting the appropriate published data as shown in Listing 16.1. This script is also available as value-added content for readers of this book; see Appendix C, "Available Online," for additional information.
    - **OutputVariable: $CloudCreated:** This variable contains the result of the script. A value of 1 means the cloud was created, and 0 means cloud creation failed.

    For additional information on creating and configuring a cloud in VMM, see the overview on creating a private cloud in VMM at http://technet.microsoft.com/en-us/library/gg610625.aspx.

LISTING 16.1 PowerShell Listing: Creating Cloud in VMM 2012

```
#Generate Job Group GUID
$JobGroupID = [Guid]::NewGuid().ToString()

#Define cloud capacity
Set-SCCloudCapacity -JobGroup "$JobGroupID" -UseCustomQuotaCountMaximum $true `
-UseMemoryMBMaximum $true -UseCPUCountMaximum $true `
-UseStorageGBMaximum $true -UseVMCountMaximum $true

#Retrieve Logical Network(s)
$resources = @()
$resources += Get-SCLogicalNetwork -Name "Contoso-LAN"

Set-SCCloud -JobGroup "$JobGroupID" -RunAsynchronously -AddCloudResource $resources

#Retrieve host group(s) and create cloud
$hostGroups = @()
$hostGroups += Get-SCVMHostGroup -Name "All Hosts"

#Create Cloud Name
$CloudName = "{Company from "Initialize Data"} {BusinessUnit from "Initialize Data"}
'
Cloud - {Status from "Initialize Data"} {ServicePackage from "Initialize Data"}"

New-SCCloud -JobGroup "$JobGroupID" -VMHostGroup $hostGroups `
-Name "$CloudName" -Description "" -RunAsynchronously

#Make sure cloud was created and publish results
$NewCloud = Get-SCCloud -Name "$CloudName"

if ($NewCloud -ne $null) {

    #Cloud created successfully
    $CloudCreated = 1;

    }

    else {

    #Cloud creation failed
    $CloudCreated = 0;

}
```

3. **Create User Role:** This has two properties that should be configured as explained here and shown in Figure 16.8:

    - **User Role Name:** {Company from "Initialize Data"} {BusinessUnit from "Initialize Data"} Self Service Users
    - **Profile Type:** Self Service User

4. **Associate User to Cloud:** This activity associates the user role created earlier in this runbook to the new cloud, as explained here and shown in Figure 16.9:

    - **User Role Name:** {User Role Name from "Create User Role"}
    - **Action Type:** Add
    - **Property:** Clouds
    - **Value:** {RoleGroup from "Create User Role"}, which will be an Active Directory security group in the format domain\group

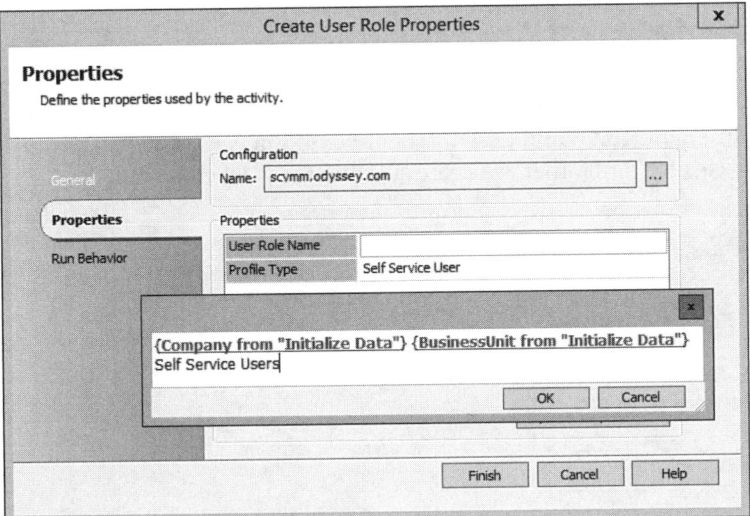

FIGURE 16.8 **Create User Role** properties.

16

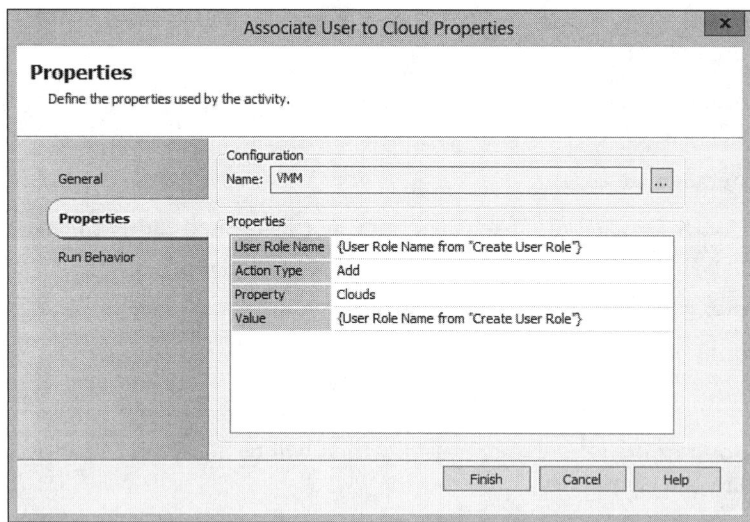

FIGURE 16.9 Properties of **Associate User to Cloud**.

5. **Update User Role Quota:** This activity updates the quota limits of the new user role. The sample shown in Figure 16.10 and described here configures the role for unlimited quotas, but you can set limits that are more suitable for your environment.

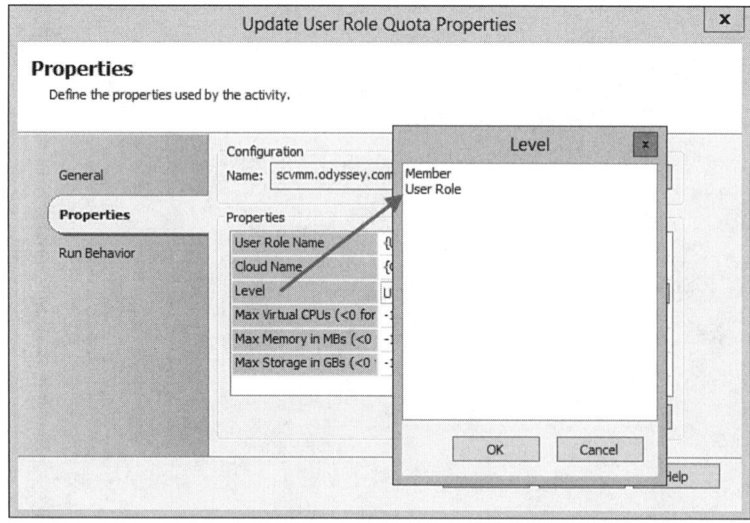

FIGURE 16.10 Level options in **Update User Role Quota** properties.

- **User Role Name:** {Company from "Initialize Data"} {BusinessUnit from "Initialize Data"} {Status from "Initialize Data"} Cloud.

- **Cloud Name:** {Company from "Initialize Data"} {BusinessUnit from "Initialize Data"} {Status from "Initialize Data"} Cloud.
- **Level:** {Company from "Initialize Data"} {BusinessUnit from "Initialize Data"} {Status from "Initialize Data"} Cloud (also shown in Figure 16.11).
- **Max Virtual CPUs (<0 for unlimited):** The number of virtual CPUs that can be assigned across all VMs in this cloud. This setting is pictured in Figure 16.11.
- **Max Memory in MBs (<0 for unlimited):** The total amount of memory that can be assigned across all VMs in this cloud.
- **Max Storage in GBs (<0 for unlimited):** The total amount of storage (in gigabytes) that can be assigned across all VMs in this cloud.

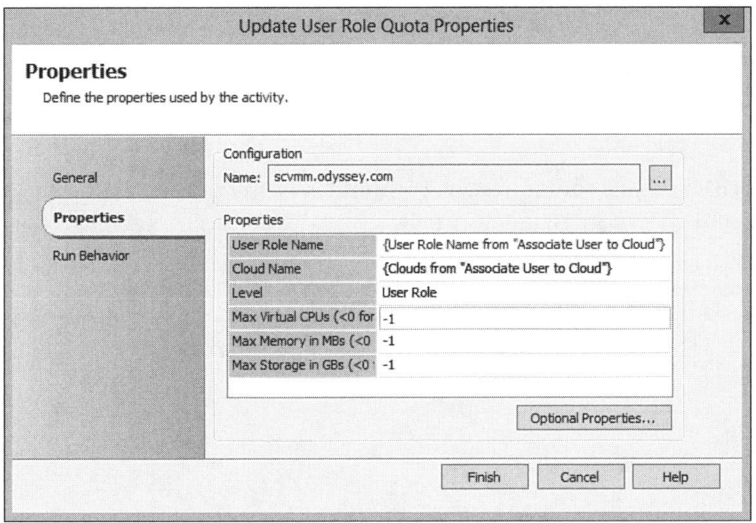

FIGURE 16.11 **Update User Role Quota** properties.

6. **Update Role Membership Properties:** This activity updates the membership of the VMMuser role—in this case, adding a group to the role as shown in Figure 16.12 and described here. Use a security group you have designated for self-service in this example.
   - **Value:** {User Role Name from "Update User Role Quota"}
   - **Action Type:** Add
   - **Property:** Members
   - **Value:** {RoleGroup from "Initialize Data"}

16

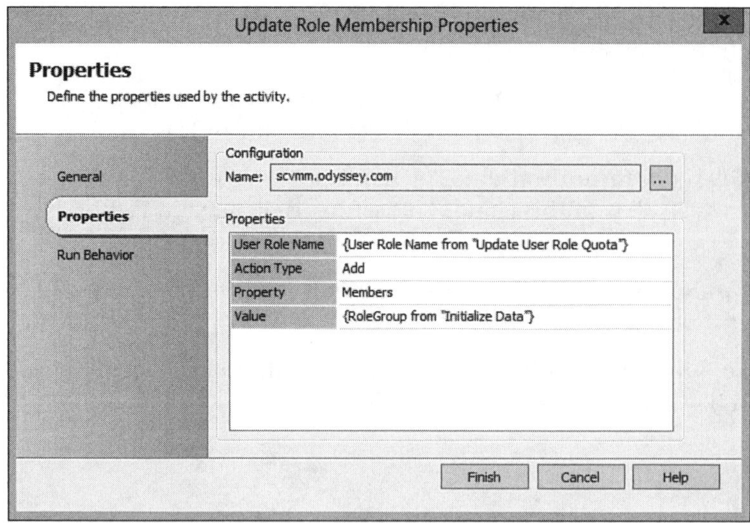

FIGURE 16.12 **Update Role Membership** properties.

7. **Add Role Actions:** This activity configures the capabilities of the self-service user role, described here and shown in Figure 16.13:

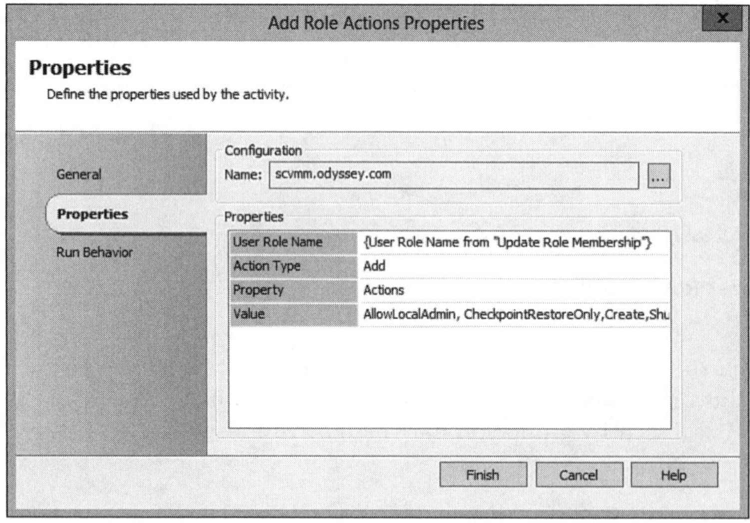

FIGURE 16.13 **Add Role Actions** properties.

- **Value:** {User Role Name from "Update Role Membership"}
- **Action Type:** Add
- **Property:** Actions
- **Value:** AllowLocalAdmin, CheckpointRestoreOnly, Create, Shutdown, Start, Stop (These values grant self-service users local admin rights, to restore [but not create] checkpoints, as well as to shut down, start, and stop VMs.)

For a complete list of actions, view the documentation for the `Set-SCUserRole` PowerShell cmdlet (in the VMM PowerShell module) at http://technet.microsoft.com/en-us/library/hh801617.aspx.

8. **Assign VM Templates:** This activity assigns VM templates to VMM user roles, as shown in Figure 16.14 and described here:
    - **User Role Name:** {User Role Name from "Update Role Membership"}
    - **Action Type:** Add
    - **Property:** VM Templates
    - **Value:** Windows 2008 R2 Template (or name of your VM template)

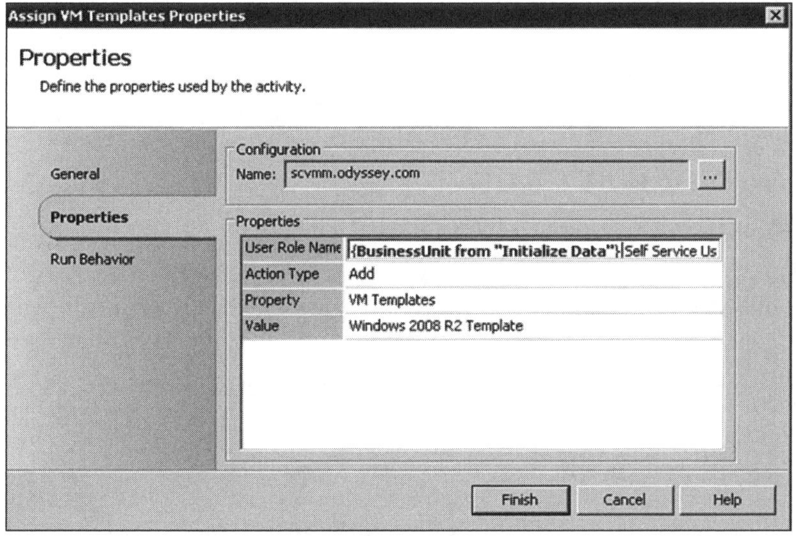

FIGURE 16.14 **Assign VM Templates** properties.

9. **Assign Service Templates:** The **Assign Service Templates** activity assigns service templates to VMM user roles, as shown in Figure 16.15 and described here:

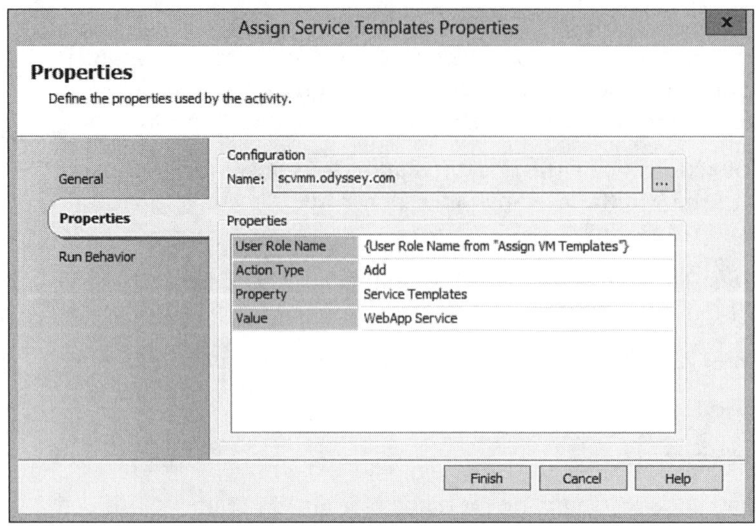

FIGURE 16.15 **Add Service Templates** properties.

- **User Role Name:** {User Role Name from "Assign VM Templates"}
- **Action Type:** Add
- **Property:** Service Templates
- **Value:** WebApp Service (or name of your service template)

10. **Add User Role Run As Accounts:** The **Add Run As Accounts** properties associates run as accounts in VMM to the newly created user role, as described here and shown in Figure 16.16:

    - **User Role Name:** {BusinessUnit from "Initialize Data"} Self Service Users
    - **Action Type:** Add
    - **Property:** Run As Accounts
    - **Value:** <comma-separated list of Run As Account display names> from the Settings -> Security -> Run As Accounts node in the VMM Admin console

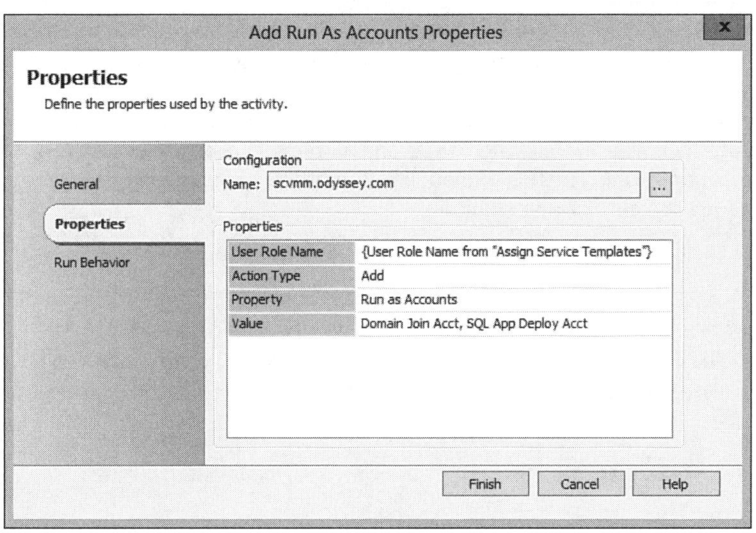

FIGURE 16.16 **Add Run As Account** properties.

Virtual Machine Provisioning

The Virtual Machine Provisioning runbook, in Figure 16.17, illustrates one way to provision a new VM from an existing VM template in VMM. You can provision new VMs in Orchestrator by using a VM template as a model, by using a VHD (using **Get VHD**), or even from an existing virtual machine (using **Create VM from VM**). The method used in this runbook is from an existing VM template.

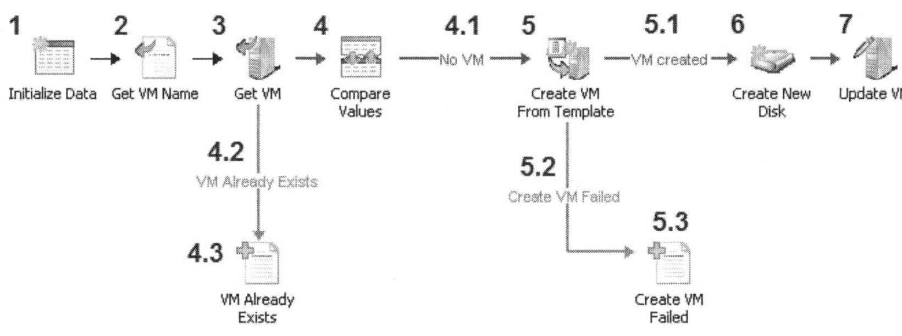

FIGURE 16.17 The Virtual Machine Provisioning runbook.

This runbook performs the following activities:

1. **Initialize Data:** This runbook begins with an **Initialize Data** activity, allowing the runbook to be initiated from outside Orchestrator or from other runbooks as part of a larger workflow.

NOTE: DEFINING A PROCESS FOR AUTOMATED VM PROVISIONING

Although a valid option for seeding the provisioning process with data is to use a text file, other methods of doing this might provide a greater degree of automation and documentation of the change process. As an example, using the VMM IP in conjunction with the Service Manager IP to automate VM provisioning based on incoming change requests (CR) is a common use case scenario. Chapter 19, "Runbook Automation in the Data Center and the Cloud," presents an example of this scenario.

2. **Get VM Name:** In this case, **Get VM Name** is a renamed **Read Line** activity from the Text File Management category. This activity retrieves the string from line 1 of the vmrequest.txt file, which is used as the VM name later in the runbook. To configure **Get VM Name**, double-click the activity and enter the following values on the Details tab:

   - **File:** c:\requests\vmrequest.txt
   - **Encoding:** ASCII
   - **Line Number:** 1

3. **Get VM:** The **Get VM** activity from the Virtual Machine Manager IP ensures that no attempt is made to provision a VM with the same name as an existing VM. The **Get VM Name** activity in Figure 16.18 is configured to query VMM for a VM with a name that matches the string retrieved from vmrequest.txt.

4. **Compare Values:** The **Compare Values** activity in this runbook compares the CPU Count of the VM retrieved by the **Get VM** activity in the previous step.

   If the **Get VM** activity in step 3 locates a VM with the same name as included in the vmrequest.txt file, the **Compare Values** activity detects a CPU count of greater than 0 and returns success, directing activity to the failure branch of the runbook; this logs an error to a text log, indicating that the VM already exists. If no VM exists, **Compare Values** returns a failure result, which then triggers the **Create VM from Template** activity.

REAL WORLD: SINGLE TASKS, MULTIPLE PATHS

You can also drop the **Compare Values** activity and instead configure link logic to compare the "Number of Objects" output of the **Get VM** activity. This is just another example of how you can achieve your automation goals in Orchestrator in multiple ways.

4.1. **Conditional Link** (No **VM**): Although the color of the link is green (since this is the success path of the runbook), the filter on this link is configured to register a match when the **Compare Values** activity reports failure. This is because you want the runbook to continue with the VM provisioning process only if a VM by this name does not already exist.

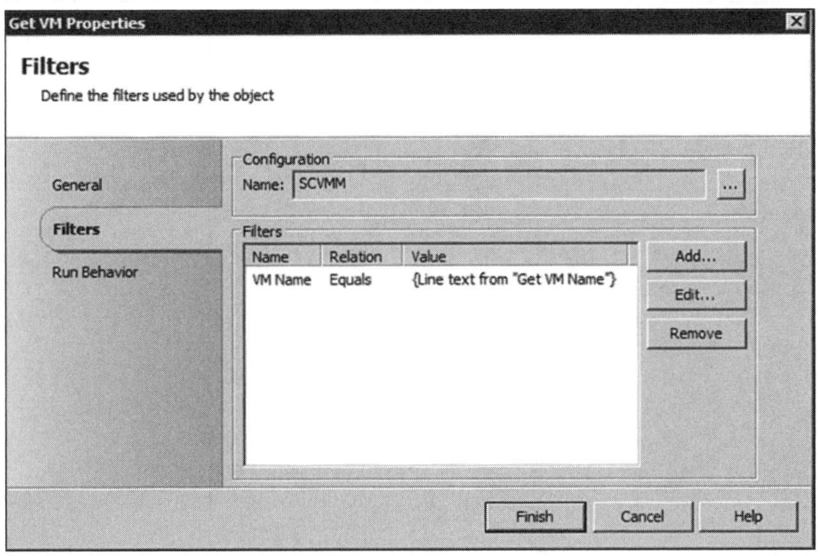

FIGURE 16.18 **Get VM** activity properties.

4.2. Conditional Link (VM Already Exists): Although the color of the link is red (because this is the failure path of the runbook), the filter on this link is configured to register a match when the **Get VM** activity reports success. This is because you do not want the runbook to continue with the VM provisioning process if a VM by this name already exists.

4.3. VM Already Exists: This **Append Line** activity writes an entry to the user-defined text error log (such as c:\logs\vmerror.txt) indicating that a VM by the name contained in vmrequest.txt already exists. The runbook then terminates.

5. Create VM from Template: The **Create VM from Template** activity creates a VM from a VM template specified in the properties of the activity. Double-click **Create VM from Template**; then on the Properties tab, configure the following values (see Figure 16.19).

- **Host Name: HOST1**
- **Path:** d:\VMs
- **VM Name:** {Line text from "Get VM Name"}
- **Source Template Name: W2K8R2_EE**

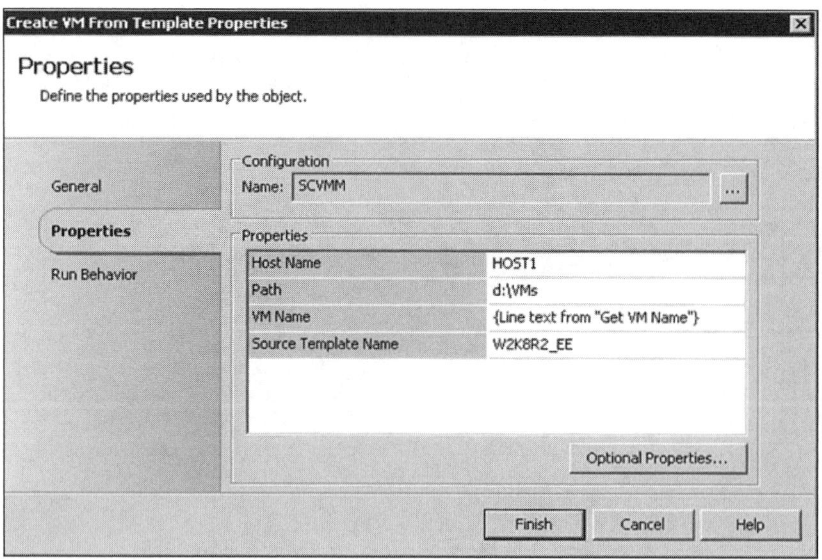

FIGURE 16.19 **Create VM from Template** properties.

5.1. Conditional Link (VM Created): This link connects the **Create VM from Template** and **Create New Disk** activities. If the **Create VM from Template** activity returns success, configuration of the new VM continues.

5.2. Conditional Link (Create VM Failed): This link connects the **Create VM from Template** and **Create VM Failed** activities. If the **Create VM from Template** activity returns failure, the logic on this link registers a match and triggers the next activity in this failure branch of the runbook.

5.3. Create VM Failed: This renamed **Append Line** activity logs an event to the c:\logs\vmerror.txt error log and writes an event indicating creation of the VM failed.

6. Create New Disk: The **Create New Disk** activity is used in this runbook to create an additional VHD and attach it to the new VM. Double-click the **Create New Disk** activity; on the Properties tab (shown in Figure 16.20), enter the following values:

- **File Name:** Auto
- **Size (GB): 5**
- **Logical Unit Number (LUN):** Auto
- **Bus:** Auto
- **VM ID:** {Get VM ID from "Create VM from Template"}
- **Bus Type:** SCSI
- **Disk Type:** Dynamic

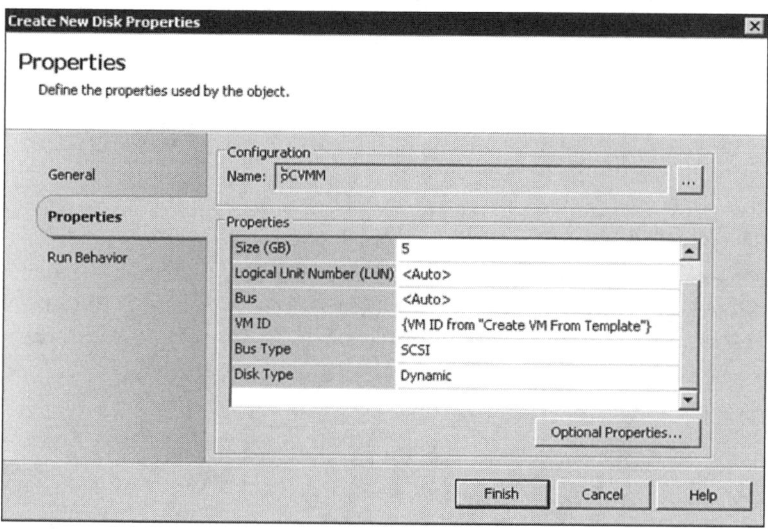

FIGURE 16.20 **Create New Disk** activity properties.

7. **Update VM:** The last activity in this branch of the runbook is the **Update VM** activity. Figure 16.21 displays the settings:

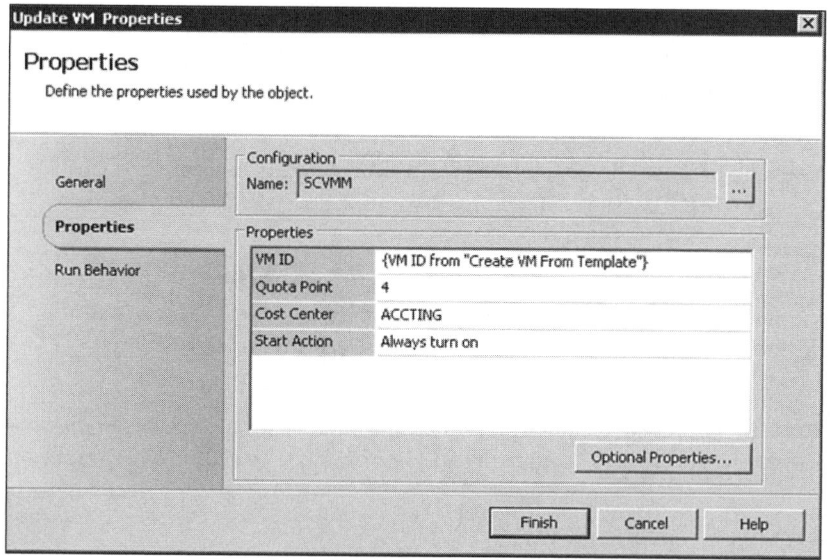

FIGURE 16.21 Define properties used by the activity.

- **VM ID:** {VM ID from "Create VM from Template"}
- **Quota Point: 4**
- **Cost Center: ACCTING**
- **Start Action:** Always turn on

VM Checkpoint and Recovery

In the workflow in Figure 16.22, Orchestrator creates a checkpoint for an existing virtual machine to provide a rollback point in case software updates cause a problem. If the Apply Updates runbook fails, the failure branch of the runbook restores the checkpoint to return the VM to its previously healthy state.

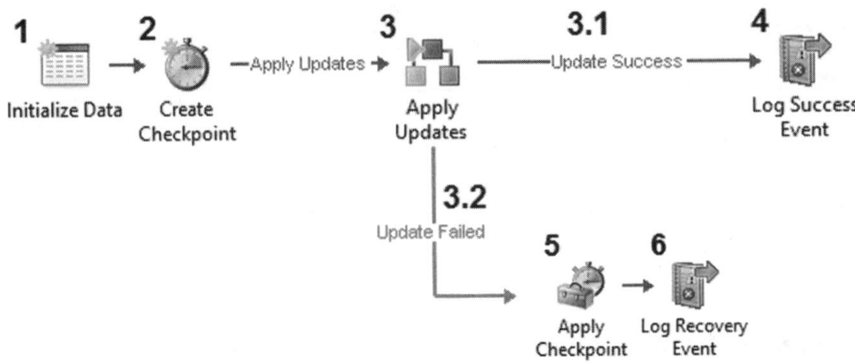

FIGURE 16.22 VM checkpoint and recovery.

If updates are applied successfully, the checkpoint should be deleted to eliminate the performance impact of the differencing disk created by a checkpoint. The steps of this runbook follow:

1. **Initialize Data:** This activity is configured with a single parameter called **VMID**; this is supplied as a parameter in a **Trigger Runbook** activity or other external call to trigger this runbook. The value supplied for the VMID parameter should be the VM ID of the VM to which updates will be applied.
2. **Create Checkpoint:** The **Create Checkpoint** activity creates a checkpoint (*snapshot* in Hyper-V) for the target VM, as configured in Figure 16.23 with the following values:
    - **VM ID:** {VMID from "Initialize Data"}
    - **Name:** {Activity Start Time from "Initialize Data"}

    This checkpoint can be used to return the VM to a known good configuration in case the application of updates results in an error condition.

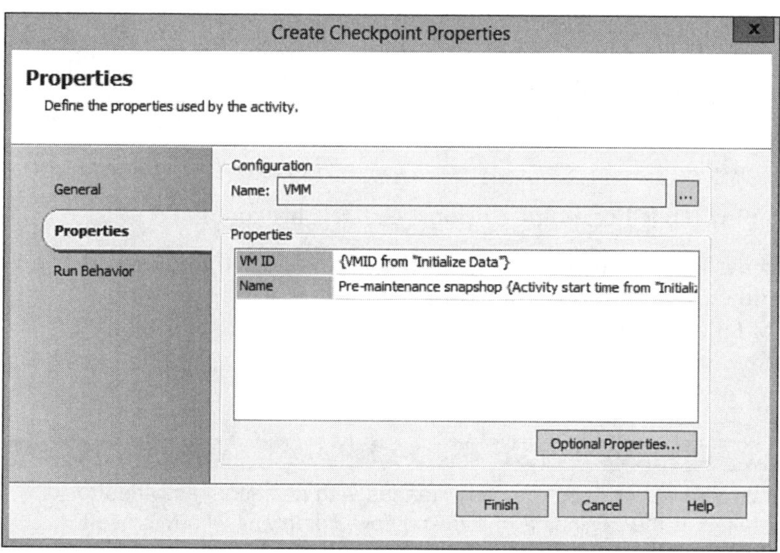

FIGURE 16.23 **Create Checkpoint** activity.

Conditional Link (Apply Updates): If the checkpoint is successful, the link triggers the next activity in the workflow. This link can be labeled ("Apply Updates," in this example), and the color can be changed to green. However, the default link filtering logic should remain at its default values.

3. **Apply Updates:** This renamed **Invoke Runbook** activity calls a separate update management workflow to apply the latest hotfixes to the targeted VM. The **Trigger Runbook** activity is configured to publish data from the child runbook indicating whether updates were applied to the VM successfully. For a refresher on how to configure data publishing between runbooks, refer to Chapter 7, "Runbook Basics."

3.1 **Conditional Link (Update Success):** If the **Invoke Runbook** activity returns published data from the Apply Updates child runbook indicating that updates were applied to the VM successfully, the runbook activity will continue down this branch of the runbook to log an event indicating a successful result.

3.2 **Conditional Link (Update Failed):** If the **Invoke Runbook** activity returns published data from the Apply Updates child runbook indicating that updates were not successfully applied to the VM, the runbook activity continues down this failure branch and attempts to return the VM to a known good state (see Figure 16.24).

4. **Log Success Event:** This renamed **Send Event Log Message** activity logs an informational event to the Windows application event log indicating that updates were successfully applied to the VM.

This runbook includes a failure branch to account for the possibility that the application of update fails or otherwise results in an error condition requiring rollback to the checkpoint created at the beginning of the runbook with **Create Checkpoint.**

5. **Apply Checkpoint:** After the checkpoint is retrieved, this renamed **Manage Checkpoint** activity is configured to apply the checkpoint to the VM, returning it to the known good state captured before the application of updates to the VM was attempted. As Figure 16.25 shows, the properties should be configured as listed here:

    - **Action:** Remove
    - **VM Checkpoint ID:** {Checkpoint ID from "Create Checkpoint"}

6. **Log Recovery Event:** This renamed **Send Event Log Message** activity logs a warning event to the Windows Application Event log indicating that the application of updates to the VM failed, along with the result of the attempt to roll back to the previous checkpoint.

REAL WORLD: CLEANING UP SNAPSHOTS

In the real world, this workflow would normally be extended with additional activities to remove the snapshot taken at the beginning of the workflow, complying with Microsoft best practices related to checkpoint management.

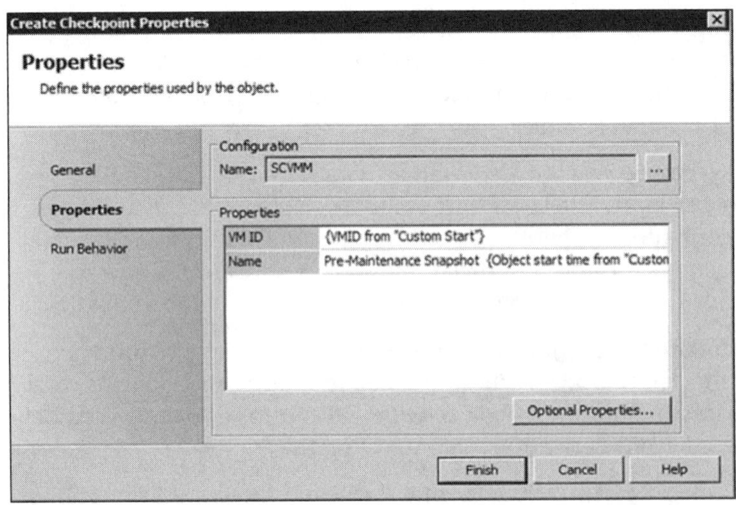

FIGURE 16.24 Update Failed link properties.

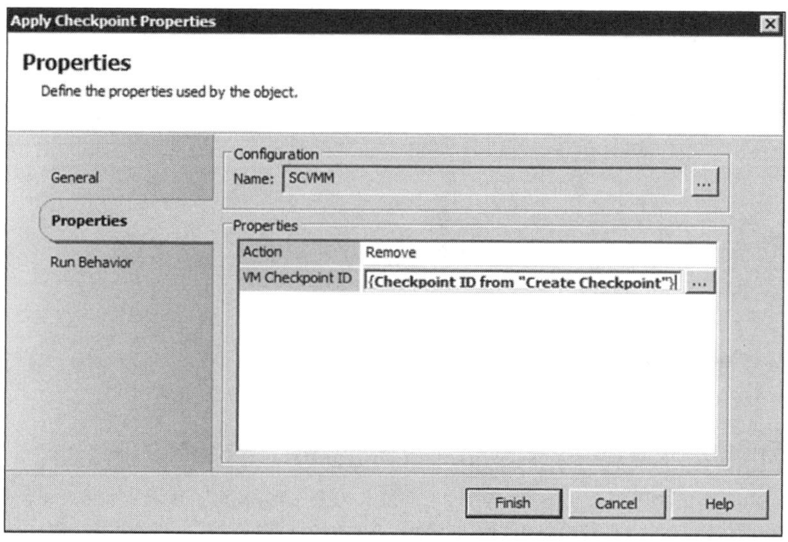

FIGURE 16.25 **Apply Checkpoint** properties.

VM Lifecycle Management

The rise of the Microsoft private cloud and highly automated and virtualized data centers introduces several scenarios to consider in VM lifecycle management. This chapter discusses two of the more common here:

- Removing unhealthy VMs (as part of a shoot-and-replace methodology)
- Retiring VMs (removing VMs beyond their "expiration date")

Removing Unhealthy VMs

In a private cloud infrastructure, instead of repairing or patching unhealthy VMs, you can deprovision them and use fully patched, healthy replacements. The sample runbook in Figure 16.26 attempts to perform a clean shutdown, remove the unhealthy VM, and then launch a provisioning workflow (similar to the earlier example in the "Virtual Machine Provisioning" section) to replace the unhealthy guest with a new VM.

If a clean shutdown of the VM is not possible, the failure branch of the runbook is invoked. It attempts to stop the VM (a dirty shutdown), remove it, and then launch the Replace VM runbook to replace the VM.

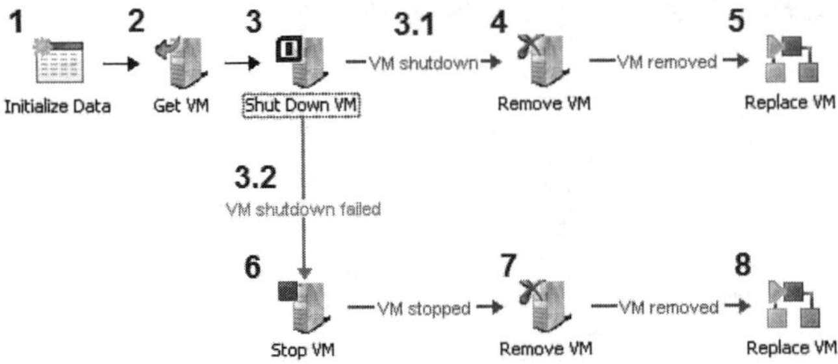

FIGURE 16.26 Replacing an unhealthy virtual machine.

TIP: MAKING YOUR RUNBOOKS AS SMALL AND EFFICIENT AS POSSIBLE

Technically, both the **Shut Down VM** and **Stop VM** activities in the runbook in this section could have been linked to the same **Remove VM** activity, making activities 7 and 8 unnecessary. They were used here for sake of simplicity for new Orchestrator users. After you create and test the runbook, you might want to attempt this alternate approach, linking **Stop VM** to activity 4 (**Remove VM**) and deleting activities 7 and 8, reducing the number of activities required in the runbook.

1. **Initialize Data:** This runbook begins with an **Initialize Data** activity, allowing the runbook to be initiated from outside Orchestrator or from other runbooks as part of a larger workflow. This custom start activity is configured with a single parameter called **VMName**, which is supplied when the runbook is started through a **Trigger Runbook** activity or another external call.

2. **Get VM:** The **Get VM** activity retrieves the VM properties of the VM, matching the name passed to the VMName parameter in **Initialize Data**. The **Get VM** activity should be configured as shown in Figure 16.27 and documented here as VM Name: {VMName from "Initialize Data"}.

3. **Shutdown VM:** This activity attempts to perform a clean shutdown of the VM specified in the VM ID retrieved by **Get VM ID**, as shown in Figure 16.28 and documented here as VM ID: {VM ID from "Get VM"}.

3.1 Conditional Link (Shutdown Successful): If **Shut Down VM** completes successfully, runbook activity continues down this branch.

3.2 Conditional Link (Clean Shutdown Failed): If **Shut Down VM** returns failure, runbook activity continues down this failure branch.

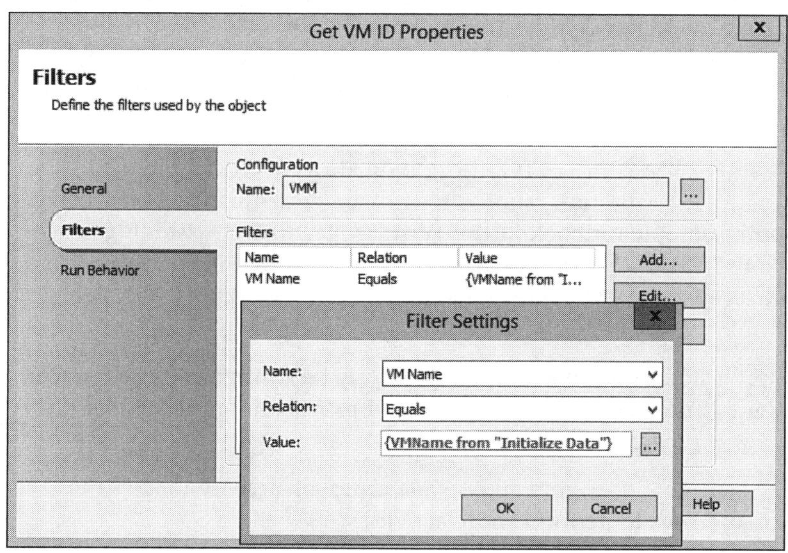

FIGURE 16.27 **Get VM** properties.

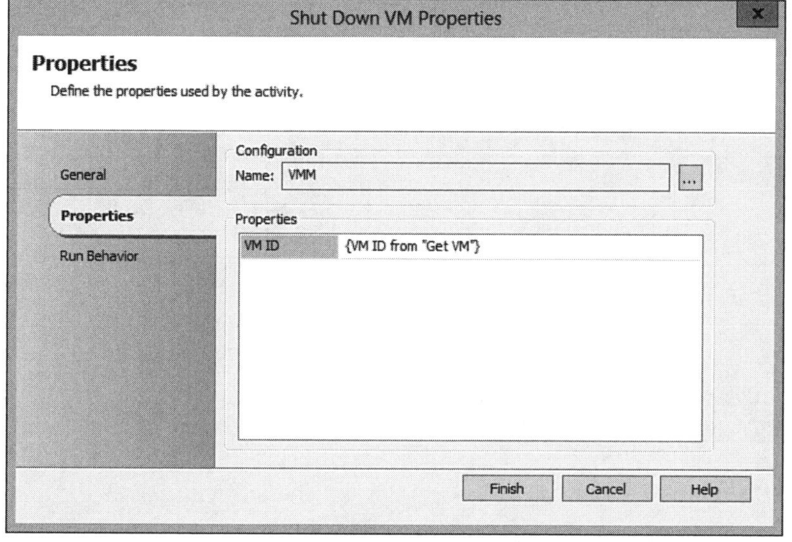

FIGURE 16.28 **Shut Down VM** properties.

4. **Remove VM:** When **Shut Down VM** returns success, the **Remove VM** activity attempts to remove the VM using the VM ID from the **Shut Down VM** activity, as shown in Figure 16.29 and documented here as VM ID: {VM ID from "Shut Down VM"}.

5. **Replace VM:** If **Remove VM** is successful, this renamed **Invoke Runbook** activity calls a VM provisioning workflow (similar to the one presented in the Virtual Machine Provisioning sample runbook in the "Virtual Machine Provisioning" section) to replace the failed VM. The runbook triggered begins with an **Initialize Data** activity that accepts the VM name as a parameter. The workflow ends when the **Invoke Runbook** activity is initiated.

   Because that VM provisioning runbook would generally be configured with its own error reporting, there is no reason to wait for the VM provisioning runbook result to duplicate error reporting here.

   If **Shut Down VM** (activity 3 in Figure 16.26) fails, runbook activity follows the failure branch and attempts to perform those activities.

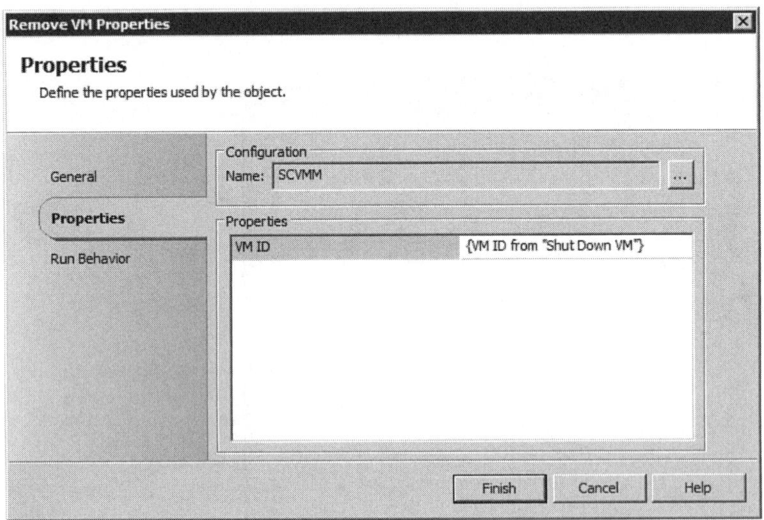

FIGURE 16.29 **Remove VM** properties.

6. **Stop VM:** Because the attempt to perform a clean shutdown of the unhealthy VM failed, the **Stop VM** activity simply stops the VM using the VM ID from the **Get VM ID** activity, as shown in Figure 16.30 and documented here as VM ID: {VM ID from "Get VM ID"}.

7. **Remove VM (2):** With the VM offline, the **Remove VM** activity is triggered to remove the unhealthy VM so that a new VM with the same name can be provisioned. The **Remove VM** activity expects a VM ID value, documented here as VM ID: {VM ID from "Stop VM"}.

8. **Replace VM (2)**: If **Remove VM** is successful, this renamed **Trigger Runbook** activity calls a VM provisioning workflow to replace the failed VM, just as the **Replace VM** activity would do in the success branch of the runbook.

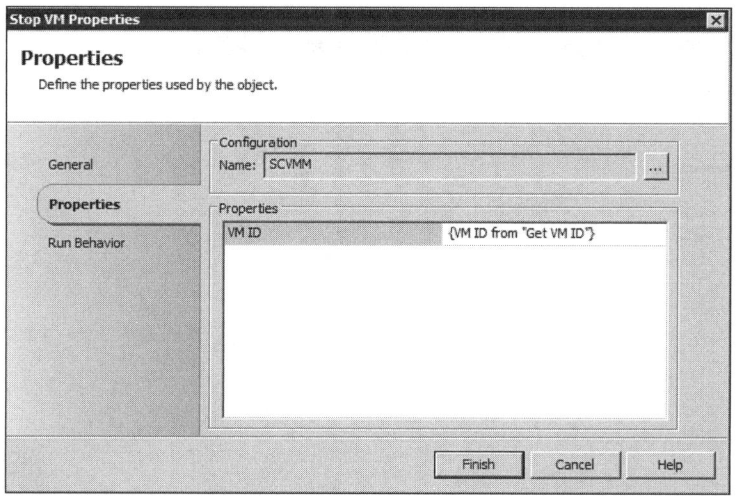

FIGURE 16.30 **Stop VM** properties.

REAL WORLD: ERROR HANDLING AND REPORTING IN ORCHESTRATOR RUNBOOKS

In a production-ready version of this runbook, this runbook would include branching and conditional links to capture and report error and failure conditions. For more information on how to build error reporting into your runbooks, see Chapter 8, "Advanced Runbook Automation."

Retiring VMs

In a self-service environment, such as that delivered as part of a private cloud solution, it is important to consider that everything has a finite lifespan. The only way to avoid the common issue of VM sprawl is to remember that everything provisioned has an end of life.

Fortunately, with VMM 2012, stamping an asset (virtual machine or service) with an expiration date is relatively easy. However, this does require some use of the VMM command shell to add a custom property, as this section demonstrates.

ABOUT CUSTOM PROPERTIES

The concept of custom properties is new to VMM 2012 and allows an administrator to add any name/value pair to a virtual machine, service, or other asset in the VMM console or via the VMM command shell. For example, you can add a custom property called **ExpirationDate** and add the date/time after which the asset should be removed from the VMM deployment.

Adding a custom property to an asset in VMM 2012 requires just several lines of PowerShell. For example, you can add custom properties such as ExpirationDate and RequestedBy to capture email contact information of the owner for future notification of expiration (see Figure 16.31).

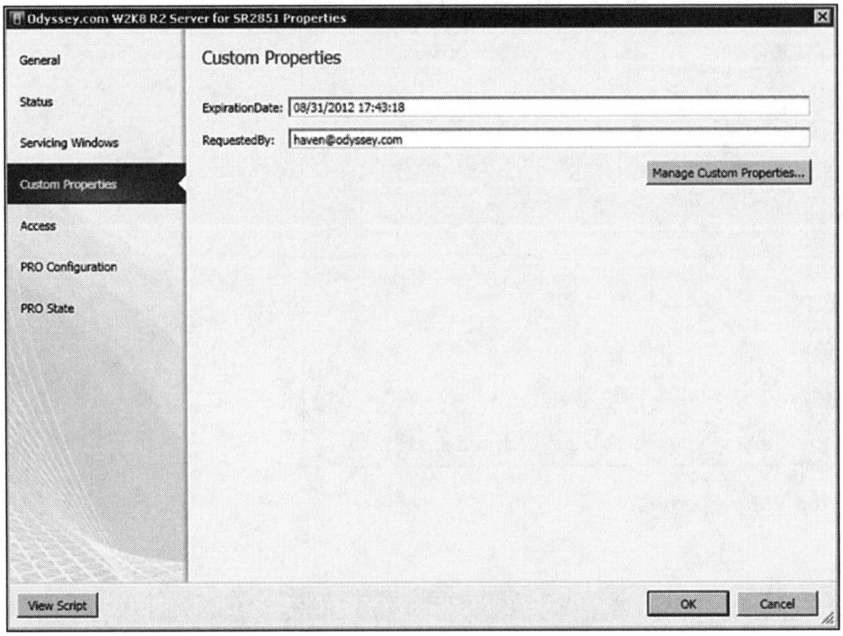

FIGURE 16.31 Custom properties for a VM.

Listing 16.2 shows the PowerShell script to use for adding these two custom properties only. This script is also available as online content for this book—see Appendix C for additional information.

LISTING 16.2 PowerShell Listing: Set Custom Properties on a VM

```
#----------------------------------------------------------------------
# Set Custom Properties on a VM
#----------------------------------------------------------------------

# Custom Property Values from Initialize Data
$RequestingUser = {RequestedBY from "Initialize Data"}
$VMName = {VMName from "Create VM from Template"}
$VMExpiration = {ExpirationInDays from "Initialize Data"}

#Retrieve the VM by name
$MyVM = Get-VM | where ($_.Name -eq $VMName)
```

```
#Set custom properties and property values on VM
$CustomPropRequestedBy = Get-SCCustomProperty -Name 'RequestedBy'
Set-SCCustomProperty -AddMember @("VM") `
-CustomProperty $CustomPropertyRequestedBy
Set-SCCustomPropertyValue -InputObject $MyVM
-CustomProperty $CustomPropRequestedBy -Value "$RequestingUser"

$CustomPropExpiry = Get-SCCustomProperty -Name "ExpirationData"
Set-SCCustomProperty -AddMember @("VM") `
-CustomProperty $CustomPropertyExpiry
Set-SCCustomPropertyValue -InputObject $MyVM `
-CustomProperty $CustomPropExpiry  -Value "$VMExpiration"
```

You can incorporate this information into an Orchestrator runbook using the **Run VMM PowerShell Script** activity (see Figure 16.32).

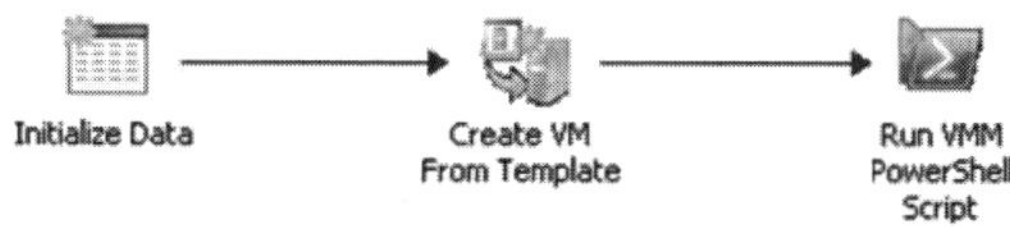

FIGURE 16.32 PowerShell to add custom properties for ExpirationDate and RequestedBy.

This sample runbook performs the following activities:

- Collects user contact information (email address) and expected life of the VM (in days)
- Creates the virtual machine from a VM template in VMM 2012
- Runs a VMM PowerShell script to add the custom properties ExpirationDate and RequestedBy

Configuration of the **Initialize Data** activity should be very familiar at this point in the book. Configure its properties as described here and shown in Figure 16.33:

- **ExpirationDate:** The date after which the VM should be deleted.
- **RequestedBy:** The email address of the requesting user.

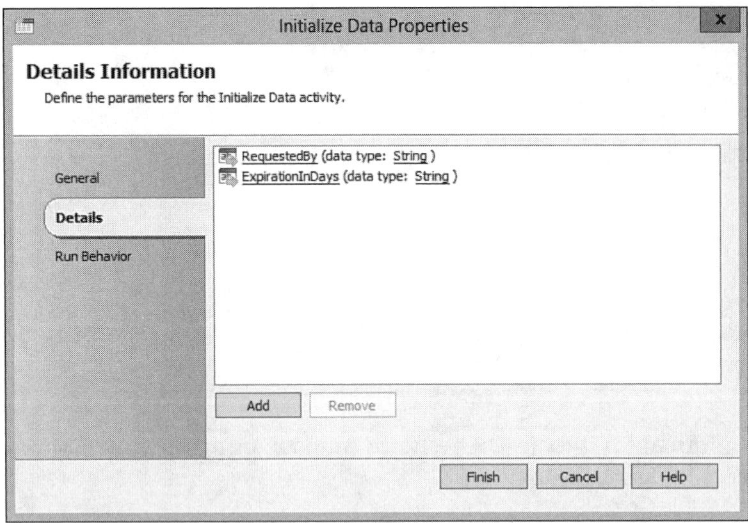

FIGURE 16.33 User inputs to add custom properties for ExpirationDate and RequestedBy.

When launched from the Orchestration console, the operator starting the runbook provides updated pieces of information—the number of days the VM is required and an email address (see Figure 16.34).

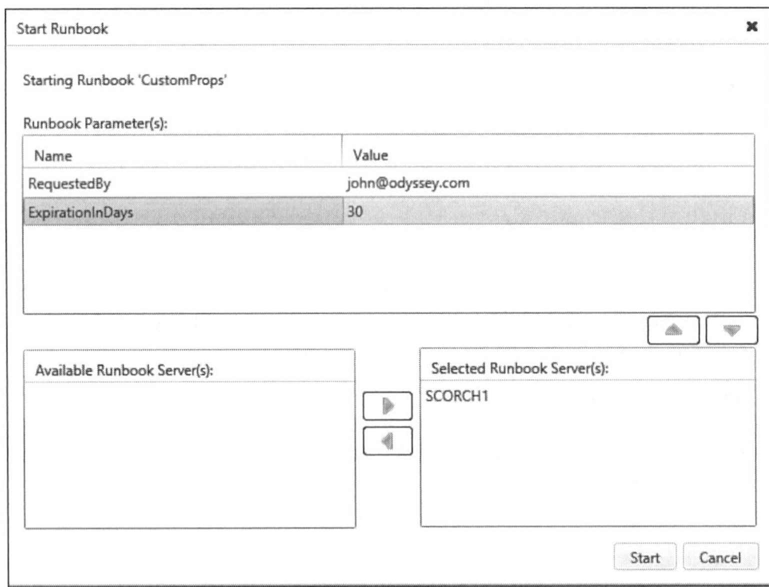

FIGURE 16.34 Runbook inputs as seen through the Orchestration console.

These two properties alone allow for automating a lifecycle management process using Orchestrator runbooks to notify users when their VMs are nearing expiration, as well as using a runbook to store the VM in a VMM library or simply perform a backup and delete.

Working with Service Templates

This section includes several examples of how to provision and configure services in VMM using the Orchestrator VMM IP:

- Deploying a service (from a service template)
- Scaling out a computer tier
- Scaling in a computer tier
- In-place servicing (also known as in-place updates)

NOTE: LAB REQUIREMENTS TO CREATE THESE EXAMPLES

These runbooks require that you have deployed Windows Server 2012 Hyper-V systems, configured them to be managed by VMM 2012 SP 1, and also deployed and configured Orchestrator to work with VMM. Implementing these prerequisites in a test environment is a relatively easy endeavor that even a Hyper-V and System Center novice can complete in about a day.

16

Deploying a Service Instance (Service Template)

The sample runbook in Figure 16.35 illustrates that using Orchestrator to deploy a service from a service template in VMM with a light touch way is surprisingly simple. This sample runbook performs the following high-level activities:

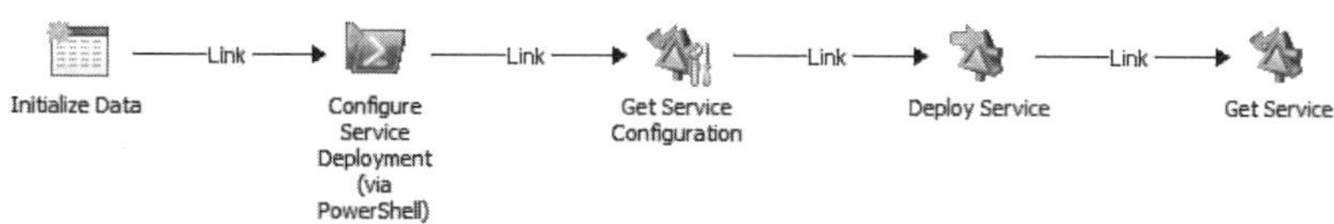

FIGURE 16.35 Runbook to deploy a service.

1. Accepts input with the name of the service instance and machine tier within the instance that needs to be scaled out (via the **Initialize Data** activity).
2. Retrieves the service template that will be used in the service deployment (using the **Get Service Template** activity).
3. Creates the configuration for the service deployment (using the **Configure Service Deployment** activity).

4. Deploys the service to the specified host or cloud (using the **Deploy Service** activity).

When you launch the runbook in the Runbook Tester or the Orchestration console, you are prompted for two pieces of information (see Figure 16.36):

- **ServiceName:** A user-defined friendly name that will be assigned to the service instance to be deployed
- **ServiceTemplate:** The name of the VMM service template you want to use to deploy a service instance

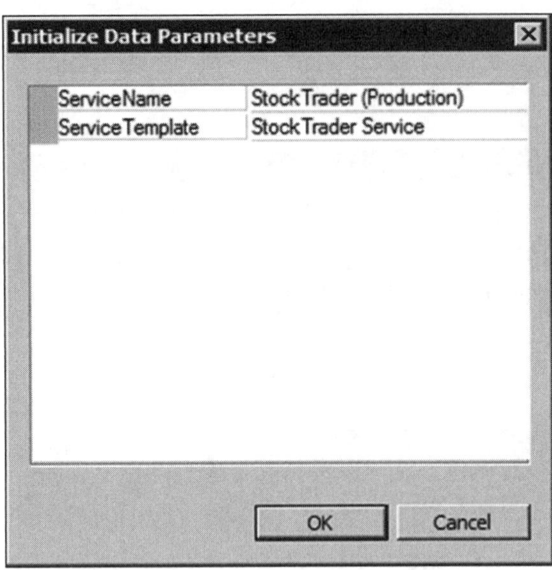

FIGURE 16.36 Parameters for deploying a service to Hyper-V with VMM (using Orchestrator Runbook Tester).

The service deployment is configured based on the user input:

- The service configuration object is retrieved (using the **Get Service Configuration** activity).
- The service is deployed (using the **Deploy Service** activity).
- When deployment is complete, the service is retrieved (using the **Get Service** activity) to ensure that deployment was successful.

If you launch the same runbook from the Orchestration console, you are prompted for the same information in a slightly different interface (see Figure 16.37).

As with any runbook, you can expand this runbook to include additional logging of runbook results and/or validation activities to verify that the service deployment was successful.

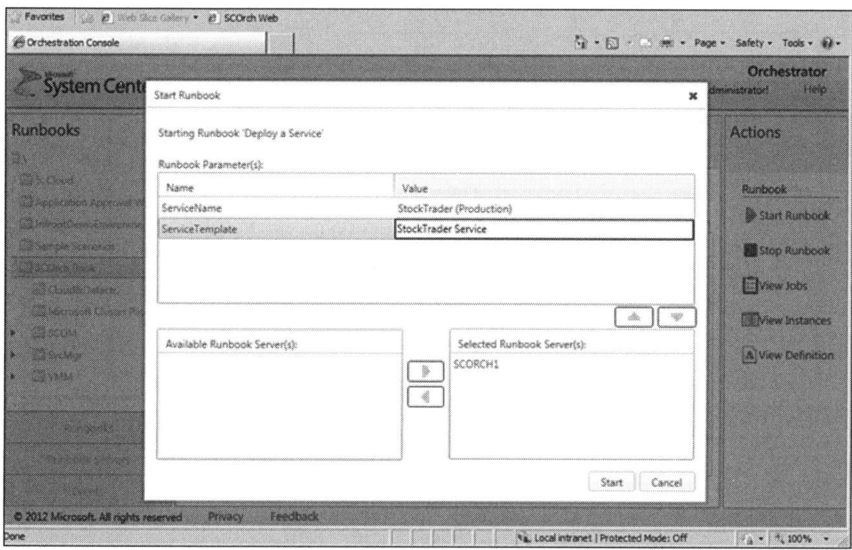

FIGURE 16.37 Deploying a service to Hyper-V with VMM (using Orchestration console).

NOTE: STEP-BY-STEP CONFIGURATION FOR DEPLOYING A SERVICE TO HYPER-V WITH VMM

For step-by-step configuration instructions for this runbook, visit "Orchestrator By Example: Deploying a Service from Template with VMM and Orchestrator" at System Center Central, at www.systemcentercentral.com/orchestrator-by-example-deploying-a-service-from-template-with-vmm-and-orchestrator-2/.

Scaling Out a Machine (Computer) Tier

One of the advantages of a private cloud infrastructure based on Hyper-V and System Center is elasticity, the capability to respond quickly to changes in demand. The runbook in Figure 16.38 scales out a computer tier by deploying another VM to the desired machine tier within the specified service instance. This sample runbook performs the following high-level activities:

1. Accepts input with the name of the service instance and machine tier within the instance that needs to be scaled out (via the **Initialize Data** activity).

2. Retrieves the running service instance (using the **Get Service** activity).

3. Retrieves the specified machine tier (using **Get Tier**).

4. Adds a VM to the machine tier specified by the user (using the **Scale Tier Out** activity).

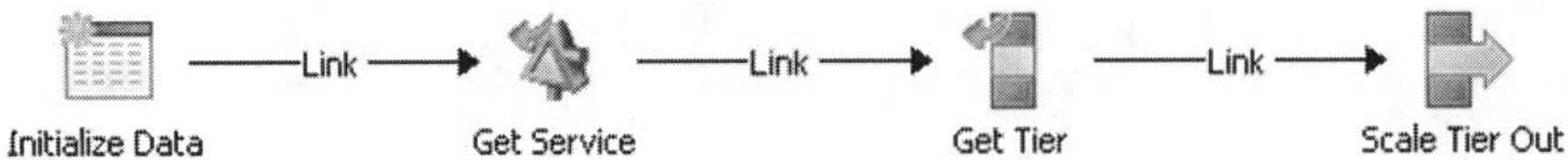

FIGURE 16.38 Runbook to scale out a machine (computer) tier.

If you launch the same runbook from the Orchestration console, you are prompted for the machine tier name and the service instance in which it is hosted (see Figure 16.39).

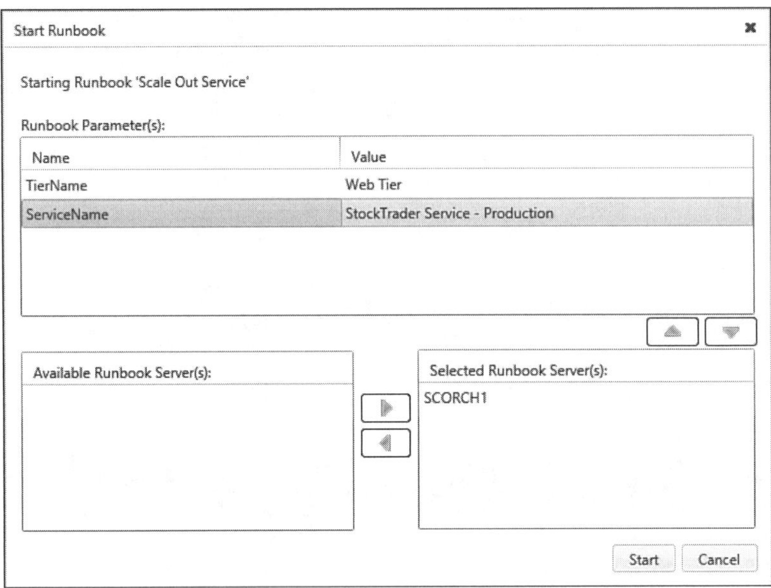

FIGURE 16.39 Scaling out a machine tier (using the Orchestration console).

NOTE: STEP-BY-STEP CONFIGURATION FOR SCALING OUT A MACHINE TIER WITH VMM AND ORCHESTRATOR

For step-by-step configuration instructions for this runbook, see "Orchestrator By Example: Scaling Out a Machine Tier with VMM and Orchestrator" at System Center Central at www.systemcentercentral.com/orchestrator-by-example-scaling-out-a-machine-tier-in-a-service-and-orchestrator/.

Scaling In a Machine Tier

The sample runbook in Figure 16.40 performs the same steps as the scale-out runbook, except that instead of adding a VM to the specified machine tier, it deletes one of them to "scale in" the service. This eliminates excess consumption and returns the resources to the resource pool (called a cloud in VMM 2012). This sample runbook performs the following high-level activities:

1. Prompts the user for the name of the service instance and machine tier within the instance that needs to be scaled out (via the **Initialize Data** activity).
2. Retrieves the running service instance (using the **Get Service** activity).
3. Retrieves the specified machine tier (using **Get Tier**).
4. Removes a VM from the machine tier specified by the user (using the **Scale Tier In** activity).

FIGURE 16.40 Runbook to scale in a machine (computer) tier.

The data inputs for this runbook in the Runbook Tester or Orchestration console look identical to those for the scale-out runbook in Figure 16.39.

NOTE: STEP-BY-STEP CONFIGURATION FOR SCALING IN MACHINE TIER WITH VMM AND ORCHESTRATOR

For step-by-step configuration instructions for this runbook, visit "Orchestrator By Example: Scaling in a Machine Tier in a VMM Service with Orchestrator" at System Center Central, at www.systemcentercentral.com/orchestrator-by-example-scaling-in-a-machine-tier-in-a-vmm-service-with-orchestrator/.

Performing In-Place Servicing

The runbook in this section performs in-place servicing (also known as a conventional update) to a service instance, in which the OS image is not replaced. This sample runbook performs the following high-level activities (see Figure 16.41):

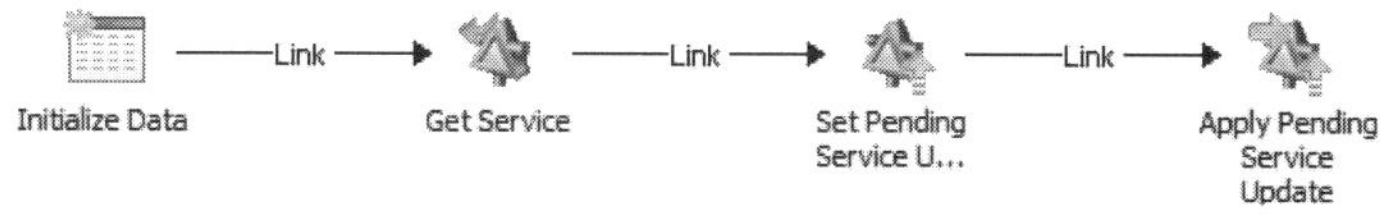

FIGURE 16.41 Runbook to update a running service instance.

1. Prompts the user for the information necessary to apply an update to a running service instance, as shown in the properties of **Initialize Data** (see Figure 16.42):

- **ServiceName:** A user-defined friendly name that will be assigned to the service instance to be deployed
- **ServiceTemplate:** The name of the VMM service template you want to use to deploy a service instance
- **TemplateRelease:** The release (version) of the template (for example, if you want to apply release 1.1 of the WebApp template to a service instance deployed from the 1.0 release)

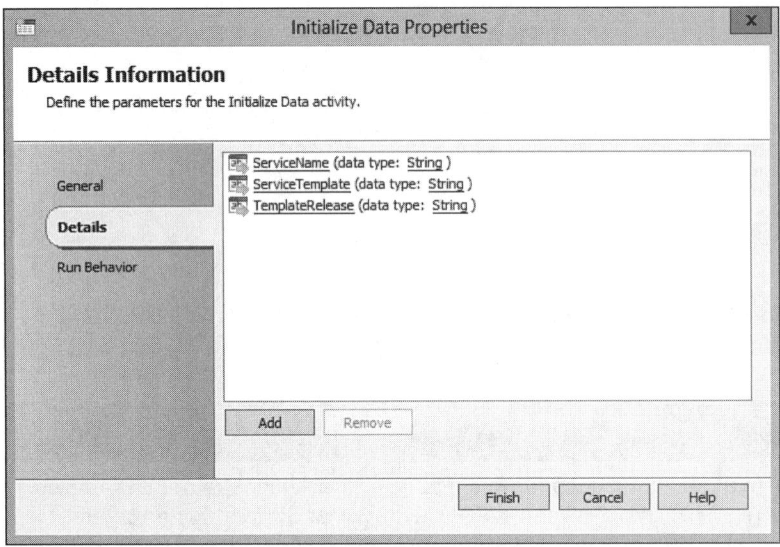

FIGURE 16.42 User inputs (**Initialize Data** properties).

2. The **Get Service** activity retrieves the running service instance based on the name provided by the user.
3. The **Set Pending Service Update** activity associates the updated service template to the running service but does not perform the actual update.
4. Finally, the **Apply Pending Service Update** activity applies the update to the service instance, performing the in-place servicing.

Technically, you can specify an earlier release of a template to roll back a recent update to the service instance. This is part of the power of the in-place servicing capabilities in VMM 2012; you can quickly roll back an update that doesn't deliver the desired end result.

If you launch the runbook from the Runbook Tester, you are prompted for the service instance, service template, and template version (called template release), as in Figure 16.43.

FIGURE 16.43 User inputs for In-Place Service Update runbook (Runbook Tester).

NOTE: STEP-BY-STEP CONFIGURATION FOR PERFORMING IN-PLACE UPDATES FOR SERVICES IN VMM AND ORCHESTRATOR

For step-by-step configuration instructions for this runbook, visit "Orchestrator By Example: Performing In-Place Updates for Services in VMM and Orchestrator" at System Center Central, at http://www.systemcentercentral.com/orchestrator-by-example-performing-in-place-updates-for-services-in-system-center-2012-vmm-sp1-and-orchestrator/.

Summary

This chapter discussed the installation, configuration, and practical application of the System Center Virtual Machine Manager IP. This is one of the more robust System Center IPs. You can leverage it in a variety of production scenarios to support provisioning, maintenance, and capacity management in pure Microsoft or hybrid (Hyper-V and VMware) virtualization infrastructures. When this IP is used in conjunction with the System Center Service Manager IP, Orchestrator can be leveraged to support an organization's change-management procedures through automation. Chapter 19 provides a detailed discussion of integrated System Center workflows.

CHAPTER 17

Integration with System Center Data Protection Manager

IN THIS CHAPTER

- Integration Pack Requirements
- Installing the Integration Pack
- Configuring the Integration Pack
- Activities at a Glance
- Activities in Depth
- Use Case Scenarios
- Troubleshooting the DPM IP

As one of the System Center integration packs (IPs), Microsoft's System Center Data Protection Manager (DPM) IP enables administrators to automate Data Protection Manager tasks and integrate Data Protection Manager with other system management tools, such as Service Manager. You can use this IP to automate many tasks in Data Protection Manager to deliver services faster and more reliably. This chapter discusses the functionality of the Microsoft System Center Data Protection Manager IP.

The chapter describes the requirements for using the DPM IP. It covers communication with Data Protection Manager, the installation procedure and configuration steps, an explanation of how each activity functions, and common use case scenarios. The chapter also presents several sample runbooks to show you how to fully leverage the DPM IP to automate your organization's server backup management processes.

Integration Pack Requirements

The DPM IP is not included in the Orchestrator 2012 installation files; it is available as a separate download from the Microsoft download website (www.microsoft.com/en-us/download/details.aspx?id=34611). The following sections discuss specific requirements.

System Center 2012 Orchestrator

The System Center integration packs were among the first integration packs that Microsoft released after acquiring Opalis in late 2009. Opalis Integration Server 6.3 offers an integration pack for DPM 2010. Orchestrator 2012 provides different Data Protection Manager integration packs, depending on the target DPM environment. Table 17.1 provides a matrix showing which Orchestrator integration pack version to use, based on the DPM environment.

TABLE 17.1 Data Protection Manager Version and Integration Pack Support

Data Protection Manager Release	Orchestrator 2012 RTM	Orchestrator 2012 Service Pack (SP) 1
DPM 2010 RTM	Orchestrator RTM DPM 2010 IP	Orchestrator RTM DPM 2010 IP
DPM 2012 RTM	Orchestrator RTM DPM 2012 IP	Orchestrator RTM DPM 2012 IP
DPM 2012 SP 1	Not supported	Orchestrator RTM DPM 2012 SP 1 IP

System Requirements

The DPM IP uses Windows PowerShell remoting on the runbook server or Runbook Designer workstation to communicate with the DPM server or computer running the DPM Administrator console and PowerShell Management Shell. The integration pack might require additional WinRM and WS-Management configuration, based on the operating system environment on which Orchestrator and DPM are running (Windows Server 2008 R2 or Windows Server 2012). See http://technet.microsoft.com/en-us/library/hh830726.aspx for information on how to configure WinRM and WS-Management.

Installing the Integration Pack

Installing the IP for DPM uses the same process as other integration packs. Follow these steps:

1. Download the IP from Microsoft's download center. The filename is System_Center_2012_SP1_Integration_Packs.EXE.
2. Run the EXE file and extract all the files (for example, to C:\TEMP\IP). This folder will contain multiple integration packs for different System Center components.
3. Use Orchestrator Deployment Manager to register and deploy the DPM IP.

Configuring the Integration Pack

All activities in the DPM IP use the connection details specified in the connection account to connect to the DPM server(s) in your implementation. If there is more than one Data Protection Manager implementation, you can create connection accounts for each implementation. Additionally, you can create multiple connections for each Data Protection Manager implementation to allow for differing permissions in the accounts used to access Data Protection Manager.

Connection accounts are critical in using the DPM IP. Perform the following steps to configure a connection account for Service Manager:

1. In the top menu of the Orchestrator Runbook Designer, select **Options -> SC12 Data Protection Manager.**
2. In the SC 2012 Data Protection Manager dialog box that opens, click **Add.**
3. In the Add Configuration dialog box, click **...** and select PowerShell Remoting. Click **OK.**
4. In the Add Configuration dialog box that opens, supply the relevant connection details. The following information is required (see Figure 17.1):
    - **Name:** The name you are giving the connection.
    - **DPM Administrator Console:** The name or IP address of a computer where the DPM Administrator console and PowerShell Management Shell are installed.
    - **DPM Server:** The name or IP address of the DPM server.
    - **User:** The Active Directory account used to connect to the Data Protection Manager server. This account must have permissions in Data Protection Manager to perform the action the runbook requests. If you don't configure an account, the runbook uses the default Runbook Server service account.
    - **Domain:** The domain in which the Active Directory account exists.
    - **Password:** The password for the Active Directory account.
    - **Authentication Type (Remote only):** The type of authentication the connection will use. This is required only if the DPM server and runbook server are installed on different machines. By default, the connection uses the authentication method implemented by the WS-Management protocol. For more information on different authentication types, see http://technet.microsoft.com/en-us/library/hh830726.aspx.
    - **Port (Remote only):** The connection uses port 5985 by default. If necessary, you can specify a new port to use when the client connects to the WinRM service on the remote server.
    - **Use SSL (Remote only):** Configure whether the connection will use SSL.
    - **Cache Session Timeout (Min.):** By default, the session times out after 10 minutes. The session then must be reconnected.

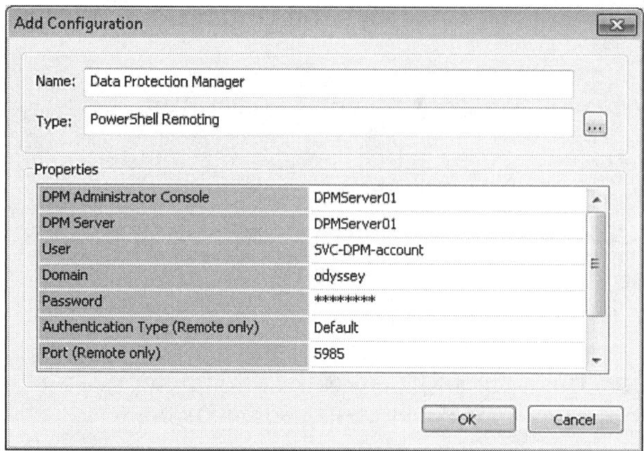

FIGURE 17.1 Configuring the DPM connection.

The Add Configuration dialog box does not provide a Test Connection button for you to test the connection details. Instead, you can build a small runbook such as the one in Figure 17.2 to test the connection.

5. Click **OK** to create the connection.

FIGURE 17.2 Runbook to test DPM connection.

Figures 17.3 and 17.4 show the configuration of the **Get DPM Server Capacity** and **Send Platform Event** activities. **Get DPM Server Capacity** requires no additional configuration except the DPM server connection. **Send Platform Event** generates a platform event with information about the DPM server capacity. To validate the connection, you can write any published DPM information from the **Get DPM Server Capacity** activity. This runbook validates the DPM connection and gives you some basic information regarding the DPM server.

Further details on how to create a connection are available on TechNet at http://technet.microsoft.com/en-us/library/hh830726.aspx.

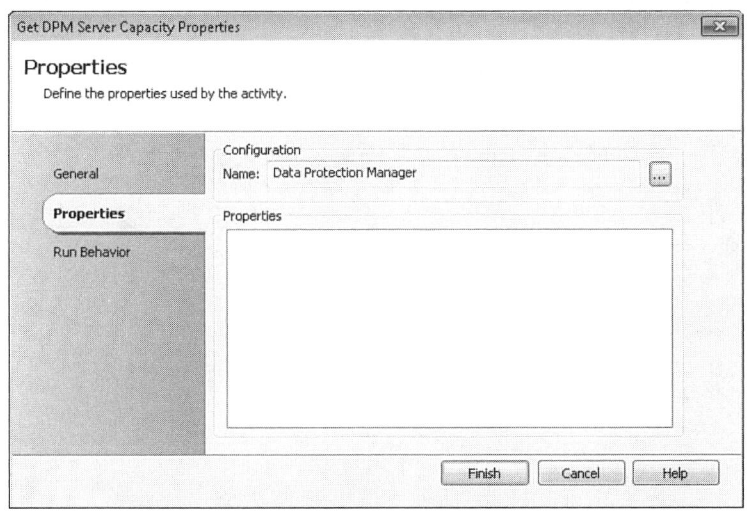

FIGURE 17.3 Properties of the **Get DPM Capacity** activity.

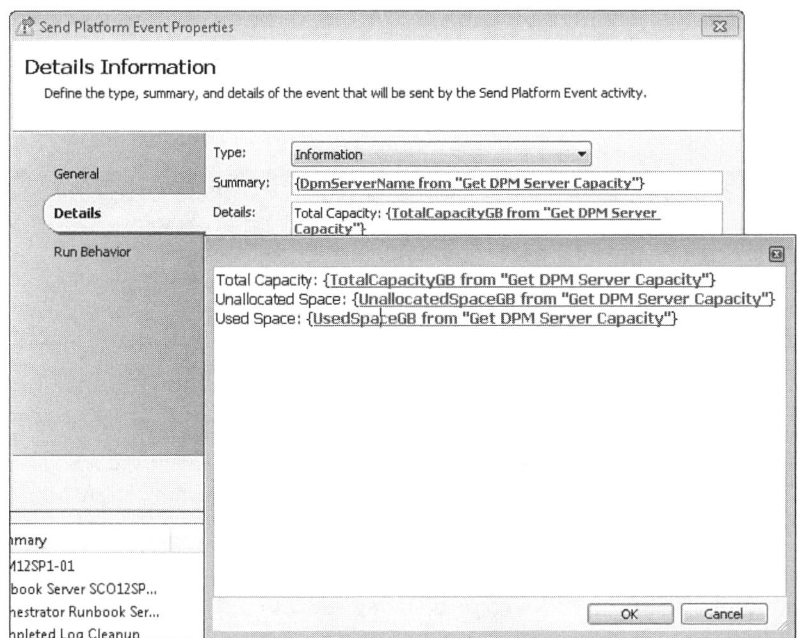

FIGURE 17.4 **Send Platform Event** activity details.

Activities at a Glance

For reference, the DPM IP includes these activities:

- Create Recovery Point
- Get Data Source
- Get DPM Server Capacity
- Get Recovery Point
- Protect Data Source
- Recover SharePoint
- Recover SQL
- Recover VM
- Run DPM PowerShell Script

Activities in Depth

This section describes each of the activities contained in this IP, to provide an understanding of what each activity does. Each activity has a link to its corresponding TechNet article, which supplies additional information on the activity and tables listing the properties and published data.

NOTE: SYNCHRONOUS BEHAVIOR

Many activities in the Data Protection Manager IP have synchronous behavior. With synchronous behavior, the activity runs for as long as Data Protection Manager needs to complete the action. For example, if a runbook includes a **Create Recovery Point** activity that takes two hours to execute, the runbook will run for at least two hours. Be sure to design your runbooks and automation solutions with synchronous behavior in mind.

- **Create Recovery Point:** This activity creates a recovery point outside of the scheduled interval configured in the Data Protection Manager protection group. Information on the elements in the activity is available at http://technet.microsoft.com/en-us/library/hh830688.aspx.
- **Get Data Source:** The **Get Data Source** activity retrieves information about data sources from a computer with the DPM agent installed or from a protection group. An example of a data source is a SQL Server database protected by DPM. See http://technet.microsoft.com/en-us/library/hh830712 for information on the elements in the activity.
- **Get DPM Server Capacity:** This activity returns storage information from a DPM server. The results from this activity can be used to determine where to store a

backup. Information on the elements in the activity is available at http://technet.microsoft.com/en-us/library/hh830699.aspx.

- **Get Recovery Point:** This activity gets all available recovery points for a specific data source. It can also be configured to return only the latest recovery point. For information on the elements in this activity, see http://technet.microsoft.com/en-us/library/hh531759.aspx.
- **Protect Data Source:** This activity adds a workload to an existing protection group. See http://technet.microsoft.com/en-us/library/hh830727.aspx for information on the elements in this activity.
- **Recover SharePoint:** This activity recovers a SharePoint farm to its original location or to a network folder. Information on the elements in the activity is available at http://technet.microsoft.com/en-us/library/hh830745.aspx.
- **Recover SQL:** This activity recovers a SQL Server database to its original location or to a network folder. Information on the elements in the activity is available at http://technet.microsoft.com/en-us/library/hh830733.aspx.
- **Recover VM:** This activity recovers a virtual machine. See http://technet.microsoft.com/en-us/library/hh830703.aspx for additional information on the elements in the activity.
- **Run DPM PowerShell Script:** If you have no suitable activity in the DPM IP, you can use the **Run DPM PowerShell Script** activity to address more complex scenarios. You can use this activity instead of using the **Run .NET Script** activity, which requires configuring remoting commands. The **Run DPM PowerShell Script** activity also provides better performance than the **Run .NET Script** activity because it reuses any open connection to the DPM server instead of opening new connections to run commands. Information on the elements in the activity is available at http://technet.microsoft.com/en-us/library/hh832010.aspx. Information on PowerShell cmdlets in System Center 2012 Data Protection Manager is available at http://technet.microsoft.com/en-us/library/hh881679.aspx.

Use Case Scenarios

The next sections present some typical use cases for the DPM IP. Each example uses at least one activity from the DPM IP and demonstrates a common use. The runbooks are explained in depth to demonstrate how to use activities to automate common DPM processes.

The following three scenarios demonstrate how to utilize activities effectively from the DPM IP:

- Create a recovery point before installing software
- Prepare a server for patch management
- Restore a SQL Server database to a network folder

Creating a Recovery Point Before Installing Software

A common request in many businesses is to make an additional backup before installing any software. As a manual process, this can consume a significant amount of time.

The runbook in Figure 17.5 creates a recovery point and then runs a silent software installation. The user inputs a server name when starting the runbook; the runbook then makes an extra backup for the server and runs the software setup. Five activities achieve this:

- The **Initialize Data** activity collects input parameters.
- The **Get Data Source** activity gets the correct data source for the protected server.
- The **Create Recovery Point** activity creates a backup for the data source.
- The **Create Alert** activity creates an alert in Operations Manager if DPM cannot create a recovery point.
- The **Run Program** activity installs the software.

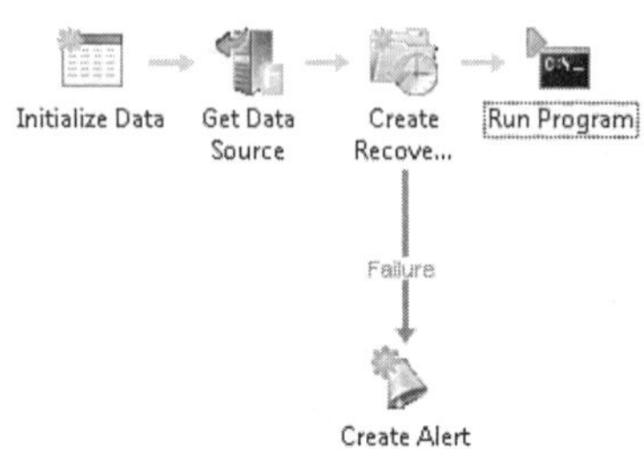

FIGURE 17.5 Runbook to create a recovery point and install software.

The following steps are required to create this runbook:

1. **Initialize Data:** To collect input parameters needed in the runbook you can use an **Initialize Data** activity. In the example in Figure 17.5, the **Initialize Data** activity is configured to collect one parameter: ServerName.

2. **Get Data Source:** This activity is required to get the correct data source ID, needed in the **Create Recovery Point** activity. In the runbook in Figure 17.5, Orchestrator is connected to a DPM server that protects C:\BACKUP on two servers. C:\BACKUP contains some important application files. The protection of C:\TEMP is configured in a protection group named C:\BACKUP.

   Figure 17.6 shows how to configure the **Get Data Source** activity. The activity is configured to get the data source for a computer with the DPM agent installed (Data Source Location equals Production Server), and Name is configured to use the input parameter from the **Initialize Data** activity. Figure 17.7 shows the Filters tab, configured to return only data sources for the protection group named C:\BACKUP.

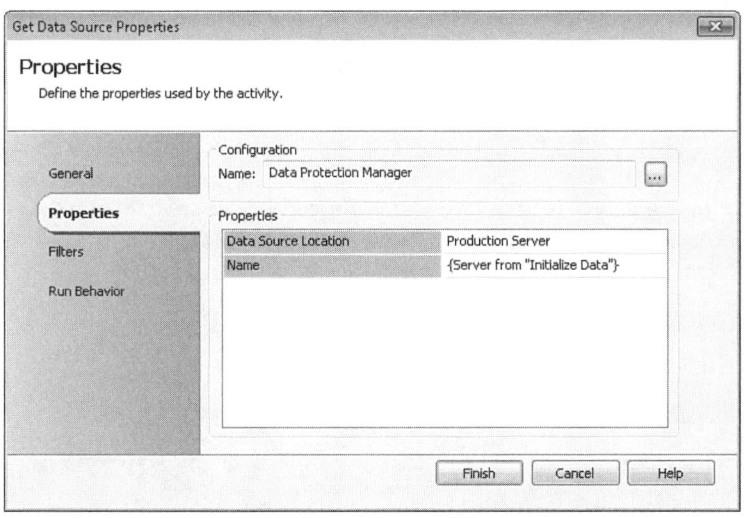

FIGURE 17.6 General configuration for the **Get Data Source** activity.

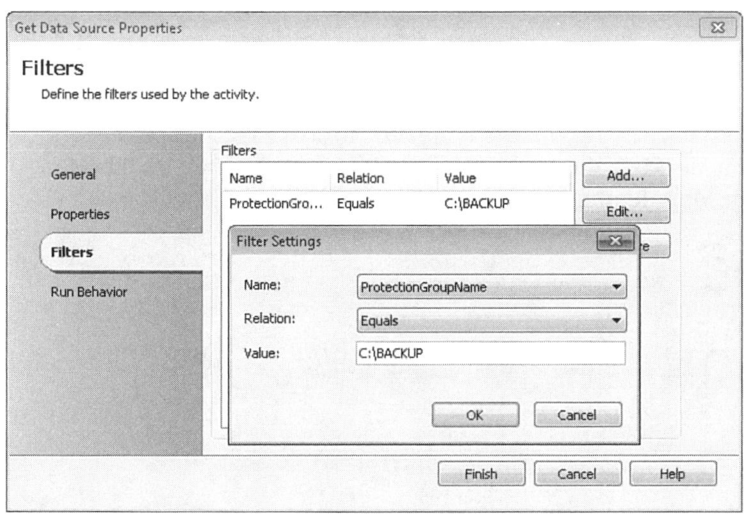

FIGURE 17.7 Filtering data sources for the protection group C:\BACKUP in the **Get Data Source** activity.

3. **Create Recovery Point:** This activity creates the recovery point for the data source returned by the **Get Data Source** activity. The only configuration made on this activity is to input the data source ID from the **Get Data Source** activity.
4. **Create Alert:** This activity is from the Operations Manager IP. If the **Create Recovery Point** activity fails, an alert is generated in Operations Manager.
5. **Run Program:** This activity runs a software setup in silent mode.

17

Preparing a Server for Patch Management

For many information technology (IT) departments, the monthly patch management process takes a considerable amount of time. Before patches and updates can be applied to production servers, backups need to be verified and applications must be shut down properly.

The runbook in Figure 17.8 puts a server into a mode where it can be updated with new patches. The runbook also verifies disk space, creates a new recovery point, and puts the computer into maintenance mode in Operations Manager. Seven activities achieve this:

- The **Initialize Data** collects input parameters.
- The **Get Disk Space Status** gets the target drive free disk space status.
- The **Start/Stop Service** stops a service.
- The **Create Alert** activity creates a generic alert for the runbook if any activity fails.
- The **Get Data Source** activity gets the correct data source for the protected server.
- The **Create Recovery Point** activity creates a backup for the data source.
- The **Start Maintenance Mode** activity sets maintenance mode in Operations Manager so that unnecessary alerts are not created during the patching process.

The runbook in Figure 17.8 can be synchronized to Service Manager and used as a runbook automation activity in a service request template. A service request can be published to the Service Manager self-service portal. Engineers can then use the portal to request a server to be ready for patching, as a service request.

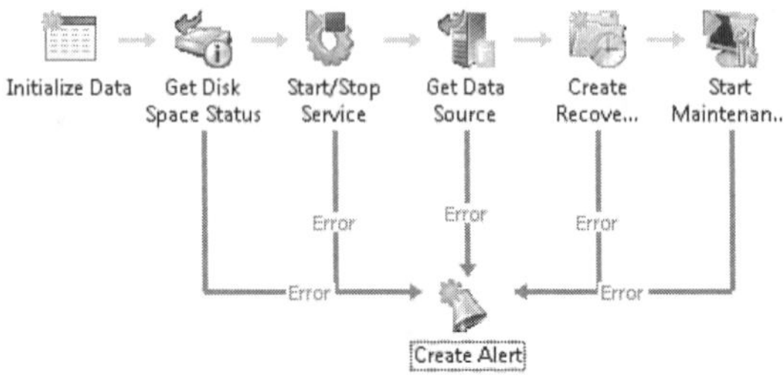

FIGURE 17.8 Runbook to get a server ready for update.

To create this runbook, follow these steps:

1. **Initialize Data:** To collect input parameters needed in the runbook, you can use an **Initialize Data** activity. In the example in Figure 17.8, the **Initialize Data** activity is configured to collect one parameter: ServerName.

2. **Get Disk Space:** This activity verifies that the system drive on the server has enough free disk space. If the system drive has enough free disk space, the runbook continues with the **Start/Stop Service** activity.

3. **Create Alert:** This activity is from the Operations Manager IP. It generates a generic alert in Operations Manager if any activity fails. This example has one **Create Alert** activity; an alternative is to use one **Create Alert** activity for each other activity. The benefit with the alternative solution is that the alert description can be more detailed, with unique information from each particular activity. In this example, the **Create Alert** activity can create only a generic alert description because it is impossible to predict which activity will fail. Therefore, it is impossible to know which activities have published data to the data bus.

4. **Start/Stop Service:** This activity stops a service that needs to be stopped before installing updates on the server. The **Start/Stop Service** activity gets the ServerName from the **Initialize Data** activity.

5. **Get Data Source:** This activity is required to get the correct data source ID, which the **Create Recovery Point** activity needs. Figure 17.6 shows the generic configuration of the activity. The **Get Data Source** activity is configured to return data sources for only one server, and the Name property on the Properties tab is configured to use the ServerName from the **Initialize Data** activity. Figure 17.9 shows the Filters configuration. The **Get Data Source** activity is configured to return data sources only when ProtectionGroupName equals CompleteBackup.

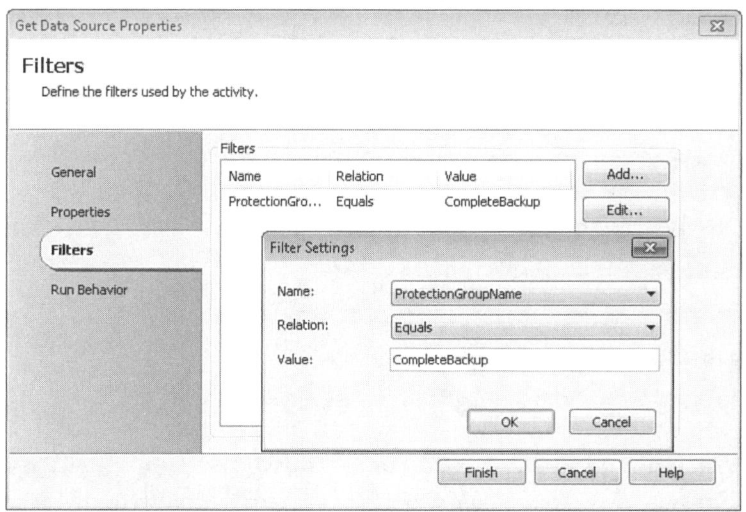

FIGURE 17.9 Filtering data sources for the protection group CompleteBackup in the **Get Data Source** activity.

6. **Create Recovery Point:** This activity creates the recovery point for the data source that the **Get Data Source** activity returns. The only configuration made on this activity is to input the data source ID from the **Get Data Source** activity.

7. **Start Maintenance Mode:** This activity is from the Operations Manager IP. The activity puts Operations Manager objects in maintenance. The **Start Maintenance Mode** activity uses ServerName from the **Initialize Data** activity. Figure 17.10 shows how the **Start Maintenance Mode** activity is configured to use the **Initialize Data** input parameter.

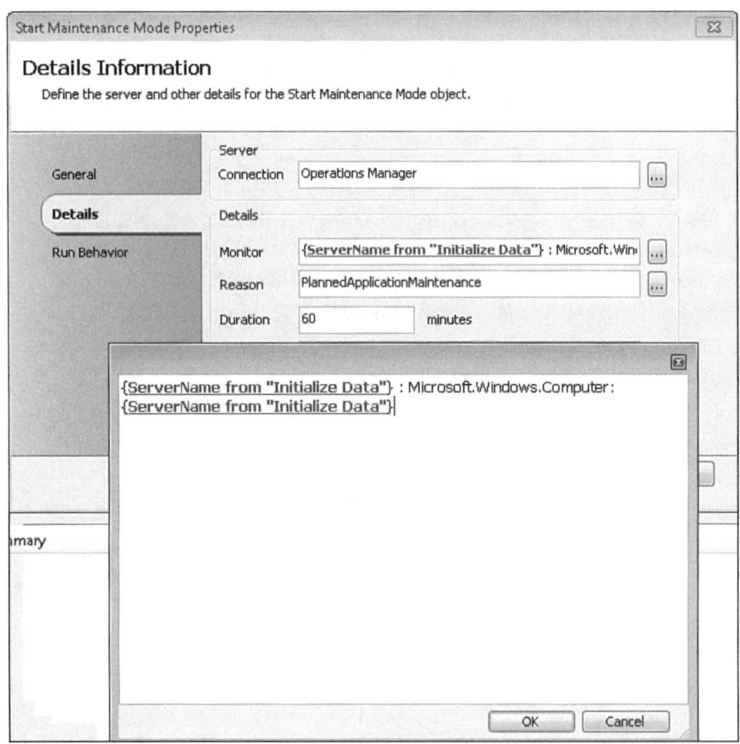

FIGURE 17.10 Configuring the **Start Maintenance Mode** activity.

Restoring a SQL Server Database to a Network Folder

Restoring data from a backup system is often a complex task that requires work from subject matter experts. Waiting for the backup team to restore data can be time consuming, especially if another team is needed to restore data. Using Orchestrator and the Data Protection Manager IP, it is possible to build a runbook to restore data, such as restoring a SQL Server database to a network folder in an effective and correct way. Engineers without knowledge of Data Protection Manager can use the runbook to restore data quickly and correctly.

The runbook in Figure 17.11 restores a SQL Server database backup to a network folder. The runbook first collects input parameters; then it obtains the latest recovery point for that SQL database and restores the database to a network folder. If recovering the SQL database is not possible, an Operations Manager alert is generated. Five activities achieve this:

- The **Initialize Data** collects input parameters.
- The **Get Data Source** activity gets the correct data source for the protected SQL database.
- The **Get Recovery Point** activity gets the latest recovery point for the data source.
- The **Recover SQL** activity recovers the latest recovery point to a network folder.
- The **Create Alert** generates an alert in Operations Manager if the recovery fails.

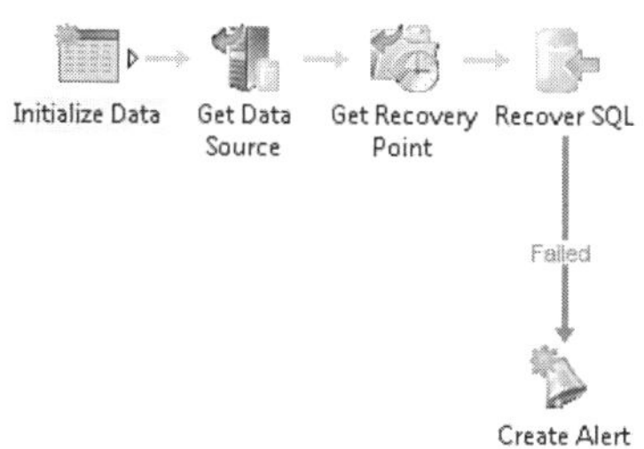

FIGURE 17.11 Runbook to restore a SQL database to a network folder.

The following steps are required to create this runbook:

1. **Initialize Data:** To collect input parameters needed in the runbook you can use an **Initialize Data** activity. In the example in Figure 17.11, the **Initialize Data** activity is configured to collect three parameters, ProtectionGroupName, ServerName, and DataSourceName. ProtectionGroupName is equal to Protection Group name in DPM. DataSourceName equals the SQL database to restore. ServerName is the production server where the SQL database is hosted.

2. **Get Data Source:** This activity gets the correct data source ID, needed in the **Get Recovery Point** activity. Figure 17.6 shows the generic configuration of the activity. The **Get Data Source** activity is configured to return data sources for only one server, and the Name property on the Properties tab is configured to use the ServerName from the **Initialize Data** activity. Figure 17.12 shows the filters configuration. The **Get Data Source** activity is configured to return data sources only when ProtectionGroupName and DatasourceName are equal to the input parameters from the **Initialize Data** activity.

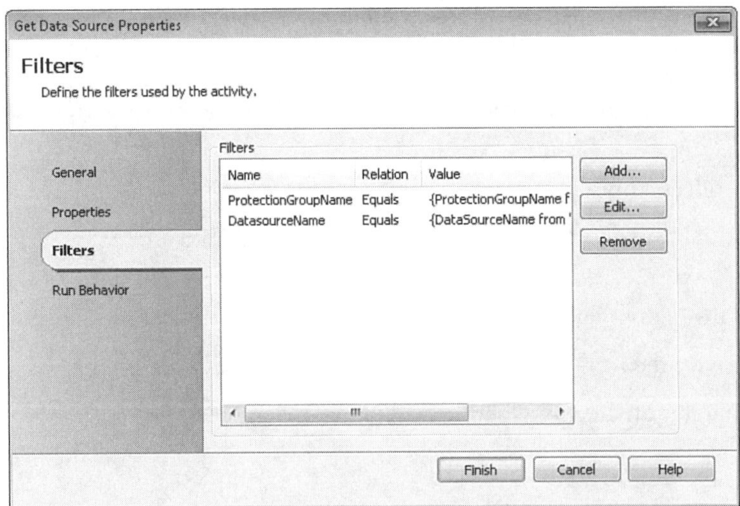

FIGURE 17.12 Filter configuration of the **Get Data Source** activity.

3. **Get Recovery Point:** This activity gets the latest recovery point for the data source that the **Get Data Source** activity returns—in this example, a SQL Server database. Figure 17.13 shows the configuration of the **Get Recovery Point** activity.

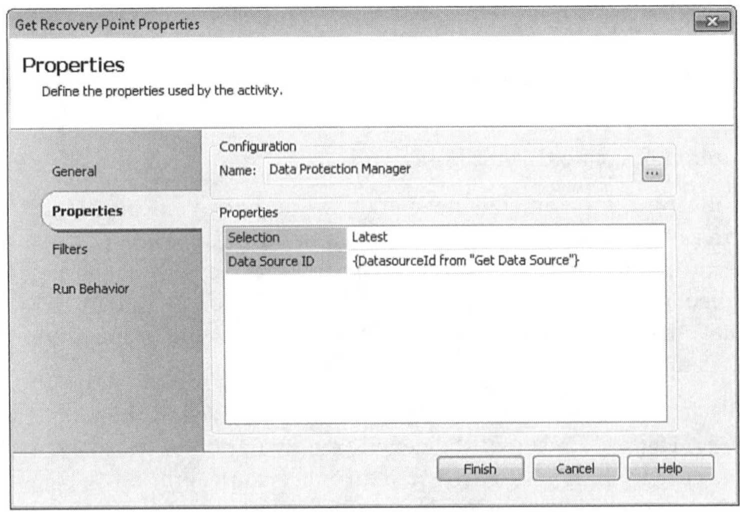

FIGURE 17.13 Configuration of the **Get Recovery Point** activity.

4. **Recover SQL:** This activity performs the actual restore of the SQL database to the network folder. Figure 17.14 shows the configuration of the **Recover SQL** activity. The activity is configured to recover to a network folder on a server named DC01. On DC01, the backup will be restored to the C:\Restore folder. The target server must be protected by DPM.

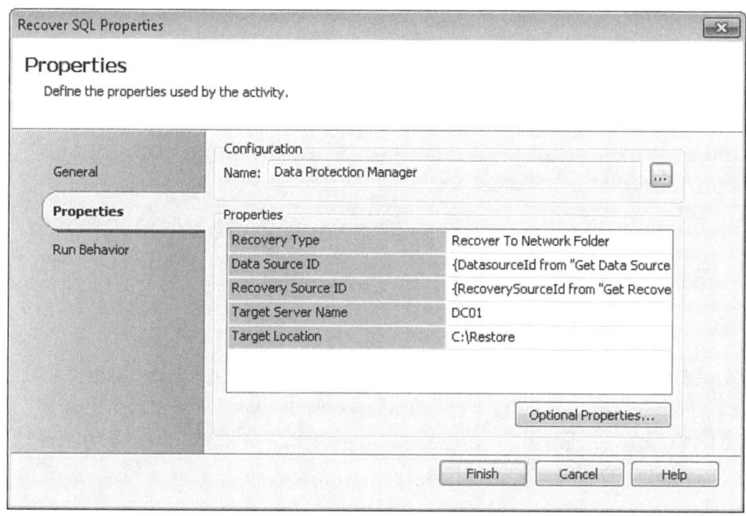

FIGURE 17.14 Configuring the **Recover SQL** activity.

5. **Create Alert:** This activity is from the Operations Manager IP. It generates a generic alert in Operations Manager if the **Recover SQL** activity fails. This example contains one **Create Alert** activity.

Troubleshooting the DPM IP

This section introduces you to methodologies for troubleshooting the Data Protection Manager IP. This integration pack relies on a number of technologies to work. When troubleshooting the integration pack, it is important to verify each layer. In general, troubleshooting the Data Protection Manager integration pack can include the following tasks:

- To verify connectivity between the runbook server and the Data Protection Manager server, you can use the following command. In this example, ODYSSEY is the Active Directory domain and SVC-DPM-ACCOUNT is the service account Orchestrator uses to connect to DPM. DPMSERVER01 is the hostname of the DPM server to which Orchestrator connects:

```
WinRM identity -remote:DPMSERVER01 -username:ODYSSSEY\SVC-DPM-ACCOUNT -password
P@ssw0rd
```

If the connection is successful, the output should be similar to Figure 17.15.

```
IdentifyResponse
    ProtocolVersion = http://schemas.dmtf.org/wbem/wsman/1/wsman.xsd
    ProductVendor = Microsoft Corporation
    ProductVersion = OS: 6.2.9200 SP: 0.0 Stack: 3.0
    SecurityProfiles
        SecurityProfileName = http://schemas.dmtf.org/wbem/wsman/1/wsman/secprof
ile/http/spnego-kerberos
```

FIGURE 17.15 Output of verification of WinRM connectivity.

If the connectivity is unsuccessful, an error number appears along with a short error description. The username and password should be for the same account Orchestrator uses to connect to the DPM server.

- The Data Protection Manager IP requires PowerShell 2.0 or later. To verify the PowerShell version, start PowerShell and run:

```
$psversiontable
```

Windows Server 2012 uses PowerShell 3.0 by default. The Data Protection Manager integration pack also requires the Data Protection Manager PowerShell snap-in. Verify that the DPM Management Shell is installed on the server configured in the DPM connection, in Orchestrator Runbook Designer.

- The DPM integration pack uses Windows PowerShell Remoting, which is based on Windows Remoting Management. To validate Windows PowerShell remoting, create a PowerShell session on the remote computer. See http://technet.microsoft.com/en-us/library/hh849717.aspx for information on creating a remote session.
- By configuring the trace logging level, you can obtain more information on the PowerShell command each Data Protection Manager IP activity runs. Chapter 11, "Security and Administration," describes how to change the trace logging level. Figure 17.16 shows an example of the PolicyModule log file on a runbook server. The runbook server has executed the runbook in Figure 17.5. Figure 17.17 shows that all records in the trace log from the DPM IP contain "DPM".

```
PolicyModule.exe.20121228165118.{0ED95D3B-732F-43F5-A
File Edit Format View Help
                Exit
    }
}

#----------------------------------------------------------------------------------------------------------
# Script for for Create Recovery Point Activity
# -DpmServer is the DpmServer.
# -DataSourceId is the data source who's recovery points will be returned.
# -ErrorDataSourceNotFound is the data source not found error message.
# -ErrorCouldNotCreateRecoveryPoint is the data source not found error message.
# ---------------------------------------------------------------------------------------------------------
function CreateRecoveryPoint()
{
    param
        (
            [String]   $DpmServer                         = $(throw "DpmServer"),
            [Guid]     $DataSourceId                      = $(throw "DataSourceId"),
                  [String]   $ErrorDataSourceNotFound                  = $(throw "ErrorDataSourceNotFound"),
            [String]   $ErrorCouldNotCreateRecoveryPoint = $(throw "ErrorCouldNotCreateRecoveryPoint")
        )

    # get data source
    $ds = Get-DataSource -DpmServer $DpmServer | where {$_.DatasourceId -eq $DataSourceId}

    if($ds -eq $null)
    {
        throw $ErrorDataSourceNotFound
    }

    # wait until idle
    while($ds.Activity -ne "Idle")
    {
        Sleep 5
    }

    # Do we have any recovery points
    if($ds.GetRecoveryPoint())
    {
        # create another recovery point
        $job = New-RecoveryPoint -Datasource $ds -Disk -BackupType expressfull -WithDataIntegrityCheck

    }
    else
    {
        # create initial recovery point
        $job = Start-DatasourceConsistencyCheck -Datasource $ds -HeavyWeight
        }

    # Wait unitl the job is finished
        While (! $job.HasCompleted)
```

FIGURE 17.16 Detailed trace logging of the DPM IP activities.

```
2012-12-28 16:51:25 [2680] 4 ThreadQueueMonitor is running

2012-12-28 16:51:25 [2680] 4 ThreadQueueMonitor is running

2012-12-28 16:51:25 [2680] 4 ThreadQueueMonitor is running

2012-12-28 16:51:25 [2680] 4 ThreadQueueMonitor is running

2012-12-28 16:51:25 [2680] 4 ThreadQueueMonitor is running

2012-12-28 16:51:25 [836] 4 AutoTrace : >> OpalisUtilityFro

2012-12-28 16:51:25 [836] 4 DPM Integration Pack: Create Po

2012-12-28 16:51:25 [836] 4 AutoTrace : << OpalisUtilityFro

2012-12-28 16:51:25 [836] 4 AutoTrace : >> OpalisUtilityFro

2012-12-28 16:51:25 [836] 4 DPM Integration Pack: # -------
# <copyright file="Script.ps1" company="Microsoft">
#   Copyright (c) Microsoft Corporation. All rights reserve
```

FIGURE 17.17 Trace logging of the DPM IP.

Summary

This chapter covered the installation and configuration requirements of the DPM IP and information on each activity it includes. It also discussed practical application of the DPM IP, with some common use scenarios. You can use the activities within this IP in many ways to automate business processes and manual tasks. When used together with the other IPs available in Orchestrator, a large percentage of common activities can be automated to provide many business efficiencies.

CHAPTER 18

Integration with Windows Azure

IN THIS CHAPTER

- Integration Pack Requirements
- Installing the Integration Pack
- Quick Introduction to PFX Files
- Configuring the Integration Pack
- Activities at a Glance
- Activity Categories in Depth
- Use Case Scenarios

A new integration pack (IP) available with System Center 2012 Orchestrator Service Pack (SP) 1, Microsoft's Windows Azure IP enables administrators to automate Windows Azure tasks and integrate Windows Azure objects with other systems and tools for on-premise SQL servers and Azure-based databases. The IP provides more than 60 activities that enable you to create, modify, and manage resources in the Windows Azure cloud. The activities in this IP act as a bridge, enabling management of public cloud resources located in Windows Azure from an on-premise Orchestrator instance. Use this IP to automate many tasks in Windows Azure to deliver services faster, consistently, and reliably.

This chapter discusses the functionality of the Windows Azure integration pack and describes the requirements to use this IP. It covers communication with Windows Azure, the installation procedure and configuration steps, and how each activity functions, along with common use case scenarios. The chapter also presents several sample runbooks to show you how to fully leverage the Windows Azure IP to automate your organization's Windows Azure operations related to certificates, deployments, cloud services, storage, and virtual machines.

WHAT IS WINDOWS AZURE?

Azure is Microsoft's application platform for the public cloud. You can use Azure in many ways: to build a web application that runs and stores data in Microsoft data centers, to store data using apps that run on-premise (not in the public cloud), to create virtual machines, and to build scalable applications. If you are unfamiliar with Azure, several links can help get you started:

- **Introducing Windows Azure:** www.windowsazure.com/en-us/develop/net/fundamentals/intro-to-windows-azure/
- **Windows Azure Execution Models:** www.windowsazure.com/en-us/develop/net/fundamentals/compute/

Integration Pack Requirements

The Windows Azure IP is not included in the Orchestrator 2012 installation files; it is available as a separate download from the Microsoft download website at www.microsoft.com/en-us/download/details.aspx?id=34611.

The Windows Azure integration pack is available and supported only on Orchestrator 2012 Service Pack 1 (updates to the Windows Azure IP are anticipated with System Center 2012 R2). To connect to Windows Azure, runbook servers need access to the Internet and the PFX management certificate file. The PFX management certificate is distributed to runbook servers manually.

Installing the Integration Pack

The process of installing the IP for Windows Azure is similar to the process for other integration packs. Follow these steps:

1. Download the IP from Microsoft's download center. The filename is System_Center_2012_SP1_Integration_Packs.EXE.
2. Run the EXE file and extract all the files (for example, to C:\TEMP\IP). This folder will contain multiple integration packs for different System Center components.
3. Use Orchestrator Deployment Manager to register and deploy the Windows Azure IP. The filename is SC2012SP1_Integration_Pack_for_Azure.oip.

Quick Introduction to PFX Files

To understand the configuration of the Windows Azure IP, you should have a basic understanding of certificates and data encryption. In general, there are two ways to encrypt data—symmetric and asymmetric encryption:

- When using symmetric encryption, the sender encrypts the file based on a symmetric key, such as a password. The sender then gives the encryption key to the receiver, who can decrypt the file. This works well when the sender and receiver are able to meet or can send the key to one another in some other way.
- With asymmetric encryption, each system or user has a pair of keys: a public key and a private key. The public key is shared, and the private key is secured. The sender uses the receiver's public key to encrypt the file. Only the receiver can decrypt the file because he or she has the private key of the key pair.

A certificate authority (CA) server is used to guarantee that the "receiver" is really the receiver and no one else. The CA server binds the public key to a certificate; this public key is connected to the private key. The certificate contains information about the owner of the certificate and the public key. Both the receiver and the sender must trust the CA server.

A Personal Information Exchange (PFX) file is an archive file format used to store private key and certificate information together in one file. The Windows Azure IP requires a PFX file with the Azure management certificate to communicate securely with Azure.

CAUTION: MORE THAN ONE CERTIFICATE IN THE PFX FILE

Although storing more than one certificate is possible in a PFX file, the Windows Azure IP cannot determine individual certificates to use in a PFX file. Remember to store only one certificate in this file.

Configuring the Integration Pack

All activities in the Windows Azure IP use the connection details specified in the connection account to connect to the Windows Azure subscription. If you will use more than one Windows Azure subscription, you can create connection accounts for each subscription.

Connection accounts are required for using the Windows Azure IP. Perform the following steps to configure a connection account for Windows Azure:

1. In the top menu of the Orchestrator Runbook Designer, select **Options** -> **Windows Azure.**
2. In the Windows Azure dialog box that opens, click **Add.**
3. In the Add Configuration dialog box, click ... and select **Azure Management Configuration Settings.** Click **OK.**
4. In the Add Configuration dialog box that opens, supply the relevant connection details. The following information is required (see Figure 18.1):
   - **Name:** This is the name you are giving the connection.
   - **PFX File Password:** This is the password for the management certification file.

- **PFX File Path:** Click ... and select the management certificate file associated with the Windows Azure subscription that you will use to connect.
- **Subscription ID:** Input the Windows Azure subscription ID to which to connect.

CAUTION: MANAGEMENT CERTIFICATE FILES

Anyone with access to the management certificate file associated with the Windows Azure subscription can authenticate a request to your Windows Azure subscription. Be sure to store the certificate file in a secured folder. Read more about generating a PFX certificate at http://msdn.microsoft.com/en-us/library/ff699202.aspx.

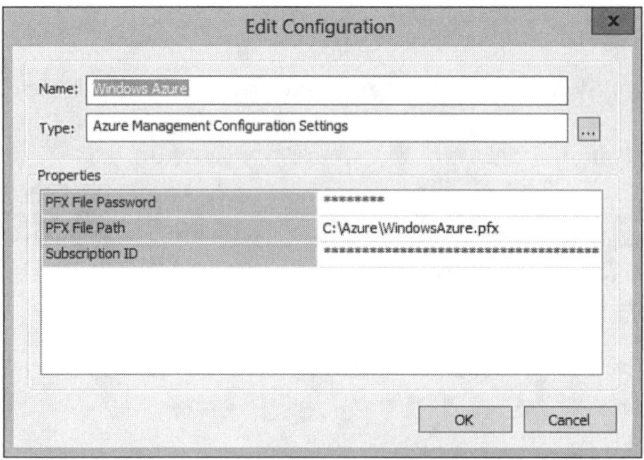

FIGURE 18.1 Configuring the Windows Azure connection.

The Add Configuration dialog box does not provide a Test Connection button for testing the connection details. However, you can build a small runbook such as the one in Figure 18.2 to test the connection.

FIGURE 18.2 Runbook to test Windows Azure connection.

5. Click **OK** to create the connection.

Figures 18.3 and 18.4 show the configuration of the **Azure Certificates** and the **Send Platform Event** activities. Azure certificates require no additional configuration other than using the Windows Azure connection and specifying **List Management Certificate** as the activity. **Send Platform Event** generates a platform event with information about the management certificate(s) configured in the Azure portal. This runbook validates the Windows Azure connection and gives you basic information about the Azure configuration. Before running the runbook, ensure that at least one management certificate is configured in Windows Azure.

FIGURE 18.3 Configuring the **Azure Certificates** activity.

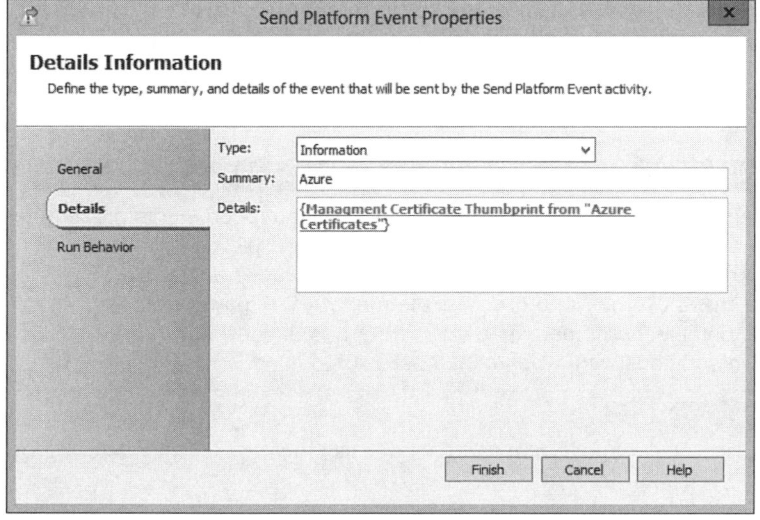

FIGURE 18.4 Configuring the **Send Platform Event** activity.

For additional detail on configuring the management certificate for Windows Azure, see http://technet.microsoft.com/en-us/library/gg481759(v=ws.10).aspx. Information on how to create a connection is on TechNet at http://technet.microsoft.com/en-us/library/jj721956.aspx.

Activities at a Glance

The Azure IP is unique, in that Microsoft has created *activity categories,* which are groupings of activities. For reference, the Windows Azure IP includes these top-level activities (activity categories):

- Azure Certificates
- Azure Cloud Services
- Azure Deployments
- Azure Storage
- Azure Virtual Machine Disks
- Azure Virtual Machine Images
- Azure Virtual Machines

Each activity in the Windows Azure IP includes required or optional properties. These properties configure how the activity executes its action. The combination of multiple properties on each activity results in a total of 64 different combinations or "activities."

Activity Categories in Depth

This section describes each of the activity categories contained within this IP to provide an understanding of what each activity does. Additional information about each activity and combinations of different configurations is available at http://technet.microsoft.com/en-us/library/jj721977.aspx.

NOTE: SYNCHRONOUS BEHAVIOR

Many activities in the Windows Azure IP have a Wait for Completion property. This property determines whether the activity should wait until the operation is complete in Windows Azure or move on to the next activity. For example, if a runbook includes a **Create Deployment** activity that takes two hours to execute, the runbook will run for at least two hours if the Wait for Completion property is set to TRUE. It is important to design runbooks and automation solutions with synchronous behavior in mind.

- **Azure Certificates:** Handles management and service certificates, such as deleting or listing certificates.
- **Azure Deployments:** Creates, deletes, gets, and swaps deployments. You can also use this category to change, update, upgrade, or roll back deployment configurations.

- **Azure Cloud Services:** Creates, deletes, and gets cloud services. You can also use this category to create affinity groups.
- **Azure Storage:** Lists, creates, deletes, and updates storage accounts and account properties.
- **Azure Virtual Machine Disks:** Adds, deletes, updates, and lists virtual machine disks.
- **Azure Virtual Machine Images:** Adds, deletes, updates, and lists virtual machine operating system images.
- **Azure Virtual Machines:** Creates, deletes, gets, restarts, starts, stops, captures, and updates virtual machine. This activity can also be used to download remote desktop files to connect to virtual machines.

NOTE: AFFINITY GROUPS

Microsoft data centers are large facilities that host thousands of servers. Network latency between two servers can be affected depending on the location of the servers in the data center. Windows Azure uses affinity groups to group servers together within the datacenter to minimize network latency. Without affinity groups where servers are in physical proximity, two servers could be randomly deployed anywhere in the data center.

Use Case Scenarios

The next sections present several typical use cases for the Windows Azure IP. Each runbook uses at least one activity from the Windows Azure IP and demonstrates a common use. The runbooks are explained in depth to demonstrate how you can use activities to automate common Windows Azure processes.

The following three scenarios demonstrate how you can utilize activities effectively from the Windows Azure IP:

- Deploy a new virtual machine in Windows Azure
- Get information about a virtual machine in Windows Azure
- Copy files from a local folder to an Azure storage container
- Deploy a new web service in Windows Azure

The Windows Azure IP often needs specific values, such as the exact name of a virtual machine. Many other IPs work with wildcards, such as all virtual machines named *Exchange*. Sometimes finding the specific value is difficult; using Windows Azure PowerShell helps you find properties and settings. Additional information regarding the Windows Azure PowerShell snap-in is at http://msdn.microsoft.com/en-us/library/windowsazure/jj156055.aspx.

Deploying a New Virtual Machine in Windows Azure

A common request in many businesses is to create virtual machines in Windows Azure. As a manual process, this can consume a significant amount of time. Using service request automation in Service Manager and integration to Windows Azure through Orchestrator lets you automate the entire process. The process can start with a service request in the Service Manager self-service portal; Orchestrator executes the service request and reports back to Service Manager.

The runbook in Figure 18.5 creates a new Azure cloud service and then deploys a new virtual machine to that service. It then creates a remote desktop shortcut file to the new virtual machine. The user provides a server name when starting the runbook; the runbook then creates the new machine. Five activities achieve this:

- The **Initialize Data** activity collects input parameters.
- The **Create Azure Cloud Service** (**Azure Cloud Services**) activity creates a new cloud service for the virtual machine. Multiple virtual machines can exist within a cloud service.
- The **Create Virtual Machine in Azure** (**Azure Virtual Machines**) activity creates a virtual machine in the cloud service.
- The **Create Alert** activity creates an alert in Operations Manager if Windows Azure cannot create a new virtual machine.
- The **Get VM RDP File** activity generates a remote desktop connection shortcut to the new machine.

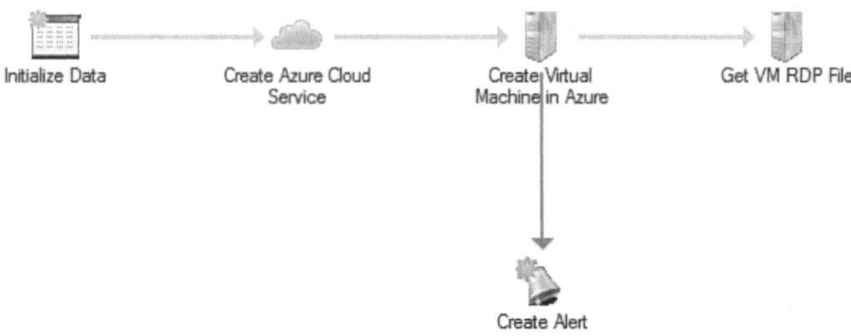

FIGURE 18.5 Runbook for creating a new virtual machine.

This runbook requires the following steps:

1. **Initialize Data:** To collect input parameters needed in the runbook you can use an **Initialize Data** activity. In the example in Figure 18.5, the **Initialize Data** activity is configured to collect one parameter: ServerName, the name of the new virtual machine.

NOTE: PARAMETER NAMES IN THE INITIALIZE DATA ACTIVITY

The **Initialize Data** activity enables you to input any parameter name you want as an input parameter. In some scenarios, a friendly name is better than a more technical parameter name, such as *New Virtual Machine Name* instead of *NVMN*. However, in other instances, it is better to use the name that successive activities in the runbook will use because this can reduce confusion among parameter names. This chapter includes examples of both technical names and friendly names.

2. **Create Azure Cloud Service:** To deploy a new virtual machine, you need a target service. If one already exists, you can use it because one service can contain multiple virtual machines. Figure 18.6 shows how to configure the **Create Azure Cloud Service** activity. This Azure Cloud Services category activity is configured to create a new cloud service named **Machines**. The new cloud service will be deployed in **North Europe**.

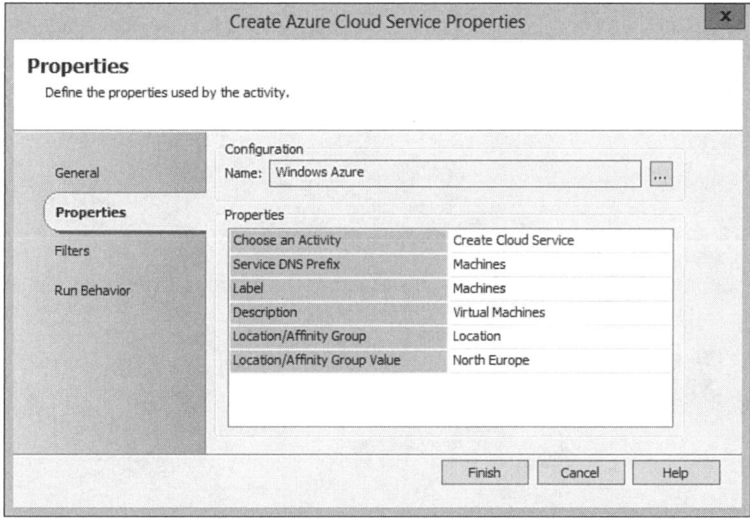

FIGURE 18.6 General configuration for the **Create Azure Service** activity.

3. **Create Virtual Machine in Azure:** This Azure Virtual Machines category activity creates the virtual machine. The activity uses the input parameter ServerName as input in a number of properties (an example is computer name). This activity is also configured to open an endpoint for port 3389, which is required to enable remote desktop connections. Figures 18.7, 18.8, and 18.9 show the configuration of this activity.

4. **Create Alert:** This activity is from the Operations Manager IP. If the **Create Virtual Machine in Azure** activity fails, an alert is generated in Operations Manager.

5. **Get VM RDP File:** This activity creates a local remote desktop connection shortcut file with a file extension of RDP. Use this shortcut to connect to the new virtual machine. Figure 18.10 shows the configuration of the **Get VM RDP File** activity. The activity uses published data from previous activities in the runbook. The RDP shortcut file is stored to a local folder named C:\Azure.

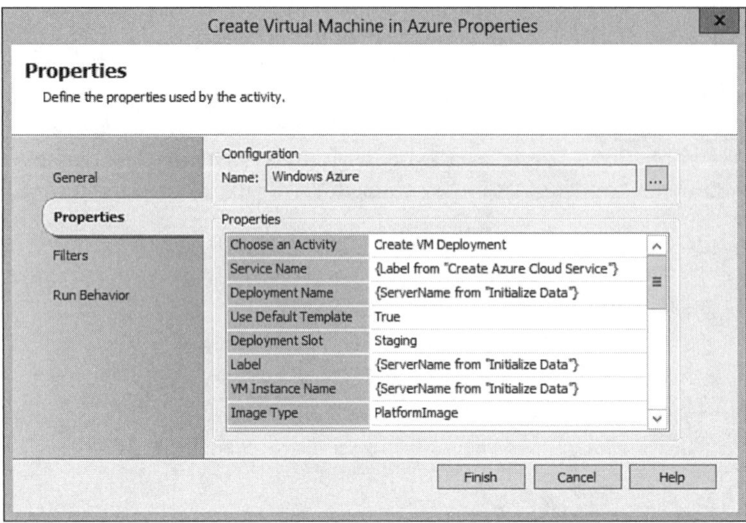

FIGURE 18.7 General configuration for the **Create Virtual Machine in Azure** activity, part 1.

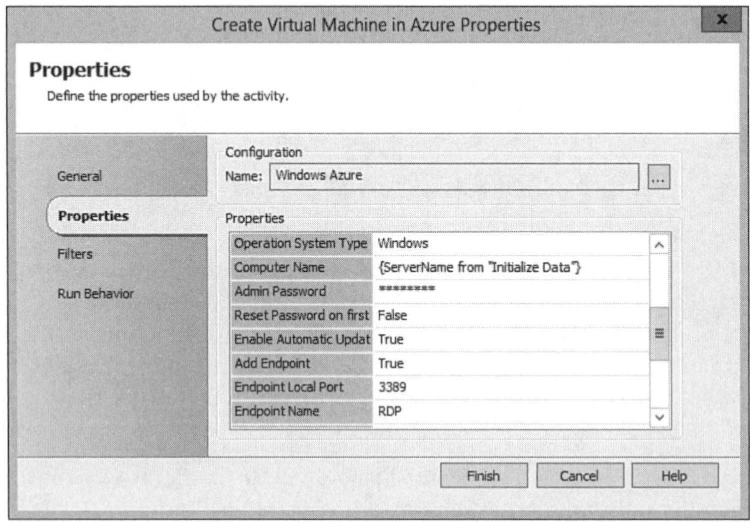

FIGURE 18.8 General configuration for the **Create Virtual Machine in Azure** activity, part 2.

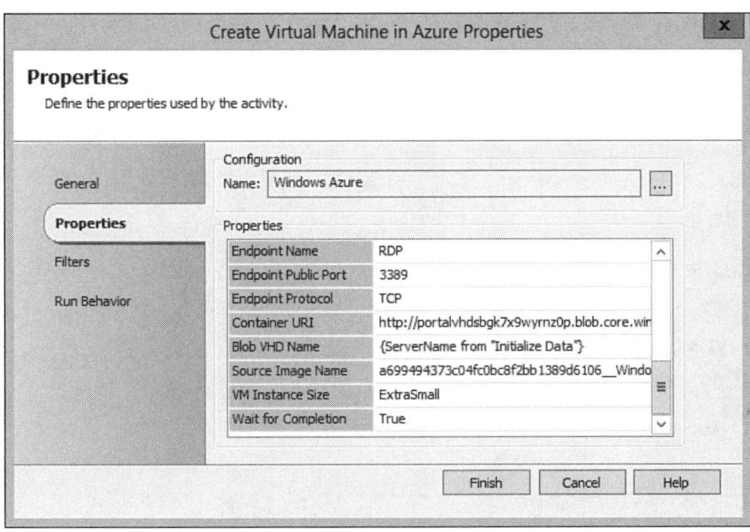

FIGURE 18.9 General configuration for the **Create Virtual Machine in Azure** activity, part 3.

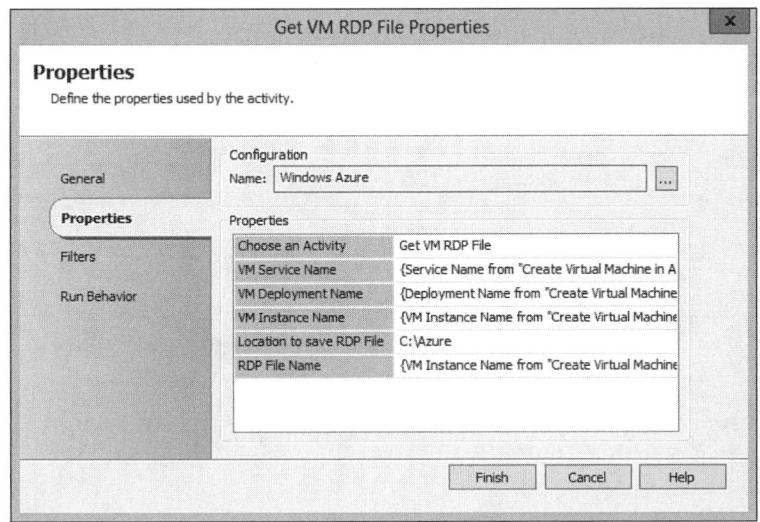

FIGURE 18.10 General configuration for the **Get VM RDP File** activity.

Getting Information About a Virtual Machine in Windows Azure

The runbook in Figure 18.11 obtains information about a virtual machine running in Windows Azure and emails the information to the recipient. The runbook can be used to request information about a virtual machine, such as by using the Service Manager self-service portal. The user inputs a server name and email address when starting the runbook; it then retrieves the machine information and emails it to the specified email address. Three activities achieve this:

- The **Initialize Data** collects input parameters—in this example, the server name and an email address.
- The **Get Azure Virtual Machine Info** activity connects to Windows Azure and reads information about the virtual machine.
- The **Send Email** activity sends an email with the information.

The runbook in Figure 18.11 can be synchronized to Service Manager and used as a runbook automation activity in a service request template. A service request can be published to the Service Manager self-service portal. Engineers or server owners can then use the portal to request server information, as a service request.

FIGURE 18.11 Runbook to get server information.

This runbook requires the following steps:

1. **Initialize Data:** To collect input parameters needed in the runbook, you can use an **Initialize Data** activity. In the example in Figure 18.11, the **Initialize Data** activity is configured to collect two parameters, ServerName and email address.
2. **Azure Virtual Machine:** This activity connects to Windows Azure and reads information about the virtual machine. Figure 18.12 shows the generic configuration of the activity.
3. **Send Email:** This activity sends an email to the email address input in the **Initialize Data** activity.

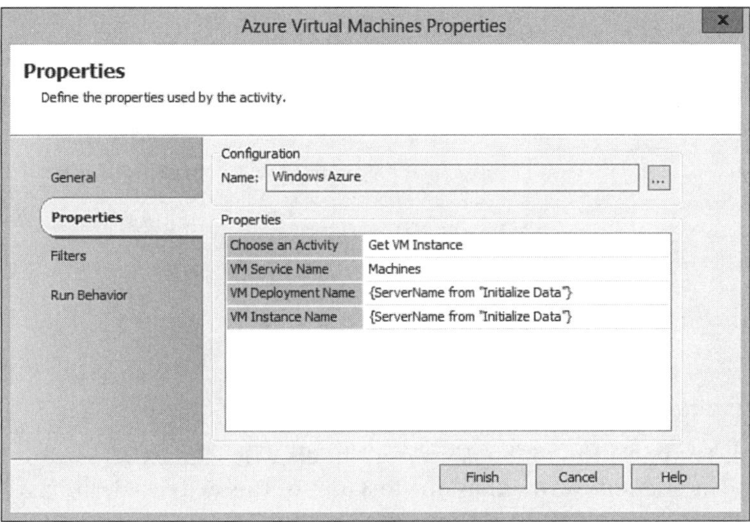

FIGURE 18.12 Configuring the **Azure Virtual Machines** activity.

Copying Files from a Local Folder to an Azure Storage Container

Synchronizing folders can be a task that requires a considerable amount of manual work, and updating files that an application uses can require a number of manual steps. Creating automatic file backup to an online storage area is a good solution for offsite backups. The runbook in Figure 18.13 archives files from a local folder to a Windows Azure storage space. The runbook creates an archive file for all files in a folder and then uploads the archive file to a container in Windows Azure. Seven activities achieve this:

- The **Monitor Date/Time** activity triggers the runbook every 12 hours.
- The **Format Date** activity formats the correct time stamp. The runbook creates a container in Windows Azure with the current time stamp as its name.
- The **Create Folder In Azure Storage** activity creates a container in Azure storage, using the results from the **Format Date** activity as the container name.
- The **Compress File** activity creates an archive file of all files in a local folder.
- The **Upload File To Azure Storage** activity copies the archive file to the new container in Windows Azure storage.
- The **Create Alert** generates an alert in Operations Manager if either of the two Windows Azure activities fails.

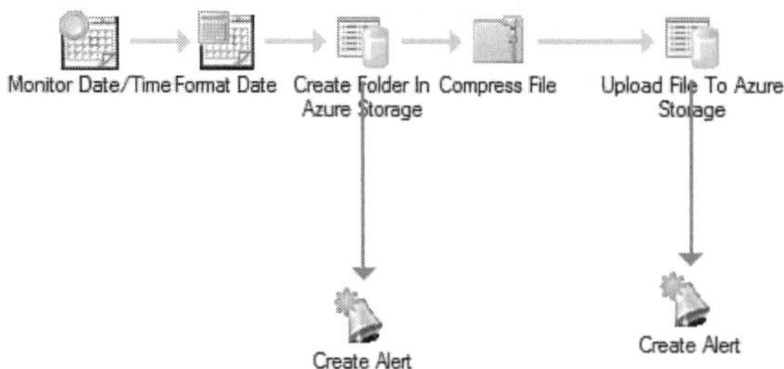

FIGURE 18.13 Runbook to copy files to an Azure storage container.

This runbook requires the following steps:

1. **Monitor Date/Time:** To trigger the runbook every 12 hours, you can use a **Monitor Date/Time** activity. The runbook always has one instance of this activity running; every 12 hours, it triggers a new instance of the runbook that will execute the remainder of the runbook.

2. **Format Date:** This activity uses a variable (Date/Time) as input and outputs the current date using this format for the day, month, and year: ddMMyyyy. Figure 18.14 shows the generic configuration of this activity.

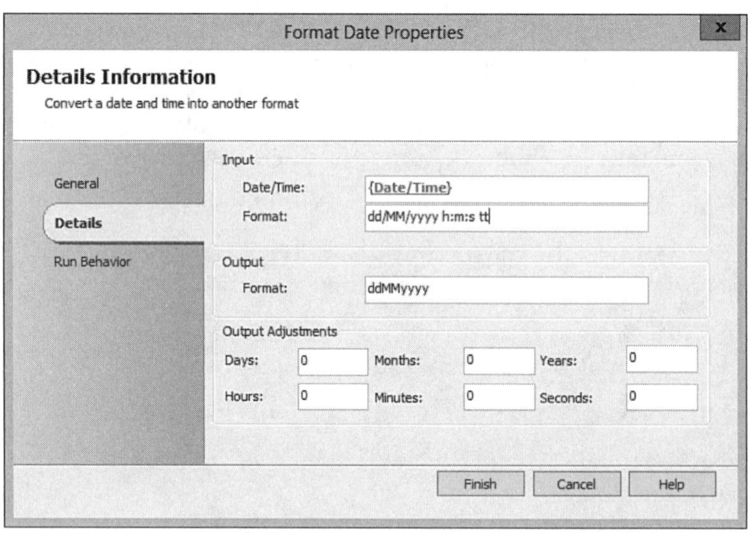

FIGURE 18.14 General configuration of the **Format Date** activity.

3. **Create Folder In Azure:** This activity creates a container in Azure using a storage account that is hard-coded in the activity. Figure 18.15 shows the configuration of the **Create Folder in Azure** activity. The new container is named with the output from the **Format Date** activity.

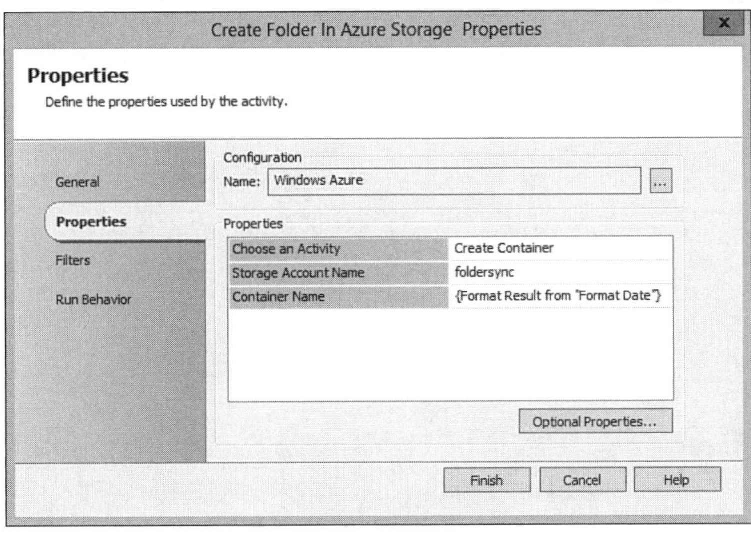

FIGURE 18.15 Configuring the **Create Folder In Azure** activity.

4. **Compress File:** This creates an archive (ZIP) file of all files in the C:\Azure\Upload folder. It names the archive file based on the output from the **Format Date** activity. Figure 18.16 shows the configuration of the **Compress File** activity.

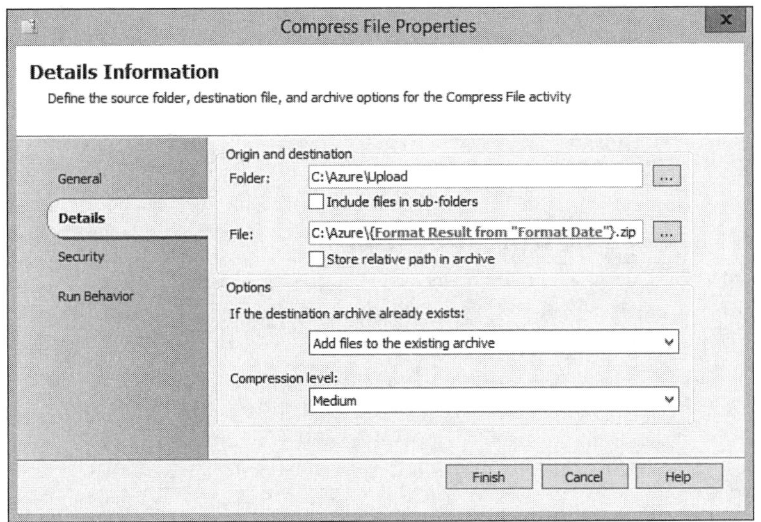

FIGURE 18.16 Configuring the **Compress File** activity.

18

5. **Upload File To Azure Storage:** This activity use the Put Blob activity property to upload the archive file created by the **Compress File** activity to Windows Azure storage. The activity gets the archive file from the previous activity with the storage account and container name. Figure 18.17 displays the configuration of the **Compress File** activity.

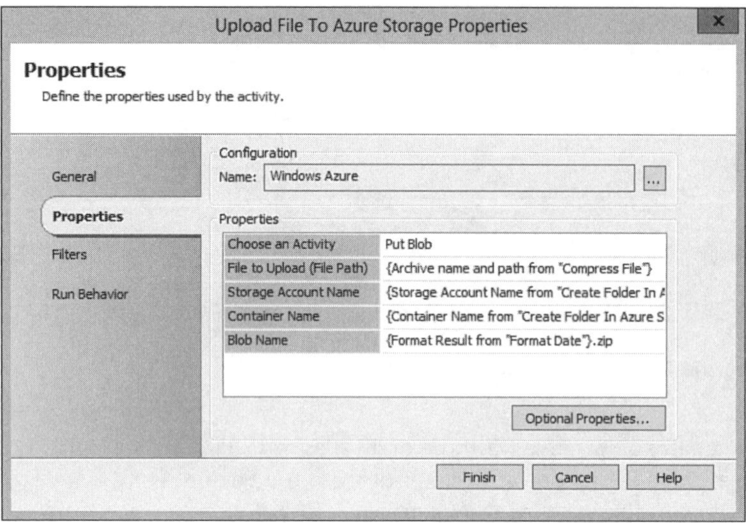

FIGURE 18.17 Configuring the **Upload File To Azure Storage** activity.

6. **Create Alert:** This activity is from the Operations Manager IP. It generates a generic alert in Operations Manager if the Windows Azure activities fail. This runbook contains two **Create Alert** activities.

Deploying a New Web Service in Windows Azure

Deploying a new version of a web service can be a task that requires a considerable amount of manual work, and updating files the application uses can require a number of manual steps. The runbook in Figure 18.18 uploads a web service package to Windows Azure storage and deploys that package. You can use this runbook when test and developer departments need to deploy new instances of a service, letting test engineers and developers handle the entire deployment cycle by themselves without involving or waiting for the information technology (IT) department. Nine activities achieve this:

- The **Initialize Data** activity collects input parameters—in this example, the deployment name and package file path.
- The **Format Date** activity formats the current time stamp. The runbook creates a container in Windows Azure using the time stamp as its name.

- The **Create Service** activity creates a new cloud service in Windows Azure.
- The **Create Container** activity creates a new container in Azure storage, using the data stamp from Format Data as name.
- The **Upload Package** activity uploads the web service package to Azure storage, targeting the new container created by the **Create Container** activity.
- The **Create Deployment** activity creates the new web service with the package uploaded by the previous activity.
- The **Get Status** (a **Get Internet Application Status** activity) checks whether the new web service is responding to requests in a correct way.
- **Return Data** publishes results for the runbook.
- **Create Alert** generates an alert in Operations Manager if any of the five Windows Azure activities fail.

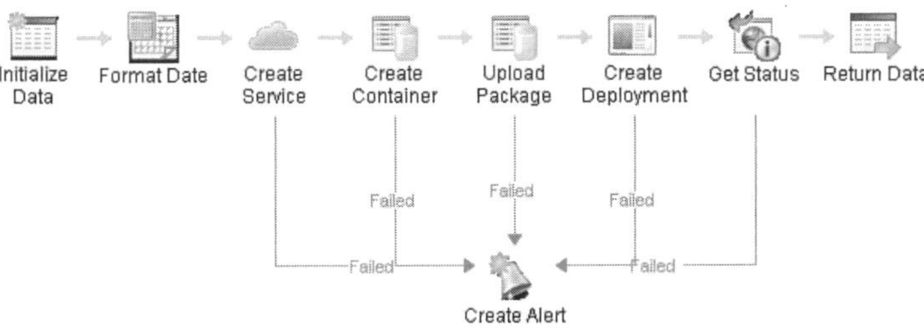

FIGURE 18.18 Runbook to upload and deploy a new web service.

This runbook requires the following steps:

1. **Initialize Data:** To collect input parameters needed in the runbook, you can use an **Initialize Data** activity. In the example in Figure 18.19, the **Initialize Data** activity is configured to collect nine parameters.
2. **Format Date:** This activity uses a variable (Date/Time) as input and outputs the current date using the day/month/year format of ddMMyyyy. Figure 18.14 previously showed the generic configuration of this activity.
3. **Create Cloud Service:** To deploy a new web service, you need a target cloud service. You can use an existing target cloud service because one service can contain multiple web services. Figure 18.20 shows how to configure the **Create Cloud Service** activity. The activity is configured to name the new cloud service using an input parameter, DNS Prefix. The activity also uses the input parameter DNS Prefix as Label and Description for the new cloud service. The new cloud service will be deployed in **North Europe.**

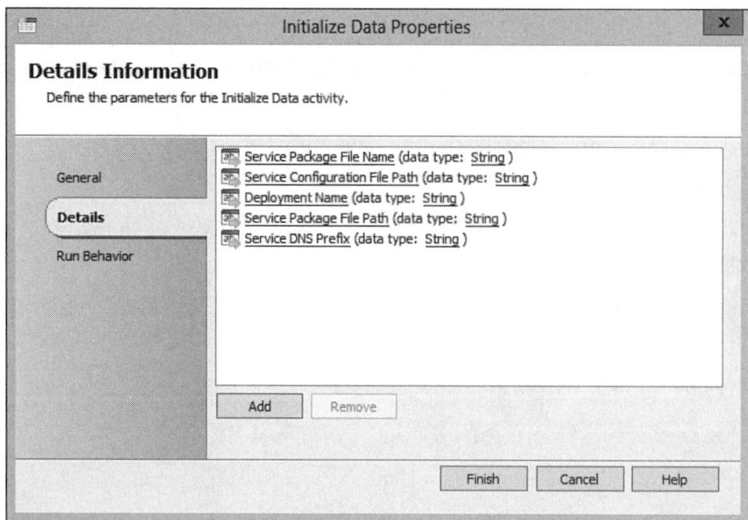

FIGURE 18.19 Input parameters for the runbook in Figure 18.18.

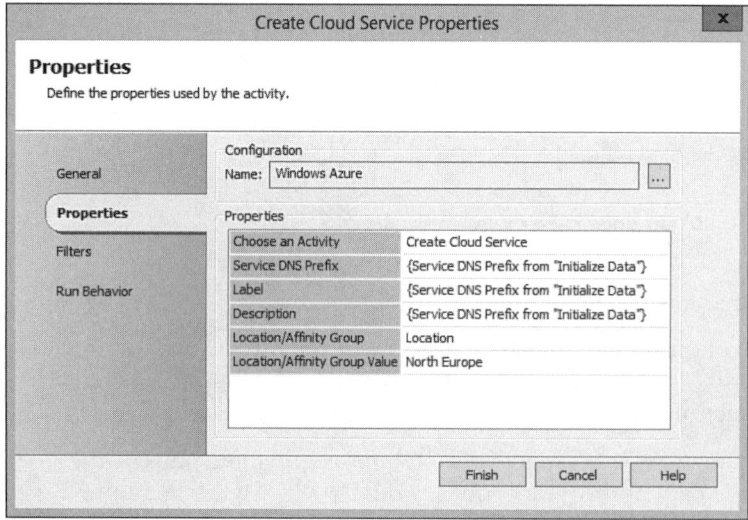

FIGURE 18.20 Configuring the **Create Cloud Service** activity.

4. **Create Container:** This activity creates a container in Azure, in a storage account that is hard-coded in the activity. Figure 18.21 shows the configuration of the **Create Container** activity. The new container is named using the output from the **Format Date** activity.

5. **Upload Service Package:** This activity use the Put Blob activity property to upload the web service package file to Windows Azure storage. The activity gets the File to Upload (File Path) and Service Package File Name from **Initialize Data** as input parameters. The Container Name and Storage Account Name are read from the **Create Container** activity. Figure 18.22 shows the configuration of the **Upload Service Package** activity.

Create Container Properties

Properties

Define the properties used by the activity.

General

Properties

Filters

Run Behavior

Configuration

Name: Windows Azure

Properties

Choose an Activity	Create Container
Storage Account Name	contososervicestorage
Container Name	{Format Result from "Format Date"}

Optional Properties...

Finish Cancel Help

FIGURE 18.21 Configuring the **Create Container** activity.

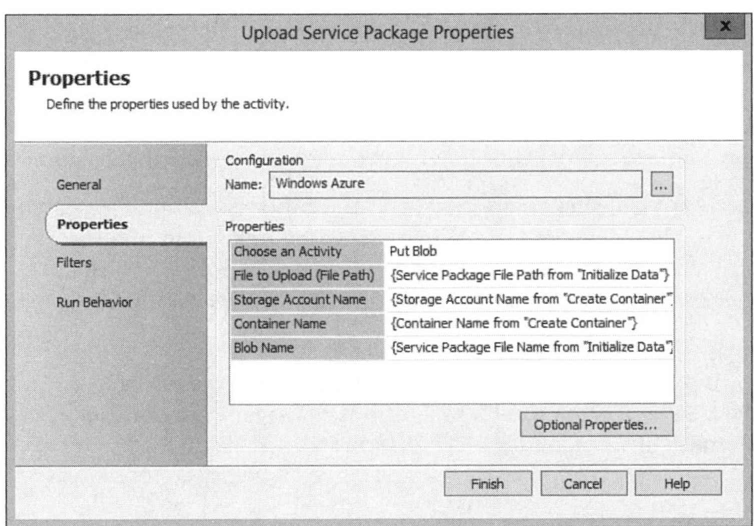

FIGURE 18.22 Configuration of the **Upload Service Package** activity.

18

6. **Create Deployment:** This activity creates a deployment of the web service. The **Create Deployment** activity obtains input parameters from the previous activity and additional input parameters from the **Initialize Data** activity. This activity is configured to Wait for Completion to ensure that the runbook does not continue until the web service is up and running in Azure. Figure 18.23 shows the configuration of the **Create Deployment** activity.

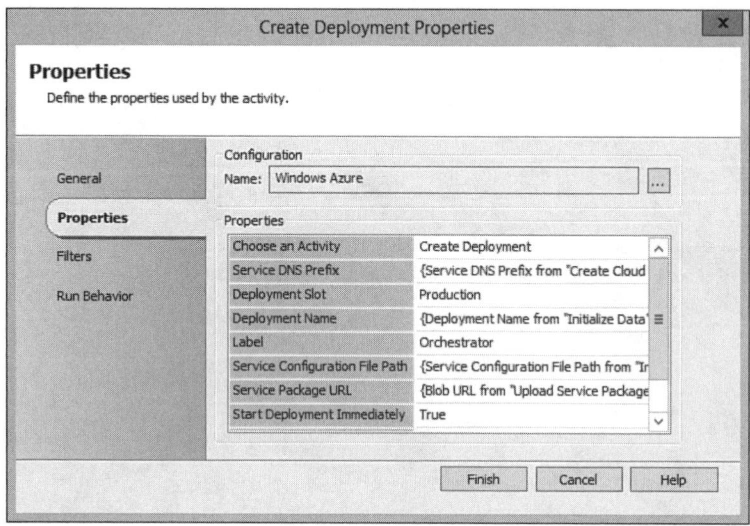

FIGURE 18.23 Configuring of the **Create Deployment** activity.

7. **Get Internet Application Status:** This activity verifies that the URL for the new web service is working. The **Create Deployment** activity publishes a deployment URL that the **Get Internet Application Status** activity uses as input. The **Get Internet Application Status** activity also verifies that the new web service welcome page contains the text **Hello World**. Figure 18.24 shows the configuration of the **Get Internet Application Status** activity. This activity is one of the standard activities.

8. **Return Data:** This activity publishes the results from the runbook. When integrated with a System Center Service Manager Service request, it can be used to publish results back to Service Manager. As a best practice, the authors recommend including a **Return Data** activity in each runbook that might be integrated with Service Manager.

9. **Create Alert:** This activity is from the System Center Operations Manager IP. It generates a generic alert in System Center Operations Manager if any of the Windows Azure activities fail.

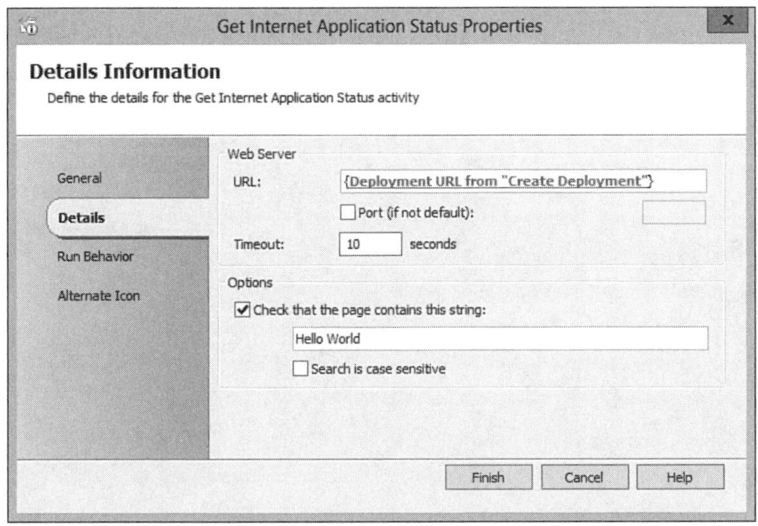

FIGURE 18.24 Configuration of the **Get Internet Application Status** activity.

NOTE: TEST WEB APPLICATIONS AVAILABLE

Microsoft's MSDN website for Windows Azure hosts test web applications that you can download and play with in Windows Azure. You can find more information and download sample applications at http://code.msdn.microsoft.com/windowsazure/. Note that Microsoft does not test or support these samples.

Summary

This chapter covered the installation and configuration requirements of the Windows Azure IP and explored each of the category activities it includes. The chapter also discussed practical application of the Windows Azure IP, with some common use scenarios. You can use the activities within this IP in many ways to automate business processes and manual tasks. When used together with the other IPs available in Orchestrator, you can automate a large percentage of common activities to provide many business efficiencies.

CHAPTER 19

Runbook Automation in the Data Center and the Cloud

IN THIS CHAPTER

The previous chapters provided examples of how you can leverage each of the System Center integration packs (IPs) and the Windows Azure IP to automate common processes. In reality, process automation can be far more complex. As information technology (IT) organizations advance their processes to support dynamic data center and private cloud initiatives, the need to develop end-to-end automation scenarios to support zero-touch automation will continue to grow. In production scenarios, policies often involve activities from multiple IPs. Occasionally, specific limitations require the use of PowerShell scripts or .NET code to augment workflows.

Fortunately, you can use the activities in the System Center IPs and the Windows Azure IP, along with the standard activities, to develop automation scenarios that address the needs of organizations to extend process automation to a level of light touch or even zero touch when appropriate.

This chapter describes some of the common requirements and considerations that go into creating runbooks in the real world. Included are several sample workflows to illustrate how activities from these IPs can be used together in the same workflows and/or with PowerShell to great effect to achieve true end-to-end automation.

Factors in Process Automation Planning and Design

When developing runbooks for production use, several common considerations go into the planning process. These include but are not limited to the following:

- **Change management:** In accordance with guidance defined in the Microsoft Operations Framework (MOF) and Information Technology Infrastructure Library (ITIL), managing change is an important part of IT operations. Changes must be documented and, in some cases, require approval from one or more persons within the organization to ensure that the change has been sufficiently planned and tested before production implementation is authorized. Using the Service Manager IP, you can incorporate change management into any workflow by adding a few simple activities.
- **Error handling and escalation:** Sometimes even well-planned changes fail. The workflow should incorporate logic to notify someone of the error condition in such a situation. Adding logging and error reporting, whether to text, to event logs, or even directly to System Center Service Manager, enables issues encountered in the automation process to be documented and then escalated to appropriate IT support personnel.
- **Asset management:** An up-to-date record of the physical and virtual assets is critical to successful configuration management, chargeback reporting, and reporting on where financial and human resources are being expended. Service Manager natively automates CMDB population, but virtually every enterprise is heterogeneous, with resources housed in many different repositories. Orchestrator can play a key role in automating the population of the CMDB from external data sources, such as third-party monitoring, human resources (HR), and enterprise resource planning (ERP) systems.
- **Self-service capabilities:** When users need resources (software, virtual machines [VMs], and so on), they typically want them right now. IT departments have learned that if users are required to wait, they might find a way to go around IT to get what they need. The results can include nonstandard applications and devices that complicate support and compromise security.
- **Capacity management:** Two promises of the cloud are "capacity on demand" and "pay for what you use." Delivering on these promises requires workflow to automate scale-out for spikes in demand, and scale-in for lulls in traffic (as Chapter 16, "Integration with System Center Virtual Machine Manager," demonstrated). Furthermore, when on-premise resources are at capacity, scaling out into the public cloud (known as *cloud bursting*) might be desirable.
- **Bulk processing:** The need to perform administrative tasks in bulk, such as when provisioning a large number of user accounts, can present special challenges that require the need to extend System Center Orchestrator to perform activities that are not possible or easily achievable with off-the-shelf IPs. Using PowerShell and the **Run .Net Script** activity, administrators can bridge gaps to facilitate reliable automation of repetitive and time-consuming administrative tasks, such as provisioning large numbers of user accounts.

Designing for the dynamic data center is about designing automation with people, process, and technology in mind.

When designing automated workflows, it is important not to focus exclusively on the technology involved in a process; you also must consider the human effort and communication required to complete that process. Some processes actually require manual steps and thus are not suitable for completely hands-free automation.

With System Center Service Manager (and potentially other help desk/ticketing systems), Orchestrator workflows can be extended to monitor for requests that come directly from the service consumer via the tools they use every day to make requests and report problems. By designing workflows with the objective of maintaining this layer of abstraction between service consumer and technology, you can achieve new levels of efficiency in IT service delivery.

Typically, the ticketing system IT uses for incident, problem, and change management and asset tracking ties together the activities of IT service delivery with those of the business processes relying on these services. By presenting the workflows as high-level processes in the ticketing system, such as "provision new user account" as a change management activity, service consumers can make requests in the user interface (UI) without concern for the underlying technology. The child runbooks within the user provisioning workflow, such as the runbooks that provision the user, setup departmental shares, and the user's virtual desktop infrastructure (VDI), are simply check boxes on a form representing procedures within the onboarding process for a new user.

When IT process automation is integrated with business process in this way, the underlying technology fades into the background, allowing business decision makers to focus on driving productivity instead of having to worry about how to navigate unfamiliar technology and difficult processes.

The Role of Orchestrator in Cloud Computing

The world of cloud computing is evolving quickly, and System Center Orchestrator is evolving with it. With the introduction of the Windows Azure IP and a significantly enhanced Virtual Machine Manager (VMM) IP in the System Center 2012 SP 1 release, Orchestrator can play an integral role in provisioning, configuration management, and capacity management in both private and public clouds.

If you are not entirely familiar with cloud computing, an explanation of what differentiates cloud computing from traditional server virtualization might be helpful. Essentially, four key attributes separate cloud computing from server virtualization:

- **Pooled resources:** In a cloud, resources are pooled to provide a larger pool of shared capacity, allowing IT or another service provider to dynamically provision and scale servers and applications.
- **Self-service capability:** When pooled resources are available, cloud computing provides a self-service approach for the business to get at those resources—more specifically, it provides a self-service IT infrastructure to business units and departments with a service level agreement (SLA). This forces a service level discussion and removes the burden to procure, provision, and manage infrastructure on a per-application, ad hoc basis.

- **Elasticity:** Elasticity refers to the capability to scale up (or scale down) dynamically as resource needs change, enabling faster delivery of capacity and cost savings through resource consolidation during lulls in demand.
- **Usage-based model:** A cloud computing environment implements a usage-based cost model, allowing subscribers to pay based on consumption. The "pay for what you use" concept is popular with subscribers for services that frequently experience sharp (but temporary) spikes in demand.

These characteristics offer obvious benefits, but they present a (potentially) radical change to IT departments that must shift from being a technology-focused organization to being a service-delivery focused organization.

The Rise of the Hybrid Cloud

The phrase *hybrid cloud* warrants some clarification. A *hybrid cloud* environment includes multiple integrated internal and/or external providers. Hybrid clouds combine aspects of both public and private clouds:

- *Private cloud* refers to a block of network, storage, and compute resources dedicated to your company within a cloud provider's data center or hoster facility. Private cloud refers a computing model, not a location.
- *Public cloud* services are offered over the public Internet and are available to anyone who wants to purchase the service. Infrastructure as a Service (IaaS) in public cloud services (such as Windows Azure) provides a platform for provisioning highly available VMs to provide distinct services, or even to provide additional capacity when private cloud resources are fully consumed.

Although these are somewhat simplified definitions of cloud computing models, they should provide a base of reference for the concepts this chapter touches on.

Use Case Scenarios

Each runbook in this section uses activities from multiple System Center IPs and the Azure IP, or incorporates PowerShell to achieve a level of process automation common to real-world scenarios.

The three scenarios shown here are explained at length, demonstrating how to automate common repetitive tasks encountered in day-to-day IT operations related to asset management, issue autoremediation, and provisioning:

- CMDB automation (dynamic asset management for data center and hybrid cloud [Orchestrator, Service Manager, and multiple third-party data sources])
- Cross-platform automation (Linux service restart)
- Cloud bursting (Orchestrator, Operations Manager, Windows Azure)

CMDB Automation (Dynamic Asset Management for Data Center and Cloud)

The Import CSV feature in System Center 2012 Service Manager imports comma-separated value (CSV) files to automatically populate data. It requires two files: the CSV file containing the data for the CMDB and the eXtended Markup Language (XML) format file that describes how Service Manager should interpret the data. The disadvantage of this feature versus the unsupported CSV Connector in the previous version (Service Manager 2010) is that this feature requires manual effort to actually import the file. The workflow in Figure 19.1 performs these high-level steps:

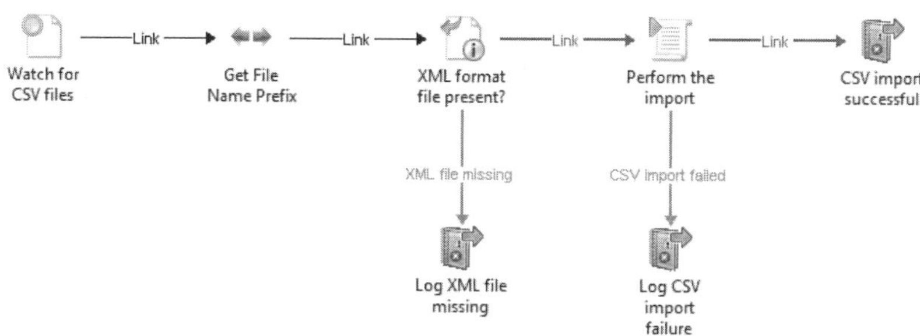

FIGURE 19.1 CMDB Automation (Asset Management) runbook.

- Watches for CSV files and monitors a user-defined directory for a CSV file.
- Verifies that the matching XML format file is present. It assumes that the filename prefix of the CSV file matches that of the XML file. For example, if your CSV file is named FileShare.csv, the XML file must be named FileShare.xml. Detection of a new CSV file (any filename with a CSV extension) triggers the runbook.
- Splits the CSV filename at the period (.) to get the filename prefix.

  Note that the **Get File Name Prefix** activity is not strictly necessary because the built-in data-manipulation function `Field` could have achieved this same goal as part of the direct property input of any activity. The authors have a personal preference for the **Split String** activity, for ease of use.
- Checks to ensure that the matching XML format file is present. If not, an error message is logged to the Windows Application event log, and the sequence ends.
- If both files are present, PowerShell remoting is used to connect to the Service Manager management server, loading the Service Manager PowerShell cmdlets.
- Runs the PowerShell script to import the CSV data file into the Service Manager CMDB.

These steps are performed in the runbook:

1. **Watch for CSV files:** This renamed **Monitor File** activity from the File Management category monitors a user-defined directory for a CSV file (see Figure 19.2). On the Triggers tab, select **Created** (see Figure 19.3).

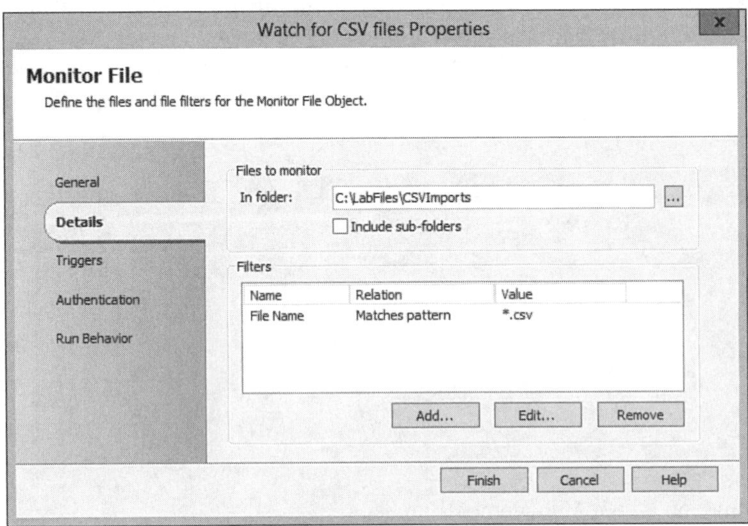

FIGURE 19.2 **Watch for CSV files** activity properties.

FIGURE 19.3 **Watch for CSV files** trigger properties.

2. **Get File Name Prefix:** This renamed **Split String** activity splits the CSV filename at the period (.) to get the filename prefix. Figure 19.4 shows the **Get File Name Prefix** configuration.

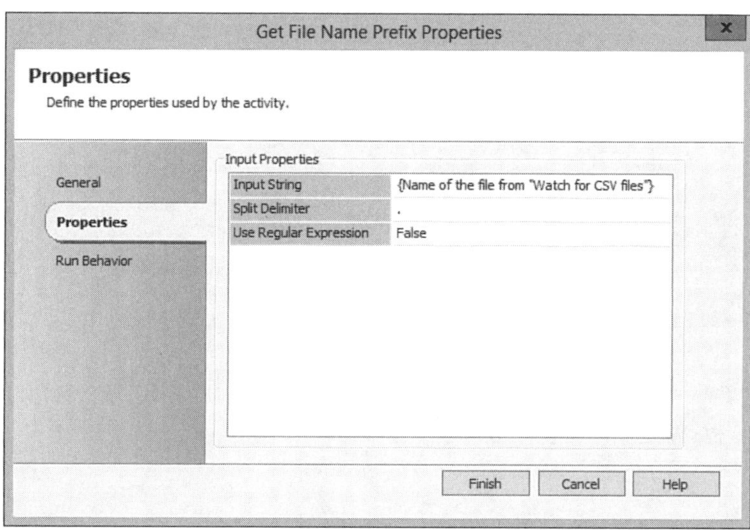

FIGURE 19.4 **Get File Name Prefix** activity properties.

3. **XML format file present?:** This renamed **Get File Status** activity checks to ensure that the matching XML format file is present. Figure 19.5 shows the configuration.

   If the matching XML file is not present, it triggers **Log XML file missing**, a renamed **Get File Status** activity, to log an error message to the Windows Application event log. The sequence then ends (see Figure 19.6).

4. **Perform the import:** After both the CSV and XML are confirmed as present, this renamed **Run .Net Script** activity (see Figure 19.7) runs a PowerShell script to initiate the CSV import process.

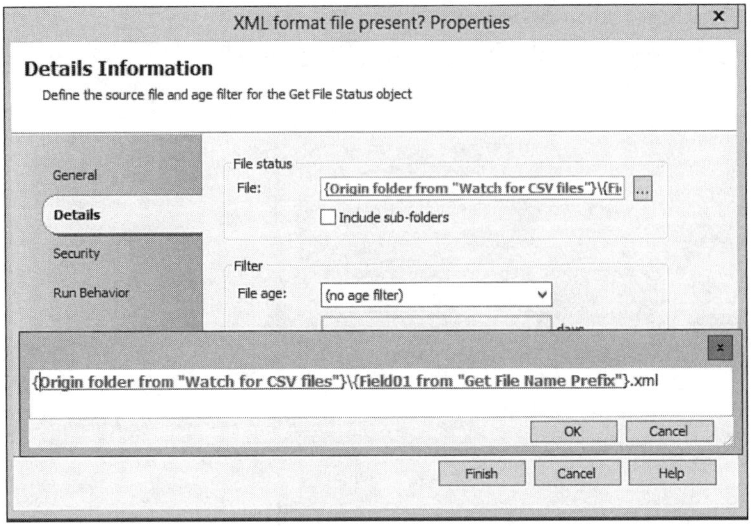

FIGURE 19.5 **XML format file present?** activity properties.

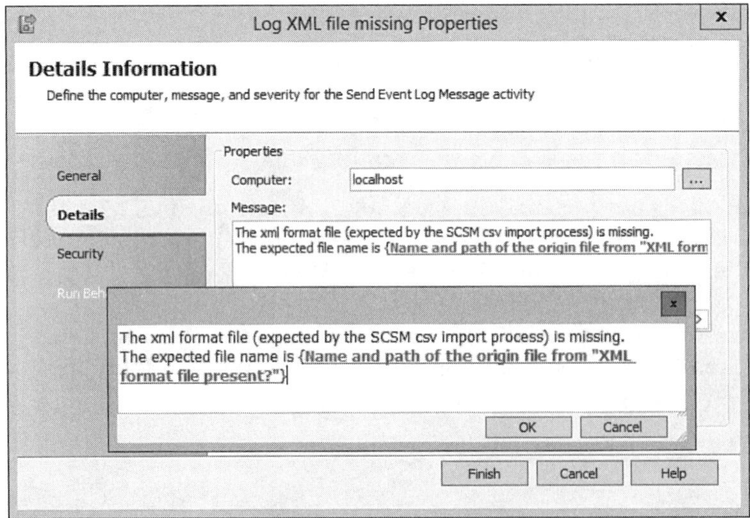

FIGURE 19.6 **Log XML file missing** activity properties.

The script in Figure 19.8 is available in the download included with this book. See Appendix C, "Available Online," for further information.

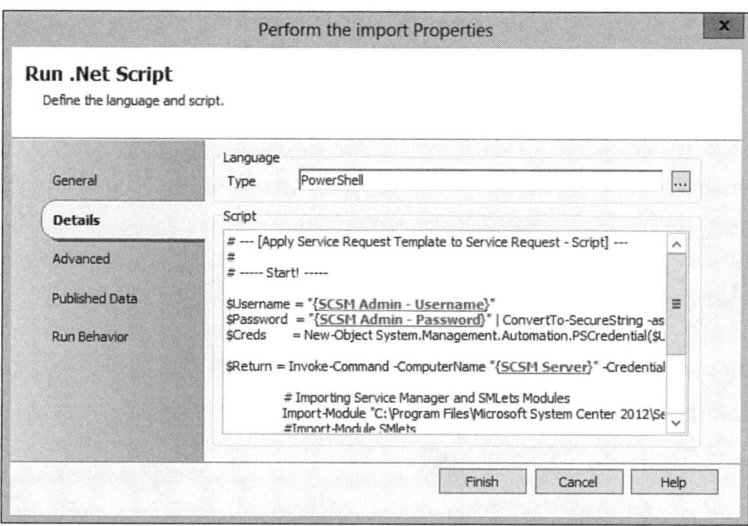

FIGURE 19.7 **Perform the import** activity properties.

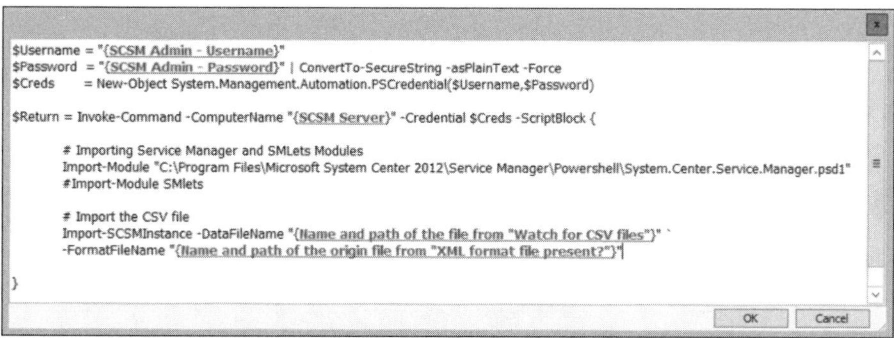

FIGURE 19.8 PowerShell script in **Perform the import** activity properties.

5. **CSV import successful:** If the import process completes successfully, this renamed **Send Event Log Message** activity logs an event to the Windows Application event log on the Orchestrator runbook server. Figure 19.9 shows the configuration of this activity.

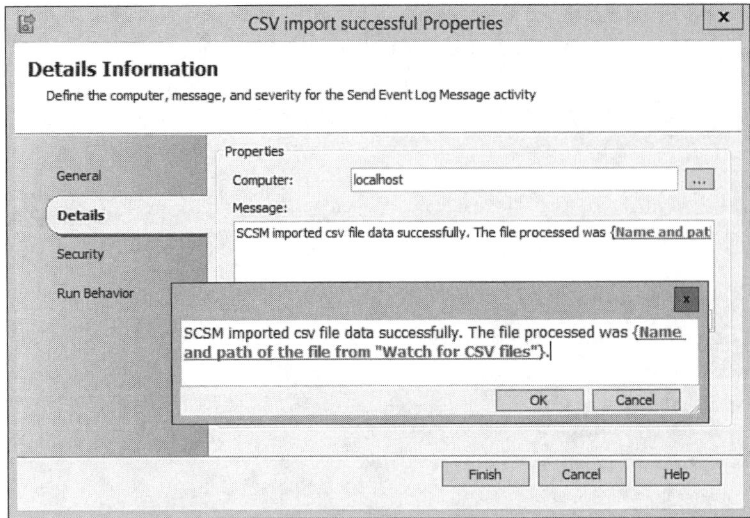

FIGURE 19.9 **CSV import successful** activity properties.

If script execution fails, a failure message is logged to the Windows Application event log on the Orchestrator runbook server. Figure 19.10 displays the configuration of the event description of the failure event.

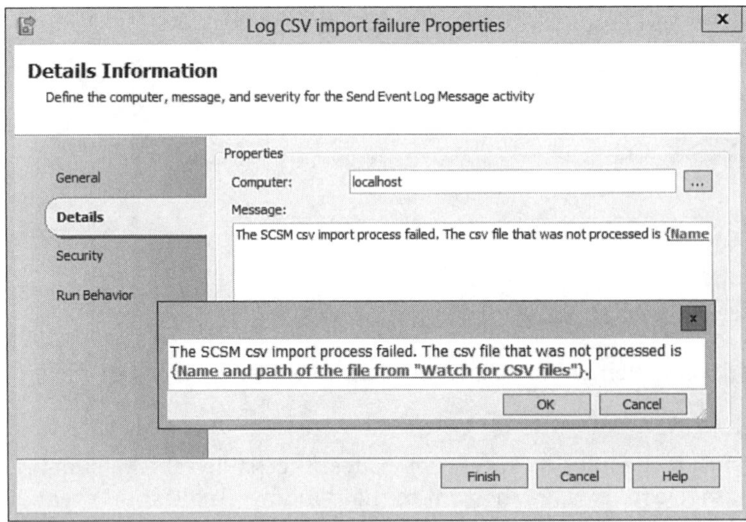

FIGURE 19.10 **Log CSV import failure** activity properties.

6. The XML file missing link triggers the next activity in this branch of the runbook if the expected XML format file is missing (see Figure 19.11).

7. The CSV import failed link triggers the next activity in this branch of the runbook if the CSV file import process fails (see Figure 19.12).

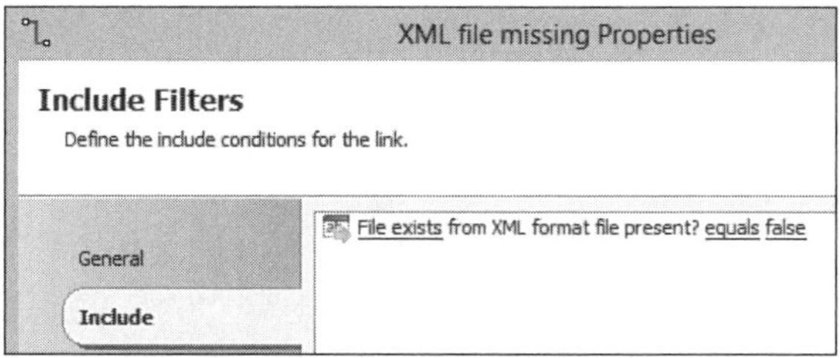

FIGURE 19.11 Link filtering logic in the XML file missing properties.

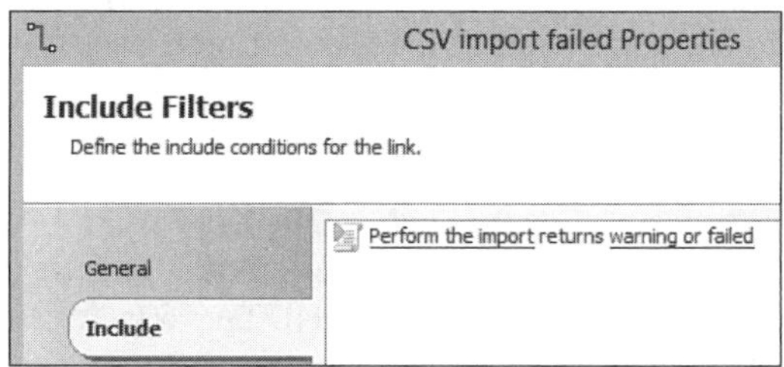

FIGURE 19.12 Link filtering logic in the CSV import failed properties.

Cross-Platform Integration (Linux Service Restart)

System Center 2012 provides strong support for the heterogeneous enterprise, and its Orchestrator component is no exception. The **Run SSH Command** activity in the System category supports automating a wide variety of administrative tasks on Linux and UNIX systems. It also makes parsing command output a simple task (output is stored in a published data property called Execution Result). This example looks at a sample runbook that checks the status of a Linux/UNIX service (daemon) and starts the service if it is not already running.

The workflow in Figure 19.13 performs the following high-level steps:

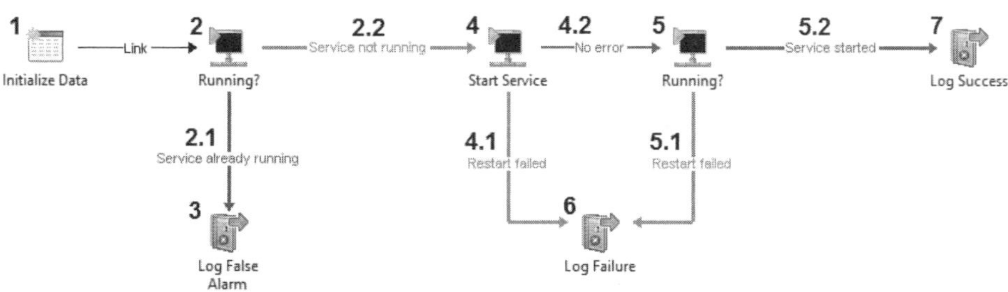

FIGURE 19.13 Linux Service Restart runbook.

- Accepts input in the form of a computer name, service name, and SSH port number.
- Checks the status of the target service on the specified computer (both provided as input) to determine whether the service is actually stopped.
- If the service is running, an event is logged to the Windows Application event log indicating a false alarm.
- If the service is not running, a service restart is attempted.
- If the restart reported success, the service status is verified again to ensure that the service is running. Based on the result, a success or failure event is logged.

REAL WORLD: ADAPTING RUNBOOKS FOR INCIDENT REMEDIATION

You can easily adapt this runbook to function as a recovery task for System Center 2012 Operations Manager. To do so, create a monitoring runbook using the **Monitor Alert** activity that then calls this runbook to remediate the failed service.

Before creating the runbook, begin by creating two variables (see Figure 19.14) to hold the username and password provided by your Linux/UNIX administrator. Notice that the option to encrypt the variable containing the Linux password was selected. This enables your Linux/UNIX administrator to supply an audited account with the necessary permissions so that Orchestrator administrators and operators do not even need to know the username and password.

If you need help in creating a variable, you can find step-by-step guidance in Chapter 8, "Advanced Runbook Concepts."

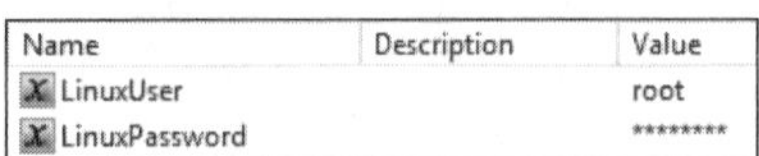

Name	Description	Value
LinuxUser		root
LinuxPassword		********

FIGURE 19.14 Variables to store the privileged Linux/UNIX credentials.

The following activities are used in the runbook:

1. **Initialize Data:** The **Initialize Data** activity accepts three input parameters (see Figure 19.15):
    - **Service:** The name of the Linux/UNIX server (daemon). This example uses the HTTP daemon, which is httpd.
    - **ComputerName:** The name or IP address of the target Linux system.
    - **SSHPort:** The listening port of the SSH daemon on the target system.

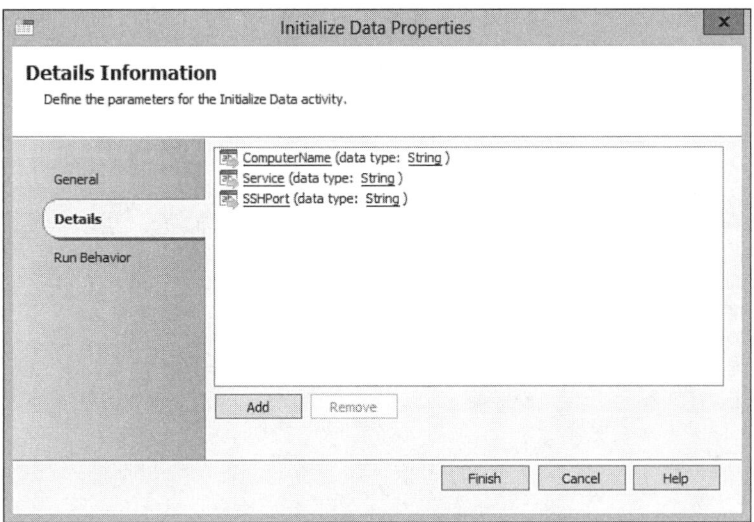

FIGURE 19.15 **Initialize Data** properties.

TIP: MAKING RUNBOOK INPUT AND VARIABLE NAMES USER FRIENDLY

Orchestrator allows both runbook input parameters (contained in the **Initialize Data** activity) and variable names to be friendly names containing multiple words with spaces between them. As an example, ComputerName can be changed to Computer Name.

2. **Running?:** To start the service, the **Running?** activity in Figure 19.16 is a renamed **Run SSH Command** activity from the System category in the Runbook Designer. The command to check service status in CentOS is service <servicename> status. For example, to check the status of the httpd service, the command is `service httpd status`.

   This activity has the following parameters:

   The Details tab contains the inputs to accept the desired computer, SSH listening port, and service for which you want to check the status (httpd, in this example):

   - **Computer:** Published data {ComputerName from "Initialize Data"}
   - **Port:** Published data {SSHPort from "Initialize Data"}
   - **Run Command:** Service {Service from "Initialize Data"} status

   The Advanced tab contains the variables created containing the username and password for the target Linux/UNIX system:

   - **Username:** Variable {LinuxUser}
   - **Password:** Variable {LinuxPassword}

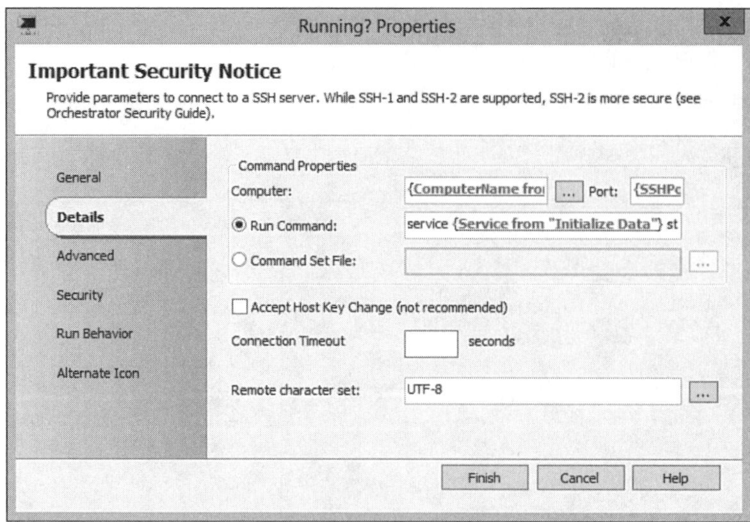

FIGURE 19.16 **Running?** activity properties.

2.1 Service already running: This branch is triggered if the specified service is currently running. Service status can be determined by searching for the string "running" in the Execution Result published data from the **Running?** activity. If the string is present, the service is running.

2.2 Service not running: This branch is triggered if the specified service is not running. The logic should be configured to monitor for the condition "Execution Result from Running? does not contain running" (see Figure 19.17).

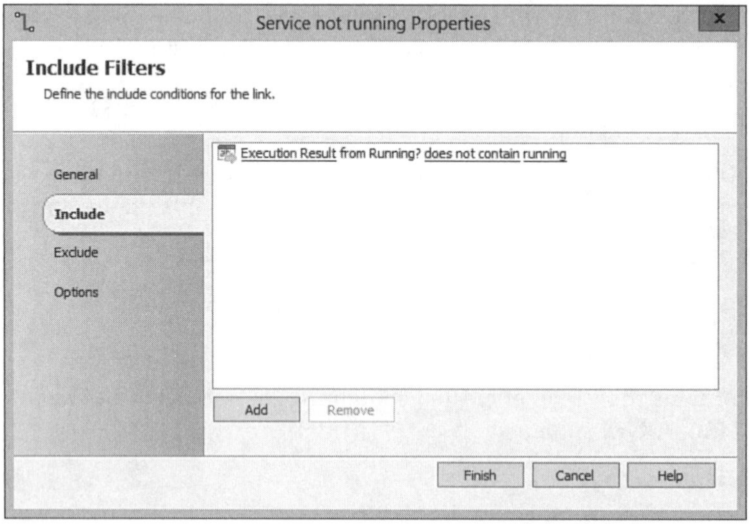

FIGURE 19.17 Link evaluation logic in **Service not running**.

3. **Log False Alarm:** This renamed **Send Event Log Message** activity sends an event to the Windows Application event log. The suggested event text is "The {Service from "Initialize Data"} service on host {ComputerName from "Initialize Data"} is already running. Exiting quietly." (see Figure 19.18).

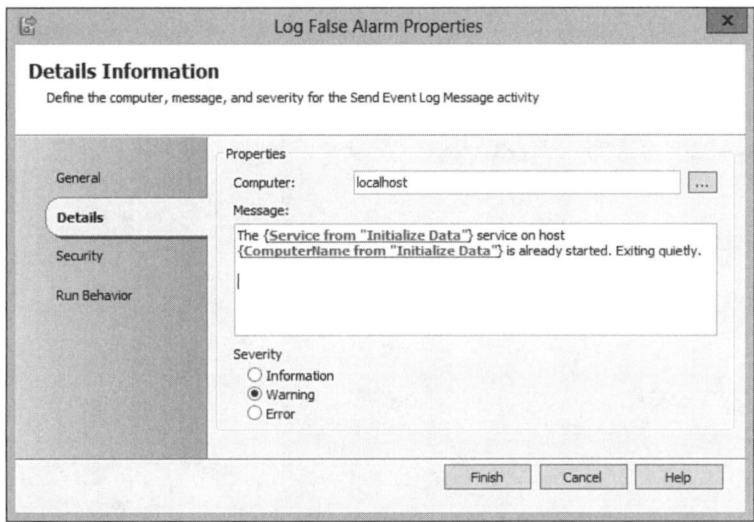

FIGURE 19.18 **Log False Alarm** activity properties.

4. **Start Service:** To start the service, the **Start Service** activity is a renamed **Run SSH Command** activity from the System category in the Runbook Designer. The command to start a service in CentOS is service <servicename> start. As an example, to start the httpd service, the command is `service httpd start`.

   This activity has the following parameters:

   On the Details tab:

   - **Computer:** Published data {ComputerName from "Initialize Data"}
   - **Port:** Published data {SSHPort from "Initialize Data"}
   - **Run Command:** Service {Service from "Initialize Data"} start

   On the Advanced tab:

   - **Username:** Variable {LinuxUser}
   - **Password:** Variable {LinuxPassword}

   The only difference between this and the **Running?** activity described in step 2 is the command that is being run.

4.1 Restart failed: Similar to the Service not running link described in step 2.2, Restart failed triggers the next activity in the runbook if the published data in the Execution Result property of Start Service does not contain the string "running" (see Figure 19.19).

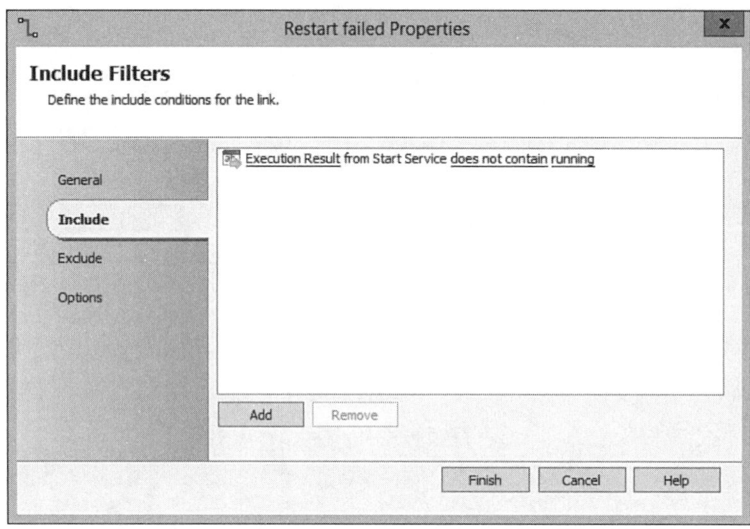

FIGURE 19.19 Restart failed link properties.

5. Running?: This renamed **Run SSH Command** activity is configured identically to the activity of the same name described in step 2. Similar to that activity, it is intended to verify that the target service is running—in this case, after a service restart is attempted.

5.1 Restart failed: This link triggers the next activity in the runbook if the published data in the Execution Result property of the **Running?** activity (step 5) does not contain the string "running".

5.2 Service started: If the service is started, this link triggers the **Log Success** activity if the published data in the Execution Result property of the **Running?** activity (step 5) contains the string "running".

6. Log Failure: This renamed **Send Event Log Message** activity sends an event to the Windows Application event log. The suggested event text is "The {Service from "Initialize Data"} service on host {ComputerName from "Initialize Data"} is failed to start. Please investigate."

7. **Log Success:** This is a renamed **Send Event Log Message** activity to the Windows Application event log. The suggested event text is "The {Service from "Initialize Data"} service on host {ComputerName from "Initialize Data"} was started successfully."

Cloud Bursting (Capacity Management for Hybrid Cloud)

One of the core tenants of the hybrid cloud is elasticity in the face of sudden spikes in demand. Cloud bursting is an application deployment model in which an application runs in a private cloud or data center and *bursts* into a public cloud when the demand for computing capacity spikes. As mentioned in the section "The Role of Orchestrator in Cloud Computing," one promise of cloud computing is that an organization pays for extra compute resources only when they are needed. The runbook in this example is largely theoretical, but it provides an example of how you can leverage runbook automation to automate capacity management in a hybrid cloud environment.

The runbook in Figure 19.20 detects an alert related to your VM or service (you must choose an applicable alert in your environment) and then calls the Deploy a New Virtual Machine in Windows Azure runbook, described in Chapter 18, "Integration with Windows Azure," to deploy a new virtual machine in a cloud service. Two activities achieve this:

- The **Monitor Alert** activity monitors for an alert of your choice that indicates that your VM or service is oversubscribed. Figure 19.21 shows the properties for this alert.
- The **Invoke Runbook (Azure VM)** activity, in Figure 19.22, calls the runbook in Figure 19.23 (and described in detail in Chapter 18), creating a new VM in the Azure cloud to scale out capacity of the on-premise service. Multiple VMs can exist within a cloud service.

FIGURE 19.20 Cloud Bursting sample runbook.

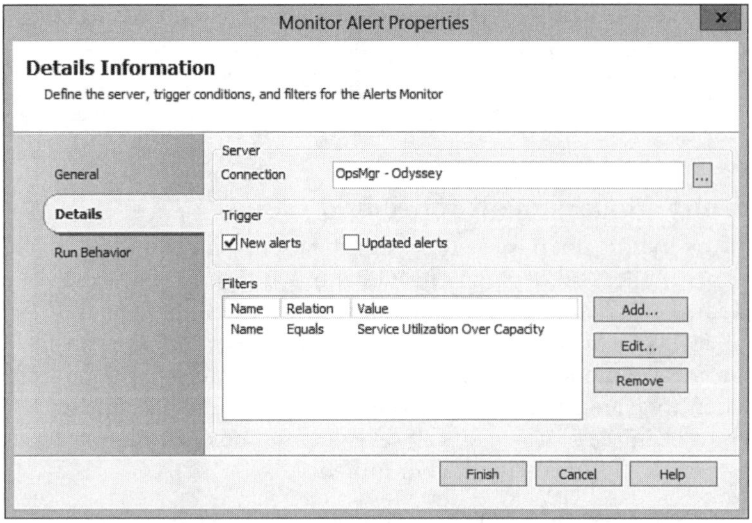

FIGURE 19.21 **Monitor Alert** activity properties.*

** The alert name in Figure 19.21 is just a placeholder for an alert name or other criteria of your choosing, relevant to your service monitoring and automation scenario. It is included here only to provide context in the sample scenario.*

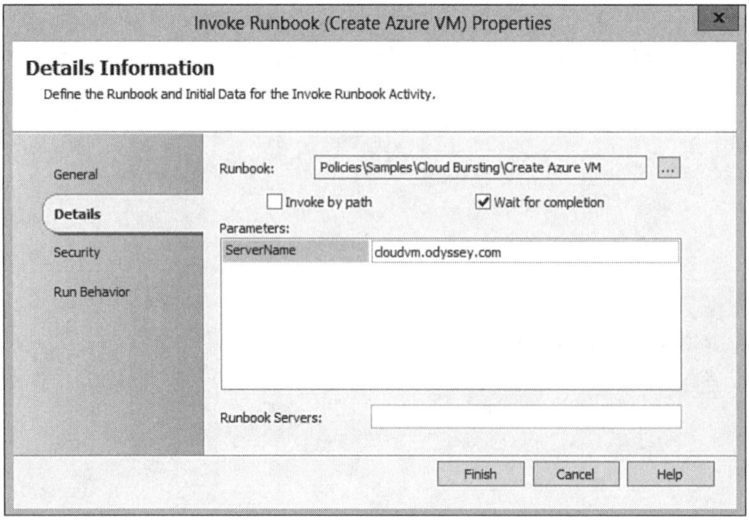

FIGURE 19.22 **Invoke Runbook (Create Azure VM)** activity properties.

The runbook in Figure 19.23 (described in detail in Chapter 18) creates a new Azure cloud service and then deploys a new virtual machine to the cloud service. It then creates a remote desktop shortcut file to the new virtual machine. It accepts a server name as input when starting the runbook; the runbook creates the new machine in an Azure cloud service.

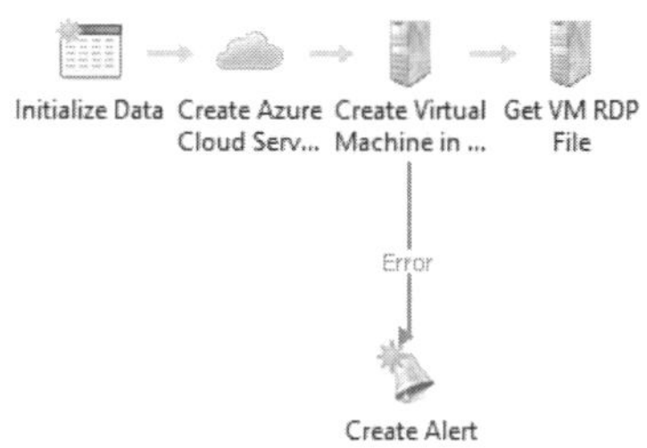

FIGURE 19.23 Runbook for creating a new VM in Azure.

Summary

Process automation is itself an import part of service delivery, but you can provide even greater efficiencies by extending process automation to automate activities in a way that is comfortable for service consumers and lower-level IT support groups. This chapter presented some examples of how to use the System Center integration packs and PowerShell to create more sophisticated process automation scenarios, delivering end-to-end automation scenarios to support your organization's service delivery improvement initiatives, dynamic data center, and private cloud initiatives. Cloud computing and IT-as-service might not be a destination on every IT department's roadmap, but all organizations can benefit from process automation designed with the end-to-end workflow (including both the technology *and* the people involved) in mind.

Process automation should not be limited to only the time-consuming and/or expensive tasks or issues; it should extend to any process in which speed, consistent results, and good documentation are desired. In the end, this approach opens the door to enabling responsive service delivery of high value to the other business units within the organization.

As another way to add value to IT operations, the next chapter discusses using the Orchestrator Integration Toolkit to create your own custom activities and publish integration packs.

CHAPTER 20

The Orchestrator Integration Toolkit

IN THIS CHAPTER

The Orchestrator activity library consists of actions you can integrate into your runbooks. Standard activities are those activities available out of the box in your library and ready for use in your workflow. These workflow activities can be extended using integration packs (IPs) that include product specific activities. You can also incorporate the System Center Orchestrator Integration Toolkit (OIT), which provides a set of tools you can use to extend the activity library with your own workflow activities and integration packs.

The OIT lets you extend your library in these ways:

- You can integrate commands, PowerShell scripts, programs, and Secure Shell (SSH) commands into custom workflow activities.
- Developers can create custom activities by integrating their own code into the Orchestrator assembly structure to define the input and output of those activities.

The toolkit includes several tools to validate activities and integrate these validated activities into the Runbook Designer:

- The toolkit includes an IP that contains activities for running and testing Orchestrator assemblies. You can use activities in the OIT to validate your own Orchestrator software development kit (SDK) assemblies in runbooks.
- The Command-Line Activity Wizard lets you quickly transform your own commands and scripts into Orchestrator workflow activities.

- The Integration Pack Wizard can package validated workflow activity assemblies as a set of activities in your integration packs. This lets you create a user-friendly interface for workflow activities and IPs, enabling you to deploy these workflow activities to different runbook servers or runbook designers in your environment.

This chapter discusses the tools available in the OIT. It covers how to use the tools and create your own workflow activities, and it provides an overview of the extensibility capabilities of System Center Orchestrator.

Overview of the Orchestrator Integration Toolkit

The Orchestrator Integration Toolkit consists of tools to help you incorporate your own logic in the Orchestrator environment. It offers options to develop and define the deployment style for any activities you create. Developers can use the SDK to create custom activities; those who are not programmers can transform scripts into activities. The capability to create your own activities provides an extra level of flexibility in System Center Orchestrator integration and automation. The various tools in the OIT offer this functionality:

- **Command-Line Activity Wizard:** This command-line utility enables you to create activities that include commands to execute Windows commands, PowerShell scripts, programs, and SSH commands.
- **Integration Pack Wizard:** This utility enables you to package your own created Orchestrator assemblies (DLLs) and dependant files into integration packs.
- **Integration Toolkit .NET IP:** The Toolkit .NET IP includes the **Invoke .NET** and **Monitor .NET** activities, which you can use to run Orchestrator activity assemblies.
- **Integration Toolkit SDK Library:** Developers use the Orchestrator SDK to write custom workflow activities.

The toolkit includes options to create and deploy your own activities. You can use different tools depending on the type of integration and how these activities will be deployed. The next sections describe the various options the toolkit provides during the different phases (planning, development, and deploying) of creating custom workflow activities. As when you build an Orchestrator runbook, you must have a target, process, and plan for your activity development.

Development Planning

Your decision to create a workflow activity comes from the automation process being built. You might need to include an action in the workflows that you cannot perform with an existing activity, or you might want to simplify reoccurring command-line actions. Some examples of when you might use the tools in the OIT follow:

- **Requirement to integrate specific actions unavailable in existing IPs:** Here you need to look for automation options. These could be scriptable, a program, or C# code that can be integrated with the Orchestrator SDK.
- **Scripts/programs that are required in multiple runbooks:** If you use one or more scripts regularly for different automations, you can create your own activities instead of repeatedly retyping (or copying) the script in an existing activity.
- **Need to interact with external systems to integrate a set of actions for use in runbooks:** Here you probably know how to code against the target to enable the action, and you need to use the Orchestrator SDK and Integration Pack Wizard.

These are just some examples of how you might use the tools to create and integrate workflow activities. Before you build an activity, you must determine its inputs, actions, and outputs. Consider these questions before you start using the tools:

- What functions are desired, and against which target?
- How many workflow activities might be necessary to enable those functions?
- How many and what inputs and outputs are required for each activity to enable the desired functionality?
- Can you use scripts, programs, or commands to execute the desired action?
- Is an application programming interface (API) available for the target system?

The answers to these questions can provide guidance for tool usage and how to configure your workflow activity. To create the activity, you will want to dive into available automation options. Answers to these next questions provide input for developing the activity:

- Will the command-line utility method be an option for this project?
    - Can you integrate existing scripts or programs into your runbook automation?
    - Does the Command-Line Activity Wizard support the scripting language?
- What type of API is available for the target system?
    - Does the API require that any specific functionality be enabled on the target system?
    - How do you want to present input, outputs, and filters for your activity?
    - Is existing code available for the desired functionality, or must you start from scratch?

The authors recommend that you document your project. You might create a document template with questions to use as input during development. This information is the input for starting your project. Treat your OIT projects as you would treat any other software development project.

Developing the Workflow Activities

The OIT includes a variety of types of tools. For example, you could use the Command-Line Activity Wizard to run programs or use the Orchestrator SDK to create your own workflow activities with Visual Studio. A brief description of each follows:

- **Command-Line Activity Wizard:** Use this wizard to execute Windows commands, PowerShell scripts, programs, and SSH commands. You can create workflow activities from nearly any command line interface (CLI) or PowerShell cmdlet or script. If you already have a large script library, consider transforming these scripts into workflow activities and integrating them into your Orchestrator activity library. The authors recommend the Command-Line Activity Wizard if you have little to no programming experience because it provides clickable steps and instructions.
- **Integration Toolkit SDK Library:** This is a developer tool used to create workflow activities, although it might be challenging for those who lack a programming background to understand the "method" usage and flexibility of this tool. Using the SDK is the most flexible and powerful approach for creating Orchestrator activities.

Using either of these tools results in an assembly (DLL) file; you can test this in your runbooks with the **Invoke .NET** activity or incorporate it into an integration pack for use with production runbooks.

Deploying Workflow Activities

When a custom activity is deployed, it is available for use in runbooks. In addition to actual usage of the activity, consider the following:

- You need to test your activities. To be able to test the execution, the activity must be available in the Runbook Designer.
- You must be able to apply updates to the code, commands, or scripts in your activities.
- You need to determine the number of activities you want to integrate into the Orchestrator activity library.

The toolkit provides two options for deploying a custom activity: using the OIT activities and creating your own IP. Creating an IP is the most comprehensive way to make your activities available to Orchestrator.

You need to know when it is appropriate to bundle your assembly in an IP or to use the Orchestrator Integration Toolkit .NET IP activities. Using the OIT IP activities is flexible; deploying an IP involves installing a Windows Installer file and updating the Orchestrator database. Consider a description of these two options:

- **Integration Pack Wizard**
  - Packages assembly and dependant files in an IP
  - Requires that IPs created with the wizard be registered and deployed using Orchestrator Deployment Manager

    - Provides a complete end-to-end solution that updates the database, with custom activities appearing in the Activities pane of the Runbook Designer
    - Enables you to deploy activities to multiple runbook servers or runbook designers across your organization and to external customers
- **Integration Toolkit .NET IP activities**
    - Provides zero footprint integration of custom created activities
    - Is the recommended deployment method for testing custom workflow activities
    - Does not require you to package the DLL file(s) in an IP; you can directly reference your file in the activity and start using it in runbooks
    - Requires that the assembly be available on every runbook server where you want to execute the custom workflow activity

Always test your assembly using the OIT IP activities. You then can further integrate your solution in a more user-friendly way using a custom IP created with the Integration Pack Wizard.

The "Command-Line Activity Wizard" and "Using the Orchestrator SDK" sections discuss the procedure for using your custom assemblies with the Integration Toolkit .NET IP activities. The "Integration Pack Wizard" section describes creating an IP using the toolkit.

Preparing the Project

After you gather all required information about the inputs, outputs, and action the activity should perform, it is time to use the OIT. Review how to integrate scripts or commands—the "Command-Line Activity Wizard" section provides an example. For SDK activity projects, review the examples described in the "Using the Orchestrator SDK" section.

The authors recommend that you use a development and testing environment for coding against APIs, executing CLI commands, and testing custom workflow activities. Test and validate your scripts and command executions before you create a custom activity. For Visual Studio Orchestrator SDK projects, use the toolkit IP activities for testing and validation. Using nonproduction resources during the testing phase of your project is best. You are automating—everything happens faster, for better or worse!

Installing the Orchestrator Integration Toolkit

You must install the OIT before you build your custom activities. This installation can be on a standalone computer; review the "Installation Prerequisites" section for information. If the Orchestrator Integration Toolkit will be installed on a computer with Orchestrator features installed, first review the system requirements for preparing the computer. The "Toolkit Installation" section discusses installing the toolkit.

Installation Prerequisites

Consider this brief overview of the Orchestrator system requirements:

- Supported operating systems to install the toolkit:
  - Windows 7 (32-bit or 64-bit), Windows 7 Service Pack (SP) 1
  - Windows 8 (32-bit or 64-bit)
  - Windows Server 2008 R2, Windows Server 2008 R2 SP 1 and above
  - Windows Server 2012
- Additional required software:
  - Windows Installer version 3.1
  - Microsoft .NET Framework 3.5, SP 1

  Toolkit installation does not fail if Microsoft .NET Framework 3.5 SP 1 is not installed because the prerequisite is not checked during installation. However, various actions in the Command-Line Activity Wizard will fail if the correct framework is unavailable on the development computer. Ensure that you have the correct version of the .NET framework installed before installing the OIT.

  - Windows Installer XML Toolset (WiX) version 3.5
  - Visual Studio 2008/2010

NOTE: WINDOWS INSTALLER XML TOOLSET 3.5

Windows Installer XML Toolset (WiX) version 3.5 is a prerequisite for System Center Orchestrator. Orchestrator 2012 SP 1 OIT supports only this specific version of the WiX. Although newer versions of WiX are available, they will not work.

Toolkit Installation

The OIT installation binaries are available as a separate download. Download the executable and extract it to an installation folder to run the installation. Follow these steps to install the Orchestrator Integration Toolkit:

1. On the computer where you are installing the OIT, navigate to the folder that contains the extracted installation files. Double-click **OrchestratorToolkitSetup.exe**. The welcome page appears (see Figure 20.1). Click **Next**.
2. Accept the license agreement, and enter your name and organization on the appropriate pages.
3. On the Ready to install page, click **Install**. The security shield icon on the Install button (see Figure 20.2) indicates that the installation will use elevated privileges.

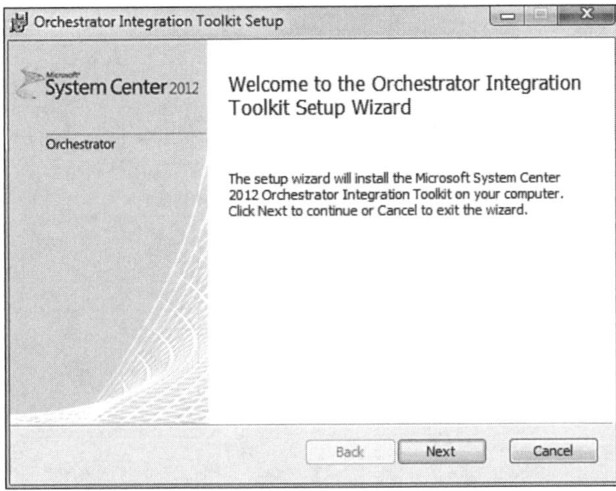

FIGURE 20.1 Splash page of the OIT Setup Wizard.

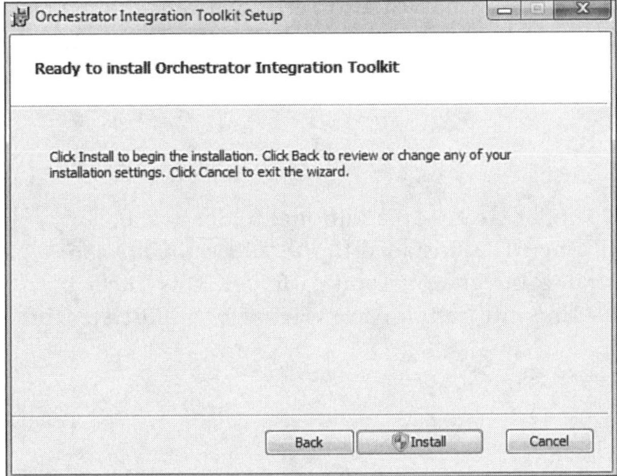

FIGURE 20.2 Ready to install the OIT.

4. Before installation begins, a User Account Control dialog box appears, notifying you of elevated privileges. Click **Yes** to continue the installation.
5. When the installation is complete (see Figure 20.3), click **Finish** to exit the wizard.

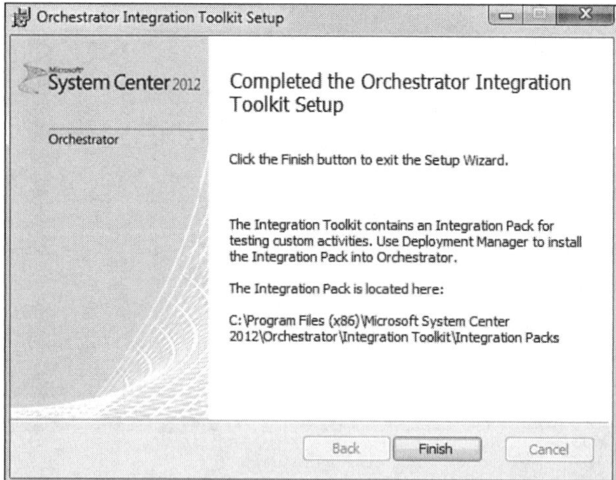

FIGURE 20.3 Setup complete page of the OIT Setup Wizard.

If you upgrade your Orchestrator infrastructure, you must also perform a version upgrade of the OIT. Uninstall the previous version, and then reinstall the OIT with the updated binaries. The uninstallation includes removal of the toolkit IP from your environment and the uninstallation of the toolkit.

Validating Toolkit Installation

Installing the Orchestrator Integration Toolkit creates an additional folder in the Orchestrator program folder. By default, the OIT is installed to the *%ProgramFiles(x86)%*\Microsoft System Center 2012\Orchestrator\Integration Toolkit\ folder. This folder includes the files used for creating and using integration packs. Figure 20.4 illustrates the folder structure.

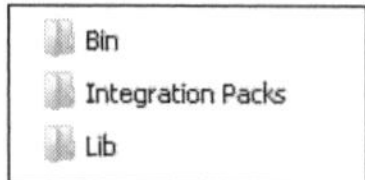

FIGURE 20.4 OIT program folder structure.

A description of these folders and files follows:

- **Bin (Integration Toolkit Utilities):** These are the executable and binary files needed to run the Command-Line Activity Wizard and Integration Pack Wizard. Two shortcuts are available in the Integration Toolkit start menu folder (see Figure 20.5).

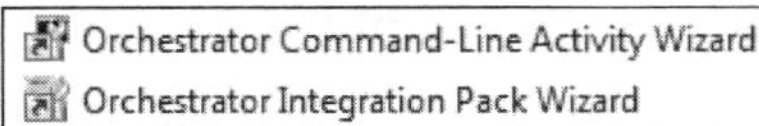

FIGURE 20.5 OIT start menu shortcuts.

- **Lib (Integration Toolkit SDK Library):** These are the assembly and eXtended Markup Language (XML) files used for developing custom activities with the Orchestrator SDK.
- **Integration Packs:** The Toolkit Integration Pack for Orchestrator (OIP file) is named System Center Integration Pack for Microsoft .NET Framework Activities. As with other IPs, you can use the Orchestrator Deployment Manager to register and deploy the OIP file.

Using the Command-Line Activity Wizard

The Command-Line Activity Wizard lets you quickly create Orchestrator workflow activities. The command, arguments, and parameters specified using the wizard are transformed into C# source code and compiled into a .NET assembly. You can test or use this assembly in your runbooks using the Integration Toolkit activities, or you can create your own IP that can be distributed and deployed like any other IP.

Assemblies created with the Command-Line Activity Wizard can include one or more commands; each command becomes an activity available for use in runbooks. These commands can be of different command types (Command, Command Line, PowerShell, or SSH command). The wizard provides flexibility when you create assemblies that consist of one or more activities targeting the same system or providing similar functionality.

The OIT utilities let you create an Orchestrator activity using any supported command that will perform the desired action. The wizard lets you quickly create your own workflow activities or migrate existing scripts to Orchestrator activities. Using the steps in the wizard, you can create a customized workflow activity in your runbook for each custom requirement. Try to create generic custom activities so that you can use them in other runbooks. This can give you a powerful custom activity library.

The next sections describe creating activities using the Command-Line Activity Wizard. The process includes gathering the information necessary to start the project, creating the assembly, and executing the custom activity in a runbook.

Starting Assembly Creation

Start creating the assembly when you have all required information. The "Development Planning" section includes questions to help obtain this information. Answers to those questions are the input for your project.

For the example in the next section, use the following as input when creating the assembly:

- **Name of assembly:** Odyssey Integration Pack
- **Assembly file:** OdysseyIP.dll
- Commands to integrate into the assembly:
  - **PowerShell example:** Create a sleep activity: `start-sleep -second`
  - **Command execution:** Create a sleep activity: `start-sleep -s`
  - **Program execution:** No information required for this example.

Creating a New Activity Assembly

This section describes the process of creating a custom assembly using the Command-Line Activity Wizard. Follow these steps:

1. Using the Start menu, navigate to **Microsoft System Center 2012 -> Orchestrator -> Integration Toolkit -> Orchestrator Command-Line Activity Wizard**.
2. On the Start page of the wizard (see Figure 20.6), either open an existing assembly or create a new assembly by clicking **Next** without specifying an existing assembly. The Command-Line Activity Wizard lets you update or add commands to existing assemblies. In this example, a new assembly is created; click **Next** without specifying an existing assembly.

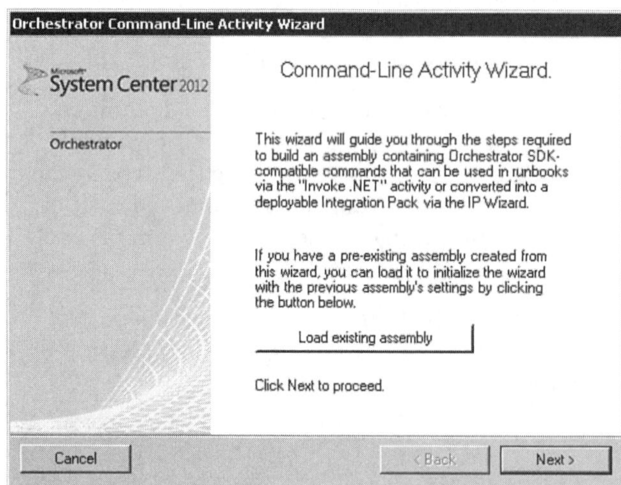

FIGURE 20.6 Command-Line Activity Wizard start page.

3. On the **Assembly Details** page in Figure 20.7, enter the **Name** and **Assembly file** information. The assembly name must begin with a letter and be followed by alphanumeric characters. This name is used as a C# namespace identifier for the assembly and your activities.

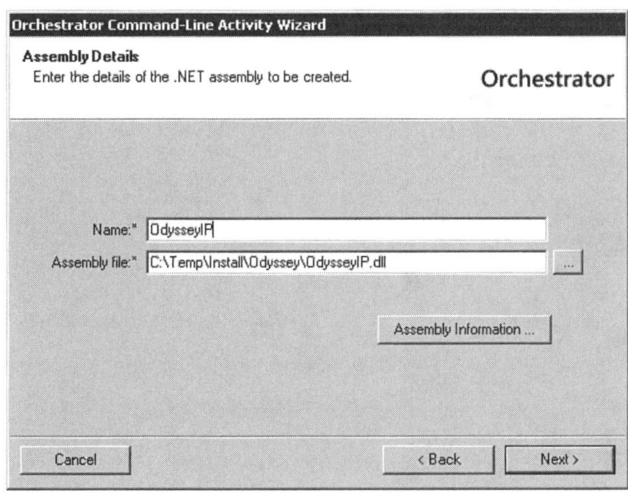

FIGURE 20.7 Assembly Details page in the Command-Line Activity Wizard.

Click **Assembly Information** to specify detailed assembly information for your project. Figure 20.8 shows this information; it appears on the Details tab when selecting file properties in Windows Explorer, with the exception of the description field. The version information appears in Windows Explorer properties as the **File version** and **Product version**. The version number has four parts and can be specified in following format: **<major version>.<minor version>.<build number>.<revision>**.

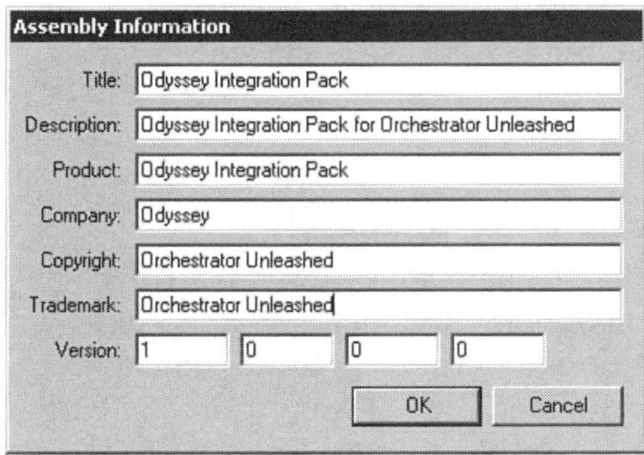

FIGURE 20.8 Assembly information page in the Command-Line Activity Wizard.

Click **OK** on the Assembly Information page, and then click **Next** to proceed to the following page in the wizard.

4. Figure 20.9 shows the Commands page, where you can add one or more commands in the assembly. To add new commands (activities), click **Add** and follow the procedure discussed in the "Adding Activities to the Command-Line Activity Assembly" section.

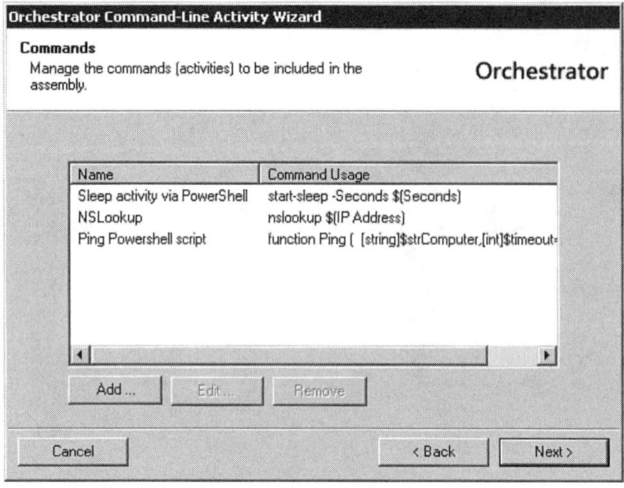

FIGURE 20.9 Commands page of the Command-Line Activity Wizard.

5. Click **Next** after adding all commands (or updating commands when updating an existing assembly). The wizard gathers the information, and the .NET activity assembly is compiled.

6. Figure 20.10 shows the page displayed after the assembly is created. To build an IP immediately from this assembly, select **Build Integration Pack** to have the IP Wizard preload the information from the assembly; otherwise, click **Finish**. You can test, validate, and run the assembly using the **Invoke .NET** activity from the toolkit IP.

Adding Activities to the Command-Line Activity Assembly

This section describes the requirements to add different commands (workflow activities) to your custom assembly and various configuration options. The toolkit supports different command types, each with its own settings. To run the wizard to create command-line activities, start your project following the procedure in the "Creating a New Activity Assembly" section, which describes adding commands on the Commands page of the Command-line Activity Wizard. Perform the following steps to add or update commands in the command-line activity assembly:

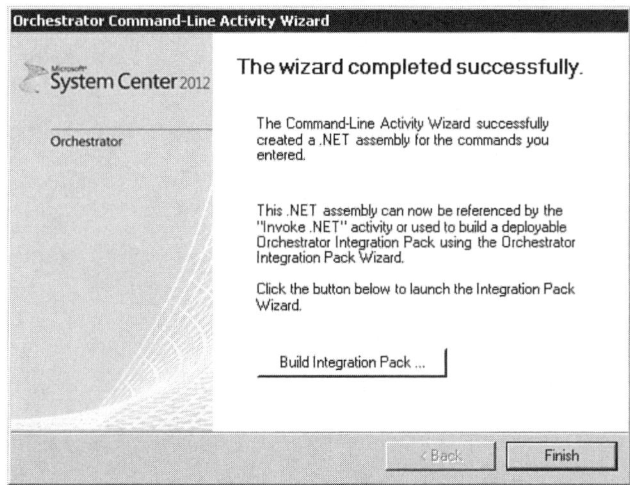

FIGURE 20.10 The wizard completed successfully.

1. On the Commands page in Figure 20.11, click **Add** to add activities to your assembly (use Edit to update an existing assembly). This opens the Add/Edit Command page. You can add one or more commands; each can be a different command type.

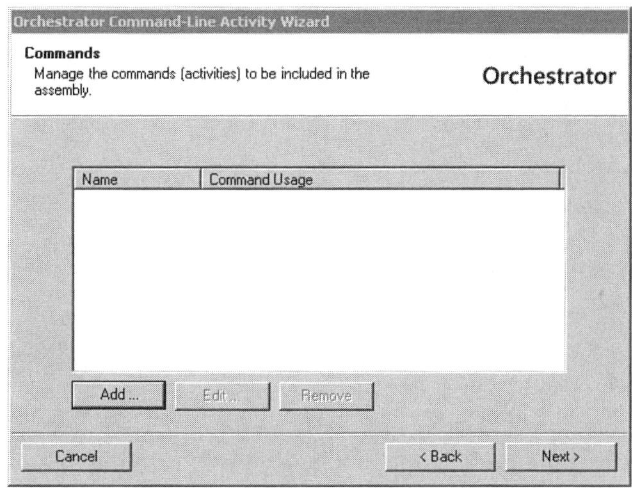

FIGURE 20.11 Commands page of the Command-Line Activity Wizard.

2. Specify the name of the command, the type, the program location (if applicable), and a description on the General tab of the Add/Edit Command page:

   - **Name:** This is the command name; it also is the name of the activity in the Runbook Designer.

20

- **Mode:** The Mode property drop-down box contains four options:

  Run Command

  Run Windows PowerShell

  Run Program

  Run SSH Command

- **Program:** This selection is active only when you select the Run Program mode. Use the ellipsis (...) button to browse to the program you want to run.

- **Description:** This is a description of the command.

Figure 20.12 is an example of a command that will be included in the custom example assembly. Use the Add/Edit Command wizards for each command you want to integrate.

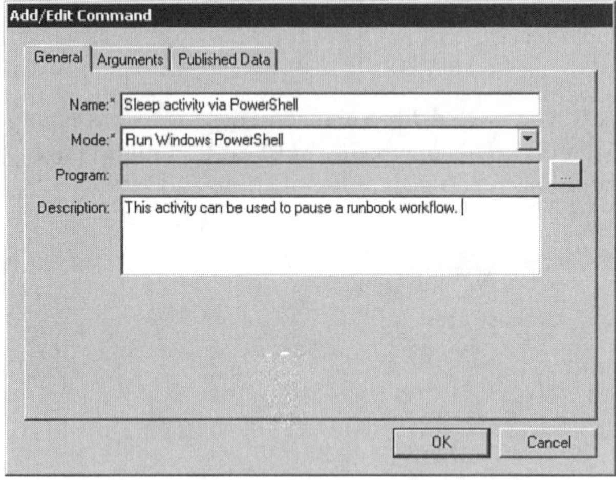

FIGURE 20.12 General tab of the Add/Edit Command page.

3. The Arguments tab of the Add/Edit Command page (see Figure 20.13) specifies the command line and parameters for each command.

   The command line is in the language (Mode selection) selected on the General tab. Specify command parameters using the Add, Edit, and Remove buttons to the right of the Parameters section. The Add and Edit buttons open the Add/Edit Parameter page (see Figure 20.14), where you can specify parameters for the command. When you are finished with the parameter definition, click **OK**.

   - **Name:** This is the parameter name; it will also be the display name of the parameter shown in the property list of the activity.

   - **Usage Mode:** Two parameter usage modes are available in the drop-down list to specify how to use the parameter in the command line:

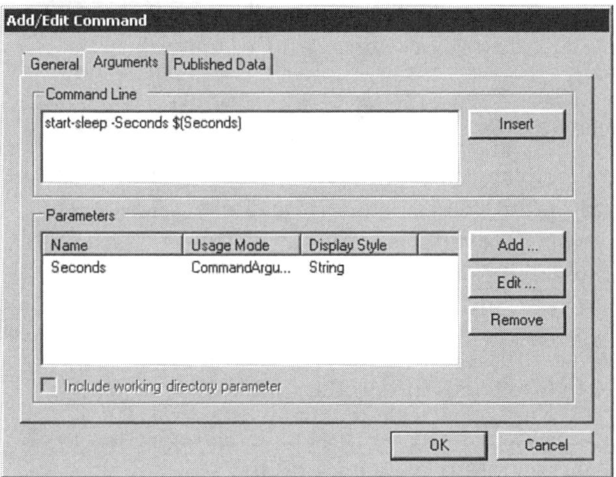

FIGURE 20.13 Arguments tab of the Add/Edit Command page.

Add/Edit Parameter
Properties
Name:* Seconds
Usage mode:* Command Argument
Display Style:* Text
Default value:
Options:
OK
Cancel

FIGURE 20.14 Properties on the Add/Edit parameter page.

Command Argument: Select this if you want to use the argument as a parameter within your command line. In the example used for this procedure, the $(Seconds) in the command `start-sleep -Seconds $(Seconds)` is the parameter for the command line.

Environment Variable: Select this mode if you plan to use the parameter as an environment variable in your command line. The environment variable is set before the command line runs. With this option selected, the command line can use the parameter as in this example: `start-sleep -Seconds %Seconds%`.

- **Display Style:** This selection defines how the parameter is presented to the user. It can be shown as Text (free form), Encrypted Text (masked text box, not logged), True/False (Boolean selection), Text with Selection (selection from a preformatted list), Date/Time (Date/Time picker control), File (File Browser control), Folder (Folder Browser control), or Computer (Computer Browser control).

- **Default value:** You can specify a default value.
- **Options:** The Options field is activated when the **Text with Selection** Display Style is selected. You can add option values here for the user to select. Click the ellipsis (...) button and enter the available values for your command-line parameter. Each option is listed and presented to the user on a separate line. When you are finished adding options, click **OK**.

4. Use the Published Data tab to publish output data to the Orchestrator data bus, making the information available to other activities in the runbook.

The dialog interface on this tab varies, depending on the Mode field selection made on the General tab. If the Run Command, Run Program, or Run SSH Command options are selected from the Mode drop-down list on the General tab of the Add/Edit Command dialog box (see Figure 20.12), the following items appear on the Add/Edit Published Data dialog box:

- **Name:** This is the parameter name; it will also be the display name of the parameters shown in the property list of the activity.
- **Source:** Choose Standard Output Stream or Standard Error Stream from the command line as the source for the published data item.
- **Mode:** Select the Match Pattern or Extract Group modes for your published data.

  Use Match Pattern to determine whether a given pattern exists within the Source; this mode returns True or False.

  Extract Group retrieves each item of data that matches the pattern you specify.
- **Pattern:** This is the regular expression that applies to the Mode you selected.
- **Description:** This optional text will display next to the published data property in the Runbook Designer.

If you selected the **Run Windows PowerShell** option from the Mode drop-down list on the General tab of the Add/Edit Command dialog box, the following items appear on the Add/Edit Published Data dialog box:

- **Name:** This is the parameter name; it will be the display name of the parameters shown in the property list of the activity.
- **Property:** Specify the name of the PowerShell property that will be saved to the published data item.
- **Description:** Specify the text that displays next to the published data property in the Runbook Designer. This information is optional.

NOTE: POWERSHELL PROPERTY

The PowerShell property name must be present as the most recent object pushed to the PowerShell pipeline. Object properties cannot be referenced.

TIP: PROVIDING DESCRIPTION INFORMATION

Although the description is optional, the authors recommend populating this because it transfers automatically into the IP Wizard when you build out the custom integration pack. Published data descriptions are useful for users who are leveraging activities when designing runbooks; they help the users understand what an element provides.

5. Click **OK** to finish adding the published data item. Repeat steps 1–4 for each published data item you want to add.
6. Click **OK** to close the Add/Edit Command dialog box and return to the Commands dialog box.

Testing and Validating the Assembly

Test the assembly using the **Invoke .NET** Toolkit IP activity. The next procedure tests the runtime of your custom workflow activities, using the assembly created in the "Creating a New Activity Assembly" section. Perform the following steps to test and validate your assembly:

1. Open the Runbook Designer and create a new runbook.
2. In the Activities pane, add the **Initialize Data** activity. To integrate your assembly in the testing runbook, drag the **Invoke .NET** activity of the Integration Toolkit category into the new runbook. In the example in Figure 20.15, the output of the **Invoke .NET** activity (**Run NSLookup**) is written to a file (**Append Line** activity).

FIGURE 20.15 Assembly test and validation runbook.

3. Use the Properties page of the **Invoke .NET** activity to configure the activities in the assembly. The General, Filters, and Run Behavior tabs are similar to those of other activities. The Class Information (see Figure 20.16) and Properties tabs are where you define the class and library to be invoked; you can select fields using the ellipsis (...) buttons on the right of the property field:

- **Assembly:** Browse to the assembly file that includes the activities you want to integrate in your runbook.
- **Class:** Use the ellipsis (...) button to select the command from the list that is displayed.
- **Setup:** The Setup field is used only by custom-developed classes using the Orchestrator SDK with the Data attribute.
- **Properties:** Use the Properties tab to provide information for each property required to execute the command.

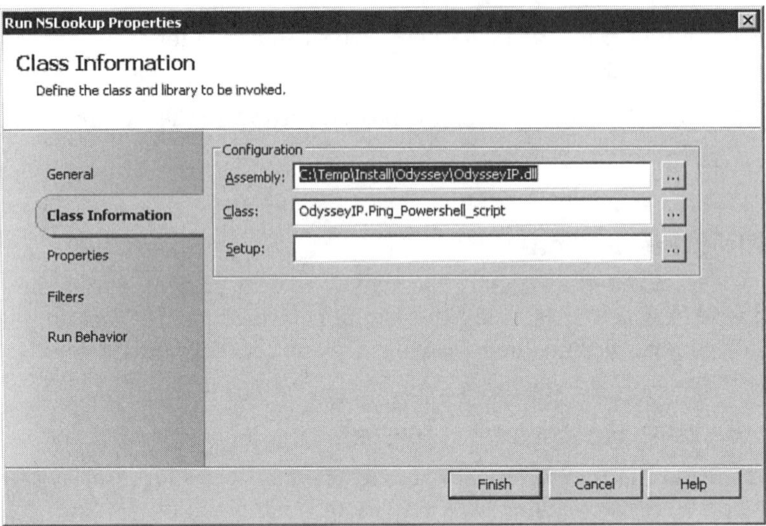

FIGURE 20.16 Class Information for the **Invoke .NET** activity.

4. Click **Finish** to save your changes. Add activities as necessary to the runbook.
5. Select **Runbook Tester** in the Runbook Designer toolbar to start the Runbook Tester.
6. Select **Run to Breakpoint** in the toolbar. The runbook starts, and your activity runs. The Run Log pane displays results of the activity.
7. Select **Show Details** under the activity name in the Run Log pane to see the detailed results, including the input properties and published data.

Converting Opalis QIK CLI Assemblies

The Command-Line Activity Wizard can convert your existing Opalis Quick Integration Kit (QIK) assemblies to Orchestrator assemblies. This is not an upgrade procedure; the wizard imports the Opalis assembly information and creates a new assembly.

Begin the conversion by starting the Command-Line Activity Wizard and loading the assembly on the Welcome page of the wizard. Specify the filename and location of the assembly. All commands used in the original Opalis assembly are listed on the Commands page of the wizard. You can make any other modifications to the assembly on the various pages of the wizard.

The process of converting Opalis QIK CLI assemblies is rather simple. When the old assembly is loaded in the wizard, you can review the prepopulated information; a new Orchestrator assembly is created based on the imported information. The "Creating a New Activity Assembly" section provides information on building assemblies using the Command-Line Activity Wizard.

Using the Integration Pack Wizard

The Integration Pack Wizard enables you to create new integration packs to deploy custom assemblies created by the Command-Line Activity Wizard or Orchestrator SDK. Using your own IP to deploy custom assembly activities provides all the advantages of using IPs, although some considerations come into play. The following describes the characteristics of creating your own IPs. You can evaluate these characteristics; using IPs might not be advisable in all cases:

- Custom activities can be registered and deployed to different runbook servers and runbook designer instances.
- Deployment Manager enables centralized administration of the IPs.
- The activities you created appear in the activity library of the Runbook Designer. The IP Wizard gives you full configuration control of the activity.
- Deploying an IP involves installing a Windows Installer file to the target.
- The assembly is packaged and can be registered/deployed, uninstalled, and upgraded like any other IP. This is the complete and most user-friendly way to make your custom activities available.

TIP: AVOIDING FREQUENT UPDATES TO THE ORCHESTRATOR DATABASE

Whereas registering an IP involves database changes, deploying an integration pack does not. If you have to frequently change the assembly (thus, also the IP), it is best not to use your own IPs to deploy and register your activities. Frequent changes to the Orchestrator database can result in unexpected behavior to the Orchestrator environment.

To reduce frequent database modifications, the authors recommend that you not packaging your assemblies into IPs during testing, unless you do so to test the complete end-to-end process of deploying your activities. If you are using a virtualized test environment, you can save the state of the Orchestrator servers before registering the IP and refer back to the saved state when modifications are required before importing the IP into production.

After testing and validating your project, deploy your assemblies using the Integration Pack Wizard. The next sections discuss creating and updating an IP using the Integration Pack Wizard.

Creating a New Integration Pack

Creating an IP with the Integration Pack Wizard is straightforward. Determine in advance what to specify in the wizard and how this will be presented in the Orchestrator environment. Follow these steps to create an integration pack using the Integration Pack Wizard:

1. Start the Integration Pack Wizard. Navigate to the Orchestrator start menu and select **Integration Toolkit -> Orchestrator Integration Pack Wizard**. The Welcome page displays (see Figure 20.17). Here you can create or update an IP:

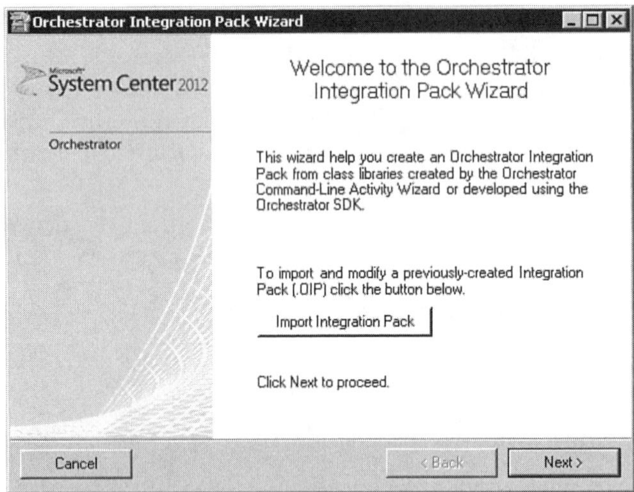

FIGURE 20.17 Welcome page in the OIP wizard.

   - Create a new IP by clicking Next and not specifying an IP to import.
   - Update an existing IP by importing it. Information for the selected IP is imported, and the assembly/IP configuration can be updated. Additional information on updating IPs is discussed in the "Updating and Converting IPs" section.

2. Use the Product Details page (see Figure 20.18) to specify details about the IP. This information controls how the activities in the IP appear in the Runbook Designer console:

   - **Product Details:** This is the name of the IP. This name is displayed in Deployment Manager.

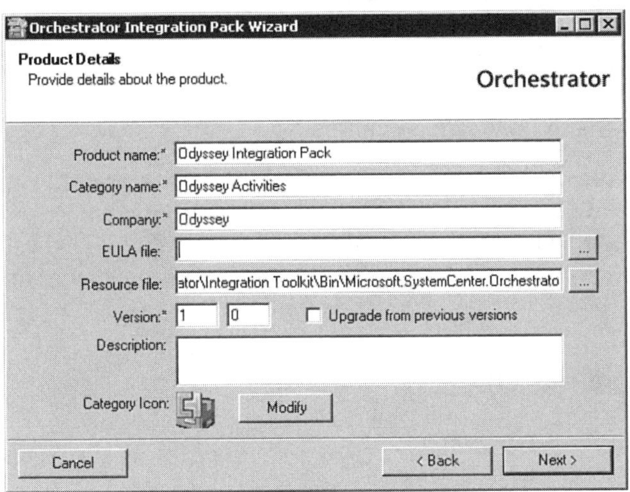

FIGURE 20.18 Product Details page in the OIP wizard.

- **Category name:** The Activity pane of the Runbook Designer is organized by category, by default. Activities in IP assemblies appear under the category name specified in this field.
- **Company:** The company name must be specified. Registered IPs appear under Control Panel -> Programs and Features on the server. The Publisher column under the Programs and Features applet displays the name specified in the company field.
- **EULA file:** To include a license agreement in your IP deployment, import an RTF-formatted text file with an extension of .EULA. This license agreement is displayed during registration of the IP; the user must accept it for registration to continue.
- **Resource file:** You can specify an assembly containing additional icons and other resources required for your project. As an example, to use your own icons for the category and activities, specify the assembly here; the icons will be selectable in the Category and Activity Icon fields. The standard toolkit resource file (Microsoft.SystemCenter.Orchestrator.Integration.Toolkit.Wizard.Images.dll) is used by default; it contains the default icon set for categories and activities.
- **Enable upgrade:** This option enables your IP to be upgraded and is selected by default when you import an existing integration pack. If not selected, new product and activity IDs are created for the IP, and the existing version of the IP will not be upgradable. This can be useful when you want a side-by-side installation of different IP versions.
- **Description:** Specify a description for the IP.

- **Category Icon:** The default icon is displayed for your IP. To modify the category, click **Modify** and select a new icon. Icons presented in this list are imported using the resource file specified on this page.

3. After entering the product information, click **Next.**

4. The Activities page displays. Figure 20.19 shows activities that are already added. Here you can reference the assembly or assemblies containing the activities you want to deploy. Assemblies created with the Command-Line Activity Wizard or the Orchestrator SDK are supported and can be added to the IP. To add a new activity to the IP, click **Add**.

FIGURE 20.19 Activities page in the OIP wizard.

5. Clicking **Add** displays the Activity Information page (see Figure 20.20), where you can select the assembly and activity you want to deploy in your IP. First select the library (your assembly); classes (activities) are then read from the assembly and can be selected in the class drop-down box.

   - **Library:** Browse to your assembly file by clicking the ellipsis (...) button to the right of the library input field.

NOTE: PATH AND ASSEMBLY NAME LENGTH LIMITATION

The length of the combined path and assembly filename cannot exceed 234 characters because of registry key name limitations. If the default path where assemblies of an IP are stored is used, you can use a maximum of 80 characters for the name of your assembly. IP registration fails when the assembly filename exceeds the maximum of 80 characters.

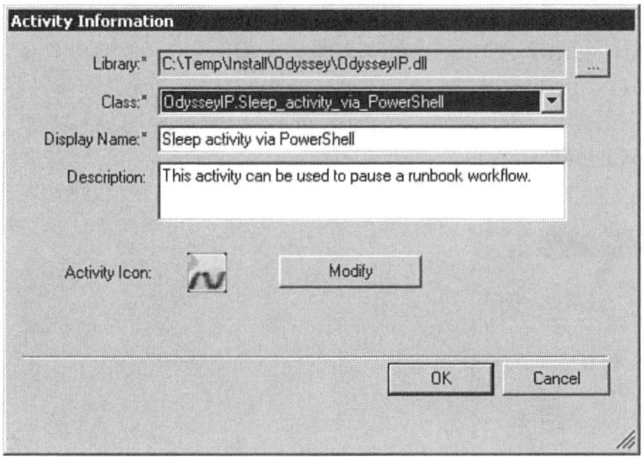

FIGURE 20.20 Activity information page in the OIP wizard.

- **Class:** Activities added to your assembly are listed in the drop-down box. Select the activity you want to add to the IP; activity information is imported from the assembly and displayed in the Display Name and Description fields.
- **Display Name:** Information is prepopulated using the Class selection. Modify the display name of the activity, if needed.
- **Description:** Information is prepopulated by the Class selection. You modify the description of the activity as necessary.

TIP: INFORMATION REGARDING COMMAND, ACTIVITY, AND CLASS

The terminology the various wizards use might seem confusing. After creating assemblies and IPs, you should run through the various wizards in the toolkit. Notice that one tool uses the word *command*; elsewhere it is named *class*. Both are different ways to define *activity*.

- The Command-Line Activity Wizard uses commands for adding activities to your project.
- Class is the terminology the Orchestrator SDK uses (activity definition in your Visual Studio project is a class).

6. Click **OK** to save your changes. You can continue adding activities to the list or add them later in an update to this IP.

REAL WORLD: BUNDLE SIMILAR ACTIVITIES IN ONE IP

As mentioned in the "Using the Integration Pack Wizard" section, the fewer IPs you need to import, the fewer database modifications take place. The authors also recommend combining activities with a similar target or purpose under one category for general usability of activities.

7. The next page of the wizard is the Dependencies and Included Files page. As Figure 20.21 shows, you can add assemblies required by the activities, scripts, or other files you plan to deploy to runbook servers and runbook designers. As an example, you can include a PowerShell script in your IP. In this assembly, you reference the path to the script, and the script action is executed.

FIGURE 20.21 Dependencies and Included Files page of the OIP Wizard.

8. On the Orchestrator Integration Pack File page in Figure 20.22, enter the path and filename of the IP that is being created. The wizard overwrites any existing filenames. If you do not specify a path, the IP is created in the Documents folder of your user profile. Click **Next** to start building the IP.

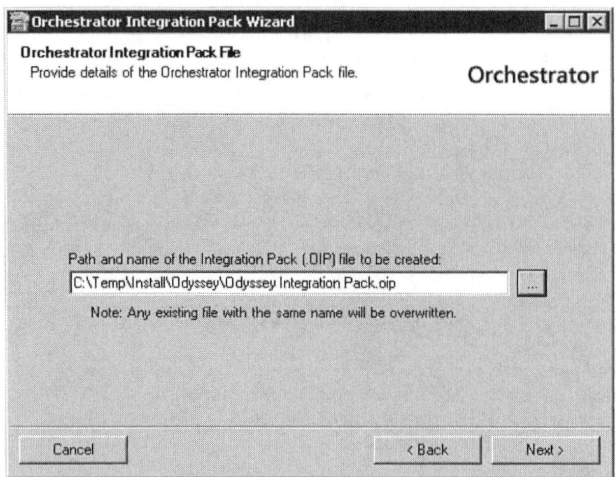

FIGURE 20.22 Orchestrator Integration Pack File page of the OIP Wizard.

9. After the IP is built, the Integration Pack Wizard completed successfully page appears. It displays the path where the IP was created (see Figure 20.23). If errors are encountered while the IP is being built, you can review the error information and go back in the wizard to make changes and retry building the IP. Click **Finish** to close the OIP Wizard.

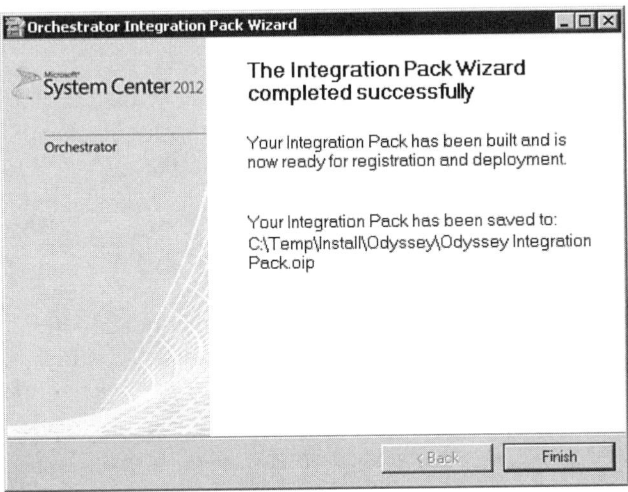

FIGURE 20.23 Final page of the OIP Wizard.

You are now ready to deploy the IP. Review the registration and deployment procedures in Chapter 5, "Installing System Center 2012 Orchestrator," on how to make the custom activities available in the runbook designer(s) and runbook server(s).

Updating and Converting Integration Packs

You can use the Welcome page of the IP Wizard to import an existing integration pack. You can upgrade IPs only by importing the existing IP in the Integration Pack Wizard and checking the **Enable Upgrade** check box. After the IP is imported, make any necessary changes. Otherwise, the IP is not upgraded, and new product ID and activity IDs are created when the IP is registered. Updating activities or the underlying assemblies results in a rebuild and reconfiguration of the IP.

TIP: UPDATING UNDERLYING ASSEMBLIES

To update the assembly without updating activity settings in the IP Wizard, save your new assembly to the same path and filename as the assembly specified in the original IP. Import the IP on the Welcome page into the wizard, and run through the wizard without making any changes. The updated assembly will be packaged in the updated IP.

The Integration Pack Wizard can convert Opalis-compatible integration packs to Orchestrator IPs. You simply import the Opalis IP on the Welcome page of the IP Wizard. Before the import occurs, the wizard displays a warning message indicating that the IP is not compatible with Orchestrator. Ignore this message and click **OK**. Product details and other configuration information are prepopulated with information from the imported assembly, which you can modify as needed for your new IP. If referencing assemblies are not yet converted to Orchestrator assemblies or the converted assemblies are not in the location specified in the imported IP, the class property will be empty on the Assembly Information page.

For additional information on converting assemblies, see the "Converting Opalis QIK CLI Assemblies" section of this chapter. For a smooth conversion of your Opalis IPs, ensure that all assemblies are converted to Orchestrator assemblies and located in the folder where the IP was created.

Using the Orchestrator SDK

Developers can use the System Center 2012 Orchestrator SDK to create custom activities. The SDK provides documentation, code samples, tools, headers, libraries, and other files that can be used to integrate custom code and create workflow activities. The Orchestrator SDK includes these resources:

- **Orchestrator SDK documentation:** The SDK documentation describes how to use the Orchestrator class libraries. This includes class library reference information; this is typically the first set of information to review when starting to build activities with the Orchestrator SDK.
- **Orchestrator SDK code examples:** The SDK provides numerous code examples that demonstrate different interfaces you can use to develop custom activities. All SDK samples in the documentation were created with Visual Studio 2010, targeting.NET Framework 3.5.
- **Orchestrator SDK assemblies:** The SDK assemblies expose the managed interfaces you can use to create Orchestrator IPs. Your Visual Studio project must reference these assemblies to be able to use SDK classes, interfaces, or enumerations. The assemblies are stored in the *%ProgramFiles(x86)%*\Microsoft System Center 2012\Orchestrator\Integration Toolkit\Lib folder.

Your Orchestrator activity project must target .NET Framework 3.5 and be created with Visual Studio 2008/2010. After creating your project, you should reference the Orchestrator SDK assemblies. How you build your SDK activity project using the available interface is dependent on the solution you want to build. Different interfaces are available in the SDK for coding activities, each with its own characteristics that control the input and output of the activity. These are the available interfaces for building Orchestrator activities:

- **Declarative:** You use the class attributes to define activity, inputs, and outputs, but the detailed implementation is left to the underlying architecture of the SDK. Inputs and outputs are statically defined.
- **Imperative:** The inputs and outputs are dynamically defined.
- **Cascading Dependencies:** Using cascading dependencies greatly simplifies the user experience when configuring complex activities because it reduces the amount of information the customer selects from, to focus only what is most relevant. You can also use this feature to include or exclude properties from displaying, based on selections in other properties. This is useful when certain properties either must be or cannot be used together.

No clear guidelines govern when to use a particular approach. Select your approach based on how you want to have the inputs and outputs appear and behave in the activity. You should understand the capabilities of each approach so that you know when to use which type of model when creating custom activities. The next sections discuss the capabilities of each approach.

Choosing a Development Approach

Creating SDK activities includes two logical parts in the coding:

- Definition of the Orchestrator activity in a SDK-defined structure (defining inputs, outputs, and action)
- Action of the activity (this is your own code that uses the activity inputs and delivers the desired output)

How you integrate your code is similar for each approach; you can add your code in the output section of the activity (as in the examples in this chapter), or you can create separate classes for each function. The activity class, input, and output definitions vary with each approach; each introduces different capabilities to control the input and output of the activity. The following sections provide a functional overview of the activity, including input, output, and filter capabilities for each approach.

Defining Activities in the Project

The activity definition is the class created in your project. The first step when creating an Orchestrator activity is to indicate to Orchestrator that it actually is an activity: Add [Activity] above the class definition. You can define one or more activities in your project and code each in a different style. This lets you create a hybrid model in which each activity has its own input and output behavior. The activity class in your project encapsulates all the functionality to define your activity: the inputs and outputs. The tables in this section list the capabilities available with the Declarative, Imperative, and Cascading Dependency approaches.

20

TIP: ATTRIBUTE INFORMATION IN EXAMPLES

Note that the examples in this section are based on the C#.NET language; attributes are represented differently in other languages. For example, in VB.NET, [Activity] is replaced by <Activity>.

Table 20.1 provides an overview of the functionality available using the Declarative approach.

TABLE 20.1 Declarative Approach

Functionality	Description	Usage

Activity definition	`[Activity]`	Specified above the class definition in your code. You can define properties in the activity definition. For example:
		`Name: [Activity ("Calculator Activity")]`
		`Description: [Activity ("Calculator Activity ", Description="Odyssey calculator activity") ]`
		`Filter Tab: [Activity ("Calculator Activity"), ShowFilters=false]`
		`Properties Tab: [Activity ("Calculator Activity"), ShowInputs=false]`
		
		If no name is specified for the activity, the name of the class is used and Boolean values are set to True by default.

Define input properties	`[ActivityInput]`	Use this attribute on public properties to define the static inputs for your activity.
Define output properties	`[ActivityOutput]`	Use this attribute on public properties to define static outputs for your activity. The public property must contain the code necessary to process and derive the output for the activity.
Define filters	`[ActivityFilter]`	Use this attribute on public properties to define the static filters for your activity.
Process data in the activity at runtime	`[ActivityMethod]`	This attribute marks a method inside an activity class as one that should be run when Orchestrator invokes the activity. You can define multiple instances to run, but you cannot control the order in which they execute. You can define one primary method and execute other methods from there.

Table 20.2 provides an overview of the functionality available for the Imperative approach.

TABLE 20.2 Imperative Approach

Functionality	Description	Usage

Activity definition	`[Activity ("Calculator") ]`	The activity attribute defines the activity class and provides the name of the activity. You need to have the activity class inherit from the `IActivity` class. For example:
		`[Activity ("Calculator")]`
		`    public class IcalculatorActivity :`
		`IActivity`
		`    {`
		`    }`

Activity design	Design()
	Activity information is specified using the following methods:
		You can use the `Design()` method and the IActivityDesigner type parameter to dynamically define activity information. For example:
		`public void Design(IActivityDesigner`
		`designer)`
		`{`
		`}`

	`AddInput()` method	Use this method to define the activity inputs. You can specify the input name and use optional methods to control input behavior. Review the Orchestrator SDK reference for a complete list of methods you can use to control your input of the activity. For example:
		`designer.AddInput("Input property X").`
		`NotRequired();`

	`AddOutout()` method	Use this method to define activity outputs. You can specify the output name and use optional methods to control input behavior. Review the Orchestrator SDK reference for a complete list of methods you can use to control your output of the activity. For example:
		`designer.AddOutput("Output property X").`
		`AsNumber();`

	`AddFilter()` method	Use the IActivityFilter interface to define the activity filters. You can specify the filter name and use methods to control the filter behavior. Review the Orchestrator SDK reference for a complete list of methods you can use to control the filter of the activity. For example:
		`designer.AddFilter("Complete").`
		`WithBooleanBrowser();`

Functionality	Description	Usage

Process data in the activity at runtime	`Execute ()`	This method executes the code in your activity and/or runs other methods. The `Execute()` method goes along with the IActivityRequest and IActivityResponse interfaces. For example:
		`public void Execute(IActivityRequest request, IActivityResponse response)`
		The input for the execution is provided by the IActivityRequest interface, and output data is published via the IActivityResponse interface. For example:
		`Int32 calcNum1 = request.Inputs["Number1 Input"].AsInt32();`
		`response.Publish("Calculator result", CalcResult);`

Table 20.3 provides an overview of the functionality available using the Imperative approach with Cascading Dependencies.

TABLE 20.3 Imperative Approach with Cascading Dependencies

Functionality	Description	Usage

Activity definition	`[Activity ("Calculator") ]`	The activity attribute defines the activity class and provides the name of the activity. You must have the `activity` class inherit from the `IActivityWithRedesign` class. For example:
		`[Activity ("Calculator")]`
		`public class CasCalculatorActivity : IActivityWithRedesign`
		`{`
		`}`

Activity design	`Design()`	You can use the `Design()` method and the IActivityDesigner type parameter to dynamically define activity information. For example:
		`public void Design(IActivityDesigner designer)`
		`{`
		`}`

Functionality	Description	Usage

	Activity information is specified via the following methods:
	`AddInput()` method
	`AddOutout()` method
	`AddFilter()` method
		Use these methods to define the activity filters, inputs, and outputs. You can specify the name and use optional methods to control the behavior, similar to the Imperative approach. To designate a property as one that causes Redesign to be called, it must be marked with the `.WithRedesign()` method. Review the Orchestrator SDK reference for a complete list of methods you can use to control your activity. For example:
		`designer.AddInput("Input property X")`
		`.WithRedesign();`

Activity redesign	`Redesign()`	This enables you to modify the list of properties displayed dynamically, depending on the user's choices. Unlike the `Design()` method, the parameters to the `Redesign()` method include an IRedesignRequest object that contains a list of all the active inputs and their values, along with the name of the property that changed. For example:
		`public void Redesign(IActivityDesigner`
		`designer, IRedesignRequest request)`
		`{`
		`}`
		The values the user chooses are set in an IInputCollection (a collection of KeyValuePair<string, IRuntimeValue>)—that is, a list of property names and their respective values. For example, to get all values set by the user:
		`IInputCollection inputs = request.`
		`RedesignInputs;`
		You can go through the collection and save the values for later usages in your redesign. For example:
		`foreach (KeyValuePair<string, IRuntimeValue>`
		`input in inputs)`
		`{`
		`if (input.Key == Simple_`
		`Advanced)`
		`{`
		`simpleadvancedvalue =`
		`input.Value.ToString();`
		`continue;`
		`}`
		`}`

<table>
<tr><th>Functionality</th><th>Description</th><th>Usage</th></tr>
<tr><td></td><td></td><td>You can set the initial set of activity properties by evaluating the ChangedPropertyName. If it is empty, the form was just opened from a previously saved state. For example:
<pre>
if (string.IsNullOrEmpty(request.
ChangedPropertyName))
{
    designer.AddInput("Select simple or
advanced").WithListBrowser("SIMPLE",
"ADVANCED").WithRedesign();
}
</pre>
You can run through the changed properties and define the specific input fields by using the <code>switch()</code> method, for example:
<pre>
switch (request.ChangedPropertyName)
{
    case ("Input property X "):
       designer.AddInput(Number1);
       designer.AddInput(Number2);
    break;
    case ("Input property Y "):
       designer.AddInput(Number1);
       designer.AddInput(Number3);
    break;

}
</pre></td></tr>
<tr><td>Process data in the activity at runtime</td><td><code>Execute()</code></td><td>The <code>Execute()</code> method executes the code in your activity and/or runs other methods, similar to the Imperative approach. The <code>Execute()</code> method goes along with the IActivityRequest and IActivityResponse interfaces. An example:
<pre>
public void Execute(IActivityRequest request,
IActivityResponse response)
</pre>
Input for the execution is provided with the IActivityRequest interface, and output data is published using the IActivityResponse interface. For example:
<pre>
Int32 calcNum1 = request.Inputs["Number1
Input"].AsInt32();
response.Publish("Calculator result",
CalcResult);
</pre></td></tr>
</table>

Defining Inputs for the Activity

Input properties are displayed on the Properties tab—or, in the case of optional properties, by clicking on Optional Properties. Similar to other activities, property values can be presented for input in different formats:

- A text box that can get a value by entering text or a subscription on published data.
- A drop-down box that contains predefined values.

The type of input and available functionality depends on how you define and add the property to the activity in your code. You can use the [ActivityInput] attribute or the `AddInput()` method of the IActivityDesigner interface to define the input properties of the activity. The Declarative approach uses [ActivityInput]; the Imperative and Cascading Dependencies approach use the `AddInput()` method. Here are the properties that can be set with the [ActivityInput] attribute (information from the Orchestrator SDK Reference):

- **Name:** Gets the name of the input property as it will be displayed in the Runbook Designer. For example: `[ActivityInput (Name="InputX")]` or `[ActivityInput ("InputX")]`
- **Default:** Gets or sets the default value to give the property. For example: `[ActivityInput ("InputX", Default="input here")]`
- **Optional:** Gets or sets whether the Orchestrator input is optional or required. For example: `[ActivityInput ("InputX", Optional=true]`
- **Options:** Sets and returns the comma-delimited set of options for the input field. For example: `[ActivityInput ("InputX", Options = "Yes,No", Default = "Yes"]`
- **PasswordProtected:** Gets or sets whether the input is password protected. Password-protected inputs are hidden by asterisks when viewed in the Runbook Designer and encrypted in the Orchestrator database. For example: `[ActivityInput ("InputX", PasswordProtected=true)]`

These properties can be set with the `AddInput()` method (information from the Orchestrator SDK Reference):

- **NotRequired:** Use this method to make the input optional. For example: `AddInput("InputX").NotRequired()`
- **PasswordProtect:** Use this method to encrypt the input and ensure that it is not displayed in plain text. For example: `AddInput("InputX").PasswordProtect()`
- **WithBooleanBrowser:** Use this method to include a Boolean browser when displaying the input for the user. For example: `AddInput("InputX").WithBooleanBrowser()`
- **WithComputerBrowser:** Use this method to include a computer browser when displaying the input for the user. For example: `AddInput("InputX").WithComputerBrowser()`

- **WithDateTimeBrowser:** Use this method to include a date/time browser when displaying the input for the user. For example:
  `AddInput("InputX").WitDateTimeBrowser()`
- **WithDefaultValue:** Use this method to set a default value when initially displaying the input for the user. For example:
  `AddInput("InputX").WithDefaultValue("input here")`
- **WithEnumBrowser:** Use this method to include a list browser with the specified enumeration. For example:
  `AddInput("InputX").WithEnumBrowser()`
- **WithFileBrowser:** Use this method to include a file browser when displaying the input property for the activity. For example:
  `AddInput("InputX").WithFileBrowser()`
- **WithFolderBrowser:** Use this method to include a folder browser when displaying the input property for the activity. For example:
  `AddInput("InputX").WithFolderBrowser()`
- **WithListBrowser:** Use this method to create a predefined selection list for the user to pick from. For example:
  `AddInput("InputX").WithListBrowser("Computer1", "Computer2")`

Compare the functionality associated with the different Orchestrator interfaces, and select the most appropriate approach. Most scenarios use the Imperative approach because it is the most flexible for defining individual properties. The only limitation with the Imperative approach arises when you want to define group properties (for correlated output data). In this case, you would use the ActivityData attribute, so you would have to use the ActivityInput attribute for those properties.

Defining Outputs for the Activity

Output properties in your custom activity define how published data is sent to the data bus. These properties must be defined at design time; otherwise, you will not have access to published data (output from the activity) in subsequent activities in the runbook. You can use the [ActivityOutput] attribute or the `AddOutput()` method of the IActivityDesigner interface to define the output properties of the activity properties.

The Declarative approach uses the [ActivityOutput]; the Imperative and Cascading Dependencies approach use the `AddOutput()` method:

- For the [ActivityOutput] attribute, you can specify the name and description of the output property. If no name is specified, the class name is used. For example:
  `[ActivityOutput("OutputX") ]`
- The following properties can be set with the `AddOutput()` method (information comes from the Orchestrator SDK Reference):
  - **AsDateTime:** Use this method to indicate that the output returns a DateTime value.

- **AsNumber:** Use this method to indicate that the output returns a numeric value.
- **AsString:** Use this method to indicate that the output returns a text value.
- **WithDescription:** Use this method to include a description of the output.
- **WithFilter:** Use this method to filter the output.

The Imperative approach provides the most functionality when defining the output for your activity. Although no browsers are associated with output properties in the Imperative approach, you do get the capability to define the output type specifically, which is not possible using the Declarative approach.

Defining Filters for Input

Filter properties defined in your activity project display on the Filters tab and provide a mechanism to limit the output returned from the activity. These are vastly similar in usage to input properties, with the exception of having criterion that must be defined so that the user can compare the output in some way to a value he or she has specified.

Filters are defined in the design area of the activity. You can use the [ActivityFilter] attribute in the Declarative approach and the `AddFilter()` method for the Imperative approach. Review the information in the "Defining Inputs for your Activity" section, which discusses defining the input for an activity.

Start Building an SDK Activity Project

Starting your Orchestrator project and its initial configuration is similar for each project. This section describes how to create a Visual Studio project. Examples documented throughout this chapter refer to this section for creating your initial environment. In this section, you create a new C# Class Library project and reference the Orchestrator assembly. Follow these steps:

1. In Visual Studio, select **File** -> **New** -> **New Project**. The New Project page opens (see Figure 20.24). Select **Class Library**, and specify a name and location. Click **OK**.
2. You must reference the Orchestrator SDK Library in your project:

   Right-click the References folder in the Solution Explorer of your project and then select **Add Reference**. Browse to the folder where the library files are installed (by default, *%Program Files(x86)%*\Microsoft System Center 2012\Orchestrator\Integration Toolkit\Lib) and select **Microsoft.SystemCenter.Orchestrator.Integration.dll**.
3. In Solution Explorer, navigate to the Class1.cs file; enter **using Microsoft.SystemCenter.Orchestrator.Integration** to declare the resource for your project. This lets you directly reference classes in the SDK without specifying the entire namespace path (see Figure 20.25). Save the .CS file. Now you can create the custom activity.

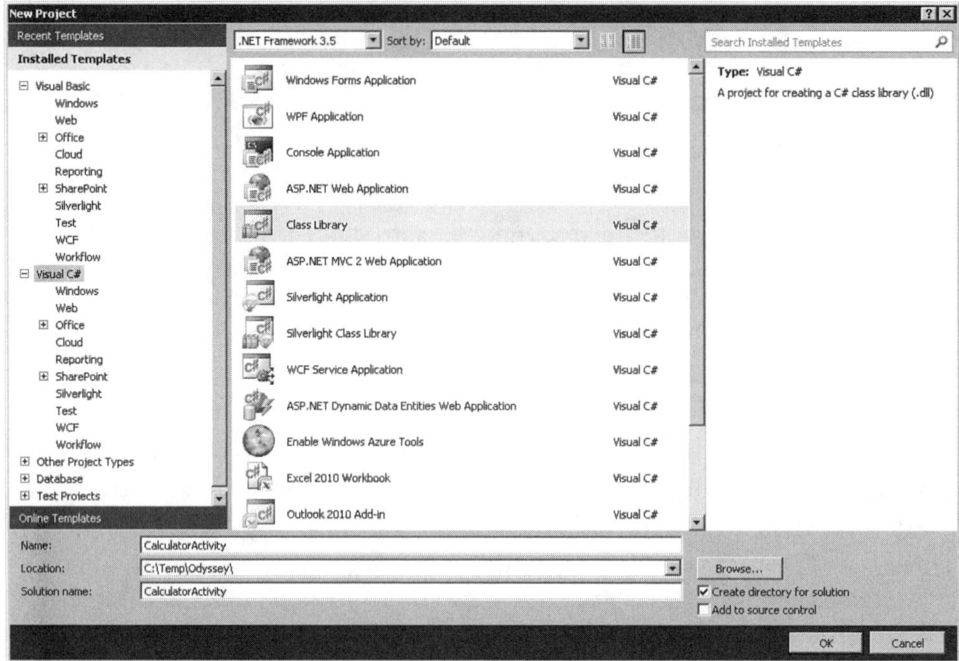

FIGURE 20.24 Visual Studio new project page.

```
using Microsoft.SystemCenter.Orchestrator.Integration;

namespace CalculatorActivity
{
    [Activity("Odyssey Calculator")]
    public class CalculatorExample
    {
    }
}
```

FIGURE 20.25 Declaration of the Orchestrator resource.

Creating a Custom Resource File

Creating resource files lets you assign your own icons to activities. This not only looks professional, but it also increases the readability of runbooks containing custom activities. To create icons for your Orchestrator projects, start with a set of bitmap (.BMP) files representing the icons you want. You must provide two sizes for each icon: 16×16 and 32×32. You can use your favorite graphics editor to create the icons, following these guidelines from the Orchestrator SDK documentation:

- **Transparency:** The transparency color for Orchestrator icons is black (0,0,0). If your icons contain black that is not intended to be transparent, change those areas to near-black (15,15,15). Visually, these will still appear to be black but are not rendered transparent. This is a key difference between Orchestrator and other products that typically use magenta as their transparency color.
- **Background:** Do not use a colored background (white or otherwise). Although these can reproduce well with one desktop color, they might not reproduce well on other backgrounds. Icons must be portable across the different Orchestrator consoles, so using transparent backgrounds is best.
- **Text:** Do not use text in an icon. Your IP might be implemented in different locales, and using words in graphics prevents localization.
- **Standardization of icon usage:** Try to utilize the same verb and noun graphics that other activities use for the same types of actions. Consistency across activities helps your runbook administrators understand what your activities do just by looking at them.
- **Product icons:** If your activities represent a theme or perform actions with a specific product, consider using a theme for your icons. That could be a consistent noun icon that represents the product, or it might be a product logo (make sure that you have rights to use it and that it displays well at 32×32 and 16×16), or it could be a colored base icon (see the new generic activity icons in the Integration Toolkit for examples).
- **Validate:** Check how your icons look after they are implemented, to check for any fuzziness (which can happen around shading and transparency edges), and fine-tune as needed.

The next procedure creates a resource file that includes your own icons to use when developing IPs or activities. Follow these steps:

1. In Visual Studio, select **File** -> **New** -> **New Project**. The New Project page displays (see Figure 20.26). Select **Win32 Project**, and specify a name and location. Click **OK**.
2. On the Welcome page in Figure 20.27, you can configure the application settings by clicking Next or do so later in the project. Click **Next** to configure the settings.
3. On the Application Settings page in Figure 20.28, select **DLL** as the application type. Click **Finish** to create the C++ project.

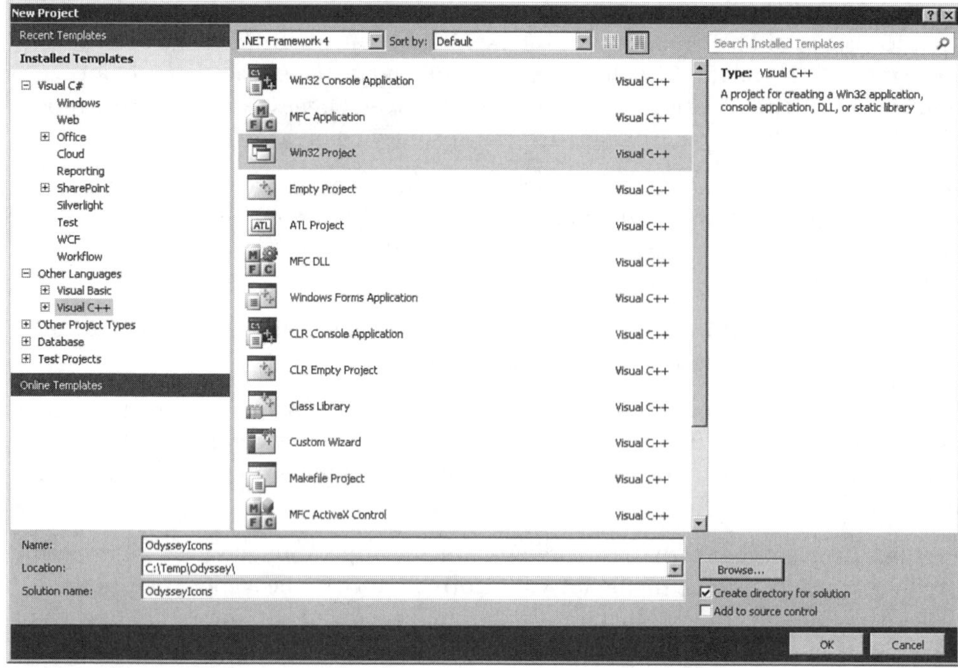

FIGURE 20.26 Visual Studio new resource assembly project page.

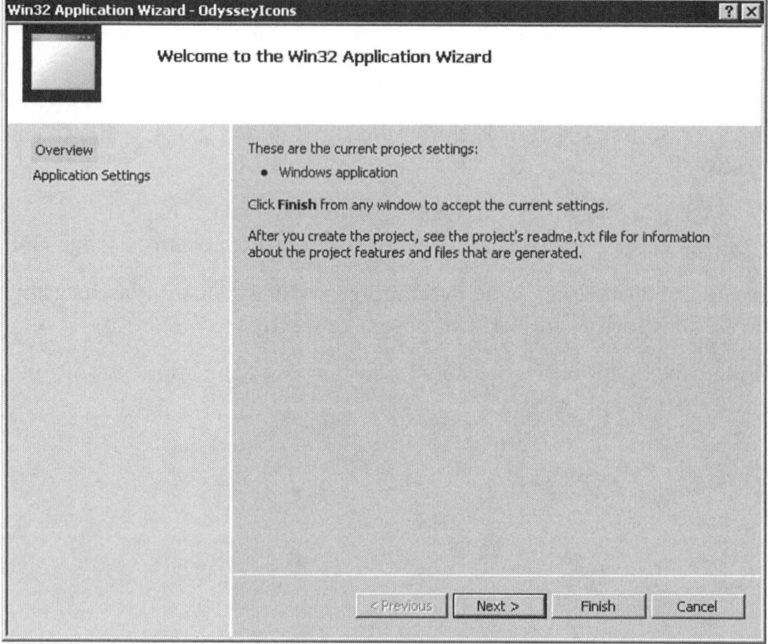

FIGURE 20.27 Welcome page of the Win32 project.

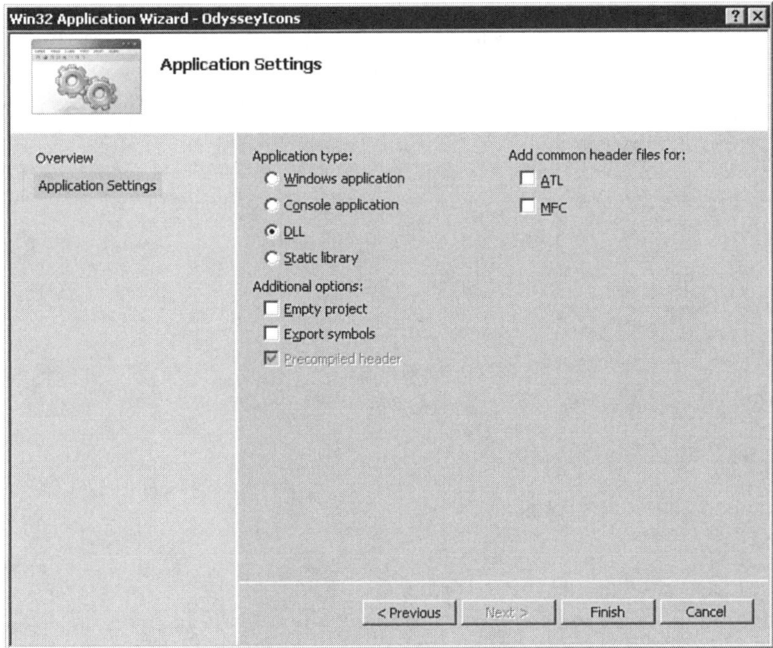

FIGURE 20.28 Application settings page of the project.

4. Navigate in Windows Explorer to the project folder. Create a folder named **Resources** under the project folder, and copy all BMP files to that folder.

5. In your Visual Studio project, navigate in Solution Explorer to the Resource Files folder. Right-click this folder; select **Add -> Resource** (see Figure 20.29).

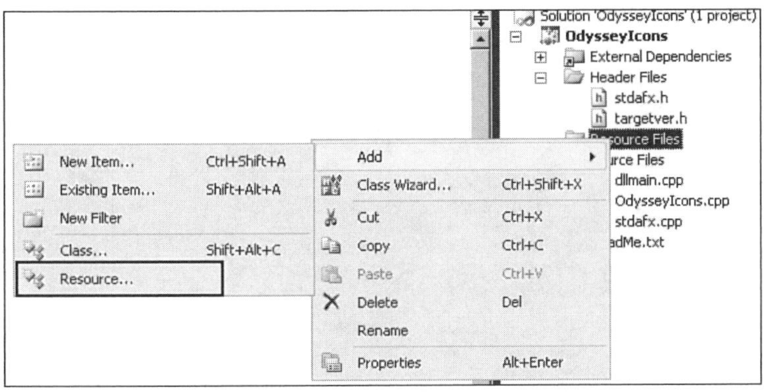

FIGURE 20.29 Menu selection to add resources in the project.

6. On the Add Resource page in Figure 20.30, select **Bitmap** and click **Import**. Browse to the folder where you saved your icon files, select them all, and click **Open**. All selected files are added as resource files to this project.

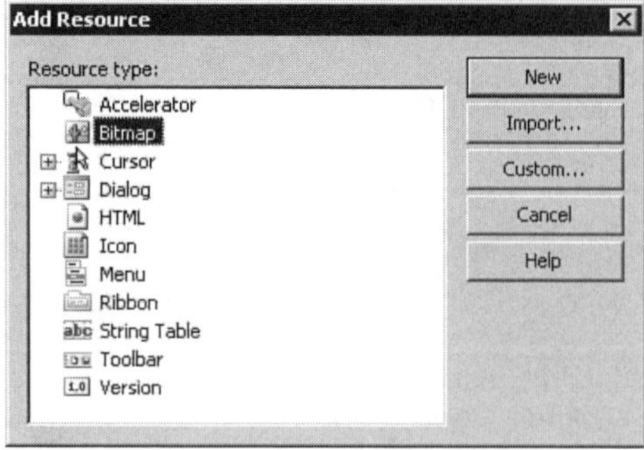

FIGURE 20.30 Add Resource page of the project.

7. In the Solution Explorer, navigate in the Resource Files folder to the *<ProjectName>*.rc file. Right-click the file and then select **View Code** to open the file.

8. In the *<ProjectName>*.rc file, navigate to the location where the bitmap files are referenced. Modify the identifiers of all the bitmaps so that they end with _16 or _32 (corresponding to the bitmap size). Figure 20.31 shows an example.

```
/////////////////////////////////////////////////////////////////////////////
//
// Bitmap
//

Alarm_16                BITMAP "C:\\Temp\\Odyssey\\OdysseyIcons\\Resources\\Alarm.bmp"
Alarm_32                BITMAP "C:\\Temp\\Odyssey\\OdysseyIcons\\Resources\\Alarm_32.bmp"
Chat_16                 BITMAP "C:\\Temp\\Odyssey\\OdysseyIcons\\Resources\\Chat.bmp"
Chat_32                 BITMAP "C:\\Temp\\Odyssey\\OdysseyIcons\\Resources\\Chat_32.bmp"
Login_16                BITMAP "C:\\Temp\\Odyssey\\OdysseyIcons\\Resources\\Login.bmp"
Login_32                BITMAP "C:\\Temp\\Odyssey\\OdysseyIcons\\Resources\\Login_32.bmp"
Network_connections_16  BITMAP "C:\\Temp\\Odyssey\\OdysseyIcons\\Resources\\Network_connections.bmp"
Network_connections_32  BITMAP "C:\\Temp\\Odyssey\\OdysseyIcons\\Resources\\Network_connections_32.bmp"
Order_tracking_16       BITMAP "C:\\Temp\\Odyssey\\OdysseyIcons\\Resources\\Order_tracking.bmp"
Order_tracking_32       BITMAP "C:\\Temp\\Odyssey\\OdysseyIcons\\Resources\\Order_tracking_32.bmp"
Run_16                  BITMAP "C:\\Temp\\Odyssey\\OdysseyIcons\\Resources\\Run.bmp"
Run_32                  BITMAP "C:\\Temp\\Odyssey\\OdysseyIcons\\Resources\\Run_32.bmp"
Saveall_16              BITMAP "C:\\Temp\\Odyssey\\OdysseyIcons\\Resources\\Saveall.bmp"
Saveall_32              BITMAP "C:\\Temp\\Odyssey\\OdysseyIcons\\Resources\\Saveall_32.bmp"
Timetable_16            BITMAP "C:\\Temp\\Odyssey\\OdysseyIcons\\Resources\\Timetable.bmp"
Timetable_32            BITMAP "C:\\Temp\\Odyssey\\OdysseyIcons\\Resources\\Timetable_32.bmp"
Yencoin_16              BITMAP "C:\\Temp\\Odyssey\\OdysseyIcons\\Resources\\Yencoin.bmp"
Yencoin_32              BITMAP "C:\\Temp\\Odyssey\\OdysseyIcons\\Resources\\Yencoin_32.bmp"
Zoom_16                 BITMAP "C:\\Temp\\Odyssey\\OdysseyIcons\\Resources\\Zoom.bmp"
Zoom_32                 BITMAP "C:\\Temp\\Odyssey\\OdysseyIcons\\Resources\\Zoom_32.bmp"
```

FIGURE 20.31 Resource file bitmap code.

9. Save your project after making changes to the .rc file, and build the solution. The result is a DLL file that you can use as a resource file when configuring your custom IPs. Figure 20.32 shows the Product Details page with the newly created OdysseyIcons.dll specified; you use the IP Wizard to select the customized icons.

FIGURE 20.32 Icon set of the custom resource file.

By using your own icon resource file, you can create unique and professional-looking integration packs. Appearance is one reason to create an icon resource file; runbook readability is another. When using the default icons, you can have several custom workflow activities, but all the activities would look the same and could be differentiated only by name. This makes it difficult to select the correct activity or troubleshoot its usage.

Declarative Approach

With the Declarative approach, you use the class attribute to define your activity input and output. Information regarding the Declarative approach is introduced in the "Choosing a Development Approach" section. This section describes an example using this approach.

Consider the example: You have a requirement for a simple calculator activity. The input is two numbers and the arithmetic operator, and the output is the calculator results. The next procedure illustrates the development process. Follow these steps:

20

1. Perform the steps explained in the "Start Building an SDK Activity Project" section to create an environment for developing your activity.
2. Consider renaming the Class1.cs file to a more descriptive name. You can specify the actual name of your activity in your code by adding the code above the class definition; see Figure 20.33, where the activity name is specified.

```
using System;
using System.Collections.Generic;
using System.Linq;
using System.Text;
using Microsoft.SystemCenter.Orchestrator.Integration;

namespace CalculatorActivity
{
    [Activity("Odyssey Calculator")]
    public class CalculatorExample
    {
    }
}
```

FIGURE 20.33 Class definition Declarative approach.

3. After creating your C# project, start defining the activity's inputs, outputs, and filters. This example has three inputs to define: two numbers and the operator value. To provide input, you need two integer properties and one string property defined in the class with a public `set` method. To define these properties as input properties, add the `[ActivityInput (<friendly name>)]` attributes to the string property. Figure 20.34 shows the code used for the activity.

```
private int calcNum1;
private int calcNum2;
private string calcOperator;
private string CalcResult;

[ActivityInput("Number1 Input")]
public int CalcNum1
{
    set { calcNum1 = value; }
}

[ActivityInput("Number2 Input")]
public int CalcNum2
{
    set { calcNum2 = value; }
}

[ActivityInput("Calc operator")]
public string CalcOperator
{
    set { calcOperator = value; }
}
```

FIGURE 20.34 Activity input Declarative approach.

4. Output coding syntax is similar to the input syntax. To provide output, use an integer property defined in the class with a public `get` method. To define it as an output property, add the `[ActivityOutput (<friendly name>)]` attribute to the integer property. In this case, some logic is coded to provide the desired result, and the result is returned as the output of the activity. This is just an example of how you can integrate your own logic into the SDK activity structure. Figure 20.35 shows how to define your output for the SDK activity.

```
[ActivityOutput("Calculator Output")]
public int CALCOutput
{
    get
    {
        switch (calcOperator)
        {
            case "+":
                CalcResult = calcNum1 + calcNum2;
                break;
            case "-":
                CalcResult = calcNum1 - calcNum2;
                break;
            case "*":
                CalcResult = calcNum1 * calcNum1;
                break;
            case "/":
                CalcResult = calcNum1 / calcNum1;
                break;
        }
        return CalcResult;
    }
}
```

FIGURE 20.35 Activity output Declarative approach.

5. You now have created an activity using Visual Studio with the Orchestrator SDK. If your project has no errors, you can build the assembly and start testing the solution. Build the assembly by right-clicking the project name in the Solution Explorer or from the Build menu item. The compiled DLL file is saved in the project bin folder in the corresponding configuration folder (debug/release). Copy the assembly to a location where it can be used in the Runbook Designer for further validation.

To validate your newly created activity assembly, you can create a test runbook and run the assembly with the **Invoke .NET** Integration Toolkit activity. If the Toolkit IP is not yet registered and deployed, review the "Toolkit Installation" section of this chapter. The next procedure describes how to test your development in the Runbook Designer. Follow these steps:

1. Open the Runbook Designer and create a new runbook. Navigate in your activity library to the Integration Toolkit category, and drag an **Invoke .NET** activity into the new runbook.
2. Double-click the **Invoke .NET** activity to open the properties from where you can select your custom assembly. On the Class Information page, click the ellipsis (...) button on the right of the Assembly textbox and browse to the DLL that was created. Click the ellipsis (...) button next to Class, and select the class name created in the assembly (your activity); see Figure 20.36 for this sample assembly.
3. Specify the input information on the Properties page (see Figure 20.37). For the purposes of this section, the values are filled in; these properties should be provided as input for your activity in the runbook.

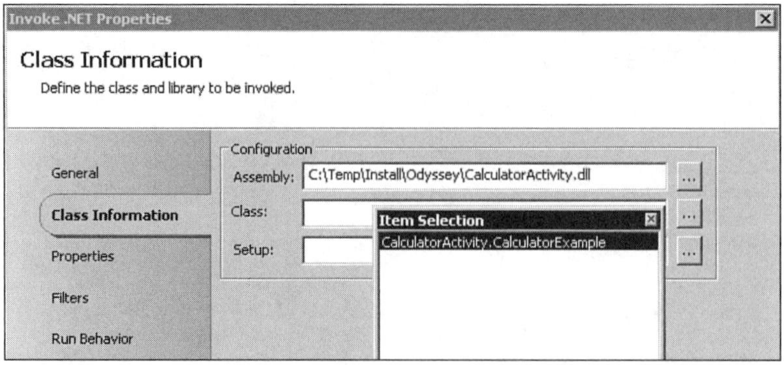

FIGURE 20.36 Invoke .NET Declarative approach.

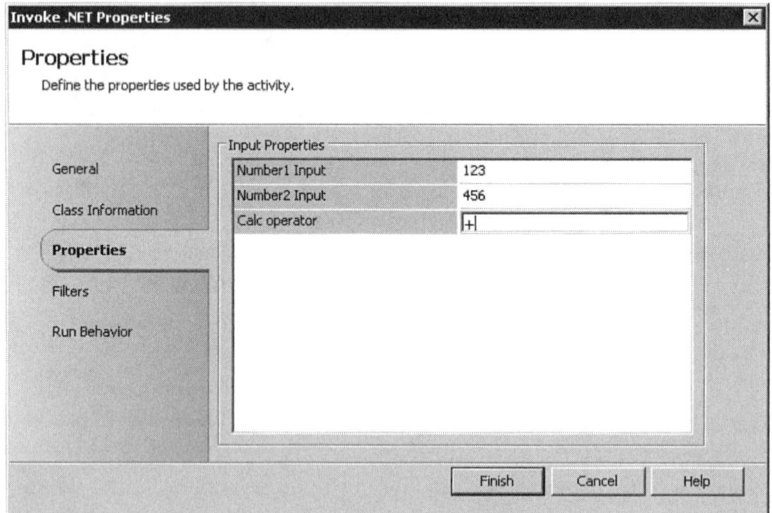

FIGURE 20.37 Property tab of the **Invoke .NET** activity.

4. After configuring your custom activity, use the Runbook Tester to validate its execution. Click **Runbook Tester** in the console and **Run** the runbook. Figure 20.38 shows the output of the activity that has calculated the sum of the two numbers provided.

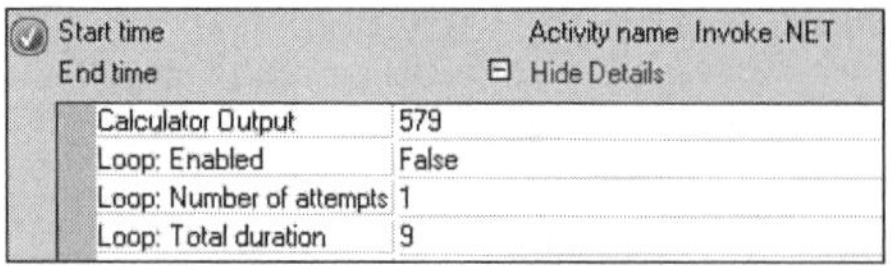

Calculator Output	579
Loop: Enabled	False
Loop: Number of attempts	1
Loop: Total duration	9

FIGURE 20.38 Activity result in Runbook Tester.

Using the Imperative Approach

The Imperative approach uses methods to define your activity input and output. You can find details regarding this approach in the "Choosing a Development Approach" section. This section shows an example.

You have a requirement for a simple calculator activity. The input is two numbers and the arithmetic operator; the result of the calculator is the output for the activity. The next procedure discusses the approach and illustrates the development process. Follow these steps:

1. Perform the steps in the "Start Building an SDK Activity Project" section to create an environment for developing your activity.

2. Rename the Class1.cs file to a more descriptive name. You can specify the actual name of your activity in your code by adding `[Activity ("Calculator")]` above the class definition, Figure 20.39 shows the activity name specified in the code.

```
using System;
using System.Collections.Generic;
using System.Linq;
using System.Text;
using Microsoft.SystemCenter.Orchestrator.Integration;

namespace OdysseyICalculator
{
    [Activity ("Calculator")]
    public class IcalculatorActivity : IActivity
    {

    }
}
```

FIGURE 20.39 Class definition Imperative approach.

3. The code in Figure 20.39 provides a starting point for defining your activity, activity inputs, outputs, and filters. In this example (see Figure 20.40), the calculator activity has three inputs: two numbers and the operator value. For the Imperative approach, output properties are also defined in the `Design` method of the class:

   - Providing input requires two integer properties and one string property, defined in the `Designer()` method. To define these properties as input properties, add the `AddInput()` method. Figure 20.40 shows the code for this activity.

   - In the same area, you can use the `AddOutput()` or `AddFiler()` to define output and filters for your project.

```
public void Design(IActivityDesigner designer)
{
    designer.AddInput("Number1 Input");
    designer.AddInput("Number2 Input");
    designer.AddInput("Calc operator");
    designer.AddOutput("Calculator result");
}
```

FIGURE 20.40 `Design` method Imperative design.

4. Defining output properties for the Imperative coding structure is similar to defining the input properties of the activity. To provide output, the IActivityRequest and IActivityResponse interfaces must be defined; you can publish the result using the `Publish()` method. For this particular example, some logic is already coded to provide the desired calculation result. This is just an example of how to integrate your own logic into the SDK activity structure. The result is published using the `response.Publish()` method; you can specify the output parameter. Figure 20.41 shows how to define your output for the SDK activity. In this example, the output parameter name is "Calculator result."

```
public void Execute(IActivityRequest request, IActivityResponse response)
{
    Int32 CalcResult = 0;
    Int32 calcNum1 = request.Inputs["Number1 Input"].AsInt32();
    Int32 calcNum2 = request.Inputs["Number2 Input"].AsInt32();
    string calcOperator = request.Inputs["Calc operator"].AsString();
    switch (calcOperator)
        {
            case "+":
                CalcResult = calcNum1 + calcNum2;
                break;
            case "-":
                CalcResult = calcNum1 - calcNum2;
                break;
            case "*":
                CalcResult = calcNum1 * calcNum1;
                break;
            case "/":
                CalcResult = calcNum1 / calcNum1;
                break;
        }
    response.Publish("Calculator result", CalcResult);

}
```

FIGURE 20.41 `Execute` method in the Imperative approach.

5. The activity, also used when describing the Declarative approach, is now transformed to the Imperative structure.

   If no errors exist, build the assembly and begin testing. Build the assembly by right-clicking the project name in the Solution Explorer or from the Build menu item. The compiled DLL file is saved in the project bin folder in the corresponding configuration folder (debug/release). Copy the assembly to a location where it can be used in the Runbook Designer.

As in the "Declarative Approach" section, you can validate your newly created activity assembly by creating a test runbook and running the assembly using the **Invoke .NET** Integration Toolkit activity. If the Toolkit IP is not yet registered and deployed, review the "Toolkit Installation" section. The next procedure describes how to test your assembly using the Runbook Designer. Perform the following steps:

1. Open the Runbook Designer and create a new runbook. Navigate in your activity library to the Integration Toolkit category, and drag an **Invoke .NET** activity into the new runbook.

2. Double-click the **Invoke .NET** activity to open the Properties page where you can select your custom assembly. On the Class Information tab, click the ellipsis (...) button to the right of the Assembly textbox and browse to the DLL that was created. Click the ellipsis (...) button next to Class, and select the class name created in the assembly (your activity), as in Figure 20.42.

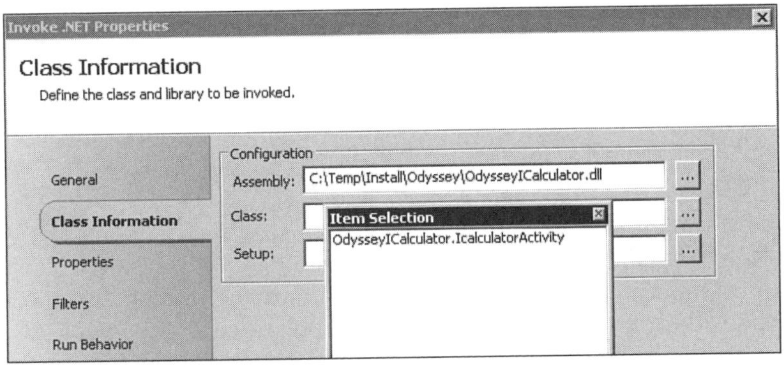

FIGURE 20.42 **Invoke.NET** activity in the runbook.

3. On the Properties page in Figure 20.43, specify input information. For testing purposes, the values are filled in; provide these properties as input to the activity in the runbook.

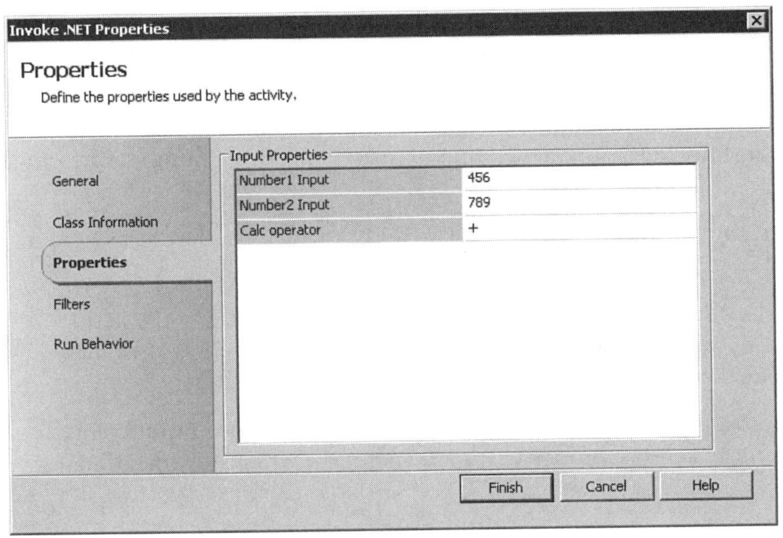

FIGURE 20.43 **Invoke .NET** activity Properties tab.

4. You now can validate execution in the Runbook Tester. Click **Runbook Tester** in the console and **Run** the runbook. In Figure 20.44, you can see that the activity has calculated the sum of the two numbers provided.

Start time | Activity name Invoke .NET
End time | Hide Details

Calculator result	1245
Loop: Enabled	False
Loop: Number of attempts	1
Loop: Total duration	9

FIGURE 20.44 Runbook Tester result for Imperative example assembly.

Cascading Dependencies Approach

The Imperative approach uses methods to define your activity input and output. Adding cascading dependencies adds flexibility to the input properties presented to the user. The input property list is updated based on the selection made on specified input properties. The section "Choosing a Development Approach" describes the details regarding the Imperative and Cascading Dependencies approach. This section describes an example of this approach.

The calculator activity example in the previous two sections is updated to demonstrate creating an activity using the Imperative approach with Cascading Dependencies. The example is updated so that when a selection is made, additional property fields display based on the selection: A simple calculator activity must be created. The user can choose between a simple and advanced calculation (this is the only property initially displayed). If the user selects Advanced, two numbers and the operator input of the activity display. The simple calculation is for demonstration purposes; the advanced calculation actually does the calculation. The output of the activity is the calculator result. The next procedure discusses the approach and illustrates the development process for this example. Perform the following steps:

1. Follow the steps in the "Start Building an SDK Activity Project" section to create an environment to start developing your activity.

2. Rename the Class1.cs file to a more descriptive name. You can specify the actual name of your activity in your code by adding the following code above the class definition. Figure 20.45 shows the activity name specified in the code.

3. The code in Figure 20.45 provides a starting point for defining your inputs. This example has one initial activity property; the others follow when Advanced calculation is selected.

    - Begin by defining static variables that simplify further usage of the string properties. The `Design()` method includes a simple trigger property for the custom activity. All input property settings are defined in the `Redesign()` method. Figure 20.46 shows an example.

```
using System;
using System.Collections.Generic;
using System.Linq;
using System.Text;
using Microsoft.SystemCenter.Orchestrator.Integration;

namespace CasDepCalculatorActivity
{
    [Activity]
    public class CDCalculatorActivity : IActivityWithRedesign
    {
    }
}
```

FIGURE 20.45 Class definition for Imperative approach with Dependencies.

```
[Activity]
public class CDCalculatorActivity : IActivityWithRedesign
{
    private readonly static string Number1 = "Number1 Input";
    private readonly static string Number2 = "Number2 Input";
    private readonly static string Simple_Advanced = "Select simple or advanced";
    private readonly static string SIMPLE = "Simple";
    private readonly static string ADVANCED = "Advanced";
    private readonly static string OPERATOR = "Calc operator";

    public void Design(IActivityDesigner designer)
    {
        designer.AddInput("CalcTrigger").WithRedesign();
    }
```

FIGURE 20.46 Class definition for Imperative approach with Dependencies.

- Figure 20.47 illustrates the `Redesign()` method for the project. All values the user provides are set in the inputs (IInputCollection) variable.

```
public void Redesign(IActivityDesigner designer, IRedesignRequest request)
{
    // Get all of the values set by the user
    IInputCollection inputs = request.RedesignInputs;
}
```

FIGURE 20.47 `Redesign` method definition for Imperative approach with Dependencies.

- Figure 20.48 contains code to read the values specified for the user (remember, all input values are stored in an IInputCollection). By reading the values each time the `redesign` method executes, the input definition becomes more flexible.
- Figure 20.49 shows the actual coding of your property list. Initially, only a selection between Simple or Advanced is available. After the selection is made and Advanced is selected, the additional activity properties are dynamically added to the list.

```
foreach (KeyValuePair<string, IRuntimeValue> input in inputs)
{
    if (input.Key == Simple_Advanced)
    {
        simpleadvancedvalue = input.Value.ToString();
        continue;
    }

    if (input.Key == Number1)
    {
        Nr1 = input.Value.ToString();
        continue;
    }

    if (input.Key == Number2)
    {
        Nr2 = input.Value.ToString();
        continue;
    }

    if (input.Key == OPERATOR)
    {
        calcoperator = input.Value.ToString();
        continue;
    }
}
```

FIGURE 20.48 Sample code to read input values.

```
// Check if this is the first time the activity is opened
// and set any default values or else set the user entered value
if (inputs.Count == 0)
    designer.AddInput(Simple_Advanced).WithListBrowser(SIMPLE, ADVANCED).WithRedesign()
        .WithDefaultValue(SIMPLE);
else
    designer.AddInput(Simple_Advanced).WithListBrowser(SIMPLE, ADVANCED).WithRedesign()
        .WithDefaultValue(simpleadvancedvalue);


// Check if the user wants do do a simple or advanced calculation

    if (simpleadvancedvalue == ADVANCED)
    {
        designer.AddInput(Number1);
        designer.AddInput(Number2);
        designer.AddInput(OPERATOR).WithDefaultValue(calcoperator);
    }

    designer.AddOutput("Calculator result");
```

FIGURE 20.49 Cascading Dependencies example.

4. Defining output properties for this project is similar to the Imperative example because you can use the Imperative coding structure to define the output of the activity. To provide output for this activity, the IActivityRequest and IActivityResponse interfaces must be defined; you can publish the result using the `Publish()` method. For this example, some logic is coded to get the desired calculation result. The result is published using the `response.Publish()` method; you can specify naming as in the Calculator result. Figure 20.50 shows how to define output for the SDK activity.

```
public void Execute(IActivityRequest request, IActivityResponse response)
{
    Int32 CalcResult = 0;
    Int32 calcNum1 = request.Inputs["Number1 Input"].AsInt32();
    Int32 calcNum2 = request.Inputs["Number2 Input"].AsInt32();
    string calcOperator = request.Inputs["Calc operator"].AsString();
    switch (calcOperator)
        {
            case "+":
                CalcResult = calcNum1 + calcNum2;
                break;
            case "-":
                CalcResult = calcNum1 - calcNum2;
                break;
            case "*":
                CalcResult = calcNum1 * calcNum1;
                break;
            case "/":
                CalcResult = calcNum1 / calcNum1;
                break;
        }
    response.Publish("Calculator result", CalcResult);

}
```

FIGURE 20.50 `Execute` method for the Imperative approach.

5. The actual input/output/filter property definition is similar to the Imperative approach.
6. Build the assembly and begin testing the solution. As with the other two approaches, you can build the assembly by right-clicking the project name in the Solution Explorer or the Build menu item. The compiled DLL file is saved in the project bin folder in the corresponding configuration folder (debug/release). Copy the assembly to a location where it can be used in the Runbook Designer.

To validate your newly created activity assembly, create a test runbook and run the assembly with the **Invoke .NET** Integration Toolkit activity. If the Toolkit IP is not yet registered and deployed, review the "Toolkit Installation" section. The next procedure describes testing your assembly in the Runbook Designer. Follow these steps:

1. Open the Runbook Designer and create a new runbook. Navigate in your activity library to the Integration Toolkit category, and drag an **Invoke .NET** activity into the runbook.
2. Double-click the **Invoke .NET** activity to open the Properties page, where you can select your custom assembly. On the Class Information tab, click the ellipsis (...) button to the right of the Assembly textbox and browse to the DLL previously created. Click the ellipsis (...) button next to Class, and select the class name created in the assembly (your activity) (see Figure 20.51).

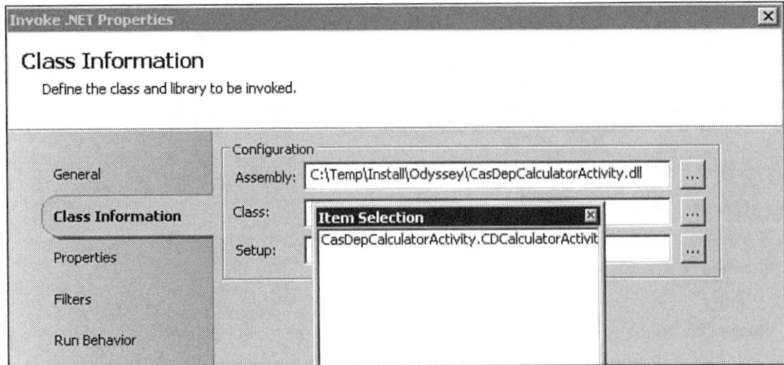

FIGURE 20.51 Assembly selection for the **Invoke .NET** activity in the runbook.

3. On the Properties page in Figure 20.52, specify the input information. In this Cascading Dependencies activity, the user must first make a selection. If Advanced is selected, the additional input properties are added to the input list, as in Figure 20.53. For testing purposes, the values are filled in; these properties should be provided as input of the activity.

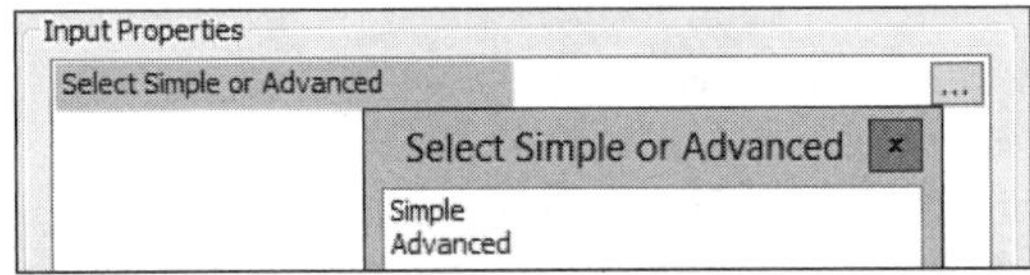

FIGURE 20.52 Cascading Dependencies input property selection.

Input Properties

Select Simple or Advanced	Advanced
Number1 Input	1234
Number2 Input	5678
Calc operator	+

FIGURE 20.53 Property tab of the **Invoke .NET** activity.

4. Validate the execution in the Runbook Tester. Click **Runbook Tester** in the console and **Run** the runbook. Figure 20.54 shows the output (Calculator result) of the sample activity that has calculated the sum of the two numbers provided.

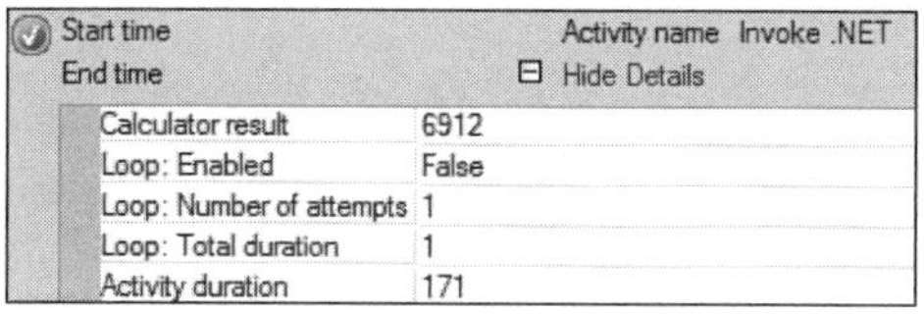

Start time		Activity name Invoke .NET
End time		⊟ Hide Details
Calculator result	6912	
Loop: Enabled	False	
Loop: Number of attempts	1	
Loop: Total duration	1	
Activity duration	171	

FIGURE 20.54 Activity result in Runbook Tester.

Summary

This chapter walked through the different utilities available in the OIT. It discussed the tools and illustrated them using sample procedures. The Command-Line Activity Wizard can help even nondevelopers create professional-looking activities. This utility offers a solution for custom activity creation in different scenarios; you can convert existing scripts, programs, and command lines to Orchestrator activities. By using the OIT SDK, you can move quickly from a beginner level to a more advanced level. Different approaches exist for coding activities; each provides its own ways to define inputs, outputs, and filters for the activity. This chapter provided guidance on the different methods in the SDK for creating activities, showed how to use the SDK for development, and discussed how to deploy custom activities.

PART IV
Appendixes

IN THIS PART

APPENDIX A
Community Solutions and Tools

IN THIS APPENDIX

- ▶ Utilities and Scripts
- ▶ Integration Packs

The System Center Orchestrator (SCOrch) community consists of enthusiastic, intelligent individuals who have created many ways to extend Orchestrator beyond the native capabilities available out of the box. This appendix covers many of the scripts, tools, and integration packs (IPs) that are freely available to help extend your implementation.

Utilities and Scripts

This section discusses the utilities and scripts that are available for System Center 2012 Orchestrator. Functionality includes managing runbooks, generating documentation, keeping the console clean, and so on.

Category Switcher

Loading many integration packs can quickly fill the Activities pane of the Runbook Designer. The name "category switcher" sounds like it might switch the category of a group of activities or move activities into different categories. Instead, it hides and unhides the categories in the Activities pane, removing clutter if desired. You can find this utility at http://orchestrator.codeplex.com.

NOTE: ACTIVITY ICONS CHANGE WHEN HIDDEN

Hiding a category not only hides the activities in the Activities pane, but also hides them in any runbook where the activities are used. The hidden activities operate correctly but do not display as expected in the runbook; instead, they show up as a generic icon with a question mark.

End User Portal for System Center Orchestrator

The End User Portal for System Center Orchestrator (EUPSCO) is a free portal for launching Orchestrator runbooks. If you are looking for a user-friendly way to present runbooks to your users without the complexity of using System Center Service Manager (SCSM), consider using EUPSCO. EUPSCO does not provide the feature-rich environment that SCSM provides, but is effective for presenting graphical forms complete with field validation.

Installation requires Internet Information Server (IIS) and SQL Server Express. EUPSCO uses the published Representational State Transfer (REST) application programming interfaces (APIs) in Orchestrator for ensured compatibility. Download the portal from http://www.eupsco.com/Downloads.

Orchestrator Health Checker

Orchestrator Health Checker is another multipurpose utility with a range of capabilities, including the ability to verify health, audit runbooks, retrieve runbook information, and execute administrative tasks such as purging logs, clearing orphaned runbooks, updating activity passwords, and stopping and starting runbooks. The utility is available at http://scorch.codeplex.com.

Orchestrator Remote Tools

Orchestrator Remote Tools is a multipurpose utility providing three useful functions:

- The User Interface (UI) Generator console provides a way to browse available runbooks graphically and generate an eXtended Markup Language (XML) template complete with parameters.
- The Remote Runbook Launcher can launch the runbooks using the XML files created with the UI Generator.
- The Remote Runbook Launcher is also available using a command-line interface.

You can find this utility at http://orchestrator.codeplex.com.

Orchestrator Visio and Word Generator

If you are need a way to document your runbook without using screenshots or re-creating the runbook layout in Visio, use the Orchestrator Visio and Word Generator utility to easily create a diagram of your runbook. The utility generates the following components in the diagram:

- Runbook title
- Activities (with thumbnail, name, and callout description)
- Smart links (with name and color)
- Looping (and intervals associated)

The utility is available at http://orchestrator.codeplex.com.

Parse Orchestrator Export

This powerful, multifunction graphical utility is designed to provide a range of capabilities, from sanitizing Orchestrator exports to cranking up object-specific logging. Specifically, the utility provides the capability to do the following:

- View exports graphically
- Automatically modify smart links to follow best practices, such as color coding for success and failure
- Modify runbook job concurrency settings en masse
- Enable or disable generic logging
- Enable or disable object specific logging
- Run analysis against runbook exports for common configuration problems
- Rename any runbook, folder, object, and global configuration

The ParseOrchestratorExport.exe utility is available at http://scorch.codeplex.com.

Sanitize Export

Whenever runbooks are exported, information is carried over that pertains to the Orchestrator environment from which the runbook was exported. SanitizeExport.exe provides a way to cleanse runbook exports of this data without having to use an intermediary (or staging) environment for cleaning runbooks. The utility creates a scrubbed version of the exported XML.

The SanitizeExport.exe utility is available at http://scorch.codeplex.com.

SCO Job Runner

SCO Job Runner is a command-line utility that provides a simple way to launch runbooks. Using the utility, you can start a runbook from anywhere the utility could be called, such as from a scheduled task, from a script, or even within System Center Operations Manager.

You can download SCO Job Runner from http://orchestrator.codeplex.com.

SCOrch Launcher

SCOrch Launcher is another command-line utility for executing runbooks through the Orchestrator web service. Like other similar utilities, SCOrch Launcher can be used by task schedulers, scripts, or other environments—such as System Center Operations Manager or Configuration Manager.

SCOrch Launcher does not require input files to operate because all required parameters can be executed on the command line. This is available at http://scorch.codeplex.com.

System Center Orchestrator Web Service PowerShell

This utility is actually a PowerShell module and a collection of PowerShell scripts that provide examples of various ways of using PowerShell to access Orchestrator through the web service. This module includes the following files:

- OrchestratorServiceModule.psm1
- Test-GetCollection.ps1
- Test-GetInstance.ps1
- Test-GetInstanceDetails.ps1
- Test-GetJob.ps1
- Test-GetRunbook.ps1
- Test-StartRunbook.ps1
- Test-StartRunbookAndGetInstanceDetails.ps1
- Test-StopJob.ps1
- Test-StopJobsOnServers.ps1
- OrchWebService.pptx

This collection can be downloaded from http://orchestrator.codeplex.com.

Integration Packs

You might find that the available integration packs from Microsoft do not fit every need. Developing additional functionality for the official integration pack could take a number of months. Activities such as **Run .Net Script** help bridge these gaps but have their own deficiencies that require workarounds.

Having recognized this problem, integration packs built by the community of Orchestrator administrators often provide that missing activity you need in your runbook. The great thing about community-driven projects is that bug fixes, functional changes, and so on are often rapidly developed and released.

CAUTION: DO NOT SKIMP ON TESTING

Microsoft does not officially support community-created and -maintained integration packs. Therefore, these IPs require heavier testing cycles than supported integration packs to ensure that they will work safely in your environment.

Working with Utilities

The integration packs in this section provide some functionality that Orchestrator does not have, such as manipulating text or working with ZIP files. They are not product or software specific. Think of them more as filling out your drawer of utilities that you can use in any runbook.

Data Manipulation Integration Pack

The Data Manipulation IP provides additional activities designed to work with data. It offers many of the popular data-manipulation functions, such as joining or splitting fields, matching patterns, and comparing data.

The integration pack is available at http://orchestrator.codeplex.com.

FTP/SFTP Integration Pack

This IP provides a number of activities related to managing FTP or SFTP activities. Activities cover commands that manage files (uploading, downloading, and more) and folders (creating, deleting, and listing). The FTP IP released with System Center 2012 Service Pack (SP) 1 contains much of the same functionality as this CodePlex version. Consider evaluating both to suit your needs.

The integration pack is available at http://scorch.codeplex.com.

Local Security Integration Pack

The Local Security IP provides activities to manage local security. Four activities provide the means of adding and removing local computer accounts, as well as adding and removing users from local computer groups. The integration pack is available at http://scorch.codeplex.com.

Port Query Integration Pack

If you need to test ports, the Port Query IP contains an activity that can test the availability of a port on a given server. It returns a value of either open or closed. The integration pack is available at http://scorch.codeplex.com.

PowerShell Script Execution Integration Pack

This integration pack provides the capability to run PowerShell scripts, with several added benefits not found in the **Run .Net Script** activity:

- It provides the capability to run scripts without having to supply credentials stored in plain text in the body of the script.
- It handles running on either x86 or x64 without additional logic in the script.

The integration pack is available at http://orchestrator.codeplex.com.

Scheduled Tasks Integration Pack

If you need to manage scheduled tasks, the Scheduled Tasks IP provides an array of activities that can handle the scenario. It offers activities to manage tasks, such as creating, deleting, and running tasks. Other activities are provided to handle triggers such as idle, logon, run once, and more.

The integration pack is available at http://scorch.codeplex.com.

Text Manipulation Integration Pack

The Text Manipulation IP brings additional activities to help perform text-manipulation actions such as replacing text, searching for blank lines, and counting the number of characters in a text string.

The integration pack is available at http://orchestrator.codeplex.com.

Standard Logging Integration Pack

The Standard Logging IP provides a means of capturing published data to a SQL table. The activities can be used to extend the logging functionality of Orchestrator if the present logging capabilities do not suffice.

The integration pack is available at http://orchestrator.codeplex.com.

Utilities Integration Pack

The Utilities IP contains several activities that can be used to handle a miscellaneous set of tasks, such as retrieving datetime, looking at the subdirectories of a file system, managing registry keys and values, and handling text. The Utilities IP is available at http://scorch.codeplex.com.

Windows PowerShell 2 Integration Pack

The Windows PowerShell 2 IP can be leveraged to do more than just run a PowerShell script. It provides the capability to manage runspaces and set credentials that do not show up as clear text in the script body.

The integration pack is available at http://sccmclictropalis.codeplex.com.

Windows Tasks Integration Pack

The Windows Tasks IP consists of two activities that can be configured to provide a variety of options.

- **File System Maintenance:** Manages files and directories
- **Multi-Server WMI Query:** Issues a WMI query to a delimited list of servers

The integration pack is available at http://orchestrator.codeplex.com.

Zip Integration Pack

The Zip IP contains two activities for zipping and unzipping files. The integration pack is available at http://scorch.codeplex.com.

Working with System Center

The IPs in this section have activities that interact with System Center products.

Configuration Manager 2007 Integration Pack

This IP provides an immense number of activities to extend the functionality of managing Configuration Manager 2007. More than 80 activities provide the capability of handling nearly every Configuration Manager scenario, ranging from assigning packages to distribution points, to synchronizing software updates. The only drawback to this integration pack is that it is not compatible with System Center 2012 Configuration Manager.

The integration pack is available at http://scorch.codeplex.com.

SCCM Client Center Integration Pack for Orchestrator 2012

Administrators familiar with SCCM Client Center will be happy to hear about this integration pack. The SCCM Client Center IP provides a set of more than 15 different activities to control the Configuration Manager client, supplementing the System Center Configuration Manager IP that contains only a single activity for client management.

The integration pack is available at http://sccmclictropalis.codeplex.com.

SCOrch Administration Integration Pack

The SCOrch Administration IP is designed to manage runbooks, providing the capability to automate exporting runbooks. Future development suggests that features will include additional activities to automate the installation and deployment of runbooks.

The integration pack is available at http://scorch.codeplex.com.

System Center Orchestrator Webservice Integration Pack

This integration pack provides a set of activities capable of managing runbooks. Activities provide the capability to start and stop runbooks and return runbook information such as instance details, runbooks in a pending status, and all runbooks in a folder.

The integration pack is available at http://scorch.codeplex.com.

Working with Other Microsoft Products

The following IPs work with other Microsoft products that are not in the System Center family.

Active Directory Integration Pack

The Active Directory IP provides an extensive number of activities (many of which overlap) to supplement the set of Active Directory activities in Microsoft's Active Directory Integration Pack. You can use this IP to perform such actions as managing multivalue properties and enumerating domains.

The integration pack is available at http://scorch.codeplex.com.

Exchange Mail Integration Pack

This useful integration pack provides the capability to manage mail. Activities in this IP can be used to read mail, move mail, send Exchange email, and more. The integration pack is available at http://scorch.codeplex.com.

Exchange Management Integration Pack

The Exchange Management IP contains more than 30 activities to help manage an Exchange environment. Activities range from managing mailboxes to managing databases. The integration pack is available at http://scorch.codeplex.com.

Microsoft Team Foundation Server 2010 Integration Pack

The Team Foundation Server IP includes activities that provide the capability to interact with work items, manage version control, and manage team projects.

The integration pack is available at http://orchestrator.codeplex.com.

Microsoft SharePoint Integration Pack

The SharePoint IP enables SCOrch to work with SharePoint libraries and lists, allowing the management of list items, attachments, and documents. Microsoft has announced a new (supported) SharePoint IP for release with System Center 2012 R2.

The integration pack is available at http://orchestrator.codeplex.com.

MSSQL Tasks Integration Pack

The MSSQL Tasks IP augments the available activities related to SQL (such as **Query Database**) by providing the capability to do such things as execute SQL scripts in sequence, manage Orchestrator variables, and dump SQL data to XML.

The integration pack is available at http://orchestrator.codeplex.com.

SQL Integration Pack

The SQL IP contains a single activity, **Run Query**, which, as the name suggests, executes a query. The activity accepts parameterized queries. The SQL IP is available at http://scorch.codeplex.com.

APPENDIX B
Reference URLs

IN THIS APPENDIX

- General Resources
- Microsoft's Orchestrator Resources
- Additional Resources
- Blogs
- System Center 2012 Resources

This appendix includes many reference URLs associated with System Center 2012 Orchestrator. URLs do change—although the authors have made every effort to verify that the references here are working links, there is no guarantee that they will remain current.

General Resources

A number of websites provide excellent resources for Orchestrator:

- Installing this System Center component is covered in Chapter 5, "Installing System Center 2012 Orchestrator." John Savill discusses how the upgrade from Orchestrator 2012 to Service Pack (SP) 1 works at http://windowsitpro.com/system-center-2012/q-how-do-i-upgrade-system-center-orchestrator-2012-system-center-orchestrator-201. Kevin Greene also goes through the steps at http://kevingreeneitblog.blogspot.com/2013/01/system-center-2012-orchestrator-scorch.html.
- CodePlex offers community software for Orchestrator, including sample workflows, objects, and code, at http://orchestrator.codeplex.com/.
- To see a complete listing of community-developed Orchestrator IPs, visit www.codeplex.com/site/search?query=orchestrator&ac=8.
- The Orchestrator Health Checker is available at https://scorch.codeplex.com/releases/view/99063. This enables you to monitor the Orchestrator environment as a whole.

- See the "Orchestrator Survival Guide" at Microsoft's TechNet Wiki, http://social.technet.microsoft.com/wiki/contents/articles/11414.system-center-2012-orchestrator-survival-guide.aspx.
- https://scorch.codeplex.com/ is the home of the community project for Orchestrator integration packs (IPs) and utilities.
- The System Center Central Orchestrator forum is at www.systemcentercentral.com/forums-archive/forums/orchestrator/.
- System Center Central also maintains an integration pack catalog, available at www.systemcentercentral.com/pack-catalog-categories/orchestrator-ip-catalog-pack-catalog/.
- To Bing for Orchestrator-related information, try www.bing.com/search?q=Orchestrator.

Microsoft's Orchestrator Resources

The following list includes some general Microsoft resources available for System Center 2012 Orchestrator:

- A general guide to Orchestrator-related resources is available at http://blogs.technet.com/b/scorch/p/orchestrator_resources.aspx.
- What's new in Service Pack 1? See http://technet.microsoft.com/en-us/library/jj614522.aspx.
- To learn what's new for Orchestrator in System Center 2012 R2, see http://technet.microsoft.com/library/dn251064.aspx.
- Download the System Center 2012 R2 Orchestrator add-ons and extensions at http://www.microsoft.com/en-us/download/details.aspx?id=39622.
- The TechNet Gallery includes the latest community content for Orchestrator—see http://gallery.technet.microsoft.com/site/search?f%5B0%5D.Type=RootCategory&f%5B0%5D.Value=SystemCenter&f%5B0%5D.Text=System%20Center&f%5B1%5D.Type=SubCategory&f%5B1%5D.Value=OpalisIntegrationPacks&f%5B1%5D.Text=Orchestrator&sortBy=Date.

  System Center content is at http://gallery.technet.microsoft.com/site/search?f% 5B0%5D.Type=RootCategory&f%5B0%5D.Value=SystemCenter&f%5B0%5D.Text=System%20Center&sortBy=Date.
- For an overview of Orchestrator 2012, see the Channel 9 recording from TechEd 2011 at http://channel9.msdn.com/Events/TechEd/NorthAmerica/2011/SIM207.
- Learn Orchestrator best practices from an MMS 2013 presentation at http://channel9.msdn.com/Events/MMS/2013/SD-B318.
- The System Center Orchestrator Engineering blog is at http://blogs.technet.com/b/orchestrator/.

- The System Center Team blog is located at http://blogs.technet.com/b/systemcenter/.
- Documentation on Orchestrator 2012 is available at http://technet.microsoft.com/en-us/library/hh237242.aspx. A downloadable version is at www.microsoft.com/en-us/download/details.aspx?id=29258.
- Orchestrator 2012 release notes are at http://technet.microsoft.com/en-us/library/jj899860.aspx.
- Microsoft's TechNet jumping-off page for deploying Orchestrator is http://technet.microsoft.com/en-us/library/hh420337.aspx.
- A guide to Orchestrator resources is at http://technet.microsoft.com/en-us/library/hh420360.aspx.
- Learn about Orchestrator's capabilities at http://technet.microsoft.com/en-us/library/hh420338.aspx.
- Orchestrator architecture is discussed at http://technet.microsoft.com/en-us/library/hh420377.aspx.
- Information regarding runbook server deployments is available at http://technet.microsoft.com/en-us/library/hh420386.aspx.
- Information about runbook designer deployments is located at http://technet.microsoft.com/en-us/library/hh420343.aspx.
- Download the Orchestrator Integration Toolkit from www.microsoft.com/en-us/download/details.aspx?id=34611.
- Read about Orchestrator security roles at http://technet.microsoft.com/en-us/library/hh912320.aspx.
- Orchestrator service accounts are discussed at http://technet.microsoft.com/en-us/library/hh912319.aspx.
- Microsoft's list of integration packs is at http://technet.microsoft.com/en-us/library/hh295851.aspx.
- Microsoft provides documentation for the System Center 2012 IPs at TechNet. http://technet.microsoft.com/en-us/library/hh830706.aspx contains links to documentation for the various IPs:
  - **Configuration Manager:** http://technet.microsoft.com/en-us/library/hh967537.aspx
  - **Data Protection Manager:** http://technet.microsoft.com/en-us/library/hh830726.aspx
  - **Operations Manager:** http://technet.microsoft.com/en-us/library/hh830690.aspx
  - **Service Manager:** http://technet.microsoft.com/en-us/library/hh832008.aspx
  - **Virtual Machine Manager:** http://technet.microsoft.com/en-us/library/hh830700.aspx

- Download the System Center 2012 IPs from www.microsoft.com/en-us/download/details.aspx?id=34611.
- Read about best practices surrounding Orchestrator architecture and runbook deployment at http://blogs.technet.com/b/privatecloud/archive/2013/05/16/automation-orchestrator-architecture-and-runbook-deployment-process.aspx.

  You might also want to check http://gallery.technet.microsoft.com/Orchestrator-Architecture-aead2e5b.
- Charles Joy's YouTube videos are at www.youtube.com/user/charlesjoyMS.
- Information regarding the ASPT tool is available at http://technet.microsoft.com/en-us/library/hh420378.aspx.
- To change the Orchestrator Users group after installation, use the PermissionsConfig tool. For information regarding this tool and examples, see http://technet.microsoft.com/en-us/library/hh463588.aspx.
- XML Notepad 2007 is an intuitive tool for browsing and editing XML documents. Read about it at http://msdn2.microsoft.com/en-us/library/aa905339.aspx, and download the tool from www.microsoft.com/downloads/details.aspx?familyid=72d6aa49-787d-4118-ba5f-4f30fe913628&displaylang=en.
- Interested in learning more about the Microsoft Operations Framework? Check out version 4.0 of the MOF at http://go.microsoft.com/fwlink/?LinkId=50015 and www.microsoft.com/download/en/details.aspx?id=17647.

Additional Resources

- The Orchestrator TechNet community forum is at http://social.technet.microsoft.com/Forums/category/systemcenterorchestrator.
- The Building Clouds blog is at http://blogs.technet.com/b/privatecloud/.
- For an overview of System Center Orchestrator 2012, see http://technet.microsoft.com/en-us/video/system-center-orchestrator-2012-an-overview.aspx.
- *Windows IT Pro* discusses how Orchestrator can help you automate day-to-day-tasks. See the article by Orin Thomas at http://windowsitpro.com/system-center-2012/understanding-system-center-orchestrator-2012.
- Watch a video by Andrew Fryer on getting started with Orchestrator 2012 to manage virtual machines at www.youtube.com/watch?v=UlQGzN-unQI.
- Kevin Holman provides a quickstart deployment guide for Orchestrator at http://blogs.technet.com/b/kevinholman/archive/2011/11/14/orchestrator-2012-quickstart-deployment-guide.aspx.
- Common activity properties are documented at http://technet.microsoft.com/en-us/library/hh228165.aspx.

- For a list of tasks you can accomplish when using monitoring activities, see http://technet.microsoft.com/en-us/library/hh225052.aspx.
- Read about using the Windows Firewall with Orchestrator at http://technet.microsoft.com/en-us/library/hh912321.aspx.
- Information on the Orchestrator web service can be found at http://msdn.microsoft.com/en-us/library/hh921667.aspx.
- Read how to configure the Orchestrator web service to use HTTPS at http://technet.microsoft.com/en-us/library/hh529160.aspx. Guidance on requesting and installing a certificate is at http://support.microsoft.com/kb/299875.
- See http://msdn.microsoft.com/en-us/library/hh921685.aspx for information on starting a runbook using the Orchestrator web service. Stopping a job is documented at http://msdn.microsoft.com/en-us/library/hh921668.aspx.
- Read about auditing at http://contoso.se/blog/?p=2980.
- You can modify migrated Opalis policies to run in Orchestrator. http://technet.microsoft.com/en-us/library/hh420340.aspx explains how.
- Joe Levy provides an example of a runbook that can patch runbook servers while maintaining high availability at http://gallery.technet.microsoft.com/Patch-Orchestrator-Runbook-8f5beba7.
- Marcus Klein discusses Exchange automation using Orchestrator 2012 at http://www.msexchange.org/articles-tutorials/exchange-server-2010/management-administration/exchange-automation-using-orchestrator-2012.html.
- Download the PowerShell Script Execution 1.1 integration pack from CodePlex at http://orchestrator.codeplex.com/releases/view/76101.
- Coauthor Anders Bengtsson of Microsoft has written a runbook validator package discussed in Chapter 10, "Runbook and Configuration Best Practices." You can download this package from http://contoso.se/blog/?p=3573.
- Download runbook examples for each of the System Center 2012 components at http://orchestrator.codeplex.com/releases/view/86195 (at the time of writing, these examples have not been updated for SP 1).
- Download Orchestrator web service PowerShell cmdlets at https://scorch.codeplex.com/releases/view/107858. These support invoking runbooks with input parameters that include special characters and have built-in help. Thanks to Ryan Andorfer for making these available.
- Read how to deploy a service from a template with VMM and Orchestrator at www.systemcentercentral.com/orchestrator-by-example-deploying-a-service-from-template-with-vmm-and-orchestrator.
- To scale out a machine tier with VMM and Orchestrator, see www.systemcentercentral.com/orchestrator-by-example-scaling-out-a-machine-tier-in-a-service-and-orchestrator/.

- To scale in a machine tier with VMM and Orchestrator, see http://www.systemcentercentral.com/orchestrator-by-example-scaling-in-a-machine-tier-in-a-vmm-service-with-orchestrator/.
- For information on performing in-place updates for services in VMM and Orchestrator, see www.systemcentercentral.com/orchestrator-by-example-performing-in-place-updates-for-services-in-system-center-2012-vmm-sp1-and-orchestrator/.
- For information on building a Wait activity, see http://contoso.se/blog/?p=2802.
- Download the SCOM Extensibility Kit 2.0 from CodePlex at http://opalis.codeplex.com/releases/view/50751.

  At the time of completing this book, the release available on CodePlex will not function in Orchestrator without first updating the source code using the PowerShell script referenced in "Migrating QIK API Custom Activities" at http://orchestrator.codeplex.com/wikipage?title=Migrating%20QIK%20API%20Custom%20Activities.
- A Microsoft Virtual Academy course discussing how to use Orchestrator with Service Manager to deploy, automate, update, and manage service offerings within your private cloud is available at www.microsoftvirtualacademy.com/training-courses/system-center-2012-orchestrator-service-manager.
- Want a jumpstart on Orchestrator? See Pete Zerger's posting at www.systemcentercentral.com/orchestrator-2012-jumpstart-day-1-runbook-concepts-components-and-databus-rules/.
- Orchestrator Mobile is a Windows Phone app that enables you to connect to and control your Orchestrator 2012 system, with the functional capability of the Orchestration console. For information, see http://gallery.technet.microsoft.com/Orchestrator-Mobile-System-81ed45d9.
- Oskar Landman, System Center Cloud and Data Center Management MVP, has written an IP that extends the capabilities of the existing Service Manager 2012 and Operations Manager 2012 IPs. Download the IP from http://gallery.technet.microsoft.com/Orchestrator-System-Center-0371cf45.

Blogs

This section lists some blogs the authors have used. Some are more active than others are, and new blogs seem to spring up overnight:

- A great source of information is System Center Central (www.systemcentercentral.com), managed by MVPs Pete Zerger, Rory McCaw, and Maarten Goet.
- If you're interested in keeping up with VMM, the VMM team has a blog at http://blogs.technet.com/scvmm/.

- Anders Bengtsson, former System Center MVP and now a Microsoft PFE, blogs on Orchestrator at http://contoso.se/blog/.
- The SCORCH Dev blog is at http://opalis.wordpress.com/
- http://systemscentre.blogspot.com/ is a blog by Steve Beaumont.
- http://itservicemngmt.blogspot.com/ is a blog that discusses basic ITSM knowledge points for people new to in ITIL.
- Kevin Sullivan's management blog is at https://blogs.technet.com/kevinsul_blog/. (Kevin is a Technology Specialist at Microsoft who focuses on management products.)
- www.systemcenterguide.com is a System Center blog by Duncan McAlynn.
- Ian Blyth, previously a Lead Technical Specialist in Microsoft U.K., blogs at http://ianblythmanagement.wordpress.com/ on System Center technologies.
- www.networkworld.com/community/meyler is a blog by Kerrie Meyler with general discussion topics, concentrating on Microsoft management.

System Center 2012 Resources

This section details some references and articles regarding Microsoft's System Center 2012:

- For an overview of System Center, see www.microsoft.com/en-us/server-cloud/system-center/default.aspx.
- The System Center 2012 Cloud and Datacenter Management page is at www.microsoft.com/en-us/server-cloud/system-center/datacenter-management.aspx.
- Key benefits of System Center 2012 Configuration Manager are discussed at www.microsoft.com/en-us/server-cloud/system-center/configuration-manager-2012.aspx.
- The TechNet Library for System Center 2012 is located at http://technet.microsoft.com/en-us/library/hh546785.aspx.
- The TechNet Manageability Center contains links to resources and TechNet magazine articles at http://technet.microsoft.com/en-us/manageability/default.aspx.
- Virtual labs for System Center components, including Orchestrator, Operations Manager, Configuration Manager, Service Manager, and Virtual Machine Manager, are at http://technet.microsoft.com/en-us/bb539977.aspx.
- Read about System Center 2012 R2, announced at TechEd NA 2012, at www.microsoft.com/en-us/server-cloud/system-center/system-center-2012-r2.aspx. You might also want to look at http://cloudcomputing.info/en/news/2013/06/microsoft-announces-windows-server-2012-r2-system-center-2012-r2-and-windows-azure-pack.html.

APPENDIX C
Available Online

IN THIS APPENDIX

- PowerShell Scripts for the Operations Manager IP
- PowerShell Scripts for the Virtual Machine Manager IP
- Scripts for Data Center Automation
- Live Links

Online content is available to provide add-on value to readers of *System Center 2012 Orchestrator Unleashed*. You can download this material, organized by chapter, from www.informit.com/store/system-center-2012-orchestrator-unleashed-9780672336102. This content is not available elsewhere. Note that the authors and publisher do not guarantee or provide technical support for the material.

PowerShell Scripts for the Operations Manager IP

Chapter 13, "Integration with System Center Operations Manager," includes runbooks for group maintenance mode using the Operations Manager integration pack (IP). This incorporates PowerShell scripts to start and stop maintenance mode, which are available online as content for this book.

PowerShell Scripts for the Virtual Machine Manager IP

Chapter 16, "Integration with System Center Virtual Machine Manager," includes a PowerShell script to create a Virtual Machine Manager (VMM) 2012 cloud. It also includes a script to set custom properties on a virtual machine (VM). These scripts are included as downloadable content for this book.

Scripts for the Data Center Automation

Chapter 19, "Runbook Automation in the Data Center and the Cloud," includes a script to import a Service Manager SMlet and CSV file. This script is also available as downloadable content.

Live Links

Reference URLs (see Appendix B, "Reference URLs") are provided as live links. These include nearly 100 (clickable) hypertext links and references to materials and sites related to Orchestrator.

A disclaimer and unpleasant fact regarding Live Links: URLs change! Companies are subject to mergers and acquisitions, pages move and change on websites, and so on. Although these links were accurate in mid-2013, it is possible that some will change or be "dead" by the time you read this book. Sometimes the Wayback Machine (www.archive.org/index.php) can rescue you from dead or broken links. This site is an Internet archive, and it will take you back to an archived version of a site...sometimes.

Index

Symbols

A

B

C

F

G

H

J

K

L

M

O

P

Q

R

S

T

U

V

W

X

Z

How can we make this index more useful? Email us at indexes@samspublishing.com